Lilacs

Lilacs

A GARDENER'S ENCYCLOPEDIA

by John L. Fiala

Revised and updated by
Freek Vrugtman

Timber Press
Portland · London

Page 1: *Syringa vulgaris* 'Gaiziņkalns'. S. Strautina
Page 2: *Syringa vulgaris* 'Minchanka'. T. Poliakova and I. Semyonova
Page 5: *Syringa vulgaris* 'Pērļu Zvejnieks'. S. Strautina

Published in 2008 by
Timber Press, Inc.

The Haseltine Building
133 S.W. Second Avenue, Suite 450
Portland, Oregon 97204-3527
www.timberpress.com

2 The Quadrant
135 Salusbury Road
London NW6 6RJ
www.timberpress.co.uk

Printed in China

Library of Congress Cataloging-in-Publication Data

Fiala, John L.
   Lilacs : a gardener's encyclopedia / by John L. Fiala.—2nd
ed. / rev. and updated by Freek Vrugtman.
      p. cm.
   First ed. published 1988.
   Includes bibliographical references and index.
   ISBN-13: 978-0-88192-795-5 (alk. paper)
   1. Lilacs. I. Vrugtman, Freek. II. Title.
   SB413.L65F53 2008
   635.9′3387—dc22
                                                    2007038225

A catalog record for this book is also available from the
British Library.

Contents

Preface to the Second Edition 9
Author's Notes to the First Edition 11
Acknowledgments 14

CHAPTER ONE **Taxonomy and Technical Considerations of Lilac Species** 17
Summary of Classification of the Genus *Syringa* 20
Alphabetical Checklist of Botanical Taxa of Lilacs 22
On Naming and Registering New Lilac Cultivars 26
Cultivar Identification and Cultivar Fingerprinting 27
Trade Designations and Trademarks Are Not Cultivar Names 28
Classification of Lilacs by Season of Bloom 30
Lilac Bloom and Climate Change—Phenology 31
Lilac Fragrance 32
Cold Tolerance and Heat Tolerance in Lilacs 33

CHAPTER TWO **Lilac Species from Europe** 37
Syringa vulgaris 37
Syringa josikaea 44

CHAPTER THREE **Lilac Species from Asia** 48
Plant Explorations in Asia Important to the Discoveries of New Lilac Species 49
Subgenus *Ligustrina*—The Tree Lilacs 67
Syringa reticulata 67
Syringa pekinensis 72
Subgenus *Syringa*, Series *Syringa* 75
Syringa vulgaris 75
Syringa oblata 75
Syringa protolaciniata 81
Syringa afghanica 83
Syringa ×chinensis 83
Syringa ×hyacinthiflora 85
Syringa ×laciniata 86
Syringa ×persica 87

Subgenus *Syringa*, Series *Pinnatifoliae* 88
Syringa pinnatifolia 88
Syringa ×diversifolia 90
Subgenus *Syringa*, Series *Pubescentes* 90
Syringa pubescens 90
Syringa meyeri 102
Syringa mairei 103
Syringa pinetorum 104
Syringa wardii 105
Subgenus *Syringa*, Series *Villosae* 105
Syringa villosa 105
Syringa emodi 106
Syringa wolfii 107
Syringa josikaea 108
Syringa komarowii 108
Syringa tomentella 112
Syringa sweginzowii 112
Syringa yunnanensis 114
Syringa tibetica 116
Syringa Villosae Group 116
Syringa ×henryi 116
Syringa ×josiflexa 117
Syringa ×nanceiana 119
Syringa ×prestoniae 119
Syringa ×swegiflexa 121

CHAPTER FOUR **Color in Lilacs** 122
Historical and Technical Considerations of Color 123
Color Charts for Lilac Flower Descriptions 124
Color Dimensions in the Garden 125
Recommendation of Lilac Cultivars by Color Classification 125
White Lilacs (Color Class I) 126
Violet Lilacs (Color Class II) 135
Blue Lilacs (Color Class III) 139
Lilac-colored Lilacs (Color Class IV) 147
Pink Lilacs (Color Class V) 153

Magenta Lilacs (Color Class VI)   165
Purple Lilacs (Color Class VII)   175
A Dozen Best According to Color   187
Lilacs of Special and Unique Color
     Classifications   188
Autumn Color in Lilacs   190
Cultivars with Golden and Variegated Foliage   191

CHAPTER FIVE   **Landscaping with Lilacs**   193
Choosing a Proper Site for a Single Plant, a Lilac
     Garden, or a Collection   193
The Smaller Garden   194
Lilacs on Hillsides, by Lakes, or at Riversides   195
Lilacs for Miniature or Rock Gardens   197
Lilacs in Japanese and Chinese Gardens   198
Lilacs in Suburban Gardens and Country
     Estates   199
A Garden Lilac Walk   200
Lilacs by Woodland Borders   201
Lilacs as Small Trees in the Garden   201
Lilacs for Hedges and Screens   202
How to Design or Remodel a Large Lilac
     Collection   203
Lilacs in the Winter Landscape   205
The Best Species Lilacs as Garden and Landscape
     Shrubs   205

CHAPTER SIX   **Companion Plants to Lilacs**   207
Magnificent Conifers and Lilacs   207
Flowering Crab Apples and Lilacs   209
Flowering Dogwoods and Lilacs   210
Flowering Cherries and Lilacs   211
Peonies and Lilacs   212
Showy Magnolias and Lilacs   212
Hostas and Lilacs   213
Combining Red, Yellow, and Orange Flowers with
     Lilacs   214

CHAPTER SEVEN   **Lilac Culture**   217
Good Drainage   217
Good Soil   218
Full Sun, the Lilac's Limelight   220
Pruning Lilacs   220
Transplanting Lilacs   222
Rejuvenating Older Lilacs   222
Tagging Lilacs and Record Keeping   224
Forcing Lilacs   226
Longevity in the Vase   230

CHAPTER EIGHT   **Lilac Diseases, Pests, and
     Problems**   231
Diseases of Lilacs   231
Insect Enemies of Lilacs   235
Miscellaneous Problems of Lilacs   240
Damage from Animals and People   242

CHAPTER NINE   **The Propagation of Lilacs**   245
Lilacs from Seed   245
Lilacs from Tissue Culture   250
Lilacs from Layered Branches   251
Lilacs from Cuttings   252
Grafting Lilacs   256
Summer Budding of Lilacs   258
Producing New Lilac Cultivars   259

CHAPTER TEN   **The Lilac Hybridizers of Yesterday,
     Today, and Tomorrow**   267
A Brief History of Plant Genetics and
     Hybridization   267
Development of the Garden Lilac in Western
     Europe   268
Lilac Hybridizing in North America   288
Lilac Hybridizing in the Russian Federation and Its
     Former Satellite Countries   328
Lilac Hybridizing in China   346

CHAPTER ELEVEN   **The Lilac in Art and
     Design**   347
Early Illustrations   347
Paintings and Prints   347
Woodcuts and Wood Engravings   349
Ceramics   349
Coins   350
Postage Stamps   350

APPENDIX A   **Noted Plant Explorers and
     Taxonomists of** *Syringa*   352
APPENDIX B   **Lilac Hybridizers and
     Originators**   357
APPENDIX C   **The World's Noteworthy Lilac
     Collections, Gardens, and Nurseries**   366

Glossary   379
Literature Cited   382
Index of Scientific Plant Names   398
Index of Lilac Cultivar Names   400
General Index   411

Preface to the Second Edition

Many years have passed since Reverend John Fiala's work was first published. Updating the information and expanding the scope of the book has not been an easy task. When writing the final drafts of *Lilacs: The Genus Syringa* and *Flowering Crabapple: The Genus Malus*, Fiala was terminally ill. Not only was he pressed for time, he also moved between Falconskeape, his summer residence and lilac garden at Medina, Ohio, and his winter quarters in Ocala, Florida, leaving him frequently without access to relevant correspondence and reference files, his notes on observations, and his plant records. This resulted in inconsistencies and shortcomings in the first edition of his book.

Several years after Fiala's death, while Falconskeape was still managed by Karen and Peter Murray, one of the service buildings burned down. It is presumed that whatever files of correspondence and notes were there went up in flames. The lack of documentation on Fiala's lilac collection and on the preparation of the original edition of his book severely hampered work on this revision.

On the positive side, emerging computer technology and word processing facilitated recording and storing notes, eliminating time-consuming retyping. Information technology, the Internet, and electronic mail have revolutionized literature searches and communication with collaborators. The use of English as the language for science and communication has also effected a wider distribution of books written in English, and although language barriers still hamper information gathering, readers will notice that the international scope of this book on lilacs has widened.

Readers familiar with the first edition of Fiala's work may wonder what happened to the eight new botanical names published at the beginning. They do not appear in this volume because *Syringa debelderi* is included in *S. pubescens* subsp. *patula* and the remaining seven taxa have not been validly published under the provisions of the *International Code of Botanical Nomenclature* (Greuter et al. 2000).

Botanical and horticultural professionals familiar with botanical nomenclature and with recommended standard abbreviations of names of authors of scientific names of plants (Brummit and Powell 1992) will note that we have restricted abbreviations to a minimum, spelling out first and middle names, where known, and leaving spaces between the initials and surname immediately following a scientific name. Also, there are several innovations to the revised and updated book.

The Villosae Group is the first cultivar group recognized in the genus *Syringa* under the provisions of the *International Code of Nomenclature for Cultivated Plants* (Brickell et al. 2004). Proposed and introduced by Marco Hoffman (2002) and registered in 2003 (Vrugtman 2004), Villosae Group encompasses the cultivars affiliated with interspecific hybrids in series *Villosae*.

In chapter one the classification of botanical taxa in the genus *Syringa* has been brought up to date, reflecting the present understanding of relationships. An alphabetical checklist of botanical taxa of lilacs has been added as a finding list; it may provide answers to the question, What happened to that name? The accepted names for each species are given according to current nomenclature. Older synonyms are also given for those who may have lilacs known to them only by these older names.

The bibliography of the first edition has been replaced by a section titled "Literature Citations," the references being linked to the text.

"The World's Noteworthy Lilac Collections, Gardens, and Nurseries" is the title of a revised and updated appendix. There are no set standards for including or excluding collections; some collections may be of worldwide or national importance, others of regional interest or holding specialized collections. Some collections may have escaped our searches; owners of a few collections prefer to remain unlisted.

A section about lilacs in arts and crafts has been added. It is not an exhaustive treatment but rather an introduction to the subject that may stimulate further research by others.

The reader will notice that in the transliteration of cultivar names from Russian to English some Cyrillic characters are transliterated by using two or more Latin characters, such as я = ya, ю = yu, ш = sh, ч = ch, and so on. Whenever this is the case the Latin characters have been underlined. For example, the Latin ya will transliterate to the Cyrillic я, rather than to the individual characters ы and a. The Latin transliteration of the Cyrillic character щ is underlined twice: shch, distinguishing it from ш = sh and ч = ch appearing side by side. This convention has been adopted from Holetich (1982). The *ALA-LC Romanization Tables* (Barry 1991) commonly in use in North America do not make provisions for reverse transliteration, for instance, from Latin script to Cyrillic script, which is desirable for a book with an international readership.

Material in some of the appendices of the first edition has been incorporated in the text of the revised book.

Although the book is published in American English, and attention has been given to preserving the original spelling of quotes and literature citations appearing in British English and Canadian English, slip-ups may have happened, for which we apologize.

This book reviews the history of the garden lilac, yet it is evident from the original introduction to the book, republished here as "Author's Notes to the First Edition," that Fiala intended to create a handbook for the present. We have retained this focus. The emphasis is on lilac cultivars that are extant, though some of these may not yet, or not any more, be readily available in the nursery trade. Information on all known garden lilacs, extant and extinct, can be found in the "International Register and Checklist of Cultivar Names in the Genus *Syringa* L." (Lilac Register, for short), a work-in-progress document published by Royal Botanical Gardens, Hamilton, Ontario (Vrugtman 2007c). Readers interested in the derivation of cultivar names of lilacs and in the essential literature references concerning the publication of cultivar names of lilacs should refer to the Lilac Register.

Readers will look in vain for a list of the best lilacs in cultivation, although the personal lilac evaluations by Fiala have been retained. The International Lilac Society has had an active Lilac Evaluation Committee since the 1980s, gathering information on lilac performance in North America, Europe, and Asia, but there has been no lilac evaluation to date by an unbiased jury using a point system. We advise the reader to look for recommendations published in *Lilacs, Quarterly Journal of the International Lilac Society,* and for regional lists published elsewhere, such as the ones by John Alexander III (1992, 1999) of the Arnold Arboretum.

FREEK VRUGTMAN

Author's Notes to the First Edition

In WRITING THIS VOLUME I have been engaged for a little more than 10 years in a labor of love. I have tried to write all about what might interest anyone who loves lilacs, from the home gardener to the connoisseur, from the park superintendent to the scientific hybridizer. May it bring you new ideas on growing them—a single bush, or as many as your garden can respectfully contain. The lilac is a simple plant to grow and needs very little extra care for so much beauty.

This volume began back when I was a boy of six or seven and oft visited my grandmother's country home in Gladwin, Michigan—some 10 miles (16 km) out of town amid the most beautiful pines, balsams, and firs of the north woods. A clear trout stream meandered about 50 feet (15 m) from her house, splashing along at hurried pace over green-mossed boulders in whose shadows the swift trout would hide as we tried to catch them by hand, rarely successful. All along this lovely river, the Sugar River, on both sides grew venerable old bushes of lilacs my aunts and uncle had planted for Grandmother. How she loved lilacs. There were more lilac bushes than I had ever seen anywhere. In bloom they were a marvelous sight. Heaven must be something like this, I thought. Ah, and their fragrance—like none other.

Grandmother was a true pioneer; she once lived with her growing family in a real log house. Now her house was a saltbox by the stream, and my Uncle Leo and two early-widowed Aunts Marie and Amelia, who were some of the greatest gardeners I ever knew, transformed the acres of lawn and gardens around Grandmother's house into one grand seed catalog come suddenly to life and bloom. Today they are all long gone—but it was from them at the age of six that I had to learn the common as well as the Latin name for all their flowers. The house, too, is gone, but some of the gardens still remain. The lilacs, moss covered from the mists of the running waters (that never froze even in winter), their old trunks more ancient than ever, continue to bloom each spring and make me a boy again. Perhaps in these pages, in your love for lilacs, you will experience some memories of youth and family. Hopefully it will bring you to love the lilacs as I do.

Few books have been written in English about the lilac. Most are long out of print and are now collector's items. A lovely little book called *Lilacs*, written by N. (Hannah) Hudson Moore and beautifully illustrated by Frederick G. Hall, was published in 1904. Probably few lilac authorities have ever seen this little volume. Reprinted from the September 1903 issue of *The Delineator*, it is filled with nostalgic tales about lilacs. If you have a copy, treasure it. A famous monograph by Susan Delano McKelvey, *The Lilac*, was published in 1928. It is a most prestigious and scholarly book about lilacs and their species origins.

Two practical guides for those who grow lilacs were published in the 1930s: *Lilac Culture* and *Lilacs in My Garden*. John C. Wister, an outstanding horticultural scholar, professor, and landscape designer, wrote *Lilac Culture*. Earlier he was responsible for a checklist of lilacs in 1927 and later (in 1942 and again in 1953) for *Lilacs for America*, which have been the backbone of lilac cultivar evaluation, color coding, and knowledge ever since. *Lilacs in My Garden* was written by the famous gardener and horticulturist Alice Harding in 1933. The well-known hybridizers Victor and Émile Lemoine named two fine lilacs in Harding's honor. One is a beautiful double white called *Syringa vulgaris* 'Souvenir d'Alice Harding' (1938), the other a double deep red-budded pink called *S. vulgaris* 'Mrs Edward Harding' (1922). Both are as lovely as the grand lady they commemorate.

Written by an Englishman, Douglas Bartrum, in 1959, *Lilac and Laburnum* has never been widely distributed in North America. It is also well done but in a more limited fashion. Subsequently, three other important publications on the lilac have been printed. *Tentative International Register of Cultivar Names in the Genus Syringa* by Owen Rogers in 1976, which updates the 1953 checklist of John Wister, is a wonderful compilation of all known lilac cultivars and species. *A Four-Year Study at Lilac Park* by Joseph Dvorak Jr. in 1978 contains marvelous line drawings. Finally, *The Edward A. Upton Scrapbooks of Lilac Information* were published by the International Lilac Society through the efforts of Owen Rogers and Isabel Zucker. The four scrapbooks are compilations of articles on the lilac, published in two volumes, one in 1980 and the second in 1986. These books, together with many individual articles published in various journals, magazines, and newspapers, have constituted all we have on the lilacs.

There has been no comprehensive volume on the many aspects of lilac species, cultivars, hybrids, the growing and propagation, landscaping with, and the hybridizing and hybridizers of lilacs, and above all, the newer lilacs and where one may view outstanding lilacs at close hand. I have undertaken to write this long journey of the lilacs. Their history is bound up with famous places, towns, and historic men and women of science who searched out and hybridized to improve the lilac. The story of the lilac is one of stamina and beauty. It is a part of our lives and world heritage. Should I have omitted some elements of value, I beg your forgiveness; should I have favored too much the newest introductions, I ask your indulgence. This I have done to show you that the lilac is not a shrub of the past but is ever new and vibrant in its development and adaptations.

In my quest for knowledge and in working to improve the lilac over the past 40 years, I have made many wonderful horticultural friends. I wish I could mention each by name, but that would be another adventure book. I am, however, indebted to several whom I must recognize, for without their efforts this book would never have been written.

To Robert B. Clark, whom I met while he was a plant taxonomist for Monroe County Department of Parks and Highland Botanical Park, Rochester, New York, and who has been a loyal and wonderful friend, a guiding hand in my lilac work, a source of constant knowledge and prodding, I owe a deep personal grati-

tude. Much of this volume is from his knowledge and research, reworked to fit the present needs. Now retired, he lives at Birchwood Gardens, his delightful retreat at Meredith, New Hampshire.

To Donald Egolf of the U.S. National Arboretum for sharing his genius in hybridizing and knowledge of horticulture, especially in lilacs, I am ever grateful. I firmly believe he is one of the world's outstanding hybridizers and plantsmen. He has been to me a friend, teacher, and guide.

To Arch McKean of Grand Beach, Michigan, a treasured friend, lilac specialist, and promoter of lilacs and lilac parks, for his friendship and knowledge of lilacs over the past decade and for sharing his lilacs with others.

There are others who have shared much with me to whom I am likewise grateful:

To Clare Short of Elyria, Ohio, friend and traveling companion, who with his sister Mary (after whom I have named a lovely early hybrid lilac) have been wonderful friends who have shared their home and their hearts over many years.

To Winifred Karl "Marty" Martin, superintendent at Holden Arboretum, who is both friend and font of knowledge on how to do things in my own little garden and an expert on lilacs and rhododendrons, and to his wonderful family.

To Joseph Dvorak Jr., who through his drawings and skill has shared his fine perceptions on lilacs that are partially presented in this volume.

To Charles D. Holetich, arboriculturist at Royal Botanical Gardens, Hamilton, Ontario, Canada, for his knowledge of lilacs and for the use of the many colored pictures he has so skillfully taken at the Gardens. I am deeply grateful for his permission to use them.

To Isabel Zucker, friend, scholar, author, and professional photographer, who has encouraged me to complete this volume before my dotage sets in. A grand person and lady of horticulture and knowledge in whose honor an equally grand lilac will soon be named

To the many individuals who have loaned me their photographs, among them Charles Gauci and the Skinner family.

Again, I must give credit to Royal Botanical Gardens at Hamilton, Ontario, for a truly dedicated and magnificent staff who love the lilac and upon whom I have greatly depended: Leslie Laking, director emeritus; Charles Holetich, who has kept up a wonderful lilac collection; Freek Vrugtman, the International Lilac Registrar; and plant taxonomist James S. Pringle, who has untangled many lilac Gordian knots as to the species that are recorded in this book.

I am deeply indebted to the Arnold Arboretum of Harvard University for its preeminent place in lilacdom—its expeditions in China seeking new plant materials, its scholarly preservation and descriptions of lilac species, and especially for the use of its historic archives and the permission to reproduce several photographs from its files.

Dear to me also, because it is so near and so much a part of my horticultural experiences, is the Holden Arboretum at Kirtland, Ohio. To the former director, R. Henry Norweb Jr., and the Norweb Family of visionary horticulturists; to the superintendent, Marty Martin, and his staff; and to Peter "China" Bristol for his knowledge, I am ever grateful. I have sought to honor the great Holden-Norweb Family by naming some of my finest lilacs after them: *Syringa vulgaris* 'Emery Mae Norweb' to honor the grand lady of the family and *S. vulgaris* 'Albert F. Holden' to honor the founder of the arboretum. They are one of America's great horticultural families and deeply fond of the lilac.

Very specially I must thank my family who have encouraged me, been my companions on lilac conventions and trips, and worked so diligently in my garden to tend and prune when I was not able and after whom I sometimes name my best lilacs and who also share my love of lilacs from our childhood. A grateful "thanks for being you" to my sisters and in-laws, Marie and Ben Chaykowski, Mollie Ann and Pat Pesata, Elsie Lenore Meile, and my sister-in-law Pauline Fiala. They have been my finest critics and helpers filling the gardens of my lifetime with their love as the lilacs do with their fragrance and bloom.

To Karen Murray and Peter Murray of Ameri-Hort Research, who are continuing my work and through whose nursery my introductions are available.

REV. JOHN L. FIALA

The Author's Notes have been edited for corrections and other needed changes for this new edition.

Acknowledgments

IT WOULD BE an impossible task to list everyone who has had an input, directly or indirectly, in providing the information contained in this revised volume. It also is impossible to distinguish between material researched for the *International Register and Checklist of Cultivar Names in the Genus Syringa*, on which I have been working since 1976, and this volume.

I am grateful for assistance received from archivists, botanists, colleagues at Royal Botanical Gardens, Hamilton, Ontario, collectors of ephemera, computer whizzes, correspondents, curators, historians, horticultural writers, horticulturists, International Lilac Society members, librarians, lilac fanciers, lilac originators, nurserymen, taxonomists, typists, data compilers, and translators, literally from around the world. William Edwards, my computer guru, introduced me to the computer in 1994; his technical advice and assistance made it all possible. Since official retirement from my job as Curator of Collections in 1992, successive administrators at Royal Botanical Gardens, Hamilton, have continued to support my research to the best of their abilities.

Special thanks to my wife, Ina, who relentlessly processed my interlibrary loans while still at work, tolerated lilac talk at home and on travels, and read the manuscript draft from cover to cover, pointing out repetitions and asking for explanations.

Most species in this volume are presented with at least one color photograph, although some, because of their rarity, are difficult to find and to photograph. I am deeply indebted to many friends for these illustrations, including Bruce Peart and Margaret Walton, Želimir Borzan, Max Peterson, Tatiana Poliakova and Irena Semyonova of Moscow for photos of Russian cultivars, Margaret Pooler, Julie McIntosh Shapiro, Sarmite Strautina, and Carla Teune.

Thanks to the Arnold Arboretum, Jamaica Plains, Massachusetts, for pictures from its archives.

Royal Botanical Gardens, Hamilton, Ontario, Canada, permitted me to reproduce a number of photographs from the C. D. Holetich Lilac Slide Collection, one of the most extensive archival collections of photographic lilac documentation, created by Charles Dragutin Holetich during the 1970s and through the 1990s.

The International Lilac Society, publisher of *Lilacs*, permitted me to make extensive use of corrections, notes, and updates pertaining to the 1988 edition and written by me that appeared in the journal from 1996 to 2007.

Missouri Botanical Garden, St. Louis, publisher of *Flora of China*, the English translation of *Flora Reipublicae Popularis Sinicae*, permitted me to make extensive use of the section on *Syringa* in volume 15.

The American Horticultural Society, publisher of the *AHS Heat Zone Map*, permitted me to reprint their map.

Linda J. Willms of Timber Press, with professional skill, has streamlined the text for this new edition while preserving much of the "essential Fiala" in chapters four to seven. I thank her for accommodating my botanical-horticultural whims.

I have done my utmost in checking and verifying the facts, nonetheless I am painfully aware of the shortcomings that remain. In the process of preparing this second edition of Fiala's book, I continuously have been revising chapters written earlier. Keeping up with current developments has been difficult, but now that my job is complete, it is up to you, the reader, to keep up with the ever-changing trends and technology that will affect the garden lilacs of the future.

Data Entry, Manuscripts, and Published Articles!
The way to find errors is to send them off to
publishers and editors. These people find the first
level of errors, but not all errors.
Your friends, your enemies, and even you, will find
the rest of the errors once your article is published.

ROBIN LEECH
(quoted with permission)

CHAPTER ONE

Taxonomy and Technical Considerations of Lilac Species

Lilacs have a fascinating history. They also display sufficient variation to make them desirable garden plants. Their natural distribution is restricted to regions with a temperate climate, with winter temperatures dropping below freezing. Although the new flower buds are initiated and developed within weeks following the end of the blooming season, a period of cold weather is prerequisite for satisfactory bloom in the following spring. Lilacs perform best in regions that satisfy these climatic requirements.

All the wild lilacs have marvelous tales to tell of their native lands and the progress made in their development as garden shrubs. Some, such as the common lilac, *Syringa vulgaris*, are well known to almost every gardener and loved for their beauty, fragrance, range of color, size of floret, and dependability. Others, beautiful in their own way, are far less known, and most would not be recognized by many people as belonging to the genus *Syringa*. By careful examination and consideration of each plant, we shall seek, as we unfold the unique history of lilacs, to appreciate the beauty they bring to gardens throughout the world. By understanding them, knowing them well, and seeing their ease of culture, we shall find them both a garden companion and a mainstay of beauty in our landscapes.

The botanical name *Syringa* derives from the Greek word *syrinx* meaning hollow stem and has given rise to common names such as *sering* in Dutch, *syrén* in Danish, *syrin* in Norwegian, *syren* in Swedish, *siren'* in Russian, *šeřik* in Czech, and *ceriņi* in Latvian. In Greek legend the nymph Syrinx was pursued by the god Pan and turned into a hollow reed from which Pan made his first flute, or pan-pipe.

One of the first common names for lilac in English was pipe tree (a name also used for *Philadelphus coronarius*, sweet mock orange) or blow stem. Ancient Greek doctors reportedly used lilac stems to inject medicines into their patients or to bleed them, and according to English botanist John C. Loudon (1783–1843), the best Turkish pipes were made from the straight stems of lilac. These early common names did not prevail for so lovely a shrub. Today it is known commonly by some form of the word *lilac*, perhaps from the Persian *lilak* or *lilaf* meaning bluish: *lilas* in French, *der Flieder* in German, *lilza* in Portuguese, and *lila* in Spanish. In Old English it was called *laylock*, *lilack*, or *lilock*.

Without names the world would be a most confusing place. Names are important for communication in daily life. By a name we are immediately aware that we mean a particular plant with all its characteristics. Names, or epithets, indicate the species or cultivar to which we wish to refer. A species (plural, also species) is the basic category in the taxonomic hierarchy; it is a native or wild population.

Species Plantarum, published in 1753 by the great Swedish botanist Carl Linnaeus (1707–1779), is the starting point of present-day nomenclature of vascular plants. It is in this work that the binomial *Syringa vulgaris* appeared for the first time; we add to it "L." or "Linnaeus," indicating that it was Carl Linnaeus who published this unique combination of genus epithet (*Syringa*) and species epithet (*vulgaris*) for the common lilac. Pre-Linnaean botanists used descriptive phrases when naming species, such as *Syringa caerulea lusitanica sive lilac Mathioli* (Morin 1621) or *Lilac Mathioli sive Syringa flore caeruleo* (Parkinson 1640), both referring to what is known today as the common lilac. In *Species Plantarum* Linnaeus used the descriptive phrase *Syringa foliis ovato cordatis*, adding *vulgaris* in the margin conceivably as a locating aid (*Species Plantarum* has an *Index Generum*, which refers the reader to the page for the genus). And

Opposite: *Syringa vulgaris* 'Liega'. S. Strautina

Syringa vulgaris habitat in Romania. Charles Holetich

so binomial nomenclature came into being; its simplicity appealed to other botanists, and it has been the convention since.

While scholars have and will continue to differ about where to place lilacs taxonomically, for simplicity we shall follow the widely accepted classification by Brummit (1992): division Spermatophyta, subdivision Magnoliophytina (formerly known as Angiospermae), class Magnoliopsida (formerly known as Dicotyledoneae), subclass Asteridae, order Scrophulariales, family Oleaceae (olive), subfamily Oleoideae, genus *Syringa*.

The Oleaceae, with about 22 genera and 500 species of woody plants, is cosmopolitan in its distribution and of economic importance. It comprises the subfamily Jasminoideae with the three genera *Jasminum* (jasmine), *Mendora*, and *Nyctanthes*, and the subfamily Oleoideae with the remaining genera, including *Olea* (olive), *Fraxinus* (ash), *Chionanthus* (fringe tree), *Osmanthus* (fragrant olive), *Ligustrum* (privet), *Forsythia* (golden bell), and *Syringa* (lilac). Of economic importance are olive, fragrant olive, jas-

mine, ash, and ornamentals including *Abeliophyllum* (white forsythia), *Chionanthus* (fringe tree), *Fontanesia*, *Forsythia* (golden bell), *Fraxinus* (ash), *Jasminum* (jasmine), *Ligustrum* (privet), *Osmanthus* (fragrant olive), *Phillyrea* (mock privet), and *Syringa* (lilac).

Members of the Oleaceae are distinguished by their twos: two-merous flowers, two anthers with two cells back to back, a two-loculed superior ovary, generally with two ovules per locule. Fiala (1988) quoted Owen Rogers, who in speaking of the Oleaceae, cautioned:

While the 2-s [*sic*] hold the family together, there are serious questions as to whether the whole assemblage is a natural evolutionary grouping. Should *Fraxinus* be included in the family at all? Suffice it to mention the problem as the first of several areas needing further work and careful study in any consideration of the family.

Classifications of living organisms are based on current knowledge and may change over the years because they reflect the opinion of the systematists who review the known facts. For instance, research by Harvard University student Benjamin Goldman-Huertas (2005) provides evidence for close affinity between the genera *Ligustrum* and *Syringa*; future taxonomists may incorporate the privets in the lilacs. A summary of classification, such as the one presented later in this chapter, is the taxonomist's shorthand for showing relationships. Each combination of botanical name (the part in Latin, printed in *italic*) and author name (the often abbreviated name of the botanist associated) is unique and can be traced in the botanical literature of the past 250 years. The *International Code of Botanical Nomenclature* (Greuter et al. 2000) provides the rules by which plants are named and classified.

James S. Pringle (1997), taxonomist at Royal Botanical Gardens, Hamilton, Ontario, Canada, provides a clear and concise explanation of the process of taxonomic research (reprinted here with permission):

The new classification summarized here is not "official" in the sense of having been designated the only legitimate classification by a vote or similar action at an International Botanical Congress. Contrary to what some people believe, no actions are taken at such conventions nor do the rules of botanical nomenclature contain provisions that give official status to some classification and prohibit the use of others. With flowering plants, there are so many families, genera, and species and such diversity in evolutionary patterns that no one plant taxonomist would feel qualified to choose among competing proposals affecting the classification of families or genera outside those with which he or she had the opportunity to become especially familiar. Strictly nomenclatural matters, related to the validity or priority of publication, are usually unequivocally dealt with by the rules of nomenclature, and seldom lead to differences of opinion. Matters of classification, in contrast, usually become less controversial as more information becomes available, but variation in nature is so complex that different researchers on the same genus may hold different opinions as to the preferable classification even when they have access to the same information.

Taxonomic papers in scholarly journals are subject to peer review, which means that qualified persons, usually knowledgeable about the genus or family that is the subject of the paper, review the manuscript before it is accepted for publication. The process does not deprive anyone of freedom of the press, but a paper that was greatly at variance with "mainstream" taxonomic concepts would not likely be accepted by such journals as *Novon* (as was one of the papers cited below), this being a relatively prestigious journal within its special field.

It will generally be acknowledged among taxonomists, moreover, that Chang, Green, and their associates have conducted more extensive studies of the systematics of *Syringa* at the species level than have any of their contemporaries, and that they have done so with significantly more specimens representing the genus than were available to their predecessors, and in cases of the Chinese botanists, with more experience with *Syringa* in the field. Also, Chang Mei-Chen was selected to be the senior author of the treatment of *Syringa* in the *Flora Reipublicae Popularis Sinicae* (Flora of the People's Republic of China), and Peter S. Green was selected as the co-author of *Syringa* for

Syringa vulgaris growing in limestone rocks in Romania. Želimir Borzan

the revised, English-language version entitled *Flora of China*. He was also selected to be the author of the treatment of *Syringa* in a forthcoming volume of the *European Garden Flora*, the successive volumes of which immediately become very useful references, routinely consulted for the identification and nomenclature. Selection for authorship by the editorial committees of such works implies recognition as a leading authority on a genus by one's fellow plant taxonomists.

Also, although the *International Code of Botanical Nomenclature* does not make Chang and Green's classification the only one that may legitimately be followed, theirs is likely to become widely regarded as "standard." Such encyclopedic references as the *Flora of China* and the *European Garden Flora* tend to be widely followed, not only because of the reputation of the respective authors but also because of the convenience of following well-known, widely available references.

Basic research on interspecific relationships of *Syringa* is bound to continue as more accurate techniques, more sophisticated equipment, and plants of the lesser-known lilac species become available to our researchers.

Summary of Classification of the Genus *Syringa*

The cultivated species of *Syringa*, their subspecies (abbreviated subsp.), botanical varieties (var.), and validly named interspecific hybrids, are listed here by subgenus and series following Pringle's (1983a, 1990, 1997) classification, but giving species status to *S. pekinensis*, based on convincing evidence provided by Li et al. (2002). Validly named interspecific hybrids are technically referred to as nothospecies; *nothos*, borrowed from the Greek, means hybrid. Some of the nothospecies were originally thought to be species, hence the notation "as a species" in some of the following citations.

Subgenus *Ligustrina* (Ruprecht) K. Koch
   S. reticulata (Blume) H. Hara
      subsp. *reticulata*

      subsp. *amurensis* (Ruprecht) P. S. Green & M.-C. Chang
   S. pekinensis Ruprecht
Subgenus *Syringa*
  Series *Syringa*
   S. vulgaris L.
   S. oblata Lindley
      subsp. *oblata*
      subsp. *dilatata* (Nakai) P. S. Green & M.-C. Chang
   S. protolaciniata P. S. Green & M.-C. Chang
   S. afghanica C. K. Schneider
   S. ×chinensis Schmidt ex Willdenow (as a species; *S. protolaciniata* × *S. vulgaris*)
   S. ×hyacinthiflora (Lemoine) Rehder (*S. oblata* × *S. vulgaris*)
   S. ×laciniata Miller (as a species; *S. protolaciniata* × ?)
   S. ×persica L. (as a species; hybrid of uncertain parentage)
  Series *Pinnatifoliae* Rehder
   S. pinnatifolia Hemsley
  Interseries hybrid
   S. ×diversifolia Rehder (*S. oblata* × *S. pinnatifolia*)
  Series *Pubescentes* (C. K. Schneider) Lingelsheim
   S. pubescens Turczaninov
      subsp. *pubescens*
      subsp. *patula* (Palibin) M.-C. Chang & X.-L. Chen
      subsp. *julianae* (C. K. Schneider) M.-C. Chang & X.-L. Chen
      subsp. *microphylla* (Diels) M.-C. Chang & X.-L. Chen
        var. *microphylla*
        var. *potaninii* (C. K. Schneider) P. S. Green & M.-C. Chang
        var. *flavanthera* (X.-L. Chen) M.-C. Chang
   S. meyeri C. K. Schneider
      var. *meyeri*
      var. *spontanea* M.-C. Chang
   S. mairei (H. Léveillé) Rehder
   S. pinetorum W. W. Smith
   S. wardii W. W. Smith
  Series *Villosae* C. K. Schneider
   S. villosa Vahl
   S. emodi Wallich ex Royle

S. wolfii C. K. Schneider

S. josikaea J. Jacquin ex H. G. L. Reichenbach

S. komarowii C. K. Schneider

   subsp. *komarowii*

   subsp. *reflexa* (C. K. Schneider) P. S. Green &
     M.-C. Chang

S. tomentella Bureau & Franchet

S. sweginzowii Koehne & Lingelsheim

S. yunnanensis Franchet

S. tibetica P.-Y. Bai

S. ×henryi C. K. Schneider (*S. josikaea × S.
   villosa*)

S. ×josiflexa I. Preston ex J. S. Pringle (*S. josikaea
   × S. komarowii*)

S. ×nanceiana McKelvey (*S. ×henryi × S.
   sweginzowii*)

S. ×prestoniae McKelvey (*S. komarowii × S.
   villosa*)

S. ×swegiflexa hort. Hesse ex J. S. Pringle (*S.
   komarowii × S. sweginzowii*)

Syringa Villosae Group

It should be noted that certain taxa in this list, such as *Syringa afghanica*, *S. pinetorum*, *S. pubescens* subsp. *microphylla* var. *flavanthera*, and *S. tibetica*, are not known to be in cultivation, or at least not known to be in cultivation outside of China. Plants cultivated under some of these names or nomenclatural synonyms thereof in Europe and North America are not true to name and have been misidentified (Pringle 1978d, Vrugtman 2004c).

Villosae Group is based on the botanical series *Villosae* C. K. Schneider. *Syringa ×josiflexa* 'Royalty' is the designated nomenclatural standard for this group. The suggested way of writing cultivar names is *Genus* (Group) 'Cultivar', for example, *Syringa* (Villosae Group) 'Royalty'. Users have the choice of leaving out the group name, for example, *Syringa* 'Royalty' (Hoffman 2003, 2004; Vrugtman 2004a). Villosae Group includes all cultivars of interspecies hybrid origin within the series *Villosae*:

S. ×henryi × S. sweginzowii (*S. ×nanceiana*)

S. ×henryi × S. tomentella

S. josikaea × S. reflexa (*S. ×josiflexa*)

S. josikaea × S. villosa (*S. ×henryi*)

S. komarowii subsp. *reflexa × S. sweginzowii* (*S.
   ×swegiflexa*)

S. komarowii subsp. *reflexa × S. villosa* (*S. ×prestoniae*)

(*S. komarowii × S. wolfii*) × (*S. sweginzowii × S.
   yunnanensis*)

(*S. komarowii × S. wolfii*) × (*S. wolfii × S. yunnanensis*)

S. ×prestoniae × S. tomentella

S. sweginzowii × S. tomentella

S. sweginzowii × S. villosa

S. tomentella × S. yunnanensis

S. wolfii × S. yunnanensis

As cultivated ornamentals, lilacs have a short history. The common lilac, *Syringa vulgaris*, appears to have been known and cherished for more than 500 years; the Persian lilac, *S. ×persica*, a hybrid of uncertain parentage, has been around for nearly 400 years; and *S. ×chinensis*, a natural hybrid between *S. protolaciniata* and *S. vulgaris*, was discovered in the botanical garden at Rouen, France, in 1777. The discovery, naming, description, and introduction of the remaining known species, subspecies, and botanical varieties are spread quite evenly over the 19th and 20th centuries. As plant exploration continues, we may not be adding new species to our list; we may, however, broaden the gene pool available for future breeding and selecting work on lilacs.

The confusion caused by the lack of accurate record keeping or the subsequent loss of archival records is regrettable. Besides being of interest to the horticultural taxonomist, lilac fancier, and historian, the information on parentage of cultivars is of interest to future plant breeders—what has worked or not worked, what combinations have resulted in superior cultivars, and what combinations appear to be dead-ends. It has become increasingly difficult to ascertain the parentage used in developing modern lilac cultivars, unless careful and accurate records have been kept. For example, among *Syringa vulgaris* hybrids we now have early hybrids using (*S. vulgaris × S. oblata* subsp. *oblata*) × *S. oblata* subsp. *dilatata*. For practical purposes some cultivars of *S. ×hyacinthiflora* have become indistinguishable from either *S. vulgaris* or *S. oblata* (Pringle 1996). Among the late-blooming cultivars are multiple hybrids involving a complex cross of four, five, and even six species or subspecies, especially in the series *Villosae*. As a result the key characteristics that link cultivars to their parentage become more and more obscure. To overcome this dilemma, Marco Hoffman proposed establishment of the Villosae Group to encompass cultivars of interspecific hybrids in the series *Villosae*.

In chapters two and three all the species, subspecies, and varietal forms of extant lilacs are discussed. Discussion of *Syringa vulgaris*, its hybrids, and some of its nearly 2000 cultivars follows in chapter four.

Alphabetical Checklist of Botanical Taxa of Lilacs

The following alphabetical checklist is not intended to be a complete inventory of all taxa in the genus *Syringa*, nor does occurrence of a name indicate that it is a currently accepted one in accordance with the *International Code of Botanical Nomenclature* or that plants of it are known in cultivation. This record is meant to provide a link between names that are found in older botanical and horticultural literature and nursery catalogs and the valid names used in the summary of classification presented earlier in this chapter (Pringle 1978d):

Syringa L.
adamiana I. B. Balfour & W. W. Smith, included in *S. tomentella* Bureau & Franchet
affinis L. Henry, included in *S. oblata* subsp. *oblata*; see also *S. oblata* var. *alba* hort. ex Rehder
afghanica C. K. Schneider, synonym *S. persica* Brandis, not L.; Schneider (1903), McKelvey (1928: 428)
amurensis Ruprecht, see *S. reticulata* subsp. *amurensis* (Ruprecht) P. S. Green & M.-C. Chang
amurensis var. *japonica* (Maximowicz) Franchet & Savatier, equivalent to *S. reticulata* subsp. *reticulata*
amurensis var. *major* hort., name not validly published
amurensis var. *rotundifolia* Lingelsheim, included in *S. reticulata* subsp. *amurensis* (Ruprecht) P. S. Green & M.-C. Chang
buxifolia Nakai, included in *S. protolaciniata* P. S. Green & M.-C. Chang; Nakai (1918: 131), P. S. Green (1989b: 121; 1995: 636); a name rejected in favor of a conserved name (status proposed)

×*chinensis* Schmidt ex Willdenow (as a species), *S. protolaciniata* × *S. vulgaris*; many synonyms, see Willdenow (1796), McKelvey (1928: 401–412)
×*chinensis* var. *alba* (Kirchner) Rehder, included in *S.* 'Correlata', synonym *S.* +*correlata* A. Braun (as a species)
×*chinensis* nothof. *bicolor* (Lemoine) Jäger; several synonyms, see Lemoine (1853), Jäger (1865: 528), McKelvey (1928: 418)
×*chinensis* nothof. *duplex* (Lemoine) Rehder; several synonyms, see Lemoine (1896), Rehder (1899), McKelvey (1928: 419–420)
chuanxiensis S.-Z. Qu & X.-L. Chen, included in *S. mairei* (H. Léveillé) Rehder; Qu and Chen (1989)
×*clarkiana* J. L. Fiala, *S. komarowii* × *S. wolfii*; Fiala (1988: 3, 7, 81), name not validly published
+*correlata* A. Braun (as a species), see *S.* 'Correlata'
debelderorum R. B. Clark & J. L. Fiala, included in *S. pubescens* subsp. *patula* (Palibin) M.-C. Chang & X.-L. Chen; Fiala (1988: 3, 6, 48), as *S. debelderi*; P. S. Green (1989a)
dilatata Nakai, see *S. oblata* subsp. *dilatata* (Nakai) P. S. Green & M.-C. Chang
×*diversifolia* Rehder, *S. oblata* × *S. pinnatifolia*; Anderson and Rehder (1935: 362), Pringle (1981: 101–103)
dubia Persoon, included in *S.* ×*chinensis* Schmidt ex Willdenow
emodi Wallich ex Royle; many synonyms, see Royle (1839), McKelvey (1928: 17), Pringle (1978a: 93–94)
emodi rosea Cornu, included in *S. villosa* Vahl; Cornu (1888), Rehder (1949b: 565)
fauriei H. Léveillé, questionably distinct from *S. reticulata* subsp. *amurensis* (Ruprecht) P. S. Green & M.-C. Chang; Léveillé (1910), McKelvey (1928: 507–508), Pringle (1990: 78; 1997: 26)
×*fialiana* R. B. Clark, (*S. sweginzowii* × *S. tomentella*) × *S. wolfii*; Fiala (1988: 3, 7), name not validly published
filicifolia Bean, included in *S.* ×*laciniata* Miller
formosissima Nakai, included in *S. wolfii* C. K. Schneider
giraldiana C. K. Schneider, included in *S. pubescens* subsp. *microphylla* (Diels) M.-C. Chang & X.-L. Chen; Diels (1901), McKelvey (1928: 129), Chang and Chen (1990: 34)

giraldii Sprenger ex Lemoine, included in *S. oblata* subsp. *oblata* 'Giraldii'

×*henryi* C. K. Schneider, *S. josikaea* × *S. villosa*; many synonyms, see Schneider (1910: 81), McKelvey (1928: 99–100)

×*heterophylla* Skinner, (*S. oblata* subsp. *dilatata* × *S. vulgaris*) × *S. pinnatifolia*; Wister (1953: 31), Pringle (1981: 103); name not validly published; probably extinct

hirsuta Nakai, included in *S. wolfii* C. K. Schneider

hupehensis, see *S. oblata* var. *hupehensis* Pampanini

×*hyacinthiflora* (Lemoine) Rehder, *S. oblata* × *S. vulgaris*; many synonyms, see McKelvey (1928: 193), Rehder (1899)

hybrida hort., included in *S.* ×*chinensis* Schmidt ex Willdenow (as a species)

hybrida hort. ex Bean, included in *S.* ×*henryi* C. K. Schneider

×*hybrida* W. R. Prince, included in *S.* ×*chinensis* Schmidt ex Willdenow

japonica (Maximowicz) Decaisne, equivalent to *S. reticulata* subsp. *reticulata*

×*josiflexa* I. Preston ex J. S. Pringle, *S. josikaea* × *S. komarowii*; Pringle (1978a)

josikaea J. Jacquin ex H. G. L. Reichenbach; many synonyms, see Reichenbach (1830), McKelvey (1928: 33–57)

julianae C. K. Schneider, see *S. pubescens* subsp. *julianae* (C. K. Schneider) M.-C. Chang & X.-L. Chen

koehneana C. K. Schneider, included in *S. pubescens* subsp. *patula* (Palibin) M.-C. Chang & X.-L. Chen

komarowii C. K. Schneider; several synonyms, see Schneider (1910: 82), McKelvey (1928: 75–76)

komarowii subsp. *komarowii*; synonyms *S. glabra* (C. K. Schneider) Lingelsheim, *S. sargentiana* C. K. Schneider; Chang and Green (1996a: 282)

komarowii subsp. *reflexa* (C. K. Schneider) P. S. Green & M.-C. Chang, synonym *S. reflexa* C. K. Schneider; Schneider (1910: 82), McKelvey (1928: 71–72), Chang and Chen (1990), Green and Chang (1995), Chang and Green (1996a: 282)

×*laciniata* Miller (as a species), *S. protolaciniata* × *S.* ?; several synonyms, see Miller (1768), McKelvey (1928: 450–463), Rehder (1945: 74), P. S. Green (1989b)

×*lamartina* Moldenke, included in *S.* ×*hyacinthiflora* (Lemoine) Rehder, *S. oblata* subsp. *oblata* × *S. vulgaris*; Moldenke (1956), P. S. Green (1984a)

×*lemoineiana* (Lemoine) J. L. Fiala, *S. sweginzowii* × *S. tomentella*; Fiala (1988: 3, 7); see also *S.* ×*swegitella* J. L. Fiala; name not validly published

luminifera hort. (?)

mairei (H. Léveillé) Rehder; synonyms *S. chuanxiensis* S.-Z. Qu & X.-L. Chen, *S. rugulosa* McKelvey; Léveillé (1916), McKelvey (1925, 1934), Green and Chang (1995), Chang and Green (1996a: 284)

meyeri C. K. Schneider; Schneider in Sargent (1911–1917, 1: 301), McKelvey (1928: 169)

meyeri var. *meyeri*; Chang and Green (1996a: 284)

meyeri var. *spontanea* M.-C. Chang; Chang and Chen (1990: 33), Chang and Green (1996a: 284)

microphylla Diels, see *S. pubescens* subsp. *microphylla* (Diels) M.-C. Chang & X.-L. Chen

microphylla var. *minor*, included in *S. meyeri* var. *meyeri* 'Palibin'; Skinner (1966: 155), P. S. Green (1979), Pringle (1979)

×*nanceiana* McKelvey, *S.* ×*henryi* × *S. sweginzowii*; McKelvey (1928: 107–108)

oblata Lindley; many synonyms, see Lindley (1859), McKelvey (1928: 175–181)

oblata subsp. *oblata*; synonyms *S. giraldii* Sprenger ex Lemoine, *S. oblata* var. *giraldii* (Sprenger ex Lemoine) Rehder, *S. oblata* var. *hupehensis* Pampanini; P. S. Green (1984a, 1984b), Chang and Green (1996a: 285)

oblata var. *affinis* (L. Henry) Lingelsheim, included in *S. oblata* subsp. *oblata*; McKelvey (1928: 188–192), P. S. Green (1984a)

oblata var. *alba* hort. ex Rehder, included in *S. oblata* subsp. *oblata*; many synonyms, see Rehder (1902), McKelvey (1928: 188–192), P. S. Green (1984a)

oblata subsp. *dilatata* (Nakai) P. S. Green & M.-C. Chang; many synonyms, see Nakai (1918), Rehder (1926), McKelvey (1928: 186–188), Green and Chang (1995: 329), Chang and Green (1996a: 285)

oblata subsp. *dilatata* f. *pendula* Rehder; Rehder (1945: 77)

oblata var. *donaldii* R. B. Clark & J. L. Fiala; Fiala (1988: 3, 6, 61, 62); name not validly published

oblata var. *giraldii* (Sprenger ex Lemoine) Rehder, included in *S. oblata* subsp. *oblata*; Chang and Green (1996a: 285) *oblata* var. *hupehensis* Pampanini, included in *S. oblata* subsp. *oblata*; Pampanini (1910), McKelvey (1928: 191–192), P. S. Green (1984a)

palibiniana Nakai, included in *S. pubescens* subsp. *patula* (Palibin) M.-C. Chang & X.-L. Chen; Chang and Green (1996a: 283)

palibiniana var. *kamibayashii* Nakai; Nakai (1922)

patula (Palibin) Nakai, see *S. pubescens* subsp. *patula* (Palibin) M.-C. Chang & X.-L. Chen; Chang and Green (1996a: 283)

pekinensis Ruprecht; Ruprecht (1857); see also Li et al. (2002); synonym *S. reticulata* subsp. *pekinensis* (Ruprecht) P. S. Green & M.-C. Chang; Green and Chang (1995: 330)

persica Brandis, not L., included in *S. afghanica* C. K. Schneider; Brandis (1874: 306), McKelvey (1928: 442)

×*persica* L., hybrid of unknown parentage; many synonyms, see Linnaeus (1753), McKelvey (1928: 434–450)

×*persica* var. *laciniata* (Miller) Weston, see *S.* ×*laciniata* Miller

pinetorum W. W. Smith; W. W. Smith (1916); McKelvey (1928: 149–150)

pinnatifolia Hemsley; Hemsley (1906), McKelvey (1928: 469)

pinnatifolia var. *alashanensis* Y.-C. Ma & S.-Q. Zhou, included in *S. pinnatifolia* Hemsley; Ma and Zhou (1981), Chang and Chen (1990), Chang and Green (1996a: 286)

potaninii C. K. Schneider, see *S. pubescens* [subsp. *microphylla*] var. *potaninii* (C. K. Schneider) P. S. Green & M.-C. Chang

×*prestoniae* McKelvey, *S. komarowii* × *S. villosa*; McKelvey (1927; 1928: 109)

×*pringleiana* J. L. Fiala, *S. komarowii* × *S. yunnanensis*; Fiala (1988: 3, 7, 73), name not validly published

protolaciniata P. S. Green & M.-C. Chang; synonym *S. buxifolia* Nakai; Nakai (1918), P. S. Green (1989b, 1995)

pteridifolia K. Koch, included in *S.* ×*laciniata* Miller

pubescens Turczaninov; many synonyms, see Turczaninov (1840), McKelvey (1928: 159–168)

pubescens subsp. *pubescens*; synonym *S. wulingensis* B. V. Skvortsov & W. Wang; Chang and Qu (1992),

Green & Chang (1995: 331), Chang and Green (1996a: 283)

pubescens subsp. *julianae* (C. K. Schneider) M.-C. Chang & X.-L. Chen; synonym *S. julianae* C. K. Schneider; see also Schneider (1907–1912, 2: 777, fig. 488 v–x), McKelvey (1928: 131–132), Chang and Chen (1990: 34), Green and Chang (1995: 331)

pubescens subsp. *microphylla* (Diels) M.-C. Chang & X.-L. Chen; synonym *S. microphylla* Diels; see also Diels (1901), McKelvey (1928: 151–152), Chang and Chen (1990: 34), Green and Chang (1995: 331), Chang and Green (1996a: 284)

pubescens [subsp. *microphylla*] var. *microphylla*; Chang and Qu (1992), Green and Chang (1995: 331), Chang and Green (1996a: 284)

pubescens [subsp. *microphylla*] var. *flavanthera* (X.-L. Chen) M.-C. Chang; Chang and Green (1996a: 284)

pubescens [subsp. *microphylla*] var. *potaninii* (C. K. Schneider) P. S. Green & M.-C. Chang; Schneider (1910: 80), McKelvey (1928: 144), Green and Chang (1995: 332), Chang and Green (1996a: 284)

pubescens subsp. *patula* (Palibin) M.-C. Chang & X.-L. Chen; many synonyms: *S. patula* Palibin, *S. palibiniana* Nakai, *S. velutina* V. L. Komarov; see also under *S. velutina* in McKelvey (1928: 135); Komarov (1900), Nakai (1926), Chang and Chen (1990: 34), Green and Chang (1995: 331), Chang and Green (1996a: 283)

×*quatrobrida* J. L. Fiala, (*S. sweginzowii* × *S. tomentella*) × (*S. komarowii* × *S. wolfii*); Fiala (1988: 3, 7, 124), name not validly published

reflexa C. K. Schneider, see *S. komarowii* subsp. *reflexa* (C. K. Schneider) P. S. Green & M.-C. Chang; Green and Chang (1995: 329)

rehderiana C. K. Schneider, included in *S. tomentella* Bureau & Franchet

reticulata (Blume) H. Hara; synonym *S. amurensis* var. *japonica* (Maximowicz) Franchet & Savatier; McKelvey (1928: 483–484), Hara (1941), Pringle (1983c)

reticulata subsp. *reticulata*; Green and Chang (1995: 330), Chang and Green (1996a: 286)

reticulata subsp. *amurensis* (Ruprecht) P. S. Green & M.-C. Chang; synonyms *S. amurensis* Ruprecht, *S. reticulata* var. *mandshurica* (Maximowicz) H.

Hara, and others; Ruprecht (1857), Green and
Chang (1995: 329), Chang and Green (1996a: 286)

reticulata var. *mandshurica* (Maximowicz) H. Hara,
included in *S. reticulata* subsp. *amurensis*
(Ruprecht) P. S. Green & M.-C. Chang

reticulata subsp. *pekinensis* (Ruprecht) P. S. Green &
M.-C. Chang; see *S. pekinensis* Ruprecht; Green
and Chang (1995: 330), Chang and Green (1996a:
286)

rhodopea Velenovský, included in *S. vulgaris* L.

robusta Nakai, included in *S. wolfii* C. K. Schneider

rothomagensis (Renault) Mordant, included in *S.*
×*chinensis* Schmidt ex Willdenow; Mordant de
Launey (1805)

rugulosa McKelvey, included in *S. mairei* (H.
Léveillé) Rehder

sargentiana C. K. Schneider, included in *S.*
komarowii subsp. *komarowii*

sempervirens Franchet, synonym *Ligustrum semper-*
virens (Franchet) Lingelsheim

siberica hort., included in *S. reticulata* subsp. *amuren-*
sis (Ruprecht) P. S. Green & M.-C. Chang

×*sinensis* hort., see *S.* ×*chinensis* Schmidt ex
Willdenow

×*skinneri* hort., *S. pubescens* subsp. *patula* × *S. pubes-*
cens subsp. *pubescens*; Skinner's Nursery (1947),
Skinner (1966: 108); name not validly published;
in cultivation as *S. pubescens* 'Skinneri'

suspensa Thunberg, synonym *Forsythia suspensa*
(Thunberg) Vahl

×*swegiflexa* hort. Hesse ex J. S. Pringle, *S. komarowii*
× *S. sweginzowii*; Hesse (1935), Wister (1942: 59;
1953: 42), Pringle (1978a: 97–100, 102–103)

×*sweginbretta* hort., formerly applied to *S. swegin-*
zowii × *S. villosa*; name not validly published

sweginzowii Koehne & Lingelsheim; several synonyms, see McKelvey (1928: 123–124); includes *S.*
tigerstedtii; Koehne and Lingelsheim (1910)

×*swegitella* J. L. Fiala, *S. sweginzowii* × *S. tomentella*;
Fiala (1988: 224), name not validly published; see
also *S.* ×*lemoineiana* (Lemoine) J. L. Fiala

tetanoloba C. K. Schneider, included in *S. sweginzowii*
Koehne & Lingelsheim

tibetica P.-Y. Bai; Bai (1979: 151)

tigerstedtii H. K. A. Smith, included in *S. sweginzowii*
Koehne & Lingelsheim; H. K. A. Smith (1948),

Boom (1957), Pringle (1978b), Chang and Green
(1996a: 283)

tomentella Bureau & Franchet; many synonyms, see
Bureau and Franchet (1891), McKelvey (1928: 1
15–121)

×*tribrida* J. L. Fiala, (*S. sweginzowii* × *S. tomentella*)
× *S. komarowii*; Fiala (1988: 3, 7, 124), name not
validly published

trichophylla T. Tang, included in *S. pubescens* subsp.
microphylla (Diels) M.-C. Chang & X.-L. Chen

×*varina* Dumont de Courset, included in *S.* ×*chinen-*
sis Schmidt ex Willdenow

velutina V. L. Komarov, included in *S. pubescens*
subsp. *patula* (Palibin) M.-C. Chang & X.-L. Chen

verrucosa C. K. Schneider, included in *S. pubescens*
subsp. *julianae* (C. K. Schneider) M.-C. Chang &
X.-L. Chen

villosa Vahl; synonym *S. bretschneideri* Lemoine; see
also Vahl (1804–1805), McKelvey (1928: 81–96)

vulgaris L.; many synonyms, see Linnaeus (1753: 9),
McKelvey (1928: 203–205)

vulgaris var. *alba* Weston; many synonyms, see
Weston (1770), McKelvey (1928: 234–236)

vulgaris var. *coerulea* Weston, included in *S. vulgaris* L.

vulgaris var. *macrantha* Borbás; Borbás (1882)

vulgaris var. *pulchella* Velenovský; synonyms *S.*
pulchella Velenovský, *S. rhodopea* Velenovský;
Velenovský (1894), McKelvey (1928: 216–217)

vulgaris var. *purpurea* Weston; many synonyms, see
Weston (1770), McKelvey (1928: 239–246)

vulgaris var. *transsilvanica* Schur; Schur (1866),
McKelvey (1928: 216)

wardii W. W. Smith; W. W. Smith (1916a), McKelvey
(1928: 173)

wilsonii C. K. Schneider, see *S. tomentella* Bureau &
Franchet

wolfii C. K. Schneider; many synonyms, see Chang
and Green (1996a: 283), Schneider (1910: 81),
McKelvey (1928: 63–69)

wolfii var. *hirsuta* (C. K. Schneider) Hatusima,
included in Chang and Green (1996a: 283),
Hatusima (1938: 103), Wister (1942: 60)

wulingensis B. V. Skvortsov & W. Wang; Skvortsov
and Wang (1958); included in *S. pubescens* subsp.
pubescens

yunnanensis Franchet; Franchet (1891), McKelvey
(1928: 29–32)

On Naming and Registering New Lilac Cultivars

The genus *Syringa* is neither the largest nor the smallest in terms of the number of species, subspecies, and botanical varieties, but from these species many cultivars have been derived through hybridization, mutation, and selection. A cultivar, as defined in article 2.2 of the *International Code of Nomenclature for Cultivated Plants* (*ICNCP*), is "an assemblage of plants that has been selected for a particular attribute or combination of attributes and that is clearly distinct, uniform and stable in these characteristics and that when propagated by appropriate means, retains those characteristics" (Brickell et al. 2004).

A cross between differing plants is called a hybrid. This term sometimes refers to a cross between two species, but it may also refer to more complex crosses where, for instance, a hybrid is backcrossed to one of its parents or crossed with a third species. Some cultivars are the result of crosses involving several species. As a consequence some authors refer to such multispecies cultivars as tribrids, quatrobrids, quintobrids, sextobrids, septobrids, octobrids, and so on, designating succinctly the number of parent species that have contributed in a given hybrid.

A cross between species may also be referred to as a nothospecies. Such crosses are either given specific epithets with the hybrid symbol (multiplication sign) prefixed, such as in *Syringa* ×*chinensis*, or are identified by a hybrid formula, for example, *S. protolaciniata* × *S. vulgaris*. To be accepted by the botanical community, new names for nothospecies must be effectively and validly published according to the provisions of the *International Code of Botanical Nomenclature* (see Pringle 1984).

From the common lilac, *Syringa vulgaris*, nearly 2000 named cultivars have been derived, most of them during the 20th century. Each cultivar is presumed distinct from all others, either in flower color, floret form, growth habit, or some other character that has been singled out as a special quality worthy of being named and recognized. Needless to say, many cultivars are so similar they should never have been named. Some even appear inferior to the wild form of the species.

At first these differences were mostly in flower color, and the earliest named lilacs were known simply by color designations such as Blue Lilac, White Lilac, or Purple Lilac. Then special qualities began to appear and be recognized, for example, *Syringa vulgaris* 'Alba Grandiflora' (white large-flowered), and so on. As new cultivars proliferated with increased refinement, lilacs began to be named for famous people ('Duc de Massa', 'Léopold III', 'Princesse Clémentine'), friends and family members ('Elsie Lenore', 'Marie Rogers', 'Mme Lemoine'), special events ('Bright Centennial', 'Russkiĭ Suvenir'), places ('Belorusskie Zori', 'City of Gresham', 'Krasnaya Moskva', 'Rochester'), or some natural resemblance ('Snowdrift', 'Sovetskaya Arktika', 'Sunset').

Today, cultivar names of lilacs are "established" and "accepted" in accordance with the *ICNCP* (Brickell et al. 2004). The starting point for cultivar and group names in *Syringa* is Susan D. McKelvey's *The Lilac: A Monograph* published in 1928. This decision, originally made by the Nomenclature Committee at

Syringa vulgaris 'Alba Grandiflora' is named for its large white flowers. B. Peart and M. Walton

the 12th International Horticultural Congress, Berlin, 1936, has been endorsed by the International Society for Horticultural Science Commission for Nomenclature and Cultivar Registration.

In 1941 the Sub-Committee on Lilacs of the Committee on Horticultural Varieties, the American Association of Botanical Gardens and Arboretums, under the chairmanship of John Wister, conducted a survey of lilacs cultivated in North America: *Lilacs for America: Report of 1941 Survey* (Wister 1942, 1943). The Sub-Committee drew up a color classification for lilacs, commonly referred to as the Wister Code. Although this classification has been useful for grouping lilac cultivars by color, it is inadequate for description and identification of cultivars.

In 1958 the 15th International Horticultural Congress, Nice, France, designated the Arthur Hoyt Scott Horticultural Foundation at Swarthmore College, Swarthmore, Pennsylvania, as International Cultivar Registration Authority (ICRA) for cultivar names in the genus *Syringa*. John Wister was appointed Registrar. In 1974 the 19th International Horticultural Congress, Warsaw, Poland, designated Royal Botanical Gardens, Hamilton, Ontario, Canada, to succeed the Scott Foundation on 1 January 1975. Freek Vrugtman was appointed International Lilac Registrar. The Registrar maintains the *International Register and Checklist of Cultivar Names in the Genus Syringa L. (Oleaceae)*.

To be worthy of a cultivar name a new lilac selection should be a "notable improvement" over already existing named cultivars. The assessment of the true qualities of a lilac should be based on observations over several seasons of bloom, preferably in different climatic areas. Naming a new cultivar on the basis of color alone simply does not take into consideration questions of the plant's growth qualities, disease resistance, ultimate height, and many other necessary garden features.

In this volume cultivar names are followed by the name of the originator and date, when known. Sometimes two or more people may have been involved in creating a cultivar. In some such instances the two are contemporaries, working at the same time at the same institution. An example is *Syringa vulgaris* 'Lebedushka' Smol'skiĭ & Bibikova, where Nikolai Smol'skiĭ and Veronika Bibikova were contemporary horticulturists

at the Central Botanical Garden in Minsk, Belarus. In other instances, the two individuals may not have known each other. *Syringa pekinensis* 'Morton' Rock & Bachtell is such an example. Kris Bachtell selected, named in 1988, and registered in 2002 this lilac, but the original plant was grown from seed collected in 1926 in China by Joseph Rock (Vrugtman 2003c). In the example of *S. oblata* subsp. *dilatata* 'Cheyenne' Hildreth, three individuals were involved in the creation of the cultivar but only the person who registered, or named, the cultivar is listed. Two plant explorers for the U.S. Department of Agriculture Bureau of Plant Industry named Palemon Dorsett and Warner Morse collected seed lot *Dorsett & Morse 6513* in 1930 in Manchuria, accessioned as Plant Introduction *90671*. Seedlings were grown and distributed. Later Aubrey Hildreth, a horticulturist for the U.S. Department of Agriculture at Denver, Colorado, selected one of these seedlings and named it (Vrugtman 1980). Appendix B lists all known cultivar originators.

Cultivar Identification and Cultivar Fingerprinting

Accurate identification of lilac plants that have lost their label or are of doubtful identity is possible only with the aid of adequate descriptions. Unfortunately, most lilac cultivars have been introduced without adequate descriptions. The earliest descriptions that are useful for verification or identification of lilac cultivars were prepared by McKelvey (1928), who based her descriptions primarily on her observations, recording in her notes where she had seen the plant, its source, and, when available, its accession number. McKelvey's color notations are based on four charts of selected colors that conform to Robert Ridgway's (1912) *Color Standards and Color Nomenclature*. Unfortunately, the color patches on these charts are most likely to have suffered the same deterioration as those in Ridgway's publication (Tucker et al. 1991). Moreover, there is no known chart providing cross-references between McKelvey's color notations and those of the more widely used *Royal Horticultural Society Colour Chart* (R. F. Wilson 1939, 1942; Royal Horticultural Society 1966, 1986, 1995, 2001).

Members of the Editorial Committee of the Commission for the Nomenclature of Cultivated Plants of the International Union of Biological Sciences recognized the need for adequate cultivar descriptions, recommending that International Cultivar Registration Authorities (ICRAs) require registrants of cultivar names to submit "[a] description in English, French, German, Russian, or Spanish, including, where applicable, details of color (with reference to color chart used), classification, chromosome data, etc." (Fletcher et al. 1958). Even more to the point are the notes for ICRAs in Appendix I of the 1995 *ICNCP* (Trehane et al. 1995), stipulating that the registrant of a cultivar name provide a

> description in a language using the Latin alphabet including, where possible, details of colour—the *RHS Colour Chart* . . . is now a widely used standard and is strongly recommended. The ICRA should try to ensure that the registrant is prompted into giving an account of characteristics that are likely to be diagnostic.

In other words, it should be clear from the description in which key characteristics the new cultivar differs from similar, older cultivars, facilitating future cultivar verification and identification.

In the past, lilac cultivar descriptions were based primarily on morphological characteristics, those of form and structure and, of course, floret color. There are, however, also chemical differences between lilac cultivars. Harnborne and Green (1980) studied flavonoids in the foliage of various species in the Oleaceae, the family to which *Syringa* belongs. Flavonoids are polyphenolic compounds. They are easily recognized as flower pigments in most flowering plant families, and their occurrence is not restricted to flowers but includes all parts of the plant.

Cultivar fingerprinting is a well-established procedure for providing reliable identifications for many cultivars of agricultural and horticultural crops such as grains, oil seeds, turf grasses, fruits, nuts, and vegetables. Microsatellite or simple sequence repeat (SSR) markers in rose (*Rosa*) cultivars, for example, provide a marker database for cultivar identification (Zhang et al. 2002). Similarly, fingerprinting techniques have been explored for hybrid poplar (*Populus* ×*canadensis*) cultivars (Rajora and Rahman 2003). Molecular

markers for cultivar fingerprinting are useful not only for verification and identification of cultivars but also offer great potential for safeguarding plant breeders' rights. Randeni (1990) surveyed cultivar fingerprinting techniques for possible future application in the genus *Syringa*. The project yielded promising results but was terminated for lack of funds.

Marsolais et al. (1993) studied random amplified polymorphic deoxyribonucleic acid (RAPD) as genetic markers for determining the origin of interspecific lilac hybrids. The results of their study demonstrated, for instance, that *Syringa* ×*chinensis* 'Red Rothomagensis' is genetically distinguishable from *S.* ×*chinensis* 'Saugeana', contradicting Robert Clark's (1977) opinion that 'Red Rothomagensis' was identical with 'Saugeana'.

One essential prerequisite for cultivar fingerprinting is access to authenticated plants. An authenticated plant has a documented link through its records, a "paper trail," to the original plant selected and named by the originator of the cultivar. Research results are only as good as the material used. Cultivar fingerprints of plants of doubtful identity can lead only to further confusion. A study of molecular markers of species and cultivars by Kochieva et al. (2004) is based on RAPD analyses of six lilac species, one interspecific hybrid, and 15 lilac cultivars. The plant material for the study was obtained from the Tsitsin Main Botanical Garden, Moscow, Russia. There is no indication that the plants used for the study were authenticated, there is no record of accession numbers of the plants used in the study, and no mention is made that voucher herbarium specimens were deposited in a herbarium.

Trade Designations and Trademarks Are Not Cultivar Names

We cannot leave the topic of how we refer to the plants we encounter in nurseries and gardens without mentioning trade designations and trademarks. Contrary to common perception, trade designations or trade names and trademarks are not cultivar names. Confusion arises when they are used as such.

The *ICNCP* defines a trade designation or trade name as "a device that is used to market a plant when the original name is considered unsuitable for marketing purposes" (Brickell et al. 2004, 105). A well-known example of a trade designation for a lilac cultivar is *Syringa vulgaris* Ludwig Spaeth. The German nursery founded by Ludwig Späth originated and introduced this plant under the name *S. vulgaris* 'Andenken an Ludwig Späth' in 1883. The cultivar name was established and accepted under the rules of the *ICNCP*. Because the alternative designation "Ludwig Spaeth" has been used by North American nurserymen for more than a century, Ludwig Spaeth has been designated a trade designation for this cultivar, but it is not a cultivar name, and therefore it is *not* a synonym of 'Andenken an Ludwig Späth'. In this volume, trade designations of plants appear in small capital letters, distinguishing them from cultivar names.

A trademark, as defined by the *ICNCP*, is "any sign, usually made from words, letters, numbers, or other devices such as logotypes, that individualizes the goods of a given enterprise and distinguishes them from the goods of its competitors" (Brickell et al. 2004, 105). Trademarks are the legal properties of their owners, and the use of trademarks is regulated by national legislation and international treaties. Registered trademarks usually bear the symbol ®, while nonregistered trademarks often bear the symbol ™. Whether registered or nonregistered, trademarks have to be maintained by usage to establish and maintain legal protection. The owner of the trademark must also be consistent in providing the "generic designation"—in the case of plants this is the cultivar name—

Syringa ×hyacinthiflora 'Monore' is the scientifically correct name for a plant sometimes sold under the trade name Blue Skies.
B. Peart and M. Walton

alongside the trademark (Trehane 2001). Following is a list of trademarks known to be in current use with lilac cultivars:

TRADEMARK	OWNER OF TRADEMARK	CULTIVAR NAME
Beijing Gold	Chicagoland Grows, U.S.A.	'Zhang Zhiming'
Blue Skies	Monrovia Nursery, U.S.A.	'Monore'
Burgundy Queen	L. E. Cooke, U.S.A.	'LECburg'
China Snow	Chicagoland Grows, U.S.A.	'Morton'
Copper Curls	North Dakota State University	'SunDak'
Elfe	Kircher Baumschulen, Germany	'Dark Night'
Elfenkönig	Kircher Baumschulen, Germany	'Sunset'
Fairy Dust	Bailey Nurseries, U.S.A.	'Baildust'
Flamingo	Kircher Baumschulen, Germany	'Edward J. Gardner'
Frau Holle	Kircher Baumschulen, Germany	'St Margaret'
Ivory Pillar	Carlton Plants, U.S.A.	'Willamette'
Josée	Pépinières Minier, France	'MORjos 060F'

TRADEMARK	OWNER OF TRADEMARK	CULTIVAR NAME
MISS SUSIE	Beaver Creek Nursery, U.S.A.	'Klmone'
MISS USA	Kircher Baumschulen, Germany	'Agnes Smith'
PHILLIP ADAMS	Australia	'Kum-Bum'
PRINCE CHARMING	Bailey Nurseries, U.S.A.	'Bailming'
REGENT, REGENT BRAND	Princeton Nurseries, U.S.A.	'PNI 7523'
RÊVE BLEU	André Briant Jeunes Plantes, France	'Delreb'
ROSENROT	Kircher Baumschulen, Germany	'Maiden's Blush'
SCHNEEWEISSCHEN	Kircher Baumschulen, Germany	'Mount Baker'
SCHÖNE VON MOSKAU	Kircher Baumschulen, Germany	'Krasavitsa Moskvy'
SIGNATURE	Lake County Nursery, U.S.A.	'Sigzam'
SNOWCAP	Carlton Plants, U.S.A.	'Elliott'
STERNTALER	Kircher Baumschulen, Germany	'Primrose'
SUGAR PLUM FAIRY	Bailey Nurseries, U.S.A.	'Bailsugar'
SUMMER CHARM	Discov-Tree R. & D., U.S.A.	'DTR 124'
THUMBELINA	Bailey Nurseries, U.S.A.	'Bailina'
TINKERBELLE	Bailey Nurseries, U.S.A.	'Bailbelle'
WATER TOWER, WATERTOWER	Chicagoland Grows, U.S.A.	'Morton'

Classification of Lilacs by Season of Bloom

To plan a garden wisely a knowledge of the season of bloom of each plant is required. Various lilac species

Wild *Syringa vulgaris* blooming in May in Romania. Želimir Borzan

bloom for a combined period of about six weeks in an ordinary season. A very warm spring will, however, bring out flowers ahead of schedule that will remain in bloom for about four weeks rather than six. Bloom also depends on climate and region. Spring in Canada and the United States is vernal-centrifugal: springtime begins in the center of the continent, continuing outward to both coasts. Likewise, it travels from south to north and upward from the valleys to the mountains. Lilacs in Iowa will be in full bloom while plants in New England are still in tight bud and will bloom a month later. In the middle states, bloom time begins in mid-April and continues to the end of May; on the East Coast it begins in late May and extends into June. On the West Coast, ocean and mountain ranges influence the climate. At Riverside, California, early cultivars commence to bloom at the beginning of March. In slightly colder areas of California where lilacs are grown for commercial purposes (for example, at Acton, Beaumont, Leona Valley, Palmdale, and Visalia) most cultivars of *Syringa* ×*hyacinthiflora* and *S. vulgaris* bloom during the first two weeks of April. In the mountains the season can be as late as May or early June. In Europe, May is lilac time. In the botanical garden in Reykjavik, Iceland, *Syringa* Villosae

Group cultivars come into bloom in July (Dora Jakobsdottir, 2000 and 2005, pers. comm. to F.V.).

Despite the intricacies of the seasons, once growing lilacs begin to bloom, they do so according to a fairly reliable pattern typical for each species. Bear in mind that the longest-blooming species is *Syringa vulgaris*, lasting for a month depending on cultivar and climate. Cultivars of this species can be early, midseason, or late midseason bloomers. Depending on the coolness of the weather, all lilacs can be expected to have a real show of color for 16 to 20 days, counting from full bud color to fading florets. This is quite a long season of bloom for a shrub. With thoughtful planning, it is possible to have some lilacs in full bloom for at least six weeks. Even in small gardens, the pleasure of a single lilac in bloom is well worth its care and planting.

Early-blooming lilacs
  S. oblata and subspecies
  S. ×hyacinthiflora (the early hybrids)
  S. vulgaris 'Rhodopea'
  S. pinnatifolia (bridging early and midseason)
Midseason-blooming lilacs
  S. vulgaris and cultivars
  S. ×chinensis and cultivars
  S. meyeri
  S. pubescens and subspecies, varieties, and cultivars
  S. ×persica
  S. ×diversifolia
  S. ×chinensis × *S. ×persica* cultivars
Late-blooming lilacs
  S. emodi
  S. pubescens subsp. *julianae* × *S. pubescens* subsp. *microphylla*
  S. villosa
  S. wolfii
  S. yunnanensis
  S. tomentella
  Villosae Group cultivars
Very late blooming lilacs (the tree lilacs)
  S. reticulata subsp. *reticulata* and cultivars
  S. reticulata subsp. *amurensis* and cultivars
  S. pekinensis and cultivars

Many of the species lilacs are not readily available or are obtainable only from an arboretum or a private collection. Most of the more complex interspecific hybrids

and their cultivars are also unobtainable, but some day the best of these will find their way into nurseries and gardens. Just being of mixed or complex ancestry does not make a lilac cultivar special or outstanding. *Syringa vulgaris* and its cultivars still reign supreme.

Many lilac species are rather insignificant in bloom. Although several are outstanding, others are not worth planting in smaller gardens; they should be reserved for larger arboreta, estates, and historical or botanical collections. Among the late-blooming lilacs so many are quite similar that one or two suffice to represent the group in any garden.

Lilac Bloom and Climate Change—Phenology

Phenology deals with the relationship between climate and periodic biological phenomena. Climate and weather influence the behavior of plants and animals—North American readers will be familiar with Groundhog Day, the legend that the groundhog or woodchuck comes out of its burrow on 2 February and is frightened back into hibernation if he sees his shadow, which according to tradition indicates six more weeks of winter if that day is sunny, and an early spring if that day is cloudy.

Because spring bloom of *Syringa ×chinensis* 'Red Rothomagensis', like that of all lilacs, is sensitive to temperature rather than daylight, it has been monitored closely for decades by scientists tracking the arrival of spring. B. Peart and M. Walton

Since the 1960s three ornamental woody perennials—*Lonicera korolkowii* 'Zabelii', *L. tatarica* 'Arnold Red' (honeysuckle), and *Syringa* ×*chinensis* 'Red Rothomagensis'—have played a significant role as highly sensitive recording instruments, pinpointing the arrival of spring. Phenomena such as the opening of the winter buds, the appearing of the first leaf, and the opening of the first flower of the lilac clone have been carefully observed and recorded at numerous stations throughout northeastern North America (Caprio 1957, Caprio et al. 1970, Hopp and Blair 1973, Hopp et al. 1973, Vittum and Hopp 1979, Dubé et al. 1984). Based on observations made at 72 sites between 1965 and 2001, Cornell University researchers determined that the blooming season of 'Red Rothomagensis' has advanced by about four days (Wolfe 2004, Wolfe et al. 2004).

Observations made in Germany on the opening of the first flowers of *Syringa vulgaris*, made by Egon Ihne, were published in 1885; alas no recent data are available for comparison.

Lilac Fragrance

In the door-yard fronting an old farm-house, near
    the white-wash'd palings,
Stands the lilac bush, tall-growing, with heart-
    shaped leaves of rich green,
With many a pointed blossom, rising, delicate,
    with the perfume strong I love.

WALT WHITMAN
"When Lilacs Last in the Door-yard Bloom'd," 1865

Fragrance is an elusive factor, very individual, emotionally colored by related experiences, and extremely subtle in its presence—from highly penetrating and noticeable to distant and elusive. The fragrance of lilacs is generally considered to be that extremely pleasing scent of *Syringa vulgaris*. It is *the* fragrant lilac above all, the best known of all lilac scents, the most cherished from early childhood memories, and the one most people seek in planting lilacs. Although several lilac species have unique and pleasing fragrances, none can equal that of the common lilac. It is strong yet not overpowering.

Not all cultivars of *Syringa vulgaris* are equally fra-

grant. In fact, some of the more recently developed cultivars with the largest florets are only faintly scented. The old *S. vulgaris* var. *purpurea* is outstanding in fragrance. Many of the older cultivars are more strongly scented than the newer doubles and latest introductions. Perhaps a special fragrance in flowers is a means of attracting insects for pollination. Could it be that in the newer, much larger flowered cultivars, color and size have gradually replaced fragrance as the attractant? Nonetheless, some newer cultivars are strongly scented, and if you are demanding about fragrance, you should investigate the scent of any lilac you intend to purchase. How often one hears, "But it doesn't smell as strongly as the old lilacs did."

Syringa oblata has a fragrance very similar to that of *S. vulgaris*, although not as strong. Most early-flowering cultivars of *S. vulgaris* × *S. oblata* parentage have pleasing fragrance. To determine personal preferences, visit a nearby lilac collection or arboretum when lilacs are in bloom. By seeing them as well as smelling them you are certain to find a cultivar pleasingly fragrant to you. Fragrance seems to be more pronounced in the early morning or late afternoon hours.

Several species have a noticeable fragrance that is very unlike that of *Syringa vulgaris*. Most of the species indigenous to China have a delightful spicy, cinnamon scent. The fragrance of *S. pubescens* subsp. *patula* is excellent, not overpowering yet captivating and pleasing. *Syringa sweginzowii* and its hybrid *S.* (Villosae Group) 'Albida' have an aromatic, spicy scent. *Syringa pubescens* smells of spicy clove; its subsp. *julianae* has its own sweet spicy scent, while subsp. *microphylla* is somewhat similar yet less pronounced. Joseph Hers (in McKelvey 1928, 171) described *S. meyeri* as being very scented, although Fiala (1988, 13) found it only faintly so. McKelvey (1928) stated that all the lilacs in series *Villosae* are "virtually odorless or rather ill-scented," yet others find them uniquely subdued, somewhat musklike spicy to displeasing.

The tree lilacs *Syringa reticulata* and *S. pekinensis* have a similar fragrance, described as a spicy musklike scent that is agreeable to some but not to others. McKelvey preferred the scent of *S. pekinensis* as "pleasing."

Gardeners should consider planting *Syringa vulgaris* and some of its more fragrant Chinese cousins in their gardens to appreciate the differences in lilac fragrances. Each is unique and pleasing in its own way.

Alexander (1996) conducted an informal, unbiased survey of 456 samples in the Arnold Arboretum lilac collection during the 1982 and 1983 blooming seasons. Four volunteer sniffers assigned fragrance ratings between 1 and 3 to each sample. Top ratings, between 2.1 and 3, were given to *Syringa pubescens* subsp. *pubescens*, *S. pubescens* subsp. *julianae*, and the cultivars 'Evangeline' (*S. ×hyacinthiflora*), 'Henri Martin' (*Syringa vulgaris*), 'Metensis' (*S. ×chinensis*), 'Pascal' (*S. ×hyacinthiflora*), 'Saugeana' (*S. ×chinensis*), and 'Serene' (*S. vulgaris*). One interesting observation is that fragrance levels of a given cultivar may vary from one blooming season to the next. As Alexander put it, "[T]he most plausible [conjecture] is that like the taste of wines, the fragrance of lilacs is just better some years." Lilac fragrance studies are continuing in the Plant Soil and Insect Science Department of the University of Massachusetts at Amherst. Lilac and privet (*Ligustrum*) fragrances appear to be very complex. They are made up of many different compounds, 185 of which have been identified at the time of writing (Theis 2007).

The reader may be disillusioned to learn that the true essential oil of the common lilac flower is not available (Steltenkamp 1979). Commercial lilac perfume and lilac fragrance in soaps are made from a mixture of extracts of nonrelated flowers (Routley 2003). The *Flora of China* reported that flowers of *Syringa reticulata* subsp. *amurensis*, Amur tree lilac, are used in China in the preparation of various perfumes (Chang and Green 1996a). The perfume QUELQUES

FLEURS, one of the famous Houbigant products created in 1912 and still sold today, contains rose, lilac, violet, and jasmine, among others (Irvine 1995).

A yellow-orange dye can be extracted from the twigs of *Syringa vulgaris*, and green and brown dyes from its foliage (Grae 1974). There was once another, albeit fraudulent economic use of *Syringa*. Resink (1907) in his treatise on tea reported that low-quality tea bricks produced in China during the late 19th and early 20th centuries occasionally would contain leaves from species other than the tea plant, *Camellia sinensis*, namely, willow, elm, lilac, rose, strawberry, and plum.

Cold Tolerance and Heat Tolerance in Lilacs

Lilacs are shrubs of colder climates. While they revel in cold winters, they have a limited ability to endure extreme cold. Ideally, they grow in U.S. Department of Agriculture hardiness zones 3 to 5 (−40°F to −10°F, or −40°C to −23°C), and reasonably well in milder sections of zone 2 (−50°F to −40°F, or −46°C to −40°C). Although they can withstand cold to −40°F (−40°C) in zone 3, they need protection from windchill that can kill flower buds. Too frequently lilacs are planted in sites where wet autumns leave them in a water pocket, freezing them in blocks of ice. This they will not tolerate; frozen ground, yes, but not frozen in ice. Come spring the plants will have died.

Lilacs do fairly well in the colder regions of zones 6 and 7 (−10°F to 10°F, or −23°C to −12°C). The warmer zones 8 and 9 (10°F to 30°F, or −12°C to −1°C) appear too subtropical for lilacs, although they have been reported to bloom well in Houston, Texas, and seem to grow but not bloom well in the northern parts of interior Florida around Gainesville. Their buds need some weeks of frost or drought to set them well for bloom. Occasionally a specimen of *Syringa ×persica* and a few of *S. reticulata* also bloom in the southern United States. It may be that some other taxa, such as *S. pubescens* subsp. *microphylla* var. *potaninii*, *S. pubescens* subsp. *julianae*, and *S. oblata*, have not been sufficiently tried in the warmer regions. Some of the taxa exhibiting more intermittent blooming, such as *S. pubescens*, *S. pubescens* subsp. *microphylla*, and *S. pubescens* subsp. *potaninii*, might be

Syringa ×hyacinthiflora 'Pascal' is more fragrant that some lilacs.
B. Peart and M. Walton

candidates for southerly regions. These intermittent bloomers apparently do not need a period of dormancy to flower. It may be that in warmer latitudes they require far more water and heavily enriched soils.

In North America some of the later-blooming species are reputedly less hardy than *Syringa vulgaris*. This may be so, but they usually require a sandy, gravelly soil rather than the heavier soil congenial to *S. vulgaris*, hence they freeze out in extremely cold weather. In Norway the late-blooming cultivars *S. villosa* 'Baldishol' and *S. josikaea* 'Holte', 'Moe', and 'Rå' were selected for their dependable performance and hardiness in cottage gardens in the high mountains—presumably, they like the combination of a good snow cover and good drainage, the habitat of alpine plants. One must visit local lilac collections and arboreta to ascertain what species will withstand the climate of a particular area. Lilacs on their own root systems are far more hardy than those grafted on privet (*Ligustrum*) stock.

In the midwestern United States, that is, around Ohio, Michigan, Indiana, and Illinois, and in the southern parts of the Canadian prairie provinces of Manitoba, Saskatchewan, and Alberta, lilacs have withstood winter temperatures that have plunged to −40°F (−40°C) in zone 3 and bloomed very well in the spring. They are exceedingly hardy shrubs and mostly bloom very well annually. Constant windchill kills and desiccates flower buds when the temperature is lower.

Fiala tried to grow lilacs in northern Florida at Ocala, on the border of zones 8 and 9, but there does not appear to be a sufficient number of frost days for them to initiate the flowering process. *Syringa oblata*, once established in good ground and with sufficient water, does manage to grow but blooms sparingly; *S. pubescens* subsp. *julianae* grows fairly well when once established (two years) and blooms sufficiently to merit growing it—good enriched ground and sufficient water in the springtime are a necessity. Selected cultivars of *S. vulgaris* appear to grow but do not bloom at this Florida location. For a hybridizer interested in developing lilacs for southern climates, *S. oblata* and *S. pubescens* subsp. *microphylla* appear to be the most promising.

The hardiness zones referred to in this volume

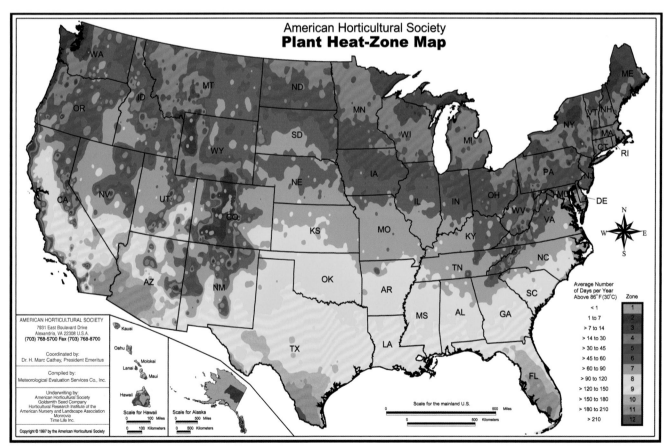

AHS Plant Heat Zone Map. Used by permission of the American Horticultural Society

are those established for North America in the U.S. Department of Agriculture Plant Hardiness Zone Map. The same zone definitions were used by the German team of Woldemar Heinze and Detlef Schreiber (1984), ecologist and geographer, respectively, when developing the hardiness map for Europe.

A Plant Heat Zone Map has been developed by the American Horticultural Society since 1997. It complements the USDA Plant Hardiness Zone Map. The Plant Heat Zone Map indexes and maps summer rather than winter temperatures. This new mapping system is especially useful and relevant for herbaceous plant growers; it is less valuable for woody plants but may be important in some situations not addressed by the USDA map. The Plant Heat Zone Map has 12 zones based on "heat days." These are days with a temperature of 86°F (30°C) or higher. The 86°F temperature is considered important in that it is identified as

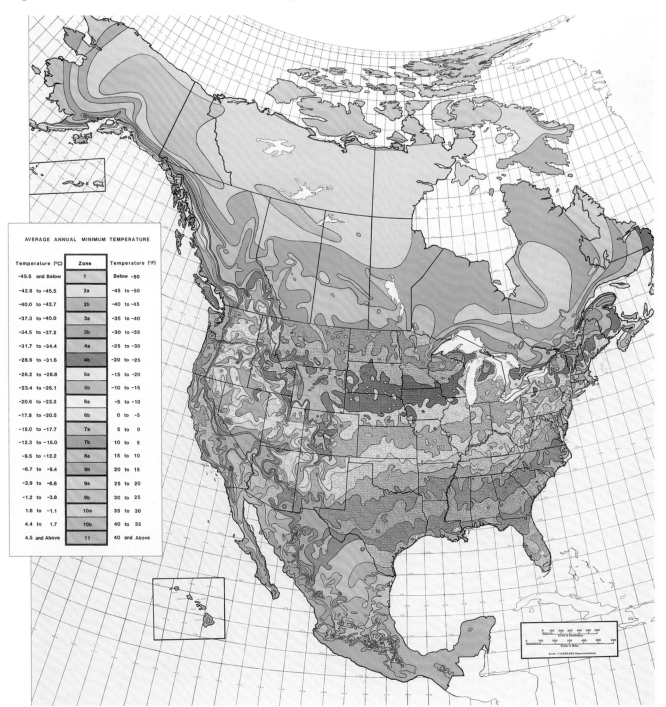

AVERAGE ANNUAL MINIMUM TEMPERATURE		
Temperature (°C)	Zone	Temperature (°F)
-45.6 and Below	1	Below -50
-42.8 to -45.5	2a	-45 to -50
-40.0 to -42.7	2b	-40 to -45
-37.3 to -40.0	3a	-35 to -40
-34.5 to -37.2	3b	-30 to -35
-31.7 to -34.4	4a	-25 to -30
-28.9 to -31.6	4b	-20 to -25
-26.2 to -28.8	5a	-15 to -20
-23.4 to -26.1	5b	-10 to -15
-20.6 to -23.3	6a	-5 to -10
-17.8 to -20.5	6b	0 to -5
-15.0 to -17.7	7a	5 to 0
-12.3 to -15.0	7b	10 to 5
-9.5 to -12.2	8a	15 to 10
-6.7 to -9.4	8b	20 to 15
-3.9 to -6.6	9a	25 to 20
-1.2 to -3.8	9b	30 to 25
1.6 to -1.1	10a	35 to 30
4.4 to 1.7	10b	40 to 35
4.5 and Above	11	40 and Above

USDA Plant Hardiness Zone Map. Courtesy of Ramon Jordan, U.S. National Arboretum, Washington, D.C.

the point at which plant proteins may experience damage. Each heat zone represents a range of average number of heat days per year. On the average, for instance, zone 1 has no heat days per year (these locations are few in the United States and are at the top of mountainous areas), zone 7 has 60–90 heat days, and zone 11 has 180–210 heat days. The Plant Heat Zone Map does not extend beyond the United States. These heat zone ratings have been introduced in American Horticultural Society publications; commercial nurseries have begun introducing the ratings in catalogs and on plant labels.

To use the two maps together, first determine the U.S. Department of Agriculture hardiness zone in which you live, then find the American Horticultural Society heat zone number for that area. That will give the range of climates in which a certain lilac can grow.

European Hardiness Zone Map. Design by D. Schreiber. Courtesy of Verlag Eugen Ulmer

CHAPTER TWO
Lilac Species from Europe

IN PRESENTING the various species of *Syringa* we will first discuss the two species native to Europe, namely, *S. vulgaris* and *S. josikaea*. The familiar common lilac, *S. vulgaris*, is widely cherished as a garden shrub. Its history and characteristics are here described. No other species among the lilacs has been so extensively developed and been the source of so many named cultivars and specialized flower forms. The principal cultivars are described in a later chapter on color in lilacs.

Ernest H. ("Chinese") Wilson, writing on the "History and Distribution of the Lilacs," gave an interesting account of the origins of the then estimated 28 lilac species (quoted in McKelvey 1928, 3):

Lilacs are an Old World group of shrubs and small trees confined with two exceptions to Asia and have no representatives in the New World. All the species are continental but one variety of the Tree Lilac (*S. amurensis* var. *japonica*) is found on the islands of Japan, and *S. velutina* occurs on Dagelet Island in the Japan Sea. Their distribution is very similar to that of the closely related genus *Ligustrum* (privet) which, however, is represented in Japan by a number of species. Of the twenty-eight species of Lilac recognized in this work, two (*S. vulgaris* and *S. josikaea*) are found in central and southeastern Europe; two (*S. emodi* and *S. afghanica*) occur in the Himalayas; two species (*S. velutina* and *S. wolfii*) of true Lilacs, together with the variety *dilatata* of *S. oblata* and two Tree Lilacs (*S. amurensis* and *S. fauriei*), are indigenous in Korea and six species of true Lilacs together with two varieties of the Tree Lilac (*S. pekinensis*) are found in northern China. The remaining fourteen are peculiar to western China. From this analysis it would appear that western China is the headquarters of the genus but in this connection it must be re-

membered that a number of species from that region are little known and when properly understood it may be necessary to reduce the number.

A remarkable piece of lilac information from a very knowledgeable man who spent most of his active life exploring for plants in China. Today, as Wilson predicted, the number of species has been reduced to 21. It is still possible that in the vastness of western China are some undiscovered native species or subspecies.

Syringa vulgaris L.
Common lilac

Syringa vulgaris is native to the Balkans, occurring in Yugoslavia, Moldavia, Serbia, Macedonia, Romania, and throughout southeastern Europe. Flowering time of the native lilacs in Macedonia is about mid-April, and in Romania about a week later (Charles Holetich, 16 April 2005, pers. comm. to F.V.).

Validly published botanical varieties are as follows:

Syringa vulgaris L. 1753
var. *vulgaris*
var. *alba* Weston 1770
var. *brevilaciniata* Jovanovič & Vukicevič 1980
var. *coerulea* Weston 1770, now included in var. *vulgaris*
var. *forsythiodes* Jovanovič & Vukicevič 1980
var. *hyacinthoides* Jovanovič & Vukicevič 1980
var. *macrantha* Borbás 1882
var. *parviflora* Jovanovič & Vukicevič 1980
var. *pulchella* Velenovský 1894
var. *purpurea* Weston 1770
var. *rhodopea* Velenovský 1922, now included in var. *vulgaris* and by some recognized as a cultivar
var. *rubra* Loddiges 1836
var. *transsilvanica* Schur 1866
var. *violacea* Aiton 1789, now included in var. *vulgaris*

The opinion of taxonomists and horticulturists may differ on accepting or rejecting some of these taxa. They are listed here mainly as historic evidence that over the centuries botanists have recognized the genetic variation in *Syringa vulgaris*. Undoubtedly, much genetic potential is still locked up in this species, waiting to be recombined by the plant breeder. No one person can do it all; we must leave some things for future generations of hybridizers.

It was not until 1794 that the actual home of *Syringa vulgaris* was rediscovered by British botanist John Sibthorp on the Eminska Planina (part of the Balkan Mountains), en route from Ruse, in northern Bulgaria, to Istanbul. The herbarium specimen collected by him is at the University of Oxford (Lack and Mabberley 1998, Lack 2000). Anton Rochel (1828), writing of the rare plants of the Banat region, in western Romania, noted lilacs growing among limestone rocks in the Alibek Mountains. Hungarian botanist János [Johann] Heuffel corroborated these findings in 1831, extending the lilac's native habitat to include the valley of the Cerna, Mount Domaglett (or Domogled; the spelling may vary), and the rocky banks along the Danube River at various ancient military posts. This was, as far as can be ascertained, their native land. Some few still claim that lilacs were the children of the cold and desolate ranges of Afghanistan and Turkey, where they bedecked the festivals of robber chiefs—but this be legend.

Centuries before the plant explorations of Sibthorp, Rochel, and Heuffel, the lilac may have been grown by local people to add a touch of beauty to their abodes. From these peasant homes of central Europe, somehow, lilacs found their way to the garden courts of Istanbul. Pierre Belon (1553) described a shrub that may, or may not, have been *Syringa vulgaris*. It was from Istanbul that the Flemish scholar and traveler Ogier Ghiselin, Count de Busbecq and ambassador of Ferdinand I of Austria to the court of Suleyman the Magnificent, brought back to Vienna in his baggage in 1562 gifts from the sultan's gardens. Among them was a plant called the lilac (Verdoorn 1944).

Syringa vulgaris blooming in May in Macedonia. Želimir Borzan

Planted in Busbecq's Viennese garden on the Bastei, the lilak or Türkischer holler, as the Austrians called it, attracted much attention. There the lilac bloomed for the first time in western Europe.

To Busbecq, man of gentle learning and connoisseur of beauty, we may owe the wisdom of again packing in his baggage in 1570 a shoot of his lilac as he, now curator of the Imperial Court Library, prepared to accompany Archduchess Elizabeth from Vienna to Paris, where she became the wife and queen of Charles IX of France. Busbecq never returned to Vienna but remained in France until his death in 1592. The story has been told over and over again. Had the lilac really made the long journey twice in his baggage—from Istanbul to Vienna and again from Vienna to Paris? We don't know; we lack reliable evidence (Lack 2000). We do know that *Syringa vulgaris* is not growing wild anywhere in modern Turkey (Yaltirik 1976, 1978), but it is grown in gardens. The nearest native habitats are in easternmost modern Greece and in adjacent Bulgaria. The entry of the common lilac into Euro-

pean gardens turned a new page in horticultural history, namely, that of the development of the garden lilac (see chapter ten).

Even though *Syringa vulgaris*, the common lilac, is indigenous to Europe, it arrived in European gardens as an exotic. The flowers were showy—even these early introductions must have stood out in any garden—and fragrant, and the shrubs were easily propagated from suckers—all factors that enhanced the popularity of the common lilac and promoted its distribution. Today we can only guess how lilacs were distributed from one garden to the next, from one town or village to the next, but we know from linguistic evidence that they were distributed. Botanist Heinrich Marzell (1885–1970), who compiled colloquial plant names in the German language and published them in four volumes, recorded just short of 500 common names for *S. vulgaris* (Marzell and Paul 1979). This does attest to the popularity and the distribution of the lilac.

From a linguistic perspective it is interesting to

Syringa vulgaris habitat in mountainous Romania. Želimir Borzan

note that about 80 of these colloquial names appear to have been derived from the Greek or Latin *syringa*. A few examples include *Cerinde, Sanderin, Sandrin, Serange, Seriinii, Sirene, Sirenen, Sirenien, Siringe, Syringe, Tsiren, Tsüren'n, Zerenen, Zeringge, Zeringle, Zerinke, Zerinte, Zirene, Ziringel, Zirinkin,* and *Ziroinen.* There was no printed or written label when a plant was passed from one person to another; the name was passed on via the spoken word, phonetically. From time to time, here and there, someone wrote down a name; in some instances it became printed evidence, documenting in a roundabout way the spread of the common lilac following its introduction as an ornamental shrub in the mid-16th century.

One of the rare reports in the literature of the common lilac being imported to a country appears in the 1756 thesis of D. E. Högman (Dahlström 1960), who stated that the first lilac plants were taken from Sweden to Turku, Finland, in 1728 by the druggist Jonas Synnerberg (1695–1775). It is very likely that Högman obtained this information from his teacher, Swedish-Finnish botanist Pehr Kalm (1716–1779).

Lilacs were brought by European settlers to the colonies in North America. Their arrival has not been recorded in the literature, but their gnarled trunks attest to their age. The first lilacs were probably brought by the Dutch and French who so loved them in their native land where they grew better than in England, although the English colonists also dearly cherished the common lilac. The sturdiness of lilacs enabled them to withstand the long sea voyage. The lilac has always been an ideal traveler, ever ready to be off on a new journey, needing little care and only remote concern. Once planted it could fend for itself and readily withstand severe cold. Lilacs became perfect settlers in the new homeland of temperate North America.

It is important to note that these were pre-Linnaean times, and there was no uniformity yet in the naming of plants. The settlers would have known the plants by their Dutch or French colloquial names. Dutch physicians among them with a knowledge of botany may have known the plants by the descriptive Latin phrases used at the time. *Syringa vulgaris,* for example, was known as *Syringa Arabum flore coeruleo* (Munting 1672) or *Syringha coerulea* (Hermann 1687, 586), *S.* ×*persica* as *Jasminum Persicum foliis integris* (Munting 1672) or *Syringha Persica foliis integris* (Her-

mann 1687, 586). Botanically educated Frenchmen may have known the common lilac (*le lilas commun*) as *Jeseminum caeruleum Arabum* (Cesalpino 1583) or *Lilac Mattioli* (Tournefort 1694, Magnol 1697).

By 1652, lilacs were commonly grown all over the colonies (Keeler 1969). In 1753 Peter Collinson, English Quaker and wool merchant of London, sent lilacs to botanist John Bartram, who complained that lilacs "are already too numerous, as roots brought by the early settlers have spread enormously" (W. Darlington 1849). Collinson considered the lilac collection of John Custis (1678–1749) in Williamsburg, Virginia, to be the best in America.

Two plantings can boast of having the oldest living lilacs in North America. The first is the Wentworth lilacs of Portsmouth, New Hampshire, planted by Royal Governor Benning Wentworth around 1750. They are massive old trees, gnarled and twisted with the centuries. Whether these are the original lilacs planted in the mid to late 1700s has not been documented.

The second planting is the group of more massive lilac patriarchs growing on Mackinac Island, Michigan. Their trunks are much larger than those of the Wentworth lilacs. That the Mackinac (pronounced

Lilacs growing on the Wentworth property show the vinelike twisting with age and the peeling bark. John Fiala

MAC-i-naw) lilacs were planted by French Jesuit missionaries working in the area in the late 1600s, or by the early permanent settlement in the 1700s, appears to be a myth. That the lilacs on the island are among the largest in North America is due to favorable growing conditions, but they are not as old as local lore would have it. In June 2007, during the annual meeting of the International Lilac Society, Charles Holetich sampled several large lilac trunks with an increment borer. Calculations based on the growth-ring counts of the extracted cores indicated that these lilacs were planted in the early 1900s, perhaps late 1800s. Nevertheless, they are truly the giants of *Syringa vulgaris*. When Carl La Rue (1948) of the University of Michigan studied the size of these lilac giants, some trunks measured over 20 inches (51 cm) in diameter; because of low branching, measurements were taken close to ground level. In 1948 the largest trunk measured 23⅗ inches (60 cm) in diameter, with several others at 21⅕, 20³⁄₁₀, 19⅕, and 18³⁄₁₀ inches (55, 51, 50, 46 cm). They appear to bethe largest in diameter of any living lilacs officially measured.

In 1767 Thomas Jefferson wrote that he "planted lilacs, Spanish broom, Umbrella and laurel" (Betts 1944); his lilacs no longer exist. George Washington recorded in his diary that on Tuesday, 22 February 1785, he "removed two pretty large and full grown Lilacs to the No. Garden gate—one on each side, taking up as much dirt with the roots as cd. be well obtained" and on Thursday, 3 March, that he "[l]ikewise took up the clumps of lilacs that stood at the corner of the South Grass plot and transplanted them to the clusters in the shrubberies and standards at the South gate." He also transplanted lilacs on 29 March, and mentioned Persian jasmine, which the editors of his diaries determined to be *Syringa ×persica* (Jackson and Twohig 1978). These lilacs, too, are long since gone. Undoubtedly, other family diaries and accounts, buried in obscure archives, include mention of the lilac fellow traveler and how it came to be so universally planted so early throughout the new land.

As early as 1771, Prince Nursery of Flushing-Landing on Long Island, New York, offered white and blue lilacs for sale (Hedrick 1950). It took another three-quarters of a century for the lilac to reach the Pacific Coast. It is most probable that Colonel James L. Warren (1805–1896), who had previously operated the Nonanum Vale Gardens near Brighton, Massachusetts, and who arrived in San Francisco on the ship *Sweden* in 1849, brought with him lilacs for the new

Mackinac Island lilacs in June. Želimir Borzan

nursery he came to establish, James L. Warren and Sons Garden and Nurseries of Sacramento and San Francisco. In 1853 Warren and Sons issued its first catalog, listing among numerous other plants *Syringa persica* var. *alba*. William C. Walker, owner of Golden Gate Nursery in San Francisco, in his 1858 catalog offered *S. persica* and *S. vulgaris*. These are in effect the earliest records of lilacs in California (Taylor and Butterfield 2003; Thomas A. Brown, 2004, pers. comm. to F.V.).

Arrive they did, in good style and health, and their progeny crossed mountains and rivers. Wrapped in burlap and wet straw, lilacs were stowed in the wagons of immigrants on the "Westward Ho!" march. Throughout the northern tier of states and settlements and on into western Canada, everywhere they left their progeny to grow and prosper. By saddlebag and stagecoach, they became kin to log cabins and sod shelters, perfumed the valleys of the Rockies, pressed onward to Oregon and Washington and the colder mountain regions of California, setting strong roots in a new and wonderful land. Their expansion to the newly opened lands of the West was simply their continued long trek from their homeland in central Europe, to Istanbul and the Middle East, then back to Europe and then onward to North America.

Floret Formation and Structure in *Syringa vulgaris* and Its Hybrids

In his lilac study, Joseph Dvorak Jr. (1978) compared *Syringa vulgaris* cultivars by floret form and thyrse structure with remarkable artistry (see pages 42–44). In the earlier lilac literature and throughout this volume, lilac florets are described mostly as being either single or double. Full descriptions of double lilacs should provide more detailed information. Owen Rogers (1998) proposed the following classification which identifies at least three different kinds of doubles:

Radial doubles, such as *Syringa vulgaris* 'Rochester'
Staminode doubles, in which the reproductive parts have turned into petaloids in some degree but with only one corolla
Hose-in-hose doubles, in which there are two or more corollas but fully functional reproductive parts

A combination of categories, for instance, hose-in-hose double plus staminode double

Translating this into a simple designation would give this notation:

S   single
D_R radial doubles; often referred to as multipetaled
D_S staminode doubles
D_{H2} hose-in-hose double, two corollas
D_{H3} hose-in-hose double, three corollas
D_{SH2} staminode and hose-in-hose double, two corollas

Syringa vulgaris is the most showy and truly the queen of the lilac species. No other species of lilac has had such attention paid to selection for unusual colorations, different floret forms, or diversity of structures, nor has any other species had so many cultivars. It is the common lilac, *S. vulgaris*, that first comes to mind whenever we speak of lilacs.

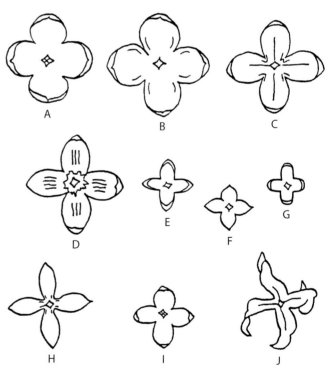

Single floret forms in lilacs. A, 'Andenken an Ludwig Späth'. B, 'Glory'. C, 'Hugo Koster'. D, 'Christophe Colomb'. E, 'Amethyst'. F, 'Marie Legraye'. G, 'Hugo de Vries'. H, 'City of Chehalis'. I, 'Susanna'. J, 'Missimo' (*S. ×hyacinthiflora*). Adapted from Dvorak 1978.

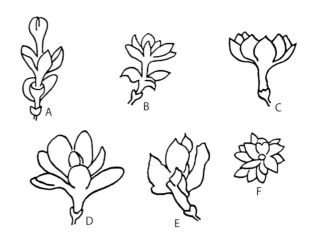

Types of *Syringa vulgaris* florets often at the end of a cluster.
A, 'Taglioni'. B, 'Prof E. H. Wilson'. C, 'Victor Lemoine'. D, 'Planchon'.
E, 'Capitaine Perrault'. F, 'Maximowicz'. Adapted from Dvorak 1978.

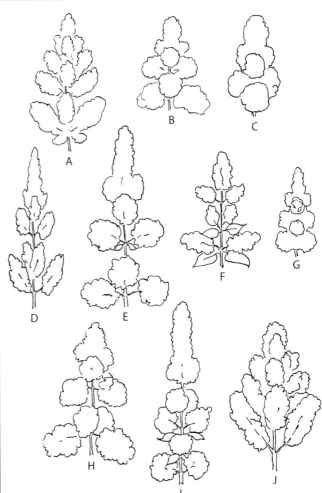

Double floret forms in lilacs. A, 'Banquise'. B, 'Président Carnot'.
C, 'Mons. Maxime Cornu'. D, 'Émile Lemoine'. E, 'Edward J. Gardner'.
F, 'Berryer' (*S. ×hyacinthiflora*). G, 'Maurice de Vilmorin'. H, 'Mme
Jules Finger'. I, 'Belle de Nancy'. J, 'Léon Gambetta'. K, 'Carolyn
Mae'. L, 'Miss Ellen Willmott'. M, 'Jeanne d'Arc'. N, 'Alphonse
Lavallée'. O, 'Dame Blanche'. P, 'Le Printemps'. Q, 'Olivier de Serres'.
R, 'Violetta'. S, 'Claude Bernard' (*S. ×hyacinthiflora*). T, 'Rochester'.
Adapted from Dvorak 1978.

Types of *Syringa vulgaris* flower clusters. A, 'Émile Gentile'.
B, 'Maurice de Vilmorin'. C, 'Christophe Colomb'. D, 'Macrostachya'.
E, 'Andenken an Ludwig Späth'. F, 'City of Chehalis'. G, 'Mme Jules
Finger'. H, 'Président Fallières'. I, 'Tombouctou'. J, 'Émile Lemoine'.
Adapted from Dvorak 1978.

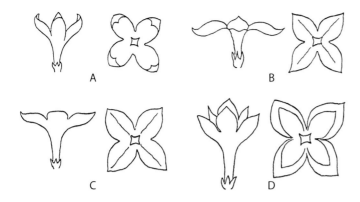

Lilac flower shapes. A, cucullate (*Syringa vulgaris* 'Lucie Baltet'). B, reflexed (*S.* ×*hyacinthiflora* 'Lamartine'). C, flat (*S. vulgaris* 'Marie Legraye'). D, cupped (*S. vulgaris* 'Amethyst'). Adapted from Dvorak 1978.

Syringa josikaea J. Jacquin ex H. G. L. Reichenbach
Hungarian lilac

Only two lilac species are native to Europe. The home of *Syringa vulgaris*, as previously noted, is in the Balkan mountain regions of Romania, Yugoslavia, and Moldavia, while the native land of *S. josikaea* appears to be in the nearby mountain country of Transylvania, more specifically what is today parts of Hungary, Czechoslovakia, Romania, and Yugoslavia, some of which was formerly the Imperial Nation of Hungary or the Austro-Hungarian Empire. The roots of *S. josikaea* lie mostly in today's nations of Hungary and Romania.

Syringa josikaea appears to have been discovered by Hungarian botanist Pál (Paul) Kitaibel (1757–1817) in what was then part of the Kingdom of Hungary [today western Ukraine]. In an undated manuscript (ca. 1800) Kitaibel stated,

> I have named temporarily so that it be not lost from memory a lilac, *Syringa prunifolia*, that grows along the roadside from Munkacs [Mukacheve] to Lemberg [Lviv], in the county of Bereg [Zakarpattia Oblast], between Hrabonitza and Pudolocz, and according to Dr. Bulla, having leaves distinctively like those of the *Prunus*.

Botanically this does not appear to have been an adequate description, so the credit for discovering this lilac goes to Rosalia, Baroness von Josika, née Countess Czaky, an ardent and knowledgeable botanist who

discovered plants of this species growing at Kolosvar, Hungary (now Cluj, Romania). It was from plants sent by the baroness to the gardens of the Imperial and Royal University in Vienna that botanist Joseph Franz von Jacquin (1766–1839) first described and named this species *Syringa josikaea*, presenting it at a meeting of German naturalists in Hamburg on 20 September 1830. Jacquin had seen several plants sent by the baroness, one of which bloomed for the first time in May 1830. Kitaibel's unpublished manuscript in the Hungarian Museum, Budapest, was sent to the Vienna university sometime between 1800 and 1810. The name proposed by him, *S. prunifolia*, would have been a more appropriate botanical name for this lilac.

In all honesty Baroness von Josika popularized a native lilac that was already known among regional botanists. To her must be given the credit of collecting specimens of this lilac and seeing to their distribution to botanists in other countries and calling attention to it as a species native to her country. At Royal Botanic Garden, Edinburgh, a Dr. Graham remarked in 1833 that "the plant received in 1832 flowered in the end of May and beginning of June. It seems, therefore, to flower later and remain longer in bloom than the other species, but does not equal any of them in beauty." John Claudius Loudon (1838) wrote, "Its leaves are shining and lucid green above, and white beneath in the manner of the balsam poplar, but of a dark green" (his description of white beneath is a poor choice). Charles Sargent (1888) made an unfounded statement when he said, "The plants of *Syringa josikaea*, now widely distributed in gardens, have all been propagated from a single plant discovered in a Hungarian garden, but not known to be wild in Europe [whereas they were collected in several places in the wild] and probably of Asiatic origin." This statement aroused considerable controversy as to the native habitat of *S. josikaea*.

McKelvey (1928) extensively reviewed the argument current at the time of her writing, namely, that *Syringa josikaea* was merely naturalized and not native in Europe, suggesting that it was brought from northern China, yet there is no evidence for such a hypothesis. She made only slight reference to the similarities between *S. josikaea* and *S. wolfii*, and she never considered that *S. josikaea* might have been a migrant with the Asiatic tribes moving westward and the Mongols settling in Hungary and areas of Transylvania (for more details see under *S. wolfii*).

As mentioned elsewhere, seeds of plants often follow the migrations of peoples. Few migrations have been as large, complete, and total as those of these Asiatic tribes to Europe. Why could not have *Syringa josikaea* been naturalized centuries before it was discovered and be a European representative of a single species to which both *S. josikaea* and *S. wolfii* are extreme forms? Considerably more scholarly, scientific, and thorough research needs to be done, as these questions cannot be settled on ethnic pride or writings from 1890 on.

McKelvey (1928) described *Syringa josikaea* as follows:

A shrub to 12 ft. [3.6 m] tall; branches upright, stout, greenish gray, lenticellate; branchlets pubescent when young, sparingly lenticellate. Winterbuds ovoid with acute apex, flower bud ⅜ in. [9 mm] long more or less, lower scales dark brown, upper reddish brown with yellowish margins, acute, puberulous, keeled and forming a four-sided bud. Leaf-scar slightly raised, shield-shaped, not conspicuous, small; bundle-trace almost straight. Leaves broad-elliptic to elliptic-oblong, sometimes obovate, 2–5½ in. [5–14 cm] long, 1–2¼ in. [2.5–5.7 cm] broad, acute to acuminate, base cuneate or rounded, ciliolate, dark green, lustrous, glabrous above, glaucescent, sometimes pubescent especially along the veins, or glabrous beneath; petiole stout or slender, ⅛–⅝ in. [3–16 mm] long, glabrous or pubescent. Inflorescence borne on leafy shoot, terminal upright, broadly pyramidal, interrupted, 4–9 in. [10–23 cm] long; rachis, pedicel and calyx tinged Carob Brown; rachis pubescent; pedicel short, pubescent; calyx pubescent with short acute teeth; flowers sometimes fascicled, corolla tube funnelform, ¼–⅜ in. [6–9 mm] long; corolla lobes erect or slightly spreading, broad at base, acute, cucullate; corolla ¼–⁵⁄₁₆ in. [6–8 mm] in diameter; color in bud Dull Dusky Purple to Dull Dark Purple to Bishop's Purple to Argyle Purple: when expanded Argyle

Syringa josikaea in the wild in Romania. Charles Holetich

Syringa josikaea, flower. B. Peart and M. Walton

Syringa josikaea 'Rubra'. John Fiala

Purple to Purplish Lilac without, Light Pinkish Lilac or Hay's Lilac within, a solid color; anthers ¹⁄₁₆ in. [1.5 mm] long, Primrose Yellow, inserted just above middle of corolla tube. Capsule oblong, smooth, ½ in. [13 mm] long, acute, or rounded at apex, each valve terminating in a short tip.

Syringa josikaea has much to offer in hybridization. Its leaves are exceptionally heavy in substance, almost leatherlike, with an attractive, lustrous-green sheen much needed in some lilac species. It is one of the few species with dark blue-violet flowers, a color also lacking in the late-blooming hybrids. Its open flowering panicles should do well when crossed with heavier-blooming, tighter-panicled species. *Syringa josikaea* crossed with *S. komarowii* subsp. *reflexa* has produced the fine hybrids known as *S. ×josiflexa* of which 'Guinevere' is the type. It grows to 8–10 feet (2.4–3 m) with a somewhat modest form. *Syringa josikaea*

Syringa josikaea 'Pallida'. B. Peart and M. Walton

crossed with *S. villosa* has given us the hybrids referred to as *S. ×henryi* of which 'Lutèce' (the old name for the city of Paris) is an excellent example. Other cultivars with *S. ×henryi* in their background are 'Floréal', 'Rutilant', and 'Prairial'. The latter is a second-generation hybrid much improved over the original *S. ×henryi* hybrids and belongs to a series now called *S. ×nanceiana* hybrids, which are pregnant with hybridizing potential. Although *S. josikaea* first-generation hybrids are not as showy as most other species crosses and so are in need of continued work and refinement, they are excellent plants with fine leaf and deep flower color. *Syringa josikaea* remains one of the best sources genetically for deep violet hybrids and excellent glossy leaves, and perhaps the only source for eventual blue-flowering, late-blooming lilacs.

Syringa josikaea requires far richer soil than most other lilac species and does fairly well even in somewhat damp soil, but not swampy. It is at best a mediocre bloomer, but with rich green foliage it is attractive in the summer garden as a background to other plants. Space should not be used in the smaller garden for this species as it has far less to offer than others. Larger gardens and collections, especially arboreta or large parks, could well plant it in large massed groups, especially in blending wooded areas into more formal space. McKelvey was quite right in suggesting that it makes an excellent hedge. It does not do well in sandy soils. It need not be grafted as cuttings strike root easily if taken immediately after bloom. From seed it is somewhat variable but acceptable. The best seedlings should be named to retain the better-blooming sorts with the deepest color and be propagated vegetatively.

'Pallida', origin unknown pre-1865, single violet.

'Rubra', origin unknown pre-1885, single magenta.

CHAPTER THREE
Lilac Species from Asia

IT IS AN ESTABLISHED FACT that *Syringa vulgaris*, the common lilac, adapts very well to the colder regions of Europe and North America. This common lilac of Balkan origins has some 20 cousins (species) whose native origins lie in the vast reaches of China. Of these different but beautiful species, so unlike in flower, leaf, and fragrance from their European relative, many deserve to be better known. Great strides are being made in their hybridization, which will lead to greater popularity. Some are wild transplants from the forests, canyons, and mountain valleys of their homeland; others have graced, as ancient garden shrubs, the temples and houses of China, perfuming the prayer rituals of Buddhist monks or the clear mountain air.

In the cold northeastern provinces of Hebei and Shandong, in montane arboreal forests, *Syringa pubescens* grows among wild roses and filberts in dense thickets of secondary growth in openings of *Picea abies* forests, while among the rich and varied shrubs of the forest floor, *S. reticulata* subsp. *amurensis* vies for a place in the sun, raising its feathery white blossoms with their spicy fragrance in late June. In the bitterly cold winter areas of the montane coniferous forests of northern Gansu and Shaanxi, the late lilac *S. villosa* is one of the five most important shrubs and ground covers. It forms thickets of seedlings mixed with older plants in full bloom. In deciduous, broad-leaved forests of mixed northern hardwoods, the lilac is, again, one of the leading shrubs in the middle plant layer just below the foliage of high trees. Reaching up to 50 feet (15 m), *S. reticulata* subsp. *amurensis* competes with 50 species in northeastern Shandong. As a border thicket at the edge of the forest, *S. villosa* forms random stands or invades forest clearings.

In eastern China's Hebei province and around Beijing, *Syringa pubescens* is common as a native of the upper oak forests of *Quercus liaotungensis*. Continu-

ing above the oaks, upward to 4600 feet (1400 m), it appears in the community of linden-birch (*Tilia–Betula*) forests, growing strongly in the rich, well-drained soils of the forest clearings. In the western provinces of Shaanxi, Gansu, and Sichuan, the tree lilac, *S. reticulata*, is the most widespread of the *Syringa* species, forming dense thickets among other shrubs on sunny slopes opposite birch-aspen (*Betula–Populus*) forests above bands of oaks. In the upper oak forest of southern Shaanxi at 4600 to 6600 feet (1400–2000 m) and above 5000 feet (1500 m) in Gansu, *S. pubescens* is common in the rich understory of cane thickets and tall shrubs, many of which are evergreens. These are definitely lilacs of the high country and open forests or forest margins (Chang and Green 1996a).

In the grasslands and deserts, *Syringa oblata*, the early lilac, is common in the sharply dissected Loess Plateau south of the Great Wall and is found everywhere in valleys and sheltered slopes. *Syringa oblata* subsp. *oblata* differs considerably from *S. oblata* subsp. *dilatata*.

From our limited knowledge of Chinese horticultural literature it does appear that lilacs were cultivated to some extent in private and public gardens. The tree lilac, *Syringa reticulata* subsp. *amurensis*, was probably most commonly grown. It was sometimes used as a temple tree, as at the monastery of Kum-Bum, and in the gardens of rich and poor, as an easily grown tree for its late bloom. Some find its fragrance unpleasant, but its malodor cannot be compared to the offensive *Rhododendron molle* or the blooming Chinese chestnut, *Castanea mollissima*. One would expect that there would be considerably more clonal variations than we now have; perhaps we must try seed from more of the species' diverse locations.

From the mountains of Yunnan and Tibet (Xizang) comes *Syringa yunnanensis*. Its flower is so insignificant that it is not cultivated even by Tibetans.

Also from Yunnan comes *S. tomentella*, and in the northeastern part of this province *S. pubescens* subsp. *microphylla* var. *potaninii* is native, as it is in Tibet and Gansu.

Sichuan is the home of *Syringa sweginzowii*, *S. komarowii*, *S. yunnanensis*, and *S. pubescens* subsp. *microphylla* var. *potaninii*. In neighboring Hubei, the province to the east, *S. pubescens* subsp. *julianae*, *S. komarowii* subsp. *reflexa*, and *S. pubescens* subsp. *microphylla* are all indigenous.

Most of the lilacs of China are known in their wild state only. The sole exception is *Syringa meyeri* var. *meyeri* which has never been found in the wild and is known only as a Chinese garden plant. *Syringa meyeri* var. *spontanea*, native to Liaoning, is also grown in gardens in Beijing and Shenyang.

The bulk of the Chinese species lilacs were discovered in the late 1880s to 1900 with a few as late as 1910 and 1925.

Plant Explorations in Asia Important to the Discoveries of New Lilac Species

Through the efforts and knowledge of plant explorers, missionaries, and botanists the many lilacs native to China and the surrounding region were discovered and introduced into collections and commercial horticulture. Since the 1700s, men and women of many countries have ventured to unexplored mountainous terrain, endured the rigors of climate and long journeys, and dealt with unfamiliar languages and hundreds of dialects to discover lilac species. Adventurous men like Grigoriĭ N. Potanin and Ernest H. Wilson discovered new species and left accounts of their exciting expeditions. The introduction of thousands of new plant species to the Western world resulted from their labors. There is hardly a garden today that does not have several of the plants they hunted out and introduced.

Many of these earliest plant collectors traveled at their own expense, were missionary-botanists, or were botanical experts employed by their countries' diplomatic missions. Most of the more recent explorations, beginning in the 20th century, have been the undertakings of some of the world's great horticultural institutions.

The Initial Era of Lilac Discoveries in China and Afghanistan

The history of the plant collectors and botanists in China, Tibet, and India can be roughly divided by the war between the West (England, France, Russia, and the United States) and China in 1860. From the beginning of plant explorations in China, as early as 1742 when Pierre d'Incarville, a French Jesuit missionary-botanist, discovered *Syringa pekinensis* in the mountains near Beijing and *S. villosa* in the same area in 1750, the history of the discovery and naming of lilac species was mostly the work of French, Russian, and English botanists who traveled or were associated with China as missionaries or military attachés. Almost 80 years later, in 1831, Russian botanist Alexander von Bunge sent lilac specimens back home. English plant collector Robert Blinkworth, working for Nathaniel Wallich of the East India Company's botanic garden at Calcutta, collected another lilac species in the Kamaon (Kumaon) region of Afghanistan; it was named *S. emodi* by Wallich in 1831.

In the next 10 years the Russian explorer and bota-

Native to China, *Syringa villosa* was discovered in the mountains around Beijing in 1750 by French Jesuit missionary-botanist Pierre d'Incarville. B. Peart and M. Walton

nist Porfirij Kirilov (1801–1864) sent seed home of two previously discovered species, *Syringa pekinensis* and *S. villosa*, and in 1840 discovered still another beautiful new lilac, *S. pubescens*, in Hebei, sending back seed and plants. Some few years later in his third exploration (1853–1856) to China, Robert Fortune sent back to England live plants of *S. oblata* and its variety *alba*, which he found growing in Chinese gardens and which today is referred to as *S. oblata* subsp. *oblata* 'Alba'. At this time two other Russian botanists, Richard Maack and Karl J. Maximowicz, independently each discovered *S. reticulata* subsp. *reticulata*.

This first 100 years was an initial phase in the discovery and collecting of lilac species. Most of these earlier explorers, although learned and able, did not collect in the volume and thoroughness of those who were to follow them in the next century, yet they added seven new species and outstanding cultivars to the growing list of known lilacs.

The Opium Wars and the Opening of China's Interior to Plant Exploration

It had been a trying time for China with the Opium Wars (1839–1842 and 1858–1860) and the Taiping Rebellion (1851–1864). The Opium Wars were a discredit to the Western powers, squeezing concessions from a rebellion-weakened Chinese government. The Manchu, aware that their empire was disintegrating, were forced to ask the help of the West. Under Captain Charles George ("Chinese") Gordon's command (1863–1864), Chinese forces crushed the Taiping Rebellion (Spence 1996). As a result of the wars with the West, China was obliged by treaty to open its interior. Plant hunters were free to follow rivers to the western interior and highlands in search of new and unknown plants. It was a grand time for the discovery of many new plant species, among which were the lilacs. Wonderful discoveries were made. A must-read is Tyler Whittle's (1970) *The Plant Explorers*; it is an exiting account of the history of plant exploration.

For collectors of lilac species the very heart of the native habitat of *Syringa* was opened to explorations—Tibet and the Chinese provinces of Gansu, Sichuan, and Yunnan. From these three provinces alone, 13 species of native lilacs were found—more than in any other area of China. To Western plant hunters the interior of China was sheer grandeur. Joseph Rock (1925–1926) wrote of

> the size of the rivers and extent of their head-waters, the many breathtaking cataracts, rapids, currents, mountain gorges, the sheer mountains and their overwhelming valleys, the flat dry plateaus cut by rivers and chasms over a thousand feet [300 m] below and the screes over which screaming winds howled endlessly.

This was the awe-inspiring interior of China that contained treasured lilac species unseen by the rest of the world. The famous Chinese poet Po Chü-i (772–846), who was made governor of this remote area in Sichuan, named Yunnan "The Land South of the Cloud" and Sichuan "The Land of the Four Rivers." This was the land that became a mecca to plant collectors, especially for the species of *Syringa*.

Some of the first men to explore interior China were amateur plant collectors like the Frenchman Prince Henri d'Orléans and the very rich Englishman

Joseph F. Rock standing by the sandstone cliffs of Li-yüan Gorge opposite He-yo-tung in Gansu Province. Photo by J. F. Rock, 3 November 1925. © President and Fellows of Harvard College, Archives of the Arnold Arboretum.

Antwerp Pratt, who "bought a luxurious houseboat on the Yangtze, hired a German assistant collector, Kricheldorf, and went sailing into Szechuan [Sichuan] in the grandest style possible!" The brilliant young linguist August Margary, an Englishman, traveled from what is now the Chang Jiang to Irrawaddy—more than 1000 miles (1600 km) of unknown country on his plant collecting journey when he was only 26. He suffered from toothaches, rheumatism, pleurisy, and dysentery. When he completed his journey, just beyond Bhamo, he died mysteriously. A British consulate investigation indicated he was probably murdered by his own litter bearers for insisting a dog be carried in his curtained litter, as they considered this to be a gross insult and outrage. Margary was "out of the ordinary." It is recorded that "when he felt lonely and depressed he would stand outside his tent singing *Clementine, Polly-wolly-doodle, The Lass of Richmond Hill* and finish off with a shouting rendering of *God Save the Queen*." Such were the lives of these freelancers among the plant collectors, an adventurous lot. The majority who came after them were of an entirely different cast.

Under the Great Annexer, Lord Dalhousie (James Andrew Broun Ramsey, Marquis of Dalhousie, 1812–1860; governor-general of India, 1847–1856), England extended its rule over India and became concerned about the extent to which Czar Alexander II (1818–1881) sent military botanists into the newly opened areas of China. Despite the open outrage of the Widow of Windsor (Queen Victoria, 1819–1901), he continued to send men who, though of a military commission, were well-trained botanists.

High among these was the capable Russian botanist Nikolai M. Przewalski (1839–1888), whose achievements took him from the rank of a literary foot soldier to a major generalship. He was essentially a naturalist botanizing along the way to reach Lhasa in Tibet. In his last attempt in 1888 he died of typhoid. Before his death, however, he left a lasting legacy of more than 15,000 plant specimens, which contained more than 1700 species of plants sent to Russia to the industrious scholar Karl Maximowicz in Saint Petersburg. Among these were many specimens of lilacs. This doyen of Russian collectors was followed by equally illustrious quasi-military botanists among

Jupar Valley, one of many "valleys of magnificent vegetation," in the Amne Machin Mountains, a branch of the Kunlan Shan in Qinghai Province (formerly part of Tibet), west central China. Rock noted the elevation as being 10,000 feet (3000 m). Photo by J. F. Rock, 26 June 1926.

whom were the brilliant Potanin, Berezovski, Kashkarov, and Roborovski. Unfortunately, much of their great work and travels remains unknown in the West because it has not been translated from Russian. Their accomplishments were extensive, including many species of lilacs.

The Plant Hunters

A new era began in 1866 with missionary-botanist Father Armand David, a Frenchman. There was a notable change in the style, character, and training of plant collectors from Europe and the West. Before David, plant collectors were adventurers, with the exception of the Russian military-botanists, with some basic training in collecting herbarium specimens who collected as they willed materials of their own choosing. After David, with a few exceptions of self-trained or academic botanists such as the Englishman Augustine Henry, the Swedish scholar Harold (Harry) K. A. Smith, the Austrians Camillo K. Schneider and Heinrich R. E. F. von Handel-Mazzetti, and the American Liberty Hyde Bailey of Cornell University, Ithaca, New York, the rest of the plant hunters were well-trained plantsmen. They collected plants for botanical study and herbaria, but this was only secondary to collecting seeds and living stock for introduction into cultivation and horticultural commerce. They were men of a professionally trained and practical cut. Rather than haphazardly skimming off the best materials, they conducted a systematic and exhaustive search for anything new and different over set and well-defined areas. These plantsmen, being better trained and more scientific, were lavishly rewarded for their efforts. Reading of their adventures in quest of new plant materials, including lilacs, is fascinating and awesome.

Missionary-Botanists

Armand David (1826–1900), born of humble parents in Espelette, a small town in the French Pyrenees, entered the Order of Lazarists. As a trained botanist, he taught botany in Italy for several years before being sent by the Lazarists on his first Mongolian Expedition to China in 1866. David carried little baggage and no food, depending on the hospitality of the people. He was methodical and painstaking as a plant collector. Although his more than 2000 species could not compare with other missionary-botanists who followed him in the Tibetan mountains, such as Abbot Jean Marie Delavay (1834–1895), who is credited with personally collecting, drying, and pressing more than 200,000 specimens, David's work was exceptionally well done and thorough. He continued collecting in China until 1874 when illness forced him to return to France, where he taught botany until his death. He collected in the mountains near Beijing and is credited as the discoverer of *Syringa pekinensis*. On his long plant expeditions he wrote, "As for food I depend on the Chinese, and I believe that with a little goodwill, one man can live wherever another can. I do not burden myself with carrying food, except a bottle of cognac, for emergencies."

Among David's contemporaries, Delavay discovered *Syringa yunnanensis* growing in the wooded areas around Lake Lanking in Yunnan. Abbot Jean André Soulié (1858–1905) collected already discovered species of *Syringa* in Tibet, where he was murdered by Tibetan monks in Yaregong. Father Giuseppe Giraldi (d. 1901), an Italian missionary-botanist, gathered and first collected plants of *S. oblata* subsp. *oblata* (as *S. oblata* var. *giraldii*) in 1891 and *S. pubescens* subsp. *microphylla* (as *S. microphylla*) in 1896 in Shaanxi. These missionary-botanists added five species and subspecies to the known lilacs.

Ernest Henry Wilson (1876–1930)

Born in the small town of Chipping Campden, Gloucestershire, England, Ernest H. Wilson showed a love and attraction for plants as a boy when working as an apprentice gardener at a Stratford nursery. From there he transferred to Birmingham Botanic Gardens and shortly after to the famous Royal Botanic Gardens, Kew. He was not much attracted to teaching botany and when recommended by Sir William Thiselton-Dyer, the Gardens' director (1885–1905), for the job of plant hunter in China for the Veitch Nursery at Chelsea, although only 23, he quickly accepted. It was the beginning of a fabulous career and a life of fulfillment in seeking new species and plants. Wilson was overjoyed. Often nicknamed "Chinese" Wilson (which he disliked) because of his many expeditions into China, he was perhaps the most outstanding of the modern plant hunters after the opening of the interior of China in 1860 at the end of the Opium Wars.

Veitch's staff instructed Wilson for six months on the practical side of plant hunting, plant identification, and transport of herbarium materials, seed collecting, and care of propagating stocks; these latter were the firm's chief interest for commercial introduction of new plants. To this was added the use of a camera. Young Wilson was an astute and able student, becoming a plant collector of the highest rank and an excellent photographer; despite its weight he always used a heavy, full-plate camera, with tripod in brass and mahogany. He was instructed by Veitch to take the long route to China via the United States so that he could stop at the Arnold Arboretum in Jamaica Plain, Massachusetts. Here he met and formed a lasting friendship with the Arboretum founder, Charles Sargent, who gave him much valuable advice on collecting in China (Shephard 2003). Later, this friendship was to result in Wilson's leaving the Veitch firm to work for the Arboretum. Another instruction of his employer was to visit Augustine Henry in Yunnan, China. This meeting also proved most beneficial to Wilson as Henry was a veteran plantsman with much knowledge to offer on plant hunting in China.

Wilson's first assignment from Veitch was to find the legendary or real *Davidia involucrata*, the dove tree, and anything of commercial value along the way. He was very successful, although he did not find *D. involucrata*, which was to come in his second journey. Wilson did discover *D. involucrata* var. *vilmoriana* (as *D. involucrata* var. *laeta*), sending seeds of it and 305 other species, plus 35 Wardian cases of tubers, corms, bulbs, rhizomes, and rootstocks together with 906 herbarium specimens—an outstanding accomplishment for his first expedition into unknown China.

Within six months of returning to England, Wilson undertook a second trip for Veitch. This time he went into Laolin (an area now part of Sichuan and Hubei, often called Wilson's exclusive territory), where he discovered rare species of poppies (*Papaver*) and other plants, among which were *Syringa pubescens* subsp. *julianae* (from Hebei) and the beautiful *S. komarowii* subsp. *reflexa* in western Hubei. Pressing deeper into Sichuan, in the areas surrounding sacred Mount Omei, Wilson discovered *S. pinnatifolia* and took seeds of the already discovered but rare *S. swe-*

ginzowii. From this one exploration Wilson was to return to Veitch four new lilacs and hundreds of other taxa. Later, in his book *Aristocrats of the Garden*, Wilson (1917, 213–229) gave an exciting account of this discovery of *S. komarowii* subsp. *reflexa*, so vivid that readers imagine themselves actually in his company of bold adventure. More detailed information on the nodding lilac can be found in an unpublished manuscript, *Wilson's Plants in Cultivation*, now in the collections of the Arnold Arboretum and summarized by Richard Howard (1980). Wilson's account of *S. sweginzowii* covering a hillside down to a valley stream is sheer artistry.

These explorations were not without danger. Wilson was not one to dwell upon himself or his accomplishments and tribulations. He described one harrowing experience: On his second journey, while searching for the regal lily (*Lilium regale*), Wilson and his party of coolies, taking an unknown and narrow path where avalanches were common, were suddenly pelted with falling stones—one boulder hit Wilson, breaking his leg in two places. Suffering greatly, a long distance from any doctor, surrounded only by his coolies who were ready to run away, he made splints from his tripod and continued carried on a litter on the narrow mountain trail. Eventually they met, coming from the opposite direction, a train of 50 mules on this high path too narrow for them to be turned—nor would the mule train wait for Wilson's small coterie to edge its way one at a time past the mules. Wilson knew he could not turn back. Racked with pain he ordered his men to lay him across the narrow path, and one by one the sure-footed mules stepped over him. Such was the life of this remarkable plant hunter. He returned with the lilacs, the regal lily, and a lifelong limp (which he called his Lily Limp). He was a wonderfully inspiring and brilliant man with a laconic sense of humor.

Upon returning from his second trip, realizing the financial difficulties being encountered at the Veitch firm, Wilson left it to join Sargent at the Arnold Arboretum, for which he made six more plant hunting trips to China. Here he had more financial backing, more freedom in collecting, and a wider scope. From each of his trips Wilson brought back additional seeds or new lilac species. On his fifth trip in 1917 he sent back seed of *Syringa oblata* subsp. *dilatata* found in

Ernest H. Wilson, the doyen of plant collectors in China, sitting on the steps of the Hunnewell administration building at the Arnold Arboretum, Jamaica Plain, Massachusetts. From 1901 to 1926 Wilson made six plant exploration trips. Photo by Charles Darling, 25 September 1922. © President and Fellows of Harvard College, Archives of the Arnold Arboretum.

Korea, and on his sixth trip in 1924–1925 he sent back seeds of *S. pinnatifolia*, which he had previously discovered in 1904 but had been unable to collect. Sargent (1911–1917) documented the value of Wilson's explorations and the extent of Wilson's accomplishments in *Plantae Wilsonianae*, in nine parts and three volumes.

Wilson was a remarkable plant hunter and was named Assistant or Keeper of the Arboretum, which delighted him. He authored several books on his plant discoveries. In 1930 he was killed in an automobile accident while driving with his wife on a highway near Worcester, Massachusetts—a tragic ending for a person of his capabilities.

Grigoriĭ Nikolaevich Potanin (1835–1920)

A man of letters, science, travel and plant collecting, Grigoriĭ Potanin was born in the city of Tomsk in Old Siberia. As a student he was one of the enthusiastic writers in Saint Petersburg, whose leader was the well-known Vissarion Belinskii (1811–1848), who greatly influenced Russian literature and politics. Potanin was a brilliant scholar and perhaps best known for his travels in China, Tibet, and Mongolia as a

The Minchow trail, as it was known to the early explorers, was built on stilts through a defile beyond Guanting in Gansu Province. It was here that mules stepped over a pain-racked Wilson as he lay across the narrow path. Note the temple in the nook of the cliff. Photo by J. F. Rock, 12 April 1925. © President and Fellows of Harvard College, Archives of the Arnold Arboretum.

quasi-military plant collector. The wealthy Irkutsk merchant and public figure in Siberia, Vladimir Platonovich Sukachev (1849–1920), participated in financing Potanin's expeditions.

Between 1876 and 1893 Potanin made four journeys to the plateau of Central Asia, traveling extensively in the plant-rich areas of Gansu. In 1885 he collected *Syringa oblata* subsp. *oblata* (as *S. oblata* var. *giraldii*) in Shaanxi and a few years later discovered *S. pubescens* subsp. *microphylla* var. *potaninii* (as *S. potaninii*) in Gansu. It was on this last rigorous journey that he discovered *S. komarowii* in Sichuan where he lost his devoted wife and fellow-worker. Although his expeditions had in mind chiefly botanical collecting and zoological observations, he brought back and wrote much ethnographic material.

After returning to Tomsk, Potanin resumed his intellectual work, particularly concerning the founding of societies for the study of Siberia and its various aspects. In later life he married a highly gifted Siberian poetess and their home became a center of literary and learned gatherings. He was active in the community and together with N. M. Iadrinstev, published papers, organized intellectual circles, and was instru-

mental in opening Irkutsk State University in 1918. Potanin worked diligently to revolutionize the intellectual life of Russians living in Siberia. Everywhere he was proclaimed as the champion of Asian study and the intellectual life of the Sibiriaks, the Russian settlers in the outlying regions of Siberia. Much of his writings, especially his exciting accounts of plant explorations into China, have not been given the attention they deserve, chiefly because they have not been translated from Russian into other languages. He was a gifted and accomplished writer. Those who grow lilacs will remember him through *Syringa komarowii* and *S. pubescens* subsp. *microphylla* var. *potaninii*, which bears its discoverer's name. Potanin died, aged 85, at his home.

Other Russian Plant Hunters

Karl Johann Maximowicz (1827–1891), also known as Carl Ivan Maximowicz, continued his explorations and in 1875 in Japan collected *Syringa reticulata* subsp. *reticulata*, calling it *S. japonica*, the name by which it was known for many years. From 1893 to 1895, distinguished Russian botanist Vladimir Leontievich Komarov, sent seeds of *S. wolfii* to Saint Petersburg,

The forested limestone crags and cliffs of Sangba Gorge near the Tebbu village of Hera in Gansu Province. The area was explored briefly as early as 1885 by Potanin, who discovered *Syringa pubescens* subsp. *microphylla* var. *potaninii* in its valleys. Photo by J. F. Rock, 07 September 1926.

enlarging the magnificent collection gathered there by nearly a century of outstanding Russian botanists and plant collectors. Miss A. Sontag, a member of the Russian legation, was the first to collect *S. patula* near Seoul, Korea, in 1895.

Joseph Francis Charles Rock (1884–1962)

A prodigy as a scholar in science and an accomplished multilanguage linguist, Joseph Rock was born in Vienna. In 1907 he was appointed to the chair of Chinese and botany at the University of Hawaii and later, economic plant collector for the U.S. Department of Agriculture. He became an American citizen in 1913. His position enabled him to travel extensively in Yunnan, where his plant collecting crossed paths with George Forrest and Francis Kingdon-Ward. Rock had a great love for China, especially in the area of southwestern Gansu he called "Tebbu land, that is, the country peopled by the Tepos south of the Min Shan which is divided in two by the Satani Alps." Tebbu land fired his imagination: "I have never in all my life seen such magnificent scenery! If the writer of Genesis had seen the Tebbu Country he would have made it the birth place of Adam and Eve!"

In his work as plant collector for Arnold Arboretum, Rock was systematic and sent back thousands of specimens, seeds, and stock. Among his collections were many forms and species of lilacs already previously discovered. He worked through all of Sichuan, which had once been controlled by the Tibetan prince of Litang. The thoroughness of his explorations would preclude the finding of other *Syringa* species in the areas of his endeavors. During the Chinese-Tibetan frontier quarrels, Tibet became extremely lawless, and in 1928, when Rock wished to botanize there, it was only through his special friendship with Drashetsongpen, a former lama turned bandit, that he was permitted to continue his work. As the border disputes continued, Rock returned to the United States. He left in Arboretum's archives a vast number of photographs of the plant explorations and commentary, most of which has yet to be published. Rock collected and brought home enough seeds of many of the lesser known lilac species to facilitate their commercial introduction.

Rock Gate, elevation 11,500 feet (3500 m), the entrance into Tebbu land in Qinghai Province. Photo by J. F. Rock, 13 June 1925. © President and Fellows of Harvard College, Archives of the Arnold Arboretum.

An iron rod chain bridge across the Wen-hsien River, northwest of Bikou village in Gansu Province. Photo by J. F. Rock, 3 April 1925. © President and Fellows of Harvard College, Archives of the Arnold Arboretum.

Rock's temporary camp by the Babao He River, elevation 10,000 feet (3,000 m), facing the western end of the snow-capped Qilian mountain range which separates Gansu and Qinghai Provinces. Rock wrote of "a land of wonderful scenery, mountains, cascades, and majestic vistas." Photo by J. F. Rock, 18 October 1925. © President and Fellows of Harvard College, Archives of the Arnold Arboretum.

Eleven Naxi assistants of Rock's expedition photographed at Liulin, Gansu Province, near Tao he River. Photo by J. F. Rock, winter 1926.
© President and Fellows of Harvard College, Archives of the Arnold Arboretum.

Rock's expedition camp "among birches, poplars, pines, and wild apple trees" in the Tao he River Valley, elevation 9200 feet (2800 m), in Gansu Province. Photo by J. F. Rock, June or July 1925. © President and Fellows of Harvard College, Archives of the Arnold Arboretum.

Rock's last campsite in the grasslands of Yobchung Valley, elevation 10,740 feet (3270 m), Gansu Province. Photo by J. F. Rock, 30 July 1926.
© President and Fellows of Harvard College, Archives of the Arnold Arboretum.

Francis Kingdon-Ward (1885–1958)

Among the later contemporaries of Joseph Rock was Francis Kingdon-Ward, the son of a botany professor at Cambridge, England, from a family of botanists. Kingdon-Ward collected plants in Yunnan, Sichuan, Upper Burma, French Indochina, and southeastern Tibet. Between 1909 and 1957 he introduced hundreds of new species. In 1913, in Yunnan, Kingdon-Ward collected herbarium specimen 312 of a *Syringa* from a "small tree or shrub of 10–15 ft. [3–4.5 m]; arid region, 10,000 ft. [3050 m]." Scottish botanist Sir William Wright Smith (1916a), a plant explorer himself, described and named the new species *S. wardii*. The species is listed in *Flora of China* (Chang and Green 1996a) as being native to southeastern Tibet and northwestern Yunnan, and has been reported in cultivation.

William Purdom (1880–1921)

About the same time another noted collector, Englishman William Purdom, who had collected for the Veitch nursery and the Arnold Arboretum, was actively working in the interior provinces of China.

Purdom discovered no new species of *Syringa* but did collect seeds of already introduced species that he thought were variations of exceptional merit. In 1914 he teamed up for one exploration with Reginald Farrer in Gansu. Later Purdom became Inspector of Forests for the Chinese government.

Joseph Hers (1884–1965)

During this active time of plant explorations from 1900 to 1930, Joseph Hers, a Belgian railroad construction engineer and administrator, working in Sichuan, collected seeds and herbarium specimens for the Arnold Arboretum in northern China from 1910 to 1924. Hers collected seed of *Syringa microphylla* and seeds that gave rise to the lilac known today as *S. pubescens* subsp. *julianae* 'Hers'.

Frank Nicholas Meyer (1875–1918)

Frank Meyer, a Dutchman by birth and later an American by choice, had worked under and was trained by the famous Dutch botanist Hugo de Vries. Meyer loved the out-of-doors and traveling; by the time he was 13 he crossed the Alps on foot and went down

A log bridge over the Tao he River near Choni in western Gansu. Wilson crossed here several times, as did Purdom. Photo by William Purdom, June 1911. © President and Fellows of Harvard College, Archives of the Arnold Arboretum.

into Italy. Later he tramped through the United States to study the vegetation of Mexico, ever collecting and always preferring to go on foot. By 1905 he was working for the United States Department of Agriculture, Bureau of Plant Industry, Office of Foreign Seed and Plant Introduction. He made four expeditions to China. He spent three years exploring for plants, combing the spice stalls of northern China, Manchuria, and northern Korea before returning to Washington, D.C. A year later he left for the Caucasus, Siberia, Russian Turkestan, and Chinese Turkestan, after which he made two more expeditions to China.

During his 1909 expedition Meyer found a beautiful lilac growing in a garden near Beijing, collected cuttings, and was responsible for its introduction into Western gardens. Camillo Schneider at the Arnold Arboretum described the new species, naming it *Syringa meyeri* for the discoverer. This unique slow-growing species has never been found in the wild, leading some to believe it is a remarkable cross involving *S. pubescens* or its subspecies *microphylla*. Today it holds species rank. The wild form has been found growing in Liaoning and has been described and named *S. meyeri* var. *spontanea* by M.-C. Chang (1990).

In 1915 Meyer found *Syringa laciniata* "growing wild at Kingchow" in the extreme east of Gansu, not far from the border with Shaanxi. "It is south of the King River, a branch of the Wei which further east runs into the Huang ho, and is north of the Tsin-ling

Range [Qinling Shandi]." Without doubt, it is indigenous there and like other plants of Chinese origin found its way from that country to Persian gardens, where, commonly cultivated, it soon came to be regarded as native to the country of its adoption. It was from this Persian adoption that early botanists classified it a subspecies of *S. persica*, whereas *S.* ×*persica* is now considered to be a hybrid of *S.* ×*laciniata*, its other parent being "unknown" or at least unidentified. During his 1915 exploration Meyer sent back to the National Arboretum in Washington, D.C., the beautiful *S. oblata* subsp. *oblata* 'Alba', for many years growing magnificently at the Glendale Center and considered one of the finest cultivars of the species. Meyer has also been credited with introducing the previously discovered *S. villosa* into cultivation.

Meyer was an extremely able and prolific plant collector who traveled the great plains of China, Manchuria, Korea, up by Lanchow, the Great Wall, and into Wilson's Gansu. Most of his enormous collections were of economical rather than ornamental importance—soy, wheat, rice, peppers, and many valuable introductions—some discovered in the open stalls of the markets. He stayed out in the open or in simple village inns, "with odors hanging about to make even angels procure their handkerchiefs. . . . with foreign tongues ever babbling strange languages and unknown dialects."

Meyer introduced the single yellow rose *Rosa xanthina* 'Canary-Bird', the Chinese elm *Ulmus parvifolia*, and several ornamental shrubs. As he was preparing to leave Hebei, something happened. No details are known, but in June 1918 his swollen body was found floating in the sluggish waters of the Yangtze River below the port of Anking, Anhui, upstream from Nanjing, Jiangsu. The river he had sailed so often claimed another of its famous voyagers. What a loss. Frank Meyer was only in his early 40s.

George Forrest (1873–1932)

George Forrest came from a humble family. Born at Falkirk, Sterlingshire, Scotland, he went to school in Kilmarnock, Ayrshire, entering pharmacy, which he disliked. He loved to walk and hunt, and preferred the outdoors. After his studies the young Forrest went to Australia to work as a roustabout in the bush country, where he remained several years. He returned to

Syringa oblata subsp. *oblata* 'Alba' lines a pathway in the German legation garden in Beijing. Meyer sent home seeds from these plants, which he described as being drought resistant and potentially valuable for hybridizing. Photo by Frank N. Meyer, 23 April 1915. © President and Fellows of Harvard College, Archives of the Arnold Arboretum.

Scotland in 1902 at 30 and took a poorly paying job in the herbarium of Royal Botanic Garden, Edinburgh. Since he could not abide crowded towns, he walked 6 miles (9.5 km) each morning and evening to his country lodging. For five hours a day, with Scottish determination, he pored over herbarium specimens from all over the world, dedicated to learning all he possibly could about plants on which he, indeed, became an expert. This work was to be a great asset in his later life as a plant collector of outstanding ability in Yunnan.

Two years later, in 1904, Forrest left for China, where he spent 28 years. The area of Tibet and Yunnan became known as "Forrest's special territory"; he guarded it well and fiercely against other plant hunters. At Yaregong, on the Tibetan border, he met and became friendly with the French missionaries, especially Soulié, a skilled physician and a linguist fluent in all the difficult frontier dialects, who from his Tibetan marches had sent more than 7000 dried plant specimens to Paris.

While Forrest was visiting Soulié the mission was attacked by Tibetan monks in a border uprising. Foreigners were seized, tortured, and killed. Soulié, captured with several other missionaries, was tortured and hacked to death. In the skirmish and murders, Forrest and 80 of the mission staff escaped with the monks in pursuit. Eventually all were caught and tortured to death except Forrest, who managed to get away. Hiding by day, he fled through the mountains south, leaving his boots behind because of their traceable prints. Nearly captured, he again escaped, wading a river over his head. Later he wrote, "At the end of eight days I had ceased to care whether I lived or died. My feet were swollen out of all shape, my hands and face torn with thorns, and my whole person was caked in mire and blood." Starvation drove Forrest to risk approaching a village where he found friendly people for a few days before the Tibetans were again upon him. He fled upriver, through canebrakes, changing his directions for six days over glacier snows and ice that lacerated his feet. At last when he thought he was safe, he came to a maize field only to step upon a farmer's panji, a sharpened bamboo stake booby trap. It completely pierced through his foot. He tore the stake loose and after some days eventually found refuge in a mission house in a town where Chinese soldiers were

stationed. It took several months for his foot to heal sufficiently for him to walk again.

In Yunnan in 1906 Forrest discovered *Syringa yunnanensis* and sent back seeds that introduced it into commerce. A less hearty soul, after such trying experiences, would have willingly sailed for home, but not George Forrest. He was a solitary, brusque man with a deep love for Yunnan, its people and customs, and he continued hunting for new species for another 24 years—years of prolific output. In 1931 from Tonghai (then Teng-yueh), Yunnan, he wrote, "When all are dealt with and packed I expect to have nearly, if not more than, two mule-loads of good clean seed, representing some 4000 to 5000 species, and a mule load means 130 to 150 lbs. [59–68 kg], that is something like 300 lbs. [136 kg] of seed.... If all goes well I shall have made a rather glowing and satisfactory finish to all my past years of labour." Indeed, it was a glowing finish to the thousands of seeds and plants he had shipped over the 28 years and a collection of more than 31,000 herbarium sheets.

As the last parcels were packed and sent on their way, Forrest went snipe hunting, which was a favorite hobby. While in the field he developed chest pains and asked to be chair-carried to a low wall. As a snipe drummed overhead Forrest raised his gun, shot, and fell to the ground dead. He was buried in the Yunnan that he so loved in fall 1931.

Reginald John Farrer (1880–1920)
Euan Hillhouse Methven Cox (1893–1977)
Reginald Farrer, born in Yorkshire, England, and E. H. M. Cox, another Englishman, were in that class of amateur plant collectors who did considerable collecting mostly in Burma (now Myanmar) and, on returning, turned their plant-collecting experiences into books of great merit and interest. Although important for their work (Farrer with his tea [*Camellia sinensis*] hunting), neither discovered or is particularly noted for plant hunting that included lilacs. They are mentioned only because of their relationship to the plant hunters who did discover or send back seeds of *Syringa* species.

Farrer will ever be known for his two books on Gansu in which he described its northwestern mountains as "stretching across the world from easterly to westerly in one unbroken rank of impregnable 18,000 foot dolomite needles, crags, castles and pinnacles." In *The Garden of Asia* (1904), *In Old Ceylon* (1908), *On the Eaves of the World* (1917), and *Rainbow Bridge* (1921), Farrer proved to be a master of words and descriptions, especially on the experiences and conditions of plant hunting in the mountainous country.

Cox, who accompanied Farrer on his first journey of plant collecting, later edited *The Plant Introductions of Reginald Farrer* (1930), which describes the considerable contributions of that collector. Cox wrote of Farrer's colorful character:

> [H]is stocky figure clad in khaki shorts and shirt, tieless and colorless, a faded toupee on his head, old boots, and stockings that gradually slipped down and clung around his ankles as the day wore on . . . the constant use of the field glasses which always hung around his neck . . . and his intense satisfaction when a plant was once in his collection bag—his enjoyment of our evening tot of rum . . . his indomitable energy . . . his frame so unlikely for searching and climbing.

There has never been his likes as an alpine gardener nor as dashing a character as a plant collector. Farrer had a fine sense of humor despite torrential rains and mountain trails: "he set out on his pony (called Spotted Fat) followed by a faithful servant whom he called The Dragon." Although Farrer was only 40, the climate and harshness of plant journeys caught up with him. Each day he could do less. Unable to eat he could take only whiskey and soda—8000 miles (12,800 km) from home, in the unrelenting rains of the Chinese-Burmese borderlands he died, as The Dragon wrote to Cox, "without giving any of us pain or trouble!"

Lilacs in China

Are there still some undiscovered lilac species to be found in China? Surely one should expect somespecies from these enormously vast, colder areas as from the other provinces of China, although much exploring has been done in recent years as is evident from the *Syringa* taxa reported in the *Flora of China* (Chang and Green 1996a). China has been a goldmine of the many species of lilacs among the richness of its native plants. What other discoveries may yet be made re-

mains untold. Great strides have been made in hybridizing these many species. They have prospered well in Canada and in the United States and more recently in Russia—what wonderful portents for the future.

Beijing
S. meyeri var. *meyeri* (in cultivation only)
S. meyeri var. *spontanea* (in cultivation)

Gansu
S. komarowii subsp. *komarowii*
S. oblata subsp. *oblata*
S. pekinensis
S. pinnatifolia
S. protolaciniata
S. pubescens subsp. *microphylla*
S. pubescens subsp. *microphylla* var. *potaninii*

Hebei
S. oblata subsp. *oblata*
S. pekinensis
S. pubescens subsp. *microphylla*
S. pubescens subsp. *pubescens*
S. villosa

Heilongjiang
S. reticulata subsp. *amurensis*
S. wolfii

Henan
S. oblata subsp. *oblata*
S. pekinensis
S. pubescens subsp. *microphylla*
S. pubescens subsp. *pubescens*

Hubei
S. komarowii subsp. *reflexa*
S. pubescens subsp. *julianae*
S. pubescens subsp. *microphylla*

Jilin
S. oblata subsp. *dilatata*
S. oblata subsp. *oblata*
S. pubescens subsp. *patula*
S. reticulata subsp. *amurensis*
S. wolfii

Liaoning
S. meyeri var. *spontanea*
S. oblata subsp. *dilatata*
S. oblata subsp. *oblata*
S. pubescens subsp. *patula*
S. reticulata subsp. *amurensis*
S. wolfii

Nei Mongol
  S. oblata subsp. *oblata*
  S. pekinensis
  S. pinnatifolia
  S. reticulata subsp. *amurensis*
Ningxia
  S. oblata subsp. *oblata*
  S. pekinensis
  S. pinnatifolia
  S. pubescens subsp. *microphylla*
Qinghai
  S. oblata subsp. *oblata*
  S. pinnatifolia
  S. protolaciniata
  S. pubescens subsp. *microphylla*
Shaanxi
  S. komarowii subsp. *komarowii*
  S. oblata subsp. *oblata*
  S. pekinensis

S. pinnatifolia
S. pubescens subsp. *microphylla*
S. pubescens subsp. *microphylla* var. *flavanthera*
S. pubescens subsp. *pubescens*
Shandong
  S. oblata subsp. *oblata*
  S. pubescens subsp. *pubescens*
Shanxi
  S. oblata subsp. *oblata*
  S. pekinensis
  S. pubescens subsp. *microphylla*
  S. pubescens subsp. *pubescens*
  S. villosa
Sichuan
  S. komarowii subsp. *komarowii*
  S. komarowii subsp. *reflexa*
  S. mairei
  S. oblata subsp. *oblata*

S. pekinensis
S. pinetorum
S. pinnatifolia
S. pubescens subsp. *microphylla*
S. sweginzowii
S. tomentella
S. yunnanensis
Tibet (Xizang)
  S. mairei
  S. pinetorum
  S. tibetica
  S. wardii
  S. yunnanensis
Yunnan
  S. komarowii subsp. *komarowii*
  S. mairei
  S. pinetorum
  S. wardii
  S. yunnanensis

Map of Chinese provinces.

The Great Botanical and Horticultural Institutions

No account of plant explorations would be complete without mention of the great world herbaria, botanical gardens, and arboreta that often were the guardians of materials obtained from these difficult expeditions and that, most often, kept meticulous record by accession number of each seedling and cutting sent them. It was through these great educational-horticultural institutions that most of the plant introductions were made and preserved for our gardens.

Foremost is the commercial nursery of Veitch in England. Singly this firm undertook to send plant collectors to Asia on several occasions and perhaps was the most significant nursery in acquiring and selling new plants from that region. It trained collectors and underwrote the financial burdens of extensive explorations, including Wilson's first two explorations (Shephard 2003).

Although several horticultural institutions became recipients of these plant treasures—in England, Scotland, France, Austria, Germany, Italy, Russia, Sweden, and the United States—a few stand out for their great contributions to the history of the lilacs. The Royal Botanic Gardens, Kew, is perhaps the paternal institution of longest horticultural standing and reputation worldwide. In the United States, Arnold Arboretum of Jamaica Plain, Massachusetts, is known for its magnificent work in horticulture, plant research, and archival and herbarium materials. Many of the original introductions of lilac species are still to be found in the Arboretum's collections. For lilacs it is the mother institution in North America. From this single source have come most of the species in commerce in North America and countless cultivars. It is one of the greatest repositories of living, authentic lilac materials in the world. In Saint Petersburg, the Komarov Botanical Institute of the Russian Academy of Science has long been renown for its herbarium, archives, and library. Also in Saint Petersburg, the Komarov Institute Botanic Garden founded in 1714 as the medicinal garden of Tsar Peter the Great has for centuries been the repository for the collections made by many famous European and Asian botanists and plant explorers, and was the main botanical garden in the former Soviet Union. In France, the archives and herbarium materials of the Jardin des Plantes of the Muséum National d'Histoire Naturelle in Paris are replete with botanical writings and specimens collected by countless scholars.

The institutions most active in modern plant explorations appear to be Arnold Arboretum; Royal Botanic Gardens, Kew; and University of Tokyo. More recently, lilac introductions have been made from South Korea through explorations by the University of New Hampshire at Durham. Elwyn Meader collected seed of *Syringa pubescens* subsp. *patula* in the Pouk Han Mountains in 1947. Selected from the resulting seedlings and introduced in 1954 was 'Miss Kim'; it subsequently received an Award of Garden Merit from the Royal Horticultural Society, London. Radcliffe Pike collected pollen of native plants of *S. vulgaris* in the mountains of Romania and brought it back to Durham, where Owen Rogers used it to pollinate flowers of *S. oblata* raised from native-collected seed, repeating the cross made originally by Victor Lemoine (1878) and resulting in *S.* ×*hyacinthiflora* 'Hyacinthiflora Plena'.

Lilac seed has been collected in China by Peter Bristol of the Holden Arboretum, Kirtland, Ohio, and others. Since the 1970s Royal Botanical Gardens, Hamilton, Ontario, has enriched its Katie Osborne

Elwyn Meader collected lilac seeds in Korea, one of which when planted was selected and named *Syringa pubescens* subsp. *patula* 'Miss Kim'. John Fiala

Lilac Garden with cultivars developed in Europe and Asia. In return, the Gardens have shared scions and cuttings of *Syringa* cultivars with public and private collections in Europe, Asia, and Australia.

McKelvey (1928) provided more detailed taxonomic information gleaned from the writings of many botanists. For those interested in updating her materials, the archives of the institutions mentioned could contribute much pertinent information on the genus *Syringa*.

Chronological Listing of Principal *Syringa* Explorations in Asia

1742 Pierre d'Incarville collects specimens of *S. pekinensis* in the Beijing mountains.

1750 Pierre d'Incarville collects specimens of *S. villosa* in the Beijing mountains.

1831 Alexander von Bunge explores the region around Beijing and sends lilac specimens back to Saint Petersburg.

1831 Robert Blinkworth collects specimens of *S. emodi* in the Kuram Valley of Afghanistan.

1831 Porfirij Kirilov rediscovers *S. pekinensis* in the Beijing mountains and sends seed to Saint Petersburg.

1835 Porfirij Kirilov rediscovers *S. villosa* and sends plant materials back to Saint Petersburg.

1840 Porfirij Kirilov collects specimens of *S. pubescens* subsp. *pubescens* in Hebei.

1853–1856 Robert Fortune sends the first live plants of *S. oblata* subsp. *oblata* and *S. oblata* subsp. *oblata* 'Alba' gathered from Chinese gardens back to England.

1855 Richard Maack and Karl Maximowicz independently collect specimens of *S. reticulata* subsp. *amurensis*.

1863 Father Armand David collects *S. pekinensis* in the Beijing mountains and is credited as its discoverer.

1870 James E. T. Aitchison collects specimens of *S. afghanica* in the Kuram Valley of Afghanistan.

1875 Karl Maximowicz collects *S. reticulata* subsp. *reticulata* in Japan, calling it *S. japonica*.

1885 Grigorii Potanin collects *S. oblata* subsp. *oblata* in Shaanxi and *S. pubescens* subsp. *microphylla* var. *potaninii* in Gansu.

1887 Abbot Jean Marie Delavay collects *S. yunnanensis* in the wooded areas around Lake Lanking in Yunnan.

1890 Pierre Bonvalot and Prince Henri d'Orléans collect *S. tomentella* in Sichuan.

1891–1894 Grigorii Potanin collects specimens of *S. komarowii* in Sichuan.

1891 Father Giuseppe Giraldi collects *S. oblata* subsp. *oblata* in Shaanxi.

1893–1895 Vladimir Komarov sends seed of *S. wolfii* to Saint Petersburg.

1895 A. Sontag collects *S. pubescens* subsp. *patula* near Seoul, Korea.

1896 Father Giuseppe Giraldi collects *S. pubescens* subsp. *microphylla* in Shaanxi.

1901 Ernest Wilson collects *S. pubescens* subsp. *julianae* and *S. komarowii* subsp. *reflexa* in Hubei.

1904 Ernest Wilson collects specimens of *S. pinnatifolia* in western Sichuan and seed of *S. sweginzowii*.

1906 George Forrest returns from Yunnan with seed of *S. yunnanensis*, introducing this species to gardens and commerce.

1907–1908 Ernest Wilson makes his third plant exploration for the Arnold Arboretum, bringing back additional seed of already-discovered species.

1908 Frank Meyer collects a lilac growing in gardens at Fengtai, Henan, bringing back cuttings to the United States; Camillo Schneider names the species *S. meyeri* for the discoverer; Meyer also collects *S. oblata* subsp. *oblata* 'Alba'.

1909–1911 William Purdom collects information and plant materials on already-discovered lilac species.

1910–1911 Ernest Wilson, on his fourth exploration on behalf of the Arnold Arboretum, collects additional seed and takes pictures of already-discovered species.

Chronological Listing of Principal *Syringa* Explorations in Asia (Continued)

1913   Francis Kingdon-Ward collects herbarium specimen of *S. wardii* in Yunnan.

1 913–1915   Frank Meyer collects additional materials and seed of already-discovered species.

1914   Édouard-Ernest Maire collects herbarium specimen of *S. mairei* in Yunnan.

1914   Francis Kingdon-Ward collects *S. pinetorum*.

1917   Ernest Wilson, on his fifth trip, sends back seed of *S. oblata* var. *dilatata* found in Korea.

1922–1923   Joseph Hers collects *S. pubescens* subsp. *microphylla* and *S. pubescens* subsp. *julianae* 'Hers', introducing them into Europe and the United States.

1924–1925   Ernest Wilson, on his sixth trip to China, sends back seed of *S. pinnatifolia* and other previously discovered species to the Arnold Arboretum.

1925–1926   Joseph Rock, working for the Arnold Arboretum, sends back lilac specimens and seed of already-discovered species from southwestern China.

1930   Palemon Dorsett and Warner Morse of the U.S. Department of Agriculture collect seed of *S. oblata* subsp. *dilatata* in Manchuria (Plant Introduction 90671).

1934   Harry Smith collects *S. tigerstedtii* (now included in *S. sweginzowii*) in Sichuan, introducing the species at the University of Uppsala, Sweden.

1947   Elwyn Meader collects seed of *S. pubescens* subsp. *patula* in the Pouk Han Mountains, Korea; 'Miss Kim' is selected from the seedlings and introduced.

1977   Robert and Jelena De Belder collect seed of *S. pubescens* subsp. *patula* in Mount Sorak National Park, South Korea.

1978   The U.S. Department of Agriculture and National Geographic Society Expedition collect *S. reticulata* subsp. *reticulata* in Japan.

1980   Peter Bristol collects seed of *S. oblata* in Sichuan.

1980   Stephen Spongberg, Bruce Bartholomew, and David Boufford, members of the Sino-American Botanical Expedition to western Hubei, sponsored jointly by the Chinese Academia Sinica and the Botanical Society of America, collect *S. komarowii* subsp. *reflexa* in the Shennongjia Forest District, Hubei.

1981–1986   Roy Lancaster on several expeditions collects *S. yunnanensis* (Sichuan, 1981, *RL 834*), *S. pubescens* (Hubei, 1983, *RL 1132*), *S. pinnatifolia* (Sichuan, 1986, *RL 1616*), *S. pubescens* subsp. *microphylla* (Sichuan, 1986, *RL 1623*), and *S. yunnanensis* (Yunnan, 1986, *RL 1684*).

1989   Frank Meyer collects *S. protolaciniata*.

1992   Chen Xin-Lu collects seed in Shaanxi from six different plants of *S. pubescens* subsp. *microphylla*, representing a range of leaf sizes, sending the seeds to Royal Botanic Gardens, Kew, England.

1993   The North America–China Plant Exploration Consortium (NACPEC) collects seed of *S. reticulata* subsp. *amurensis* in Heilongjiang.

1993   Charles Baring and William McNamara collect seed of *S. emodi* in the Great Himalayan National Park, India.

1994   Kris Bachtell, Peter Bristol, and Paul Meyer, members of NACPEC, collect seed of *S. pubescens* subsp. *patula*, *S. pekinensis*, and *S. villosa* in Beijing Municipality.

1996   Chen Xin-Lu sends scions of *S. pekinensis* and *S. pubescens* to Royal Botanical Gardens, Hamilton, Ontario (*RBG 960006* and *RBG 960005*).

1996   NACPEC collects *S. komarowii* subsp. *reflexa* and *S. pubescens* subsp. *microphylla* in Shaanxi.

1997   NACPEC collects *S. reticulata* subsp. *amurensis* and *S. wolfii* (*NACPEC 97023*) in Jilin.

1997   Stephen Spongberg and Andrew Bell collect two as-yet-unidentified species of *Syringa* during their expedition to Yunnan and Sichuan (*S&B 113, 243*).

There were undoubtedly other plant explorations to China that included native collections and perhaps garden lilacs of which we are unaware. It is significant that the many species and cultivars of lilacs discovered and introduced over 240 years by men and women from many nations make this plant, indeed, an international shrub.

In the following pages are presented the different species of lilacs that are readily accepted as such by most authorities today. The accepted names for each species are given according to the latest nomenclature. Older synonyms are also given for those who may have lilacs known to them only by these older names. Most species are presented with at least one color photo, or more. Some because of their rarity are difficult to find and to photograph.

Subgenus *Ligustrina*—The Tree Lilacs

The subgenus *Ligustrina* derives its name from the resemblance of its flowers to those of privet (genus *Ligustrum*). At one time these late-flowering tree lilacs were considered by some botanists not to belong to the genus *Syringa*. Today we recognize their identity with the lilacs. The tree lilacs, their botanical classification and naming, have been troublesome for taxonomists for many years. As recently as the late 1990s Chang and Green (1996a) recognized one species in this subgenus, namely, *S. reticulata*, with three additional subspecies—*reticulata*, *amurensis*, and *pekinensis*. More recently, however, Li et al. (2002) demonstrated convincingly that subspecies *pekinensis* should be given species status.

1a Shrubs or trees 4–10(–15) m, with smooth, cherrylike
     bark; fruit capsule apex blunt. . . . .*S. reticulata*
   2a Leaves mostly longer than 7 cm, hairy, especially
       on the midrib and main veins on the undersurface
       . . . . *S. reticulata* subsp. *reticulata*
   2b Leaves mostly less than 7 cm, glabrous above,
       petiole stoutish, 1–2 cm; veinlets slightly sunk
       . . . .*S. reticulata* subsp. *amurensis*
1b Shrubs or small trees 2–5(–10) m, with exfoliating bark;
     petiole slender, 1.5–3 cm; veinlets not sunk on the
     upper surface of the leaf; fruit capsule apex acute to
     acuminate . . . .*S. pekinensis*

Syringa reticulata (Blume) H. Hara

Shrubs or trees 4–10(–15) m, glabrous. Petiole stoutish, 1–2 cm; leaf blade ovate, ovate-lanceolate, elliptic-ovate, oblong-lanceolate, or suborbicular, 2.5–13 × 1–6(–8) cm, papery or thickly so, or rarely pubescent below, base rounded, truncate, subcordate, or cuneate, apex acuminate to caudate-acuminate or acute. Panicles lateral, one to many paired on same branch, 5–20(–27) × 3–20 cm. Pedicel to 2 mm. Calyx 1–2 mm. Corolla wheel shaped, white, 3–5 mm; tube as long as calyx or slightly longer. Capsule long elliptic to lanceolate, 1.5–2.5 cm, smooth or minutely lenticellate, apex blunt. Flowering May–August, fruiting August–October.

 Habitat: Mixed forests on slopes, grasslands, near gullies; 100–1200 m. Heilongjiang, Jilin, Liaoning, Nei Mongol; Japan, Korea, eastern Russia.

This description and range accommodate the whole of the species; two subspecies are recognized.

Syringa reticulata subsp. *reticulata*
Japanese tree lilac
Synonyms: *Ligustrum reticulatum* Blume, *S. japonica* (Maximowicz) Decaisne, *S. amurensis* var. *japonica* (Maximowicz) Franchet & Savatier

The binomial *Syringa reticulata* (Blume) H. Hara applies to both the Japanese tree lilac (subsp. *reticulata*) and the Amur tree lilac (subsp. *amurensis*). Referring to the Japanese tree lilac as *S. reticulata* is quite acceptable, but referring to it as *S. reticulata* subsp. *reticulata* is more precise and distinguishes it from the Amur tree lilac. Subspecies *reticulata* is endemic to Japan.

 McKelvey (1928) relayed the story of the introduction of *Syringa reticulata* subsp. *reticulata* which,

> first appeared in *The Gardeners' Chronicle* of 1886 where a letter from Professor C. S. Sargent is quoted: "Mr. W. S. Clark, at that time President of the Agricultural College at Sapporo, in Japan, sent to the [Arnold] Arboretum in 1876, seed of an Oleaceous plant, described by him as a small tree. The plants raised from these seeds flowered last summer [1885] for the first time, and proved to be *Syringa japonica*."

Syringa reticulata subsp. *reticulata* is the finest of the tree lilacs. It is a lovely, upright-growing tree to 30 feet (9 m), rather round-topped, with dark leaves and large plumes of feathery white blossoms that resemble huge panicles of privet. It blooms in June or early July, depending on latitude and altitude. The protruding yellow anthers give added elegance. It has the same fragrance as the Peking lilac (*S. pekinensis*). The Japanese and Amur lilacs have a most appealing reddish brown glossy bark that peels on younger branches, not unlike cherry bark. The bark of Japanese lilac is somewhat more reddish to deep rich brown than that of the Amur lilac; both are prominently lenticellate. Both are splendid forms of a charming tree that will delight you and all who visit your garden. McKelvey found very little difference between the two. It might be difficult to find subsp. *amurensis* as very few nurseries carry it, preferring subsp. *reticulata* instead.

There are a number of selections of *Syringa reticulata* subsp. *reticulata*.

'Cameo's Jewel', Moro 1995. An open-pollinated seedling of 'Ivory Silk'. Foliage mottled and margined golden yellow, becoming cream marked by midsummer.

'Chantilly Lace', J. Herrmann ca. 1990. "Margins on young leaves pale yellowish green, maturing to creamy yellow; width of margins irregular, varying from 5 to 20 mm. Central portion of leaf blades blotched dark green with light green (see photo on page 192). Plants in most aspects somewhat smaller than the green form. In exposed sunny locations var-

Syringa reticulata subsp. *reticulata*, bark. John Fiala.

Syringa reticulata subsp. *reticulata*, habit. Falconskeape, Medina, Ohio. John Fiala.

Syringa reticulata subsp. *reticulata*, flowers. B. Peart and M. Walton

iegated foliage is prone to sunburn" (Vrugtman 1988, 1989).

'China Gold', Fiala 1990. Foliage variegated to golden, turning pale yellow-green by summer. Habit more upright than the green form. New-growth branchlets reddish.

'Cole', Cole 1977. Single white. Habit narrower than the green form.

'Elliott' (marketed in North America as SNOW-CAP), Carlton Plants Nursery 2000. A compact selection with uniform branching habit.

'Golden Eclipse', Bakker 2000. "Leaves unfold with bright golden variegated and undulated margins, and a dark green center. As the season progresses the golden margins fade [eclipse] to a lighter green; the foliage shows excellent resistance to sunburn" (Vrugtman 2003b).

'Ivory Silk', Pokluda 1973. Introduced by Sheridan Nurseries, Ontario. More compact and globose

in crown than most selections, it is hardy in USDA hardiness zones 3–7, blooms heavily already at an early age, grows to 20 feet (6 m) with a 12-foot (3.6-m) spread in 15 years, is drought resistant and free of pests and disease. It was awarded the coveted Penn-

Syringa reticulata subsp. *reticulata* 'Chantilly Lace', flowers. B. Peart and M. Walton

Syringa reticulata subsp. *reticulata* 'Chantilly Lace', habit. B. Peart and M. Walton

Syringa reticulata subsp. *reticulata* 'Golden Eclipse'. B. Peart and M. Walton

Syringa reticulata subsp. *reticulata* 'Ivory Silk'. flowers. B. Peart and M. Walton

sylvania Horticultural Society's Gold Medal in 1996 and is the 2000 Theodore Klein Plant Award Winner of the University of Kentucky Nursery and Landscape Program (Gressley 2000).

'**PNI 7523**' (marketed in North America as REGENT or REGENT BRAND), Flemer 1988. Plants under this name are grown from seed, upright in habit, and quite vigorous; probably a topovariant.

'**Sigzam**' (marketed in North America as SIGNATURE), Zampini 1999. Habit rounded, upright, 18–20 feet (5.4–6 m) tall, 15 feet wide (4.5 m). Foliage blue-green, turning bronze in autumn. Thyrses rich creamy white. Fruit inconspicuous. Very similar to 'Ivory Silk' with the exception of the flowers, which are formed in rounded instead of pyramidal thyrses. Blooms mid-July, a week later than 'Ivory Silk'. Use as a small street tree, or ornamental tree in the landscape. USDA hardiness zone 3.

'**Summer Snow**', Schichtel 1990. Selected for its smaller, more compact, subglobose habit, glossy bark, and large creamy white thyrses. Suited for urban tree planting

'**Willamette**' (marketed in North America as IVORY PILLAR), Carlton Plants Nursery 2000. Habit more upright and narrow than other cultivars, attaining a pyramidal shape although not quite a pillar.

The Japanese lilac cultivars are all of relative recent vintage, hence there is little comparative information available on their performance. David Gressley (2000), at the Holden Arboretum, reported that 'Ivory Silk' "tends to grow in an upright form with a rounded top. Lower branches tend to angle upward at somewhat less than 45 degree angles." About 'Summer Snow' Gressley (2000) wrote,

> [I]ts inherent advantage lies in the ability to maintain a single leader habit. Although rounded in youth, the canopy matures to an upright rounded form, just a bit broader than 'Ivory Silk'. Lower branches appear to angle closer to 45 degrees from the leader. Floral quantity and quality, fragrance and bark texture of 'Summer Snow' are comparable to 'Ivory Silk' with neither taxa able to claim a clear superiority over the other.

The Japanese lilac is quite similar in size, habit, leaf, and inflorescence to the Amur tree lilac. In tree form *Syringa reticulata* subsp. *amurensis* is more rounded and broader than *S. reticulata* subsp. *reticulata*. McKelvey (1928) stated that the Japanese tree lilac,

> [d]iffers from [Amur tree lilac] in its more tree-like habit and larger size, up to 30 ft. [9 m] tall; in its later blooming season (this applies to the cultivated plant); in its slightly larger, ovoid winter-buds with noticeably ciliate margins to the scales; in its slightly larger leaves, flowers and flower clusters; in the occasionally subcordate base of the leaf and in the pubescence covering, at least when young, its under surface; and in its usually oblong and verrucose capsule.

Syringa reticulata subsp. *reticulata* makes a most pleasing street tree. In the Netherlands it is planted widely in city streets. In Cleveland, Ohio, some decades ago, under an enterprising Shade Tree and Parks

Director, several streets in the newer developments were planted with the subspecies. After 30 years they were lovely small trees requiring practically no pruning or spraying, forming an avenue of bright summer green and magnificent in bloom. The one problem is that children love to peel their attractive bark. Excellent advice on using the Japanese tree lilac for urban island and median-strip planting is given by William Flemer III (1984) of Princeton Nurseries, Princeton, New Jersey.

Syringa reticulata subsp. *amurensis* (Ruprecht) P. S. Green & M.-C. Chang
Amur tree lilac, Manchurian tree lilac

Synonyms: *S. amurensis* Ruprecht, *Ligustrina amurensis* Ruprecht, *L. amurensis* var. *mandshurica* Maximowicz, *S. reticulata* var. *amurensis* (Ruprecht) Pringle, *S. reticulata* var. *mandshurica* (Maximowicz) H. Hara, *S. fauriei* H. Léveillé (which appears to be only questionably distinct according to Pringle 1990)

> Trees 4–10(–15) m. Petiole stoutish, 1–2 cm; leaf blade broadly ovate, elliptic-ovate to oblong-lanceolate. Calyx 1.5–2 mm. Corolla 4–5 mm. Capsule blunt at apex. Flowering June–July, fruiting August–October.
>
> Habitat: Mixed forests on slopes, grasslands, near gullies; 100–1200 m. Heilongjiang, Jilin, Liaoning, Nei Mongol; Korea, eastern Russia.

This is the continental subspecies, also referred to as Manchurian lilac (Olmsted et al. 1923), found native throughout northern China. It was probably first found in 1855 by two Russian botanists traveling independently, Richard Maack and Karl Maximowicz. Ruprecht (1857, 25) quoted Maack:

> It was gathered by me first on June 20 [1855], on the right valley wall of the Chingan Range, later, now and again, in Central Amur near the mouth of the Garin on the left valley banks of the Ongma Chongko [?]. It grew on the banks of the valleys and at the foot of the banks in mixed forests. I collected it on June 20 in full boom and later on July 26, with unripe and barren fruit in the right valley wall of Sargu by the river Girri. It is called *furagda* by the Goldi at the mouth of the Ussuri and below it.

Maximowicz (1859) described it as "a tree entirely glabrous, leaves ovate, acuminate, subtruncate . . . same color on both sides, the calyx lobes very short." He noted it as coming from the lower Amur near Borbi and from several places in the Bureja Mountains, where in some places it was common in deciduous woods, and in others it grew on the margins of coniferous forests.

Gustav Radde (quoted in Bretschneider 1898), who explored Siberia from 1855 to 1859, also described the subspecies:

> Trunks having the thickness of a leg, little inclined to grow into a shrub, and usually reaching at the most a height of 20–30 feet [6–9 m]. It avoids proximity to conifers and was not seen in the interior of the mountains. It only rarely extends to the banks of the rivers (for instance the left bank of an unnamed stream as a gigantic specimen 35 feet [10.5 m] tall, hidden however, by *Ulmus*, etc.). Common in the valleys of Chotschio which open to the west and southwest . . . It does not appear in the plains.

Syringa reticulata subsp. *amurensis*, habit. B. Peart and M. Walton

Syringa reticulata subsp. *amurensis*, flowers. B. Peart and M. Walton

Syringa pekinensis Ruprecht
Peking lilac, Chinese tree lilac

Synonyms: *S. reticulata* subsp. *pekinensis* (Ruprecht) P. S. Green & M.-C. Chang, *Ligustrina amurensis* var. *pekinensis* (Ruprecht) Maximowicz, *S. amurensis* var. *pekinensis* (Ruprecht) Maximowicz

> Shrubs or small trees 2–5(–10) m. Petiole slender, 1.5–3 cm; leaf blade ovate to ovate-lanceolate or suborbicular. Calyx 1–1.5 mm. Corolla 3–4 mm. Capsule apex acute to acuminate. Flowering May–August, fruiting August–October.
> Habitat: Woods on slopes, valleys, along gullies; 600–2400 m. Gansu, Hebei, Henan, Nei Mongol, Ningxia, Shaanxi, Shanxi, northern Sichuan; usually cultivated as an ornamental in northern China.

McKelvey (1928) was uncertain who first discovered this species. Although several plant explorers collected in this region—Pierre d'Incarville in 1742, Porfirij Kirilov from 1831 to 1840, Alexander Tatarinov from 1840 to 1850, Father Armand David in 1863—it was

Franz Ruprecht, the famous student of the Russian flora, who first described the species in 1857.

Syringa pekinensis was introduced into cultivation by Emil Bretschneider, who collected seed in the Beijing mountains. Seed was received in Paris at Jardin des Plantes in 1880, in England at Royal Botanic Gardens, Kew, in 1881 (according to Bean), and in Germany at Botanical Garden and Botanical Museum Berlin-Dahlem in 1885. On 23 January 1882 seed was received at the Arnold Arboretum.

Seedlings of Peking lilac are vigorous, but they take their time before producing their first bloom. First bloom of the Arnold Arboretum seedlings was recorded in 1889. Although the original tree at the Arnold Arboretum (*AA 1746*) is no longer alive, the Central Experimental Farm in Ottawa, Ontario, Canada, received two plants from the Arboretum in 1902, most likely seedlings grown from seed collected from the original introductions. Joan Speirs (2004, pers. comm. to F.V.) reported that one of these two plants is in the arboretum:

> It is a huge lovely tree and appears to fit the description for the [sub]species and is readily distinguishable for *Syringa reticulata* subsp. *reticulata* and subsp. *amurensis* by leaf size and shape and later bloom time than the other two subspecies. This is the only specimen of this subspecies at the Farm.

McKelvey's (1928) description, a bit more detailed than others, stated,

> In cultivation a large slender, round-topped shrub or small tree up to 15 ft tall, but said to attain 40 ft as a wild plant; bark on old wood fissured, on branchlets reddish brown, marked by numerous large and conspicuous lenticels, sometimes exfoliating in papery flakes, fissuring early. Winter-buds ovoid with acute apex . . . Leaves firm in texture, lanceolate, ovate, ovate-lanceolate, elliptic-ovate . . . 1–3½ in. long, ¾–2¼ in. broad . . . dark green above, paler beneath . . . Inflorescence commonly from one pair of lateral buds at end of branchlet . . . 4–7 in. long; rachis spreading horizontally . . . corolla-lobes narrow . . . color Marguerite Yellow (XXX.); . . . stamens twice as long as limb, . . .

Syringa pekinensis, flowers. B. Peart and M. Walton

Syringa pekinensis, bark. John Fiala

Syringa pekinensis, leaves. B. Peart and M. Walton

anthers Primrose Yellow.... Capsule ¾ in. long, oblong... sparingly verrucose.

Decaisne (1979), quoting Father Armand David's description of the fragrance of the Peking lilac, described it thus: "The white flowers exhale the fragrance of honey."

For the garden *Syringa pekinensis* is a rapidly growing tall shrub or tree with dark foliage and heads of very small creamy white flowers covering the tree in wonderful clusters in mid to late June; although in some localities it will be as early as mid-May, in others it will be as late as early July, depending on latitude and altitude. As the tree ages, its most outstanding characteristic is the beautiful peeling bark, which is especially attractive against winter snow. In growing this subspecies from seed, some plants are greatly superior in the peeling and papery curls of the bark. One must be certain to obtain a specimen from such a plant.

Although *Syringa pekinensis* is a strong and rapid grower in its first decade, it is rather shy blooming. In the United States it is not planted as extensively as is *S. reticulata* subsp. *reticulata* and its cultivars because of its reputation for slow flowering. For many decades *S. reticulata* subsp. *reticulata* appeared to be the better small tree, with exciting cherrylike bark, better form, and larger blossom. In recent years, however, growers have given increased attention to the Peking tree lilac and its variability. Several cultivars of *S. pekinensis* are known:

'**Cleaves**', Cleaves 2000. Selected for its unusually large foliage.

'**DTR 124**' (marketed in North America as SUMMER CHARM), Wandell 1992. Slightly smaller than the species, ovoid in stature, reaching 30 feet (9 m) high and 15 feet (4.5 m) wide, producing creamy white fragrant thyrses in June (U.S. Plant Patent 8951, 18 October 1994).

'**Jin Yuan**', B.-H. Dong & J.-Y. Chen 1990s. Name registered in 2003. Selected for its yellowish golden inflorescences. Florets single, very fragrant. Not yet reported in cultivation in North America or Europe, it has appeared also under the names 'Bei Jing Huang' (Zhang and Cui 2000) and 'Beijing Huan' (Zhang and Dirr 2004).

'**Morton**' (marketed in North America as CHINA SNOW), Rock & Bachtell 1991. Selected for its tolerance to drought, extreme cold (USDA hardiness zones

5–8) and deicing salts, its narrow habit of growth, and attractive bark. Trees are very floriferous, the thyrses creamy white and very fragrant. The original tree, grown from seed collected by Joseph Rock in Gansu, China, in 1926, has reached 40 feet (12 m) high and 25 feet (7.5 m) wide at its home in the

Syringa pekinensis 'Pendula', habit. B. Peart and M. Walton

Syringa pekinensis 'Pendula', flowers. B. Peart and M. Walton

Morton Arboretum, Lisle, Illinois. Formerly listed as WATER TOWER (McKelvey 1928, 496–497; Bachtell 1991; Vrugtman 2003c).

'Pendula', Temple 1887. This very rare, excellent medium to small tree was selected for its weeping growth habit. It needs ample room in the garden for maturity. The leaves turn color in autumn. Temple's original plant was one of the seedlings raised from the seed lot received by the Arnold Arboretum from Emil Bretschneider in 1882. It is more weeping in name than in actual growth, although we have seen a few specimens that were noticeably so while still very young. To propagate this cultivar it must be grafted, preferably at eye height, to retain its weeping characteristic, or obtained as rooted cuttings and staked, but never grown from seed. Seed of this cultivar produces a high percentage of albino seedlings, far more so than in any other lilac.

'SunDak' ('Sundak'; marketed in North America as COPPER CURLS), D. Herman 1999. Selected at North Dakota State University, Fargo, for its coppery orange, peeling bark and large white thyrses. Persistent seed capsules add winter interest.

'Zhang Zhiming' (marketed in North America as BEIJING GOLD), Zhang Z.-M. & Bachtell 2003. Selected for its light yellow or primrose-yellow, although not quite gold, well-scented inflorescences.

Cultivating Tree Lilacs

All tree lilacs thrive in rich, well-drained soils. If a large tree is desired, prune away all lower and smaller branches (Gressley 2000). Alternatively, two- or three-trunked trees provide winter interest because of the appearance of the bark and the interesting branching pattern. Plant tree lilacs in front of a background of tall conifers to highlight the display of bloom. Place them as single specimens at the turn of a winding walk. Surround them in a shrub planting with the very latest-to-bloom Villosae Group cultivars, with which they will often overlap in bloom. Tree lilacs are exotic in solitary or triangular plantings. They are healthy trees seldom, if ever, bothered by insects or diseases. Their seed panicles are very large and most interesting in autumn.

Many specimens of *Syringa reticulata* are grown from seed by nurserymen and show considerable variation in size, quality of bloom, and richness of bark. Tree lilac seeds take weeks longer, a month or more, to germinate and do so over a long period of time, never evenly as does *S. vulgaris* seed. One must be patient. Some seedlings are definitely better than others, whereas others are poor in all aspects. Frequently, no distinction is made between the two subspecies. A great deal of selection can to be done to develop better cultivars. Those selected should be propagated only by cuttings and not from seed.

The tree lilacs from China and Japan are full of mysteries. *Syringa reticulata* has never been successfully crossed with any other lilac species, although several attempts have been made. Some crosses produced infertile embryos. In 1900 Louis Henry, at the Jardin des Plantes in Paris, crossed both subspecies *reticulata* and *amurensis* with *S. villosa*, *S. pubescens*, and *S. vulgaris*, resulting in infertile seed. In 1930 Karl Sax unsuccessfully crossed *S. reticulata* with *S. reflexa*; Clapp attempted a *S. vulgaris* cross. In 1950 Albert F. Yeager attempted the cross *S. reticulata* × *S. pubescens* subsp. *patula* 'Miss Kim'. In 1964 Frits Schneider crossed *S. reticulata* subsp. *reticulata* × *S. vulgaris* 'Night', without success. Kudryatseva and Bibikova (1969) attempted *S. reticulata* subsp. *reticulata* crosses with *S. vulgaris*, *S. josikaea*, *S. oblata*, *S. reflexa*, *S. villosa*, and *S. wolfii* without success. In 1967 F. L. Skinner tried to cross *S. ×prestoniae* with *S. reticulata* subsp. *reticulata*. In 1973 Fiala attempted the cross *S. reticulata* subsp. *reticulata* × (*S. sweginzowii* × *S. tomentella* × *S. wolfii*) (Pringle 1981).

Subgenus *Syringa*, Series *Syringa*

Syringa vulgaris L.
Common lilac

Geographically, *Syringa vulgaris* is a European species and was discussed in chapter two. Systematically, it is part of the series *Syringa*, so it deserves to be mentioned here. Although geographically *S. vulgaris* is far removed from its Asian cousins, genetically it is not; it is one of the two parents of *S. ×chinensis* and *S. ×hyacinthiflora*, which are part of series *Syringa* and of horticultural interest. See drawings of the leaves and a flowering branch on page 76.

Syringa oblata Lindley
Early blooming lilac, broadleaf lilac

Shrubs or small trees to 5 m; branchlets glabrous, puberulent, or pubescent. Petiole 1–3 cm; leaf blade ovate, ovate-orbicular, to reniform, slightly broader than long or slightly narrower than long, 2.5–10(–14) × 2.5–8(–15) cm, glabrous or pubescent, villous to glabrescent, base subcordate or truncate to broadly cuneate, apex abruptly acute to long acuminate. Panicles erect, lateral, congested or lax, 4–16(–20) × 3–8(–10) cm. Pedicel to 3 mm, glabrous or pubescent. Calyx 2–3 mm. Corolla purple, lilac, or sometimes white; tube subcylindric, 0.6–1.7(–2.2) cm; lobes ovate-orbicular to oblong or obovate-orbicular, 4–8(–10) mm, spreading. Anthers yellow, inserted on corolla tube to 4 mm from mouth. Capsule obovate-elliptic, ovate, to oblong-lanceolate, 0.7–1.5(–2) cm, smooth.

Habitat: Woods, thickets, valleys, along streams, roadsides, gravelly mountains; 100–2600 m. Gansu, Hebei, Henan, Jilin, Liaoning, Nei Mongol, Ningxia, Qinghai, Shaanxi, Shandong, Shanxi, northwestern Sichuan; Korea. Widely cultivated elsewhere in China.

Syringa oblata blooms earlier than *S. vulgaris*. The European species ordinarily blooms from mid-May to the first week in June, while the Asian species, which includes its two subspecies, blooms from one to nearly two weeks earlier. *Syringa oblata* is a sturdy lilac, and where late frosts are not exceedingly bothersome, it and its many hybrids, the cultivars of *S. ×hyacinthiflora*, can be a real spring opener! At Medina, Ohio, where late frosts are unpredictable and often devastating, *S. oblata* always managed a delightful early display despite the frosts. Cultivars of *S. ×hyacinthiflora* are somewhat less reliable, although there will always be a spring when all the lilacs fail because of the frost. *Syringa oblata* and *S. ×hyacinthiflora* cultivars are strong and healthy growers and seem somewhat less affected by scale, that plague of lilacs, although they are by no means foolproof as garden plants.

Syringa oblata is geographically a widespread species, occurring in 12 provinces of China's interior and throughout Korea; some of the more recent plant collectors have brought back seed that show some differences from the described subspecies. Early collections of *S. oblata* came principally from gardens in China and were the first to be described, often with the note, "found only in Chinese gardens." These were the first introductions of *S. oblata* into commerce.

Two subspecies are recognized (Green and Chang 1995, Chang and Green 1996a):

1a Shrubs or small trees to 5 m; leaf blade ovate-orbicular to reniform, usually slightly broader than long, base truncate to subcordate; corolla tube 0.6–1.4 cm, lobes 4–6 mm; capsule 1–1.5(–2); earlier flowering
.... *S. oblata* subsp. *oblata*
1b Shrubs 1–3 m; leaf blade ovate to ovate-orbicular, usually slightly narrower than long, base truncate to broadly cuneate; corolla tube 1–1.7(–2.2) cm, lobes 5–8(–10) mm; capsule 0.7–1.2(–1.5); later flowering
.... *S. oblata* subsp. *dilatata*

Syringa oblata subsp. *oblata*
Early blooming lilac

Synonyms: *S. giraldii* Lemoine, *S. oblata* var. *alba* Rehder, *S. oblata* var. *giraldii* (Lemoine) Rehder, *S. oblata* var. *hupehensis* Pampanini, *S. vulgaris* var. *oblata* (Lindley) Franchet

Shrubs or trees to 5 m. Leaf blade ovate-orbicular to reniform, base truncate to usually subcordate, apex abruptly acute to acuminate. Calyx ca. 3 mm. Corolla purple or sometimes white; tube 0.6–1.4 cm; lobes ovate-orbicular to obovate-orbicular, 4–6 mm. Anthers inserted on corolla tube to 4 mm from mouth. Capsule 1–1.5(–2) cm. Flowering April–May, fruiting June–October.

Habitat: Woods, thickets on slopes, valleys, along streams or roadsides; 300–2600 m. Gansu, Hebei, Henan, Jilin, Liaoning, Nei Mongol, Ningxia, Qinghai, Shaanxi, Shandong, Shanxi, northwestern Sichuan. Widely cultivated in several other provinces.

Once called the broad-leaved lilac, *Syringa oblata* subsp. *oblata* was observed by Alexander von Bunge (1833) as early as 1831, although he referred to it as *S. chinensis*. Even then he observed that these lilacs are common in Chinese gardens. Robert Fortune returned to England from his third trip to China (1853–1856) with seed of subsp. *oblata*. John Lindley (1859) quoted Fortune as saying,

The Chinese informed me it came from the north and was common in the gardens of Peking . . . it is

more tree-like in general outline; the leaves, also, are very striking, being large, rather fleshy and oblately cordate. The species blooms profusely, and its fine bunches of purple flowers are very ornamental. There is a white variety equally interesting [*S. oblata* subsp. *oblata* 'Alba'] found in the same country which I have succeeded in getting home alive . . . both these varieties will be found perfectly hardy.

John Lindley, J. D. Hooker, and C. S. Sargent noted the close similarity between this species and *Syringa vulgaris*. Sargent (1912) added, "In gardens this plant becomes a tall, broad shrub, but the brittleness of the branches, which are often broken down by snow or ice, reduces its value." We do not find this so in the midwestern United States. Although its branches are somewhat more brittle than those of *S. vulgaris*, it is a fine shrub. Its height, alone, makes it less desirable for home gardens.

Plants of *Syringa oblata* subsp. *oblata* are somewhat similar to those of *S. vulgaris*, they bloom earlier, are

Syringa oblata subsp. *oblata*: (1) fruiting branch, (2) flower with corolla opened showing calyx, stamens, and distal portion of style. *Syringa vulgaris*: (3) flowering branch, (4–6) leaves. *Syringa* ×*chinensis*: (7) sterile branch. Drawing by Lu Jinwei; redrawn by Cai Shuqin. Reprinted by permission from Wu and Raven 1996, p. 239.

more frost resistant, and their flowers are far less significant and are borne in loose panicles that have a wonderful fragrance. Many of the hybrids have a pale to deeper purple autumn leaf color, which is most attractive in the landscape. They are strong growers, many of them becoming small, multitrunked trees.

Several white-flowered cultivars of *Syringa oblata* subsp. *oblata* are known.

'Alba', origin unknown, single white. Synonyms: *S. oblata* var. *alba* hort. ex Rehder, *S. oblata* var. *affinis* (L. Henry) Lingelsheim, *S. affinis* L. Henry. Quite common in cultivation in China, in the provinces north of the Chang Jiang (Yangtze), this cultivar is similar in all respects to plants of *Syringa oblata* subsp. *oblata* except that it is a bit more slender with a more open habit, has smaller leaves heavily truncated at the base, and, of course, bears white flowers. This plant was brought back from China by Robert Fortune in 1856. In 1894 Louis Henry wrote about a white form of *S. oblata* without giving it a name. The plants he described growing at the Muséum National d'Histoire Naturelle, Paris, were raised from seed sent in 1880 by Emil Bretschneider. The plants flowered in 1891. Henry (1894) noted that the seedlings show no color variations and therefore he looked upon them as a wild form of *S. oblata*.

'Frank Meyer', Meyer & Fiala 1988, single white. Frank Meyer collected a medium-sized white-flowering variant in 1908 near Beijing (McKelvey 1928). The original plant raised from seed sent by Meyer, recorded as Plant Introduction *23031*, is a beautiful white-flowering lilac growing near the old greenhouse at the U.S. Department of Agriculture Glendale Plant Introduction Center. Because it is such an excellent white plant, Fiala (1988) proposed giving it the cultivar name 'Frank Meyer' so it would not be lost or confused with any other form. Later it was feared lost for some years but was reported in cultivation at the Raulston Arboretum, Raleigh, North Carolina (Lawrence C. Hatch, 2 April 2003, pers. comm. to F.V.). Peter Green (1984a), following a visit to China and the plant nursery at the 18th century Summer Palace of the Qing Emperors at Chengde, Hebei, wrote of a white lilac: "I was able to confirm that this white plant needs to be propagated vegetatively while the other plants referred to above [*Syringa oblata*] had been raised from seed." He went on to state,

This white lilac was clearly *Syringa oblata* var. *alba* hort. ex Rehder (*S. oblata* var. *affinis* [L. Henry] Lingelsheim), a variety which was lost in cultivation in Britain at one time but may perhaps have been lost in the west, and in need of reintroduction. One suspects that it is entirely dependent on clonal reproduction and is perhaps a cultivar or, botanically, no more than a form.

Fiala (1988) did not believe that vegetative propagation alone led to the conclusion that a plant was a cultivar since in many species and subspecies there are sufficient incidental variations to merit certain seedlings being propagated for their superior qualities vegetatively rather than by seed. Green may not have been aware of the splendid specimen of 'Frank Meyer' at the Glendale Plant Introduction Center, grown from seed collected by Meyer.

It appears that three or four forms of white *Syringa oblata* subsp. *oblata* of independent origin are known,

Syringa oblata subsp. *oblata*. B. Peart and M. Walton

Syringa oblata subsp. *oblata* 'Alba'. B. Peart and M. Walton

namely, Robert Fortune's introduction, which may or may not be the same as the Chengde white lilac of Peter Green, and two others grown from seeds—those described by L. Henry at the Museum in Paris, and 'Frank Meyer'.

White-flowered forms of subsp. *oblata* do not appear to have been used in hybridizing until the 1980s by Donald Egolf at the U.S. National Arboretum where 'Frank Meyer' was used extensively with dramatic results. It is unfortunate that most of the results of this breeding program appear to have been ignored or lost. There is a great need for good, white early-flowering hybrids.

'Giraldii', Sprenger 1903, single purple to pinkish. Synonyms: *S. villosa* "Giraldi" Sprenger, *S.* "Giraldi" Lemoine, *S. affinis* var. *giraldi* C. K. Schneider, *S. oblata* var. "Giraldi" (Sprenger) Rehder. The history of the Giraldi lilac is best summarized from McKelvey (1928, 182–186) as follows. Father Giuseppe Giraldi (d. 1901) collected seeds of a lilac in Shanxi, China. From these seeds plants were grown by German nurseryman Carl L. Sprenger. Sprenger named them *S. villosa* "Giraldi" in his *3rd List of Plants* issued in 1903, while the Lemoine nursery listed them as *S.* "Giraldi" in catalog 155 of the same year. Subsequently, Alfred Rehder (1926) named and described them as *S. oblata* var. "Giraldii" (Sprenger) Rehder (in *Flora of China* quoted as *S. oblata* var. *giraldii* [Lemoine] Rehder). Under the currently accepted classification of the genus by Chang and Green (1996a), *S. oblata* var. *giraldii* has been "absorbed" in *S. oblata* subsp. *oblata*. Since all cultivars resulting from the cross *S. oblata* × *S. vulgaris* go by the name *S. ×hyacinthiflora*, the connection to the history of the Lemoine "Early Lilacs" and to John Wister's "EH-G" or "Early Hybrids of Giraldi," namely, *S.* "Giraldi," would be lost without providing a connection by establishing and accepting the cultivar name 'Giraldii'.

Syringa oblata subsp. *dilatata* (Nakai) P. S. Green & M.-C. Chang

Synonyms: *S. dilatata* Nakai, *S. dilatata* var. *alba* W. Wang & Skvortsov, *S. dilatata* f. *alba* (W. Wang & Skvortsov) S.-D. Zhao, *S. dilatata* var. *longituba* W. Wang & Skvortsov, *S. dilatata* var. *pubescens* S.-D. Zhao, *S. dilatata* var. *rubra* W. Wang & Skvortsov, *S.*

dilatata var. *violacea* W. Wang & Skvortsov, *S. oblata* var. *dilatata* (Nakai) Rehder

> Shrubs 1–3 m, many-branched. Leaf blade ovate to ovate-orbicular, 3–10 × 2.5–8 cm, base truncate to broadly cuneate, or rarely subcordate, apex short to long acuminate. Panicles lateral, lax, 5–10 × ca. 8 cm. Calyx ca. 2 mm. Corolla lilac or red-lilac to violet-lilac, sometimes white; tube 1–1.7(–2.2) cm; lobes oblong-elliptic, 5–8(–10) mm. Anthers inserted at middle of corolla tube. Capsule 7–12(–15) mm. Flowering May–June, fruiting September.
>
> Habitat: Gravelly mountains; 100–700 m. Jilin, Liaoning; Korea.

Japanese botanist Takenoshin Nakai first noted this lilac in its fruiting stage in 1911 but did not associate it with *Syringa oblata* (Nakai 1911). In 1918 he described it, naming it *S. dilatata*. Nakai's specimens were from plants found in the mountains of Korea. Alfred Rehder (1926) recognized the affiliation with *S. oblata* and proposed the name *S. oblata* var. *dilatata*. Chang Mei-Chen and Peter Green (1996a) raised it to a subspecies and identified two botanical formas: f. *alba* with white flowers, and f. *oblata*, cultivated in northern China, with red-lilac or violet-lilac flowers.

Seed of this subspecies was sent to Arnold Arboretum in 1917 by E. H. Wilson who was collecting in the Diamond Mountains of Korea from 1917 to 1918. Two separate forms are evident among the plants grown from Wilson's seed collections: one without heavy leaves, grown at the Arnold Arboretum, and the other with the characteristic leathery leaves, grown at Walter Hunnewell's Estate in Wellesley, Massachusetts. Of this new variety of *Syringa oblata* Wilson noted on a herbarium specimen that it was collected from a shrub 6 feet (1.8 m) tall with wine-colored autumn foliage, and that this lilac was "common on slate rocks and limestone from 35 miles [56 km] west of Yeiko [Korea]." Again, in the *Journal of the Arnold Arboretum*, Wilson (1919) remarked,

> On the mudshales and limestone a little to the northwest of Keijyo [Korea], grows a lilac (*Syringa dilatata* Nakai), which opens its panicles of palest lilac flowers early in the spring. It is a bush of good habit, often 12 feet [3.6 m] high and nearly as broad, with dark green leathery foliage which col-

ors finely in autumn. Examples 2 feet [60 cm] high bear flowers.

Wilson assumed the leathery-leaved lilac he had found was the same as that described by Nakai, but neither Nakai's description nor McKelvey's (1928) include this heavy, leathery leaf texture. Could it be that Wilson in reality described a different form of *S. oblata*? Heavy, leathery leaves are a very desirable characteristic for a garden plant, but subsp. *dilatata* does not have such leaves. Also, the blossom color of the subspecies is deeper than the color as described by McKelvey (1928) of the plants then growing at the Arnold Arboretum from the seed collected by Wilson:

> This [Wilson's] variety differs considerably from the type [*S. oblata* subsp. *oblata*] in general appearance. The habit of the plant is more graceful, with many slender branchlets tinged when young Bay (II). Its leaves glabrous, ovate, long-acuminate, and as a rule truncate at the base; they are borne on very slender petioles, frequently an inch [2.5 cm] long .... The flowers are handsomer with longer and more slender corolla-tube, ... the habit of the Korean plant is spreading rather than upright [as in subsp. *oblata*]. In color the

flowers are ... when expanded Pale Laelia Pink (XXXXVIII) tinged Hay's Lilac (XXXVII) .... The winter-buds are obovoid with acute apex .... The leaf-scar much raised, shield-shaped, conspicuous, large.

In a footnote McKelvey stated that she took her description of the flowers from two separate plants—one at the Arnold Arboretum and the other at the Hunnewell Estate. This leads to some confusion as the original plants growing at the Arnold Arboretum fit the typical description of *S. oblata* subsp. *dilatata*,

Syringa oblata subsp. *dilatata*, flowers. B. Peart and M. Walton

Syringa oblata subsp. *dilatata*, habit. Highland Botanical Park, Rochester, New York. John Fiala

whereas the Hunnewell specimen represents the native *S. oblata* subsp. *dilatata* ['Nakai'] described by Wilson. The former has ordinary leaves and pale flowers; the latter has leathery leaves and somewhat darker flowers and better bush form altogether.

'**Birchwood**', R. B. Clark 1988, single pink. Fine autumn color. Not yet in the trade.

'**Cheyenne**', Hildreth 1971, single bluish. A low grower with fine autumn color. Selected from plants grown from seed collected by Palemon Dorsett and Warner Morse, U.S. Department of Agriculture, in Manchuria in 1930, Plant Introduction *90671* (Vrugtman 1980a).

'**Donaldii**', Egolf & Fiala 1988, single purple. Seed of wild provenance was collected from four trees of known origin in Korea and sent to the National Plant Germplasm System prior to 20 December 1976 from Seoul National University College of Education in South Korea. Subsequently, the seeds were accessioned at the U.S. National Arboretum as *S. oblata* subsp. *dilatata* (*NA 39951*), where the plants produced from this seed lot are growing (USDA-ARS-GRIN, 24 March 2003). Robert B. Clark and John L. Fiala (1988) proposed the name *S. oblata* var. *donaldii*, which, however, is not validly published (Vrugtman 2004). We propose the cultivar name 'Donaldii' to honor Donald Egolf, who grew plants in his research collection as vegetatively propagated progeny of his plant appear to be growing in at least four lilac

collections in North America. The following description is based on 5- and 6-year-old plants growing at the National Arboretum (*NA 39951*), where the herbarium specimen is located. Shrubs 3–4 m, slightly less broad, well branched from the ground (even more so than other cultivars of *Syringa oblata*). Branches reddish brown with small but conspicuous lenticels. Leaves ovate, apex acuminate, leaf base round but at times truncate though less frequently so; very smooth above with margins mostly undulate; leaf texture heavy, leathery; leaves on average 16.8 × 10.5 cm (individual measurements: 19 × 12 cm, 16 × 10 cm, 18 × 11 cm, 15 × 9 cm, and 16 × 10 cm; this with good and regular culture), to Fiala's knowledge a leaf size not

Syringa oblata subsp. *dilatata* 'Cheyenne', flowers. B. Peart and M. Walton

Syringa oblata subsp. *dilatata* 'Cheyenne', habit John Fiala

Syringa oblata subsp. *dilatata* 'Donaldii'. John Fiala

found in any other members of *S. oblata*; leaves dark green above, pale whitish green beneath, often with fine pubescence beneath. Autumn foliage color ranges from a deep black-purple, changing to red-purple and shades of carmine; the shiny leaves are among the last to be shed. Inflorescences from terminal and lateral buds. Flower buds purple, opening to pale purplish to deeper purple. Flowers moderately fragrant in open, spreading thyrses with a modest to sparse number of florets.

'**Nakai**', Wilson & Fiala 1988, single pinkish. Of the Hunnewell plant McKelvey (1928) stated, "At its best, this is to me one of the most beautiful of all Lilacs" and added, undoubtedly now referring to the Arnold Arboretum specimen, "although every specimen is not of equal decorative value. Those at the Arnold Arboretum are inferior up to the present time to a plant growing at Mr. Walter Hunnewell's." Fiala (1988, 61) believed that the Hunnewell specimen represents a selection of *S. oblata* subsp. *dilatata* that should be given cultivar status, namely, *S. oblata* subsp. *dilatata* 'Nakai', to prevent it from being lost among the ordinary or inferior seedlings of the subspecies. His claim that the Hunnewell specimen had been moved to the Arnold Arboretum could not be confirmed (John Alexander III, 2004, pers. comm. to F.V.). An unpublished note by Theophilus D. Hatfield (1855–1929), head gardener at the Hunnewell Estate, claimed:

> Through Mr. Sargent's generosity, a very good collection of lilacs has been added, and these, for the most part, occupy the garden, formerly given up to tender Rhododendrons. Among the species, three have been added, which are of merit. *Syringa dilatata*, which I believe really is *S. oblata* var. *dilatata*. It is a free-blooming lavender-flowered variety of graceful habit.

This may or may not have been the plant on which McKelvey based her description. Fiala established plants of 'Nakai' at his Falconskeape garden from a yet unknown source; plants of it were released in 1988 to a private lilac collection, but 'Nakai' appears to have been neither distributed nor made available commercially; it is still awaiting introduction (Vrugtman 2003a). No record referring to this plant could be

Syringa oblata subsp. *dilatata* 'Wild Fire', autumn color.
John Fiala

found at the Hunnewell Estate (David Dusenbury, 2004, pers. comm. to F.V.).

'**Wild Fire**', Fiala 1984, single lilac. Leaves turn wine and bronze colors in autumn. Fine autumn color.

Since all forms of *Syringa oblata* and their hybrids bloom earlier than *S. vulgaris*, it is essential to avoid planting them in frost pockets or against warm buildings that prematurely advance their already early buds, or in sheltered spots. They need open, well-ventilated, sunlit sites. They are not fussy. Since they are excellent growers, strong and robust by nature, do not overfertilize. Most need little extra help. Use them in the backgrounds (*S. oblata* subsp. *oblata* 'Giraldii' hybrids) or as early focal shrubs (*S. oblata* subsp. *oblata* hybrids). To keep the taller sorts low, they must be pruned periodically. If left to grow too tall they become small trees with flower spikes correspondingly smaller and difficult to appreciate. Fine lilacs cannot be purchased as early hybrids in the nursery container trade; instead, they must be bought from a nursery specializing in newer lilacs grown on their own roots. Do not settle for less; if you do, you deserve the poor lilac you will receive. Plant explorers have gone through great sacrifices to bring us these species; hybridizers have worked hard for many years to produce new cultivars.

Syringa protolaciniata P. S. Green & M.-C. Chang
Afghan lilac

Synonym: *Syringa buxifolia* Nakai

Shrubs 0.5–3 m; branchlets four-angled, glabrous. Leaves 3- to 9-parted to -divided or entire, 1–4 × 0.4–2.5 cm; stalkless or with petiole to 2.5 cm, glabrous; leaf blade and lobes lanceolate, elliptic, ovate, or obovate, glabrous and with conspicuous glandular dots below, base cuneate, apex obtuse or acute. Panicles lateral, usually many paired on upper parts of branches, 2–10 cm; rachis, pedicel, and calyx glabrous. Pedicel 2–6 mm, slender. Calyx 1.5–2 mm. Corolla lilac or purple, 1–2 cm; tube subcylindric, 7–12 mm; lobes ovate to narrowly elliptic, spreading. Anthers yellow-green, inserted on corolla tube to 2 mm from mouth. Capsule slightly four-angled, 0.8–1.5 cm, smooth. Flowering April–June, fruiting June–August.

Habitat: Woods, steep slopes; 800–1200 m. Eastern and southern Gansu, eastern Qinghai; sometimes cultivated in northern China.

As Green (1995) pointed out, "The degree of leaf laciniation varies in this species, and lobed or even entire leaves may be found on a single shoot."

'Kabul', origin unknown, single violet. The corolla lobes are longer and therefore narrower in proportion

Syringa 'Purple Haze'. Julie McIntosh Shapiro

to their length, being (6–)7–9 mm long and 3–4 mm broad, as opposed to 5–7 × 3–4 mm in the plants descended from the original Chinese introduction of *Syringa protolaciniata*, which was grown under the misapplied name *S. laciniata* auct., "auct." meaning "not necessarily its actual author." It is known to be hardy at the Arnold Arboretum, USDA hardiness zone 3b (Vrugtman 1990). It appears to have been introduced from gardens in Kabul, Afghanistan, and has been grown for some years under the misapplied name *S. afghanica* (not *S. afghanica* C. K. Schneider) (Green 1998).

'Purple Haze', Alexander III 2005, single purple. This cultivar resulted from what appears to be the first controlled cross—*S. protolaciniata* × *S. oblata* subsp. *dilatata*—made at the Arnold Arboretum in 1991. For once we have excellent documentation— one would expect that when dealing with Harvard University. The female parent (*S. protolaciniata*) can be traced back via the Arnold Arboretum and the University of Copenhagen Botanic Garden to material collected by Klaus Ferdinand in Barbur Jabul, Afghanistan; the pollen parent (*S. oblata* subsp. *dilatata*) to material collected by Ernest Wilson in North Kankyo, Korea. Alexander reports that 'Purple Haze' is a vigorous shrub with a globose habit; its foliage is similar to that of *S. ×chinensis*, but the leaves are occasionally lobate or laciniate; its flowering time coincides with that of *S. ×hyacinthiflora* cultivars. The fragrant thyrses are 10–14 × 5–7 cm; individual florets measure 18–19 mm in diameter with the corolla lobes being slightly reflexed. It is a promising addition to the assortment of garden lilacs (Vrugtman 2005b).

Syringa protolaciniata: (1) flowering branch, (2) opened corolla showing stamens, (3) infructescence. *Syringa pinnatifolia*: (4) flowering branch, (5) flower with corolla opened showing calyx, stamens, and pistil. Drawing by Lu Jinwei; redrawn by Cai Shuqin. Reprinted by permission from Wu and Raven 1996, p. 240.

Syringa afghanica C. K. Schneider

Habitat: Afghanistan (Nuristan), Pakistan (Kuram Valley) (Grohmann 1974).

In 1870 James Aitchison collected a single lilac specimen in the Kuram Valley on the low outer hills near Shalizan, Afghanistan, at 7500 feet (2250 m). This plant has remained an enigma to taxonomists and lilac specialists. Aitchison labeled it *Syringa persica*. Camillo Schneider used Aitchison's plant when he described a plant he called *S. afghanica* (McKelvey 1928):

> [W]e have to picture the wild plant as a small, gnarled and much ramified, dwarf shrub, with very finely leaved foliage . . . ; also the inflorescences are small, dense, terminal, compound panicles, lengthened and composed of terminal and lateral panicles. . . . flowers lilac.

Harsukh and John F. Duthie collected *S. afghanica* in the late 1890s in the Kuram Valley (Grohmann 1974). Ian Hedge and Per Wendelbo (1970) reported seeing it in the same region in June 1969. Wendelbo remarked, "It is not possible to solve the problem whether *S. afghanica* is, indeed, a good species" (Murray 1968).

James S. Pringle (1978d) shed considerable light on the causes of the original confusion, concluding that *Syringa ×laciniata* has been most often confused for *S. afghanica*. Although *S. afghanica* is not known to be in cultivation, it has been included here because the name *S. afghanica* may still be found in some collections and in some nurseries for plants that are not true to name.

Syringa ×chinensis Schmidt ex Willdenow
Chinese lilac

In 1794 Austrian nurseryman Franz Schmidt commented that Dutch nursery catalogs listed "*S. chinensis*," but since there is no assurance that this lilac would be hardy in Austria, he did not acquire it; neither did he add a description. Two years later German botanist Carl Willdenow (1796) published a description and the name *S. chinensis* for a new species of lilac. That is not surprising as there were only a few lilac species in

those days with which to compare it. McKelvey (1928) stated, "Much has been written in regard to both the proper classification and the native country of *S. chinensis*," presenting a thorough review of the literature known to her. According to the current state of knowledge it is presumed that *S. ×chinensis* is a hybrid between *S. protolaciniata* and *S. vulgaris*. Molecular investigations of the genus *Syringa* may present data leading in yet another direction—today's classification is always based on today's knowledge. See the drawing on page 76.

We do not know why it was originally named *Syringa chinensis*. It is often said to have occurred as a natural hybrid at the botanical garden at Rouen about 1777, hence its common name Rouen lilac. It is quite possible since plants of *S. persica* var. *laciniata* (today *S. protolaciniata*) and *S. vulgaris* were growing in the garden, and the blooming periods of these lilacs overlap. Open pollination between these two taxa could have happened at any other garden where the two lilacs were growing in close proximity. That the two taxa are compatible was demonstrated by Émile Lemoine, who crossed *S. persica* var. *laciniata* with *S. vulgaris* "double-flowered selection," resulting in the semidouble *S. ×chinensis* 'Duplex'.

Among the *Syringa ×chinensis* cultivars are some of the loveliest and most useful garden shrubs. They are easy to grow, reach 12–15 feet (3.6–4.5 m) after many years, form upright rounded bushes of equal width or wider, sucker very little, have rather slender branchlets, and flower from the branch extremities on several lateral buds, giving the inflorescence a long-flowered effect. They are excellent for mass effect and color, producing enormous amounts of bloom.

'Bicolor', Lemoine 1928, single white with a small but prominent, deep-purple eye and golden anthers. An outstanding plant. Makes a large shrub for backgrounds, very fine.

'Duplex', Lemoine 1897, double lilac, very good.

'La Lorraine', Lemoine 1899, single magenta. Fine background shrub.

'Orchid Beauty', Hilborn pre-1945, single magenta.

'Président Hayes', Lemoine 1889, single magenta. Beautiful but little known.

'Red Rothomagensis', Baldwin pre-1934, single purple. A genetically distinct clone propagated and

Syringa ×*chinensis*. B. Peart and M. Walton

Syringa ×*chinensis* 'Président Hayes'. B. Peart and M. Walton

Syringa ×*chinensis* 'Orchid Beauty'. John Fiala

Syringa chinensis 'Saugeana'. B. Peart and M. Walton

distributed in North America exclusively for use at phenological observation stations (Hopp et al. 1973, Marsolais et al. 1993).

'Saugeana', Saugé 1822, single pinkish to purple. The Saugé lilac has not yet been surpassed.

Certainly the named cultivars should be more widely propagated by nurserymen and more widely grown. As hybridizers continue to make this cross of *Syringa protolaciniata* with newer forms of *S. vulgaris* we can expect exciting hybrids, even doubles. Note that *S.* ×*chinensis* var. *alba* (Kirchner) Rehder is *not* a white-flowering selection of *S.* ×*chinensis*. It is a synonym of *S.* 'Correlata', the graft chimera *S.* ×*chinensis* + *S. vulgaris*. However, all the plants we have seen under these names in more recent years, and the plants we have inquired about, turned out to be either *S.* ×*chinensis* or *S. vulgaris*, but never the graft chimera, which contains tissue of both "parents."

Syringa ×*chinensis* and its cultivars, like *S.* ×*laciniata* and *S.* ×*persica* and their cultivars, are most useful in larger groups, where they give a massive show of color, or in hedges, or as single specimens, where they are truly grand. An excellent use of *S.* ×*chinensis* and *S.* ×*persica* can be seen in Royal Botanical Gardens, Hamilton, Ontario, and in Highland Botanical Park, Rochester, New York. These groupings embody the best that can be achieved with good landscaping design. The unique *S.* ×*chinensis* 'Bicolor' on the hillside path at Highland Botanical Park provides an excellent show. Cultivars of *S.* ×*chinensis* are all heavy bloomers, perhaps because they produce little or no seed, are not offensively perfumed, are graceful in form, and are subdued in color range. Should you need a thick boundary hedge, or a screen to hide service areas, play courts, or a neighbor's building, they are excellent choices. Small birds delight in building their nests in the slender branches of these lilacs, which are too thin for a cat to climb. They sucker very little. All are beautiful, and the newer hybrids have not diminished the utility and beauty of the very first introductions. These cultivars are not suited for small city gardens, but if you have space, by all means plant them all.

Syringa ×hyacinthiflora Rehder
Hyacinth lilac, early flowering lilac, American hybrid lilac

Syringa ×hyacinthiflora is a cross between *S. oblata* and *S. vulgaris*. Although lilac specialists may make a distinction between "Early Hybrids" (*S. oblata* × *S. vulgaris*), "Early Hybrids of Giraldi" (*S. oblata* subsp. *oblata* 'Giraldii' × *S. vulgaris*), and "Early Hybrids of Dilatata" (*S. oblata* subsp. *dilatata* × *S. vulgaris*), all cultivars resulting from these crosses, and in many instances subsequent crosses and backcrosses, are classified as *S. ×hyacinthiflora*. In the early to mid-20th century these groups may have been relatively distinct, but with continued crossing and backcrossing the morphological dividing lines are no longer definite. James S. Pringle (1996) pointed out that few if any cultivars of *S. ×hyacinthiflora* introduced since the mid-20th century have resulted from first-generation crosses between native-collected *S. oblata* subsp. *oblata*, *S. oblata* subsp. *oblata* 'Giraldii', or *S. oblata* subsp. *dilatata* and *S. vulgaris*. These newer cultivars are more likely to have resulted from third-, fourth-, or later-generation crosses. Pringle concluded, "Reliable determination of whether a lilac cultivar is *S. vulgaris* or *S. ×hyacinthiflora* will not be achieved by having anyone 'look' at it, nor will even an assessment of strong probability be possible through this approach."

Twenty years after Robert Fortune returned to England from China with seed of *Syringa oblata* subsp. *oblata*, Victor Lemoine had added the species to his collection and used its pollen on the one known lilac with double, albeit puny flowers, *S. vulgaris* 'Azurea Plena', introducing the resulting "*S. hyacinthiflora plena*" in his 1878 catalog. Alfred Rehder (1899) published the name *S. ×hyacinthiflora*, which covers all hybrids and cultivars resulting from the cross *S. oblata* × *S. vulgaris*. For the original and first cultivar we have preserved the name *S. ×hyacinthiflora* 'Hyacin-

thiflora Plena'. Walter Clarke (1876–1953), of W. B. Clarke and Company in San Jose, California, used *S. oblata* subsp. *oblata* to produce such outstanding *S. ×hyacinthiflora* beauties as 'Blue Hyacinth', 'Bountiful', 'Esther Staley', and 'Fantasy', among others. John Rankin (1891–1967) added 'Lewis Maddock', the earliest of all pinks.

Syringa oblata subsp. *oblata* 'Giraldii' reached the Lemoine nursery about 1900. It was used by Émile Lemoine in crosses with *S. vulgaris*, which resulted in early lilac hybrids. Among Lemoine's first introductions were *S. ×hyacinthiflora* 'Lamartine' and *S. ×hyacinthiflora* 'Mirabeau' in 1911, with 13 more to follow. These are the cultivars classified by John Wister (1953) as EH-G or "Early Hybrids of Giraldi." Cultivars of *S. oblata* subsp. *oblata* 'Giraldii' parentage distinguish themselves by their tall, vigorous, and upright growing habit; unless restrained by heavy pruning they become small trees.

Syringa ×hyacinthiflora 'Lamartine'. B. Peart and M. Walton

Syringa ×hyacinthiflora 'Mirabeau'. B. Peart and M. Walton

Syringa ×*hyacinthiflora* 'Maiden's Blush'. B. Peart and M. Walton

Syringa ×*hyacinthiflora* 'Pocahontas', flowers. B. Peart and M. Walton

Syringa ×*hyacinthiflora* 'Pocahontas', habit. John Fiala

Syringa ×*hyacinthiflora* 'The Bride'. B. Peart and M. Walton

Working to produce shorter plants, Frank L. Skinner of Dropmore, Manitoba, used *Syringa oblata* subsp. *dilatata* to add the new strain of lower-growing "Early Hybrids of Dilatata" or EH-D of incomparable beauty. Among these must be singled out *S.* ×*hyacinthiflora* 'Maiden's Blush', *S.* ×*hyacinthiflora* 'Pocahontas', and *S.* ×*hyacinthiflora* 'The Bride' (see chapter ten for more details).

Syringa ×*laciniata* Miller
Cut-leafed lilac

Originally described as a species, cut-leafed lilac is a cross of *Syringa protolaciniata* with an unknown *Syringa*. One of the most beautiful and useful hybrids, *S.* ×*laciniata* has had a confusing past; its parentage is

obscure, its place of origin is not known, and its history of introduction into cultivation and subsequent distribution have not been recorded. McKelvey (1928) did an extensive review of the literature known at the time; however, based on more recent scientific findings, *S.* ×*laciniata* has been assigned a new place in the series *Syringa*.

Philip Miller (1768) considered it to be a true species; Weston (1770) considered it to be a botanical variety of *Syringa persica*, which was not considered to be a hybrid at the time. Did the early botanists and horticulturists always look at the same taxon? Could it be that some looked at what is known today as *S. protolaciniata* and others at *S. ×laciniata*?

Syringa ×laciniata is an outstanding lilac worthy of a place in any garden. It is a tall plant, to 12 feet (3.6 m), with an equal spread at maturity. In the spring its willowy, somewhat arched branchlets are covered with lavender-purple buds opening to a lighter pale-lavender bloom, borne in many somewhat small clusters along the slender branches, giving the total effect of a long flowering wand. It is a modest shrub, easy of culture, undemanding, a fine annual bloomer, and relatively free of pests. The plant bears both entire and laciniate foliage, often on the same stem. The leaves of both types are not large and are dark to medium green. The plant needs good soil, drainage, and sunlight.

Syringa ×persica L.

Shrubs 1–2 m, slightly broader; branches slender, upright to arching. Leaf blade lanceolate to ovate-lanceolate, entire, rarely lobed or laciniate, 2–6.5 × 0.5–1.5 cm. Panicles lateral, 5–10 × 5–7.5 cm. Corolla pale lilac, fragrant.

Originally described as a species, this lilac is a hybrid of uncertain parentage. It was one of the two lilacs

Syringa ×laciniata, flowers. B. Peart and M. Walton

Syringa ×laciniata, leaves. B. Peart and M. Walton

Syringa ×persica. B. Peart and M. Walton

Syringa ×persica makes a wonderful border screen at Royal Botanical Gardens, Hamilton, Ontario, Canada. John Fiala

recognized by Linnaeus (1753) as species—quite understandably so, because at the time there was only one other lilac to compare it with, *Syringa vulgaris*.

Although the name "*Jasminum persicum*" appears on a 1660 list of plants grown at the Jardin des Plantes in Paris, it was the Dutch botanist and medical doctor Abraham Munting who first described this lilac in 1672 as "*Jasminum Persicum foliis integris*." Paul Hermann, professor of botany and director of the botanical garden of the University of Leiden from 1680 to 1695, listed "*Syringha Persica foliis integris*" in 1687, apparently referring to the same plant at the Jardin des Plantes; perhaps this is the earliest use of the name *Syringa*. *Syringa* ×*persica* is known only as a cultivated plant.

'**Alba**', single, origin not known, ca. 1770, very good background shrub.

'**Taff's Treasure**', Taffler pre-1999, single, purple.

Subgenus *Syringa*, Series *Pinnatifoliae*

Syringa pinnatifolia Hemsley

Synonym: *S. pinnatifolia* var. *alashanensis* Y.-C. Ma & S.-Q. Zhou

Shrubs 1–4 m; branchlets generally four-angled, along with petiole, rachis, pedicel, and calyx glabrous. Leaves pinnately compound; petiole 0.5–1.5 cm; leaflets 7–11(–13), opposite or nearly so, stalkless; leaflet blade ovate-lanceolate to ovate, 5–30 × 3–13 mm, glabrous or adaxially sparsely pubescent, base cuneate to subrounded and usually oblique, apex acute to acuminate or obtuse. Panicles slightly nodding, lateral, 2–6.5 × 2–5 cm. Pedicel 2–5 mm. Calyx ca. 2.5 mm. Corolla white or light red, somewhat tinged with lilac, 1–1.6 cm; tube slightly funnelform, 0.8–1.2 cm; lobes ovate or oblong. Anthers yellow, inserted on corolla tube to 4 mm from mouth. Capsule oblong, 1–1.3 cm, smooth. Flowering May–June, fruiting August–September.

Habitat: Thickets on slopes; 2000–3100 m. Gansu, Nei Mongol, Ningxia, eastern Qinghai, southern Shaanxi, western Sichuan.

Syringa pinnatifolia has been listed in China as an endangered species since 1989 (Song et al. 1989; Fu 1992; Bao Bojian, 14 March 2005, pers. comm. to F. V.). Although reported from six provinces in north-western China, the actual number of individual plants of *S. pinnatifolia* appears to be quite small. Roots and stems of *S. pinnatifolia* have been collected for medicinal use throughout its native range for decades, resulting in vastly diminishing numbers of plants (Song et al. 1989). *Syringa pinnatifolia* and the Chinese herbal medicine made of it is known as *tu chen xiang* (Cui et al. 2004). When grown at lower elevations and in regions with hot summers this lilac performs best in partial shade (Hong-Xia Cui, 16 March 2005, pers. comm. to F.V.). Should you ever lose a plant of *S. pinnatifolia* from your collection, roots and all, you may guess why. (*Tu chen xiang* is also the common name for the resin of *Aquilaria sinensis*, the source of an extract used in an unrelated Chinese traditional medicine [Yip 2005]).

Syringa pinnatifolia is the sole member of series *Pinnatifoliae*. "It is distinct from all other lilacs," according to William B. Hemsley (1843–1924) of Royal Botanic Gardens, Kew, who was the first to describe it in 1906:

At first sight this new lilac might be taken for a variety of the Persian, as it certainly resembles *Syringa persica* var. *laciniata*, but on closer examination it proves to be a distinct species. It differs in all the leaves being distinctly pinnate, that is, divided to the midrib into separate leaflets; in the lanceolate acute leaflets of much thinner texture, and very minutely fringed on the margin; in the rounded lobes of the calyx; and in the relatively longer corolla tube. *Syringa pinnatifolia*, as I propose naming it, was imported by Messrs James Veitch and Sons, through their collector, Mr. E. H. Wilson, who discovered it in the extreme West of China, at an elevation of 9000 feet [2700 m]. Like many of his discoveries, it appeared to be quite rare, and no seed was collected, but a young plant was brought home safely. Mr. Wilson describes it as an elegant bush, 6–8 feet [1.8–2.4 m] high, with very slender branches and white flowers. It has not yet [1906] flowered in this country, so far as I know, but judging from the dried specimens I venture to predict that this new Lilac will prove a welcome acquisition.

Hemsley mentioned the fruit as unknown, "*Capsula ignota*" (McKelvey 1928).

In May 1904 Ernest H. Wilson collected for the Veitch firm at Mupin, Sichuan, where he discovered this species. He returned to Mupin in June 1908 for the Arnold Arboretum, again gathering *Syringa pinnatifolia*. He described the shrubs as "7–10 feet [2.1–3 m] tall with pink flowers, growing in thickets at an altitude of 7500 feet [2250 m]." Seed of a specimen collected in October 1910 was received at the Arnold Arboretum in February 1911; the plant raised from it flowered for the first time in 1917 (McKelvey 1928). See the drawing on page 82.

The flower color has created some confusion. Bean (1910) reported that the flowers were "white with a slight tinge of lilac." Wilson (1917) mentioned them as being "a pale mauve-colored" whereas previously he called them "pink." The Lemoine nursery in Nancy, France, in their English catalog 197 (1923–1924) listed *Syringa pinnatifolia* as "[a] most curious species of Lilac with very distinct pinnate leaves, small white flowers in terminal panicles." This is incorrect; as McKelvey (1928) noted, "[T]he flower clusters are produced from lateral, not terminal buds." Referring to the *Ridgway Color Standards* McKelvey determined the color as "Clear Dull Green-Yellow to Light Chalcedony Yellow (XVII)." She noted that most of the plants in cultivation were "white."

McKelvey (1928) reported that a specimen of *Syringa pinnatifolia* growing at the Arnold Arboretum (*6860*) resembled some of the rose species, such as *Rosa omeiensis* Rolfe, in habit and in foliage:

It is a round-topped shrub, 5 feet [1.5 m] tall, with stout, spreading somewhat angular branches and a distinctive bark which peels off in thin, paper-like layers from the old wood. The foliage unfolds early in the spring and is retained until well into autumn and its pinnate character distinguishes it from all other Lilacs. The small creamy or pure white flowers, with anthers clearly visible in the wide throat, have a somewhat unpleasant fragrance. The clusters are small and inconspicuous and slightly nodding. They open during the first two weeks in May—or considerably earlier than those of most of the Lilac species—and are too small and hidden by the foliage to make the plant of much value as a decorative garden shrub. It is interesting rather than ornamental and, because of its somewhat picturesque habit, might be of value as a tub plant.

Syringa ×*persica* closely resembles this species but only in foliage, being far superior to *S. pinnatifolia* in bloom. *Syringa pinnatifolia* is not suitable for home gardens but rather for the largest botanical gardens. Specimens can be found in a few lilac collections in North America and Europe. The species is also listed by a few commercial nurseries.

Karl Sax (1947) crossed *Syringa pinnatifolia* with *S.* ×*laciniata*, producing seedlings described as vigorous and including plants of possible horticultural value. Plants of this hybrid are growing at Arnold Arboretum; Morden Research Centre, Morden, Mani-

Syringa pinnatifolia, habit. Brooklyn Botanic Garden, Brooklyn, New York. John Fiala

Syringa pinnatifolia, leaves and flowers. John Fiala

toba; Highland Botanical Park, Rochester, New York; and Royal Botanical Gardens, Hamilton, Ontario (Pringle 1981). It may open new vistas to hybridists for the future.

Syringa ×diversifolia Rehder

A truly unique hybrid is *Syringa ×diversifolia* (Anderson and Rehder 1935), resulting from the interseries cross *S. pinnatifolia* × *S. oblata* subsp. *oblata* (formerly known as *S. oblata* var. *giraldii*). It was first discovered as a chance seedling. Karl Sax crossed *S. pinnatifolia* with *S. oblata* subsp. *oblata*, obtaining progeny almost identical to the type of *S. ×diversifolia*. It is not an outstanding garden plant but could well point directions for possible new crosses by hybridizers for the future. Two cultivars are known.

'**Nouveau**', Sax & Upton 1944, single pinkish. Grown, selected, and named by Edward A. Upton (1980, 1986) from seed received from Karl Sax in 1936.

'**William H. Judd**', Sax & Skinner pre-1949, single white. Appears to have been grown, selected, and named by Frank L. Skinner from seed of a cross (*S. pinnatifolia* × *S. oblata* subsp. *oblata* 'Giraldii') given to him by Sax (Wister 1953). Perhaps hybridizers could explore the possibilities of crossing other forms of *S. oblata*, or even *S. vulgaris*, with *S. pinnatifolia*.

Subgenus *Syringa*, Series *Pubescentes*

Syringa pubescens Turczaninov

Shrubs 1–5 m; branchlets four-angled or subcylindrical, along with petiole, rachis, pedicel, and calyx glabrous, puberulent, pilose, or pubescent. Petiole 0.5–2 cm; leaf blade ovate, ovate-elliptic to lanceolate, or obovate to suborbicular, 1.5–8(–13) × 1–6 cm, upper surface glabrous, pilose, or pubescent, lower surface pilose, pubescent, villous, to glabrous, base cuneate to rounded, apex acute to caudate-acuminate or obtuse. Panicles erect, lateral, rarely terminal, 5–16 × 2.5–7 cm; rachis four-angled or subcylindrical. Pedicel absent or short. Calyx 1.5–2 mm. Corolla purplish red, purple, lilac, pink, to white, 0.8–1.8 cm; tube subcylindric or slightly funnelform, 0.6–1.7 cm; lobes oblong or ovate, spreading. Anthers purple or purple-black,

rarely yellow, inserted on corolla tube at or to 3 mm from mouth. Capsule long elliptic to oblong-lanceolate, 0.7–2 cm, obviously lenticellate.

Habitat: Slopes, grasslands, woods, thickets, along rivers; 300–3400 m. Gansu, Hebei, Henan, western and northwestern Hubei, Jilin, Liaoning, southern Ningxia, eastern Qinghai, Shaanxi, western Shandong, Shanxi, northeastern Sichuan; Korea.

This description and stated area of distribution cover the species, including the subspecies and botanical varieties. Four subspecies are recognized, which can be separated with the following key (Green and Chang 1995, Chang and Green 1996a):

1a Branchlets and inflorescence axes more or less four-angled . . . . .go to 2

    2a Branchlets and inflorescence axes distinctly four-angled, usually glabrous; anthers inserted on corolla tube 1–3 mm from mouth; flowering May–June, fruiting June–August . . . . *S. pubescens* subsp. *pubescens*

    2b Branchlets and inflorescence axes slightly four-angled, usually puberulent or pubescent; anthers inserted on corolla tube to 1 mm from mouth; flowering May–July, fruiting August–October . . . . *S. pubescens* subsp. *patula*

1b Branchlets and inflorescence axes subcylindrical . . . . go to 3

    3a Calyx purple, glabrous; anthers inserted on corolla tube to 1 mm from mouth; flowering May–June, fruiting October . . . . *S. pubescens* subsp. *julianae*

    3b Calyx purple, mostly puberulent, sometimes densely pubescent or subglabrous; anthers inserted on corolla tube to 3 mm from mouth; flowering May–June (in cultivation often blooming again August–September), fruiting July–October . . . . *S. pubescens* subsp. *microphylla*

Syringa pubescens subsp. *pubescens*
Synonym: *S. wulingensis* Skvortsov & W. Wang

Shrubs to 5 m; young shoots glabrous; branchlets and inflorescence rachis distinctly four-angled, usually glabrous. Leaves ovate to usually broadly ovate, occasionally elliptic, (1.5–)2.5–3.5(–7) cm × (1–)1.7–2.5(–4) cm, glabrous above, glabrous to pilose below especially on the midrib and pri-

with very short, obtuse calyx lobes." Emil Bretschneider (1898), citing Otto von Möllendorf, who collected this species in China in 1881 in the mountains west of Beijing, and Turczaninov, who described the material of Kirilov and Bunge collected in 1831, stated,

This shrub, from 6 to 8 feet high [1.8–2.4 m], is found in the lower regions of the mountains, has smaller leaves, 1½ inches [4 cm] long, ovate white beneath, pubescent on the midrib. Flowers are also small. The small seed capsules are covered with warts. In Chinese it is called *Siao ting hiang* (the Clove-like lilac) because of the resemblance of the flower bud to the Clove.

Syringa pubescens belongs to the series *Pubescentes*; all of its members have great similarities. A mature plant at the Arnold Arboretum is some 12 or more feet (3.6 m) high with numerous slender branches, as broad as it is tall. Its foliage and buds unfold early in the spring and it is a dependable and profuse bloomer. "Color in bud Purplish Lilac (XXXVII); when expanded Purplish Lilac without" (McKelvey 1928). We see it mostly as a pale lilac with a pale pinkish wash. The delicate flowers are not showy, nor the individual clusters large, but since many pairs of buds are produced on the same branchlet the total inflorescence is long. *Syringa pubescens*, like many of the Asian species, has its own distinct spicy clovelike fragrance. Truly, it is a plant for the discriminating lilac collector.

A photograph (*7286* and *5925*) at the Arnold Arboretum of *Syringa pubescens* taken by Frank Meyer on Xiaowutai Mountain in Hebei "shows the difficult conditions under which the plant sometimes grows" (McKelvey 1928). Meyer's notation with the photograph reads: "A medium size wild lilac with rather small leaves found in rocky places at altitudes from 5000 to 8000 feet [1500–2400 m]. It is intolerant of heavy clay soils."

Soon after its discovery *Syringa pubescens* was introduced into the nursery trade. Dieck, owner of the Zöschen Nursery, near Merseburg, Germany, offered it for sale in 1887. Bretschneider's seed was received at Royal Botanic Gardens, Kew, in 1880, and the plants first bloomed there in 1888; he also sent seed to the Arnold Arboretum in 1882, where the seedlings bloomed first in 1886. *Syringa pubescens* is not known

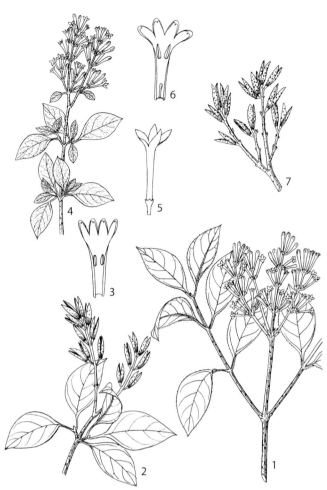

Syringa pubescens: (1) flowering branch, (2) fruiting branch, (3) opened corolla showing stamens. *Syringa pubescens* subsp. *microphylla*: (4) flowering branch, (5) flower, (6) opened corolla showing stamens and distal portion of style, (7) infructescence. Drawing by Lu Jinwei; redrawn by Cai Shuqin. Reprinted by permission from Wu and Raven 1966, p. 237.

mary veins, apex acute to obtuse. Panicles more or less dense, 4–8(–10) cm, glabrous to pilose. Corolla purplish lilac outside, paler inside; tube 10–15 mm; lobes 2–4 mm. Anthers inserted on corolla tube 1–3 mm from mouth. Flowering May–June, fruiting June–August.

Habitat: Slopes, thickets of ravines, along rivers; 900–2100 m. Hebei, Henan, eastern Shaanxi, western Shandong, Shanxi.

Porfirij Jevdokimovic Kirilov, who traveled through Mongolia in 1831 with Alexander von Bunge, is believed to have discovered *Syringa pubescens* growing on cliffs at the foot of the mountains in northernmost Hebei. Nicolai Turczaninov first described *S. pubescens* in 1840 as "a *Syringa* with ovate acute leaves, pubescent on the midrib beneath, ciliate on margins,

Syringa pubescens subsp. *pubescens*, habit. B. Peart and M. Walton

Syringa pubescens subsp. *pubescens*, flowers. B. Peart and M. Walton

to be a heavy seed setter; the plant at the Arnold Arboretum is said to produce very little or no seed at all; elsewhere, it either produces no seed or a very small quantity.

At Kew, Sir Joseph Dalton Hooker reported the plant to be hardy, but Bean (1980) stated,

> It is only a second-rate lilac in this country, owing to the frequent injury of the young growths and panicles by late frosts. In the United States, where the summer heat is greater, and the seasons better defined, it is very beautiful.

So it is, one of our finer lilacs and a choice specimen for any garden.

No cultivars or hybrids of *Syringa pubescens* subsp. *pubescens* have been recorded to date. Isabella Preston crossed *S. vulgaris* with *S. pubescens* (subsp. *pubescens*), but in June 1928 she stated, "I examined the seedlings raised and could find no evidence of *S. pubescens* (subsp. *pubescens*) influence." Frank L. Skinner (1966) reported crossing *S. pubescens* (subsp. *pubescens*) × *S. oblata* subsp. *dilatata* in 1962; although the resulting seed germinated well, there are no reports of selections or introductions. It would seem that the possibility of crosses among the similar subspecies *pubescens*, *julianae*, *microphylla* and the latter's variety *potaninii* might not be as difficult and could produce some exciting hybrids.

Syringa pubescens subsp. *julianae* (C. K. Schneider) M.-C. Chang & X.-L. Chen

Synonyms: *S. julianae* C. K. Schneider, *S. verrucosa* C. K. Schneider

> Shrubs to 2 m, broad; young shoots puberulent. Petioles 2–12 mm; leaf blade narrowly ovate to elliptic, (2.5–)4–5(–7) × (1.5–)2.3–2.5(–3) cm, scattered pilose above, pilose below, densely pilose on midrib and primary veins, apex acute. Panicles more or less open, (3–)4–6(–10) cm, densely pilose. Corolla violet-purple outside, paler inside; tube 7–8 mm. Anthers inserted on corolla tube to 1 mm from mouth. Flowering May–June, fruiting October.
>   Habitat: Hubei.

This beautiful lilac was discovered by Ernest Wilson on a mountain cliff in western Hubei in 1901. The taxonomist Camillo Schneider thought so much of it that he named it for his wife. Although one of the loveliest lilacs, *Syringa pubescens* subsp. *julianae* is relatively unknown beyond the collections in public gardens. It blooms a little later than most plants of *S. vulgaris*, generally opening in late May into the first week of June in Ohio, and always escapes even the latest frosts. The rather small, fragrant (spicy aromatic) flower clusters are borne in profusion all along the slender upper twiggy branches. The florets, violet-purple on the outer surfaces of the corolla and petals, and white to whitish blushed the palest lavender within, have violet anthers. This contrast of colors is strikingly beautiful. It is not unusual to find flowers with five or six corolla lobes rather than the customary four. *Syringa pubescens* subsp. *julianae* should be in every garden where there is space for a corner shrub or specimen. It needs room, however, as its branches can spread to 5–6 feet (1.5–1.8 m).

Subspecies *julianae* does not fare well in heavy clay soils but needs a well-drained, gravel-sand, humus-enriched location. Remember, Wilson found it on a mountain cliff. It is very intolerant of waterlogged or wet situations, but it does accept dry sites. Perhaps this is why it is not often found in the heavy clay of the midwestern and central states, whereas it thrives in the soils of New England. We have grown it most successfully on a well-drained site mulched frequently with very well rotted sawdust to 2 inches (5 cm). It needs no pruning and is not bothered by lilac pests or scale. This does not mean that it is totally immune to them, but in our 35 years with this species we have not experienced difficulties. At Medina, Ohio, it has been completely hardy to at least −30°F (−34°C).

Although *Syringa pubescens* subsp. *julianae* appears to be somewhat self-sterile, it hybridizes freely with *S. pubescens* subsp. *microphylla*. It is one of the few lilacs that grows in northern Florida, where it blooms fairly well but not as profusely as it does in northern North America.

'George Eastman', Fenicchia 1978, single pinkish to magenta. One of the reddest cultivars of the subspecies, this upright-growing shrub has rich, wine-red buds and deep cerise-pink flowers. The rich reddish pink is the same on the outer and inner sides of corolla and petals, although the florets fade with age to a lighter pink. It is slower growing than either its par-

Syringa pubescens subsp. *julianae*. John Fiala

ent stock or *Syringa pubescens* subsp. *julianae* 'Hers'; it needs well-drained gravelly soil and should not be transplanted too often but allowed to develop a good root system. It augurs to be a progenitor of a whole new series of *S. pubescens* subsp. *julianae* cultivars.

This chance seedling was named for George Eastman (1854–1932) of Eastman Kodak fame, who bestowed a gift upon the city of Rochester, which became known as Durand-Eastman Park. It is a magnificent piece of property close to the southern shore of Lake Ontario, with hills, rivers, and small lakes, resembling the mountains and hills of China with their mirror lakes—the ideal spot for lilacs. It was on this land that Bernard Slavin, then park superintendent, mapped out some of Rochester's most beautiful horticultural collections. Here, the rare dove tree, *Davidia involucrata*, flourishes with its fluttering dovelike blossoms; the Asian crab apples paint the hillsides with color every spring; and magnificent specimens of *Acer griseum* display their cinnamon and bright orange peeling bark. The setting in which these transplanted Asian treasures are growing is a natural one. Springtime comes gradually and winters are tempered by Lake Ontario.

Along one of the streams, as it rounds a bend paralleled by a curving road, are a number of lilac seedlings. For want of a better name they were called "*Syringa* species." In time they grew. Spreading shrubs, slender of branch, arching, they rooted in the well-drained, gravelly sandy soil high along the stream banks and bloomed in shades of pale and deeper lavenders each year. In the springs of 1971 and 1972, a few of their seedlings attracted the attention of park superintendent Richard A. Fenicchia and park taxonomist Robert B. Clark. Were these dark reddish purple lilacs something different? They were shown to Fiala in 1971, who was given a cutting of one of them (there appeared to be two separate plants, both a slightly different reddish purple), a rosy, carmine-red-budded plant. The cutting was successfully rooted and grown at Medina, Ohio.

Meanwhile, circumstances forced the widening of the road at Durand-Eastman Park, and the remaining lilacs were removed. Some of the reddish seedlings were propagated at the park nursery. Happenstance

Syringa pubescens subsp. *julianae* 'George Eastman'. B. Peart and M. Walton

and wet weather worked their way, and the seedlings were eventually lost. The remaining survivor was the single plant at Falconskeape in Medina. It was propagated and plants were sent to the U.S. National Arboretum, Washington, D.C., to Birchwood Gardens, Meredith, New Hampshire, and to the George Landis Arboretum, Esperance, New York. Cuttings were sent to Wedge Nursery in Minnesota and to California. By the late 1980s the National Arboretum, Birchwood Gardens, and Falconskeape plants appeared to be the only survivors. The clone was named and its future appears assured; 'George Eastman' is commercially available and has been reported from lilac collections in North America and Europe.

'**Hers**', Hers pre-1953, single pinkish. The details have been lost, but it is presumed that the original plant, also referred to as Hers' variety and Hers' form, was grown from seed collected by Joseph Hers (1884–1965), a Belgian railroad construction engineer and administrator as well as amateur botanist who collected seeds and herbarium specimens for the Arnold Arboretum in northern China between 1910 and 1924. 'Hers' has wide, weeping branches; a 10-year-old specimen at Falconskeape measured 12 feet (3.6 m) across and was about 5 feet (1.5 m) tall. Each spring it was covered with cascading deep purple-violet buds that opened a lighter lavender, both on the outside and inner side of corolla and petals. And what a lovely fragrance! It is a plant most worthy of a quiet Buddhist garden or a prayer house. The notable difference between 'Hers' and the subspecies is in flower color: the subspecies flower is a paler lavender on the outside and a blushed, pale lavender-white on the inside, while the flower of 'Hers' has a far deeper purple corolla and outer petals opening to a light lavender floret inside the petals. 'Hers' is a notable wide weeper with willowy sweeping branches whereas the subspecies *julianae* is far more upright, although it, too, is a wide shrub. Some taxonomists believe that 'Hers' does not differ from the subspecies, but when the two are growing side by side the difference is visible.

Three hybrids are known, all crosses between *Syringa pubescens* subsp. *julianae* 'Hers' and *S. pubescens* subsp. *julianae* 'George Eastman'. *Syringa pubescens* subsp. *julianae* 'Pink Parasol' (Fiala 1983) has dainty, baby pink flowers with recurved, parasol-like florets on an upright plant. A taller and better grower than

'George Eastman', it shows the great diversity obtainable by intensive breeding in this lovely subspecies. *Syringa pubescens* subsp. *julianae* 'Pink Parasol' has been introduced commercially. Two subsequent selections with the same parentage but producing larger thyrses have not yet appeared on the market: *Syringa pubescens* subsp. *julianae* 'Epaulettes' (Fiala 1984) is a single magenta with broad-shouldered blooms, and *S. pubescens* subsp. *julianae* 'Sentinel' (Fiala 1984) is a single lilac to magenta.

Syringa pubescens subsp. *julianae* 'Hers'. B. Peart and M. Walton

Syringa pubescens subsp. *julianae* 'Epaulettes'. John Fiala

Syringa pubescens subsp. *julianae* 'Pink Parasol'. John Fiala

Syringa pubescens subsp. *microphylla* (C. K. Schneider) M.-C. Chang & X.-L. Chen

Synonyms: *S. microphylla* Diels, *S. giraldiana* C. K. Schneider, *S. microphylla* var. *giraldiana* (C. K. Schneider) S.-Z. Qu & X.-L. Chen, *S. pubescens* var. *tibetica* Batalin, *S. schneideri* Lingelsheim, *S. trichophylla* T. Tang

Three botanical varieties of this subspecies have been recognized (Green and Chang 1995, Chang and Green 1996a):

1a Leaves pilose above, pilose to villous below especially on midrib; corolla white tinged with pink
. . . . *S. pubescens* var. *potaninii*
1b Leaves glabrous above to pubescent or subglabrous except for midrib, sometimes pilose toward base below . . . . go to 2
2a Corolla purplish red; anthers purple to purple-black . . . . *S. pubescens* var. *microphylla*
2b Corolla white; anthers yellow
. . . . *S. pubescens* var. *flavanthera*

The differences between *Syringa pubescens* subsp. *microphylla* varieties *microphylla* and *potaninii* are small, and both resemble *S. pubescens* subsp. *pubescens*. Do not blindly trust labels; when in doubt take a close look at the plants and at the distinguishing characteristics provided here.

Syringa pubescens subsp. *microphylla* var. *microphylla*

Shrubs 2 m, broad; young shoots finely puberulent, occasionally glabrous. Leaves narrowly to broadly ovate, to narrowly to broadly elliptic; apex obtuse to acute, very slightly acuminate; glabrous above, rarely scattered pilose; glabrous below, except for the midrib and primary veins toward their bases, rarely pilose. Panicles more or less dense, 4–10(–12) cm, pinkish lilac, paler within. Anthers inserted on corolla tube to 3 mm from mouth. Flowering May–June (often reblooming in cultivation August–September), fruiting July–October.

Habitat: Woods in valleys, near rivers, grasslands at mountain tops; 500–3400 m. Gansu, southwestern Hebei, western Henan, western Hubei, southern Ningxia, eastern Qinghai, Shaanxi, Shanxi, northeastern Sichuan.

This lilac was first described (as *Syringa microphylla*) by Ludwig Diels (1901) based on two fruiting specimens collected in October 1896 by Father Giuseppe Giraldi. It had been collected earlier by other plant explorers and was probably first collected by Hungarian Ludwig Lóczy in 1879. Subsequently, Joseph Hers collected many specimens of it between 1919 and 1923. With one of his specimens he recorded that the flowers were used as a substitute for tea. In another note Hers referred to it as the four-season lilac because of its remontant (perpetual) habit of flowering. He sent specimens from several areas back to the United States. In the United States this lilac bloomed for the first time at the Arnold Arboretum in 1915: "It is far from being one of the handsomest of the Lilacs, but if it keeps up its habit of flowering a second time in autumn it will be at least interesting even if other lilacs are more beautiful" (Sargent 1917).

All in all, it is somewhat slow growing to about 8 feet (2.4 m) and with considerable breadth since many branches spread horizontally. McKelvey (1928) wrote of it:

The branchlets, yellow-green in color, are long, "whispy," and so slender as to droop under the weight of the flower-clusters . . . flower-clusters are small, rarely over 3 inches [7.5 cm] long . . . [but produced] from lateral buds, they appear from many pairs of buds on the same branchlet and intermingle, producing what appears to be large and showy inflorescences, sometimes 10 inches [25 cm] or more long. The individual flower . . . has a very sweet fragrance. This plant has the curious habit of blooming twice in one season.

The fragrance is delicate and exquisitely unique. Some individuals claim it has little or no fragrance, but because it is a variable subspecies, there is little wonder that plants from widely different areas would differ.

On 15 October 1992, Chen Xin-Lu of Beijing collected seed in the wild from six different plants with different leaf sizes in Shaanxi, near Caiziping in the Hu Xian district. Chen described the habitat as rocky, open, and arid. Seed was sent to Royal Botanical Gardens, Hamilton, Ontario, and passed on to Royal Botanic Gardens, Kew. Seedlings grown from this collection have been distributed to public lilac

Syringa pubescens subsp. *microphylla* var. *microphylla*. B. Peart and M. Walton

Syringa pubescens subsp. *microphylla* 'Superba' used as a clipped, formal hedge at Royal Botanical Gardens, Hamilton, Ontario, Canada. John Fiala

Syringa pubescens subsp. *microphylla* 'Superba'. B. Peart and M. Walton

collections, but subsequent evaluations are not yet available.

In spite of having somewhat brittle wood, *Syringa pubescens* subsp. *microphylla* var. *microphylla* is a strong grower, but in moist seasons it does not stop growing and the late growth does not ripen, leaving a twiggy effect in the spring. *Syringa pubescens* subsp. *potaninii* displayed this same messy habit at Falconskeape in Medina, Ohio. These dead branchlet tips can be annoying but are soon forgotten as the plant bursts into bloom. The plant does well in loamy, sandy gravel. There is little difficulty in producing new plants from early spring softwood cuttings. This lilac does not appear to sucker and, other than removing the slight winter dieback at the tips of the smallest branchlets, it requires little if any pruning.

'**Superba**', Cassegrain 1933, single pinkish. This cultivar has better, pinkish, and slightly larger florets than var. *microphylla*. Although it sets much seed as a result of its long blooming period, most of it is sterile. It should prove a fine parent in hybridizing as its pollen is fertile.

Syringa pubescens subsp. *microphylla* var. *flavanthera* (X.-L. Chen) M.-C. Chang

Leaves glabrous above to pubescent or subglabrous except for midrib; sometimes pilose toward base below; florets white; anthers yellow.

Habitat: Shaanxi (Foping Xian). This botanical variety has not yet been reported in cultivation.

Syringa pubescens subsp. *microphylla* var. *potaninii* (C. K. Schneider) P. S. Green & M.-C. Chang

Shrub to 4 m, upright to spreading; young shoots finely puberulent. Leaves ovate to elliptic, (2.5–)3–5(–6) × (1.5–)2–2.5(–3.5) cm, puberulent to glabrous above, occasionally scattered pilose; scattered to densely pilose below, especially on the midrib and main veins toward the base, apex acute, slightly acuminate. Panicles more or less dense, 6–10 mm, finely puberulent. Corolla pinkish lilac outside, paler inside; tube 8–10 mm; lobes 2–3.5 mm.
Habitat: Gansu.

The Russian plant explorer Grigoriĭ Potanin discovered this lilac growing in the deeply dissected Loess Plateau of southern Gansu, in June 1885. Writing some years later, Camillo Schneider (1910) named it after its discoverer. Reginald Farrer, while collecting plants near the Tibetan border in 1914 in southeastern Gansu, collected this lilac, describing it as

[A] tall, slender, and very graceful lilac of 6–8 feet [1.8–2.4 m], which I have only once seen, far up, on the shady side in a collateral of the great Siku Gorge, growing in a big colony amid blocks of mossy detritus from the cliff-wall overhead. Its flowers, so far as I could judge it at the end of June, seemed small and rather poor, in small insignificant panicles; it may however improve in cultivation.

Otto Stapf (1924), commenting on a plant grown from seed collected by Farrer, wrote, "[I]t may be that the 'insignificant' panicles were merely the last of the season. At any rate the inflorescences of the plant raised by Major Stern from Farrer's seed hardly warrant the term 'insignificant'."

Today, *Syringa pubescens* subsp. *microphylla* var. *potaninii* is a very significant lilac. Although relatively unknown by the general public, it is well established in public collections. It is more upright, vaselike in habit rather than spreading. Var. *potaninii* closely resembles var. *microphylla* but is somewhat variable in color, from whitish purple to a light rose-purple with a general overall appearance of pinkish fading to near white. The calyx is a light purple, and the anthers pale purplish yellow. In some soils it flowers more magenta than purplish, perhaps in response to differences in soil pH. The wood is somewhat brittle, and the plant should be encouraged early to form a shrub of more than one main trunk. It does not sucker; cuttings will root easily in the spring. The leaves vary remarkably, even on the same branch. Most of the plants of var. *potaninii* observed by Fiala, including the one at Falconskeape, Medina, Ohio, were the creamy rose to pink type. The buds are a deeper rose, and the opening florets a creamy rose mixed with white. As the flower fades it is more whitish than rose. The branches, upright in growth, resemble pink flowering plumes. There is such a great similarity between varieties *potaninii* and *microphylla* that plants growing side by side at Falconskeape were difficult to tell apart except by the shrub habit and close inspection for minute morphological differences.

Like variety *microphylla*, variety *potaninii* is a long-season grower. Often, the branchlet tips do not sufficiently harden and are killed by frost, leaving a twiggy, broomlike effect in the spring. Since the plant flowers on lower, matured lateral buds, winter kill does not seem to affect its blooming, only its appearance. Perhaps in less fertile soils and with drier summers, late-summer growth may not occur. Its natural habitat is gravelly, well-drained mountainsides. It does not tolerate heavy, waterlogged soils. It has great tolerance for long summertime droughts. In the spring it is a very delightful shrub, one for real shrub connoisseurs.

Syringa pubescens subsp. *microphylla* var. *potaninii*. John Fiala

It is, unfortunately, not readily available except from some private lilac collections or larger arboreta. It rarely produces seed but does carry sterile seed pods. There are no known cultivar selections.

Syringa pubescens subsp. *patula* (Palibin) M.-C. Chang & X.-L. Chen

Korean lilac

Synonyms: *Ligustrum patulum* Palibin, *S. koehneana* C. K. Schneider, *S. palibiniana* Nakai, *S. patula* (Palibin) Nakai, *S. pubescens* var. *hirsuta* Skvortsov & W. Wang, *S. velutina* V. L. Komarov

> Shrubs to 3 m, young shoots slightly pubescent to glabrous. Leaves ovate or broadly ovate to usually elliptic or broadly elliptic, (3–)5–9(–11) cm × (2–)2.5–5(–6) cm, glabrous above, usually glabrous below, except for short pilose on midrib and primary veins toward the leaf base, apex slightly acuminate. Panicles more or less dense, 5–9 (–15) cm, pilose. Corolla red-lilac outside, white inside; tube 7–8(–10) mm; lobes 2(–3) mm long. Anthers inserted on corolla tube to 1 mm from mouth. Flowering May–July, fruiting August–October.
>
> Habitat: Grasslands, woods; 300–1200 m. Jilin (Changbai mountain area), Liaoning; Korea.

This lilac was first collected in Seoul, Korea, by A. Sontag of the Russian legation, who found it on 20 May 1895, near Tap Tong. The Russian botanist Ivan Palibin first determined it as *Ligustrinum patulum*. Vladimir Komarov (1900), who collected it as *Syringa velutina* in northern Korea in 1897, described it as

> a shrub 6–12 feet [1.8–3.6 m] tall, branched, with slender erect branches, with gray bark marked by many lenticels, the leaves papery . . . the inflorescence all densely short-pilose . . . panicles uninterrupted, pyramidal, the pedicels almost lacking or as long as the calyx, the calyx velvety white-pilose.

Collecting in different areas, Komarov found the plant occurred quite frequently among rocks, on rocky slopes, or in mountain gravel. It was also collected in northern Korea by Takenoshin Nakai, and by Ernest Wilson on his expeditions in 1917–1918. Taxonomists, in keeping with the rules of nomenclature, have returned to its first recorded mention by Palibin but have corrected the genus name. Today it is known as *S. pubescens* subsp. *patula*.

This lovely, modest shrub is neither coarse nor a rampant grower. Its pale, light lavender, feathery blossoms have a delightfully spicy fragrance uniquely its own. Although the flower panicles are not large, this lilac is a reasonable heavy bloomer, shortly after the peak of the *Syringa vulgaris* season. Where room allows, several of these medium to smaller shrubs should be planted simply for their fragrance throughout the garden. Subspecies *patula* sets seed rather abundantly and should prove to be an excellent source for hybridizing with other species. In the autumn its rather pale green, somewhat smaller leaves turn a beautiful shade of mauve and soft violets. Grown from seed, many interesting variations develop, which can be intensified by selective breeding. Remember that *S. pubescens* subsp. *patula* comes from the high mountains, so give it good, well-drained soil.

'Cinderella', Moro 1998, single pinkish.

Syringa pubescens subsp. *patula*. B. Peart and M. Walton

Syringa pubescens subsp. *patula* 'De Belder'. John Fiala

'**De Belder**', De Belder & J. L. Fiala 1988, single lilac. Synonym: *Syringa debelderorum* R. B. Clark & J. L. Fiala, as *S. debelderi*. Robert De Belder (1921–1995) and his wife, Jelena De Belder-Kovačič (1925–2003), amateur horticulturists and proprietors of Arboretum Kalmthout and Domain Hemelrijk (Essen) in Belgium, collected seeds of a lilac in Mount Sorak National Park, South Korea (De Belder 1998). Some of the seeds were distributed to the Arnold Arboretum and the U.S. National Arboretum (*NA 42179*). Robert Clark and John Fiala named and described *S. debelderi* (Fiala 1988, 48). Because the name was chosen to honor the De Belders, the epithet was subsequently corrected to *S. debelderorum* (Green 1989). Since the plants appear to be well within the morphological range of *S. pubescens* subsp. *patula*, and since the plant at Falconskeape (*NA 42197-F3810*) has been vegetatively propagated and introduced, Vrugtman (2004d) proposed the cultivar name 'De Belder'.

Shrubs to ca. 70 × 40 (for 6-year-old plants); canes and branches slender, slow growing and somewhat twiggy. Leaves to 7 × 5 cm, opposite, dull medium green, leaf blade elliptic-ovate to oblong, slightly pubescent to glabrous above, slightly whitish pubescent beneath, base broad-cuneate to rounded, apex narrowly acuminate; primary and secondary veins conspicuous and raised beneath. Panicles terminal and lateral, to 6 × 3.5 cm. Flower buds lavender-purple;

Syringa pubescens subsp. *patula* 'Excellens', habit. B. Peart and M. Walton

Syringa pubescens subsp. *patula* 'Excellens', flowers. B. Peart and M. Walton

tubes paler lavender, ca. 4 mm long; florets single, opening to a medium to pale lavender-purple; fragrance is slight but not pronounced. Capsules 1–1.4 cm long, warty, often with four seeds. Plants are slow growing and self-fertile. 'De Belder' appears to be entirely hardy to −4°F (−20°C), or USDA hardiness zone 6; we lack reports on hardiness in colder zones.

'**Excellens**', Lemoine 1936, single white. Rare and very fine.

'**Miss Kim**', Meader & Yeager 1954, single violet. Elwyn Meader of the University of New Hampshire, Durham, gives the following account of how he discovered and named this cultivar:

It was 11 November 1947, a holiday in Seoul, Korea, where I was stationed as horticulturist for the U.S. Army Military Government, that meant a day free for hiking in the nearby Pouk Han Mountains. Early that morning a companion and I set out through the old city's North Gate with C-rations and canteens tied to our belts.

Up hill and down dale we followed well-trodden trails until we had scaled Paik Un Dae (White Cloud Peak), 892 m [2927 ft.] in height. There stunted pines and shrubs grew in crevices where sufficient soil had clung to the craggy granite. On a cliff high above I spotted a lonesome, upright shrub, shoulder high, neatly ensconced in a wide crack of rock. Two inches [5 cm] of snow had collected under the plant despite bare ground at lower elevations. As I examined its twigs and seed pods I knew it must be a lilac. Could the dried capsules still contain any seeds in such a wind-swept place? A diligent search rewarded me with a few, most had gone with the wind!

Back home in 1948 I planted my twelve precious seeds which I'd collected that previous Veterans' Day in Korea. Seven thrifty seeds sprouted. Five grew into tall upright plants like their parent in the Korean mountains. Two, however, although strong and vigorous enough, were rather dwarf by comparison. All seedlings proved hardy and in time bloomed late, a full week or so after *Syringa* (Villosae Group) 'James Macfarlane'. The fragrant single flowers, purple in bud and when first open, fade to a blue-ice whiteness before falling.

One of the two low-stature seedlings bore dark green leaves with wavy margins. The foliage remained free of mildew all summer and turned Burgundy red in autumn for a delightful display. I named it 'Miss Kim', since Kim is a most common family name in Korea. There are thousands of Misses Kim, many could easily win a Beauty Contest if such were ever held in that country.

'Miss Kim' was released in 1954 by the New Hampshire Agricultural Experiment Station and became the first named cultivar of *Syringa pubescens* subsp. *patula*. In view of the extremely limited sampling of lilacs growing wild in the Pouk Han Mountains, further plant explorations for valuable germplasm might well be considered. If space in the garden requires choosing between subspecies *patula* and 'Miss Kim', by all means choose the cultivar.

Syringa pubescens subsp. *patula* 'Miss Kim', habit. John Fiala

Syringa pubescens subsp. *patula* 'Miss Kim', floral buds. B. Peart and M. Walton

Syringa pubescens 'Skinneri'
Synonym: *S.* ×*skinneri*

Frank L. Skinner (1966) made the cross *Syringa pubescens* subsp. *patula* ("*velutina*") × *S. pubescens* subsp. *pubescens* in 1945, introducing the resulting seedling in 1947 as *S.* ×*skinneri*. Only one plant resulted, which was subsequently propagated vegetatively. The flowers are white with a pinkish blush.

Syringa meyeri C. K. Schneider
Meyer lilac, dwarf Korean lilac

> Shrubs to 1.5 m, densely branched, compact; branchlets slightly four-angled, puberulent. Petiole 0.6–1.5 cm, glabrous or puberulent; leaf blade elliptic-ovate or elliptic-obovate, sometimes ovate, broadly ovate, or suborbicular, 1–5 × 0.8–3.5 cm, glabrous or pilose along veins beneath, palmately five-veined or nearly so, base cuneate to subrounded, apex acute to short acuminate or obtuse. Panicles erect, lateral, congested or lax, 2.5–10 × 2.5–4 cm; rachis and pedicel puberulent. Pedicel 1–2 mm. Calyx dark purple, ca. 2 mm, glabrous or puberulent. Corolla blue-purple, purplish red, purplish pink, or white, 1.7–2 cm; tube subcylindric, 0.5–1.5 cm; lobes oblong, spreading. Anthers light brown at first, becoming black, inserted below mouth of corolla tube. Capsule long elliptic, 1–2 cm, obviously lenticellate.
>
> Habitat: Slopes. Liaoning.

Two botanical varieties have been recognized (Green and Chang 1995, Chang and Green 1996a):

1a Inflorescence congested; corolla tube ca. 15 mm; leaf
    blade 2–5 × 1.5–3.5 cm . . . . *S. meyeri* var. *meyeri*
1b Inflorescence more loose; corolla tube 5–8 mm; leaf
    blade 1–2 × 0.8–1.8 cm . . . . *S. meyeri* var. *spontanea*

Syringa meyeri var. *meyeri*

> Leaf blade elliptic-ovate or elliptic-obovate, sometimes ovate or suborbicular, 2–5 × 1.5–3.5 cm. Flowers congested. Corolla blue-purple; tube ca. 1.5 cm. Flowering April–June, fruiting August–September.
>
> Habitat: Beijing and Shenyang, known only in cultivation.

The beautiful *Syringa meyeri* var. *meyeri* (commonly called just *S. meyeri* in the nursery trade) is known only as a cultivated plant. It was first found in gardens of the Fengtai district of Beijing. It is a low, compact shrub, growing only to 5 feet (1.5 m) with sturdy upright branches. It flowers in smaller clusters of pale lilac to lilac-purple, even to a whitish lavender. In some ways it is quite similar to *S. pubescens*. The Chinese call it *Shau-ting-hsien*, according to Frank Meyer, who was the first to send cuttings back to the U.S. Department of Agriculture in 1909. Meyer related that it is much used for forcing in China. With the two sets of *S. meyeri* cuttings Meyer sent home, he also noted that one has a slightly different color: "There are two white-flowering ones among them. Keep them protected from heavy frosts. It has a future for the western people as a very graceful, spring-flowering shrub of dwarfy habit."

Syringa meyeri has proven to be entirely hardy and has the habit, observed also in *S. pubescens* subsp. *microphylla*, of blooming again in late summer or very early autumn. *Syringa meyeri* is most clearly distinguished from other species in series *Pubescentes* by the venation of leaf, with two pairs of veins paralleling the margins.

Joseph Hers also collected *Syringa meyeri* from a garden in Chengchow in northern Henan on 20 April 1920. On his herbarium specimen (*Hers 85*) at the Arnold Arboretum, Hers noted that the Chinese name is *Nan-ting-siang* (the South Syringa) and described it thus: "A slow grower, never higher than 4 or 5 feet [1.2–1.5 m]; very scented, dark lilac. Rarely found on its own roots, more often grafted on *Ligustrum*. Its name seems to imply a foreign or southern origin" (McKelvey 1928).

'Palibin', origin unknown pre-1920, single pink. A beautiful, delightful small lilac, at one time called *Syringa palibiniana* (Green 1979). It is the most dwarfed or slow growing of all lilacs, reaching up to 4, rarely 5 feet (1.2–1.5 m) only after many years if left unpruned. It makes a fine, deep green hedge with or without pruning. Its bright, dark, green leaves, glossy, small, and somewhat leathery, give it added value throughout the season. In the spring it is covered with deep purple buds that burst into a lavender-pinkish tinged blue bloom. In blossom alone it bears some similarity to *S. pubescens* subsp. *microphylla*, which is more pink and a much taller shrub. It spreads moderately by underground suckers and is rather easy to root from early spring shoots taken in the first weeks of June. The plant suckers well if given a good mulch of well-rotted sawdust. It likes loose soil somewhat on the dry side. Peter Green reported in 1978 that the "new" Korean lilac in the Rock Garden at Royal Botanic Gardens, Kew, after 30 years was only 4 feet [1.2 m] high and 6½ feet [1.9 m] across. To assure retention of the dwarf form it should be propagated from cuttings. It adapts well as a Japanese bonsai specimen. Very few nurseries offer this cultivar. Only relatively recently has it been used in hybridization. 'MORjos 060F' (marketed as JOSÉE), a lovely plant from France, originated in the 1960s by Georges Morel, a plant physiologist, virologist, and biochemist, and was introduced by Pépinières Minier of Beaufort-en-Vallée in 1974. It resulted from the cross (*S. pubescens* subsp. *microphylla* × *S. pubescens* subsp. *patula*) × *S. meyeri*. Fiala used 'Palibin' in his hybridization work (see *S. pubescens* subsp. *julianae*). It will certainly prove an excellent cultivar for future hybridists.

Syringa meyeri var. *spontanea* M.-C. Chang

Synonyms: *S. meyeri* var. *spontanea* f. *alba* (W. Wang, Fuh & Chao) M.-C. Chang, *S. microphylla* var. *alba* W. Wang, Fuh & Chao, *S. microphylla* f. *alba* (W. Wang, Fuh & Chao) Kitagawa

Leaf blade suborbicular or broadly ovate, 1–2 × 0.8–1.8 cm; flowers loose; corolla purplish red, purplish pink, or white; tube 5–8 mm. Flowering May, fruiting September–October.

Habitat: Slopes; ca. 500 m. Liaoning; cultivated in Beijing, Shenyang, and other areas.

See the drawing on page 104.

Forma *spontanea*. Flowers purplish red to purplish pink.

Syringa mairei (H. Léveillé) Rehder

Synonyms: *Ligustrum mairei* H. Léveillé, *S. chuanxiensis* S.-Z. Qu & X.-L. Chen, *S. rugulosa* McKelvey

Syringa meyeri 'Palibin'. B. Peart and M. Walton

Shrubs or small trees to 2(–4) m; branchlets cylindrical, usually densely villous. Petiole 3–7 mm; leaf blade ovate, broadly elliptic to suborbicular or obovate, 2–9 × 2–5 cm, leathery, rugose and pubescent above, densely villous beneath, base cuneate to subrounded, apex acute to obtuse; midrib and veins conspicuously impressed. Panicles lateral, rarely terminal, 6–14 cm; rachis pubescent. Pedicel minute. Calyx purplish red, ca. 2 mm, puberulent. Corolla purplish red, white when expanded, 0.9–1.5 cm; tube slender, subcylindric, 6–11 mm; lobes ovate to oblong-elliptic, spreading. Anthers yellow, inserted near or slightly below mouth of corolla tube. Capsule oblong-lanceolate, 1–2 cm, nearly smooth. Flowering July, fruiting July–November.

Habitat: Thickets on slopes or along roadsides; 1900–2600 m. Western Sichuan, southeastern Tibet (Xizang), northern Yunnan.

The species is named for the French plant collector Édouard-Ernest Maire (1848–1932), who collected herbarium specimens in Yunnan in July 1914. The French botanist Augustin A. Hector Léveillé examined the herbarium specimen and described it in 1916 as a new privet, *Ligustrum mairei*. McKelvey (1928: 148) examined a duplicate herbarium specimen of the same collection and described it as a new lilac, naming it *Syringa rugulosa*, in 1925. Alfred Rehder, realizing that the earlier description and epithet by Léveillé had priority, published the new combination *S. mairei* in 1934. *Syringa mairei* has not yet been reported in cultivation.

Syringa pinetorum W. W. Smith

Shrubs to 1–3 m; branchlets cylindrical, villous to puberulent, gradually glabrescent. Petiole 2–7 mm; leaf blade ovate, ovate-lanceolate, to lanceolate, 1.5–2.5(–4) × 0.8–2(–3) cm, papery, sparsely pubescent or subglabrous above, pilose along veins or glabrescent below, base cuneate to broadly cuneate, apex acute to acuminate. Panicles erect, lateral, loose, 4–11 × 3–6(–8) cm; rachis, pedicel, and calyx usually puberulent. Pedicel to 3 mm. Calyx 1.5–3 mm. Corolla lilac or pale red, 1–1.5(–2) cm; tube cylindric, 6–10(–15) mm; lobes ovate to elliptic, spreading. Anthers yellow, inserted on corolla tube to 3 mm from mouth. Capsule long elliptic to lanceolate, 0.8–1.5 cm, nearly smooth. Flowering May–July, fruiting July–September.

Habitat: Valleys, under pines; 2200–3600 m. Western Sichuan, southeastern Tibet (Xizang), northwestern Yunnan.

This species was described from a herbarium specimen (*12472*) collected in 1914 by Francis Kingdon-Ward, who found it growing "in open pine forests," hence the species epithet *pinetorum*, "of the pine forest."

McKelvey (1928) reported, "There are in cultivation in this country [United States] plants bearing the name *Syringa pinetorum*, which were propagated at the Arnold Arboretum from seed collected by [George] Forrest and distributed by Royal Botanic Garden, Edinburgh. These plants are clearly *S. yunnanensis*." This has been confirmed by Fiala (1988), Pringle (1990), and Green and Chang (1995). As recently as 2004 more than 20 public and private collections on

Syringa meyeri var. *spontanea*: (1) flowering branch, (2) opened corolla showing stamens. *Syringa pinetorum*: (3) flowering branch, (4) opened corolla showing stamens. Drawing by Lu Jinwei; redrawn by Cai Shuqin. Reprinted by permission from Wu and Raven 1996, p. 238.

three continents were still listing *S. pinetorum* in their inventories, although to our knowledge this species was not yet in cultivation (Vrugtman 2004c).

Syringa wardii W. W. Smith

Shrubs or small trees to 5 m, young shoots pubescent. Petiole 2–3 mm; leaf blade suborbicular, 1.2 × 2.2 cm, glabrous above, paler, glabrous or puberulent beneath, base rounded to truncate, very short attenuate onto petiole, apex rounded or obtuse, sometimes very short apiculate-acuminate; primary veins four or five on each side of midrib, faintly reticulate below. Panicles erect, lateral, loose, 6–10 × 3–7 cm; rachis pubescent. Pedicel 1–3 mm. Calyx ca. 2 mm, almost truncate, teeth minute. Corolla 1.5–1.7 cm; tube cylindric, 1–1.2 cm; lobes ovate, obtuse, 4–5 mm. Anthers inserted slightly above middle of corolla tube. Capsule long elliptic, 1–1.4 cm, nearly smooth. Flowering May–June, fruiting September.

Habitat: Arid scrub on slopes, in woods; 2400–3000 m. Southeastern Tibet (Xizang), northwestern Yunnan.

The species is named for Francis Kingdon-Ward, who collected a herbarium specimen of this lilac in 1913. Until a few years ago it was known only from Kingdon-Ward's herbarium specimen. *Syringa wardii* has only relatively recently been reported in cultivation.

Subgenus *Syringa*, Series *Villosae*

Syringa villosa Vahl
Synonyms: *S. bretschneideri* Lemoine, *S. emodi* var. *rosea* Cornu, *S. villosa* var. *rosea* Cornu ex Rehder

Shrubs to 4 m, glabrous or puberulent to villous. Petiole 0.8–2.5 cm; leaf blade ovate, broadly elliptic, to obovate-oblong, 4–11(–18) × 1.5–6(–11) cm, glabrous above, abaxially pilose or barbate only along veins, occasionally glabrous, base cuneate to subrounded, apex acute or short acuminate. Panicles erect, terminal, rather compact, 5–13(–17) × 3–10 cm. Pedicel 0.5–1.5 mm. Calyx 2–4 mm. Corolla lilac-red to pink to white, 1–2 cm; tube slender, subcylindric, 0.7–1.5 cm; lobes ovate to elliptic, spreading. Anthers yellow, inserted near mouth of corolla tube or slightly protruding. Capsule oblong, 1–1.5 cm, smooth or nearly so. Flowering May–June, fruiting September.

Habitat: Near gullies, riverbanks, thickets; 1200–2200 m. Hebei, Shanxi.

Pierre d'Incarville (1706–1757), the Jesuit botanist-missionary, had a keen eye for new plants as well as a zeal for religion. He sent to Paris, somewhere around 1750, a very interesting collection of dried plants and seeds. Being a pupil of the great French botanist Bernard de Jussieu (1699–1776), to whom he sent his plant collection, he carefully separated those plants collected in Beijing from those of the surrounding area. Among the specimens gathered in the Beijing mountains was one of a yet unknown lilac. This lilac was described in 1804 by the Danish botanist Martin Vahl and named *Syringa villosa*.

In 1835 *Syringa villosa* was rediscovered in Beijing

Syringa wolfii: (1) flowering branch, (2) opened corolla showing stamens and distal portion of style, (3) infructescence. *Syringa villosa*: (4) flowering branch, (5) opened corolla showing stamens, (6) fruiting branch. Drawing by Lu Jinwei; redrawn by Cai Shuqin. Reprinted by permission from Wu and Raven 1996, p. 235.

by the Russian botanist Porfirij Kirilov. Emil Bretschneider introduced *S. villosa* into cultivation in 1889, well over a century after its original discovery. He sent seeds to Jardin des Plantes, Paris; Royal Botanic Gardens, Kew; Arnold Arboretum, Massachusetts; and Saint Petersburg, Russia. The Lemoine nursery in Nancy, France, offered the species for sale for the first time under the name of *S. bretschneideri*, honoring Bretschneider, from whom it received the seed in 1890. In the hands of hybridizers, *S. villosa* would become one of the parent species of the interspecific hybrids *S. ×henryi* and *S. ×prestoniae*, and cultivars in the Villosae Group.

In the garden, the flowers of *Syringa villosa* are distinctly pink, although when using a color chart there is a tinge of bluish lavender not readily apparent to the unaided eye but more often captured on color film. In Europe, *S. villosa* is grown more often as a small tree. McKelvey (1928) wrote,

Syringa villosa. B. Peart and M. Walton

While visiting the Central Experimental Farm at Ottawa, Canada, in June 1927, I saw a collection of hedges grown for demonstration purposes. One of *Syringa villosa*, planted in 1911, is now about 20 feet [6 m] broad and about 15 feet [4.5 m] tall. It forms a handsome hedge, but is not so striking as one of *S. josikaea*.

Syringa emodi Wallich ex Royle
Himalayan lilac

Shrubs to 5 m; branches upright; branchlets rather robust; bark silvery gray, lenticellate. Leaves elliptic-oblong, to 9 × 5 cm, dark green and glabrous above, silvery gray and slightly pubescent beneath when young. Panicles terminal. Corolla white or purple; tube 1 cm; lobes short, valvate, linear-oblong, hooded at the tips. Anthers about one-half protruding. Flowering May–June, fruiting September–October.

Habitat: Slopes; 2000–3000 m. Afghanistan, Pakistan, western Himalaya, Kashmir (Ladakh), Nepal (Kihara 1957, Stewart 1972, Grohmann 1974, Hara et al. 1982, Dhar and Kachroo 1983).

Robert Blinkworth, plant collector for Nathaniel Wallich, director of the East India Company's botanic gardens at Calcutta, was first to collect *Syringa emodi* in the western Himalaya around Kuram Valley, Afghanistan. In 1831 Wallich listed the species from the dried specimen collected by Blinkworth, naming it *S. emodi*. Subsequently, it was described and illustrated by John F. Royle (1839). Although E. H. Wilson (1917) stated that it "is among the last of the true Lilacs to flower and is less hardy than any other. . . . In its pale foliage it is distinct from other Lilacs and it is one of the very few species which thrive better in

Syringa emodi 'Aurea'. John Fiala

Great Britain than in New England," *S. emodi* thrives as well in the midwestern United States and in Canada, as it does in England, the Netherlands, Denmark, Poland, and even Iceland and Australia.

In late spring the flower buds on occasion may be touched by frosts. *Syringa emodi* is a broad, round shrub with heavy foliage and large leaves, opening late in the spring and among the last to fall in the autumn. It is a dirty bloomer in that its spent flowers do not fall neatly, and there is an unevenness to their opening. Thus there are faded and opening florets on the same raceme, giving an untidy appearance. Alas, it passes this untidy trait to its offspring; hybridizers have not been able to do well with it. In long summer droughts it often sheds many of its leaves. It is a shrub for well-drained but moist loamy soils of mountain freshets or riverlet banks. Its most striking characteristic is its extremely lenticellate bark, marked on the branchlets with long, pale, vertical fissures, which on older and grayer branches display a fishnet pattern.

Although not an attractive garden and landscape plant, *Syringa emodi* may have some merit to the hybridizer; it may be able to transmit its interesting bark and its white floret color to its hybrids. Good white-blooming late hybrids will always be in demand. The value of this species has yet to be proven. Only 'Aurea' can be found occasionally in lilac collections.

'Aurea', origin unknown pre-1886. A single white, gold-leaved cultivar first described in 1886. It is probably the best of all the gold-leaved and variegated oddities found in *Syringa*, retaining its gold color for most of the season before turning a pale green. At best it is a lilac for botanical collections. There is a good specimen in the collection at Highland Botanical Park, Rochester, New York.

'Elegantissima', van der Bom 1876. A single white with yellow-margined leaves. Very difficult to obtain.

'Variegata', origin unknown pre-1877. A single, white.

Syringa wolfii C. K. Schneider

Synonyms: *S. formosissima* Nakai, *S. formosissima* var. *hirsuta* (C. K. Schneider) Nakai, *S. hirsuta* (C. K. Schneider) Nakai, *S. hirsuta* var. *formosissima* (Nakai) Nakai, *S. robusta* Nakai, *S. robusta* var. *rupestris* Baranov & Skvortsov

Shrubs to 6 m; branchlets green when young, becoming gray with age, glabrous or pubescent. Petiole 1–3 cm, glabrous or pubescent; leaf blade elliptic-oblong, elliptic, or obovate-oblong, 3.5–12(–18) × 1.5–7(–10) cm, glabrous or sparsely pubescent above, villous below, base cuneate to subrounded, apex usually acute to acuminate. Panicles erect, terminal, 5–30 × 3–18 cm; rachis, pedicel, and calyx villous or pubescent, occasionally subglabrous. Pedicel to 2 mm. Calyx 2–3.5 mm. Corolla pale purple to purple-red, 1.2–1.8 cm; tube funnelform, 1–1.4 cm; lobes oblong-ovate to ovate, upright or spreading. Anthers yellow, inserted near or slightly below mouth of corolla tube. Capsule oblong, (1–)1.2–1.7 cm, smooth. Flowering June, fruiting August.

Habitat: Mixed forests, thickets, woods, along rivers; 500–1600 m. Heilongjiang, Jilin, Liaoning; Korea, eastern Russia.

Camillo Schneider described *Syringa wolfii* in 1910 from a living specimen growing at the Forestry Insti-

Syringa wolfii. B. Peart and M. Walton

tute in Saint Petersburg. He named the species in honor of the institute's director, Egbert L. Wolf (1860–1931). Schneider believed the species was native to China, although at the time its exact native location was not known. Vladimir Komarov, who traveled extensively in Manchuria and Korea from 1893 to 1895, undoubtedly, was the first to send seed of *S. wolfii* to Europe (via Saint Petersburg) albeit under the name *S. villosa* var. *hirsuta*. In August 1917 E. H. Wilson gathered seed in Korea, which he sent to the Arnold Arboretum, this being the first authenticated introduction to North America. See the drawing on page 105.

It is evident from the synonyms listed for *Syringa wolfii* that is has been difficult to clearly define the species. It is strikingly similar to *S. josikaea*, although *S. wolfii* is handsomer in bloom than the best forms of *S. josikaea*. In flower color the two are very similar. Some botanists believe that they are extremes of the same species. McKelvey (1928) objected, stating, "A vast territory exists between their habitats, and *S. wolfii* may be regarded as the Asiatic representative of the European plant."

Syringa wolfii is a lovely species, not for the small garden and perhaps best in the hands of hybridizers who make great strides with it as a parent plant. It imparts to many of its hybrids the glossy dark green leaf plus vigor. Some fine cultivars, including *S.* (Villosae Group) 'Spellbinder', have resulted from the cross *S. komarowii* × *S. wolfii*. The flower color of *S. wolfii* varies in different plants from a pale lavender to a pale darker purple; in clay soils the same clone is often more pinkish lilac to a pale pink-purple. Some plants bear heavier inflorescences than others when grown from seed produced by selfing.

Syringa josikaea J. Jacquin ex H. G. L. Reichenbach
Hungarian lilac

Although *Syringa josikaea* belongs geographically in chapter two, systematically it is part of the series *Villosae*, so it is justified to add a note here. It is similar to *S. wolfii* as previously noted. Curiously, as McKelvey (1928) noted under *S. josikaea*, certain botanists were of the opinion that *S. josikaea* was merely naturalized and not native in Europe, suggesting that it was

brought from northern China, yet there is no evidence for such a hypotheses.

Syringa komarowii C. K. Schneider

Shrubs to 1.5–6 m; branchlets cylindrical, glabrous or pubescent. Petiole 1–3 cm; leaf blade ovate-oblong, oblong-lanceolate, elliptic, to elliptic-obovate, 5–19 × 1.5–7(–9) cm, glabrous or pubescent along midrib above, pubescent or denser along veins below, base cuneate, apex acute to long acuminate. Panicles nodding to pendulous, terminal, compact or lax, 4–25 × 3–13 cm; rachis, pedicel, and calyx densely pubescent to glabrous. Pedicel to 1.5 mm. Calyx 2–3 mm. Corolla purple-red, red, to pale lilac outside, white inside, 1–2.2 cm; tube funnelform, 0.8–1.5(–2) cm; lobes ovate to ovate-oblong, spreading or usually upright. Anthers yellow, inserted on corolla tube to 2 mm from mouth or somewhat protruding. Capsule ripening usually reflexed, long elliptic, 1–1.5(–2) cm, smooth or sparsely lenticellate. Flowering May–June, fruiting July–October.

Habitat: Thickets, woods, near rivers and gullies; 1000–3400 m. Southern Gansu, western Hubei, southern Shaanxi, Sichuan, northern Yunnan.

This volume follows the original spelling of the epithet used by Schneider, who derived it from the German transliteration Komarow, though some argue it should be *komarovii* since the English transliteration of the Russian (Cyrillic) name is Komarov.

Wilson (1917) believed *Syringa komarowii* to be an extreme form of the very variable *S. reflexa*. Today we recognize them as two subspecies of *S. komarowii*, which can be separated with the following key (Green and Chang 1995, Chang and Green 1996a):

1a Corolla dark; corolla lobes mostly more or less erect; inflorescences usually more or less compact
.... *S. komarowii* subsp. *komarowii*
1b Corolla pale; corolla lobes usually spreading; inflorescences somewhat pyramidal, often interrupted
.... *S. komarowii* subsp. *reflexa*

Syringa komarowii subsp. komarowii
Synonyms: *S. glabra* (C. K. Schneider) Lingelsheim, *S. komarowii* var. *sargentiana* (C. K. Schneider) C. K. Schneider, *S. sargentiana* C. K. Schneider, *S. villosa* var. *glabra* C. K. Schneider

Syringa komarowii. John Fiala

Syringa tibetica: (1) flowering branch, (2) flower. *Syringa yunnanensis*: (3) flowering branch, (4) opened corolla showing stamens. *Syringa komarowii*: (5) flowering branch, (6) opened corolla showing stamens, (7) infructescence. Drawing by Lu Jinwei; redrawn by Cai Shuqin. Reprinted by permission from Wu and Raven 1996, p. 234.

Differs from subsp. *reflexa* in that the inflorescences usually are more or less compact, the corolla somewhat deep purple-red, red, to lilac-red outside, and the lobes mostly more or less erect. Habitat: Thickets, woods, near rivers; 1000–3400 m. Southern Gansu, southern Shaanxi, Sichuan, northern Yunnan.

Syringa komarowii, one of the finest native species from China, was first collected most likely by the plant explorer Grigoriĭ Potanin, who sent his materials to the botanical garden in Saint Petersburg, Russia. Camillo Schneider (1910), who described and named it from those materials, recorded that it was collected in Sichuan on 18 July 1893.

As a shrub to 10 feet (3 m) tall, a bit more in very good soils, *Syringa komarowii* subsp. *komarowii* is ideal for background planting; its habit is more rounded than weeping. It rarely suckers but can be readily grown from seed. Use subspecies *komarowii* in mass planting in front of Russian olive (*Elaeagnus an-*

Syringa komarowii subsp. *komarowii* in native habitat, mountains of Sichuan, China. C. Teune.

gustifolia). It will not grow too tall, and the feathery plumes go well with the soft-textured olive. The contrast of its pinkish lavender blossom, and in summer its good green foliage against a background of silvery olive is well worth the effort.

The species has much to offer as a garden plant and as a parent in hybridizing. Many of the plants labeled *Syringa komarowii* do not have the intense drooping character of the inflorescence pictured in McKelvey's (1928) book. Undoubtedly, there are many misnamed lilacs in horticultural collections. An exceptionally fine form of *S. komarowii*, described originally by Charles Sargent as *S. wolfii*, is growing at the Arnold Arboretum. In some respects subspecies *komarowii* in leaf and vigor appears to be a better plant than subspecies *reflexa*, but the latter is more showy in bloom.

Syringa komarowii is an outstanding species for hybridizing. Recent introductions are *S.* (Villosae Group) 'Lark Song', resulting from (*S. sweginzowii* × *S. tomentella*) × *S. komarowii*, and *S.* (Villosae Group) 'Spellbinder', resulting from *S. komarowii* × *S. wolfii*.

Syringa komarowii subsp. *reflexa* (C. K. Schneider) P. S. Green & M.-C. Chang

Synonyms: *S. reflexa* C. K. Schneider, *S. komarowii* var. *reflexa* (C. K. Schneider) Jien ex M.-C. Chang

Differs from subsp. *komarowii* in that the inflorescences are somewhat pyramidal, often interrupted; the corolla somewhat light red or pale lilac outside; and the lobes usually spreading. Habitat: Woods near gullies; 1800–2900 m. Western Hubei, northeastern Sichuan.

Syringa komarowii subsp. *reflexa* was described in 1910 by Camillo Schneider from two herbarium specimens collected in Hubei, one by Augustine Henry between 1885 and 1889, the other by Ernest Wilson in 1901. Schneider (1910) wrote: "A shrub related to *S. villosa*; ... inflorescence to 14 × 3 cm large ... flowers violet (?)." It was the reflexed fruit rather than the pendulous thyrses that prompted Schneider's choice of the descriptive epithet *reflexa* (McKelvey 1928).

Wilson in collecting this lilac again in 1907 near Fang-hsien noted at one location that the flowers were reddish while at another they were a rosy pink. Seed collected by Wilson in October 1910 (*4460*) was sent to the Arnold Arboretum and from there to Royal

Botanic Gardens, Kew. This was the first introduction into cultivation in North America and Europe.

The Lemoine nursery was the first to offer *Syringa komarowii* subsp. *reflexa* for sale in 1917 (catalog 191, English edition, page 25), describing it as having "reflexed lobes of a soft mauve color." It is a genetically variable species, not only in color but also in flower and inflorescence. When subsp. *reflexa* is grown from protected, selfed seed, the resulting seedlings show variations in color—shades of light pinks, tinged mauve to a pale lavender—and in the degree of drooping of the inflorescence.

Wilson discovered *Syringa komarowii* subsp. *reflexa* growing along the margins of the forest and mountain wood thickets. In 1917 he wrote:

> The most distinct of all Lilacs is the new [*Syringa komarowii* subsp. *reflexa*] with narrow, cylindrical flower clusters from 9 to 12 inches [23–30 cm] long which arch downward from near the base and thus hang somewhat like the inflorescence of the Wisteria. The expanding flower buds are bright red and the open flowers are pale rose color. . . . A strong-growing shrub from 8 to 12 feet [2.4–3.6 m] high, with erect stems and oblong lance-shaped leaves, its season of flowering is mid-June.

Wilson went on to suggest that in the hands of the hybridist *Syringa komarowii* subsp. *reflexa* "may be the forerunner of a race totally different in aspect from present day Lilacs." Three years later Isabella Preston, at the Central Experimental Farm, Ottawa, crossed subsp. *reflexa* with *S. villosa*, creating her famous *S.* ×*prestoniae* hybrids. She also crossed subsp. *reflexa* with *S. josikaea*, resulting in *S.* ×*josiflexa*.

Subspecies *reflexa* does not relish hardpan, clay, or undrained soils. As it is a native of forest borders, give it well-drained woodsy loam mixed with gravel, and put it on a little drier hillside. Use it as a focal plant in your garden.

Often one sees so-called typical representatives of a species, lilacs that were grown from seed sent back by plant explorers—perhaps only a few seeds were collected, and the description made from a rather poor representative of the species. This may have been the case with *Syringa komarowii* subsp. *reflexa*. The black-and-white pictures from the Arnold Arboretum Archives clearly indicate the variability of subspecies *reflexa* seedlings. Not only is this true of plant vigor and form but especially in floriferousness, size of florets and thyrses, and the various shades of color. To our knowledge no one has done mass seeding of controlled self-pollinated subspecies *reflexa*. Some far superior seedlings would undoubtedly be found if such a self-pollination were to occur.

James S. Pringle (1977), taxonomist at Royal Botanical Gardens, Hamilton, Ontario, described several hybrid crosses made there in series *Villosae*. It is the most extensive hybridization program and description of results of so many interspecific crosses that it merits special recognition. Pringle described the results of the many crosses and discussed the merits of each cross, its potential for hybridizing, and its value as a garden plant. Among these crosses were those involving *Syringa komarowii* subsp. *reflexa* as one of the parents: *S. emodi* × *S. komarowii* subsp. *reflexa*, *S.* × *henryi* × *S. komarowii* subsp. *reflexa*, *S. komarowii* subsp. *reflexa* × *S. yunnanensis*, *S. sweginzowii* × *S. komarowii* subsp. *reflexa*, and "*S. wolfii* hybrid" × *S. komarowii* subsp. *reflexa*. In all, it is an extraordinary and thorough hybridizing of *S. komarowii* subsp. *reflexa* within the series *Villosae*. Plants have remained numbered but none has been introduced and named, although some appear to have considerable promise for hybridizers.

'**Alba**', Upton 1933. A white form was discovered by Edward A. Upton growing in his nursery at Goodrich, Michigan, and introduced by him in 1933. The flowers are a clear, creamy white, with both narrow and drooping clusters typical of the species. In habit it is identical to the pink form except that the leaves are paler green. It is a wonderful shrub for both the garden and the hybridist but unfortunately extremely rare.

'**Slavin**', Slavin and Fiala pre-1988, single pink. One of the loveliest forms of subspecies *reflexa* observed by Fiala was a seedling grown by the late Bernard Slavin when superintendent at Highland Botanical Park, Rochester, New York. Fiala proposed the name *S. komarowii* subsp. *reflexa* 'Slavin' (*BHS 5*) so that it may not be lost. Some might argue that it is a hybrid, but Fiala believed it to be a superior selection of subspecies *reflexa*. Kent Millham (22 February 2005, pers. comm. to F.V.), horticulturist at Highland

Syringa komarowii subsp. *reflexa*. B. Peart and M. Walton

Syringa komarowii subsp. *reflexa* 'Slavin'. John Fiala

Botanical Park, writes that in fact there are two selections, *BHS 5* and *BHS 6*, which are very similar, that the original lilacs are large, well-established plants in the Park that are not in danger of being lost, and that they have been propagated and are awaiting further evaluation and perhaps introduction.

Syringa tomentella Bureau & Franchet

Synonyms: *S. adamiana* I. B. Balfour & W. W. Smith, *S. alborosea* N. E. Brown, *S. rehderiana* C. K. Schneider, *S. tomentella* var. *rehderiana* (C. K. Schneider) Rehder, *S. wilsonii* C. K. Schneider

Shrubs to 1.5–7 m; branchlets sparsely to densely pubescent. Petiole 0.8–1.5 cm, along with rachis, pedicel, and calyx pubescent, villous, or glabrescent; leaf blade ovate-lanceolate to elliptic-lanceolate, rarely ovate or obovate, 2.5–11 × 1.5–5 cm, appressed pubescent or glabrous above, hairy as on branchlets or barbate along veins below, base cuneate to subrounded, apex acute to acuminate. Panicles erect, terminal or sometimes lateral, loose, 10–25 × 4–12 cm. Pedicel 1–1.5 mm. Calyx 2.5–3 mm. Corolla lilac-red, pink, or white, 1–1.7 cm; tube slightly funnelform, 0.8–1.4 cm; lobes ovate to elliptic, spreading. Anthers yellow,

Syringa tomentella: (1) flowering branch, (2) opened corolla showing stamens and distal portion of style, (3) infructescence. *Syringa sweginzowii*: (4) flowering branch, (5) opened corolla showing stamens. Drawing by Lu Jinwei; redrawn by Cai Shuqin. Reprinted by permission from Wu and Raven 1996, p. 236.

reaching mouth of corolla tube or slightly protruding. Capsule oblong-elliptic, 1.2–2 cm, obviously lenticellate or smooth. Flowering June–July, fruiting September.

Habitat: Woods on slopes, thickets of valley, along gullies; 2500–3500 m. Western Sichuan.

Louis Bureau and Adrien Franchet first described the discovery of *Syringa tomentella* (Bureau and Franchet 1891). This species was collected by Pierre Bonvalot and Prince Henri d'Orléans in Sichuan, on entering To-tsien lu and the borders of Yunnan. A somewhat fuller description is given by Wilson (1917):

> I saw this plant in flower for the first time on 9 July 1908 on the frontiers of eastern Thibet [Xizang] at an altitude of 9000 feet [2700 m], and I thought then that I had never before seen such a handsome species of Lilac. It had foot-high [30-cm], broad panicles of pink to rosy lilac colored flowers and on other bushes they were white. The plants were 8 to 15 feet [2.4–4.5 m] high, much-branched yet compact in habit, and the wealth of flower clusters made it conspicuous from afar.

The plant of *S. tomentella* at the Arnold Arboretum justifies Wilson's description. It was not until 1904 that this species was introduced into cultivation (Rehder 1949). The Arnold Arboretum received its first plant in 1907 from the Veitch nursery in London.

Syringa tomentella and *S. villosa* are closely related; often the latter is sold as the former. *Syringa tomentella* produces fine hybrids and should be used considerably more by hybridizers, especially in crosses with the fine- or small-leaved species of series *Villosae*. It is a better species than the summer leaf-shedding *S. villosa*. For larger parks and arboreta *S. tomentella* should be planted more often, especially in mass groupings. It is not a plant for the smaller garden; for larger gardens some of its newer hybrids are preferable.

Syringa sweginzowii Koehne & Lingelsheim

Synonyms: *S. tetanoloba* C. K. Schneider, *S. tigerstedtii* H. K. A. Smith

Shrubs to 2.5–4 m; branchlets four-angled, glabrous. Petiole 0.5–2 cm, glabrous or pilose; leaf blade ovate, ovate-elliptic, to lanceolate, 1.5–4(–8) × 1–3(–5) cm, shiny and glabrous above, barbate along veins or glabrous below, base cuneate to subrounded, margin tinged purplish red when young, apex acute to acuminate. Panicles erect, terminal or lateral, 7–25 × 3–15 cm; rachis generally four-angled, including pedicel and calyx purple-brown, puberulent or glabrous. Pedicel to 2 mm. Calyx 1.5–2 mm. Corolla pink, lilac, to white, 0.9–2 cm; tube slender, sub-cylindric, 0.6–1.5 cm; lobes ovate-oblong to lanceolate, spreading. Anthers yellow, inserted on corolla tube below or near mouth. Capsule long elliptic, 1.5–2 cm, smooth. Flowering May–June, fruiting September–October.

Habitat: Thickets, woods, near river sides or gullies; 2000–4000 m. Western Sichuan.

In 1910 Bernhard Koehne and Alexander von Lingelsheim described *Syringa sweginzowii* from a living specimen in the arboretum of the dendrologist Maximilian (Max) von Sivers (1857–1919), Römershof-Skriveri, near Riga, Latvia. They do not state who discovered this new species. However, Grigorii Potanin, on behalf of the Russian Geographical Society, made an expedition from 1891 through 1894 into western Sichuan. In his company, as zoologist for the expedition, was Mikhail Berezovski. Potanin brought back seed, as did Berezovski, together with specimens of this lilac. It is most likely that Sivers's plant came from either of these sources and it might be safe to assume that *S. sweginzowii* was first discovered by Potanin and Berezovski in May and June of 1893 in western Sichuan.

In this same neighborhood Ernest Wilson collected specimens and seed of *Syringa sweginzowii* in 1904. He recorded in his field notes and diary that the one specimen (*4080*) was growing at an elevation of 11,000 feet (3350 m), a bush 6 feet (1.8 m) tall, in a ravine in the descent to the Yalong river at Nagachuka, Sichuan. A second specimen (*4569*) was a bush 6 feet tall growing at an altitude of 8,000–10,000 feet (2400–3000 m) in northern Sichuan, toward Sunpan, in August 1910 (McKelvey 1928). See the drawing on page 112.

In England, *Syringa sweginzowii* was exhibited first in June 1915. The Arnold Arboretum received its first plant in November 1910 from the nursery of Regel and Kesselring at Saint Petersburg, Russia. It flowered in 1912 (Anonymous 1912):

[*Syringa sweginzowii*] does not produce the extremely large individual flowers associated with the modern garden forms of the common Lilac, yet they possess a delicacy and refinement which makes them extremely beautiful. It is one of the loveliest of all Lilacs.

The flowers of the Arnold Arboretum plant are a pale yellowish pink. Clusters are open and never crowded, and carry a delicate fragrance.

At Medina, Ohio, *Syringa sweginzowii* is a neat, upright growing shrub of about 10 feet (3 m) with somewhat small leaves. Its deep garnet-colored stems (a brownish reddish) are covered in spring with dawn flushed pink florets in open, billowy clusters. The reddish stems and pale pink flowers are a very attractive combination. This hardy plant and outstanding garden performer is somewhat fussy about its location and soil. It is neither rampant growing nor big-leaved as are *S. villosa* or *S. tomentella*; furthermore it does not like open, windswept locations (although it is a native mountaineer) or hard clay soils. Placed in very light shade to protect it from the hottest suns, it thrives wonderfully. Give it well-drained soil or a fertile hilltop that simulates its habitat in China. *Syringa sweginzowii* belongs to the later-blooming species, opening its flowers midway between the last of *S. vulgaris* and the beginnings of the Villosae Group hybrids. Its fragrance is a haunting, aromatic, spicy scent that brings one back to the spice stalls of the bazaars of old Cathay, altogether unlike the scent of *S. vulgaris*. It is certainly one of our finer lilac species.

In 1930 Lemoine introduced *Syringa* (Villosae Group) 'Albida'. It develops into a tall slender plant, flowering at the end of May with a profusion of many-branched panicles of most elegant character. The long-tubed flowers with reflexed lobes are a very delicate pale pink passing to white. They, too, are very pleasantly sweet-scented. In more recent years 'Albida' has been extensively used in hybridizing with *S. komarowii*, giving us the beautiful tribrid (three-species) cultivar *S.* (Villosae Group) 'Lark Song', and with *S. wolfii* the cultivars *S.* (Villosae Group) 'Springtime' and *S.* (Villosae Group) 'Sunrise'. *Syringa sweginzowii* and *S.* (Villosae Group) 'Albida' are both excellent hybridizing parents and should be more used in crosses

Syringa sweginzowii. B. Peart and M. Walton

Syringa sweginzowii 'Superba'. B. Peart and M. Walton

Syringa (Villosae Group) 'Albida'. B. Peart and M. Walton

with *S. ×prestoniae* cultivars for their openness of bloom and their outstanding fragrance.

'**Superba**', Lemoine 1915, single pink. RHS Award of Merit 1918.

Syringa yunnanensis Franchet
Yunnan lilac
Synonyms: *S. yunnanensis* var. *pubicalyx* Jien ex P.-Y. Bai, *S. yunnanensis* f. *pubicalyx* (Jien ex P.-Y. Bai) M.-C. Chang

Shrubs to 2–5 m; branchlets cylindrical or slightly four-angled, usually glabrous. Petiole 0.5–2 cm, glabrous; leaf blade elliptic, elliptic-lanceolate, to oblanceolate, 2–8(–13) × 1–3.5(–5.5) cm, glabrous or rarely pubescent along veins below, base cuneate or rarely subrounded, apex acute or short acuminate. Panicles erect, terminal, 5–18 × 3–12 cm; rachis and pedicel puberulent or rarely woolly. Pedicel 0.5–1.5 mm. Calyx 1–2.5 mm, glabrous or rarely woolly. Corolla white to lilac-red, 0.7–1.2(–1.7) cm; tube funnel-form, 5–8(–13) mm; lobes oblong, spreading. Anthers yellow, usually inserted on corolla tube up to 2 mm from mouth. Capsule oblong, 1.2–1.7 cm, slightly lenticellate. Flowering May–June, fruiting September.

Habitat: Thickets, woods on slopes, gullies; 2000–3900 m. Southwestern Sichuan, southeastern Tibet (Xizang), northwestern Yunnan.

The relatively unknown *Syringa yunnanensis* is closely related to the Himalayan lilac, *S. emodi*. It was discovered in 1887 by Abbot Jean Marie Delavay, growing in the woods by Lake Lanking near the city of Talifu in Yunnan, southwestern China. This upright, rather narrow shrub, 10–12 feet (3–3.6 m) tall, bears pale whitish purplish, rose-tinted flowers on terminal leafy shoots that are rather insignificant. Frequently, it has five corolla lobes rather than the usual four. Although several plant collectors were in this same area before Delavay, namely, Marie Joseph François Garnier in 1868, William Gill in 1877, Szeczenyi in 1880, and Alexander Hosie in 1883, no collection of this species was made until John Anderson gathered the plant in 1868 (Bretschneider 1898). However, it was from Delavay's specimen that Adrien René Franchet first described *S. yunnanensis* in 1891. See the drawing on page 109.

George Forrest has been credited with introducing

Syringa yunnanensis in native habitat, mountains of Sichuan, China. C. Teune

Syringa yunnanensis 'Rosea'. B. Peart and M. Walton

Syringa yunnanensis. Sir William Wright Smith, professor of botany at the University of Edinburgh, and regius keeper of Royal Botanic Garden, Edinburgh, wrote (16 December 1926, to Susan McKelvey),

> The earliest reference to our having *S. yunnanensis* appears in our catalogue of Plantae Chinenses Forrestianae (*Notes from the Royal Botanic Garden, Edinburgh,* vol. VII. 1912, nos. *F. 2294, F. 2636, F. 4655*). George Forrest at this time was collecting for A. K. Bulley, who was the first director of the Bees Nursery Company. This company and the Botanic Garden here raised plants from seeds collected by Mr. Forrest in these early expeditions. The plants apparently did very well and seed of *S. yunnanensis* appeared in our Seed List for December, 1920, showing that the plants had made considerable progress by that date.

The Arnold Arboretum received its first plant of *S. yunnanensis* from Bees Nursery of Neston, Cheshire,

England, in September 1908, labeled "*Ligustrum* no. 21" (McKelvey 1928).

Syringa yunnanensis, like most of the late-blooming species, does not sucker. It is easy to root from green cuttings taken after it has bloomed. Until relatively recently *S. yunnanensis* has been little used in hybridizing, as none of its characteristics appears really outstanding except the openness of its inflorescence (this can be found in better species). The small florets of *S. yunnanensis* are a bane to hybridizers. *Syringa yunnanensis* seems to transmit a small floret, an open inflorescence, a narrow growth habit, and a deeper lavender color to its progeny. With continued and selective hybridization some few, refined hybrids should appear.

This plant needs a well-drained situation. For very large estates, arboreta, or for hybridizers, this species has historical or scientific value. Until better hybrids are developed, it is not a lilac to be considered by most. At best, *Syringa yunnanensis* remains an insignificant lilac species. In the past, it was widely distributed in North America under the erroneous name *S. pinetorum* W. W. Smith; it may still be grown under that name at some arboreta and in private collections (McKelvey 1928, Pringle 1990, Green and Chang 1995, Vrugtman 2004c).

'Alba', Hillier ca. 1949, single white.

'Rosea', Hillier ca. 1946, single pinkish.

Syringa tibetica Pei-Yu Bai

Shrubs to 2.5–4 m, densely pubescent. Petiole 1–1.3 cm; leaf blade oblong or oblong-elliptic, 7–10 × 3.5–5 cm, sub-glabrous above except along veins or sparsely pubescent, densely pubescent or pubescent below only along veins, base cuneate to subrounded, apex acute or short acuminate. Panicles terminal, 7–13 cm. Pedicel 1–2 mm. Calyx 2–3 mm. Corolla white; tube 5–7 mm; lobes lanceolate, reflexed. Anthers yellow, entirely protruding from corolla tube. Capsule not seen. Flowering June.

Habitat: Margins of woods; 2900–3200 m. Tibet (Xizang).

First described and named by Bai Pei-Yu (1979), this species has not yet been reported in cultivation. See the drawing on page 109.

Syringa Villosae Group

Proposed in 2003 by Marco Hoffman (2003, 2004), Villosae Group is based on the botanical series *Villosae* C. K. Schneider. The group includes all cultivars of interspecies hybrid origin within the series. *Syringa ×josiflexa* 'Royalty' is the designated nomenclatural standard for Villosae Group. Fiala (1988, 78) was well aware of the problem of uncertain parentage when he wrote,

> *Syringa villosa* crossed with *S. reflexa* begot the Preston hybrids . . . and the Preston hybrids crossed with *S. josikaea* begot . . . and with *S.*

Syringa (Villosae Group) 'Royalty'. John Fiala

tomentella begot . . . and with *S. sweginzowii* begot . . . and with *S. wolfii* begot . . . and their progeny crossed with *S. yunnanensis* crossed with *S. komarowii* . . . and so we came to have today a whole new group of late-blooming multibrids (crosses with several species). The begots begot until we have an array of progeny so numerous that taxonomists can no longer identify, yet alone describe, who begot what and when and by whom.

Villosae Group is designed to accommodate all these cultivars of mixed parentage within the series *Villosae* C. K. Schneider. The concept is already in use by European garden writers and the nursery industry (Albrecht 2005). More about this group in chapter four.

Syringa ×henryi C. K. Schneider

The original cross *Syringa josikaea* × *S. villosa* was made by Louis Henry at the Jardin des Plantes in Paris, and seedling selections appear to have been exhibited for the first time at the Société Nationale d'Horticulture de France in 1890. Camillo Schneider (1910) first described the new hybrid, naming it for its originator. *Syringa* (Villosae Group) 'Lutèce' is the nomenclatural type of *S. ×henryi*. McKelvey (1928) wrote of this cross:

> The *Syringa ×henryi* hybrids, which are very similar in general habit and in foliage to the parents *S. villosa* and *S. josikaea*, are distinguished in their flowers by the form of the corolla tube, which is less cylindric than that of *S. villosa* and less funnelform than that of *S. josikaea*, by the size of the anthers, which are smaller than those of *S. villosa* and larger than those of *S. josikaea*, and by the position in the corolla tube where they are inserted slightly higher than those in *S. josikaea* and slightly lower than those in *S. villosa*. In color the flowers vary a little on different plants but all contain considerable blue in their coloring matter and in this show their *S. josikaea* ancestry.

Several cultivars of *Syringa ×henryi* can be found in lilac collections and in the nursery trade:

'Alba' (*S.* Villosae Group), Lemoine 1934, single pinkish.

Syringa (Villosae Group) 'Lutèce'. B. Peart and M. Walton

Syringa (Villosae Group) 'Summer White'. B. Peart and M. Walton

'**Crayton Red**' (*S.* Villosae Group), Crayton pre-1931, single purple, very fine.

'**Julia**' (*S.* Villosae Group), Wickman 1993 (not Preston), single pinkish.

'**Lutèce**' (*S.* Villosae Group), L. Henry pre-1901, single violet, a large treelike plant, good.

'**Summer White**' (*S.* Villosae Group), Lape 1975, single white.

Syringa ×*josiflexa* Preston ex J. S. Pringle

The original cross *Syringa josikaea* × *S. reflexa* was made in 1920 by Isabella Preston at the Central Experimental Farm, Ottawa, Ontario. The first named selection of the progeny of this cross is *S.* (Villosae Group) 'Guinevere'; it is the nomenclatural type of *S.* ×*josiflexa*. Although the epithet *josiflexa* was used informally, it was not validly published until 1978. Pringle (1978a) wrote:

> The hybrid origin of *Syringa* ×*josiflexa* 'Guinevere' is readily apparent in its morphology. Its greater resemblance is to *S. josikaea*, because of the erect axis of its inflorescence and its relatively deeply colored corollas. The corolla color of young buds was recorded as 77B (*Royal Horticultural Society Colour Chart* 1966); older buds were predominantly close to 77C, paler distally; in open flowers, the lower portion of the tube was 77C, the upper portion 77C, and the limb 76B–77D. The influ-

Syringa (Villosae Group) 'Agnes Smith'. B. Peart and M. Walton

ence of *S. reflexa* appears in the widely divergent primary branches of the inflorescence, which are more cernuous distally than those of *S. josikaea*, and in the greater admixture of pink in its corolla color.

Since the currently accepted classification by Chang and Green (1996a) no longer recognizes *Syringa reflexa* as a species but places it in *S. komarowii* as a subspecies, it is understood that all progeny of the cross *S. josikaea* × *S. komarowii* will carry the name *S.* ×*josiflexa*. Selected *S.* ×*josiflexa* cultivars are as follows:

'**Agnes Smith**' (*S.* Villosae Group) (marketed as Miss USA), Rogers 1970, single white.

'**Anna Amhoff**' (*S.* Villosae Group), Yeager 1959, single white.

'**Bellicent**' (*S.* Villosae Group), Preston pre-1942, single pinkish.

'**Guinevere**' (*S.* Villosae Group), Preston 1925, single magenta.

'**Jesse Hepler**' (*S.* Villosae Group), Rogers 1978, single purple.

'**Marie Rogers**' (*S.* Villosae Group), Rogers 2005, double white-violet.

'**Royalty**' (*S.* Villosae Group), Preston 1936, single purple.

Syringa (Villosae Group) 'Bellicent'. B. Peart and M. Walton

Syringa (Villosae Group) 'Guinevere'. B. Peart and M. Walton

Syringa (Villosae Group) 'Anna Amhoff'. B. Peart and M. Walton

Syringa (Villosae Group) 'Jesse Hepler'. B. Peart and M. Walton

Syringa ×nanceiana McKelvey

In its catalog 199 (1925–1926) the Lemoine nursery introduced a new lilac named *Syringa* "Henryi Floréal," progeny obtained from the cross *S. ×henryi* 'Lutèce' × *S. sweginzowii* 'Superba'. McKelvey (1928) proposed the name *S. ×nanceiana* (meaning "from the city of Nancy") for all hybrids between *S. ×henryi*

Syringa (Villosae Group) 'Floréal'. John Fiala

Syringa (Villosae Group) 'Rutilant'. B. Peart and M. Walton

(*S. josikaea* × *S. villosa*) and *S. sweginzowii*. 'Floréal' is the nomenclatural type of *S. ×nanceiana*.

McKelvey (1928) wrote,

> The following notes were made upon its winter-buds: oblong with acute apex, flower bud ⁵⁄₁₆ in. [8 mm] long, scales reddish brown with dark margins, acute, keeled and forming a markedly four-sided bud, lustrous, glabrous. Leaf-scar much raised, shield-shaped, inconspicuous, medium size; bundle-trace crescent-shaped. In their form these buds resemble those of the parent *S. sweginzowii*. The form of the flowers and flower-cluster is much like that of the parent *S. ×henryi*. The foliage appears to be close to *S. ×henryi* although slightly smaller. This promises to be a valuable and distinct hybrid Lilac.

The oldest cultivars of *Syringa ×nanceiana*, originated at Lemoine nursery, are

'**Floréal**' (*S*. Villosae Group), Lemoine 1925, single pink.

'**Rutilant**' (*S*. Villosae Group), Lemoine 1931, single purple.

Syringa ×prestoniae McKelvey
Preston lilac

This cross between *Syringa villosa* and *S. komarowii* was first made in 1920 by Isabella Preston at the Central Experimental Farm, Ottawa, Canada, where the most extensive collection of her cultivars is maintained. Using seed of *S. villosa* with pollen of *S. komarowii* (then as *S. reflexa*), she created a whole new race of late-blooming lilacs now called in her honor *S. ×prestoniae*, or simply, the Preston hybrids. For her work Preston will forever be known as the Grande-dame of the Hybrids.

Many Preston hybrids were named to honor Shakespearean women. One must get acquainted with these lovely lilacs to appreciate the work of this gifted woman. Some may argue that Preston named too many similar cultivars. Nevertheless, they do make a historic and beautiful contribution to the development of the late-blooming lilacs. Preston named 71 of her initial seedlings. Most of her introductions have pink to lavender-pink flowers. Many are quite similar, but one type has upright panicles, another drooping. Because of the similarity of color, only a few of her cultivars are carried even by the finest lilac specialty nurseries. An additional 35 cultivars of *Syringa* ×*prestoniae* have been added by other breeders, including J. Herbert Alexander Sr., Władysław Bugała, William A. Cumming, John L. Fiala, Owen M. Rogers, Frank L. Skinner, and Albert F. Yeager.

The Preston hybrids are noticeably different from their cousins, the French hybrids or *Syringa vulgaris*

Syringa (Villosae Group) 'Isabella', habit. B. Peart and M. Walton

Syringa (Villosae Group) 'Isabella', flowers. B. Peart and M. Walton

cultivars, in flower, leaf, plant habit, and particularly in their own exotic fragrance. They bloom a week or so later than the *S. vulgaris* cultivars. They are large shrubs, even small trees. Among the best *S.* ×*prestoniae* cultivars are the following (see chapter four for more Preston hybrids):

'Isabella' (*S.* Villosae Group), Preston 1928, single lilac.

'Paulina' (*S.* Villosae Group), Preston 1927, single purple.

'Ursula' (*S.* Villosae Group), Preston 1928, single pinkish lavender.

'W. T. Macoun' (*S.* Villosae Group), Preston 1927, single pinkish.

Left to themselves, these hybrids, part of the Villosae Group cultivars, often are somewhat rampant growers, reaching 10–12 feet (3–3.6 m). They do not sucker, they have attractive green foliage mostly free of insects and pests, and they are heavy bloomers plagued with an abundance of seed—keep these clipped if possible. In limited surroundings they are most effective as a single garden tree. Prune them to three or no more than five trunks when still young, removing all spontaneous lower shoots, keeping them growing upward; soon they will develop in a small spreading tree. Placed where they will provide shade, they do an excellent job for the small patio.

Some of these late-blooming lilacs are delightful when potted as very young plants in large earthen tubs and set out on the patio. Keep them trimmed after blooming and they will perform well for a number of years. They root from green cuttings rather well. Their colors range mostly in the pinks and pale lavender-pinks but among the newer introductions are beautiful whites and deeper purples. Myriads of butterflies and hovering hummingbirds will visit the pale pink, cerise, white, and lavender flowers of your lilacs.

A word of caution. In 2002 two new cultivars appeared on the market, *Syringa* (Villosae Group) 'Charisma' and *S.* (Villosae Group) 'Shantelle'. They are characterized by slow growth and bunched branchlets, a habit that suggests their suitability as hedge plants. Their blooming habit, single and purple, is identical to that of *S.* (Villosae Group) 'Royalty'; in fact they appear to have derived independently from lilac witches'-broom on 'Royalty', caused by phytoplasmas. The *ICNCP* (Brickell et al. 2004), Chapter 2, Article 2.8, Example 4, recognizes that "[p]lants of a clone which are derived from aberrant growth may form a cultivar." Similarly, plants derived from aberrant growth are not excluded from protection under plant breeders' rights legislation, if applied for. There is, however, a significant difference between planting a cultivar derived from a genetic mutation or sport in one's garden, or adding a lilac infected with lilac witches'-broom to one's lilac collection, whether garden, park, or nursery. The latter may not be a wise thing to do. The best protection is knowing about the plants one obtains and about their sources (Vrugtman 2004b, Hibben 2005). Some nurseries have discontinued producing and selling such cultivars.

Syringa ×swegiflexa hort. Hesse ex J. S. Pringle

The original cross *Syringa reflexa* (that is, *S. komarowii*) × *S. sweginzowii* was made prior to 1935 at Hermann Hesse's nursery in Weener (Ems), northwestern Germany. Although the epithet *swegiflexa* had been used in horticultural literature, it was not validly published until 1978. Referring to two specimens (*Pringle 1586* and *Pringle 1581*) deposited at Royal Botanical Gardens, Hamilton, Ontario, Canada, Pringle (1978a) wrote,

Syringa ×swegiflexa bears a stronger resemblance to *S. sweginzowii* than to *S. reflexa*. Its inflorescences, however, are less open than those of *S. sweginzowii*, and its corollas are deeper pink. The buds and the tubes of the open corollas were 69B–70D (*Royal Horticultural Society Colour Chart 1966*) on the plant represented by *Pringle 1586*, and close to 62D on the plant represented by *Pringle 1591*; in both cases, the limbs of the open corollas were nearly white. The leaves are larger and more closely spaced than those of *S. sweginzowii*, but smaller than those of *S. reflexa*.

Syringa ×swegiflexa has two cultivars:
'Carlton' (*S.* Villosae Group), Preston pre-1948, single pinkish.
'Fountain' (*S.* Villosae Group), Preston pre-1953, single pinkish.

Syringa ×swegiflexa. B. Peart and M. Walton

CHAPTER FOUR
Color in Lilacs

THE MOST IMPORTANT ornamental quality of lilacs is color, followed by fragrance. Color is the magnetic first appeal of any flower, leading to further appraisal of texture, substance, form, pattern, and singleness or doubleness. Colors are never seen alone but in relationship to other colors seen at the same time. One of the best-known American colorists, Faber Birren (1900–1988), stated, "Beauty is not out there in man's environment, but here within man's brain. The perception of color, including feelings and emotion, is the property of human consciousness."

The range of colors found in lilacs makes their description difficult. Two factors contribute to deeper or lighter hues and to intensity of one color over another when found in combination. These are weather (climatic conditions at blooming) and edaphic constitution (the condition and composition of soil and subsoil). In cool, damp weather, colors are deeper and more intense, often deeper blue or purple. Hot sun brings out the magenta in lilac pigmentation and fades it to lighter colors and off-white. The gravelly, lighter soils of New England, often heavily enriched

Syringa ×hyacinthiflora 'Maiden's Blush' in lighter soil and warmer weather has delicate, pale pink flowers devoid of lavender. John Fiala

122

with limestone, give different shades and hues than do the heavier clays of the Midwest or the rich loams of the Pacific Northwest. You must see a specimen blooming in your particular area and in your kind of soil to judge accurately what it will look like in your garden. Descriptions given in general accounts are accurate in a wider sense, but subtle variations of color and tints arise from the factors mentioned.

Color hues in lilacs also change daily as their buds swell and show color, begin to burst into bloom, and as the thyrse begins to unfurl its florets, first at the bottom and then a daily march upward until it is in full bloom. This "unfolding of the colors" is part of the nostalgic magic and captivating charm of the lilac. One person may prefer a certain lilac in swelled buds, another in half-bloom with buds of one color and blossoms another, while still other individuals prefer the color of a lilac in full bloom. Often the buds, the reverse of the petals, or the outer petals are a deeper or entirely different color than that of the open floret.

Historical and Technical Considerations of Color

The history of color is fascinating. It occupied the ancient Greeks Pythagoras (6th century BC), Plato (ca. 428–ca. 348 BC), and Aristotle (384–322 BC), and the Roman Pliny (AD 23–79), all of whom discoursed on color. Aristotle stated, "Simple colors are the proper colors of the elements—water, fire, air, and earth." Centuries later Leonardo da Vinci (1452–1519) wrote, "White for light, yellow for earth, green for water, blue for air, red for fire and black for darkness." Sir Isaac Newton (1642–1727) studied the nature of light and devised the first color wheel. Jakob Christof Le Blon (1667–1741), German printmaker and painter, defined the "red-yellow-blue basic color theory" in 1725, a theory and means of organizing color still favored by artists.

Certain qualities of color need to be considered,

Syringa ×*hyacinthiflora* 'Maiden's Blush' in heavier soil and colder weather has flowers with considerable lavender color. John Fiala

particularly if we are hybridizing lilacs or judging their flowers for color. Modern colorists agree that three qualities of color are requisite for understanding what we see. First is hue, the specific name of a color. Scientifically speaking, hue is measured as dominant wavelength and its position in the spectrum, recognized as violet (the shortest wavelength), blue, green, yellow, orange, and red (the longest wavelength). The second quality of color is saturation, also called chroma or purity. Saturation is the intensity of the color, its brightness or dullness. Tone is a color not at its full intensity. And the third color quality is reflectance or value. Tint is a light value, shade a dark value.

Scientists tell us there are no black pigments found in flowers. The pigmentations that color lilac florets are produced by flavonoids, which include white to yellow flavones, and anthocyanins, which are responsible for the reddish and violet to bluish colors. The dark colors of lilacs result from very high concentrations of pigment in the cells of the petals—when painting with watercolors and one is using too much water the color looks washed out. Horticulturally, this is called lack of substance; in terms of color it is known as low saturation or low chroma. High-saturation flowers look dark; low-saturation flowers are light in color. Plant breeders know that line breeding will intensify any color.

The human eye is able to distinguish about two million different colors, that is, combinations of hue, saturation, and reflectance. There are standard methods of measuring and defining colors. We compare unknown colors with known ones to identify and classify the unknowns.

The simple color classifications devised for lilacs by John Wister (1942, 1953) and his Committee on Horticultural Varieties of the American Association of Botanical Gardens and Arboretums presented a logical sequence of color categories composed of seven basic classes: I, White; II, Violet; III, Bluish; IV, Lilac; V, Pinkish; VI, Magenta; VII, Purple. No attempt was made to describe the hundreds of variations or nuances found in lilacs. Although time has proved the Wister code a useful system of classification for lilac colors by general color grouping, it is inadequate when it comes to describe, identify, or just confirm the identity of a cultivar.

Color Charts for Lilac Flower Descriptions

Anyone attempting to identify a lilac cultivar that lost its label, or even to verify a questionable one, will discover that many descriptions of lilac cultivars are inadequate. Susan McKelvey was one of the first students of *Syringa* to recognize that, without adequate color notation, subsequent identification would be difficult if not impossible. She added to her monograph four color charts with color patches that conformed to Robert Ridgway's (1912) *Color Standards and Color Nomenclature*. Each color patch has its name and Roman numeral. McKelvey (1928) commented on the difficulty of describing the color of a lilac floret caused by the rapid changes taking place from the moment a floret is fully expanded.

In 1939 and again in 1942 the British Colour Council and Royal Horticultural Society of London published a two-volume color chart created by Robert Wilson and consisting of 800 color patches. Five thousand copies were produced. The chart, however, is too old to be useful today.

Tucker et al. (1991) surveyed color charts for biological descriptions published between 1776 and the 1980s; they recommended the *Royal Horticultural Society Colour Chart*. The 1966 edition had 808 color chips, some of which were dropped from the 1986 edition. Also, some of the red-purple hues of the later edition did not match the previous version. The Society produced 7000 copies of the original chart.

The most recent editions of the *Colour Chart*, published in 1995 and 2001, contain 76 additional colors and are superior to the earlier, less comprehensive 1966 and 1986 editions. With a total of 884 colors, the 1995 chart matched the 1966 edition quite well. The 2001 chart equals the 1995 edition in quality but is expensive and rarely available where most needed, namely, in the hands of the people who describe old and new lilac cultivars and those who participate in the Lilac Performance Survey of the International Lilac Society.

The various color charts can be summarized as follows:

Horticultural Colour Chart 1 and 2. 1939 and 1942. London. British Colour Council and Royal Horticultural Society. Also known as the (Robert F.) Wilson Colour Chart. 800 color patches, each with a unique name. 5000 copies printed.

RHS Colour Chart. 1966. London. Royal Horticultural Society. 792 color patches, each with a number rather than a name. 7000 copies printed. Accompanying this edition is a Table of Cross-References of the RHS Colour Chart to the Horticultural Colour Chart, the British Colour Council Dictionary of Colour Standards, the British Colour Council Dictionary of Colours for Interior Decorations, the Nickerson Colour Fan, and the International Commission on Illumination. Cross-references to the latter are of particular importance since the colors are expressed in coordinates obtained with a Hilger and Watts J.40 Colourmeter, with check measurements made on a Beckman spectrophotometer.

RHS Colour Chart. 1986. London and Leiden. Royal Horticultural Society and the Flower Council of Holland. 808 color patches. A reprint of the 1966 edition, but some of the colors, particularly in the red-purple hues, no longer match the 1966 ones.

RHS Colour Chart. 1995. London and Leiden. Royal Horticultural Society and the Flower Council of Holland. 884 color patches. A true reprint of the 1966 edition with 76 new colors that were previously hard to match, primarily dark purples, bright orange, bronze, grays, and greens.

RHS Colour Chart. 2001. London and Leiden. Royal Horticultural Society and the Flower Council of Holland. 884 color patches. Identical to the 1966 and 1995 editions.

RHS Mini Colour Chart. 2005. London and Leiden. Royal Horticultural Society and the Flower Council of Holland. 244 color patches, each one carefully chosen to represent the broad spectrum of color found in the full version.

The color determination system most extensively used today by floriculture and paint industries is the Munsell system (Munsell 1952). It divides color into steps as the eye would see them and describes color in the terms of hue, value, and chroma. Each of these three qualities is described by a number, hence any color can be described by a simple number standing for the color's relationship to hue, chroma, and value.

Color Dimensions in the Garden

When looking at landscapes the eye becomes farsighted when focusing on red, yellow, or orange. These colors appear closer, whereas green, brown, and violet recede, appearing more distant. Colors also affect size. Light colors tend to expand, and therefore, light-colored objects appear larger, whereas the deeper colors contract and appear smaller. In terms of visibility, yellow is the brightest hue, followed by vibrant orange. Most plants depend on flower color to attract insects for pollination; bees, for instance, identify four colors, with blue being their preferred color.

Johann Wolfgang von Goethe (1749–1832), German poet and scientist, developed a science of colors in his 1400-page *Zur Farbenlehre* (1810). He opposed the theory of Isaac Newton's *Opticks* (1704). Goethe claimed that color sensations reaching the human brain were shaped by our perception, by the mechanics of vision, and by the way the brain processes information. What we see of an object depends on the object, the lighting, and our perception.

Color in lilacs is an interesting subject since pigmentation is often more intense or entirely different on the outer layer or dorsal side of the petal than on the inside or ventral side, giving the floret a two-toned effect. Clear colors should be preferred to washed-out ones, good saturation to weak. With the many cultivars and hybrids, plus the intensification of breeding programs, we are certain to have newer and more distinct combinations of colors.

Recommendation of Lilac Cultivars by Color Classification

Among the about 2000 named lilac cultivars of various colors it would be very difficult for most gardeners, even experts, to select the "best" for their gardens without some assistance. In the following pages a wide range of lilac cultivars is discussed according to color classification. Fiala has attempted to present a list of recommendations for each of the colors as a guide for those who wish to use them. For more than 40 years he observed many lilac cultivars and discussed the merits of many of them with lilac experts, but he did not see every single lilac recommended. For the few recommended sight unseen, he accepted the judgment of correspondents.

The purpose of these recommendations is to upgrade the selection of lilacs for modern gardens and planting. Perhaps we are a bit too nostalgic about the "old sorts," suckers gleaned from the old homestead grounds or given to us by friends. Much breeding and selecting work since the 1930s has been done in North America, Europe, and Asia. The achievements of those who worked to improve the garden lilac must not be ignored.

Many cultivars on the recommended lists are relatively unknown to the majority of nurseries; they can be found only in specialized nurseries. The International Lilac Society, its publications, and its members are a good source of information. Also, visit botanical gardens and arboreta that have lilac collections.

In the recommendation of the various lilac cultivars, not only the bloom but also habit, form, vigor, and susceptibility to disease have been given weighted consideration. For instance, Lemoine's famous *Syringa vulgaris* 'Mont Blanc' is not included because it is a rather poor grower with pallid foliage and requires considerable pruning. One of the aims of the International Lilac Society and its Lilac Evaluation Committee is to identify the best cultivars, publish the evaluation reports in *Lilacs*, the quarterly journal of the society, and promote the introduction, propagation, and distribution of these cultivars.

White Lilacs (Color Class I)

White is the essential element in the lilac garden, the one color that coordinates and ties together all other colors. A garden planting cannot have too many white-flowering plants. White is the best color to use when it is necessary to separate clashing colors or to bring out the richness of any color placed close to it. A special kind of unity is obtained with the color white in the garden.

White is the color most reflective in the twilight hours. After sundown as shadows fall, the deeper col-

ors in the garden disappear first, then the pinks, then the vibrant lemon yellows, but white somehow remains to reflect the moonlight. White lilacs give the night garden a whole new dimension. Today we have many excellent white lilacs with new introductions appearing almost every year. In planning your lilac planting, remember that there are early-, midseason-, and late-season white lilacs; one can have flowers from early May to mid-June.

Among the earliest to bloom are the *Syringa* ×*hyacinthiflora* cultivars (*S. vulgaris* × *S. oblata*) such as 'Gertrude Leslie', 'Sister Justina', and 'The Bride'. White lilacs, however, come into their glory with the *S. vulgaris* midseason bloomers. Among these are many fine old and new cultivars, although sources of many of the newer ones are difficult to find.

Historically, we have seen that the earliest white lilacs had rather small florets with an ashen or bluewash cast, not the pure whites of today. Often they were akin to the old *Syringa vulgaris* var. *alba* Weston 1770, tall, treelike, with pallid leaves. It was not until Victor Lemoine and his son, Émile, introduced far better white lilacs that real progress began. Hybridizers have made even greater strides at improving the white lilacs—using mostly Lemoine introductions. White has been purified, floret size increased, leaves are now a healthy dark green, and the shrub has been lowered to average height. White lilacs are mostly judged by their mass effect to contrast with other colors in the garden. One could plant a whole garden of 100 or more white cultivars and have a beautiful and varied garden.

Recommended *Syringa vulgaris* cultivars in class I (white):

'Aloise', single, Fiala 1986, smaller florets but extremely heavy bloomer annually, fine
'Avalanche', single, Fiala 1983, large florets, very showy, very fine to excellent
'Banquise', double, Lemoine 1905, very good
'Bernard Slavin', single, Fenicchia 1972, multipetaled, very good
'Bloemenlust', single, Piet 1956, fine, very limited production for forcing
'Candeur', single, Lemoine 1931, large-flowered, very fine to excellent, showy

Syringa vulgaris 'Banquise'. B. Peart and M. Walton

Syringa vulgaris 'Excellent'. B. Peart and M. Walton

'Carley', single, Havemeyer 1953, large florets, outstanding to excellent

'Early Double White', double, Clarke 1944, very
good, nearly unobtainable

'Edith Cavell', double, Lemoine 1916, very showy,
excellent

'Emery Mae Norweb', double, Fiala 1980, deep
creamy buds, excellent

'Excellent', single, Eveleens Maarse 1938, very showy,
fine

'Father John', single, Brown 1993 (syn. Brown 7525-
17), very showy, excellent

'Flora 1953', single, Eveleens Maarse 1953, one of the
finest whites, excellent

Syringa vulgaris 'Flora 1953'. John Fiala

'Fraîcheur', single, Lemoine 1946, very fine but most difficult to find

'Galina Ulanova', single, Kolesnikov 1976, very showy, fine

'General Sheridan', double, Dunbar 1917, very lacy but new shoots obscure bloom, fine

'Geraldine Smith', single, Rankin 1963, good to very good

'Gerrie Schoonenberg', single, Eveleens Maarse 1948, very good

'Gertrude Clark', single, Fiala 1984, multipetaled, very fine

'Glacier', double, Fiala 1981, very showy, very fine

'Gloire d'Aalsmeer', single, J. D. Maarse 1938, very good

'Heather', single, Havemeyer pre-1942, good, annual bloomer, medium florets

'Joan Dunbar', double, Dunbar 1923, older cultivar but still good

'Käte Härlin', single, W. Pfitzer Sr. 1909, old but good

'Königin Luise', single, Pfitzer 1921, very good

'Lebedushka', single, Smol'skiĭ & Bibikova 1964, very large florets, showy, very fine

'Madeleine Lemaire', double, Lemoine 1928, very fine but difficult to obtain

'Marie Finon', single, Lemoine 1923, very fine, large florets

'Marie Legraye', single, Legraye pre-1879, very old but still good

Syringa vulgaris 'Galina Ulanova'. B. Peart and M. Walton

Syringa vulgaris 'Fraicheur'. B. Peart and M. Walton

Syringa vulgaris 'General Sheridan'. B. Peart and M. Walton

Syringa vulgaris 'Gerrie Schoonenberg'. B. Peart and M. Walton

Syringa vulgaris 'Madeleine Lemaire'. B. Peart and M. Walton

Syringa vulgaris 'Heather'. B. Peart and M. Walton

Syringa vulgaris 'Marie Finon'. B. Peart and M. Walton

Syringa vulgaris 'Joan Dunbar'. B. Peart and M. Walton

Syringa vulgaris 'Marie Legraye'. B. Peart and M. Walton

'Maud Notcutt', single, Eveleens Maarse 1956, fine

'Miss Ellen Willmott', double, Lemoine 1903, very dependable bloomer, fine

'Mme Abel Chatenay', double, Lemoine 1892, old but good

'Mme Felix', single, Felix & Dykhuis 1924, very good

'Mme Florent Stepman', single, Stepman-Demessemaeker 1908, large spike, very fine, an older cultivar, also used for forcing

'Mme Lemoine', double, Lemoine 1890, very good but not Lemoine's finest

'Mme Léopold Draps', single, Draps 1945, very good

'Monique Lemoine', double, Lemoine 1939, very fine and showy

'Monument', single, Lemoine 1934, one of the last Lemoine whites, very good

'Mother Louise', double, Fiala 1969, florets of exceptional quality, very fine

'Nanook', single, Eveleens Maarse 1951, very good, difficult to obtain

'Oakes Double White', double, origin not known (perhaps a renamed older cultivar), pre-1963, very good

'Panna Dorota Gołąbecka', double, Karpow-Lipski 1952, very good, difficult to obtain

"Primrose H" (marketed in Germany as STERNTALER), sport of 'Primrose' from the Holden Arboretum, perhaps different

"Primrose L," sport of 'Primrose' from the garden of Albert Lumley, perhaps different

'Prof. E. H. Wilson', double, Havemeyer 1943, beautiful white rosettes, excellent

'Riet Bruidegom', single, Eveleens Maarse 1950, very fine

'Rochester', single, Grant 1971, magnificent multipetaled, outstandingly beautiful, one of the very finest, slow grower, difficult to obtain and difficult in propagation, excellent

Syringa vulgaris 'Mme Abel Chatenay'. B. Peart and M. Walton

Syringa vulgaris 'Mme Felix'. B. Peart and M. Walton

Syringa vulgaris 'Mme Florent Stepman'. B. Peart and M. Walton

'Satin Cloud', single, Fiala 1985, very showy, very
    fine to excellent
'Sculptured Ivory', single, Fiala 1985, very fine
'Slater's Elegance', single, Slater 1973, huge florets,
    beautiful, excellent, very difficult to obtain but
    among the very finest single whites
'Snow Shower', single, H. E. Sass 1953, very good,
    difficult to obtain

Syringa vulgaris 'Riet Bruidegom'. B. Peart and M. Walton

Syringa vulgaris 'Oakes Double White'. B. Peart and M. Walton

Syringa vulgaris 'Slater's Elegance'. B. Peart and M. Walton

Syringa vulgaris 'Prof. E. H. Wilson'. B. Peart and M. Walton

Syringa vulgaris 'Snow Shower'. B. Peart and M. Walton

'Souvenir d'Alice Harding', double, Lemoine 1938,
exceptionally fine, excellent, one of the best
doubles
'Souvenir de Mme Louis Gielis', single, Gielis 1950,
heavy bloomer, very fine

'Sovetskaya Arktika', double, Kolesnikov 1974,
showy, very fine
'St Joan', double, Blacklock 1957, extremely beauti-
ful, among the best, excellent
'St Margaret' (marketed in Germany as FRAU
HOLLE), double, Blacklock 1957, beautiful,
among the best, excellent
'Swansdown', single, Fiala 1984, large thyrses, multipetaled, very showy and very fine
'Taglioni', double, Lemoine 1905, large white triple
slippers, fine
'Vestale', single, Lemoine 1910, large florets, moderate bloomer, very good
'White Lace', single, Rankin 1964, small florets,
extremely showy, very good
'White Swan', single, Havemeyer 1943, good, depend-
able bloomer

Syringa vulgaris 'Sovetskaya Arktika'. B. Peart and M. Walton

Syringa vulgaris 'St Margaret'. B. Peart and M. Walton

Syringa vulgaris 'White Lace'. John Fiala

Syringa vulgaris 'White Swan'. B. Peart and M. Walton

Other recommended lilacs in class I (white):

S. ×*chinensis* 'Bicolor', single, Lemoine 1928, a lovely white lilac with a pert deep purple eye, a large shrub for backgrounds, very fine

S. 'Chinese Magic', single, Fiala 1978 (*S. pekinensis* × *S. reticulata* subsp. *amurensis*), creamy flowers, more spreading, small tree, very good for background or naturalizing plantings

S. emodi 'Elegantissima', single, van der Bom 1876, foliage with yellow margins, very difficult to obtain

S. ×*hyacinthiflora* 'Angel White', single, Lammerts 1971, very fine

S. ×*hyacinthiflora* 'Gertrude Leslie', double, Skinner 1954, very early, good

S. ×*hyacinthiflora* 'Mount Baker' (marketed in Germany as SCHNEEWEISSCHEN), single, Skinner 1961, very good, showy

S. ×*hyacinthiflora* 'Sister Justina', single, Skinner 1956, very fine, showy

Syringa ×*hyacinthiflora* 'Gertrude Leslie'. B. Peart and M. Walton

Syringa ×*hyacinthiflora* 'Mount Baker'. B. Peart and M. Walton

Syringa ×*hyacinthiflora* 'Angel White'. B. Peart and M. Walton

Syringa ×*hyacinthiflora* 'Sister Justina'. B. Peart and M. Walton

S. ×*hyacinthiflora* 'The Bride', single, Skinner 1961, very fine, among the best early-flowering white hybrids

S. komarowii subsp. *reflexa* 'Alba', single, Upton 1933, beautiful hanging racemes, extremely rare

S. oblata 'Frank Meyer', single, Meyer & Fiala 1988, excellent

S. pekinensis 'Pendula', single, Temple 1887, very rare, excellent

S. ×*persica* 'Alba', single, origin not known, ca. 1770, very good background shrub

S. pubescens subsp. *patula* 'Excellens', single, Lemoine 1936, very fine, most difficult to obtain true cultivar

S. reticulata subsp. *amurensis*, a smaller tree with cherry bark, flowers single from creamy white to pure white, late blooming

S. reticulata subsp. *reticulata*, single, a medium-sized tree, late blooming, for background use only, very effective, very good

S. reticulata subsp. *reticulata* 'Cole', single, Cole Nursery 1977, very good, habit narrower than the green form

S. reticulata subsp. *reticulata* 'Ivory Silk', single, Pokluda 1973, very fine upright form

S. (Villosae Group) 'Agnes Smith' (marketed as Miss USA), single, Rogers 1970 (*S.* ×*josiflexa*), one of the finest, magnificent, a choice hybridizer's prize, excellent

S. (Villosae Group) 'Albida', single, Lemoine 1930 (*S. sweginzowii* × *S. tomentella*), tall shrub, slender branchlets, fine fragrance, very good

S. (Villosae Group) 'Anna Amhoff', single, Yeager 1959 (*S.* ×*josiflexa*), very fine, late blooming

S. (Villosae Group) 'Elaine', single, Preston 1948 (*S.* ×*josiflexa*), good

S. (Villosae Group) 'Hunting Tower', single, Skinner 1953 (*S. villosa* × *S. sweginzowii*), very good

S. (Villosae Group) 'Snowdrift', single, Fiala 1983 (*S.* ×*prestoniae*), an abundance of small florets, practically no seed, wonderful glossy leaves, fine

S. (Villosae Group) 'Summer White', single, Lape

Syringa (Villosae Group) 'Elaine'. B. Peart and M. Walton

Syringa (Villosae Group) 'Hunting Tower'. B. Peart and M. Walton

Syringa (Villosae Group) 'Swanee'. B. Peart and M. Walton

1975 (*S.* ×*henryi*), very fine to excellent, very showy

S. (Villosae Group) 'Swanee', single, Morden Research Centre 1937 (*S.* ×*prestoniae*), very good

Violet Lilacs (Color Class II)

Lavender or lilac is the original color of *Syringa vulgaris*. In 1770 British botanist Richard Weston named the lavender, purplish, and violet lilacs *S. vulgaris* var. *purpurea*. What Weston combined in variety *purpurea* was split about a century and a half later into the two classes violet (II) and lilac (IV). In color charts they are distinct, but in reality both are a lavender-purplish. They differ in that those in class II are more purple-blue and range from very light to very deep purple, whereas those in class IV are a purple mixed with pinkish tones or a real lavender shade.

Recommended *Syringa vulgaris* cultivars in class II (violet):

'Agincourt Beauty', single, Slater 1968, very large florets, outstanding very deep purple, excellent

'Burgemeester Loggers', single, Eveleens Maarse 1960, very good to fine

'Burgemeester Voller', single, Eveleens Maarse 1948, slight lavender cast, very good

'Cavour', single, Lemoine 1910, large florets, very good

'Champlain', double, Lemoine 1930, very fine

'De Miribel', single, Lemoine 1903, long conical thyrses with deep bluish tones, very fine

'Dr Edward Mott Moore', single, Fenicchia 1972, multipetaled, showy, excellent

Syringa vulgaris 'Burgemeester Loggers'. B. Peart and M. Walton

Syringa vulgaris 'Champlain'. B. Peart and M. Walton

Syringa vulgaris 'Agincourt Beauty'. B. Peart and M. Walton

Syringa vulgaris 'De Miribel'. B. Peart and M. Walton

'Dr John Rankin', single, Fiala 1985, very fine, smaller florets

'Fred Payne', single, Havemeyer 1943, large florets, very good

'Henri Robert', double, Lemoine 1936, pale violet, very fine

'Hosanna', double, Fiala 1969, very pale violet, very good

'Jessie Gardner', single, Gardner 1956, very good

'Koningsloo', single, Draps 1938, large florets and showy, very good

'Kosmos', single, Shtan'ko & Mikhaïlov 1956, very fragrant, showy, very fine

'Le Nôtre', double, Lemoine 1922, very showy and very fine to excellent

'Lipchanka', single, Romanova & Egorova ca. pre-1980s, dark violet, heavy bloomer, very fine

'M. I. Kalinin', single, Kolesnikov 1941, violet to lilac, fragrant large clusters, fine

'Maximowicz', double, Lemoine 1906, pale violet, showy, excellent

'Mood Indigo', single, Clarke 1946, fine to excellent

'Pauline Fiala', single, Fiala 1983, dark violet with white eye, very heavy bloomer, very fine to excellent

'Russkaya Pesnya', double, Vekhov 1996, large florets, showy, fine

'Sesquicentennial', single, Fenicchia 1988, very heavy bloomer, showy, excellent

Syringa vulgaris 'Kosmos'. B. Peart and M. Walton

Syringa vulgaris 'Fred Payne'. B. Peart and M. Walton

Syringa vulgaris 'Henri Robert'. B. Peart and M. Walton

Syringa vulgaris 'M. I. Kalinin'. B. Peart and M. Walton

'Souvenir de Mevrouw Dr Kenis', single, Nelen 1936, pale violet, very good

'Topaz', single, Zhogoleva 1976, very large florets, very fine

'Violet Glory', single, Castle 1969, huge florets of deep violet, excellent

'Violetta', double, Lemoine 1916, deep violet, very showy, excellent

Syringa vulgaris 'Topaz'. B. Peart and M. Walton

Syringa vulgaris 'Maximowicz'. B. Peart and M. Walton

Syringa vulgaris 'Russkaya Pesnya'. B. Peart and M. Walton

Syringa vulgaris 'Violetta'. B. Peart and M. Walton

Other recommended lilacs in class II (violet):

S. ×hyacinthiflora 'Louvois', single, Lemoine 1921, large florets, very showy, very fine

S. ×hyacinthiflora 'Pocahontas', single, Skinner 1935, better classified as violet than purple, very fine to excellent

S. ×hyacinthiflora 'Touch of Spring', single, Fiala 1982, very floriferous, very fine

S. josikaea, single, more violet than lavender, one of the better species for the background, very good

S. josikaea 'Pallida', origin not known, pre-1865, single violet.

S. ×laciniata, single, very floriferous, tall growing, excellent

S. meyeri, single, very attractive small-leaved shrub, very good

S. pubescens, single, medium lavender-violet, very fine to excellent

S. pubescens subsp. *patula*, single, variable in color and size, very fine

S. pubescens subsp. *patula* 'Miss Kim', single, Meader & Yeager 1954, very pale violet with lavender-bluish cast, one of the outstanding selections of this subspecies, excellent

S. (Villosae Group) 'Ariel', single, Preston 1942 (*S. ×prestoniae*), good

S. (Villosae Group) 'Eventide', single, Fiala 1980, large florets, very showy, excellent

S. (Villosae Group) 'Jaga', single, Bugała 1970, a second-generation *S. ×prestoniae*, very fine

S. (Villosae Group) 'Jessica', single, Preston 1928 (*S. ×prestoniae*), very good

S. (Villosae Group) 'Kim', single, Preston 1942, good

S. (Villosae Group) 'Lutèce', single, L. Henry pre-1901, medium violet, large, treelike, good

S. (Villosae Group) 'Nike', single, Bugała 1970, a second-generation *S. ×prestoniae*

Syringa (Villosae Group) 'Kim'. B. Peart and M. Walton

Syringa (Villosae Group) 'Jessica'. B. Peart and M. Walton

Syringa (Villosae Group) 'Nike'. B. Peart and M. Walton

Blue Lilacs (Color Class III)

Pure blue is a difficult color to obtain in any of the lilac species. Some of the earliest selections of *Syringa vulgaris* were bluish or bluish lavender or light purple. None of these is a pure blue. 'Coerulea Superba', Ellwanger & Barry 1868, contains a considerable amount of blue. Victor Lemoine is the father of the blues so far as lilacs are concerned. In 1932 he introduced 'Firmament', which is considered the beginning of fine, light blues. In rapid succession came a number of blues: 'Ami Schott', a lovely double in 1933, and 'Madame Charles Souchet', a clear, pale blue with but a touch of lavender in 1949. Theodore A. Havemeyer added 'Mrs A. Belmont' in 1953 and 'True Blue' in 1956. These and 'Rhodopea', a small-flowered deep blue lilac, once thought to be a species, are the foundation of the modern blues. Since 1965 the blues were crossed with the white 'Rochester', producing an array of improved blues—light, medium, and dark blues, starred blues, eyed and rayed blues—often combined with the multipetals of 'Rochester'.

Much work remains to be done for far better and clearer blues in both the early and the late hybrids. A hybridizer could spend a lifetime improving these and leave a legacy of fine lilacs in blue.

Specially recommended *Syringa vulgaris* cultivars in class III (blue):

'Alekseĭ Mares'ev', single, Kolesnikov 1951, large bluish to lilac florets, showy, very fine

'Ambassadeur', single, Lemoine 1930, bluish, very fine

'Ami Schott', double, Lemoine 1933, medium blue with deeper tones, showy, excellent

'Bleuâtre', single, Baltet 1894, very old, small florets, fragrant, good

'Blue Angel', single, Havemeyer & Eaton 1954, difficult to find, good bluish, fine

'Bluebird', single, Fiala 1969, large florets, medium blue, very showy large spikes, excellent

'Blue Danube', single, Fiala 1986, the bluest of its day, very fine

'Blue Delight', single, Castle 1969, very good to fine

Syringa vulgaris 'Blue Danube'. John Fiala

Syringa vulgaris 'Alekseĭ Mares'ev'. B. Peart and M. Walton

Syringa vulgaris 'Blue Delight'. B. Peart and M. Walton

'Blue Giant', single, Fiala 1977, light blue very fine

'Bluets', single, Fiala 1979, a good grower

'Boule Azurée', single, Lemoine 1919, medium-sized florets of good blue, very fine

'Charles Sargent', double, Lemoine 1905, mixed shades of blue brushed lavender, very fine

'Crépuscule', single, Lemoine 1928, large florets, showy, excellent

'Dawn', single, Havemeyer pre-1942, very good to fine

'Decaisne', single, Lemoine 1910, darker blue with purple shades, very fine

'Diplomate', single, Lemoine 1930, pale blue dusted lavender, fine

'Duc de Massa', double, Lemoine 1905, huge spikes, showy, very fine to excellent

'Dwight D. Eisenhower', single, Fenicchia 1969, multipetaled, pale blue brushed lavender, heavy bloomer, very showy, excellent

Syringa vulgaris 'Charles Sargent'. B. Peart and M. Walton

Syringa vulgaris 'Decaisne'. B. Peart and M. Walton

Syringa vulgaris 'Bluets'. John Fiala

Syringa vulgaris 'Boule Azurée'. B. Peart and M. Walton

Syringa vulgaris 'Duc de Massa'. B. Peart and M. Walton

Syringa vulgaris 'Émile Gentil'. John Fiala

Syringa vulgaris 'Dwight D. Eisenhower'. B. Peart and M. Walton

Syringa vulgaris 'Fałe Bałtyku'. B. Peart and M. Walton

'Eleanor Berdeen', single, Berdeen 1979, bluish and pinkish bicolor, excellent

'Émile Gentil', double, Lemoine 1915, pale lavender-blue, very fine

'Fałe Bałtyku', single, Karpow-Lipski 1961, bluish with pale lavender tones, very good

'Firmament', single, Lemoine 1932, pale blue of outstanding quality, showy, excellent

'Flow Blue', single, Fiala 1980, mixed shades of blue, very good

'Georges Claude', double, Lemoine 1935, large thyrses, quality, very fine

'Golubaya', single, Kolesnikov pre-1963, blue dusted lilac-purple, tall grower, showy, very fine

'Heavenly Blue', single, Blacklock 1943, difficult to find, very good

'Hugo Mayer', single, Eveleens Maarse 1950, a Dutch blue with lavender dusting, very fine

'Jules Simon', double, Lemoine 1908, very fine

'Lawrence Wheeler', single, Gardner 1968, difficult to find, very good

'Lynette Sirois', double, Berdeen 1968, blue flushed lavender, very fine

'Madame Charles Souchet', single, Lemoine 1949, large florets of outstanding pale to medium blue, showy, quality, excellent

'Madame Hankar-Solvay', single, Klettenberg 1935, good color, fine but difficult to find

'Marat Kazeï', single, Smol'skiĭ & Bibikova 1964, very good

'Maréchal Lannes', double, Lemoine 1910, bluish purple, excellent

'Margot Grunewald', double, Grunewald 1913, very good

'Maurice Barrès', single, Lemoine 1917, medium blue of quality, excellent

Syringa vulgaris 'Maréchal Lannes'. B. Peart and M. Walton

Syringa vulgaris 'Jules Simon'. B. Peart and M. Walton

Syringa vulgaris 'Margot Grunewald'. B. Peart and M. Walton

Syringa vulgaris 'Madame Charles Souchet'. B. Peart and M. Walton

Syringa vulgaris 'Maurice Barrès'. B. Peart and M. Walton

'Mechta', single, Kolesnikov 1941, large florets and panicles with reddish buds, bluish to lilac, very showy, excellent

'Minister Dąb-Kocioł', single, Karpow-Lipski 1961, firm blue color, very good to fine

'Mrs A. Belmont', single, Havemeyer pre-1942, large florets of blue brushed with lavender tones, white eye, very fine

'Mrs Elizabeth Peterson', single, Havemeyer 1953, a unique blue color, deep blue changing to deep violet, very beautiful purple tones, excellent

'Nadezhda', double, Kolesnikov pre-1974, large thyrses, very fine to excellent

'Nebo Moskvy', double, Kolesnikov 1963, a blue of great merit, showy, fine

"No. 71" (syn. 'Dr Lemke'), double, Lemke 1953, bluish to lilac, very fine

'Olivier de Serres', double, Lemoine 1909, large floret of medium to dark blue, very showy, excellent

'P. P. Konchalovskiĭ', double, Kolesnikov 1956, large thyrses, showy, excellent

Syringa vulgaris 'Mechta'. B. Peart and M. Walton

Syringa vulgaris 'Nebo Moskvy'. B. Peart and M. Walton

Syringa vulgaris 'Nadezhda'. B. Peart and M. Walton

Syringa vulgaris 'P. P. Konchalovskiĭ'. B. Peart and M. Walton

Syringa vulgaris 'President Lincoln'. B. Peart and M. Walton

Syringa vulgaris 'Sumerki'. B. Peart and M. Walton

Syringa vulgaris 'Prof. Hoser'. John Fiala

'Président Grévy', double, Lemoine 1886, fine blue with large starry florets, immense panicles, excellent

'President Lincoln', single, Dunbar 1916, medium blue, tall, leafy grower, very good

'Prof. Edmund Jankowski', single, Karpow-Lipski 1958, very good

'Prof. Hoser', double, Hoser ca. 1930, double white and double magenta, showy, full spikes, very fine; claimed to be a graft chimera, 'Dame Blanche' + *S. vulgaris* 'Président Poincaré'

'René Jarry-Desloges', double, Lemoine 1905, very good

'Rhodopea', single, pre-1928; once considered a species (*S. rhodopea*), thus many forms with varying shades and depth of blue are found under this name, some truly blue, medium-sized florets, fragrant, fine to very fine, depending on individual plants

Syringa vulgaris 'True Blue'. B. Peart and M. Walton

Syringa vulgaris 'Woodland Blue'. B. Peart and M. Walton

Syringa ×*hyacinthiflora* 'Charles Nordine'. B. Peart and M. Walton

Syringa ×*hyacinthiflora* 'Descanso King'. B. Peart and M. Walton

'Saturnale', single, Lemoine 1916, difficult to find, very fine

'Savonarole', double, Lemoine 1935, very difficult to find, beautiful shades of blues, very fine to excellent

'Sea Storm', single, Fiala 1984, large florets and thyrses of shades of deep blue tinged with violet, showy, recurved petals, heavy bloomer, very fine to excellent

'Sumerki', single, Kolesnikov 1954, dark violet-blue of considerable merit, very fine

'True Blue', single, Havemeyer 1956, large florets and thyrses, outstandingly showy pale blue, excellent

'Wedgwood Blue', single, Fiala 1981, Wedgwood blue with lilac-pink buds, beautiful hanging racemes, very showy, somewhat lower grower, excellent

'Woodland Blue', single, Hancock 1967, difficult to obtain, good to very good

Other recommended lilacs in class III (blue):

S. ×*hyacinthiflora* 'Big Blue', single, Lammerts 1953, bluish very fine

S. ×*hyacinthiflora* 'Blue Boy', single, Sobeck 1966, brushed lavender, good

S. ×*hyacinthiflora* 'Charles Nordine', single, Skinner 1953, bluish lavender, very fine

S. ×*hyacinthiflora* 'Descanso King', single, Sobeck 1966, blue with lavender tones, very good

S. ×*hyacinthiflora* 'Doctor Chadwick', single, Skinner pre-1963, bluish with lavender tones, fine

S. ×*hyacinthiflora* 'Laurentian', single, Skinner 1945, bluish with lavender tones, very good

S. ×*hyacinthiflora* 'Peggy', single, Preston 1931, brushed lavender, very good

S. ×*hyacinthiflora* 'Spring Dawn', single, Clarke 1960, lavender tones, very fine

S. oblata subsp. *dilatata* 'Cheyenne', single, Hildreth 1971, low growing, very fine

S. (Villosae Group) 'Desdemona', single, Preston 1927 (*S.* ×*prestoniae*), lavender tones, very fine

S. (Villosae Group) 'Elinor', single, Preston 1928 (*S.* ×*prestoniae*), blushed lavender-blue, fine

Syringa ×*hyacinthiflora* 'Peggy'. B. Peart and M. Walton

Syringa ×*hyacinthiflora* 'Doctor Chadwick'. B. Peart and M. Walton

Syringa (Villosae Group) 'Desdemona'. B. Peart and M. Walton

Syringa ×*hyacinthiflora* 'Laurentian'. B. Peart and M. Walton

Syringa (Villosae Group) 'Elinor'. B. Peart and M. Walton

Lilac-colored Lilacs (Color Class IV)

As previously mentioned, class IV lilacs are similar to class II lilacs in color, yet distinct. While the violet lilacs are purple-blue, the lilac-colored lilacs are either pinkish purple or true lavender.

Specially recommended *Syringa vulgaris* cultivars in class IV (lilac):

'Alice Chieppo', double, Fiala 1984, very early, fragrant, heavy bloomer, showy, excellent

'Alphonse Lavallée', double, Lemoine 1885, considerable bluish tones, good

'Ametist 2', single, Shtan'ko & Mikhaĭlov 1956, silvery lilac, bluish cast, very fine

'Anna Nickles', single, Stone 1963, fragrant, large florets, very fine

'Belorusskie Zori', single, Smol'skiĭ & Bibikova 1964, very fragrant, large-flowered, fine

Syringa vulgaris 'Anna Nickles'. B. Peart and M. Walton

Syringa vulgaris 'Alphonse Lavallée'. B. Peart and M. Walton

Syringa vulgaris 'Ametist 2'. B. Peart and M. Walton

Syringa vulgaris 'Belorusskie Zori'. B. Peart and M. Walton

'Betty Stone', single, Stone 1963, fragrant, large florets, very fine

'Carolyn Mae', double, J. Sass 1942, good to very fine, difficult to obtain

'Centenaire de la Linneenne', single, Klettenberg 1936, lavender-violet, good but no longer available

'Christophe Colomb', single, Lemoine 1905, very fine to excellent

'Directeur Doorenbos', single, Eveleens Maarse 1955, very good

'Émile Lemoine', double, V. Lemoine 1889, still one of the finest lilac doubles, excellent in every way

'Gortenziya', single, Kolesnikov 1930, fragrant, very good

'Henri Martin', double, Lemoine 1912, large thyrses, very fine

Syringa vulgaris 'Directeur Doorenbos'. B. Peart and M. Walton

Syringa vulgaris 'Carolyn Mae'. B. Peart and M. Walton

Syringa vulgaris 'Gortenziya'. B. Peart and M. Walton

Syringa vulgaris 'Christophe Colomb'. B. Peart and M. Walton

Syringa vulgaris 'Henri Martin'. B. Peart and M. Walton

'Hippolyte Maringer', double, Lemoine 1909, very
  good
'Indiya', single, Kolesnikov 1955, large florets, fragrant, moderate bloomer, good
'Izobilie', double, Kolesnikov pre-1959, very showy,
  fine
'Jacques Callot', single, Lemoine 1876, very fragrant,
  good

'Kapriz', double, Kolesnikov 1952, very good
'Komsomolka', double, Kolesnikov 1974, very fine
'Kremlevskie Kuranty', single, Kolesnikov 1974,
  large florets, showy, very fine

Syringa vulgaris 'Hippolyte Maringer'. B. Peart and M. Walton

Syringa vulgaris 'Kapriz'. B. Peart and M. Walton

Syringa vulgaris 'Indiya'. B. Peart and M. Walton

Syringa vulgaris 'Komsomolka'. B. Peart and M. Walton

'Léon Gambetta', double, Lemoine 1907, very showy, excellent

'Leonid Leonov', single, Kolesnikov 1941, very showy with purplish cast, excellent

'Lullaby', double, Fiala 1984, very large thyrses, very fine

'Marlyensis Pallida', single, origin not known, pre-1864, very fragrant, pale lavender, very good

'Marshal Zhukov', single, Kolesnikov 1948, fragrant, showy, very fine

'Maurice de Vilmorin', double, Lemoine 1900, very showy, excellent

Syringa vulgaris 'Marlyensis Pallida'. B. Peart and M. Walton

Syringa vulgaris 'Léon Gambetta'. B. Peart and M. Walton

Syringa vulgaris 'Marshal Zhukov'. B. Peart and M. Walton

Syringa vulgaris 'Lullaby'. John Fiala

Syringa vulgaris 'Maurice de Vilmorin'. B. Peart and M. Walton

Syringa vulgaris 'Michel Buchner'. B. Peart and M. Walton

Syringa vulgaris 'Pamyat' o S. M. Kirove'. B. Peart and M. Walton

Syringa vulgaris 'Pioner'. B. Peart and M. Walton

'Michel Buchner', double, Lemoine 1885, showy, very fine

'Mollie Ann', single, Fiala 1983, large florets, very heavy and showy bloomer, excellent

'Mrs John S. Williams', single, Havemeyer pre-1953, large florets, showy, excellent

'Ogni Donbassa', double, Rubtzov, Zhogoleva, Lyapunova & Gorb 1956, very good to fine

'Pamyat' o S. M. Kirove', double, Kolesnikov 1943, very showy large thyrses, excellent

'Pioner', single, Kolesnikov 1951, very fragrant, fine

'Prince of Wales', single, Dougall 1874, fragrant, petals recurved, fine to very fine

'S. V. Lavrov', double, Lavrov pre-1974, quality bloom, very good

'Sonnet', single, Fiala 1983, very fine

'Tadeusz Kościuszko', double, Karpow-Lipski 1958, very good

'Victor Lemoine', double, É. Lemoine 1906, of exceptional merit, showy, excellent

'William Robinson', double, Lemoine 1899

Other recommended lilacs in class IV (lilac):

S. ×*hyacinthiflora* 'Excel', single, Skinner 1932, very good to fine

S. ×*hyacinthiflora* 'Nokomis', single, Skinner 1934, very good to fine

S. ×*hyacinthiflora* 'Norah', single, Preston 1931, good

S. *josikaea*, single, a deep color more purple than lilac, good, fine glossy leaves, somewhat sparse in bloom

S. ×*persica*, single, pale lilac, an outstanding large background shrub, very showy, fragrant

S. *pubescens* subsp. *julianae*, single, white to whitish blushed pale lavender inside, violet-purple outside, upright and wide growing, fine

S. (Villosae Group) 'Adriana', single, Preston 1928 (S. ×*prestoniae*), very good

S. (Villosae Group) 'Agata', single, Bugała 1970, second-generation S. ×*prestoniae*, very fine

S. (Villosae Group) 'Charmian', single, Preston 1928 (S. ×*prestoniae*), good

Syringa (Villosae Group) 'Agata'. B. Peart and M. Walton

Syringa ×*hyacinthiflora* 'Excel', habit. B. Peart and M. Walton

Syringa ×*hyacinthiflora* 'Excel', flowers. B. Peart and M. Walton

Syringa (Villosae Group) 'Charmian'. B. Peart and M. Walton

Syringa ×*hyacinthiflora* 'Nokomis'. B. Peart and M. Walton

Syringa (Villosae Group) 'Jagienka'. B. Peart and M. Walton

Syringa ×*hyacinthiflora* 'Norah'. B. Peart and M. Walton

S. (Villosae Group) 'Isabella', single, Preston 1928 (*S.* ×*prestoniae*), very fine to excellent

S. (Villosae Group) 'Jagienka', single, Bugała 1970, second-generation *S.* ×*prestoniae*, very fine

Pink Lilacs (Color Class V)

Pink colors in lilacs are very difficult to classify since so many cultivars contain varying shades of lavender and magenta, and sometimes even blue. Clear pinks are rare. Pink is an elusive shade in lilacs that changes with the weather, with the brightness of the sun, and with soil pH (acid or alkaline soils have much to do with shades and intensity of color). Often, true pinks shift to lavender or bluish pinks in colder seasons or heavier soils.

The many pink cultivars of *Syringa vulgaris* listed here have been divided into two subgroups: the soft, clear pinks that seem to have no admixture of lavender, violet, or blue, and the mixed pinks that appear predominantly pink but upon closer scrutiny have lavender, magenta, or bluish casts. When the mixed pinks are side by side with the deeper purples, rich magentas, violets, blues, or whites, they appear to be real pinks, but when placed next to the true pinks or lavenders, they are not as pink as they appear.

No exhaustive and scientific study has ever been made of the color of lilacs; perhaps they are too elusive to be categorized. Pink is a color that needs the attention of hybridizers. Frequently, the pink florets are rather small. Many of the pink doubles have tightly knit thyrses with a too compact appearance. Other pinks fade to a washed-out white when in full sun. A soft, filtered umbrella of high shade retains their delicate tones. In half-bloom they are most beautiful with the contrast of deeper pink buds and the unfolding light pink florets. Prune the pink cultivars heavily to encourage strong young growth on the bush.

Although there are some fine newer pink introductions, some of the oldest and finest pinks are well over a century old. *Syringa vulgaris* 'Lucie Baltet', introduced by the Baltet nursery of Troyes, France, in 1888, with bronze-pink buds opening to a delicate pale pink, is still among the finest. *Syringa vulgaris* 'Macrostachya', introduced by Renaud of Nantes, France, in 1874, with its long, pale pink thyrses, is another excellent albeit older true pink.

Pink lilacs are for close viewing, where their truly delicate shades and tones can best be appreciated. They are spectacular when planted with dark purple lilacs.

Recommended *Syringa vulgaris* cultivars in class V (true pink):

'Alenushka', single, Shtan'ko & Mikhaïlov 1956, difficult to obtain, very fragrant, very fine
'Archiduchesse Charlotte', single, Brahy-Ekenholm 1861, very rare, old, beautiful, very good
'Catawba Pink', double, Utley 1980, very good
'Charm', single, Havemeyer pre-1942, large florets, very good

'Cora Lyden', double, Lyden 1963, a beautiful lilac, very fine
'Cynthia', single, Berdeen 1971, pale pink of great quality, very fine to excellent
'Hermann Eilers', single, origin not known, pre-1913, good

Syringa vulgaris 'Catawba Pink'. B. Peart and M. Walton

Syringa vulgaris 'Charm'. B. Peart and M. Walton

'Holy Maid', single, Fiala 1984, pale lovely pink, outstandingly beautiful, excellent
'I. V. Michurin', double, Kolesnikov 1941, fragrant,
   very fine
'Lavaliensis', single, origin not known, pre-1865, used
   for forcing
'Lee Jewett Walker', single, Berdeen 1981, very pale
   pink, of exceptional beauty, excellent
'Lilarosa', single, origin not known, 1887, very good
   background, fragrant, small florets but showy,
   good
'Lois Amee Utley', double, Fiala 1986, very showy,
   very fine to excellent
'Lourene Wishart', double, Fiala 1980, very clear, fine
   pink, heavy bloomer, excellent
'Lucie Baltet', single, Baltet 1888, low growing, very
   fine to excellent
'Macrostachya', single, Renaud 1874, long clusters of
   pale pink, very fine
'Maiennacht', single, Löbner pre-1947, pale pink,
   very good
'Marie Frances', single, Fiala 1983, pale pink, multipetaled, very showy, excellent
'Marshal Vasilevskiï', double, Kolesnikov 1963, very
   fine quality, very good

Syringa vulgaris 'Lee Jewett Walker'. John Fiala

Syringa vulgaris 'Lilarosa'. B. Peart and M. Walton

Syringa vulgaris 'Cynthia'. B. Peart and M. Walton

Syringa vulgaris 'Lucie Baltet'. B. Peart and M. Walton

Syringa vulgaris 'Macrostachya'. B. Peart and M. Walton

Syringa vulgaris 'Martha Kounze'. B. Peart and M. Walton

Syringa vulgaris 'Mme Antoine Buchner'. B. Peart and M. Walton

Syringa vulgaris 'Marshal Vasilevskii'. B. Peart and M. Walton

'Martha Kounze', double, Havemeyer pre-1953, excellent, very showy

'Melissa Oakes', single, Oakes 1977, pale pink, very fine to excellent

'Mme Antoine Buchner', double, Lemoine 1909, very fine to excellent

'Montaigne', double, Lemoine 1907, high quality, pale pink, very fine

Syringa vulgaris 'Montaigne'. B. Peart and M. Walton

'Mrs Harry Bickle', single, Rolph 1956, pale pink
feathery spikes, very fine

'Olimpiada Kolesnikova', double, Kolesnikov 1941,
very fine

'Pink Lace', single, J. Sass 1953, pale to medium pink,
very fine to excellent

'Pink Mist', single, Havemeyer & Eaton 1953, large
florets, very good

'Pomorzanka', single, Karpow-Lipski 1962, very fine
quality, very good

'Radiance', double, Fiala 1985, very fine to excellent

'Stephanie Rowe', single, Berdeen 1979, very pale
pink long clusters, difficult to obtain, very fine to
excellent

Syringa vulgaris 'Pink Lace'. B. Peart and M. Walton

Syringa vulgaris 'Mrs Harry Bickle'. B. Peart and M. Walton

Syringa vulgaris 'Pink Mist'. B. Peart and M. Walton

Syringa vulgaris 'Olimpiada Kolesnikova'. B. Peart and M. Walton

Syringa vulgaris 'Stephanie Rowe'. John Fiala

Recommended *Syringa vulgaris* cultivars in class V (mixed pink):

'Capitaine Perrault', double, Lemoine 1925, very fine

'Comte Horace de Choiseul', double, Lemoine 1887, old but still good

'Edward J. Gardner' (marketed in Germany as FLA-MINGO), double, Gardner pre-1950, pale pink of outstanding beauty, excellent

'Elsie Lenore', single, Fiala 1982, enormous florets and panicles, outstandingly showy, a colchicine-treated seedling of 'Sensation', excellent

'Général Pershing', double, Lemoine 1924, of considerable merit, very fine

'Katherine Havemeyer', double, Lemoine 1922, very heavy thyrses, lavender pink, very fine

'Konstantin Zaslonov', single, Smol'skiĭ & Bibikova 1964, very good

'Konstanty Karpow', single, Karpow-Lipski 1953, very good

Syringa vulgaris 'Katherine Havemeyer'. B. Peart and M. Walton

Syringa vulgaris 'Comte Horace de Choiseul'. B. Peart and M. Walton

Syringa vulgaris 'Edward J. Gardner'. B. Peart and M. Walton

Syringa vulgaris 'Konstanty Karpow'. B. Peart and M. Walton

'Little Miss Muffet', single, Fiala 1965, low growing, perhaps should be classified magenta (VI), large florets on small bush, very good

'Marie Marcelin', double, of unknown origin, pre-1953, very fine

'Midwest Gem', double, H. P. Sass 1942, medium pink, fine

'Miriam Cooley', single, Klager 1931, very fine, of great quality

'Olive May Cummings', double, Berdeen 1979, pinkish to violet, very good

'Romance', single, Havemeyer & Eaton 1954, rosy lavender, large florets of outstanding merit, very fine

Syringa vulgaris 'Marie Marcelin'. B. Peart and M. Walton

Syringa vulgaris 'Midwest Gem'. B. Peart and M. Walton

Syringa vulgaris 'Olive May Cummings'. B. Peart and M. Walton

Syringa vulgaris 'Romance'. B. Peart and M. Walton

'Ukraina', single, <u>Zhogoleva</u> 1974, large florets, fragrant, very fine and showy

'Utro Moskvy', double, Kolesnikov 1938, very fine lilac-pink with silvery tones

Other recommended lilacs in class V (pink):

S. ×*hyacinthiflora* 'Anabel', double, Hawkins 1956, very early, good; often misspelled "Annabel"

S. ×*hyacinthiflora* 'Berryer', double, Lemoine 1913, lavender tones, tall grower, good

S. ×*hyacinthiflora* 'Bountiful', single, Clarke 1949, very showy, great quality, excellent

S. ×*hyacinthiflora* 'Buffon', single, Lemoine 1921, lavender tones, recurved, very good

S. ×*hyacinthiflora* 'Catinat', single, Lemoine 1922, good

S. ×*hyacinthiflora* 'Churchill', single, Skinner 1945, very fine

Syringa vulgaris 'Ukraina'. B. Peart and M. Walton

Syringa ×*hyacinthiflora* 'Anabel'. B. Peart and M. Walton

Syringa vulgaris 'Utro Moskvy'. B. Peart and M. Walton

Syringa ×*hyacinthiflora* 'Berryer'. B. Peart and M. Walton

S. ×*hyacinthiflora* 'Claude Bernard', double, Lemoine 1915, very fine

S. ×*hyacinthiflora* 'Daphne Pink', single, Skinner 1959, very fine

S. ×*hyacinthiflora* 'Fénelon', single, Lemoine 1936, good

Syringa ×*hyacinthiflora* 'Claude Bernard'. B. Peart and M. Walton

Syringa ×*hyacinthiflora* 'Buffon'. B. Peart and M. Walton

Syringa ×*hyacinthiflora* 'Daphne Pink'. B. Peart and M. Walton

Syringa ×*hyacinthiflora* 'Catinat'. B. Peart and M. Walton

Syringa ×*hyacinthiflora* 'Churchill'. B. Peart and M. Walton

Syringa ×*hyacinthiflora* 'Fénelon'. B. Peart and M. Walton

Syringa ×hyacinthiflora 'Fraser'. B. Peart and M. Walton

Syringa ×hyacinthiflora 'Vauban'. B. Peart and M. Walton

Syringa ×hyacinthiflora 'Lewis Maddock'. B. Peart and M. Walton

S. ×hyacinthiflora 'Fraser', single, Skinner 1945, fine bloomer, very good

S. ×hyacinthiflora 'Kate Sessions', single, Clarke 1942, large florets, very fine

S. ×hyacinthiflora 'Lewis Maddock', single, Rankin 1963, very early, very fine pink

S. ×hyacinthiflora 'Maiden's Blush' (marketed in Germany as ROSENROT, in Denmark as

ROSARÖD), single, Skinner 1966, pale to medium pink, outstanding, excellent

S. ×hyacinthiflora 'Orchid Chiffon', single, H. E. Sass 1953, very good

S. ×hyacinthiflora 'Vauban', double, Lemoine 1913, good

S. komarowii, single, very fine medium pink, excellent

S. komarowii subsp. *reflexa*, single, beautiful hanging racemes, medium to dark pink to lavender-pink depending on the individual plant selection, excellent

S. meyeri 'Palibin', single, origin not known, pre-1920, deep purplish red buds opening to pinkish lavender flowers, variable, very fine small growing and showy, excellent

S. pubescens subsp. *julianae* 'George Eastman', single, Fenicchia 1978, deep carmine buds, outstanding pink, upright grower, excellent

S. pubescens subsp. *julianae* 'Hers', Hers pre-1953, more lavender than pink, arching branches, very fine species cultivar, excellent, needs room

S. pubescens subsp. *julianae* 'Pink Parasol', single,

Syringa (Villosae Group) 'Ethel M. Webster'. B. Peart and M. Walton

Fiala 1983, recurved petals of pale pink, fine grower and bloomer, excellent

S. pubescens subsp. *microphylla* var. *potaninii*, single, delicate pink, softwooded, blooms over the entire summer

S. pubescens subsp. *microphylla* 'Superba', single, Cassegrain 1933, very fine, needs good drainage

S. (Villosae Group) 'Alice Rose Foster', single, Alexander 1968 (*S.* ×*prestoniae*)

S. (Villosae Group) 'Basia', single, Bugała 1970, a second-generation hybrid of *S.* ×*prestoniae*

S. (Villosae Group) 'Carlton', single, Preston pre-1948 (*S. komarowii* subsp. *reflexa* × *S. sweginzowii*), pale pink, good

S. (Villosae Group) 'Coral', single, Morden Research Centre 1936 (*S.* ×*prestoniae*), very good

S. (Villosae Group) 'Enid', single, Preston 1938 (*S.* ×*josiflexa*), good

S. (Villosae Group) 'Esterka', single, Bugała 1970 (*S.* ×*prestoniae*), very good

S. (Villosae Group) 'Ethel M. Webster', single, Preston 1948 (*S.* ×*prestoniae*), second generation, very good

S. (Villosae Group) 'Fountain', single, Preston pre-1953 (*S.* ×*prestoniae*), pale pink, good

Syringa (Villosae Group) 'Fountain'. B. Peart and M. Walton

Syringa (Villosae Group) 'Goplana'. B. Peart and M. Walton

Syringa (Villosae Group) 'Miss Canada'. B. Peart and M. Walton

Syringa (Villosae Group) 'James Macfarlane'. B. Peart and M. Walton

Syringa (Villosae Group) 'Prairial'. B. Peart and M. Walton

S. (Villosae Group) 'Goplana', single, Bugała 1970
(*S.* ×*prestoniae*), very fine

S. (Villosae Group) 'Heloise', single, Skinner 1932
(*S.* ×*prestoniae*), very good

S. (Villosae Group) 'Irving', single, Preston pre-1953
(*S.* ×*swegiflexa*), good to fine

S. (Villosae Group) 'James Macfarlane', single,
Yeager 1959, excellent

S. (Villosae Group) 'Lark Song', single, Fiala 1968
[(*S. sweginzowii* × *S. tomentella*) × *S. komarowii*],
medium-sized shrub, extremely floriferous, practically no seed pods, excellent

S. (Villosae Group) 'Miss Canada', single, Cumming
1967 (*S.* ×*josiflexa* 'Redwine' × *S.* ×*prestoniae* 'Hiawatha'), an excellent late lilac

S. (Villosae Group) 'Prairial', single, Lemoine 1936
(*S.* ×*henryi* × *S. tomentella*), medium pink, heavy
bloomer, very fine

Syringa (Villosae Group) 'Quartet'. John Fiala

Syringa (Villosae Group) 'Romeo'. B. Peart and M. Walton

Syringa (Villosae Group) 'Spellbinder'. John Fiala

S. (Villosae Group) 'Quartet', single, Fiala 1984 [(*S. sweginzowii* × *S. tomentella*) × (*S. komarowii* × *S. wolfii*)], medium-sized shrub, extremely floriferous annually, pale pink, excellent

S. (Villosae Group) 'Romeo', single, Preston 1938 (*S. ×prestoniae*), very good

S. (Villosae Group) 'Spellbinder', single, Fiala 1968

Syringa (Villosae Group) 'Telimena'. B. Peart and M. Walton

(*S. komarowii* × *S. wolfii*), very fine pale pink, very floriferous and showy, excellent, medium-sized shrub

S. (Villosae Group) 'Springtime', single, Fiala 1968 [(*S. sweginzowii* × *S. tomentella*) × *S. wolfii*]

S. (Villosae Group) 'Telimena', single, Bugała 1970 (*S. ×prestoniae*), very fine to excellent

S. (Villosae Group) 'Ursula', single, Preston 1928 (*S. ×prestoniae*), violet shades, one of the best, excellent

Magenta Lilacs (Color Class VI)

Magenta (VI) and purple (VII) are the classes with the darkest lilacs. Magenta denotes "fuchsia, a bright purplish-red color," one with carmine tones, a crimson or purplish red. Purple denotes a color having "components of red and blue," a deep tone of reddish crimson-blue. You must have the flowers in front of you to appreciate the difference a bit of blue can make in these very deep reddish purple colors. Since very few women are color-blind to red and blue, they are perhaps better judges as to which cultivar belongs where, but some men also have good color perception in these categories. Many of the deep pink, magenta, and purple lilac cultivars are wrongly classified. By using the *Royal Horticultural Society Colour Chart*, either the 1995 or 2001 edition, one can determine their exact shade.

Recommended *Syringa vulgaris* cultivars in class VI (magenta):

'Amor', single, Löbner pre-1947, very good to very fine

'André Csizik', single, Eveleens Maarse 1950, very good

'Arch McKean', single, Fiala 1984, large florets, showy, excellent

'Botaniste Pauli', single, Klettenberg 1935, very good but no longer found in nurseries

'Bright Centennial', single, Robinson 1967, deep reddish color, very fine to excellent

'Capitaine Baltet', single, Lemoine 1919, large florets, showy, very fine

'Charlotte Morgan', double, Seabury ca. 1928, fine but not readily obtainable

Syringa vulgaris 'André Csizik'. B. Peart and M. Walton

Syringa vulgaris 'Amor'. John Fiala

Syringa vulgaris 'Bright Centennial'. B. Peart and M. Walton

Syringa vulgaris 'Capitaine Baltet'. B. Peart and M. Walton

Syringa vulgaris 'Charlotte Morgan'. B. Peart and M. Walton

'Congo', single, Lemoine 1896, bright deep reddish, heavy bloom, very old but excellent

'Corinne', single, Baltet pre-1900, still very fine

'Downfield', single, Havemeyer pre-1942, very fine

'Eden', single, Oliver 1939, deep reddish purple, fair to good

'Frederick Douglass', single, Fenicchia 1972, multi-petaled, very fine

Syringa vulgaris 'Corinne'. B. Peart and M. Walton

Syringa vulgaris 'Congo'. B. Peart and M. Walton

Syringa vulgaris 'Downfield'. B. Peart and M. Walton

'Fryderyk Chopin', single, Karpow-Lipski 1958, very
fine, not found in nurseries

'G. J. Baardse', single, Eveleens Maarse 1943, medium
florets, very good, showy

'Georges Bellair', double, Lemoine 1900, one of the
better magenta doubles, very fine

'Gismonda', double, Lemoine 1939, very fine large
thyrses

'Glory', single, Havemeyer 1943, enormous florets,
shy bloomer, many suckers, good

'Henry Wadsworth Longfellow', double, Dunbar
1920, very good

'James Stuart', single, Havemeyer pre-1942, large florets, heavy bloomer, very fine

'Lady Lindsay', single, Havemeyer pre-1942, large,
recurved florets, very red, fine

'Leon Wyczółkowski', single, Karpow-Lipski 1958,
very good

Syringa vulgaris 'Glory'. B. Peart and M. Walton

Syringa vulgaris 'Georges Bellair'. B. Peart and M. Walton

Syringa vulgaris 'Henry Wadsworth Longfellow'. B. Peart and M. Walton

Syringa vulgaris 'Gismonda'. B. Peart and M. Walton

Syringa vulgaris 'James Stuart'. B. Peart and M. Walton

'Magellan', double, Lemoine 1915, good reddish, not easily found

'Maître Georges Hermans', double, Lambrechts 1952, fine reddish lavender, difficult to find

'Marceau', single, Lemoine 1913, very fine, very large deep reddish florets

'Maréchal Foch', single, Lemoine 1924, very large, reddish pink florets, tall, excellent

'Masséna', single, Lemoine 1923, large reddish florets, excellent

'Mister Big', double, Havemeyer & Eaton 1954, fine, not easily obtainable

Syringa vulgaris 'Lady Lindsay'. B. Peart and M. Walton

Syringa vulgaris 'Magellan'. B. Peart and M. Walton

Syringa vulgaris 'Maréchal Foch'. B. Peart and M. Walton

Syringa vulgaris 'Marceau'. B. Peart and M. Walton

Syringa vulgaris 'Mme F. Morel'. B. Peart and M. Walton

'Mme F. Morel', single, F. Morel 1892, very old but
    showy, very good
'Mrs Edward Harding', double, Lemoine 1922, very
    heavy large spikes, fine
'Mrs John W. Davis', double, Havemeyer pre-1942,
    very fine
'Mrs Watson Webb', single, Havemeyer pre-1942,
    very fine to excellent, large spikes
'Paul Deschanel', double, Lemoine 1924, enormous
    panicles, large florets, excellent
'Paul Thirion', double, Lemoine 1915, very fine, deep
    reddish pink, very fine to excellent

Syringa vulgaris 'Paul Deschanel'. B. Peart and M. Walton

Syringa vulgaris 'Mrs Edward Harding'. B. Peart and M. Walton

Syringa vulgaris 'Paul Thirion'. B. Peart and M. Walton

Syringa vulgaris 'Mrs Watson Webb'. B. Peart and M. Walton

Syringa vulgaris 'Planchon'. B. Peart and M. Walton

'Planchon', double, Lemoine 1908, very good

'Président Loubet', double, Lemoine 1901, very fine mixed pinkish red shades

'Président Poincaré', double, Lemoine 1913, very fine, heavy, large spikes

'Prince Baudouin', single, Klettenberg 1935, good to fine but no longer available

'Priscilla', single, Havemeyer 1944, very large florets with lavender cast

'Radzh Kapur', single, Kolesnikov 1974, very large florets, fine

'Réaumur', single, Lemoine 1904, very fine to excellent

'Red Feather', double, Ruliffson 1953, good

'Ruhm von Horstenstein', single, Wilke 1928, very good

Syringa vulgaris 'Président Poincaré'. B. Peart and M. Walton

Syringa vulgaris 'Priscilla'. B. Peart and M. Walton

Syringa vulgaris 'Réaumur'. B. Peart and M. Walton

Syringa vulgaris 'Radzh Kapur'. B. Peart and M. Walton

Syringa vulgaris 'Ruhm von Horstenstein'. B. Peart and M. Walton

Syringa vulgaris 'Stefan Makowiecki'. B. Peart and M. Walton

Syringa vulgaris 'Voorzitter Dix'. B. Peart and M. Walton

'Saint Jerzy Popieluszko', single, Fiala 1985, very fine to excellent, showy reddish

'Souvenir de Georges Truffaut', double, Lemoine 1953, fine

'Souvenir de Louis Chasset', single, Lemoine 1953, very fine

'Stefan Makowiecki', single, Karpow-Lipski 1958, fine

'Talisman', single, Fiala 1984, very showy, fine to very fine

'Voorzitter Dix', single, Eveleens Maarse 1950, fine

'Zarya Kommunizma', single, Kolesnikov 1951, very large deep reddish florets, fine

Other recommended lilacs in class VI (magenta):

S. ×*chinensis* 'La Lorraine', single, Lemoine 1899

S. ×*chinensis* 'Orchid Beauty', single, Hilborn pre-1945

S. ×*hyacinthiflora* 'Ada', single, Preston 1953, good

S. ×*hyacinthiflora* 'Alice Eastwood', double, Clarke 1942, very good

S. ×*hyacinthiflora* 'Esther Staley', single, Clarke 1948, tall grower, heavy bloom, excellent

S. ×*hyacinthiflora* 'Fantasy', double, Clarke 1960, very fine

Syringa vulgaris 'Zarya Kommunizma'. B. Peart and M. Walton

Syringa ×hyacinthiflora 'Alice Eastwood'. B. Peart and M. Walton

S. ×*hyacinthiflora* 'Katherine Jones', single, Clarke 1953, good

S. ×*hyacinthiflora* 'Missimo', single, Clarke 1944, very fine

S. ×*hyacinthiflora* 'Montesquieu', single, Lemoine 1926, fine

S. ×*hyacinthiflora* 'Patricia', double, Preston 1931, good

S. ×*hyacinthiflora* 'Pink Cloud', single, Clarke 1947, very fine

Syringa ×*hyacinthiflora* 'Montesquieu'. B. Peart and M. Walton

Syringa ×*hyacinthiflora* 'Esther Staley'. B. Peart and M. Walton

Syringa ×*hyacinthiflora* 'Patricia'. B. Peart and M. Walton

Syringa ×*hyacinthiflora* 'Fantasy'. B. Peart and M. Walton

Syringa ×*hyacinthiflora* 'Pink Cloud'. B. Peart and M. Walton

S. ×*hyacinthiflora* 'Summer Skies', single, Clarke 1948, very fine

S. ×*hyacinthiflora* 'Sunset' (marketed in Germany as Elfenkönig), double, Clarke 1949, very fine to excellent

S. ×*hyacinthiflora* 'Sweetheart', double, Clarke 1953, very fine

S. komarowii, single, very fine to excellent, color variations when grown from seed

S. pubescens subsp. *julianae* 'Epaulettes', single, Fiala 1984, very fine, showy

S. pubescens subsp. *julianae* 'Sentinel', single, Fiala 1984, upright very good, lilac to magenta

S. (Villosae Group) 'Dancing Druid', single, Fiala 1968, presumably (*S. yunnanensis* × *S. tomentella*) × (*S. komarowii* × [*S. sweginzowii* × *S. tomentella*]), very good

S. (Villosae Group) 'Germinal', single, Lemoine 1939 (*S.* ×*henryi* × *S. tomentella*), fair

S. (Villosae Group) 'Guinevere', single, Preston 1925 (*S.* ×*josiflexa*), good

S. wolfii, single, very good, one of the better species, does have variations of color when grown from seed, propagate selected seedlings vegetatively

Syringa ×*hyacinthiflora* 'Summer Skies'. B. Peart and M. Walton

Syringa ×*hyacinthiflora* 'Sweetheart'. B. Peart and M. Walton

Syringa (Villosae Group) 'Germinal'. B. Peart and M. Walton

Purple Lilacs (Color Class VII)

Viewers are attracted by deep purple lilacs. More people will choose the deepest purples over any other color. In a classification that has several shades of deep purple, mostly the deep reddish blue-purples, it is often difficult to ascertain whether some of the deep violets belong to class VII or class II; therefore, some cultivars could appear in both classes.

Often the darkness of purple lilacs is not conveyed in the garden; they should be contrasted with white or light pink lilacs. Dark lilacs need to be viewed at close range. They lose their effectiveness at any great distance. Use them as a close-up focal point; come upon them suddenly in the garden as you round a path, or place them alongside the patio or as a solitary shrub. Accent them by planting low, white companion plants at their feet. Try a dark lilac underplanted with true blue hostas—a unique color contrast—or with *Malus* 'Silver Moon', 'Prairie Rose', 'Prince Georges', or some of the newer *Malus* cultivars that are late bloomers, or with many of the early low perennials.

Many of the really dark lilacs are late bloomers, so choose only the late-blooming white or pink lilacs to accompany them. Good later-blooming whites are 'Emery Mae Norweb', 'Gertrude Clark', 'Prof. E. H. Wilson', 'St Joan', 'St Margaret', or the delicate pink-shaded white 'Krasavitsa Moskvy' and the uniquely colored 'Professor Robert B. Clark'—all cultivars of *Syringa vulgaris*. Do not use the early *S.* ×*hyacinthiflora* cultivars with the late-blooming *S. vulgaris*.

If the deep purples are shaded for a few hours from the hottest afternoon sun, they will retain their deep purple color much longer. Hot suns fade their colors to a washed-out purple. These deep purples are particularly beautiful at Royal Botanical Gardens, Hamilton, Ontario, where they are grown in the semishade of tall trees.

Some of the deep purples can be fussy growers, slow and at times weak, needing a little extra care with water and weed-free soil. The newer introductions are fine and strong growers. All the deepest-colored lilacs are not found in this class VII alone, many more are in class II, and some would fit in both. Class VII has the deep reddish-blue purples, whereas class II has the deep violets or violet-blues without the admixture of reddish blue.

Recommended *Syringa vulgaris* cultivars in class VII (purple):

'A. B. Lamberton', double, Dunbar 1916, good
'A. M. Brand', single, Brand 1940, large florets, very fine
'Adelaide Dunbar', double, Dunbar 1916, very good
'Alesha', single magenta, Sakharova 1973, large florets more cherry red than purple, fine
'Andenken an Ludwig Späth' (marketed in North America as LUDWIG SPAETH), single, Späth 1883, good, surpassed by newer cultivars
'Anna Elisabeth Jaquet', single, Piet 1907, very fine, very showy heavy bloomer
'Anne Shiach', single, Havemeyer & Michie 1943, very fine to excellent, difficult to find
'Anne Tighe', double, Yeager 1945, very fine

Syringa vulgaris 'A. B. Lamberton'. B. Peart and M. Walton

Syringa vulgaris 'A. M. Brand'. B. Peart and M. Walton

Syringa vulgaris 'Adelaide Dunbar'. B. Peart and M. Walton

Syringa vulgaris 'Andenken an Ludwig Späth'. B. Peart and M. Walton

Syringa vulgaris 'Anna Elisabeth Jaquet'. B. Peart and M. Walton

Syringa vulgaris 'Anne Shiach'. B. Peart and M. Walton

'Archevêque', double, Lemoine 1923, unique color,
  fine
'Arthur William Paul', double, Lemoine 1898, good
'Bishop McQuaid', single, Fenicchia 1972, multi-
  petaled, very fine to excellent
'C. B. van Nes', single, van Nes 1901, very good
'Calvin C. Laney', single, Dunbar pre-1923, very
  good
'Charles Joly', double, Lemoine 1896, very good,
  somewhat small thyrses
'Chris', single, Berdeen 1969, very good
'Col. Wm. R. Plum', single, Brand pre-1942, good

Syringa vulgaris 'Charles Joly'. B. Peart and M. Walton

Syringa vulgaris 'Arthur William Paul'. B. Peart and M. Walton

Syringa vulgaris 'Calvin C. Laney'. B. Peart and M. Walton

Syringa vulgaris 'Col. Wm. R. Plum'. B. Peart and M. Walton

Syringa vulgaris 'De Croncels'. B. Peart and M. Walton

'Danton', single, Lemoine 1911, very good
'De Croncels', single, Baltet pre-1876, very deep lavender toned pink with coppery buds, rather low growing, abundant bloom, very fine
'De Saussure', double, Lemoine 1903, very good
'Dianah Abbott', single, Berdeen 1976, very fine to excellent
'Diderot', single, Lemoine 1915, very good to fine
'Dr Brethour', single, Paterson 1960, very fine to excellent
'Dusk', single, Havemeyer pre-1942, very good

Syringa vulgaris 'Diderot'. B. Peart and M. Walton

Syringa vulgaris 'De Saussure'. B. Peart and M. Walton

Syringa vulgaris 'Dusk'. B. Peart and M. Walton

'Dzhavakharlal Neru', single, Kolesnikov 1974, good
and becoming available
'Edith Braun', single, Rankin 1968, one of the finest,
excellent
'Edmond Boissier', single, Lemoine 1906, very fine
'Ethel Child', single, Child pre-1978, very good
'Ethel Dupont', single, Havemeyer pre-1942, very
good
'Ethiopia', single, origin unknown, pre-1929, very
good to fine, very dark
'Etna', single, Lemoine 1927, very fine to excellent
'Étoile de Mai', double, Lemoine 1905, combination
of purple and white, good
'Flower City', single, Fenicchia 1983, large florets
with a light silvery reverse, very floriferous, ex-
tremely showy, exceptional

Syringa vulgaris 'Dzhavakharlal Neru'. B. Peart and M. Walton

Syringa vulgaris 'Edmond Boissier'. B. Peart and M. Walton

Syringa vulgaris 'Edith Braun'. B. Peart and M. Walton

Syringa vulgaris 'Ethiopia'. B. Peart and M. Walton

'Frank Klager', single, Klager 1928, very fine
'Frank Paterson', single, Paterson 1960, very showy,
   tall grower, excellent
'Fürst Bülow', single, Späth 1921, very fine and very
   showy
'Hallelujah', single, Havemeyer & Eaton 1954, very
   fine
'Helen Schloen', single, Paterson 1962, very fine

Syringa vulgaris 'Fürst Bülow'. B. Peart and M. Walton

Syringa vulgaris 'Frank Klager'. B. Peart and M. Walton

Syringa vulgaris 'Hallelujah'. B. Peart and M. Walton

Syringa vulgaris 'Frank Paterson'. B. Peart and M. Walton

Syringa vulgaris 'Helen Schloen'. B. Peart and M. Walton

'Jane Day', single, Havemeyer pre-1942, very good

'Krasnaya Moskva', single, Kolesnikov pre-1960, fine, moderate bloomer

'Laplace', single, Lemoine 1913, good

'Léopold III', single, Klettenberg 1935, very good but no longer available

'Margaret Fenicchia', single, Fenicchia 1997, very outstanding to excellent

'Margaret Rice Gould', single, Brand pre-1953, very good

'Mildred Luetta', double, Hetz 1950, very fine to excellent

'Miss Aalsmeer', single, H. Maarse pre-1943, very fine

'Mme Pierre Verhoeven', single, Verhoeven 1936, very good

Syringa vulgaris 'Margaret Rice Gould'. B. Peart and M. Walton

Syringa vulgaris 'Jane Day'. B. Peart and M. Walton

Syringa vulgaris 'Laplace'. B. Peart and M. Walton

Syringa vulgaris 'Mildred Luetta'. B. Peart and M. Walton

Syringa vulgaris 'Monge'. B. Peart and M. Walton

'Monge', single, Lemoine 1913, outstandingly showy, excellent

'Mrs Flanders', single, Havemeyer pre-1942, smaller florets but outstanding color, excellent

'Mrs R. L. Gardner', single, Gardner 1956, very fine

'Mrs W. E. Marshall', single, Havemeyer 1924, small florets but perhaps the darkest-colored lilac, almost black, excellent

'Murillo', double, Lemoine 1901, very fine

'Negro', single, Lemoine 1899, very good

'Pasteur', single, Lemoine 1903, very good

'Paul Hariot', double, Lemoine 1902, very fine

Syringa vulgaris 'Pasteur'. B. Peart and M. Walton

Syringa vulgaris 'Mrs W. E. Marshall'. B. Peart and M. Walton

Syringa vulgaris 'Paul Hariot'. B. Peart and M. Walton

'Polesskaya Legenda', single, Smol'skiĭ & Bibikova
    pre-1959, fine

'Prodige', single, Lemoine 1928, very large florets,
    excellent

'Sarah Sands', single, Havemeyer 1943, excellent

'Stadtgärtner Rothpletz', single, Fröbel 1905, very
    fine heavy bloomer. A misnamed double dark lilac
    which has been sold under this name in North
    America since the 1920s is not the correct 'Stadt-
    gärtner Rothpletz'; the single true-to-name culti-
    var is extinct (Vrugtman 1980b).

'Toussaint-Louverture', single, Lemoine 1898, long
    spikes, very fine

'Triste Barbaro', single, originator unknown, pre-
    1938, very good

'Vesper', single, Fleming 1979, excellent, very showy

'Vésuve', single, Lemoine 1916, very fine, showy

'Volcan', single, Lemoine 1899, showy, very fine

Syringa vulgaris 'Toussaint-Louverture'. B. Peart and M. Walton

Syringa vulgaris 'Vesper'. B. Peart and M. Walton

Syringa vulgaris 'Prodige'. B. Peart and M. Walton

Syringa vulgaris 'Sarah Sands'. B. Peart and M. Walton

Syringa vulgaris 'Volcan'. B. Peart and M. Walton

Syringa vulgaris 'Znam<u>y</u>a Lenina'. B. Peart and M. Walton

Syringa vulgaris 'Zulu'. B. Peart and M. Walton

Syringa ×hyacinthiflora 'Dark Night'. B. Peart and M. Walton

'Woodland Violet', single, H. E. Sass pre-1953, very good

'Znam<u>y</u>a Lenina', single, Kolesnikov pre-1959, one of the finest red lilacs, a heavy bloomer, excellent

'Zulu', single, Havemeyer pre-1942, violet, large florets, very showy, excellent

Other recommended lilacs in class VII (purple):

S. ×hyacinthiflora 'Dark Night', single, Sobeck 1966, very good

S. ×hyacinthiflora 'Grace', single, Preston pre-1950, good

S. ×hyacinthiflora 'Lavender Lady', single, Lammerts 1953, very good

S. ×hyacinthiflora 'Lavender Lassie', single, Morey 1967, very good

S. ×hyacinthiflora 'Max Löbner', single, Löbner ca. 1947, very good

S. ×hyacinthiflora 'Muriel', single, Preston pre-1936, good

S. ×hyacinthiflora 'Purple Gem', single, Clarke 1960, very fine

S. ×hyacinthiflora 'Purple Glory', single, Clarke 1948, very fine to excellent

S. ×hyacinthiflora 'Purple Heart', single, Clarke 1948, very fine, showy

S. ×hyacinthiflora 'Splendor', double, Clarke 1948, very fine

S. ×hyacinthiflora 'Tom Taylor', double, Skinner 1962, very fine

Syringa ×hyacinthiflora 'Grace'. B. Peart and M. Walton

Syringa ×hyacinthiflora 'Lavender Lady'. B. Peart and M. Walton

Syringa ×hyacinthiflora 'Max Löbner'. B. Peart and M. Walton

Syringa ×hyacinthiflora 'Purple Glory'. B. Peart and M. Walton

Syringa ×hyacinthiflora 'Tom Taylor'. B. Peart and M. Walton

S. (Villosae Group) 'Alice', single, Preston 1928 (*S. ×prestoniae*), very good

S. (Villosae Group) 'Donald Wyman', single, Skinner 1944 (*S. ×prestoniae*), very good

S. (Villosae Group) 'Francisca', single, Preston 1928 (*S. ×prestoniae*), very good

S. (Villosae Group) 'Lynette', single, Preston 1938 (*S. ×josiflexa*), very good

S. (Villosae Group) 'Maybelle Farnum', single, Yeager 1961 (*S. ×josiflexa*), very fine

S. (Villosae Group) 'Nellie Bean', single, Yeager 1961 (*S. ×josiflexa*), very fine

S. (Villosae Group) 'Paulina', single, Preston 1927 (*S. ×prestoniae*), very good

S. (Villosae Group) 'Royalty', single, Preston 1936 (*S. ×josiflexa*), good

S. (Villosae Group) 'Viola', single, Preston 1928 (*S. ×prestoniae*), very dark

Syringa (Villosae Group) 'Alice'. B. Peart and M. Walton

Syringa (Villosae Group) 'Maybelle Farnum'. B. Peart and M. Walton

Syringa (Villosae Group) 'Francisca'. B. Peart and M. Walton

Syringa (Villosae Group) 'Royalty'. B. Peart and M. Walton

A Dozen Best According to Color

It is almost an impossible task to recommend the dozen best lilacs from one's own experience. Some plants stand out as exceptional, but what may be outstanding in New England may be average in the Midwest or poor on the Pacific Coast. Climate and soil play important roles in vigor, habit, color, fragrance, and hardiness. Some newer cultivars may find impossible to obtain, especially the cultivars selected from the progeny of the multipetaled *Syringa vulgaris* 'Rochester' crosses. They are exceedingly lovely and soft-colored. It would be easy to fill a garden from the work of a single hybridizer, but it is better to seek a variety of forms, single and double, early and late. Many of the newer lilacs and the Russian introductions are still relatively unknown. Several nurseries in North America, Europe, and Tasmania have been expanding the selection of good garden lilacs. Here are a dozen or more of the best from each color class, as chosen by Fiala.

Best White Lilacs (Class I)
  'Agnes Smith' (*S.* Villosae Group)
  'Alba' (*S. komarowii* subsp. *reflexa*)
  'Avalanche' (*S. vulgaris*)
  'Bicolor' (*S. ×chinensis*)
  'Candeur' (*S. vulgaris*)
  'Carley' (*S. vulgaris*)
  'Edith Cavell' (*S. vulgaris*)
  'Flora 1953' (*S. vulgaris*)
  'Monument' (*S. vulgaris*)
  'Mother Louise' (*S. vulgaris*)
  'Rochester' (*S. vulgaris*)
  'Slater's Elegance' (*S. vulgaris*)
  'Souvenir d'Alice Harding' (*S. vulgaris*)
  'Sovetskaya Arktika' (*S. vulgaris*)
  'St Joan' (*S. vulgaris*)
  'Summer White' (*S.* Villosae Group)

Best Violet Lilacs (Class II)
  'Agincourt Beauty' (*S. vulgaris*)
  'Dr John Rankin' (*S. vulgaris*)
  'Le Nôtre' (*S. vulgaris*)
  'Louvois' (*S. ×hyacinthiflora*)
  'M. I. Kalinin' (*S. vulgaris*)
  'Miss Kim' (*S. pubescens* subsp. *patula*)

'Pallida' (*S. josikaea*)
  'Pauline Fiala' (*S. vulgaris*)
  'Pocahontas' (*S. ×hyacinthiflora*)
  'Sesquicentennial' (*S. vulgaris*)
  'Violetta' (*S. vulgaris*)
  S. pubescens subsp. *patula*

Best Blue Lilacs (Class III)
  'Ami Schott' (*S. vulgaris*)
  'Blue Danube' (*S. vulgaris*)
  'Dwight D. Eisenhower' (*S. vulgaris*)
  'Laurentian' (*S. ×hyacinthiflora*)
  'Madame Charles Souchet' (*S. vulgaris*)
  'Maréchal Lannes' (*S. vulgaris*)
  'Mrs Elizabeth Peterson' (*S. vulgaris*)
  'Olivier de Serres' (*S. vulgaris*)
  'P. P. Konchalovskii' (*S. vulgaris*)
  'Saturnale' (*S. vulgaris*)
  'Sea Storm' (*S. vulgaris*)
  'Sumerki' (*S. vulgaris*)
  'True Blue' (*S. vulgaris*)
  'Wedgwood Blue' (*S. vulgaris*)

Best Lilac-colored Lilacs (Class IV)
  'Carolyn Mae' (*S. vulgaris*)
  'Isabella' (*S.* Villosae Group)
  'Leonid Leonov' (*S. vulgaris*)
  'Lullaby' (*S. vulgaris*)
  'Mollie Ann' (*S. vulgaris*)
  'Mrs John S. Williams' (*S. vulgaris*)
  'Victor Lemoine' (*S. vulgaris*)
  S. ×persica
  S. pubescens subsp. *julianae*

Best Pink Lilacs (Class V)
  'Edward J. Gardner' (*S. vulgaris*)
  'Elsie Lenore' (*S. vulgaris*)
  'Émile Lemoine' (*S. vulgaris*)
  'Ethel M. Webster' (*S.* Villosae Group)
  'George Eastman' (*S. pubescens* subsp. *julianae*)
  'Hers' (*S. pubescens* subsp. *julianae*)
  'Holy Maid' (*S. vulgaris*)
  'Lark Song' (*S.* Villosae Group)
  'Lee Jewett Walker' (*S. vulgaris*)
  'Lois Amee Utley' (*S. vulgaris*)
  'Lourene Wishart' (*S. vulgaris* Fiala, not Margaretten)
  'Lucie Baltet' (*S. vulgaris*)

Best Pink Lilacs (Class V) (continued)
'Maiden's Blush' (*S. ×hyacinthiflora*)
'Marie Francis' (*S. vulgaris*)
'Mary Short' (*S. ×hyacinthiflora*)
'Miss Canada' (*S.* Villosae Group)
'Mme Antoine Buchner' (*S. vulgaris*)
'Pink Parasol' (*S. pubescens* subsp. *julianae*)
'Romance' (*S. vulgaris*)
'Spellbinder' (*S.* Villosae Group)
'Springtime' (*S.* Villosae Group)
'Ursula' (*S.* Villosae Group)
'Utro Moskvy' (*S. vulgaris*)
S. komarowii subsp. *komarowii*
S. komarowii subsp. *reflexa*

Best Magenta Lilacs (Class VI)
'Arch McKean' (*S. vulgaris*)
'Capitaine Baltet' (*S. vulgaris*)
'Crayton Red' (*S.* Villosae Group)
'Epaulettes' (*S. pubescens* subsp. *julianae*)
'Frederick Douglass' (*S. vulgaris*)
'Georges Bellair' (*S. vulgaris*)
'Maréchal Foch' (*S. vulgaris*)
'Missimo' (*S. ×hyacinthiflora*)
'Mrs John W. Davis' (*S. vulgaris*)
'Mrs Watson Webb' (*S. vulgaris*)
'Paul Deschanel' (*S. vulgaris*)
'Paul Thirion' (*S. vulgaris*)
'Pink Cloud' (*S. ×hyacinthiflora*)
'Sunset' (*S. ×hyacinthiflora*)
S. komarowii

Best Purple Lilacs (Class VII)
'Anne Shiach' (*S. vulgaris*)
'De Croncels' (*S. vulgaris*)
'Donald Wyman' (*S.* Villosae Group)
'Dr Brethour' (*S. vulgaris*)
'Edith Braun' (*S. vulgaris*)
'Etna' (*S. vulgaris*)
'Flower City' (*S. vulgaris*)
'Frank Paterson' (*S. vulgaris*)
'Monge' (*S. vulgaris*)
'Mrs W. E. Marshall' (*S. vulgaris*)
'Nellie Bean' (*S.* Villosae Group)
'Prodige' (*S. vulgaris*)
'Purple Gem' (*S. ×hyacinthiflora*)
'Purple Glory' (*S. ×hyacinthiflora*)

'Sarah Sands' (*S. vulgaris*)
'Tom Taylor' (*S. ×hyacinthiflora*)
'Znamya Lenina' (*S. vulgaris*)
'Zulu' (*S. vulgaris*)

Lilacs of Special and Unique Color Classifications

A few lilacs belong in classes all their own; others have unique characteristics not ordinarily found in lilacs. Many could be mentioned, but here are some that are both outstanding and distinctive. The rayed and striped patterns in florets are a breakthrough to an entirely new series of pattern colors; most are from seedlings of *Syringa vulgaris* 'Rochester'.

'Albert F. Holden', single, Fiala 1980, deep purple buds opening to deep purple florets with a silver, showy two-color effect
'Atheline Wilbur', semidouble, Fiala 1979, deep rose-lavender buds opening to multipetaled florets of orchid, rose, and violet, excellent
'Blue Delft', single, Fiala 1982, deep blue buds opening to multipetaled florets that are rayed and striped dark and light blue, excellent
'General Sherman', single, Dunbar 1917, lavender buds opening to florets of pearled, pale pinkish lavender turning to creamy lavender, Dunbar's finest selection
'Krasavitsa Moskvy' (marketed in the United States as BEAUTY OF MOSCOW, in Germany as SCHÖNE VON MOSKAU), double, Kolesnikov 1974, pinkish lilac buds opening to double florets of very pale lavender tint on white; one of the finest lilacs in commerce, excellent in every way
'Mrs Trapman', single, Havemeyer 1943, a unique shade of old rose and lavender not usually seen in lilacs, somewhat small florets
'Ostrander', double, Klager 1928, outstanding combination of deep carmine with heliotrope and silver
'Pat Pesata', single, Fiala 1981, deep pink-lavender buds opening to multipetaled pale blue florets, edged, starred and eyed white, pearled pink over pale blue, very showy
'Porcelain Blue', single, Fiala 1981, multipetaled, pale pearled blue, excellent

'Primrose', single, G. Maarse 1949, butter cream yellow-green buds opening to small florets of pale creamy yellow, a yellowish color not yet found in any other lilac

'Professor Robert B. Clark', single, Fiala 1983, clear pale pink buds opening to very large multipetaled florets of pale pearled white, very effective and unique

'Rhapsody', single, Fiala 1983, unique color translucent blue and pearled pink, pink buds, very fine to excellent

Syringa vulgaris 'General Sherman'. B. Peart and M. Walton

Syringa vulgaris 'Krasavitsa Moskvy'. B. Peart and M. Walton

Syringa vulgaris 'Porcelain Blue'. B. Peart and M. Walton

Syringa vulgaris 'Primrose'. B. Peart and M. Walton

'Sensation', single, Eveleens Maarse 1938, deep purple buds opening to smaller florets of deep purple edged in white, a mutation of 'Hugo de Vries', periclinal chimera, outstandingly effective and unique

Syringa vulgaris 'Sensation'. B. Peart and M. Walton

Syringa vulgaris 'Silver King'. B. Peart and M. Walton

Syringa vulgaris 'Tiffany Blue'. John Fiala

'Siebold', double, Lemoine 1906, deep pink buds opening to double florets of pale pinkish creamy white, dwarf, excellent but difficult to find

'Silver King', single, Lemke 1941, lavender buds opening to florets of pearled silvery lavender, unique and very effective

'Tiffany Blue', single, Fiala 1984, outstanding shades of pearled blue colors, showy, large florets, excellent

Autumn Color in Lilacs

Although lilacs are not known for autumn leaf coloring, there are some notable exceptions. A few cultivars of *Syringa vulgaris* mostly in the whites, present a reasonable display of lemon yellow foliage, for example, 'White Lace'. Among the *S. pubescens* subsp. *patula* cultivars, autumn color is a most attractive change to

The leaves of all forms of *Syringa pubescens* subsp. *patula* turn soft reddish and mauve-purple in autumn. John Fiala

Syringa meyeri 'Palibin' leaves are an attractive reddish bronze in autumn. John Fiala

soft pastels of reddish and mauve purples; 'Miss Kim' displays a definite and consistent purplish fall color.

Syringa meyeri 'Palibin' has an attractive reddish bronze color, and many *S. ×hyacinthiflora* cultivars have wine and bronze leaves, for example, 'Lamartine' and 'Laurentian'.

Syringa oblata displays good fall colors. *Syringa oblata* subsp. *dilatata* seedling selections can be quite striking; they turn a deep purple to a reddish bronze.

The possibility of developing colorful seed pods on lilacs and autumn leaf color might be a future endeavor for an enterprising hybridizer. There are some fair yellow-podded *Syringa vulgaris* cultivars as well as a few of a light purplish hue.

Cultivars with Golden and Variegated Foliage

From time to time lilacs appear with gold or a combination of gold, white, and green variegations in their foliage. Most of them are novelties and not of genuine garden value. In the 18th century Philip Miller (1768) listed "white-blotch'd Lilac, *Lilac; flore albo, foliis ex albo variegatis*" and "yellow-blotch'd Lilac, *Lilac; flore albo, foliis ex luteo variegatis*," cultivars that disappeared long ago.

Several gold-variegated cultivars of *Syringa vulgaris* are known, but others await introduction. For example, 'Wittbold Variegated', found in the 1960s by Alan F. Block, a nurseryman from Romulus, Michigan, is reported to be growing in the Lumley collection at Lilacland, Pelham, Massachusetts, but has yet to be introduced. Colin Chapman (2001) reported a yet unnamed, single, purple, variegated seedling of *S.* (Villosae Group) 'Elinor', recorded as "62(a)/91." Frank and Corinna Moro (2003) reported several yet unnamed variegated late lilacs.

Pure gold-leaved forms include *Syringa emodi* 'Aurea' and the induced mutation *S.* (Villosae Group) 'Kum-Bum', which is of limited ornamental value in the garden. Tree lilacs with variegated foliage or golden foliage are relative newcomers; having made their first appearance in the 1990s, not much can be said about differences between cultivars and their performance. All gold-leaved plants need full sun. Most become a pale green as the season advances. Gold-leaved lilacs are a curiosity for the most part and cannot replace the named green-leaved cultivars. Since there is little demand for gold-leaved lilacs, they are almost impossible to find except as a rootlet or cutting from a large collection, arboretum, or lilac specialist.

Recommended gold-variegated cultivars of *Syringa vulgaris*:

'Aucubaefolia', Gouchault 1919, double bluish, the most widely known gold-variegated form of the species, appears to be a mutation of the double, bluish 'Président Grévy'

'Aurea', unknown origin pre-1880, single violet

'Dappled Dawn', Hauck 1966, single bluish, common in collections, available commercially

Syringa vulgaris 'Aucubaefolia'. B. Peart and M. Walton

Syringa vulgaris 'Dappled Dawn'. B. Peart and M. Walton

Syringa vulgaris 'Lutens'. B. Peart and M. Walton

Syringa reticulata subsp. *reticulata* 'Chantilly Lace'. B. Peart and M. Walton

'Lutens', Barankiewicz 1994, single pinkish to purple

'Quadricolor', Behnsch pre-1890, single lilac

Recommended gold-leaved cultivars of other *Syringa* species and interspecific hybrids:

S. emodi 'Aurea', origin not known, pre-1886, single, white

S. emodi 'Variegata', origin not known, pre-1877, single, white

S. ×hyacinthiflora 'Corinna's Mist', Moro 2001, single, pinkish

S. ×persica 'Taff's Treasure', Taffler pre-1999, single, purple

S. reticulata subsp. *reticulata* 'Cameo's Jewel', Moro 1995, single, white

S. reticulata subsp. *reticulata* 'Chantilly Lace', J. Herrmann ca. 1990, single, white

S. reticulata subsp. *reticulata* 'China Gold', Fiala 1990, single, white

S. reticulata subsp. *reticulata* 'Golden Eclipse', Bakker 2000, single, white

CHAPTER FIVE
Landscaping with Lilacs

I<small>N NORTHERN AND COLDER CLIMATES</small> the lilac is one of the most effective flowering shrubs. Among the earliest to bloom, its flowering period extends over a number of weeks, progressing from colorful buds to full bloom. It is a tough and hardy shrub, not often bothered by frosts and relatively free from major pests; it can be depended upon to be a mainstay of the spring landscape. Lilacs come in a wide range of colors (except yellows, oranges, and bright reds). In size and form they seem to be tailored to meet the needs of all gardens, large or small. They adapt well for a variety of practical needs, such as screens, hedges, trees, and specimen plantings. A well-grown lilac in full bloom, with its captivating fragrance, no matter what cultivar or color, is a breathtaking sight.

Lilacs are great as single specimens for close viewing and fragrance. They are outstanding where space allows them to be massed in groups of threes or fives, as background shrubs, for framing a view, or for hiding certain areas from view. No other spring shrub is so versatile for landscape use. To achieve the best effect, it is important to understand the lilac's needs, habit of growth, and ultimate size. Too often one sees beautiful lilacs crowded into a small space. Some lilac species and many newer and slower-growing cultivars are well suited for single-story homes while other lilacs are adapted for the largest estates.

Lilacs are specially well used when planted with companion plants and shrubs that enhance them either at flowering time by forming a fine background for the lilacs in bloom or, later in the season, by providing color against the green foliage of the midsummer lilacs. Several of these companion plants are discussed in chapter six. Whenever possible, plant some of your most scented lilacs where their fragrance might be carried by the prevailing winds across your garden.

In a garden of limited size, lilacs are best treated as specimen shrubs or dwarf hedges. In larger gardens, they can be used in various other ways not only for their bloom but also for their attractive deep green color in the landscape during the rest of the growing season.

Should you be planning a major collection of lilacs, or an arboretum with lilacs, you and members of your community may be wondering how such a development will affect the local environment. In Canada and the United States you may require an environmental assessment of your plans. NatureServe, the international agency overseeing the Invasive Species Assessment Protocol, has ranked the invasiveness of the common lilac, *Syringa vulgaris*, "insignificant" because it "rarely spreads to new areas" and when it does so, it "can be eradicated with relative ease when removal is desired" (NatureServe 2006).

Choosing a Proper Site for a Single Plant, a Lilac Garden, or a Collection

Where a lilac is planted is as important as how it is planted. There is a great difference between planting one lilac and a collection of lilacs, as in a lilac walk, or using lilacs in conjunction with other landscape plants. Select a location with good drainage, such as the top of a slope rather than the bottom, in mostly full sunlight and not crowded in by other large shrubs and trees.

For a single plant you can generally enrich the soil and provide good drainage. For a larger planting of several lilacs you must be more careful to provide the correct site. Follow the rules: good drainage, good soil, good sun, and proper care. Group lilacs in uneven numbers. Use colors that will not clash; use plenty of white-blooming lilacs mixed with other colors. Lilacs are perhaps best when grown with complementary flowering trees and shrubs and other plants, and with a background of choice evergreens that enhance their bloom. Never plant lilacs in straight rows centered in all directions like an apple orchard.

If you are planning a collection of lilacs, a walk, or an arboretum, then you should visit all the arboreta, parks, and large collections possible, especially those in your own area. It will be a delightful case of motivated learning. By carefully observing lilacs in bloom, you will be able to judge which cultivars and species are pleasing and which are not, and which might be suitable in your own garden. Take note of the lay of the land, its slopes and views, the kind of soil in which lilacs grow best, the drainage, and the exposure to sun. Notice how some of the best plantings limit what can be appreciated in an eyeshot and how they lead one on and on. Provide enticing previews from, perchance, a hilltop, with the invitation to come down into the sloping glen for a closer view, as at the Katie Osborne Lilac Garden (Hamilton, Ontario, Canada). Curve your lilac walk for interest, as at the Arnold Arboretum (Jamaica Plain, Massachusetts), or at Ewing Park (Des Moines, Iowa), to encourage further exploration. Or gradually unfold the lilac wonders with landscaped grassy walks and progressive vistas, as at the Holden Arboretum (Kirtland, Ohio). Or wander through the lilacs, as at Highland Botanical Park (Rochester, New York), Centennial Lilac Garden (Niagara Falls, Ontario), or Lilacia Park (Lombard, Illinois). Each of the great collections presents special in-

sights on to how and where one should plant lilacs. A lilac needs at least 10 feet (3 m) of space or more in each direction, even then they are somewhat crowded.

The Smaller Garden

For the smaller garden choose among *Syringa meyeri*, *S. oblata* subsp. *dilatata*, *S. pubescens*, *S. pubescens* subsp. *julianae*, *S. pubescens* subsp. *microphylla* var. *potaninii*, *S. pubescens* subsp. *patula*, and the slow-growing and dwarf cultivars of *S. vulgaris*. Use them as modestly growing background shrubs, as dwarf hedging (*S. meyeri* 'Palibin'), or as single specimens. From among the *S. vulgaris* cultivars consider 'Little Miss Muffet', 'Lucie Baltet', or 'Pixie' and from *S. ×hyacinthiflora* consider 'Purple Gem' or 'Purple Glory', none of which exceeds 5 feet (1.5 m) when grown on its own roots.

Syringa meyeri 'Palibin' is an outstanding, very small lilac of exceptional quality and bloom. There are many other cultivars listed throughout the various chapters that with a little pruning can well be kept at no more than 6–8 feet (1.8–2.4 m). *Syringa meyeri*, *S. meyeri* 'Palibin', and other dwarf lilacs perform well as potted shrubs for a roof garden or patio. *Syringa pubescens* and *S. pubescens* subsp. *julianae*, with their arching branches, and some of the lower-growing cultivars and species are well suited for Japanese gardens.

Lilacs line the path leading to Colonel Plum's original barn at Lilacia Park, Lombard, Illinois.
John Fiala

Introduced in the late 1800s, the short-growing *Syringa vulgaris* 'Lucie Baltet' is still among the finest cultivars for small gardens, including rock gardens. B. Peart and M. Walton

Syringa vulgaris 'Flora 1953' is a well-chosen specimen for home gardens. John Fiala

Lilacs on Hillsides, by Lakes, or at Riversides

One of the most effective uses of lilacs is in clumped groups on hillsides or slopes, where their blooming reflects in a tranquil lake or riverside. Lilacs will succumb if their roots are flooded, even for a brief time, by spring freshets. The secret to planting lilacs by lakes or rivers is to locate them on higher ground or atop banks that are well drained all year. The only lilac reputed to tolerate some wetness is the European *Syringa josikaea*, but never in standing water. Lilacs must have dry feet, free of flooding and free from the inroads of muskrat tunnels at their roots. Generally, a high spot or slope can be found or created along the water's edge where lilacs may hang their panicles to be reflected in the lake.

White lilacs reflect far better than any other color. *Syringa komarowii* subsp. *reflexa* 'Alba', *S. vulgaris* 'Miss Ellen Willmott' and the older *S. vulgaris* 'Macrostachya', and *S.* ×*hyacinthiflora* 'Lewis Maddock', with its carmine buds and pale pink blooms, are simply beautiful in their watery reflections. The blues and dark purples are poor reflectors. Stick to the whites.

Often some of the species lilacs can be naturalized at the water's edge. There used to be a planting of *Syringa pubescens* subsp. *julianae* seedlings made by Bernard Slavin at Durand-Eastman Park, Rochester, New York, that had self-sown and taken over a sweep of the river banks high above the water and had become a thicket of naturalized seedlings—a sight to behold in bloom and a natural landscaping masterpiece. These species lilacs rooted their arching branches and self-sowed the banks. From one of these seedlings came the beautiful selection *S. pubescens* subsp. *julianae* 'George Eastman'. Certainly on high banks, *S.* ×*chinensis*, *S.* ×*persica*, the beautiful *S. pubescens*, *S. pubescens* subsp. *microphylla*, or *S. pubescens* subsp. *patula* could well be used massed in such a waterside natural planting.

If you have a hillside, flaunt it with an array of lilacs. On gentle, fertile slopes lilacs can make a spectacular display, especially if there is the opportunity to look slightly down on them from an opposite rise or from above. This is marvelously done at Arnold Arboretum and Royal Botanical Gardens, Hamilton.

With a natural outcropping of granite or stone or a valley beyond, the vista is even more attractive, for instance, at Lilacland in Pelham, Massachusetts. Avoid northern and northwestern sides of slopes; they are generally too cold and receive less sun. Often the windchill factor and false spring bursts damage lilac buds on the very tops of hillsides. It may be that you will have to add some background of conifers or flowering trees.

The very deep purples have little, if any, carrying power over distance, so they need an abundance of white lilacs or silver-leaved shrubs behind them. Most

Lilacs reflecting their images in water at Lilacland, the Lumley estate in Pelham, Massachusetts. John Fiala

of the deep purple lilacs are later bloomers. Russian olive (*Elaeagnus angustifolia*), with its silvery leaves, is a breathtaking background for dark-blooming purple lilacs.

Generally, the species lilacs, the later Villosae Group cultivars, and many of the newer interspecific hybrids are better for creating a naturalized effect along hillsides and water's edge than are the heavier-blooming Villosae Group cultivars. A planting of 'Isabella' or 'Ursula' or a massing of 'Agnes Smith', 'Anna Amhoff', or 'Lark Song', or 'Summer White'—all Villosae Group cultivars—would be most impressive reflected in a waterside planting or on a hillside or slope. The old hillside plantings of *Syringa* ×*chinensis* 'Bicolor' at Highland Botanical Park indicate what can be expected from fine cultivars with time. Several parks such as Highland Botanical Park, Royal Botanical Gardens, Arnold Arboretum, and Holden Arboretum are laid out on hillside slopes. Thus one can appreciate what can be accomplished on a smaller, or larger, scale elsewhere. One must project the landscape vision to what is expected of the lilac planting at maturity, 20 or more years hence. Mostly we plan and plant for the next generation to appreciate and view, so it must be planned well for the beauty and the wonderful fragrance of the flowers.

The massed planting of lilacs at Grape Hill Gardens in Clyde, New York, is both breathtaking in its beauty and extremely well done. John Fiala

Lilacs for Miniature or Rock Gardens

Most of us think of lilacs as rather large, sometimes unmanageable shrubs. Since the 1950s, as hybridizers have transformed the blossom into wonderful size and colors, they also have worked wonders with the form and shape of the lilac bush, producing excellent, tidy, miniature plants. They have custom tailored the lilac for smaller gardens, including rock gardens. There are now lilacs that rarely grow more than 3–4 feet (90–120 cm) tall. You can have the beauty and fragrance of lilacs in your landscape but on a much smaller scale.

Syringa meyeri 'Palibin' is a slow-growing cultivar that is easily confined to a height of 4 feet (1.2 m) or less. The Chinese love it for their small, walled, patio gardens. It has lovely lavender blossoms that cover the plant in spring, while throughout the rest of the year it is most attractive with small, deep green, glossy leaves, similar to those of a larger boxwood. It is an excellent choice for a hedge, border, or in the rock garden. It never looks unkempt, needs very little pruning, is excellent with golden alyssum (*Aurinia saxatilis*) or rock plants, and will occasionally produce a moderate bloom in late summer or early fall if weather conditions are ideal. Try it with the earliest white clematis spilling over rocks at its feet or plant it against an old stone wall where its deep purple buds and lav-

Rarely reaching 5 feet (1.5 m) tall, *Syringa meyeri* 'Palibin', seen here at the University of Guelph Arboretum, Guelph, Ontario, Canada, is the dwarfest lilac. John Fiala

ender blossoms give a splash of bright color to the meandering gray-tan wall with very late yellow daffodils around it.

Syringa oblata subsp. *dilatata* usually will not exceed 5–6 feet (1.5–1.8 m). Very early in spring it is covered with beautiful, feathery, lavender-bluish flowers with a wonderful fragrance. In the fall it has the added attraction of deep reddish lavender-purple leaves; it is one of the few lilacs with autumn color. Hummingbirds seem to delight in building their small, silky nests in its branches. Subspecies *dilatata* requires very little pruning, although as is true of all lilacs, it benefits from some trimming and thinning.

Syringa pubescens subsp. *patula* 'Miss Kim' and *S. pubescens* subsp. *patula* 'Klmone' (marketed as MISS SUSIE) are fine selections and much more attractive than the wild subspecies from the Korean mountains. Under ordinary garden conditions they will not exceed 5–6 feet (1.5–1.8 m). Both have an aromatic fragrance; in the fall their foliage turns russet, wine, and red-purple. 'Miss Kim' or 'Klmone' can be used very successfully in smaller city gardens and in rock gardens. They serve well as a focal point in any garden.

Cultivars in the Fairytale Series (*Syringa meyeri* 'Palibin' × *S. pubescens* subsp. *microphylla* 'Superba'), originated by Neal Holland of North Dakota State University, Fargo, include 'Bailbelle' (marketed as TINKERBELLE), 'Baildust' (FAIRY DUST), 'Bailina' (THUMBELINA), 'Bailming' (PRINCE CHARMING), and 'Bailsugar' (SUGAR PLUM FAIRY). All of these grow to just 5–6 feet (1.5–1.8 m) tall and are admirably suited for the smaller garden.

Dwarf or low-growing cultivars of the common lilac, *Syringa vulgaris*, never seem to outgrow their bounds, need little pruning, and are magnificently fragrant and good bloomers. They are enchanting when planted along a miniature garden path or in a rock garden. 'Lucie Baltet' is a very old favorite with coppery-pink florets. 'Purple Gem', 'Purple Glory', and the more difficult to grow 'L'Oncle Tom' are very deep purple. The deep purple dwarfs are very slow growers and a bit more difficult to establish, not tolerating wetness one bit. 'Little Miss Muffet', introduced in 1977, rarely exceeds 3–4 feet (90–120 cm) when grown on its own roots. Grafted on rootstock, these dwarfs grow much larger. 'Little Miss Muffet' has a rather large thyrse of deep magenta reddish violet,

Like all deep purple dwarfs, *Syringa vulgaris* 'L'Oncle Tom' is slow-growing and difficult to establish. B. Peart and M. Walton

Low-growing *Syringa vulgaris* 'Little Miss Muffet' is ideal in a miniature or Japanese garden. John Fiala

opening to lavender-pink flowers. 'Mount Domogled', a dwarf form of *S. vulgaris* brought to the United States in 1935 by Edgar Anderson, who collected it near Băile Herculane on the southern face of Mount Domogled in Romania, has flowers that are quite fragrant. 'Prairie Petite', developed by Glenn Viehmeyer and introduced in 1998, rarely exceeds 3 feet (90 cm) in height and width. Originally intended primarily for further breeding of small garden lilacs, this cultivar has been introduced commercially.

Although dwarf and slow-growing lilac cultivars used to be rather difficult to find in nurseries, modern micropropagation techniques have drastically changed the nursery scene. These small lilacs definitely have a place, and an important one, in our modern smaller gardens. They are lovely combined with the many fine dwarf conifers and rock plants now available.

In choosing suitable lilacs, knowledge of the newer introductions and observation of growth habits and forms of these lilac cultivars will aid considerably in achieving the overall effect one seeks to create in the smaller, miniature or rock garden. Like all lilacs, the dwarf cultivars need excellent drainage, full sun, good soil, and very moderate pruning. It is a pity that so beautiful and versatile a shrub as the dwarf or low-growing lilac is neglected by so many landscapers due to lack of knowledge of these plants. Alas, commercial garden landscapers tend to rely on local nurs-

Lilacs in a rock garden setting at Royal Botanical Gardens, Hamilton, Ontario, Canada. John Fiala

ery sources for their choice of plants. Some of the nurseries known to specialize in lilacs are listed in appendix C.

Lilacs in Japanese and Chinese Gardens

Although China is the center of origin of the genus *Syringa*, only a few species, subspecies, and varieties appear to be grown in Asian gardens. Why should they not be a part of every Chinese garden? How could they be out of place in their own native setting? These questions can be answered only by garden or landscape architects or garden historians from China or Japan, or those who studied the traditions of oriental gardens and their plants. The five essays in *On Chinese Gardens* by Chen Congzhou (1984), eminent expert on ancient architecture and garden culture, are highly recommended to readers who want to explore the history and philosophy of Chinese gardens.

Simulating an oriental landscape scene in an occidental setting is a different matter. What could be more oriental than the captivating fragrance of *Syringa pubescens*, the delicate subspecies *julianae* or *patula*, or the feathery spikes of subspecies *microphylla* var. *potaninii*? Only the winds, rains, soil, hills, and rocky outcrops of their native China that have been their home for eons.

How magnificently the Peking lilac, *Syringa pekinensis*, blooms in the walled gardens of old Beijing as it has for centuries on the fringes of the Beijing mountains, shedding white-plumed blossoms like a blessing on China's valleys below. It is a marvelous tree for the background or as a single specimen. Another tree lilac, *S. reticulata* subsp. *reticulata*, has a somewhat better shape—it is a bit rounder. Other lilacs that can be skillfully incorporated in an oriental garden are the showy *S. komarowii* and the beautiful semiweeping *S. komarowii* subsp. *reflexa*. Both are background shrubs for such gardens as they eventually become too large for a specimen planting.

When planting a lilac in a Japanese garden, it is important to select both the plant and its exact location with discretion. Generally Japanese gardens have considerable shade and screening, whereas lilacs demand sunshine to perform their best. A few of the feathery hybrids can often be very proper in such landscaping; 'Spellbinder' and 'Sunrise' from the Villosae Group are two such examples. 'Pendula' makes a good distant background for a Japanese garden, and the very rare *Syringa pinnatifolia* is a real treasure at the crossing of two paths.

Lilacs in Suburban Gardens and Country Estates

Larger gardens of close to an acre (0.4 ha) or more belong in a special category where the gardener can do marvelous things with special lilac plantings. Suburban gardens and estate properties differ from other home sites in that they are too large to be called a city lot or a yard, and cannot simply be dismissed as a farm. They are in a class all their own that requires creating a larger vista of beauty. They also offer more opportunities for massed plantings that allow special effects and the challenges of using a wider variety of plants. Larger gardens enable gardeners to develop areas of naturalized landscaping. Often, these larger properties have lakes, ponds, hillsides, or beautiful valleys. In these situations the lilacs' proper places and how to use them most effectively demand serious consideration, either as single specimens, in massed plantings, reflected in watersides, or as hedges, boundary lines, or walks. Here, too, they can be framed by conifers, flowering trees, and hosts of other plants.

In these gardens, lilacs are planted for close-up beauty and fragrance as well as for creating more distant vistas of color. For close viewing use the larger-flowered kinds, especially some of the newer cultivars that are so striking in their colors and hues. For vistas use three to five of the same cultivar or color for a mass planting. A friend of Fiala's who loved the newer large-floreted and deep-colored lilacs that are not always as fragrant as some of the older kinds solved this problem by planting an occasional very fragrant older lilac in the background to fill her garden with their wonderful scent.

Some prima donnas of the lilac world are admirably suited for close-up inspection or as focal points. Consider a stately 'Maréchal Foch' standing sentry by a garden path in pale pink epaulettes with deeper carmine chevrons, or an 'Émile Lemoine'. Equally outstanding is the ballerina-pink bloom of 'Lucie Baltet' in coppery pink. Do not overlook the Dutch sport so aptly named 'Sensation' with its deep purple florets edged in white Dutch lace; it must be seen to be appreciated. The rayed and starred pale blue of 'Pat Pesata' is unique and beautiful, as is the pale blue of 'Dwight D. Eisenhower'. Then there are the pristine whites of 'Carley', 'Flora 1953', or 'Slater's Elegance', or the abundant bloom of 'Aloise', or the doubles 'Souvenir d'Alice Harding' and 'St Joan', or the incomparable beauty of 'Rochester', if you can wait the many years it requires to reach maturity. They are truly outstanding as single specimens for close viewing. In the deep red-purples, plant as specimens 'Agin-

Syringa ×hyacinthiflora 'Asessippi' at Meadowlark Hill, the estate of Max and Darlene Peterson, in Ogalla, Nebraska. John Fiala

Lilacs line a pathway. B. Peart and M. Walton

court Beauty', 'Anne Shiach', 'Arch McKean', or 'Sarah Sands'. In chapter four we have listed some of the finest lilacs by color. All are equally beautiful in either single or double blossoms, but the single lilacs are a better choice if you prefer large flowers and deep purple colors.

A Garden Lilac Walk

Nothing is more pleasing than to be able to come upon rare specimens of lilacs along a winding grassy path. Arnold Arboretum has for many years had a splendid Lilac Walk, displaying many cultivars and species planted along the roadway and adjacent to a hillside of lilacs. Ewing Park (Des Moines, Iowa) and many others have outstanding walks where one can see both the massed effect and the close-up character of individual lilacs. Among the finest private walks

is the one at Lilacland in Pelham, Massachusetts. The newer plantings at the Holden Arboretum are likewise examples of excellent planning, careful selection of some of the finest cultivars, and ease in viewing.

Historically, lilac walks were planted along a winding path, rather close together and for some distance without interplanting of other shrubs or trees, but in the summertime and fall they are simple shrubs quickly passed over. If you feel that your lilac walk ought to be a bit more updated, interplant the lilacs with other flowering trees and shrubs and conifers for a constant succession of interest in bloom and fruit throughout the year. To achieve this most pleasing effect, lilacs need to be grouped in threes, fives, or sevens at vantage points along the walk. Place them where they tempt the visitor to continue to discover new combinations and cultivars along the way. A group of early-blooming lilacs can be separated by a few choice conifers from very late blooming ones, which in turn can be separated by some other flowering trees or shrubs from the midseason kinds. On occasion, plant a single outstanding specimen such as 'Sensation' or 'St Joan' with a garden bench for your guests to rest and view that particular lilac. Interspersed among the many lilac plantings could be flowering crab apples, conifers, *Davidia*, *Magnolia*, *Aesculus pavia*, *Viburnum*, or even beds with *Paeonia* and *Hemerocallis* (see chapter six for details on these and other companion plants). With careful choice of cultivars and species, one can extend the length of bloom of a good lilac walk for several weeks.

Lilacs by Woodland Borders

Often, the landscape tie of a lawn and a garden with a neighboring woodland is not an easily created transition. The English had a solution, creating the ha-ha, a walled ditch or sunken hedge that created a barrier (especially for livestock) without impairing the view. Lilacs can assist in transition if they are placed between the garden and the naturalized forest.

Species lilacs are the ideal planting at the wood's edge with adequate sun. In their native China, many of the species lilacs are shrubs of the forest edge, where they often form small thickets. *Syringa vulgaris* in its native Balkan mountain habitat also is at home in open woodland spaces among stony outcrops and in rocky areas. In a larger garden or park such lilacs can play a similar role. Plant the rather tall, treelike early hybrids in small clumps of threes, all of one cultivar some 20–30 feet (6–9 m) from the woodland's edge. Combine them with intervals of flowering dogwoods or some of the better flowering crab apples and you will have a wonderful, natural-looking buffer zone of bloom between the heavy forest and its surrounding areas. One does not look for massive continuous bloom in such cases but for pockets of bloom along the landscape horizon.

White birch trunks with pale pink or lavender lilacs can be a great combination. 'Lamartine', 'Lewis Maddock', or 'Louvois' backed by flowering dogwoods (*Cornus florida*) are sheer elegance. The heavier-flowering *Syringa vulgaris* cultivars are too overpowering with their massive bloom. Try some of Frank Skinner's cultivars or use *S. oblata* subsp. *dilatata* in pale lavender, feathery drifts. *Syringa komarowii*, *S. pubescens*, *S. pubescens* subsp. *julianae*, *S. sweginzowii*, and many of the fine *S.* ×*chinensis* cultivars such as 'Bicolor' are excellent choices. Do not crowd them together, but leave spaces for open small meadows in which to naturalize large drifts of spring bulbs, especially late-blooming daffodils. For summer and autumn color, sow in these open spaces wildflowers such as daisies (*Chrysanthemum*) and later drifts of hardy asters. If you plant some of the *S. oblata* subsp. *dilatata* hybrids, not only will your spring woodland be perfumed but in autumn these lilacs will give a display of deep wine and purple foliage.

Another fine woodside lilac is *Syringa pubescens* subsp. *patula* with its aromatic fragrance and pale mauve autumn foliage. If space allows plant an occasional small tree lilac such as *S. reticulata* subsp. *reticulata* alone or in groups of three. Many of the late-blooming cultivars in the Villosae Group or the newer multibrid 'Springtime' are excellent when used in this fashion. However, do not overdo the buffer area with lilacs; they do not add anything but green shrubbery the rest of the year—and there are other beautiful shrubs as well that could be planted among them.

Lilacs as Small Trees in the Garden

Lilacs can make excellent small trees if properly trained and pruned. The tree lilacs, *Syringa reticulata* and its subspecies, and *S. pekinensis*, which bloom in late June or early July, can grow too large for the smaller garden. Instead, plant one of the early hybrids such as *S. oblata* subsp. *oblata* 'Giraldii', which is more apt to make an excellent small tree if trimmed back to two or three trunks. The early hybrids is more rangy and taller growing than the *S. oblata* subsp. *dilatata* hybrids and range in color from pinks to lavenders with few whites. They do not sucker so readily.

Each year prune out all the lower and weak branches, and soon you will have a fine spreading tree. The blossoms will not be at eye level and will be considerably smaller due to minimal pruning, but you will have lilacs with wonderful fragrance and an interesting tree. An occasional specimen treated this way can provide shade for the patio and be underplanted with a circle of ferns and *Impatiens* surrounded by a circular brick mosaic.

Early hybrid lilacs make excellent small patio trees. With age their trunks assume the typical twist so characteristic of *Syringa vulgaris* and their somewhat shaggy bark is also very attractive. With a little care, even an occasional borer seems to do little harm if good culture and ordinary pest control are practiced. Some of the taller *S. vulgaris* cultivars, such as 'Mme Antoine Buchner', 'Mrs Trapman', 'Sarah Sands', or the unique 'Sensation' and 'Silver King', do well treated in this manner. If there is space, plant three of these small trees together, about 20 feet (6 m) apart, prune high, and plant a magnificent bed of *Hosta* cultivars in their shade.

Lilacs for Hedges and Screens

Lilacs have been used successfully as screens, hedges, and backgrounds. Their height and density of branches admirably suit them for such purposes. There is also an aesthetic use of lilac hedges and screens in carrying the eye through long vistas to a focal point.

We no longer depend on *Syringa vulgaris* or *S. villosa*; there are newer, excellent cultivars. Many of the lesser-known lilacs make excellent smaller hedges and screens, such as *S. josikaea S. komarowii*, *S. pubescens* subsp. *microphylla*, and the newer cultivars in the Villosae Group. Large parks and estates will benefit by boldly incorporating these plants in their landscapes. Some of the older *S.* ×*chinensis* cultivars have been used with excellent results on the hillsides as a screen at Highland Botanical Park, while *S.* ×*persica* in a long row is magnificent at Royal Botanical Gardens,

A hedge featuring *Syringa* ×*chinensis*. B. Peart and M. Walton

Syringa meyeri 'Palibin' makes a natural low-growing hedge at the University of Guelph, Guelph, Ontario, Canada. John Fiala

Syringa vulgaris used as a property screen along a New York highway. John Fiala

Hamilton. Envision a winding background hedge of 'Agnes Smith' or a screen of a dozen plants of *S. pubescens* subsp. *julianae* 'Hers' as a spreading background to smaller plantings of flowers or spring bulbs. Far more use should be made of the best of the Villosae Group cultivars as screens and taller hedges. They are strong and rugged shrubs; given room to develop, good ground, and a side dressing of compost and fertilizer, they will be a success.

To see lilacs in smaller gardens and on large estates visit the Shelburne Museum (Shelburne, Vermont) at lilac time, and the fine old lilac plantings at Woodstock, Vermont; Cooperstown, New York; and Portsmouth, New Hampshire.

How to Design or Remodel a Large Lilac Collection

During 1979–1980 at the Holden Arboretum, under the farsighted direction of R. Henry Norweb Jr. (1918–1995), a whole new vision of lilacs in a new arboretum design was accomplished with astounding results—a tribute to the director and staff. The design was the work of Charles L. "Pete" Knight (1911–2001), landscape architect and senior partner of the Cleveland firm of Knight and Stoller. The new Lilac Walk was laid out on 7 acres (2.8 ha), featuring about 260 lilacs, including about 125 plants that were 40 or more years old, saved and transplanted from the original collection. A large transplanting and holding operation had to be undertaken, necessitating considerable labor and expense.

The soil at Holden was found to be a shallow, heavy clay with shale not far below. This is a real problem for most plants, especially lilacs. To overcome the effect of poor drainage, raised beds were constructed. Mounds were built; in cross section they consisted of a 3-inch (7.5-cm) layer of sandy gravel, 9–12 inches (23–30 cm) of topsoil, 3 inches (7.5 cm) of well-rotted manure, topped by a bark mulch. Twenty-five years later David Gressley (31 January 2005, pers. comm. to F.V.), horticulturist at the arboretum, reported:

Having maintained the Demonstration/Display Gardens from 1987 until 2003, I can tell you that the plan is largely successful. The raised beds and subsurface drainage appear to be largely intact, have maintained their integrity. Several areas were amended with a silica-based soil mix to improve soil drainage under my administration. One area in particular required extensive renovation because the original grade consisted of a compacted gravel surface used for vehicle traffic. The resulting hardpan resulted in water retention in the root zone. After further amending and grade raising, the problem was abated, at least for the time being. The beds were mulched with composted leaf mold for several years which seemed to increase the vitality of the plants.

The complete redesigning and replanting of the Holden Arboretum lilac collection is an example that will be of interest to any other arboretum, large park, or large private collection planning a lilac display or contemplating the rejuvenation of an older collection. A fine collection of lilacs will attract thousands of visitors annually to see them in bloom.

The basic layout of the Katie Osborne Lilac Garden at Royal Botanical Gardens, Hamilton, is somewhat different. Shortly before his retirement as arboriculturist, Charles D. Holetich (1995) wrote in his final *Horticultural Leaflet*:

Where Old Guelph Road underpasses Highway 403 was the location of the first lilac collection of Royal Botanical Gardens. In the fall of 1960 and spring of 1961, the collection (approximately 100 different lilacs) was moved to its present location in the Arboretum, which was cleared from existing woods. Apart from occasional leveling for the grass path, the existing ground contours are those of the original natural landscape. In 1965, the collection caught the interest of a Gardens' friend whose subsequent generosity resulted in a greatly expanded garden. In the Katie Osborne Lilac Garden at present [1995] are displayed 802 different kinds of lilacs, which makes it the largest such collection in the world. It stands in memory of one who was fond of lilacs and had a special interest in Royal Botanical Gardens, Hamilton. Different exposures within the Lilac Dell are used to grow specific groups of lilacs such as single or double French Hybrids, Prestoniae hybrids, early flowering hybrids, species, etc. Though the lilacs are sun-loving plants, occasional trees from the original forest were left as an aesthetic contribution to the rolling grounds, this creating a pleasant environment throughout the year.

The landscape designs for the Holden Arboretum and Royal Botanical Gardens take their places with other well-designed lilac collections in the United States and Canada, such as the Arnold Arboretum, Highland Botanical Park, Ewing Park, and the Jardin botanique de Montréal.

In designing an arboretum with a special collection, one of the first requirements is the establishment of parameters of financial expenditures for the entire program. Since the Holden design was envisioned as a new type of lilac walk it included many other genera and species of trees and shrubs. The design must incorporate existing natural boundaries, topography, soils, microclimates, the existing planting, and the relationship with other areas adjacent to the lilac planting. All existing features need to be mapped in relationship to future access requirements. High and low tree forms, and medium and low massings need to be considered in relationship to wooded areas and lawns

or meadows. The site must be attractive at all seasons, especially in the spring and early summer, when everyone is aware of growing plants and flowers. Evergreens should be included for winter interest and background for floral displays, as well as other genera that are spectacular in fruit or fall foliage. Because of limited area, only the choicest species and cultivars should be displayed. A working collection elsewhere should carry the more complete lilac inventory. Last but not least, a plan should allow for viewing of plant groupings arranged in the most pleasing combination of size, texture, and color, not just as specimens, while still permitting close inspection of individual plants for identification, study, and enjoyment.

Criteria for lilac selection should include mature height of plants, texture of foliage, color of bloom, hardiness, phenological aspects (bloom date, fall color if any, and so on), and the several types (species; early-, mid-, or late-season blooming; hybrids). The overall design should include circulation criteria (width and gradient of drives, walks, and paths, and access for maintenance equipment), relation of turf panels to planting beds, the possible inclusion of water (pools or swales, or both), filler plants among the lilacs, and fall and winter effect. Lilacs and permanent plantings

Lilacs at Highland Botanical Park, Rochester, New York, in peak bloom in late May. John Fiala

Lilacs at Shelburne Museum, near Burlington, Vermont. John Fiala

A mass planting of *Syringa pubescens* subsp. *patula* 'Miss Kim' at Centennial Lilac Garden, Niagara Falls, Ontario, Canada. John Fiala

need to be spaced for their size at maturity. Filler plants are expendable and must be removed before crowding the lilacs.

It is hoped that in years to come a few large arboreta and parks here and there will be planning and designing large, authenticated collections of lilacs.

Lilacs in the Winter Landscape

Winter is a good time to take a close look at the diversity of buds, bark, and seed pods and review last season's growth, assess shaping (pruning) strategies, and needs for nourishment. Fat, thick growth indicates that all is well; thin, spindly growth indicates a need for pruning and more food.

Be kind to the winter birds and place feeders on the heaviest lilac branches. Perchance, they will return there to nest and warble songs mid the lilac blooms of May. Look also to what insect pests or rodents feast unknown to you upon your lilacs. Scale and borer holes give testimony to summertime negligence in spraying and pruning.

Winter is a time for marking with bright tags lilac root suckers that are to be dug and used to produce new plants. At the same time, mark old lilacs for removal, plan new beds, and see the heavy framework of both trees and shrubs.

The Best Species Lilacs as Garden and Landscape Shrubs

In presenting this evaluation of the species as garden plants, we have in mind gardens that have enough room to grow one or several lilacs. If only one lilac can be included, then we strongly recommend one of the finer cultivars of *Syringa vulgaris*.

The largest arboreta and botanical gardens should have space enough to carry a good collection of all the species lilacs, good or indifferent. There are good reasons for having such a collection: botanists like to see specimens from different sites of the natural range of the species, and horticulturists and breeders are interested in collections from the wild that show morphological differences that may widen the gene pool available for future hybridizing. It is interesting to note that the North American Plant Collections Consortium of the American Association of Botanical Gardens and Arboreta (2001: p. x), now the American Public Gardens Association,

(1) coordinates plant collections development in botanical gardens in order to ensure that rare, unusual, or threatened collections held in only a few botanical gardens are replicated elsewhere for safe keeping and to minimize duplication so that new collections preserve plant groups not currently found in botanical gardens, and (2) ensures that plant collections are well maintained and of high quality by increasing genetic diversity in them and by improving collection management practices in order to maintain, document, and protect important collections.

Recommended lilac species for landscapes large and small:

Subgenus *Ligustrina* (tree lilacs)

S. pekinensis. Too large for the home garden unless used as a specimen tree. Better suited for the largest gardens, arboreta, and botanical gardens.

S. reticulata subsp. *reticulata.* A small upright tree. The finest tree lilac for smaller home gardens.

S. reticulata subsp. *amurensis.* A small rounded tree. Almost identical to subsp. *reticulata* but not as desirable for home gardens.

Subgenus *Syringa*, Series *Syringa*

S. oblata subsp. *dilatata.* Lower growing than other forms of *S. oblata.* One of the first lilacs to bloom. Has wonderful mauve-purple foliage in the autumn.

S. protolaciniata. Rarely seen, even in botanical collections.

S. vulgaris. Has brought forth the finest cultivars, but progeny from plants or seeds collected in the native range of the species may not be worth a spot in your garden.

Subgenus *Syringa*, Series *Pinnatifolia*

S. pinnatifolia. An interesting shrub but only for the largest gardens and arboreta. Rarely seen today even in botanical collections.

Subgenus *Syringa*, Series *Pubescentes* (little-leaved lilacs)

S. meyeri. Slow growing. Excellent for the garden.

S. pubescens subsp. *pubescens.* A fine lilac for the garden although it needs some width to show its full beauty.

S. pubescens subsp. *julianae.* One of the finest lilacs for the garden but needs room to develop.

S. pubescens subsp. *microphylla* var. *microphylla.* A very heavy bloomer. Excellent for the larger garden

S. pubescens subsp. *microphylla* var. *potaninii.* Good cerise buds and intermittent bloom. Not an excellent garden shrub because its wood is too brittle.

S. pubescens subsp. *patula.* Very delicate, refined. Excellent in every way.

Subgenus *Syringa*, Series Villosae (large-leaved, late-blooming lilacs)

S. emodi. For the largest collections and arboreta only. Not for the home garden.

S. josikaea. A fine, deep green-leaved lilac good for large gardens.

S. komarowii subsp. *komarowii.* A fine lilac for large or small gardens.

S. komarowii subsp. *reflexa.* Has showy, drooping blossoms. Needs room to show its excellent form. A truly unique lilac.

S. sweginzowii. A slender, tall grower. Good accent shrub. Very fine.

S. tomentella. Good for larger gardens, estates, and arboreta. Not for the home garden.

S. villosa. For larger gardens only. For home gardens, its cultivars in the Villosae Group are far superior.

S. wolfii. A fine plant for the larger garden, but its hybrids are far superior.

S. yunnanensis. A poor plant all around for the home garden. Only for the largest species collections and for hybridizers.

CHAPTER SIX
Companion Plants to Lilacs

L<small>ILACS POSSESS</small> an outstanding and unique beauty. They are very attractive because of the masses of color, bloom, and captivating fragrance in springtime. However, they are enhanced by many different companion plants. Some plants are particularly suited by their form, background color, bloom, or compatibility and harmony to grow together with lilacs.

Magnificent Conifers and Lilacs

Among nature's most beautiful trees one must certainly count the conifers—pines (*Pinus*), spruces (*Picea*), hemlocks (*Tsuga*), firs (*Abies*), cedars (*Cedrus*), false cypresses (*Chamaecyparis*), yews (*Taxus*), and a host of others. In large gardens mature conifer specimens rise like pillars into the sky, bold sentries of the landscape, keeping a watchful eye over all they survey. Others are magnificent weepers spreading farther each year. Cones on evergreens with their subtleties of color, texture, and form add an extra dimension. The evergreens can be a tremendous asset as backgrounds to plantings and shrub borders, and especially for lilacs.

Discover by observation of conifers, as in lilacs, which species and cultivars are best suited for your own location, then proceed with your planning and planting. Some conifers are limited by climate, others by size or space. There are many selections of dwarf and miniature evergreens to choose from. The Gotelli Collection of Dwarf and Slow-Growing Conifers and the Watnong Pinetum Collection at the U.S. National Arboretum in Washington, D.C. (Cutler 1997), and the collection at the Arnold Arboretum are among the finest in the world to see these smaller forms ideally suited for limited garden space.

Some conifers, such as pines, spruces, hemlocks, and firs, can be grown in nearly any garden. The selection of a particular variety suited for your location need be your only concern. For backgrounds, property dividers, and windbreaks, they have served for centuries, often without respect for their individual character and beauty (like soldiers lined up for duty). In our gardens they must become individuals, respected each for what they are and how they share their grace and character with the whole garden.

Ewing Park, Des Moines, Iowa, is among the great lilac collections that use conifers and lilacs together extremely well. Conifers do not dominate these parks and gardens—they attend and enhance the lilacs planted around them: the blue- and pink-flowering lilacs with blue-toned conifers, the whites with dark green or even golden backgrounds, and the pale lavender tones with medium green conifers. The deep purple lilacs, with flashing dark tresses, must have lighter backgrounds of intermediary, early-flowering shrubs or small trees. Their bloom is lost when planted directly against dark conifers.

Conifers make an excellent background for lilacs at Royal Botanical Gardens, Hamilton, Ontario, Canada. Note also the low underplanting. John Fiala

Pink-flowering lilacs like *Syringa* ×*hyacinthiflora* 'Mary Short' go well with blue or dark green conifers. B. Peart and M. Walton

Some of the exotic weeping forms of hemlock or spruce do well as a distant background for lilacs. All large conifers serve as distant backgrounds for anything planted in front of them; they need room for development. In planting lilacs, one can generally use only the eastern, southern, and southwestern sides of evergreen back-planting; the lilacs need sunlight. Never plant lilacs on the northern side of evergreens or other trees. This rule holds true for most flowering trees.

Consider some of these conifers for your lilacs: *Abies concolor* (one of the finest), *A. homolepis* var. *umbellata*, *A. koreana*, *A. procera*, *Cedrus libani* 'Glauca' (where winters are not so severe it is excellent), *Chamaecyparis obtusa* 'Gracilis', *C. pisifera* 'Boulevard', *Cryptomeria japonica*, *Juniperus scopulorum* 'Gray Gleam', *Picea omorika*, *P. pungens* 'Koster', *Pinus bungeana* (the lovely lacebark pine—all clones are not equally attractive), *P. cembra*, *P. densiflora* 'Oculus-draconis' (dragon-eye pine, leaves marked with two yellow bands—lovely planted behind white lilacs),

P. resinosa, *P.* ×*schwerinii*, and *P. strobus* (one of the best). *Taxus baccata* 'Fastigiata', *T. cuspidata* 'Capitata', *Thuja occidentalis*, and *Tsuga canadensis* are fine for smaller gardens.

Use early hybrid lilacs against an evergreen background since so few other flowering trees bloom as early as do the lilacs. Use the newer, outstanding mid-season *Syringa vulgaris* cultivars (see "Classification of Lilacs by Season of Bloom" in chapter one) as plants flanked by some of the choicest conifers. The combinations are endless and your garden will be a landscaper's delight. Do not forget some of the truly outstanding blue-flowering lilacs against the many kinds of newer and beautiful blue Colorado spruce (*Picea pungens*) selections. Pink lilacs are resplendent against a background of dark conifers such as *P. pungens* 'Moerheim'. Need to know more about conifers? See Martin and Tripp's (1997) *Growing Conifers: Four-Season Plants* and other publications, including those of the American Conifer Society.

Flowering Crab Apples and Lilacs

Top priority for spring blossom among flowering shrubs and trees to plant with lilacs must be given to the flowering crab apples (*Malus*). Although most flowering crab apples bloom a week to 12 days prior to the peak of lilac bloom, there is enough overlap of expanding buds and bloom. Of particular appeal in this lilac–crab apple combination is the change in the crab apples from brilliant red buds to soft pink and pure white bloom, creating a backdrop for the striking lilac colors—blues, lavenders, pinks, and deep purples. A few later-blooming crab apples exist, and they too are excellent with all the lilacs. *Malus* 'Prairie Fire' is a moderately upright tree with red-purple buds, fragrant red-purple blossoms, and deep purplish red fruit, while *M.* 'Silver Moon', one of the latest-blooming crab apples, is a vase-shaped, very disease-resistant tree with pinkish white buds, white blossoms, and persistent bright red fruit. Combining crab apples and lilacs at various stages of bud, half, and full bloom is an art of knowing which cultivars complement each other.

Flowering crab apples can be divided into two main groups. The older cultivars are mostly large and spreading trees. For example, *Malus floribunda* (Japanese crab apple) with red buds, mildly fragrant white blossoms, and yellow and red fruit is a heavy annual bloomer that can be used in a background or as a specimen tree. *Malus hupehensis* (tea crab apple) is a spreading vase-shaped tree with pink buds, mildly fragrant white blossoms, and yellow-green fruit. A heavy bloomer in alternate years, it has a unique habit that is outstanding in the landscape. Both species have received the RHS Award of Garden Merit.

The newer cultivars are much smaller but heavy-blooming trees with smaller, more colorful fruit. Suitable for smaller spaces, they generally have more variety of form, ranging from upright through round-headed to many types of weepers. *Malus* 'Evereste' is a small conical tree with pink buds, white blossoms, and yellow-red fruit. Ideally suited for a small garden, it received the RHS Award of Garden Merit in 1996.

Many of the newer cultivars are polyploids and interspecific hybrids, and their disease resistance is a great improvement over many of the older cultivars. Two very disease-resistant introductions from Fiala are *Malus* 'Red Peacock' and *M.* 'Sinai Fire', both with bright red buds, white blossoms, and brilliant orange-red fruit. Other disease-resistant Fiala introductions include *M.* 'Autumn Glory' with bright red buds, white blossoms, and bright orange-red fruit; *M.* 'Maria', one of the best deep red weepers; *M.* 'Molazam' (MOLTEN LAVA), a graceful weeper with winter yellowish bark; and *M.* 'Serenade', an upright semi-weeping tree whose yellow fruit turns orange with red cheeks.

In a background planting, be it of crab apples or lilacs, the plants may be somewhat closer together than those in the foreground. At two-thirds maturity, the branches of background plants must appear close but not intergrown. Specimens planted in front must have room for full development of individual plants. Even given ample growing space, plants will require some periodic pruning. The form and position of mature trunks, especially in flowering crab apples, is a science and an art that Japanese gardeners have learned to appreciate.

Flowering crab apples are two-season trees: one of beautiful springtime bloom lasting at most two weeks,

Blooming together in late spring are the white-flowered *Malus* 'Silver Moon' and the deep purple-flowered *Syringa vulgaris* 'Sarah Sands'. John Fiala

Fragrant companions *Syringa vulgaris* 'Lilarosa' (foreground) and *Malus baccata* (background), Siberian crab apple, at Grape Hill Gardens, Clyde, New York. John Fiala

Lilacs and crab apples at Falconskeape Gardens in Ohio. John Fiala

can provide suggestions for plants that do well in a given region.

Flowering Dogwoods and Lilacs

Where the northern winters are somewhat less severe, *Cornus florida* (Florida dogwood) stands out as one of the loveliest native American trees, which awakens in spring with bracts of white. It is also a wonderful autumn foliage tree with scarlet and orange-gold foliage intermingled with brilliant red berries. Flowering dogwoods are excellent companions for early-blooming lilacs.

Dogwoods are somewhat difficult to get started. They need woodsy hillsides, extremely good drainage, and rather light sandy-gravelly soil. In fact, what suits lilacs is good for dogwoods too. Dogwoods are smaller trees of the forest edge and do better with a bit of shade, although they will take full sun. Start them in the spring as small plants. Do not waste money on specimen trees, which are very difficult to transplant. Be certain the trees are on their own roots, if at all possible, and come "balled and burlapped" with an unbroken root-ball; never buy them bare-rooted. Although Florida dogwood generally is hardy to zone 5, most of its cultivars were selected in the milder zones and will be prone to winter damage in the northern regions. Even native plants in the colder part of the natural range of the species are not always bud hardy, producing misshapen bracts after a severe winter.

Dogwoods are excellent at a wood's edge, leading into a lilac path or garden. They are the perfect intermediary between the deeper woods, especially when the woods are predominantly of pines (*Pinus*), hemlocks (*Tsuga*), or other conifers. Plant dogwoods as nature would, in small groups or as a single specimen.

From the native eastern dogwood, *Cornus florida*, several choice white-flowering cultivars have been derived, including 'Big Giant', 'Cherokee Princess', 'Cloud Nine', 'New Hampshire', and 'White Cloud'. Among the pink- and red-flowering dogwoods are some fine cultivars: 'Apple Blossom', 'Cherokee Chief' (deeper pink-red), 'Royal Red', 'Spring Song', and 'Sweetwater'. There are also some very pale blush pinks and some having a creamy yellowish tint when placed next to the pure whites.

the other of brilliant colored fall fruit that covers two to four months, depending on the cultivar. A few can be considered fragrant, although generally their fragrance is not as strong as that of the lilacs with a couple of exceptions. *Malus baccata* var. *jackii* is known for its white buds and white flowers followed by good red fruit. Among the better crabapple cultivars are 'Adams', 'Centzam' (CENTURION), 'Chrishozam' (CHRISTMAS HOLLY), 'Coral Cascade', 'David', 'Donald Wyman', 'Indian Magic', 'Mary Potter', and 'Sentinel'. All of these have been selected for their disease resistance, flowering beauty, attractive fruit, and year-round dependability, but all are not of equal merit. For additional information on crab apples, see Fiala's (1994) *Flowering Crabapples: The Genus Malus*. The International Ornamental Crabapple Society is also a good source of information. Local nurseries

Should you have your own native seedlings, they can be grafted with some of the better flowering cultivars. On planning a landscape using dogwoods with lilacs, one must project into the future and picture ultimate sizes of the fully grown specimens. Dogwoods, like lilacs, do not like to be crowded into tight spaces.

Where the climate is not so extreme, *Cornus kousa* (kousa dogwood) is a good choice for planting among early lilacs. Some excellent cultivars of *C. kousa* were named and introduced by Polly Hill of Barnard's Inn Farm, now the Polly Hill Arboretum, West Tisbury, Massachusetts. They include *C. kousa* var. *chinensis* 'Big Apple', with very showy bloom and outstanding fruit; 'Gay Head', with showy bloom and fruit; and 'Square Dance', a more vertical than spreading tree with spectacular bloom and fruit. 'Madame Butterfly', selected by David Leach of Madison, Ohio, flaunts bracts that resemble swarms of butterflies (Spongberg 1984). All are good companions with the early hybrid lilacs and with *Syringa oblata* cultivars.

Cornus nuttallii (Pacific dogwood) does best in the Pacific Northwest. Its true flowers are purple and green, surrounded by four to eight, but usually six, showy bracts. 'Eddie's White Wonder' (*C. florida* × *C. nuttallii*) is a hybrid offspring. Try Pacific dogwoods with your lilac planting.

If you have an area where you wish to naturalize your plantings, try the combination of native dogwoods with some of the species lilacs such as *Syringa pubescens* subsp. *julianae* 'Hers', or underplant the dogwoods with drifts of *S. pubescens* with its fragrant bloom. A lovely combination is *S. pubescens* subsp. *microphylla* var. *potaninii* backed by dogwoods. For a magnificent effect, try a massed planting of *S.* ×*chinensis* intermingled with dogwoods frolicking along the forest edges. The pale blues and lavenders of the early hybrid lilacs are excellent with dogwoods, although these lilacs in time, too, can become trees. *Syringa oblata* subsp. *dilatata* is excellent with early dogwoods.

Flowering Cherries and Lilacs

As with dogwoods, where soil is sandy-gravelly and winters less severe, flowering cherries (*Prunus*) are excellent companions for the early lilacs. What applies to dogwoods seems to be good advice for flowering cherries.

Flowering cherries do not bloom during the regular lilac season. Rather, most of them are at their peak when the lilacs are still in bud. They make a fine display with *Syringa oblata* and its cultivars, and their white and pale pink flowers are good companions for early lilac hybrids such as 'Fénelon', 'Lamartine', 'Lewis Maddock', 'Maureen', 'Pink Cloud', and 'Sunset', or the deeper purple-flowered 'Pocahontas'.

Prunus 'Hally Jolivette' (*P. subhirtella* × *P.* ×*yedoensis*) is a delightful flowering cherry with pale pinkish to white double blossoms and a low-growing habit. It is excellent with *Syringa oblata* subsp. *dilatata*. The two plants seem to bloom together in Ohio. Although cultivars of *P. mume* such as 'Alphandii', 'Beni-chi-

Pink-flowered *Syringa* ×*hyacinthiflora* and white-flowered dogwood at wood's edge in Lilacland, the Lumley estate in Pelham, Massachusetts. John Fiala

Syringa ×*hyacinthiflora* 'Maureen' is one of many early blooming lilacs that can be planted with flowering cherries to make a fine display in spring. B. Peart and M. Walton

dori', 'Omoi-no-mama', 'Peggy Clarke', and 'Pendula' are magnificent, their hardiness limits them to zone 6 or milder.

Peonies and Lilacs

Herbaceous peonies and tree peonies (*Paeonia*) can be excellent companions to lilacs. For early hybrid lilacs—hybrids of *Syringa oblata* subsp. *oblata* and *S. oblata* subsp. *dilatata*, that is, *S. ×hyacinthiflora* cultivars—use the earliest species peonies and their hybrids such as *P. mlokosewitschii*, *P. officinalis*, 'Playmate', 'Moonlight', and several of the Saunder cultivars. Lilacs look best in a bed with peonies of one cultivar. Too much variety gives a spotted effect.

A single choice lilac surrounded by a well-kept bed of 7–10 choice peonies, all of one kind, can be beautiful. A fine example would be the grand old lilac 'Lucie Baltet', with its delicate shades of coppery pink surrounded by a massed bed of pink or red peonies. With specimen lilacs in pink or dazzling white, use brilliant red peonies such as 'Alexander Woollcott', the wonderful double 'Ballerina', the very rare 'Burgundy' (a real gem), 'Burma Midnight', 'Camellia', the brilliant 'Cardinal's Robe', 'Carina', 'Chalice', 'Cytheria', the exotic 'Early Windflower', the outstanding 'James Cousins', 'Marie Fischer', or the excellent 'Moonrise'. With most lilacs, the pink peonies are always wonderful companions: 'Frosted Rose', 'Laura Magnuson', 'Pageant', 'Starlight', 'Sylvia Saunders', or 'Victoria Lincoln'.

Among the *Paeonia* Lactiflora Group cultivars (the common garden peony) are many wonderful choices, ranging from white through pinks, oranges, reds, and shades of lavender: 'America' (a large scarlet), 'Angel Cheeks', 'Ann Cousins', 'Best Man', 'Bonanza', 'Bridal Gown', 'Bridal Icing', 'Cheddar Gold', 'Cheddar Surprise', 'Claire de Lune' (pale yellow), 'Coral Charm', 'Coral Sunset', 'Dinner Plate', 'Elk Grove', 'Emma Klehm', 'Ethel Mars', 'Fairy's Petticoat', 'Goshen Beauty', 'Helen Hayes', 'Highlight', 'Honey Gold', 'Jay Cee', 'Minnie Shaylor' (old, but good), 'Mister Ed', 'Moon River', 'Paul Bunyan', 'Pink Jazz', 'Princess Margaret', 'Raspberry Sundae', 'Snow Mountain', 'Sylver', 'Top Brass', or 'Vivid Rose'. 'Blush Queen' planted in front of pink lilacs is an excellent combination.

Japanese and Chinese tree peonies and the beautiful Saunder hybrids are magnificent companions for lilacs. Surround 'Agincourt Beauty', 'Albert F. Holden', 'Atheline Wilbur', 'Monge', or 'Victor Lemoine' with white tree peonies 'Chichibu', 'Gessekai', 'Renkaku', 'Shiro Kagura', 'Stolen Heaven', or 'Wings of the Morning'. You might wish to use a bed of one of the very fine pale lavender tree peonies such as 'Guardian of the Monastery', 'Kenreimon', 'Marie Laurincen', or 'Mt Fuji'.

Lilacs and peonies are a wonderful combination when cultivars are used that bloom together—the deep purple edged white lilac 'Sensation' surrounded by a bed of the very rare herbaceous peony 'Picotee', white edged purple-pink, or by the pure white of 'Early Windflower' or 'Late Windflower' (they are indistinguishable late or early and are truly magnificent rarities), or the beautiful 'White Innocence'. Another focal point is lilac 'Maiden's Blush' surrounded by the early hybrid peony 'Ballerina', 'Pink Lady', 'Rose Crystal', or if one can find it and divide it enough, the very, very rare 'Eclipse'. The American Peony Society is a good source of information on the genus *Paeonia*, its species, hybrids, and cultivars.

Showy Magnolias and Lilacs

One of the early spring flowering shrubs outstanding with lilacs is *Magnolia*. Magnolias grow well together with lilacs throughout zone 5 and in sheltered areas of zone 4. Not all magnolias are equally hardy, and one must select them with care. They vary from pure white, pink, lavender, and rich red-purple to soft cream and one deep yellow. *Magnolia ×loebneri* 'Merrill', with pure white flowers, blooms early enough to plant with the early hybrid lilacs. Most of the choicest magnolias bloom later, just in time for *Syringa vulgaris*. They like the same deep, well-drained, enriched loam.

Among the best and hardiest magnolias are cultivars of *Magnolia liliiflora*. Known as the "de Vos and Kosar magnolia hybrids," these cultivars were developed by Francis de Vos and William F. Kosar and introduced by the U.S. National Arboretum in the mid-1950s. The de Vos cultivars are 'Ann', 'Judy', 'Randy', and 'Ricki'; the Kosar hybrids are 'Betty', 'Jane', 'Pinkie', and 'Susan', all in various tones of lavender, pink, and red-purple. Because of their relatively diminutive stature and because their names honor arboretum secretaries or wives and daughters of staff, they have been nicknamed the Eight Little Girls. The Girls may bloom intermittently throughout the summer. Their hardiness, to zone 3, tolerance of poorly drained, heavy clay soils or dry areas, and compact size, reaching a height of 10 feet (3 m) and a spread of 8½ feet (2.5 m), make them popular choices. All are excellent with the white lilacs.

Many of the *Magnolia ×soulangiana* cultivars are outstanding: 'Amabilis', pure white; 'Lennei', with enormous deep purple flowers; and 'Verbanica', white flushed pink. All are excellent with most colors of lilacs.

Magnolia ×loebneri 'Ballerina' is a magnificent rose blushed white. *Magnolia* 'Spring Snow' is a truly outstanding white, and M. 'Woodsman' and the newer M. 'Pristine' with M. 'Elizabeth' a pale cream-yellow. Indeed, you are fortunate if you can obtain any of these beauties. Other magnolias suitable for planting with lilacs are M. *liliiflora* 'O'Neill', a deep wine purple; M. *wiesneri* (syn. M. *watsonii*); or the cherished M. *denudata* (syn. M. *yulan*), much revered as a classic in China. Some of the less publicized and obtainable yet beautiful magnolias include 'Royal Crown'; M. *salicifolia*, thoroughly hardy and beautiful; M. *sprengeri* var. *diva*, a pink-lavender; and M. ×*thompsoniana* 'Urbana'. *Magnolia sieboldii*, the Oyama magnolia, is a small tree or large shrub, exquisite in bloom and very outstanding.

The deep yellow *Magnolia acuminata* 'Miss Honeybee' is a rather large shrub that in time may become a small tree. Rare and outstanding, it is excellent with the white-cream lilacs such as 'Aloise', 'Carley', 'Flora 1953', 'Mother Louise', 'Prof. E. H. Wilson', 'Souvenir d'Alice Harding', or 'St Joan'.

The Magnolia Society maintains a magnolia cultivar register, and its journal, *Magnolia*, is a good source of information.

Hostas and Lilacs

Have you ever watched hostas in the spring unpack their shipshape, squared-away leaves as they come popping from their winter rest? Their busy unfurling, unfolding suddenly erupts in a clump of bright new leaves, rich greens, blues, blue-greens, grays, golden with white, white with bright green, or gold, in all kinds of shapes and textures, from large, broad leaves to puckered and crinkled leaves to small lanceolate leaves. What a marvelous display in colors, textures, and shapes.

Hosta and *Syringa* go well together. The leaves of the hostas complement the flowers of the lilacs. Both hostas and lilacs revel in rich soils with good moisture during the hot summer months. Hostas appreciate filtered sun or high shade. They crowd out grass and weeds, and are rather low in maintenance, although slugs may be a problem. In the Northern Hemisphere put in a glorious bed of hostas on the northern or western side of lilacs, never on southern or eastern exposures.

The giant-leaved *Hosta sieboldiana* 'Elegans', with its broad, rounded leaves overlaid with a heavy blue luster, is a real conversation piece when well grown. Imagine seven or eight of these plants around some of the beautiful blue lilacs. Do not be content with the older, so-called blue lilacs such as 'President Lincoln'. Use really blue lilacs like 'Ami Schott', 'Blue Delft', 'Crépuscule', 'Dwight D. Eisenhower', 'Pat Pesata', 'Porcelain Blue', 'Prof. Hoser', or 'True Blue'. Then get out your *Hosta* specialty catalogs and consider the blue-gray hostas 'Krossa Regal' with large leaves and summer spikes to 6 feet (1.8 m) and 'Rough Waters' with puckered leaves, or the true blues 'Big Daddy' and 'Tokudama', both with cupped leaves, or the blue-green 'Blue Umbrellas'. For a low, blue, flat glaucous mound use the flattering 'Blue Boy'. Place the shorter

Creamy white lilacs such as *Syringa vulgaris* 'St Joan' are ideal for planting with yellow-flowered *Magnolia acuminata* 'Miss Honeybee'. B. Peart and M. Walton

Like other white-flowered lilacs, *Syringa vulgaris* 'Carley' is attractive when underplanted with gold hostas. B. Peart and M. Walton

Syringa vulgaris 'Capitaine Baltet' footed with hostas at the Bernard McLaughlin estate, South Paris, Maine. John Fiala

plants up front and the large-leaved ones near the base of the lilacs but not too close. *Hosta* 'Samuel Blue' has very wrinkled blue leaves.

Blanket the foreground of pink lilacs with some of the true-blue hostas. With white and lavender lilacs use the gold-leaved hostas or those with gold and green. Two fine, neat, gold hostas for edging are 'Gold Drop' and 'Gold Edger'. *Hosta* 'Ellerbroek' has wide, deep green leaves edged in gold and is marvelous in front of a white lilac as is *H. sieboldii* 'Louisa' with small narrow leaves edged in white. *Hosta sieboldiana* 'Frances Williams' has large irregular yellow margins on heavy seersuckered blue-green leaves and is terrific when established around lilacs 'Emery Mae Norweb', 'Primrose', or 'Rochester'. Other yellow-leaved hostas include *H.* 'August Moon', seersuckered; *H.* 'Cardwell Yellow', bright yellow; and *H.* 'Sum and Substance', huge, heavily textured leaves that are essentially pest-proof.

Some of the bright green hostas are a lovely foundation for the lilac parade. *Hosta* 'Birchwood Green' gives a delightful display of flowering spikes later in the season; *H. montana* 'Big Boy' has giant leaves; and the old standby *H.* 'Royal Standard' takes sun well.

Among the many hostas with variegated leaves are *Hosta* 'Celebration', a cream center with a green margin, good for rock gardens or as low-growing ground cover; *H.* 'Fascination', a showstopping combination of green blotched white-yellow; *H.* 'Flamboyant', a broad cream margin with dabs of green, chartreuse, white, and yellow; and *H.* 'Gold Standard', a light green center with a dark green margin.

The lovely and fragrant lilac 'Albida', the beautiful *Syringa pubescens* subsp. *julianae* 'Hers', and the later-flowering 'Agnes Smith', 'Anna Amhoff', 'Lark Song', and 'Summer White' are all good combinations with hostas. For more information on hostas, also known as plantain lilies, see the publications of the American Hosta Society.

Combining Red, Yellow, and Orange Flowers with Lilacs

One of the ever useful and unusual flowering shrubs or small trees that can be most successfully combined with certain, but not all, colors of lilacs is the shrubby form of *Aesculus pavia* (red buckeye). Generally, it is found in red shades, but the color of its cultivars ranges from brilliant red to soft carmine, deep pink, and salmon suffused coral with varying shades between. These newer red buckeye cultivars are excellent and brilliant companions to the midseason-blooming *Syringa vulgaris* cultivars and species lilacs. Combine white and pink in front of the red of *A. pavia* for a memorable sight indeed. A clump of three red buckeyes kept in shrub form and planted rather close surrounded by five or seven white lilacs behind and to their side can be an outstanding focal point in any landscape. Use coral and pink *A. pavia* with blue lilacs, the palest pinks with the violet- and lavender-toned lilacs.

The early hybrid lilacs bloom before *Aesculus pavia* blooms. *Syringa pubescens* subspecies and varieties (for example, subsp. *microphylla*, subsp. *microphylla* var. *potaninii*) and *S. sweginzowii* are compatible as are some of the late-blooming hybrids and cultivars in the Villosae Group, such as 'Agnes Smith', 'Dawn', 'Fountain', 'Isabella', 'Lark Song', and 'Springtime'.

Aesculus pavia is native from Florida to Louisiana and north to Virginia and West Virginia; it is somewhat tender in the harsher areas of zone 5 where it needs winter protection. Why not try to grow it from seed? It blooms at a very early age, often when a foot (30 cm) high, is attractive, and will last for years. Its fruit is also attractive. Three cultivars of red buckeye merit mention: 'Atrosanguinea', with dark red flowers; and 'Humilis' and 'Koehnei' with a low-growing to prostrate habit.

Bright yellows and oranges with lilacs might seem a contradiction, but they, too, can be very effective if the right combinations are made. Only white lilacs and very deep purple lilacs go well with these bright colors. Since most of the bright yellow and orange spring-flowering shrubs are rather early and most of the deep purple lilacs are rather late, it is a rare combination. Mostly we are left with the white lilacs. Surround them with the bright yellow of the Knaphill-Exbury azaleas (*Rhododendron*) 'Gold Dust', 'Golden Oriole', 'Klondyke', or 'Toucan', or the brilliant orange of 'Gibraltar'—making for beautiful landscaping in bloom. Lilacs grow equally well in the acidic bed of the azaleas, especially if the bed is made of well-rotted sawdust or peat mixed with sand, but if you are

fearful of such a planting, you can always give the lilac area behind the azaleas a somewhat less acidic soil.

White lilacs surrounded by the princely tree peonies in yellow are equally magnificent. Use either the Itoh Group cultivars or the Saunder hybrids in their wonderful shades of yellow and flares. Among the Saunder hybrids are *Paeonia* 'Age of Gold', *P.* 'Roman Gold', *P.* 'Silver Sails', and the indescribable *P.* 'Savage Splendor' with its mixed colors. Likewise, a beautiful landscape can be created by surrounding the deep yellow cream-budded lilac 'Emery Mae Norweb' or the white-flowered lilacs 'Carley', 'Flora 1953', 'Mother Louise', 'Rochester', 'Slater's Elegance', or 'Souvenir d'Alice Harding' with a bed of Itoh Group peonies. Toichi Itoh crossed a herbaceous peony with a tree peony; the resulting hybrid bloomed for the first time in 1954, after his death. His achievement was not recognized in Japan. The Itoh peonies, also referred to as yellow intersectional hybrids, were further developed in the United States. These hybrids produce vigorous plants with striking deep yellow flowers. A few examples are *P.* 'Yellow Crown', *P.* 'Yellow Dream', *P.* 'Yellow Emperor', and *P.* 'Yellow Heaven'.

Beautiful specimens of white lilacs surrounded by a bed of *Aurinia saxatilis* (syn. *Alyssum saxatile*) make a most memorable picture well worth duplicating. If your lilacs are in a somewhat raised planting with a

White-flowered *Syringa vulgaris* 'Mme Lemoine' goes very well with yellow and orange Exbury azaleas at the Bernard McLaughlin estate, South Paris, Maine. John Fiala

Syringa vulgaris 'Olivier de Serres', one of the best blue-flowered lilacs, is very attractive with an underplanting of blue-purple perennials. B. Peart and M. Walton

Syringa vulgaris 'Sensation' underplanted with deep purple ajuga at Highland Botanical Park, Rochester, New York. John Fiala

short stone wall, allow *Alyssum idaeum* to spill over the wall.

Many of the early-flowering perennials are wonderful companions to lilacs, although they may have to be interplanted with something else for later bloom. Often a green bed surrounding blooming lilacs can be most effective, especially if it be *Hemerocallis* cultivars that later will parade a show of their own in midsummer with the green of lilacs as their display curtains. The daylilies then use the dark lilacs as background for their grand summer parade.

Perhaps you like to change your plant combinations from year to year. Do this with bulbs (especially lilies), annuals, or hardy herbaceous perennials. Many of the late-flowering tulips put on a wonderful display with lilacs as a background. Most annuals are not early enough, but among the perennials the combinations appear endless. One combination Fiala particularly remembered was a bed of blue bugle (*Ajuga genevensis*) with thousands of blue-purple flowers carpeting a magnificent blooming *Syringa* 'Olivier de Serres'.

CHAPTER SEVEN

Lilac Culture

As beautiful and useful as lilacs are, people are surprised to learn how undemanding are their cultural requirements. Nor are these splendid plants particularly susceptible to disease or pests. Keep lilacs free of weeds, give them room to grow, avoid competitive trees and shrubs, plant them out of windswept locations, and avoid unusually warm sites that force buds into premature bloom. Add a couple handfuls of ground limestone every third year around each lilac and they will remain happy. Good lilac culture has but four basic requirements: good drainage, good soil, good sunlight, and good pruning. Given these, lilac bushes will grow and blossom each year with little additional care (T. A. Havemeyer in McKelvey 1928, 519–521).

Good Drainage

Lilacs above all are shrubs or small trees requiring good drainage. They are inhabitants of the fertile hills and the fringed mountain woodlands. In their native habitat they never venture into swampy areas, nor are they found where drainage is not perfect year-round. They are exuberant growers in sandy, gravelly loams that have good drainage. Under such conditions they send forth strong shoots and luxuriant foliage.

In the garden, lilacs may be planted with no further thought in sites with controlled drainage and a gravelly-sandy loam resembling that of their native home. In such well-drained soils simply dig an ample hole, about twice the diameter of the root-ball, enrich the soil at the bottom with organic matter, plant the lilac, and add additional rich soil to cover the crown, mounding the lilac very slightly.

In gardens with clay or heavy soils, however, planting is not so simple. In such sites, a planting hole as just described, no matter how large or how amended,

is fatal. The clay walls make an underground crypt that holds water and saturates whatever soil is put into it. Planting, or rather entombing, a lilac in such a hole is certain death. The clay walls make an impenetrable barrier for collected water. The roots of the lilac soon begin to decay and in a matter of a few weeks are a mass of blackened fibers and rotting roots. This does not mean you cannot grow lilacs, and grow them well, in clay and heavy soils, but it does mean you cannot plant them in the traditional way and expect them to survive. In heavy soils, enriched clays, and clay-loams or soils that have heavy clay or rock understrata, lilacs must be planted on top of the soil rather than in it.

In these more difficult soils, drainage is the first consideration. If the garden has a hillside or slope, it is wise to plant the lilacs on it. Always plant them in the top third of the slope and never in the lower half which weeps from the water moving from the top down. In the absence of a slope, stake out a bed and its contours on a level area out of the way of any natural waterways. Place a layer, 6–8 inches (15–20 cm) deep, of sand and gravel directly on the surface of the heavier soil. Over this foundation add a 6- to 8-inch layer of sandy-gravelly loam. Top both layers with 4 to 6 inches (10- to 15-cm) of manure or humus. Never use fresh cow, horse, or chicken manure. Such manure must be mixed with an equal amount of woodchips or sawdust and allowed to rot for two or three years before being incorporated in any garden.

On top of this organic layer place another 6 inches (15 cm) of good soil mix. Use well-drained, organically enriched garden soil with plenty of sandy pea-sized gravel in it. To make your own garden soil, combine equal parts of good loam, sharp sand, and humus. Slope the sides of the mound gently. Set your lilacs on top of the mound. Do not plant them in the manure layer; instead, let their roots grow down into it. Cover the roots of the lilacs with 8 inches (20 cm) of good garden soil. Then spread 3–4 inches (7.5–10 cm) of mulch, such as wood chips or saw dust, over the entire mound.

Although making a raised bed is a bit of work, lilacs are planted only a few times in a lifetime. If you do it,

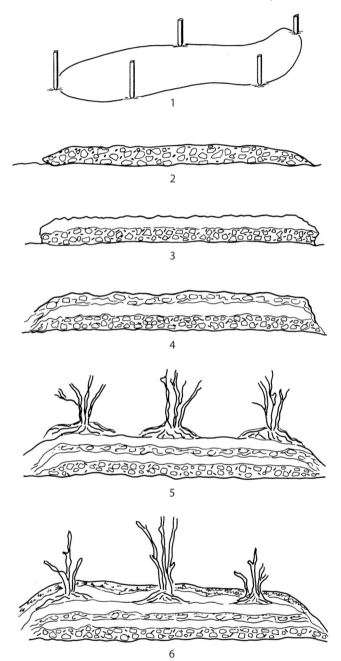

Preparing an aboveground lilac bed on a poorly drained site: (1) Stake out the shape of the bed. (2) For the first layer, cover the surface of the bed with a layer of sand and gravel. (3) Make the second layer using garden loam mixed with sand and gravel. (4) Spread manure or humus to make the third layer. (5) Top the organic material with a layer of good soil and set the lilacs on top. (6) Cover the roots of the lilacs with more good garden soil, then mulch the entire mound. Drawing by John Fiala.

do it well. The final bed will be about 30 inches (75 cm) tall. In large areas, raise the bed to 3 feet (90 cm) or more. In time these beds will settle to 6 inches (15 cm) and some roots will reach the heavier soil below, but not the fibrous feeding and nourishing roots that the lilac needs to survive and flourish.

The type of raised bed for lilacs described here has gently sloping sides so that grass or underplanting looks natural and at home. Do not plant lilacs on man-made mountain peaks that look like ancient burial grounds. The raised planting area should appear to naturally rise from the ground as a slight mound or rolling terrain. With this manner of planting, it is more economical to make a longer raised bed that will accommodate several lilacs in two or three alternately spaced rows. Always plant the tallest-growing cultivars in the background and in the center of the bed with the lower-growing ones to the front and sides. The lowest-growing lilacs, such as 'Little Miss Muffet', 'Lucie Baltet', 'Purple Gem', and 'Purple Glory', are always placed up front.

Every three or four years add medium to your raised areas in the form of mulches and good topdressing. Lilacs will thrive beautifully in such mounded plantings, provided they have at least 6 inches (15 cm) of good soil covering the root areas. You may prefer to plant them far apart, enough for a mowed grassy walk between them, or a bit closer and then underplanted with fine companion plants. Be mindful that your lilacs will spread with age (like most of us). The whole story about this Balkan beauty *Syringa vulgaris* and its Chinese cousins, the species lilacs, can be summed up by pointing out that they may on occasion have their feet in swiftly flowing mountain freshets and streams but they never, absolutely never, will stand in rice paddies or swamps. No, never! They must always have dry feet.

Good Soil

Lilacs thrive, exuberate, luxuriate, and radiate beauty and health when they have well-drained, good soils. It need not necessarily be the very best but at least good corn-growing, potato-producing, flower-blooming soil. It should be fairly rich in organic matter if lilacs are expected to grow well and bloom for many years. No, a bucket or so of sphagnum or peat will not do. An abundance of good garden soil is required to allow lilacs to grow many years. You cannot expect good bloom without strong annual growth of shoots. Unlike flowering crab apples and many shrubs, lilacs do not bloom from blossom spurs that remain year after year. New shoots carry the lilac blossom load for each coming spring. A fine display of flowers is obtained from good growth and by pruning.

When lilacs are well established, new growth will exceed 6 inches (15 cm) of pencil-thick shoots. Such shoots will produce fat, strong flower buds for the next season. If growth is thin and long, say 16 inches (40 cm) or more in one season, it may be that the lilacs are in too rich a soil, suffer too much shade and are reaching for the sun, or need pruning and thinning. In any case these thin shoots often do not bloom, and if they do the flowers are thin and small, and tend to droop. In the common lilac, *Syringa vulgaris*, and the early hybrids, *S. ×hyacinthiflora*, next spring's flowers are set early on this year's spring-summer growth, whereas in the late-blooming species and their hybrids the bloom comes from the new spring growth. In both cases the bloom depends on the health of last year's growth and vegetative buds.

Soil is better when enriched with good organic materials that give it tilth (tone or texture) rather than commercial fertilizers. The latter, although they add nutrients, do not build up the tilth of the soil, which provides drainage capacity, air-holding ability, and the environment needed by beneficial soil organisms. Of course, using moderate amounts of fertilizer is far better than allowing the soil to become depleted of nitrogen, phosphorus, and potash, becoming so poor that not even weeds will grow in it.

A word about weeds—good healthy weeds. They are a fine indicator of good soil. Spindly weeds, especially those with reddish and off-color leaves, are an indication of poor soil—hardpan clays and mineral-deficient ground that will not grow good lilacs. Better to use such soils for parking areas or tennis courts.

Do not despair if you have poor soil. Enrich it with mulches and mix sand-gravel with it. Plant rye or wheat to turn under when a foot (30 cm) high, building up organic content. Get barnyard manure, straw, and sawdust, add nitrogen fertilizer to help the mix rot, till it into the soil, and let the site sit for a year.

Repeat this performance a few years in a row and, lo, the tennis area or parking lot is magically transformed into garden soil. Be mindful it takes blood, sweat, and constant effort, but it wins the war against clay, hardpan, and just no-good soils. Now you know why lilacs and other plants will not grow in the ground excavated from your basement piled around the foundation of your home with a 2-inch (5-cm) topping of so-called garden soil.

Should the soil be too sandy or stony, beware. It may lack sufficient humus or organic matter for plants to grow really well. In hot weather, nutrients leach out of sandy soils quickly and roots dry up readily. But again, organic matter will save the soil. Incorporate large amounts of organic matter such as straw, manure, compost, wood chips, and sawdust, adding nitrogen to aid their decay. Clay-soil owners are not the only ones who must learn to work miracles in building up their soil tilth; even sand dunes succumb to hard and persistent enrichment. Fiala saw beautiful lilacs growing all along the coast of Maine in sandy soils enriched by nature and by hand, despite salt winds and cold northeasterlies. What gardeners in southern regions have known for a long time, namely, that lilacs are difficult to grow in regions with hot, humid climates and do not tolerate wet conditions in poorly drained soils with a high clay content, has been confirmed by research at North Carolina State University (Lasseigne 2004).

When adding large volumes of dry, organic materials to soils, such as dry peat, shredded bark, sawdust, wood chips, and dry straw, remember that these materials do not initially hold water readily. It takes a long time before they absorb water. Because they are resistant to wetting, small plants, including seedling lilacs, small rooted cuttings, or newly planted lilacs can quickly dry out for lack of moisture, especially on hot days, even though you may have watered them very recently. Research has shown that 70–78 percent moisture saturation is achieved within 5 days with peat-vermiculite medium, but 45 days are required for milled pine bark medium to achieve a saturation of 58–78 percent. This difference accounts for the failure of lilacs in some nurseries that use holding beds composed of such mixes. Allow a lot more time for these amendments to become wettable before planting. It is well to have them piled for a year and beginning to decay before adding them to your soil. You do not want to lose all your fine lilac seedlings or rooted cuttings, do you?

Full Sun, the Lilac's Limelight

Visiting the truly magnificent lilacs of the Katie Osborne Lilac Garden at Royal Botanical Gardens, Hamilton, Ontario, Canada, and seeing beautiful specimen lilacs grown with loving care in partial high shade can be deceiving. This carefully grown garden is an exception. Generally lilacs love full sun for at least two-thirds of the day. They will sulk and refuse to set their flower buds well if relegated to a place in the shadows. Lilacs are star performers—they insist on having the leading place in the sun. They do not like shade or root competition from greedy trees or rapacious shrubs. The lilac needs room, air, and sunlight to display its majesty.

In gardens with good ground, rolling slopes, and trees trimmed to cast deep shade for a small part of the day only, gardeners can replicate the splendid

planting at the Katie Osborne Lilac Garden. Theirs is superb culture. It requires work that many gardeners cannot undertake, a knowledge of root systems, and splendid selection of individual sites. The limited shade keeps the darker lilac colors from fading and in excellent condition. However, for most lilac growers the rule must be, plant your lilacs in nearly full sun. They will be beautiful, bloom their hearts out, and never disappoint the gardener come spring.

Pruning Lilacs

How shall lilacs be pruned? First, consider what landscaping effect is to be achieved. Tall, background lilac trees are pruned differently from shrubs used as single specimens or in massed effect, and smaller, eye-level shrubs usually require more severe pruning. Each purpose demands a somewhat slightly different approach, yet prune one must.

Is it possible to avoid pruning or do very little at most? Certainly. Many wild-growing lilacs bloom around abandoned or burned-out buildings or have

In nearly full sun *Syringa* (Villosae Group) 'Frederick Law Olmsted' (white-flowered) and *S.* (Villosae Group) 'Monore' BLUE SKIES (bluish purple–flowered) produce spectacular clusters of flowers in early spring. B. Peart and M. Walton

kept faith over a stone cellar whose frame house has long vanished. Yet through it all, "Lilacs last in the door-yard bloom'd," as Whitman put it. How do they bloom in such circumstances? Not in a magnificent and grand style, neither at their best nor in full beauty. For good bloom a certain amount of pruning is required, even if it be cutting lilacs when in bloom with longer than usual stems.

How much should one prune in any one season? Certainly, prune out all diseased or infested canes, all old, unnecessary and declining stems, wild, thin suckers, and all twiggy, small branches. The latter are a sign of poor growth and indicate a need for nourishment and pruning. The next good rule of thumb is to cut out one-quarter to one-third of the oldest branches and suckers each year. This allows a bush to renew itself with good strong canes and growth every four years. Leave the strongest trunks that will form the frame of the shrub. Eliminate all but the strongest suckers, leaving them to replace older canes and for new plants that will be later separated from the plant. Some lilacs sucker a great deal, others only rarely. Prune some of the height off so that the bush will not become a tree. Keep the bloom at eye level by holding the height to about 8 or 9 feet (2.4–2.7 m).

If you are seeking lilacs as trees or background plants, then pruning is usually directed to retaining only two or three main stems and cutting off all other shoots, removing all lower branches, and allowing the plant to grow upward, treelike. Cultivars of *Syringa oblata* subsp. *oblata* (formerly known as variety *giraldii*) and the Villosae Group (including cultivars of *S.* ×*prestoniae* and *S.* ×*josiflexa*) are best suited for this kind of background use, although *S.* ×*prestoniae* cultivars make wonderful shrub specimens pruned as most lilacs to lower form. *Syringa vulgaris*, excepting only the oldest common lavender (var. *purpurea*) and white forms (var. *alba*), do not make good small trees. If used as background or hedge materials, they are best pruned at the base to a moderate but higher bush form, cutting away suckers and weaker growth. Many of the dwarf and low-growing lilacs require little pruning except to keep them from getting too old by replacing the oldest trunks with newer shoots.

Generally, all lilacs are greatly improved by annual pruning and rejuvenation. Cutting off old seed pods scores no points as pruning; this does not count as sufficient removal of actually growing old wood. It is tidy, cosmetic work, helpful if done immediately after blooming, but it is not pruning.

Do not avoid pruning for a decade before you are forced into it. It then becomes a horrendous, major job, hard work, and a considerable disfigurement to the landscape. If you have been derelict, by all means do the job. The lilacs will certainly survive, but you may not.

Syringa ×*hyacinthiflora* 'Lamartine' pruned to tree form at Tyler Arboretum, Media, Pennsylvania. John Fiala

Syringa vulgaris 'Primrose' trained to a standard (a single stem in tree form). B. Peart and M. Walton

Transplanting Lilacs

Lilacs, even 40-year-old plants, can be transplanted at most any time of the year if done properly. The best time, however, is when they are dormant or not growing, generally in the fall, late summer, or early spring (in that order of preference). Tests have shown that late fall and the hot days of late July–August are excellent times to transplant lilacs, even better than early spring. However, you must be alert to what you are doing and to aftercare.

When transplanting lilacs, take as many of the fibrous, close-to-the-surface feeding roots as possible. Lilacs are rather shallowly rooted and top feeders. Most of their feeding roots are in the top 1½ feet (45 cm) of soil; their anchoring roots go deeper but are not as necessary as the feeding roots. In transplanting,

Lilac bushes dug up at Holden Arboretum were first planted in a wood chip holding bed, where they grew heavy roots before being transplanted to a permanent location. Charles Gauci

A pruned *Syringa vulgaris* 'Alphonse Lavallée' at Holden Arboretum two years after being transplanted. Charles Gauci

a small portion of the roots will necessarily be lost. Compensate for this loss by removing a proportionate part of the top of the plant, cutting it back or heavily pruning it.

Tests during the gigantic relandscaping of the lilac collection at the Holden Arboretum in Ohio produced some amazing insights into transplanting lilacs. Charles Gauci and Winifred Martin found that lilacs, even 30-year-old bushes, lifted by forklifts and held for several months in a gravel-sand bed mulched with straw, continued to grow fibrous feeding roots. They were watered daily in the heat of the summer. After being replanted several months later they continued excellent growth.

In the home garden the same results can be had if lilacs are given ample drainage after transplanting (gravel-sand), watered frequently, and moderately top-pruned. Excellent drainage and a good flow of water and air around the roots are necessary. Gravel plus wood chips plus straw mulch immediately on the roots do much to provide this. Do not just pack good soil, tramped down—that is water saturated on the roots. Lilacs need moist air drainage too. The key to successful transplanting of lilacs rests in a good soil ball of undamaged fibrous roots, good drainage, a good sand-gravel underlay, and good watering. Lilacs will not transplant well if they are set in a water hole for any length of time, so avoid water-saturated, soil-filled mud holes at all times. Firm your lilacs down after transplanting but do not trample them. You are moving beloved friends, not tramping out grapes for wine.

Rejuvenating Older Lilacs

When older bushes begin to decline—main trunks are filled with borers, growth is poor, blossoms are small, and new wood is sparse—then drastic measures aimed at rejuvenation must be undertaken. First, look to the soil conditions. Is the lilac growing in poor, depleted, worn-out soil? This is the principal reason for lilac decline in plants 30 or more years old. Over the years, without mulches and care, the soil not only is depleted but also is compacted and thus poorly drained. The lilacs have taken a heavy toll on the available soil nutrients. Hand in hand with rejuvenating pruning, one must also do some serious soil improvement, adding manures, mulches, and topdressing in abundance. Feed your older lilacs well.

At times lilacs fail with age because unnoticed changes have been made in drainage and roots begin to decay. Seek out these changes in your lilac plantings. Pollution, soil depletion, age, and disease are all factors in decline. Each must be considered individually. However, drastic rejuvenation by cutting old lilacs to the ground together with soil enrichment most often is all that is needed for a whole new plant.

After attending to the soil one must often cut out all the oldest wood to the ground to allow the lilac to renew itself by growing new suckers. If you perform this pruning over a three-year period, the plant will not look so forlorn. Never underestimate the stamina of old lilacs. Most often they will renew themselves vigorously, and in a few years you will have a new, young shrub. Pruning does not always work. Then you have to say to your lilac friend, "Alas! poor Yorick. I knew him, Horatio," as you dig out the dead centenarian root (Shakespeare, *Hamlet*, act 5, scene 1). One can never quite tell, as with people, if the lilac is merely old or actually dying.

When lilacs cease growing well they begin to "blueberry" or "twig" their annual growth. This short stubby growth produces small flowers or none at all. When this happens it is time to consider removing the whole main stem and letting the newer stronger suckers take over. As mentioned, before making such a pruning decision look to the condition of the soil and consider the need for good growing conditions. Blueberrying is frequently a sign of compacted, waterlogged soils with insufficient tilth, air, and drainage. Often the more drastic measures of improving the plant's environment must be taken rather than pruning.

Caution and beware! If your lilacs are of that unhappy kind grafted on privet (*Ligustrum*) or common lilac rootstock, you cannot prune or rejuvenate them by cutting back to the ground. Alas, you will, if so foolish as to buy such grafts, find the chicanery of plant magic has transformed your once beautiful lilac into a privet shrub, or a French lilac into a common lilac bloom. How? Because you have removed the grafted cultivar top, and the rootstock is all you have left. Someone may ask what kind of lilac you have as they gaze at a privet, *Syringa villosa*, or *S. ×persica* plant upon which your choice lilac once grew. This is very good reason why one should plant only own-root lilacs. If you buy grafted lilacs, which the gods forbid, but if you insist, then you must plant them deep to form their own roots above the graft and remove any rootstock growth from below the graft. This undergrowth from the mothering rootstock left unremoved will soon starve off the grafted top. May this never happen to you.

If you live in the United States, you may want to check with the Cooperative Extension Service of the state university in your state. It is quite likely that information on hardiness, pests and diseases, and general cultivation of lilacs is available, either in printed form or on the Internet. An example of this type of publication is the *Lilacs for Cold Climates* (Jull 2006), available both in print and electronic form, from the University of Wisconsin.

New suckers are flowering two years after a 30-year-old plant of *Syringa vulgaris* 'Mauve Mist' was renewed by drastic cutting back to the ground. John Fiala

Tagging Lilacs and Record Keeping

Always tag your lilacs with their correct names: when they were planted, where you obtained them, who was the originator, and their species or hybrid parentage. Not only you but also your friends and visitors will want to know what that beautiful shrub is called.

Two kinds of record keeping should be kept up in any large or refined collection of lilacs. First, each shrub should have a name tag—a good, durable tag that will last a long time as we do not get around to renew tags often. Some long-lasting tags are embossed and individually stamped. Because they are rather expensive, such tags are not feasible for most of us. A good plastic disk tag is available that can be fastened by coated wire to the shrub's outer branches. A round, 4-inch (10-cm), bright yellow plastic disc is ideal. It has ample room on which to write with ordinary pencil that lasts some few years and can be rewritten with ease, is easily seen because of the bright color, and can be used on both sides. In time it needs to be rewritten—about every three years.

Set the tags on the same sides of all your shrubs and trees, so they can be found more readily, especially if plants are large. Fasten the tags securely yet loose enough to allow continued growth of substantial branches without becoming embedded—not on weak branches that will be later pruned away. Use both sides of the tag and include species, cultivar name, hybrid cross, introducer, source of plant material, or whatever other information you wish. Introduce your garden shrubs with class and due respect—calling each by its proper name. They are offended if treated as nobodies.

As to wire ties, they must be plastic coated. Copper and other wires wear through and often cut branches; plastic-coated wire lasts indefinitely. Also, copper wire on aluminum tags is a poor combination, as you learned in high school physics.

The second kind of record keeping is more important than tagging. It is a book that records all your plants and exactly where each is planted—a garden log. Herein by map, by card, or by number, you should record the exact location, species, name, source, graft or cutting, bud or seedling, originator, date planted,

A permanent marker identifies *Syringa* (Villosae Group) 'Desdemona' in a public garden. B. Peart and M. Walton

International Lilac Society, Inc.

LILAC PERFORMANCE FORM

Botanical and cultivar name _____

Plant obtained from _____

Location _____ Specimen observed at _____

_____

Age (if known) _____ yrs.   Height _____ m   Spread _____ m   Growing space _____ m

Branching habit: ☐ Strongly ascending   ☐ Moderately ascending   ☐ Spreading

Density: ☐ Thick   ☐ Moderate   ☐ Thin

Growth: ☐ Long (40+ cm/yr)   ☐ Moderate (20–40cm/yr)   ☐ Short (1–20cm/yr)

Pruned or thinned: ☐ Regularly   ☐ Occasionally   ☐ Never   Rejuvenated: ☐ Yes   ☐ No

Propagation of specimen: ☐ Grafted   ☐ Budded   ☐ On own roots   ☐ Unknown

Flowers: ☐ Single   ☐ Double   Average diameter of corolla _____ cm

Average number of corolla lobes: ☐ 4   ☐ 8   ☐ 12   ☐ Other _____

Tip of corolla lobe: ☐ Pointed   ☐ Rounded   ☐ Other _____

Shape of corolla lobes at peak of bloom: ☐ Cupped   ☐ Flat   ☐ Reflexed

Fragrance: ☐ Strong   ☐ Moderate   ☐ Slight   ☐ Lacking

Flower cluster: Length _____ cm   Width at the base_____ cm

    ☐ Rigid   ☐ Lax   ☐ Dense   ☐ Sparse   ☐ Pointed   ☐ Rounded   ☐ Other _____

Visual color description: Bud _____   Flower cluster in bloom _____

    Corolla tube _____   Lobes _____   Lobe margins_____

Color chart designation: ☐ RHS   ☐ Nickerson   ☐ Munsell   ☐ Other_____   Code _____

Amount of bloom: ☐ 40+ clusters   ☐ 20–40   ☐ Fewer than 20

Flowering habits: ☐ Good annually   ☐ Alternately   ☐ Good occasionally   ☐ Unknown

Blooming time: From _____ to _____ (from opening of first to fading of last cluster)

Lasting quality of cut bloom: ☐ 5 days   ☐ 3 days   ☐ 1 day   ☐ Unknown

Leaf size (from medium length shoot): Average length _____ cm   Average width _____ cm

Soil at cultivar site: ☐ Clay   ☐ Sandy   ☐ Loamy   ☐ Other_____

Drainage: ☐ Good   ☐ Poor   Soil pH (if known) _____

Exposure: ☐ Sunny   ☐ Semi-shade   ☐ Shade

    ☐ East   ☐ South   ☐ North   ☐ West   ☐ Level ground

Pests and disease observed during past 5 years: ☐ Borer   ☐ Hornet   ☐ Scale

    ☐ Mildew   ☐ Other _____

Extreme minimum temperature observed during past _____ years at or near the collection: _____ °F or _____ °C

Other comments _____

_____

_____

_____

_____

_____

Completed by _____

Address _____

Date _____

C. Holetich, R.B.G.

nursery from which it was purchased, and all pertinent information on hybridization of that plant, its offspring, and so forth. This record is the nerve center of a collection and the collector's knowledge.

For large collections, assign a special number, an acquisition number, to each plant. Many large arboreta keep an indexed file for each plant. Hybridizers do not need to be told how important accurate record keeping is. You may even wish to include a photo close-up of each flower in bloom, plant form, and so on. Seedlings must always be marked, "Seedling of," and never given their seed parent's name. Never label a plant with a name that is not certain or whose origin is doubtful. For instance, today there are several cultivars named *Syringa vulgaris* 'Lucie Baltet', each a bit different but all beautiful. Are they mutations of the original plant, or are they seedlings? When similar lilacs are given the same name, nothing but confusion ensues, and you and your garden become suspect.

When friends want a rootlet of an unnamed seedling, simply tell them, "It is an unnamed seedling," and do not even mention the parent as they will soon call it by the parent's name. Try to avoid buying lilacs just by color and then adding your own name from a description you read in a catalog. Keep your own garden record book with information as accurate as you would have in your own family ancestry. Your garden friends are part of your family history. Teach your children and family members to call their favorite lilacs by their proper names. Pass your record book on with your property. It is a sacred trust. Are lilacs not the garden friends you once planted with loving care?

Some people are blessed with a photographic memory; they can recite the history of every lilac in their collection, describe its habit, the color and shape of the florets, its relative time of bloom, what fungus disease it is affected by or which one it is resistant to, and much more. Admirable as it may be, this method of keeping records is not infallible, and it does not outlast its keeper. Charles Holetich, former chairman of the International Lilac Society's Lilac Evaluation Committee, designed the Lilac Performance Form (see page 225). Printed two-sided on 5 × 8 inch (127 × 203 mm) cards, many hundreds of these forms have been sent out, on request, to individuals and institutions growing lilacs. Although the primary purpose of the Performance Form is to provide a database for the Lilac Evaluation Committee, the form is well-suited for keeping a record of performance of one's own lilacs. Since there is no copyright on this form it can be reprinted on customary North American 8½ × 11 inch sheets, or the European DIN A4 (210 × 297 mm) sheets of paper, and arranged in a ring-binder.

Forcing Lilacs

About forcing lilacs, Dutch nurseryman Dirk Eveleens Maarse wrote, "To those who know the lilac forcing, cut-flower market, there is no 'other way' to force lilac bloom than the 'Dutch Way'!" The methods established by the lilac and flower growers of the Netherlands since the 1940s have stood the test of producing excellent bloom at the proper season without fail. Unfortunately, North Americans rarely, if ever, see cut lilacs at Christmas or any other time. The florist market here has commercially spent all its efforts on producing thousands of poinsettias, whereas in Europe lilacs are a fragrant, traditional Christmas flower. For those who have a special interest, especially for those who could be in the Netherlands shortly before the Christmas season, a visit to the forcing houses and garden center at Aalsmeer is an experience of tremendous interest and of exacting horticultural skills under hundreds of acres of glass.

Thousands of lilacs are sold throughout Europe each Christmas. Plants to be forced must be handled with great skill and in a special way, beginning two to three years in advance with special pruning to produce long-stemmed bloom. These plants are kept in huge pots, or burlapped, or dug at the proper time and brought into the greenhouses for special forcing treatment. Sometimes, hot-water baths are used to break dormancy; sometimes a special dormancy-breaking gas is substituted. Plants are exposed for a designated amount of time to controlled heat and light in order to break into peak bloom precisely at Christmas.

A Brief History of Commercial Lilac Forcing

Commercial forcing of lilacs had its beginnings in the mid-1770s near Paris, France. *Syringa* ×*persica* was grown in pots and forced into bloom in dark cellars; the resulting flowers were white. 'Marlyensis' was added at a later date. All through the 19th century pot-grown, flowering lilacs were sold in Paris 10 months of the year, September through June. They were in particularly great demand during the Christmas and New Year holidays. The Paris firm of Moinet had become the largest establishment in the world forcing lilacs; in the mid-1890s it had a workforce of as many as 80 employees.

Another French florist company to force lilacs was that of Souchet-Laurent. Commencing with Sébastien Laurent (1812–1888), the Laurent and Souchet families at Vitry-sur-Seine in the Val de Marne on the outskirts of Paris for five generations produced winterflowering crops from mid-October to April. Laurent took up lilac forcing sometime prior to 1853, and some of his nine siblings, or their spouses, would join him in this venture. 'Marlyensis', the Marly lilac, was one selection they used; *S. ×chinensis* and *S. ×persica* may also have been grown in the early days. When named cultivars came on the market they were tried for forcing, but since lilac forcing was a competitive business in the Marne Valley, lilacs would be referred to only by numbers rather than by their cultivar names, which were kept a family secret. Laurent was a member-for-life of the National Horticulture Society of France and an innovator and promoter of new and better methods of lilac forcing. Laurent's granddaughter, Marie L. Laurent (1869–1940), married Eugène Souchet (1862–1929), adding Souchet to the company's name. Eugène and his son, Charles (1894–1977), introduced ether treatment and built the ether chambers, which were still standing in 1982.

Toward the end of the 19th century other lilac-

Syringa vulgaris 'Mme Casimir Périer', a double white introduced by the Lemoine nursery in 1894, was a popular forcing lilac for many years. B. Peart and M. Walton

forcing firms arose in other communities of Paris— Vaugirard, Glacière, and Saint Marcel—and competed for a share in the market. The lilac cultivars used for forcing underwent changes over the years, depending on suitability for forcing and consumer preferences. Known to be grown at the Souchet-Laurent firm, at one time or other, were 'Andenken an Ludwig Späth', 'Katherine Havemeyer', 'Maréchal Foch', 'Mme Casimir Périer', 'Mme Florent Stepman', 'Mrs Edward Harding', 'Président Fallières', and 'Souvenir d'Alice Harding'. During favorable seasons, as many as 60,000 flowering branches were produced. Quality standards were high. At the 1933 Horticulture Exhibition in Paris the Souchet-Laurent firm received an award for the forced lilacs it displayed.

Charles Souchet and his wife were well acquainted with the Lemoines. In 1949 the Lemoine nursery released a single bluish lilac under the name 'Madame Charles Souchet'; the cultivar had been selected by the Souchets from a number of unnamed seedlings at the Lemoine nursery. By the mid-1970s, however, the demand for forced lilacs had declined; fewer lilacs were used in funeral wreaths, and other forced flowers competed on the florist market. Although in the unheated churches lilacs would stay fresh a full month, central heating kept houses and apartments warmer, shortening the life span of lilac flowers.

Julien Souchet (b. 1927), son of Charles, was the last member of the Laurent and Souchet families to manage the firm. Just a year after the death of Julien's parents, the firm closed its doors and the estate was divided among the seven children (Bellanger 2005; Jean-François Gonot, 2004–2005, pers. comm. to F. V.; Gilles M. G. C. Souchet, 2004–2005, pers. comm. to F.V.).

Belgian florists learned the technique of forcing lilacs from the French. When the first forced lilacs appeared in florist shops of Amsterdam, they were an immediate hit with the buyers. Dutch florists recognized the opportunity and got into the business. In 1870 the first greenhouses were constructed in Aalsmeer. The Dutch growers experimented with the new crop, initially growing potted lilacs. By 1894 they produced flowering branches, primarily *Syringa ×chinensis* cultivars, gradually switching to cultivars of *S. vulgaris*.

For some time in the early 1900s the anesthetics ether and chloroform were used in the treatment of lilacs prior to forcing (Johannsen 1900, É. Lemoine 1903–1904). The firm of Friedrich Harms at Hamburg, Germany, one of the leading producers of forced lilacs, used the method with good results (Harms 1902). In an earlier publication, Harms (1897) commented on the albeit unsatisfactory experiments in the use of artificial pigments such as eosin, methyl blue, methyl aniline violet, and orange II.

Although other centers of lilac forcing developed, such as in Hamburg, Berlin, Frankfurt, Stuttgart, and Saint Petersburg, none rivaled the concentration of growers in the Aalsmeer-Boskoop region and the quality and quantity of branches produced. Forced lilac branches are available from the end of October to early May. In 1926 six million branches were produced; by 1936 the output had risen to 12 million. Production declined during the depression years of the 1930s and World War II; in 1945 a recovering industry was producing 4.5 million branches, and about 12 million in 1983 (Potter 1913; McKelvey 1928, 537–547; Souchet 1931). Primary export countries during the last two decades of the 20th century were Germany, France, the United Kingdom, Switzerland, Finland, the Gulf States, and the United States. In 1982 the United States imported 505,000 lilac stems from the Netherlands (J. L. Green 1984, van den Berg 1988).

The Lilacs for Forcing

Not all cultivars are equally good for forcing even though they may produce superior blooms when grown outdoors. Lilac breeding and selection work in France, Belgium, Germany, and the Netherlands has provided an ample flow of new *Syringa vulgaris* cultivars to be tried for their forcing qualities, such as straight stems, full thyrses, clear colors, good fragrance, and longevity in the vase.

For his doctoral dissertation, Wietse Sijtsema (1962) investigated the various aspects and merits of forcing cut branches of lilacs into flower using 'Andenken an Ludwig Späth', 'Marie Legraye', and 'Mme Florent Stepman'. He found that cut branches of the latter could be forced into bloom but that the florets always turned out to be smaller than those "forced on the shrubs." This method had no commercial advantages.

The florist industry classifies forced lilacs in two groups: white and blue. All lilacs with colored florets

are referred to as blue. About 5 percent of the forced lilacs marketed are blue. At the beginning of the 21st century the main cultivars available in Aalsmeer include 'Andenken an Ludwig Späth' (single purple), 'Dark Koster' (single bluish), 'Hugo Koster' (single lilac), 'Lavaliensis' (single pinkish), 'Lila Wonder' (single bicolor, violet heart with white margin), 'Mme Florent Stepman' (single white), 'Ruhm von Horstenstein' (single magenta), and 'White Sire' (single white).

Lilac cultivars currently of minor importance, because they are either being phased in or out, or have become obsolete for forcing are 'Bloemenlust' (single white), 'Charles Joly' (double purple), 'Charles X' (single magenta), 'Engler Weisser Traum' (single white), 'Helena Agathe Keessen' (single white), 'Hermann Eilers' (single pinkish), 'Maréchal Foch' (single magenta), 'Margaretha' (single white), 'Marie Legraye' (single white), 'Marlyensis' (single lilac), 'Mme Casi-

Syringa vulgaris 'Dark Koster', a popular forcing lilac. B. Peart and M. Walton

Syringa vulgaris 'Hugo Koster', a popular forcing lilac. B. Peart and M. Walton

mir Périer' (double white), 'Mme Felix' (single white), 'Mme Lemoine' (double white), 'Président Grévy' (double bluish), 'Sensation' (single purple and white), and 'Snow White' (double white).

Consumer tastes never remain constant, neither do the costs of production: 8.2 million stems were traded at the Dutch flower auctions in 1997, 6.4 million in 1999, 4.2 million in 2002 (90 percent of them of 'Mme Florent Stepman'), and up again to 5.5 million in 2005. Research and development must keep pace with crop production and marketing.

The decline in production and sales of forced lilac stems in the 1980s and 1990s raised the question whether there existed additional cultivars suitable for forcing, that is, cultivars that would produce straight stems of desired length with full thyrses and florets of lasting quality and quantity in attractive colors and with good disease resistance. A study was initiated in 1997 and a preliminary selection made. Fifty-eight cultivars were grafted on *Syringa vulgaris* rootstock in February 1998 and planted out in May, followed by propagation through tissue culture and testing for *Verticillium dahliae* susceptibility. Those plants that had developed sufficiently were placed in the greenhouse in January 2001 and forced into bloom, followed by two growing seasons in the field. A second forcing trial followed in February 2003 (Krijger 2003). Cultivars that showed the most promise in these preliminary trials were the following:

'Bright Centennial', single magenta
'Esther Staley', single magenta
'Geraldine Smith', single white
'Heather', single white
'Independence', single white
'John Kennedy', double white
'Marshal Zhukov', single lilac to magenta
'Monument', single white
'Nadezhda', double bluish to lilac
'Necker', single pinkish
'Oaks Double White', double white
'Primrose', single white
'Romance', single pinkish
'Sister Justina', double white
'Sovetskaya Arktika', double white
'Victorie', single white
'White Swan', single white

Further production trials will be needed, followed by marketing trials. As always, ultimately it is the consumer's taste and purchasing power that will determine which of the cultivars will be successful, providing the grower with the necessary monetary returns.

Although *Syringa vulgaris* seedlings have been the favored rootstock for lilacs used for forcing, there has been a continuous search for clonal rootstock that provides uniformity in growth and disease resistance, and that is readily propagated through tissue culture. Several rootstocks, originally selected in the 1940s or 1950s at the Eveleens and Maarse firm in Aalsmeer, were put on trial again in the 1980s by nurserymen Hendrik Maarse and Hendrik J. Keessen. One selection was made and named 'Robuste Albert'.

The Aalsmeer Flower Auction

In March 2005, the Aalsmeer flower auction (or VBA) introduced the bicolored 'Lila Wonder', the first new forcing lilac since the 1920s. Discovered in 1997 as a sport of 'Dark Koster' by Gerard Bunnik of Albert Maarse nursery, it took eight years to test the new clone and produce 3000 shrubs for forcing. The first branches auctioned sold for €2.85 (about U.S. $3.75) each (Vrugtman 2007a).

Climatic and edaphic conditions around Aalsmeer are perfect for lilac forcing: mild winters and a long growing season in combination with low-lying fields, the fertility of which is renewed regularly with the silt dredged from the lakes and canals in the area. Lilac shrubs for forcing require two full growing seasons outdoors in the field, so half the shrubs remain over winter in the field; the other half are dug up and brought into the greenhouse for forcing.

Rising production costs have resulted in a lower demand for forced lilacs at the Aalsmeer flower auctions; many growers have switched to other forcing crops such as snowball (*Viburnum*) and forsythia. About 40 lilac growers remain in Aalsmeer; an average-sized nursery handles about 60,000 lilac shrubs, forcing 30,000 a year, requiring three people to do the work (Boon 2005, Vrugtman 2005a).

The topic of Aalsmeer would by incomplete without mentioning "de klok." The Flower Auction Aalsmeer consists of five auction halls, four for flowers and one for plants. Thirteen auction clocks are stationed throughout the halls. The plant hall, which accommodates 600 bidders, has four clocks. Altogether, the five auction halls provide space for 2000 buyers. Auctioning goes by the Dutch auction system: the lights around the clock's edge run backward from 100 to 1. These lights indicate the price. The clock, therefore, runs from the highest to the lowest price, which is always per unit, that is, per single flower or plant. If the light indicates the price that a buyer will pay, the buyer quickly hits the button, stopping the clock at that price. The number on this buyer's card appears on the clock's face, indicating that he or she was the first to push the button and, therefore, is the buyer. The buyer then tells the auctioneer, via the desk intercom, how much of the consignment he/she will buy; the remainder is again put up for auction. Data about concluded transactions are immediately entered into the central computer, from which invoices for buyers, payments for growers, and statistics are processed. For each clock, some 1500 transactions can be effected per hour—one transaction every 2.4 seconds.

Longevity in the Vase

Only rarely are cut flower stems moved directly from the grower to the consumer. More often the stems are bundled, packed, and shipped via the Aalsmeer flower

Made for a meeting of the International Lilac Society, this outstanding floral arrangement naturally includes lilacs. John Fiala

auction and the wholesaler to the retailer before reaching the consumer. Longevity in the vase is an important factor in testing and selecting lilac cultivars for forcing. Proper treatment of cut flowers in transit and at their destination also enhances their longevity.

Research on this topic has been conducted for many years at various institutes. The most useful current advise for the retailer comes from the federation of Dutch growers of forced shrubs (Trekheesters Aalsmeer) via the Internet (www.syringa.nl) and can be summarized as follows:

1. What to watch for when you buy

   Lilacs are marketed per branch. A distinction is made between two and four buds.

   Forced shrub branches are marketed by length, in 4-inch (10-cm) increments.

   Forced shrubs are optimal for marketing when the buds are colored.

2. How to care for forced shrubs in your shop

   Upon arrival in your shop, cut—with a knife or pruning shears—about 2 inches (5 cm) off the end of the stem and put the branches in clean water.

   Add shrub nutrient such as CHRYSAL CLEAR; this nutrient prolongs vase life and enhances full flowering of the shrubs.

   Do not put the branches in a zinc pail.

   Check the water level regularly because a bunch of forced shrub branches may use up to half a liter of water per day.

   Avoid drafts.

   Keep forced shrubs in water at a temperature of approximately 41°F (5°C).

3. Tips for full flowering at the consumer's

   Forced shrubs benefit from care; use the following tips to get full bloom:

   Cut 2 inches (5 cm) off the branches to enhance water uptake.

   Place the flowering branches in a clean vase; do not use a zinc vase. Preferably use a glass vase to be able to check the water level. Forced shrubs may use up to 2 cups (0.5 liter) of water per day.

   Put the branches in clean water, adding a shrub nutrient such as CHRYSAL CLEAR.

   Avoid drafts and bright sunlight.

   Vase life is considerably prolonged if the flowering branches are placed in a cool spot at night.

CHAPTER EIGHT

Lilac Diseases, Pests, and Problems

L ILACS ARE MOSTLY TROUBLE-FREE shrubs, but occasionally problems do occur. Fortunately, only a few of these can cause significant damage. Generally the diseases affecting lilacs are not as serious or as troublesome as are insect pests. Pollution and people also can be threats to lilacs. In this chapter we look at how these various lilac enemies affect the plants and what can be done to control the damage they create.

Diseases of Lilacs

A few diseases can be devastating when they strike. Most serious are the bacterial blights. In warm humid sites, powdery mildew can be a problem.

Bacterial Blight

Lilac blight (caused by the bacterium *Pseudomonas syringae* pv. *syringae*) is not a problem every year or in every locality, but enough of it is seen in lilac plantings to arouse concern. It requires both knowledge of the causative agent and a method for dealing with the disease.

Lilac blight is more common in the moist regions along the North American Pacific coast and throughout the heavier clay soils of the Midwest than it is in the eastern United States and Canada. It is believed to be associated with the longer, more variable, frost-pocketed springs experienced in those areas compared to the later arrival and more even advance of spring-time in the East. It is definitely associated with wet, humid, frosty nights and warm days accompanied by cold spring rains. The general symptoms resemble those of fire blight (caused by *Erwinia* species), which is also a bacterial disease.

On new foliage, initial symptoms look like water-soaked blotches. A bit later these areas begin to wilt and turn dark brown. Affected areas and blossoms may also turn black. Early symptoms on young shoots are a black striping around the shoot or a blackening of one side of the shoot. Ordinarily the discoloration does not extend very far but is enough to wilt, then blacken the new growth, leaves, and buds. Affected shoots have a noticeable black, droopy quality.

One means of controlling bacterial blight is by pruning out stems to provide better air circulation. Because you are dealing with a bacterial disease that enters the plant through wounds, sterilize tools in alcohol or strong household bleach. Bacteria ooze from the infected tissue, especially in rainy weather, so it is best to avoid any kind of pruning during wet, humid conditions. Apart from appearance, once the infection has set in, immediate pruning is of no real value. Where adverse environmental conditions prevail, avoid using a high-nitrogen fertilizer in the spring as it causes an excess of soft, flush new growth. Avoid overhead irrigation in spring.

The only control spray recommended and cleared for use on lilacs under these conditions is Bordeaux mixture, the old standby, used at the rate of 2 pounds (1 kilo) copper sulfate and 2 pounds hydrated lime mixed thoroughly with 50 gallons (190 liters) of water. Apply it as soon as you see any symptoms of blight. After the weather warms and the blight is past, cut off all dead and blackened areas and burn them. The lilacs will respond with new growth and should be fine next year. Tidy up and prune for more open plants and watch for overcrowding from other shrubs that block airflow. When plants are young and have plenty of space between them, they are not as readily infected as when they are older and begin to crowd for space. This blight results in the loss of leaves and flower buds.

Phytophthora Blight

Phytophthora blight (caused by the fungus *Phytophthora syringae*) is less often seen in lilacs than bacterial blight but is similar. Its lesions are brown rather than black. It kills shoots and root sprouts to a greater extent, very often to the ground line. This soil-borne fungus is typically a wet-weather disease, although after long periods of drought it can also do serious damage. Plants under stress appear more susceptible.

For some control, pruning and thinning are recommended. Susceptible plants may be sprayed with Bordeaux mixture when the leaves are opening and again when they are fully opened. This precaution need not be taken unless the disease was serious in the previous year. Often, pruning or removing excessive foliage of the afflicted plant and adjacent shrubs to create airflow is the best measure. A good practice is to avoid growing lilacs in mixed plantings or close to rhododendrons or elderberry (*Sambucus*), both of which are very susceptible to phytophthora infection. Considerable spread of the disease may occur in such mixed plantings.

Sudden Oak Death

Sudden oak death (SOD) or ramorum blight (caused by the fungus *Phytophthora ramorum*) was first observed in California in 1995. The pathogen has spread rapidly to many parts of North America and to Europe, mostly by the movement of infected plants. By 2006 the pathogen had been diagnosed in nearly 100 species of native and cultivated plants, including *Syringa vulgaris*. Symptoms observed on infected host plants are leaf spots, leaf scorch, stem cankers, or twig blight. However, these symptoms are very similar to those of less serious diseases. Plants infected with *Phytophthora ramorum* may decline over a couple of growing seasons. Positive determination of the presence of the fungus can be made only by the use of a serological test (ELISA, that is, enzyme-linked immunosorbent assay) in a plant disease diagnostic laboratory. In the United States, this disease has been classified as a "regulated pest"; state departments of agriculture will work with nursery operators to quarantine and eradicate affected sites. Canada has implemented a Sudden Oak Death (*Phytophthora ramorum*) Certification Program (Shishkoff 2006).

Stem Blight

Stem blight (caused by the fungus *Ascochyta syringae*) is reportedly common in South England. It has been reported in North America, also. Treat as for other blights. Avoid overhead irrigation in spring.

Verticillium Wilt

Verticillium wilt (caused by the fungus *Verticillium albo-atrum*) is not common in lilacs as it is in some other trees and shrubs. The initial symptom is a loss of glossiness of leaves, which later turn pale and wilt. Premature defoliation of branches is common, with affected branches dying to the ground. Ordinarily there is some discoloration of the wood or xylem of the affected stem. Verticillium wilt differs from phytophthora blight in that there are no external lesions on wilting stems. Sudden wilting occurs with no external symptoms. You must cut into the bark to detect the infection. The fungus is soil-borne. No preventive measure is known. Remove and burn the entire plant, which in time will die anyway. Do not replant lilacs in soils where verticillium wilt thrives.

Powdery Mildew

Spores of mildew (caused by the fungus *Microsphaera syringae*) germinate on the leaf surface and the fungus growth, or mycelium, continues mostly on the surface although it will penetrate the leaf surface to draw nourishment from the epidermal layer, generally entering through leaf stomata. In late summer and fall mildew often appears as a dry, white, powdery film on lilac foliage. Usually it is associated with damp, wet weather and warm humid nights. If it appears in the flush of the growing season, it can somewhat stunt the growth of the leaves and cause a yellowing, but this is not usual. Mostly older leaves are affected with the white, sometimes cottony film. It is not difficult to control, but it is unsightly. Rarely does it do any harm to an otherwise healthy plant.

To get rid of mildew effectively, use wettable sulfur

at the rate of 3 pounds in 100 gallons of water (1.4 kg in 380 liters). For complete control, two or three applications should be made beginning as soon as the fungus spots appear, then again at three-week intervals. Noticeable results are evident with one spraying but two or three are recommended for complete kill of late fungus spores.

Powdery mildew is at most a superficial disease, although it may be very unsightly. All lilacs can host mildew, with some cultivars being far more susceptible than others; severity of infestation will vary from one region to another, from one climate to another. In growing lilac seedlings, one can detect at a very early age those that are highly susceptible among the seedlings. Discard them. Generally *Syringa vulgaris* cultivars appear to be more susceptible than other lilac species and their hybrids and cultivars. Rarely does one find mildew on the tree lilacs, *S. reticulata* and its subspecies and *S. pekinensis*.

Owen Rogers (pers. comm. to J. L. F.) of the University of New Hampshire summarizes mildew on lilacs very well:

1. Leave it alone. The plant will survive if otherwise healthy.
2. Spray with chemicals if the shrub is very visible or valuable.
3. Replace the cultivar with one that is more resistant.

All this advice is excellent. You must be the ultimate judge as to how disturbed you wish to become about mildew. Some very beautiful cultivars, such as Lemoine's *Syringa vulgaris* 'Rosace', are extremely susceptible, others are relatively immune.

Armillaria Root Rot

This disease, also known as shoestring root rot or honey mushroom, is caused by a group of at least 12 species of *Armillaria*, the most common being *A. melea*. These fungi rot the roots of many different trees and shrubs such as fir, oak, pine, rhododendron, lilac, and dogwood. They have been found also on raspberry and strawberry. Plants which are not in prime

Syringa reticulata subsp. *reticulata* is very resistant to mildew. B. Peart and M. Walton

condition are more likely to be attacked. Symptoms of this root rot appear as stunting, yellowing, or browning of foliage, which may be shed. Leaves may look unhealthy and become sparse over a period of several years or may show no evidence of any problems but suddenly die.

Armillaria root rot can be distinguished from other problems by examining the lower trunk and roots. If armillaria is present, a white, generally felt-like fungus growth can be seen between the bark and the wood when the bark is carefully peeled from the wood. At the edge of a diseased area, the white fungus growth normally assumes a characteristic fan shape. The fungus also forms blackish, stringlike strands about ¹⁄₁₆ inch (1.5 mm) in diameter or less which can often be seen between the bark and the wood, and/or on the surface of the roots, and/or in the adjacent soil. The shoestring-like strands resemble roots. Honey-colored mushrooms may develop around the base of the affected plant.

There is no cure for severely affected plants. They should be removed and destroyed as soon as possible. Control is directed toward stopping further spread of the disease, or protecting the replacement planting from infection. Do not replant lilacs in the same location.

Lilac Witches'-Broom from *Phytoplasma*

Witches'-broom is a condition in which a plant forms thick, twiggy growths in large masses at the branch ends. The appearance of this growth gives the condition its name. It occurs in a wide variety of shrubs and

Syringa (Villosae Group) 'Royalty' is quite susceptible to witches'-broom. Note the many branchlets arising from a single bud.
John Fiala

trees. Often these witches'-brooms, hanging from one to hundreds on larger trees and shrubs, may look singularly attractive, especially in the winter landscape and on trees—but not on lilacs. It is definitely an unhealthy condition. The tree or shrub soon becomes a mass of twiggy, broom growths, fails to bloom and gradually weakens until it dies. The brooms usually die back during the winter, leaving no new growth or terminal buds for the following year. Although most of this brooming in lilacs is caused by pollution (see discussion later in this chapter), some authorities maintain that true brooming disease is initiated by a virus attack on the plant. *Candidatus Phytoplasma fraxini* has been identified as the causal agent (Griffiths et al. 1999).

Studies conducted by Craig R. Hibben, research plant pathologist at Brooklyn Botanic Garden Research Center in Ossining, New York, indicate that lilac witches'-broom (LWB), which includes proliferations of axillary shoots, shortened internodes, and stunted leaves, may be caused by phytoplasma, originally referred to as mycoplasmal organisms or MLOs (Hibben et al. 1985, Hibben et al. 1986, Hibben 1986). These phytoplasma plant pathogens, which resemble bacteria without a cell wall, were detected in phloem sieve tubes of leaves stained by Dienes' stain and viewed via transmission electron microscopy (Sinclair and Griffith 1994). Hibben has found an increasing number of cases of LWB in the late-blooming *Syringa* Villosae Group cultivars, especially in 'Royalty'.

Hibben's research also indicates a similarity between LWB and ash yellows in white ash, *Fraxinus americana*: "Ash yellows is a widespread and lethal disease in northeastern United States of ash, and it is also caused by MLO." His studies have contributed much to the knowledge of the spreading and fatal disease of LWB. Ideally, such work will point to the cause and possible cure or preventative methods. *Syringa vulgaris* and *S. oblata* appear to be somewhat, but not entirely, untouched by the disease, which is most prevalent in series Villosae, especially in the Villosae Group cultivars.

We have seen an increase of witches'-broom, perhaps coincidental, in a few years after heavy damage to lilacs by cicadas. The cicadas, which penetrate plant branches to lay eggs, prefer the late lilac hybrids and the ash. The only control for the disease is to destroy the plants. It is the most practical method of preventing its spread.

Although LWB, the infectious properties of phytoplasma, and the susceptibility of *Syringa* (Villosae Group) 'Royalty' have been known since the mid-1980s, two phytoplasma-induced lilac cultivars appeared on the market in 2002. 'Charisma' and 'Shantelle' were derived from witches'-broom on 'Royalty' (Vrugtman 2004b). As tempting as it might be to add dwarf (stunted) lilac cultivars to a collection, they are still diseased plants.

Insect Enemies of Lilacs

The major insect pests of lilacs are oyster shell scale and lilac borer. Other pests may attack lilacs also, but are much less common. Still a few other insect pests injure lilacs on occasion, but are not specific to lilacs. Damage from these occurs when in a large infestation they attack several species of plants. Two that are sometimes mentioned as troublesome in Europe but unknown in America are *Otiorhynchus lugdunensis* a beaked nocturnal insect, which at times does considerable damage to leaves and buds, mostly in the British Isles, and *Lytta vesicatoria*, also known as Spanish fly or blister beetle, which comes in swarms destroying foliage in some parts of England. The rose chafer has also been reported from British gardens. In Russia, Leonid Kolesnikov (1955) noted that "the worst of the lilac pests is *Cetonia aurata* L., a species of bronze beetle which devours the florets of lilacs especially the white flowering varieties."

Lilac Scales

Scale is the number one insect enemy of lilacs. Left unattended it can destroy a whole garden of lilacs. Two forms of scale attack lilacs: oyster shell scale (*Lepidosaphes ulmi*) and San Jose scale (*Aspidiotus perniciosus*). Oyster shell scale is a small gray or brown insect that lives under a tough shell very reminiscent of a very, very small oyster shell, hence its common name. It is by far the most prevalent of the two scales. The other form that occasionally infest lilacs is the San Jose scale. It is a bit larger and rounder than the oyster shell scale and is scalloped.

Since scales of all kinds thrive on a variety of hosts, especially ash and willows, they are constantly being introduced into the garden by wind-blown mites and on the feet of birds as they hop from branch to branch. Gardeners must be on constant guard to attack this troublesome pest as soon as it manifests itself on either lilacs or any of the many host trees and shrubs. Because it is almost impossible to eliminate scale from large growing ash or willows, do not plant lilacs close to or on the windward side of these hosts.

For some unknown reason, scale seems to more rapidly infest plants that are in a somewhat weakened condition, those that are poor growers, surrounded by weeds, or neglected. Scales start slowly on a twig or at the base of a cane and soon spread over the whole plant. Mostly they invade the two- or three-year-old canes at their base, then quickly climb upward, sideways, and anywhere they can. Do not be fooled into thinking that they are permanently encrusted in one section simply because you cannot see them moving. On days when temperatures are above 60°F (16°C) they loosen hold and very slowly begin to travel. In the mite stage, when they are nearly microscopic white woolly specks, they are great little travelers both on the host shrub and in the air, ever seeking new plants to infest. If left alone they soon encircle a cane, particularly at the branch junctures, and so sap its vitality that the cane and often the whole plant soon dies. They are particularly noticeable in the fall after the leaves are gone and reveal the full infestation.

Make no mistake, scale is one of the toughest insects to fight. When it is not on the move, it will not die under its protective shield no matter how it is sprayed. The shell appears glued to the branch and cannot be washed away. If, perchance, it should die, it seems always to leave enough eggs to continue the infestation, hidden in a bark crevice or under a branch juncture. Hence control must always include more than one spraying.

If only a few scales are present, they can be effectively rubbed off with a sharp stick, blade, or plastic label. For a larger infestation an inclusive spray must be used for the adult scale in its crawling stage and for the emerging mites as well. Such spraying must be applied at the right time in spring (or fall) when the scale begins to move about at above 60°F (16°C). For serious infestations (all scale is serious), spray in late May with a registered insecticide. Always follow directions on whatever scalecide or insecticide you use. Spray again in late summer (August or early September) to catch later mites. Often the May spray should be followed with a summer scalecide in June to catch eggs and mites hatched after the May spraying. If the control is rather complete in the spring and there appear to be no more scale infestations, the fall spray may be omitted. Dormant oil spray appears to be ineffective in controlling scale.

Often scale appears rather suddenly as a white cottony mass that has taken over a whole lilac cane or an entire plant. Drastic measures must be taken at once. With severe infestations the most practical measure, and the best, is to remove the infested canes right to ground level. If done early enough, plants will recover with new growth in time. After cutting out diseased canes, be certain to clean up the area by removing dried grass, weeds, and anything else that might be hiding infestations closer to the ground.

Plants that are scale-free for a year or two are not immune from further attacks. Scales come suddenly

Upright-growing *Syringa reticulata* subsp. *reticulata* 'Ivory Silk' is drought resistant and free of pests and diseases. B. Peart and M. Walton

when least expected. Gardeners must be vigilant. Continually examining all plants regularly is essential. Part of the program of ridding a garden of scale should include not only regular spraying, but also removing grass and weeds around the plants that harbor scale.

An infestation often follows a heavy application of cow manure. We know of no reason that well-rotted cow manure should be blamed for subsequent scale attacks, but the two seem to go hand in hand. Some older lilac growers are so fearful of cow manure that they refuse to use it at all. This of course is pure nonsense, but vigilance must be practiced at all times. Perhaps it will be found that some element in the sap is the special attractant to scale both in lilacs and other plants such as ash and willow.

Spray and prune for an open, healthy shrub. Often people ask why some particular cultivar always seems to be infested with scale. It may be that they are using an ineffective spray at the proper time, or an effective one at the wrong time—when scale are not moving. Some lilac cultivars, such as 'White Hyacinth' or 'Lady Lindsay', are always infested. We suspect that birds transmit a considerable amount of scale in the mite stage; this scale-proneness of specific cultivars is an area waiting for experimentation. Early hybrids appear less susceptible to scale than the ordinary *Syringa vulgaris* cultivars. The late species hybrids, the Villosae Group cultivars, and some of the newer hybrids are not altogether immune from scale. *Syringa pubescens* and its subspecies seem to be very little bothered as are the tree lilacs, *S. reticulata*, its subspecies, and *S. pekinensis*.

Lilac Borer

Inspect your lilacs carefully in June, especially the older canes and heavy branches. Look close to the ground on old shaggy trunks, particularly around old wounds. If you see a very roughened area with a tiny bit of sawdust floss coming from a small hole or wound, you have found the work and home of the lilac borer (*Podosesia syringae*). Should you be able to open that tiny hole, you would find comfortably ensconced the larva of the insect—a little wormlike, cream-colored creature, grublike, with a brown head. It overwinters in its burrow. It spends the summer eating out galleries to make its way, becoming fat on the growing green wood of the cambium of the lilac. Very late the following May, or early June where spring arrives later, it emerges as a wasplike adult leaving the casting of its pupa, the winter coat, hanging near the hole. The pupal case is its spring calling card stuck to the branch or bark of the lilac. The adult borer waspy-looking moths are out and mating, ready to lay their eggs. Spray immediately for excellent results. Adult emergence varies according to different locations, mid-June in the midwestern United States and perhaps into early July farther north and east.

The adult borer looks very much like a wasp and would be mistaken for one by most people although in reality it is a clearwing moth. They are day fliers camouflaged by using the defense of looking and acting like a wasp. Their wings are rather purplish with rusty colored wing bases. Soon after emerging they mate and begin to lay their eggs on the heavier trunks, canes, and branches (there is really nothing for them to bore into or overwinter on new shoots or thinner canes). They love ready-made open wounds, especially those inflicted by mowers close to the base of the shrubs. The tiny, yellowish eggs hatch in 7–10 days and the lively little larvae immediately begin to burrow into the heartwood of the cane. At first, being small, they work closely under the outer layer of the cambium bark and then, as they grow stronger, they attack the heartwood and move deeper within.

Often, during the month of late May to early June, a small cocoon can be found in the previous year's borer hole. This cocoon contains a small parasitic enemy of the lilac borer, the ichneumon wasp (order Hymenoptera, family Ichneumonidae, *Megarhyssa* sp.). It, too, will emerge from its cocoon about the same time as the borers and lay its eggs to hatch and feed attached to the growing lilac borer larva, which will eventually die. In a survey at Ohio State University, about 37 percent of lilac borer larvae were infected with this parasite. At times nature does work in favor of the lilac grower. One can hope that the ichneumon wasp inhabits the garden, but you cannot count on perfect control. If it is present and the borers are few, do not spray lest you rid the garden of one of its most useful, beneficial parasites.

A partial control of the lilac borer, which avoids harmful chemicals or the killing of the ichneumon wasp, can be achieved with pheromones of the clear-wing moth borer (order Lepidoptera, family Sesiidae). This pheromone attractant was pioneered at the Ohio Agricultural Research Center in Wooster. Lilac borers, like other clearwing borers, use a sex pheromone attractant, a powerful, volatile chemical produced by the female to attract a mate. The compound 18-carbon acetate is highly attractive to lilac borer males that are then caught in pheromone traps set throughout the garden. It will not only entrap the lilac borer but also several other kinds of borers, such as the dogwood, rhododendron, and peach tree borers, thereby greatly reducing mating success and eliminating the need for strong chemicals. Ask for such pheromone traps at your garden nursery stores before considering applying heavy chemical sprays.

Most lilacs can withstand a few lilac borers, but when they increase in number the gardener had better do something to control them. With the newer means of borer control, these insects should pose practically no problem to the lilac grower.

Cicadas

In the years of the emerging cicada, or locust (family Cicadidae, *Cicada septendecim*), severe damage can be done to lilacs and many other trees and shrubs, especially on one- and two-year-old wood. Cicadas do not damage older wood or bark as it is too hard and rough for their egg-laying process. The cicada lives in the ground as a fat white grub for a considerable number of years (10 to 17 or 20, depending upon the particular variety) eating rootlets below the frost zone, often slowing the growth process of the plant considerably. In the central and midwestern United States where cicadas are common, as many as a hundred or more grubs may be feeding on a single plant. As upon a signal, in the proper year, they begin their ascent, usually in late July and August. Emerging from the ground in their nymphal form, they crawl upon the nearest weeds, small shrubs, and trees, where they shed their nymphal skins and emerge as adults. The adult is a very large, strong, horseflylike insect, with clear wire wings. The adults converge in hordes, hundreds hanging on tall weeds, and smaller shrubs, with a fearful droning sound that can be heard for great distances, made by rubbing their coarse wings together, as they seek to mate. When disturbed they are rapid in flight making a strong whirring sound that frightens even birds, who rarely eat them.

The female finds a tender one- or two-year-old branchlet of particular shrubs or trees. Some species are preferred to others; lilacs appear an acceptable species but not a preferred one. The female slits the branchlet—razorlike longitudinally—laying her eggs into the slits and then, in her downward descent, she scores the branch around, weakening it. Soon it will brown and die, then be broken by the wind and fall to the ground bringing with it the now-hatched larvae. These will crawl from their nesting branch, burrow into the soil, eating plant roots as they descend into the soil below the frost level. They can and, where plentiful, do considerable damage to the growing roots. Thus two-fold damage is experienced: the damaged branches which either die, or are totally disfigured by slit scars and eventually must be removed, and by the loss of the feeding roots. Lilacs are rarely totally killed. They are greatly damaged for that year with the loss of next spring's buds as the damage occurs so late in the summer that new growth rarely can be renewed.

Katydid music may be nostalgic to some few poets, but the cicada's deafening dirge is a death-roll for garden shrubs. You will see the destruction in split, old branches that either die or may be temporarily healed but later will eventually be weak or deformed and must be removed.

No effective spray control is known as the adults are so numerous and so active in flight and movement. To protect choice lilacs (or other small trees or shrubs), when your extension sounds the warning, cover your plants with cheesecloth until the mating and egg-laying are over—about three weeks. Where damage has been done, cut off the egg-bearing branches as soon as possible and burn before the larvae emerge or the branch begins to brown.

So formidable, hard-shelled and noisy an insect has few natural enemies. Most birds are afraid of them. A variety of the digger wasp (*Sphecius speciosa*), which is black or rust colored, with a yellow-banded abdomen, preys on cicadas with which it provisions its nest. Unfortunately in horde years there are too few digger wasps to amount to any kind of control. One or two off-year cicadas, and there are always a few, as with humans, who are out of tune with the species, sterilely rubbing their humming wings in the high trees in late summer, are harmless. When they appear in hordes, by the thousands, then gardener, beware.

Lilac Leaf Miner

In some parts of France and England but rarely in the Americas, lilac leaf miner (*Gracillaria syringella*) can be a vexing problem. It lays its eggs in groups of 3–12 on the underside of lilac leaves (and some other choice species) where in six days the young caterpillars emerge and make their way into the leaf between the lower and upper surfaces, mining them as they gorge on tissue and destroy the chlorophyll. If one separates the two surfaces, the small caterpillars can readily be seen. In a few weeks they emerge, roll up the leaf surface with webs of thread until they are fully grown. They let themselves down to earth by silken threads, enter the ground where they spin cocoons and pupate. The adult, small moths reappear in about a fortnight, mate, lay their eggs on the underside of the leaf and the cycle repeats. As many as three generations may appear, one in April, another in May, and still another in August. As the caterpillars emerge from the eggs an insecticide spray is probably the most effective control.

Nematodes

Root nematodes generally are not a danger to lilacs. However, an examination of *Syringa* ×*persica* roots in the 1980s at the University of Illinois found an extremely high population of the lesion nematode, *Pratylenchus* species—indeed some of the highest populations of nematodes ever seen. The plants were moved to another field and as of 1988 had not been markedly infested. No other reports of nematodes found on any other lilac species or cultivar are known. It may be a meaningful caution for not using *S.* ×*persica* as an rootstock on lilac grafts (as is the practice in some nurseries).

European or Great Hornet

This inch (2.5-cm) long hornet (*Vespa crabro* var. *germana*), resembling a yellow-jacket with orange markings over a reddish brown abdomen, has proved to be a real lilac pest in some parts of the eastern United States and Canada, especially in New Jersey and eastern Pennsylvania. So far this hornet has not been reported in the West. Although it comes from Europe, little is heard of damage there. In late summer and early fall, this giant hornet singles out mostly two-year-old lilac canes, slits, strips, and peels them, carrying off the tender bark to insulate its nest. The insects are amazing to watch. The great diligence and vigor with which they work in cutting away the bark is astonishing. Often they girdle and strip whole branches, which of course die. They do not eat the bark, but chew it and mix it with saliva to make a papier-mâché that is used for nest protection and building.

The wasps do not seem to be affected at all by poisonous sprays. They are vicious in their work, brook no interference, and have a nasty sting. The only effective control appears to be to identify their nest by following their flight, usually in a tree hollow, but as often in the ground or hanging in a high tree or bush. At night, to include all members of the colony and to keep from their stings, the nest should be burned and destroyed. Encircle the entire nest and attaching branches with a large plastic garbage bag, close the mouth of the bag tightly, then snip off the branch. At this point, you can put the whole bag in a freezer overnight to kill the wasps. You may also set a bonfire to burn them.

Although a single colony of this hornet is comparatively small, it can do considerable damage to a planting of lilacs in a very short time. The hornets do not necessarily limit themselves to lilacs, but they do prefer lilac bark if available at all. The ravished canes are entirely lost, but the plant will send up new shoots the following spring. However, if one does not destroy the colony the same damage recurs each year with a total loss of bloom. This is not a hornet to be taken lightly.

Japanese Beetle

The Japanese beetle (order Coleoptera, family Scarabaeidae, *Popillia japonica*) is a most discouraging garden pest, which fortunately is usually not interested in lilacs. It skeletonizes the leaves by devouring all the leaf tissue and, where extremely tender, the whole shoot. It is a scarab beetle, ½–¾ inch (13–19 mm) long. Its hard wing-covers and head are a lustrous greenish copper. In severe infestations, Japanese beetles can quickly divest a whole plant of its leaves and young shoots. Their larvae live in the soil, doing considerable damage to both grass and shrub rootlets. The larvae are plump, white grubs that, if not poisoned in the soil, soon lead to an infestation of garden moles which feed upon the underground grubs.

Special sprays for this beetle have been developed and are readily available under several names. A most effective control measure is the new beetle trap using a sex pheromone attractant, but if you place the trap near the beetle's favorite feeding ground, you may just increase the population density.

Fall Webworm

Fall webworms (order Lepidoptera, family Arctiidae, *Hyphantria cunea*) are a disfiguring nuisance to all shrubs on which they settle. Unfortunately, lilacs are attractive to them. The moths lay their eggs in late summer and early autumn on the undersides of the leaves. The eggs soon hatch into tiny caterpillars that immediately begin to spin a silky, protective web around themselves and their supply of leaves for food. When they devour all the leaves within the first web, they enlarge it to include greater pastures and for night protection where they return each evening. As the caterpillars grow, eventually to 1½ inches (4 cm) long, they are seen as a mass of greenish, gray-brown worms moving in a silken nest filled with their debris. They forage beyond their tents in the daytime, denuding and devouring whole branches of leaves, with their nests high in the outer extremities, often beyond reach. Birds fear becoming entangled in the web. Several large webs may be found on a single shrub. Even-

Syringa vulgaris 'Wedgwood Blue' is a compact grower selected by John Fiala for its fragrant blue flowers. The buds are lilac-pink before opening. B. Peart and M. Walton

tually the caterpillars fall to the ground, enter a pupal stage and soon another generation is ready to emerge and mate. The whole egg-laying process repeats as often as two or three times per year in good weather.

An easy method of control where there are not too many webs is to gather the nest tents toward evening, when all the pests have returned for protection, into a large paper bag, or plastic garbage bag, and burn them, destroying the entire colony. Where infestations are high and difficult to reach and while still very small, the best control is to spray the leaves with some webworm poison. You may also use a small ladder and a long limb pruner to snip the branches. Look for the tiny eggs and caterpillars in mid to late summer. Mostly they go unnoticed until their web, which begins as a silken mass in the crotch of a branch, becomes enlarged, extremely unsightly and messy.

Miscellaneous Problems of Lilacs

Lilacs are sturdy plants and will stand a great deal of abuse, attack of disease or insects and come back if given proper treatment. A few environmental conditions do, however, exist that must be considered. Among these are airborne pollutants, animal-rodent problems and man-made hazards.

Lilac Witches'-Broom from Pollution

Previously in this chapter we looked at the diseases that might cause witches'-broom; however, most witches'-brooms in lilacs are caused by pollution. Some authorities maintain that true brooming disease is initiated by a virus attack on the plant. Occasionally one finds a broom caused by mite or insect infestations. Along one of the oldest interstate highways in the United States, the Pennsylvania Turnpike, one can see hundreds of thousands of trees and shrubs in every stage and condition of pollution brooming. Some are rather interesting especially if you travel in the winter when all the leaves are gone and can see the brooms clearly. It seems to affect every species of tree and shrub growing along this old Pike. The various kinds and types of brooming would make an interesting folio of silhouettes.

In some of the older arboreta experiencing urban pollution, we are seeing an increased incidence of leaf-roll necrosis and brooming. Insect and virus brooming on lilacs is rare. Fiala reported seeing some incidence of it on mixtoploid plants when working with colchicine. It appears to be a problem of radical chromosome disruption. Much work at the Arnold Arboretum selecting seed of witches'-broom on pines has resulted in an interesting and valuable collection of dwarf pines and conifers. It would be interesting to see if broom seed in lilacs might not also produce natural dwarfs.

Leaf-roll Necrosis and Pollution

Leaf-roll necrosis is an airborne condition caused, so far as can be ascertained, by pollution. Studies at the Brooklyn Botanic Garden (Walker 1975) and Morton Arboretum have shown that lilacs, as well as many other ornamental shrubs and trees, deteriorate because of sulfur dioxide and other toxic gases which are the product of motorcar emissions and industrialization. Plants suffering from leaf-roll necrosis show a marked leaf curl around the leaf margins, gradual defoliation, and an unthrifty condition of the entire plant. Eventually they die. In areas of heavy pollution, as experienced in the central areas of most large cities, only a very limited number of extremely pollution-tolerant shrubs and trees will grow. Sadly lilacs are not among them. All their species and cultivars are more or less susceptible to pollution but a few are more tolerant. Planting less susceptible cultivars, however, does not guarantee that they will not eventually fall victim to pollution.

Heroic and regulatory efforts to curb and lessen pollution are the only preventive measures. Not only lilacs but also most of our finest flowering trees and shrubs are victims of encroaching pollution along highways and city streets. The cost of industrial modernization appears to be a marked reduction in places and kinds of trees and shrubs one may safely plant. Sites for large arboreta should be selected away from freeways and urban pollutants.

Frost Chilling or Freezing of Lilacs

A common problem in the western and midwestern United States is damage to leaves and buds caused by chilling and freezing. In these areas unseasonably warm weather often pushes buds beyond a safe level, so subsequent frosts damage the leaves and particularly the small buds. This occurs when the buds are not yet in the real color stage. The buds appear to be in good form but fail to advance. It may be a week before one realizes that they have been frozen and will not open. Often part of the bud will freeze and the upper portions continue to advance resulting in a misshapen and partially floreted thyrse.

Some lilac cultivars appear to be more susceptible to frost damage than others. Many of the early hybrids, cultivars of *Syringa* ×*hyacinthiflora*, seem to escape this damage, whereas some of the earlier cultivars of *S. vulgaris* are very prone to freeze damage in the bud stages. Generally neither leaves nor buds turn brown, but the leaves have a characteristic curl or pinched effect around the edges where they have frozen. Leaf development is hindered. There is no remedy for the vagaries of the weather, but in some gardens improvement of air flow may alleviate this damage by eliminating frost pockets.

Lilac blights, wilts, frozen buds, and frost damage all seem to appear together in a given spring. All are results of radical temperature fluctuations. In the midwestern United States it is not uncommon to have early spring days in the range 50–60°F (10–16°C) while night temperatures drop suddenly to 25°F (−4°C). This is the kind of weather, especially if accompanied by rains and sleets, that accelerates these plant diseases and troubles. It is amazing how sturdy lilacs really are in coping with such extremes. The eastern seaboard of North America appears not to

Syringa vulgaris winter twig with terminal floral and lateral vegetative buds. Želimir Borzan

have such radical day-night variations, although the region does have occasional killing frosts. It has a milder and later entrance of spring.

Although lilacs are very rugged and withstand extremely cold weather, premature balmy days of spring cause some trouble. Avoid planting lilacs in warm areas near the house that will prematurely force buds. See to good airflow and a location that has a windbreak from windchill. Often it is colder than one may think in windchill areas. A good windbreak will do marvels for lilacs. Table 1 indicates the windchill at selected temperatures and wind speeds.

Table 1. Windchill at selected temperatures and wind speeds.

WIND IN MPH (KMH)	TEMPERATURE IN °F (°C)						
0	40°F (4°C)	30°F (−1°C)	20°F (−7°C)	10°F (−12°C)	0°F (−18°C)	−10°F (−23°C)	−20°F (−29°C)
5 (8)	37°F (3°C)	27°F (−3°C)	16°F (−9°C)	7°F (−14°C)	−6°F (−21°C)	−15°F (−26°C)	−26°F (−32°C)
10 (16)	28°F (−2°C)	16°F (−9°C)	2°F (−17°C)	−9°F (−23°C)	−22°F (−30°C)	−31°F (−35°C)	−45°F (−43°C)
15 (24)	22°F (−6°C)	11°F (−12°C)	−6°F (−21°C)	−18°F (−28°C)	−33°F (−36°C)	−45°F (−43°C)	−60°F (−51°C)
20 (32)	18°F (−8°C)	3°F (−16°C)	−9°F (−23°C)	−24°F (−31°C)	−40°F (−40°C)	−52°F (−47°C)	−68°F (−56°C)
25 (40)	16°F (−9°C)	0°F (−18°C)	−15°F (−26°C)	−29°F (−34°C)	−45°F (−43°C)	−58°F (−50°C)	−75°F (−59°C)
30 (48)	13°F (−11°C)	−2°F (−19°C)	−18°F (−28°C)	−33°F (−36°C)	−49°F (−45°C)	−63°F (−53°C)	−78°F (−61°C)
35 (56)	11°F (−12°C)	−4°F (−20°C)	−20°F (−29°C)	−35°F (−37°C)	−52°F (−47°C)	−67°F (−55°C)	−83°F (−64°C)
40 (64)	10°F (−12°C)	−6°F (−21°C)	−22°F (−30°C)	−36°F (−38°C)	−54°F (−48°C)	−69°F (−56°C)	−87°F (−66°C)

Graft Incompatibility

Often an older grafted lilac begins to languish. First, branches do not renew themselves with new growth, then soon thereafter the bottom branches and finally the main trunk die for no apparent reason. This usually occurs in older, single-trunked lilacs that have never formed their own root system. If you dig out the old root you will find that at the line of the lilac graft upon privet rootstock, the scion lilac has outgrown the union with the rootstock and is marked by a large knob. This overgrowth has disturbed the union and prevented the passage of food from the root to the upper plant. You will find no roots have developed on the upper part of the union.

Either the graft was made too high or the plant was planted too shallowly. This provides a good reason not to plant grafted, but rather own-root, lilacs. However, not all grafted lilacs are the same. Good nurseries graft on white ash (*Fraxinus americana*) rootstock that is merely a nurse-root for a year and replant grafts deeper to form own roots. They do not offer these plants for sale until they have formed their own roots. This procedure creates no problems for the gardener since the ash understock falls away before the plant is put up for sale. If you have to plant grafted lilacs, always plant them with the graft union at least 4 inches (10 cm) below the soil surface. In time, the lilac can possibly develop its own root system.

Damage from Animals and People

Several kinds of mammal damage are frequently seen on lilacs. People and their machines also injure lilacs. Most or all of this type of damage can be prevented or reduced if we understand the nature of the predator and take the appropriate action.

Deer Damage

Undoubtedly the greatest damage done by animals is that done by deer where they are numerous, especially in late fall and winter. Deer browse-damage lilacs by eating the tips of young branches (those most likely to bloom well) even to a foot or a foot and a half (30 to 45 cm) high. Great damage is done by the bucks in the fall and early winter during their velvet stage and the rutting season. They viciously attack lilac shrubs, stripping the main trunk of its bark with their antlers, totally ruining the shrub for the next few years until it is able to regenerate. The shrub always dies back to good wood, usually to the ground. Fortunately bucks prefer eastern arborvitae or northern white-cedar (*Thuja occidentalis*) to lilacs.

There are several remedies for deer damage. The best is extensive hunting. If you prefer less vigorous measures and have only a few bushes you can erect a three-legged tepee made of 4-inch (10-cm) boards, sturdy enough so wind and deer do not knock it over. Deer are reputed to fear the smell of blood or clipped human hair. Most garden stores carry dried blood repellent, and clipper hair can be obtained from your barber. Tie nylon bags of dried blood or hair clippings at strategic points on the shrubs. These are half-measures and must be applied before the fall rains and the deeper freezes begin, and renewed after heavy rains.

Some deer-repellent sprays have been developed with limited value. In Maryland where deer pests have reached epidemic proportions, some control has been had by mixing hot sauces with VAPOR-GARD, an emulsifying agent with excellent sticking properties. Fill a spray tank halfway with water, add 2 ounces of VAPOR-GARD per gallon (57 gm per 4 liters), mix thoroughly, then add 2–4 ounces of hot sauce per gallon (57–113 gm per 4 liters). Use only VAPOR-GARD in this solution, and mix the ingredients in this particular order. If not, the hot sauce does not emulsify and washes off the plant. Should this happen what residue is left may act as an attractant rather than a repellent. If mixed properly, the hot sauce should stay in solution for two hours within which time you must spray your plants. Apply the spray only when temperatures are above 40°F (4°C). Hot sauces, such as Louisiana hot sauce and Tabasco pepper sauce, are readily available at grocery stores. Their main ingredients are extracts of cayenne peppers, *Capsicum annuum* and *C. frutescens* cultivars.

Some people claim that aluminum foil hung in the branches to blow in the wind frightens deer. Take your choice—spray or foil—but nothing is as effective as hunting the deer where allowed. What the bucks miss with their antlers and simulated battle antics, the does and yearlings delight in browsing on, just to let you know they have been there and done your winter pruning—their way. All in all, beautiful and innocent looking, deer can be a real nuisance!

Rabbit, Mouse, and Mole Damage

When your lilacs are older, three or more years, damage done by rodents will be minimal. As small plants or young seedlings whose succulent bark can be reached, especially as the snow mounds over them and rabbits can reach the outer more tender branches and buds, expect damage unless you spray them in advance with hot sauce spray or some other rodent repellent, or have placed small wire fencing around them. Rabbits cut yearling growth just to sharpen and keep their teeth from overgrowing. Being rodents they must constantly have their teeth trimmed through use, otherwise they will overgrow and the rabbit will starve to death as the overly long teeth make it impossible for them to properly open their jaws and feed. Lilacs are ideal winter teeth conditioners for them.

Field mice and moles nibble and debark the canes under the snow and weeds. Their winter feasting is not revealed until spring, when leaf buds fail to swell and begin to dry. On close examination one sees their girdling work on the lowest branches and cane base near the ground. How one then wishes he or she had cleared away the sod from small plants and protected them with wire, foil, or the newer antirodent tubes available in garden stores. Very small plants may not recover; well-rooted ones most often put forth new shoots from below the ground in spring.

Occasionally a woodchuck or groundhog (*Marmota monax*) coming out of hibernation in the spring will polish and sharpen his teeth and long claws on a nearby lilac bush, stripping and ripping its bark, gnawing and being rather fearsome in the damage. Like deer they will shred your lilac plants, not stopping at one. They are, however, more controllable. This time the woodchuck has to go. How? That is your problem; I merely point out the culprit.

In lilac seed beds, nurseries, and beds that are heavily mulched with rich humus and good soil, beware of moles. They revel in seed beds. They glory in undermining the choicest seedlings, as they widen and plough open their underground burrows with their furry little snouts and clawed paws until you wonder why your seedlings and young lilacs have wilted and dried. Moles can do a great deal of damage in a few hours. They especially delight in well-watered, cooler ground in the heat of summer.

Use what you must but get those moles out. Of course they are after the grubs in the soil, so rid your soil of grubs and you will have no moles, the experts say. Not necessarily so. Moles are really out to get seedlings and small plants. Some advocate using a noisy wooden windmill or a wooden flapping bird. These are supposed to make moles nervous so they move away. From experience I vouch moles have nerves of steel—or have none at all. Whatever you use, poison bait, traps, noise makers, you must get rid of moles.

A word of caution in getting rid of rodent pests: be careful of your own pets. You may catch or poison dear Ole Rags or Kitty Cat if you are not careful. Since mole runs have so many exits, cyanide gas and smoke bombs are not of much use; cyanide gas is extremely dangerous. Your best bets are the commercial poisoned peanuts or pellets which must be used over a long period of time.

Mower Damage

Considerable damage can be found in every arboretum or lilac garden due to unskilled operation of lawn mowers. Often canes and trunks are skinned and injured by hurried attempts at coming too close to plants in an effort to save time. One of the great advantages of having a large weed-free circle of mulched soil around each plant is that it prevents needless attempts at coming too close to plants with mowers. These nicks, cuts, and debarking can be tolerated on rare occasions by more robust trees or shrubs but not by lilacs. Usually they do not show the injury damage until a week or so later when the whole cane begins to wither and die.

Do not let careless or nearsighted maintenance workers close to your lilacs with mowers. Far more damage is done to plants than is imagined. When grass and weeds surround lilacs it is difficult to see where the actual trunk is, as often it may twist or turn close to the ground. This advice also holds for hand grass blades and for twine power whips that can quickly debark a tender lilac cane. Lilac bark, except on the oldest trunks, is easily injured. Small lilacs should be staked or marked with tall white markers that can be easily seen from a tractor or mower. Only park superintendents and collection curators know how many choice plants have been eliminated by mowers when not adequately marked. Fortunately most healthy, larger lilacs will sprout again from the roots, but not all.

Chemical Weed Killers

You can kill the weeds in your garden as well as all your lilacs in one clean swoop if you are not careful with the use of weed killers. Some weed killers are fine for the first year or two, but you cannot continue to use them without gradually building up a toxicity in the soil that eventually will take its toll on plants. Read carefully all instructions before buying or using any weed killers. Consult your extension agent or your arboretum or park supervisor as to what is safe for what plants in your area. These individuals are a better source of advice than the store or garden center clerk who is anxious for a sale.

Damage from weed killers shows itself initially as undeveloped, curled, deformed new growth with chlorosis (yellowing) of the leaves. The yellow or white leaves fall from older branches as well. Plants languish and die. Once the chemical is within the plant, there is no cure, even by moving or soaking it. Be careful of the chemical mists that drift to your lilac plantings and to all your garden from roadside spraying crews. There should be a national law forbidding roadside spraying. It can be devastating to the homeowner. Here you must be adamant. Put up "No Spraying" signs well in advance of summer road spraying programs and in front of your garden. County road crews are notorious for their inability to see and read signs. If you know the day they are to spray your area, stand at attention on your property line and forbid such spraying. Protect your plantings, your garden, your family and pets.

If you must use weed killers at all, follow directions very carefully. Use a face mask for your own safety. Spray only on windless days and close to the ground to prevent drifting. A somewhat safe way to clear a small area is to securely attach an old hand towel to a garden rake or a paint roller with a long handle and drag it over the weeds you wish to eliminate being careful not to touch any plant parts or root suckers. It works. Be forewarned, if you find your plants turning yellow or white before autumn, do not think you have discovered a new leaf mutation; you probably have discovered the effects of an overdose or misuse of weed killer.

Not all weed killers are suitable for the same plants. Weed killers are generally cumulative in the soil and eventually can build up lethal proportions; they kill by entering the plant through any portion of it. They also are dangerous chemicals for humans as well, and are easily carried as fine mist by the wind to plants and the air you breathe. They remain lethal in the spraying tank no matter how you clean it. (If you cannot follow this sound advice you perhaps ought not be a gardener at all. Buy your lilacs from the florist or enjoy them at the park or nearest arboretum.)

Imbedded Tagging Wires

Often smaller lilacs are wire-tagged rather tightly. As the shrub grows, small branches become trunks. The wires become ingrown and girdle the cane or branch. The plant may die but ordinarily an unsightly bulge develops where the plant seeks to overgrow the enmeshed wire. Tags should always be loose and allow for growth. Place all your name tags on the same side of all your trees, for ease in finding them. Also, be careful in staking plants so that the tie is firm. Wind-tossed and shaken canes can often be debarked and damaged by loose ties.

Encroaching Trees and Shrubs

In large beds of lilacs, especially if they must be hand mowed or weeded, one must be on guard for encroaching plants, shrubs, and trees. Certain of these can be a real nuisance, either from seedlings or by runners. Particularly difficult are the brambles (*Rubus*), black locust (*Robina pseudoacacia*), sumac (*Rhus typhina*), multiflora rose, and periwinkle (*Vinca minor*). These aggressors must be dealt with forthright and totally eliminated.

CHAPTER NINE

The Propagation of Lilacs

Lilacs can be propagated from seed, cuttings, layering, grafting, budding, and tissue culture. Each method has its advantages and problems, but for most home gardeners, cuttings and layering offer the best results, while commercial lilac growers, who need lots of plants to sell in the shortest amount of time, will want to propagate lilacs by tissue culture. Fiala experimented with grafting lilacs in his Ohio garden, but this technique requires lots of experience, so home gardeners who only need a plant or two generally do not bother with it. Growing lilacs from seed is time consuming and therefore of greatest interest to hybridizers wanting to create new plants.

Lilacs from Seed

Growing plants from seed is the most common means of plant propagation. Pollination is the transfer of pollen (male ♂) from the anthers to the stigma (female ♀) of a flower. It is followed by fertilization, the fusion of the male and female gametes, and seed formation. Pollen may be carried from anther to stigma either by wind, insects, birds, animals, or people. If a plant's blossom is pollinated by pollen produced by the same plant, it is referred to as self-pollination or selfing; the plant is selfed. If a plant's blossom is pollinated by pollen produced by another plant, it is referred to as cross-pollination.

The seed, once set, ripens and falls to the ground. Some of it is eaten by worms, insects, birds, or animals, or harvested by people. A few seeds are covered by leaves or sheltered in an earthen crevice. Of these, a few remain intact and find a favorable spot to germinate beneath or at some distance from the mother plant. Those eventually finding a suitable place freeze and thaw in moist conditions. This treatment breaks any inherent dormancy of the seed, preparing it for germination. When a seed germinates, the embryo develops into a seedling. In the spring a tiny percentage of all the seed produced by a plant will sprout and grow into new plants. (For more detailed information on the various stages from flower pollination to seed germination, consult Hartmann et al. 2002.)

Whether a lilac is selfed or cross-pollinated with another lilac, the offspring will show variation, since each garden lilac has inherited a mixed set of genes from several generations of ancestors. Seedlings that show desirable characteristics, be they habit of the plant, color of florets, or features of foliage or seed pod, may be propagated vegetatively, tested for the stability of the desired characteristics, and named as new cultivars.

Every cross between two different lilacs produces a hybrid. In an intraspecific hybrid, both parents belong to the same species. Most cultivars of *Syringa vulgaris* have resulted from intraspecific hybridization, as have most of the French Hybrids. The exceptions are cultivars that originated as bud mutations or sports. In an interspecific hybrid, the parents belong to different species. For instance, cultivars of *S.* ×*hyacinthiflora* and cultivars in the Villosae Group are interspecific hybrids; their parentage involves two or more lilac species.

When one picks seed from any given plant, there is no way of knowing whether that seed resulted from self-pollination or cross-pollination. Normally, in open-pollinated seed it is impossible to tell which plant may have been the pollen parent. In a controlled cross made by a hybridizer, only selected pollen is transferred to the stigmata of selected, emasculated florets (all stamens have been removed) which are then protected to assure that the parents are known. Usually controlled crosses yield seedlings equal or inferior to their parents, only a few may show some desirable traits that have been recessive in the parent

An open-pollinated seedling selection, *Syringa vulgaris* 'Azurea Plena', was used by Lemoine to create *S.* ×*hyacinthiflora*. B. Peart and M. Walton

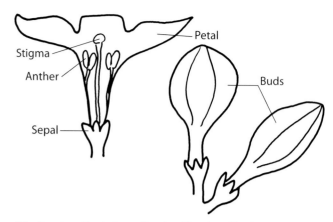

Lilac floret and buds for pollination. The closed buds are ready to have their anthers removed so self-pollination does not occur.
Drawing by John Fiala

plants, especially where exceptionally fine parents (often also the product of hand pollination) have been chosen. Crossing very superior parent plants with outstandingly unique characteristics may better the chances for success. Luck does play a role; horticultural breakthrough can happen when the right genes combine. Examples are Lemoine's use of *Syringa vulgaris* 'Azurea Plena' in creating *S.* ×*hyacinthiflora*, and the more recent creation of *S. vulgaris* 'Rochester'.

Hybrids and Controlled Crosses of Lilacs

Hybridizers select two outstanding lilac parents and carefully plan the cross. The flower bud must be carefully opened before any pollen, including its own, can reach the stigma. Just prior to opening the flower bud, remove the petals (the cylindrical corolla tube) very carefully with forceps (tweezers). Since the two stamens are inserted near or above the middle of the corolla tube, they can be removed with the corolla tube

without injury to the pistil. The pistil has a filiform style, shorter than the stamens, with a two-lobed stigma. The stigma is dusted with the desired pollen, using a fine-hair brush, glass rod, or similar implement. Emasculate and pollinate several florets on the same thyrse and remove all remaining florets and flower buds. After pollination carefully cover the thyrse to prevent unwanted pollen from reaching the newly pollinated stigmata. This is usually done with waxed paper bags which are sufficiently weatherproof to last for a week or more until the chances for open pollination have past. Remove the protective bag when no longer required; high temperatures within the bag may dry the pistil and cause mold. Mold is deadly to seed formation.

Always label each thyrse with the name or code of the seed (pod) parent (the one you emasculated) first, and the pollen parent (the one that supplied the pollen you just transferred) second. The formula is "pod parent × pollen parent." Open-pollinated seed should also be marked, namely, "pod parent × open." Enter the information of your crosses, with date and location, also in your record book.

If one is making crosses within an already heavily crossed species, dramatic results can be expected, but rarely happen. In *Syringa vulgaris*, for example, colors can be deepened, fragrance increased, resistance to sun-fading improved, floret size increased, new color patterns developed (rayed, eyed, edged, and so on), and a number of other desired characteristics can be brought out or strengthened.

If one is crossing two different species the results may be quite unexpected. Even more interesting plants

Syringa (Villosae Group) 'Lark Song' was bred by John Fiala. B. Peart and M. Walton

can arise from crossing several species. Some contemporary lilac hybridizers are no longer working on crosses using two different species but are working with hybrid plants that contain up to six different species (multibrids). The progeny of these crosses give rise to considerable variety. It is almost impossible to identify the genetic species in these complicated crosses unless excellent records are kept. For instance, 'Lark Song' resulted from a cross between (*Syringa sweginzowii* × *S. tomentella*) and *S. komarowii*; thus, it has the inherent characteristics of three species (a tribrid) in its make-up. 'Springtime' and 'Sunrise' are crosses of (*S. sweginzowii* × *S. tomentella*) × *S. wolfii*, also tribrids. Crosses of 'Lark Song' × 'Springtime' have four species (quatrobrids). Crosses of quatrobrid seedlings with *S.* × *prestoniae* (*S. villosa* × *S. komarowii* subsp. *reflexa*) are quintobrids (they contain five species). These newer multibrids become increasingly difficult to follow genetically and taxonomically unless well documented. Even the best taxonomist cannot ascertain the number of species they contain. Hybridizers are already creating cultivars involving eight species (polybrids). Further advances in interspecific breeding of lilacs are possible.

How good are all these multibrids as garden plants? Where compatible species have been crossed and recrossed, a veritable Pandora's Box of new forms, color shades, and plant variations has been opened. Further recombinations of genetic factors in new ratios may bring forth recessive factors, never seen before in a lilac. The more species crossed, the wider and more unpredictable the variations. What may be of value to the hybridizer or taxonomist may be worthless to the gardener concerned with landscape effect, or to the commercial grower. Unlike *Syringa vulgaris*, which has thousands of selected cultivars after intensive inbreeding, the remaining species of lilacs are mostly raw material with little or no inbreeding, hybridization, and selectivity of cultivars. It is doubtful that, as beautiful as these species are, they will ever approach the intensification of outstanding characteristics found in common lilac cultivars.

Collecting Lilac Seed

Cut off all unwanted seed pods immediately after blooming. Leave only the few you labeled and wish to save for seed. The lilac fruit is a two-celled capsule; each capsule contains four shiny brown seeds. When seed has been separated from the capsules (if dry this need not be done immediately but can wait for a winter day), store it in a bag or container in a cool place away from heat or sunlight after dusting it lightly with a fungicide. Lilac seed will germinate fairly even in the second year after collecting, but not well thereafter, if at all. Winter-picked capsules are generally worthless as they have already shed their seeds; any remaining seeds will have been attacked by mold and fungus in the wet capsule.

Planting Lilac Seed

Three methods for handling lilac seeds are possible. The first method is to prepare a seed bed early in the fall of good, well-drained, sandy-loam soil. Separate the dry seed from the capsules; this must always be done or else the capsule will waterlog and the seed will rot. Scatter the seed evenly over the bed. Cover lightly with ¼ inch (6 mm) of fine soil or sand. After the first freeze cover the entire bed with a very light mulch, an inch or two (2.5–5 cm) of straw or other light mulching material, to keep the soil from alternately thawing and freezing. Do not cover too heavily or the mulch will become waterlogged and stay wet all winter. Avoid using leaves since they may increase the chance for disease. In the spring remove the mulch to uncover small seedlings sprouting here and there. Shade your seedbed or frame at once from direct sunlight to prevent sun scorch.

The second method is to collect, dry, and clean seed in the fall. Save it in a plastic bag in a cool dry place until February. If refrigerated, store seed in a small glass jar and not in plastic to avoid the fluorinated hydrocarbon gas (freon) emitted by most older refrigerators. Even in small quantities, it is lethal to dry or growing seed. In February plant the seed in trays containing a sterile, damp medium that neither is soggy nor holds too much water, but allows good air circulation. A suitable medium is made of sterilized potting soil or milled sphagnum moss (*Sphagnum* species), mixed with a bit of coarse, washed sand. Water once, drain well, and cover with a clean plastic bag. Place the seed trays in a cool but not freezing place around 55–60°F (13–16°C). Dust the seed surface with a registered fungicide. Depending on the species, the seed should germinate in two to four weeks.

After the seeds have sprouted, or if you see no sprouts within three weeks, move the trays to a sunlit window, under grow lights, or into a greenhouse where the temperature remains 65–70°F (18–21°C) with ample sun or artificial light. Alternatively you may leave them in the cool area until you place them outdoors; if held for any length of time this, however, increases the risk of rotting and mold. Brought into sunlight and warmth the seed germinates and grows rapidly within about 10 days. Once the seedlings are growing, the trays should be uncovered and kept barely moist, never soggy, or all the plants will rot. Dust weekly with a fungicide to prevent damping off. The best preventive measure for this disease is good air circulation and not overwatering. Seed germination varies. *Syringa villosa* and its hybrids are more precocious than *S. vulgaris*, whereas *S. reticulata* seeds take about a month to six weeks. If you discover albino seedlings, with white first leaves and pink stems, do not bother planting them in seedling beds. They

Syringa vulgaris mature fruit. Želimir Borzan

have no chlorophyll and will eventually die. Do not confuse them with variegated leaves, those that have some little green in them. The latter will grow and perhaps be worth saving.

The third method is to store the dry seed in a glass jar in the refrigerator or a cool place. In spring when danger of frost is past, plant the seed directly outdoors in prepared seed beds within a lath or shade house, or in a shaded area, or in flats that can be moved at will. Cover the sown seed lightly and water well. Keep the seed bed or flats shaded and watered at all times. Outdoors you must water lightly almost daily; drying spring winds can cook seedlings. Cover your seed beds or flats with screen, or those pesky sparrows will soon make a dirt-bath out of your seed beds. For an earlier start you can sow your lilacs seeds in flats and grow them under artificial lights or place them in a sunny window or greenhouse. Dust them every 10 days with a fungicide. Set out the little plants either in a shade house or in a shaded nursery bed after danger of frost is over.

Caring for Seedlings

Once germinated, lilacs are tough, sturdy little seedlings, rather easy to grow. Cover them with screen or fencing when very small. Do not plant lilac seedlings too close together; give them a foot and a half (45 cm) at first; even this is a bit close and you will have to transplant every other one. Finally, transplant them after their second year to nursery rows in the open where they will have good soil, drainage, and sun, about 4–5 feet (1.2–1.5 m) apart, slightly closer if space is limited, and leave them until they bloom in about another two or three years. Do not overfertilize or you will be misled as to the real quality of the bloom and plant. Leave them after first bloom for another three years for evaluation.

Some seedlings may be discarded after the second flowering season. Keep evaluating them for several years. They either get better or worse with age—as do all of us. From open-pollinated seed, you will get only a very few seedlings that are worthy of being named; most can be discarded and destroyed. Do not perpetuate inferior plants by giving them away.

Once you begin hybridizing in earnest, not merely planting seed, you are on an endless and consuming,

Two-year-old seedlings of *Syringa oblata* subsp. *dilatata* 'Donaldii' show typical, large leathery deep green leaves with undulating margins. John Fiala

creative venture that grows and grows until it fills all your available time and land. May all your progeny not give you heartaches. In the long run you may be better buying the best named cultivars at whatever price. But then you will miss all the surprise associated with originating and creating new lilacs. (Addition technical information on lilacs from seed can be found in Schopmeyer 1974 and USDA 2005.)

Lilac Cultivars from Seed?

The answer is "No, lilac cultivars are clones." However, there are exceptions. Article 2.15 of *The International Code of Nomenclature for Cultivated Plants* (Brickell et al. 2004) reads, "An assemblage of plants grown from seed that is repeatedly collected from a particular provenance and that is clearly distinguishable by one or more characters (a topovariant) may form a cultivar." There are at least two topovariants among the lilac cultivars. The first, *Syringa reticulata* subsp. *reticulata* 'PNI 7523' Flemer 1988, is a single, white tree lilac marketed in the United States as Regent and Regent Brand Japanese tree lilac. Plants are grown from seed. The second, *S. villosa* 'Legacy' United States Department of Agriculture-Natural Resources Conservation Service, Bismarck, North Dakota, 1999, is a single, pinkish-flowered tall shrub grown from breeder's seed or certified seed. Plants of this late lilac appear to be well suited for planting in multirow farmstead and field shelterbelts, as wildlife habitat, and for recreational site plantings on the Great Plains (Vrugtman 2007b).

Lilacs from Tissue Culture

Micropropagation is used to rapidly increase the availability of new cultivars, and when propagation by conventional methods, such as rooting soft and hardwood cuttings and grafting, is not economical. There appears to be no species of lilac that cannot be propagated in this manner. Own-root plants of saleable size can be obtained within two years. For the home gardener and smaller operations that cannot afford the expense of a tissue-culture laboratory, the older, traditional methods of lilac propagation are presented. There will always be a few of us who prefer to propagate some of the lilac cultivars in a smaller way.

Great strides have been made in the methods of micropropagation. For lilacs it was merely a factor of adapting what had already been achieved in other plant species, making it economically feasible. Fiala had in his garden a tissue-culture plant of 'Lucie Baltet' that was equally as rapid-growing as those obtained by any other method. Unless a root-stock confers some benefit, such as greater hardiness in wet or clay conditions, or better disease control in plants for greenhouse forcing, self-rooting is an advantage for lilacs that have been tissue-cultured. There does not appear to be the problem in lilacs of great numbers of mutations due to the micropropagation process, as often found in genera such as *Heuchera* and *Hosta*.

Shoot multiplication is probably considered standard methodology for woody plant micropropagation; it is the one used for *Syringa*. The original method (Minocha 1979, Hildebrandt and Harney 1983, Haskell et al. 1986, Hildebrandt 1986) used a

growing shoot tip in a medium of high cytokinin concentrations to promote growth and to overcome apical dominance. This produced a many-branched shoot system. The individual shoots are either rooted or used for further development.

Shoots can also be obtained by encouraging a single shoot and dividing that for multiplication. The ease of manipulating the specific cultivar will determine the means of micropropagation by axillary development.

Toshio Murashige of the Department of Plant Sciences at the University of California, Riverside, has been a pioneer in the development of tissue-culture techniques. He stated that micropropagation involves four basic types of manipulations or stages (Murashige 1974). In Stage I an aseptic culture must be established; that is, an "explant," part of a stock plant, must be cleaned, disinfected and placed on a tissue-culture medium. A growing plant tissue must be obtained, free from all microbial contamination. This goal is usually the most difficult aspect to achieve in micropropagation, as simple as it may appear.

In Stage II, propagule or shoot multiplication often coincides with Stage I. Its objective is to obtain rapid increase in shoots or other structures that ultimately give rise to plants. Explants in shoot multiplication respond to the high concentration of cytokinin of the medium by proliferating new shoots. As many as one million shoots a year can be obtained by this method from single growing tip. Stage III involves the rooting of each plantlet, either *in vitro* using auxins (plant hormones) or *ex vitro/in vivo* by treating each shoot as a mini-cutting. Each cutting is typically treated with a rooting hormone and stuck in a plug tray with a fairly porous growing medium. Stage IV involves the acclimatization of the tissue-cultured plant to lower humidity, together with increased lighting found in a greenhouse or in outdoor conditions.

Stages II and IV, rooting and acclimatization, can be combined in lilacs, saving time, labor, and money. The hardening process of tender plantlets will require varying amounts of time, but should take no longer than one month.

Micropropagation, as briefly detailed, is not a technique for the home gardener, who is not equipped with sterile laboratory facilities. Most ornamental plants are now increased through tissue culture. Specialized facilities and streamlined procedures have brought about radical changes in the nursery industry. Since its early beginnings in the 1960s micropropagation has been greatly advanced and industrialized (Elke Haase, 2005, pers. comm. to F.V.; Virginia Hildebrandt, 2005, pers. comm. to F.V.). Readers more deeply interested are advised to consult the current literature for up-to-date information (for example, Kyte and Kleyn 1996). The importance of micropropagation of lilacs may be judged by the statistics for Germany—55,000 plants in 1988 to 455,000 plants in 2000 (Preil 2002).

Lilacs from Layered Branches

Layering is one of the oldest means of propagating plants. A branch is covered with soil so that new roots are produced (see figure this page). Occasionally a branch is close enough to the ground or can be bent; nick or wound the bark in two or three places at the lowest point of the branch, preferably below a leaf-bud, and dust the wounds with a rooting compound. Cover the branch with 3–4 inches (7.5–10 cm) of soil and keep damp to encourage callus and root formation. You can mound the layering site slightly with good soil to which sharp sand has been added, and place a good stone or brick on it to prevent the branch from snapping up out of the soil. Keep the soil moist. Secure the branch with a wire hoop or wooden peg.

In a year roots should have formed, but wait two years for good root formation. Cut the plant off the branch of the mother plant. Leave the layering in place for yet another year to form a more extensive root system, then transplant it to a permanent place or a nursery row, or pot it up. Layering is a longer process than propagating by suckers, but for some species and cultivars that do not sucker, it is an easy way of propagation.

Stool Layering of Lilacs

Stool layering is an old method which researchers at the East Malling Research Station, Kent, England, have refined in light of better knowledge of plant physiology. Called the Old Wood Method, it is used to obtain a number of new plants from a single older plant, hence the name. A plant is hilled for layering.

The bark is nicked, or wounded, then dusted with rooting compound. In four to six months a callus forms over the wound from which roots will grow. The hilling soil must be kept damp at all times to provide moisture and air for the rooting process. Plants are left hilled for a year.

Another method refined at East Malling produces plants sooner, with a stronger root system. The older canes of a strong lilac are pruned back to 4- to 6-inch (10- to 15-cm) stubs, forcing the mother plant to produce strong new growth. Several shoots will sprout and form pencil-thick growths the first year. These are then notched (bark wounded) slightly and dusted with rooting compound. Rooting medium is hilled up around the new, year-old growth some 4–5 inches

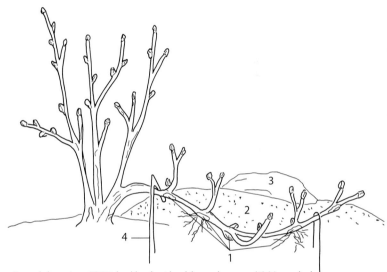

Branch layering: (1) Nicked bark at bud-branch areas. (2) Mounded soil covering wounded branch. (3) Rock holding branch in place. (4) Peg securing branch. Drawing by John Fiala.

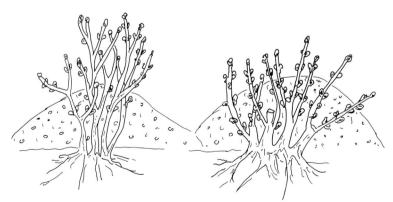

Stool layering. The Old Wood Method (left) uses wood that is two years old or older. The New Wood Method (right) uses shoots that are only one year old. Both methods require good well-drained loam-sand soil. Drawing by John Fiala.

(10–13 cm). The medium is kept damp but not wet so the forming roots have both adequate air and water. Use a mixture of two parts humus (well-rotted leaf mold), one part sharp sand, and one part good garden loam for the medium. Do not pack heavy soils or fine sand around the plant. Hill the plant so that only the top two buds are above ground (up to a foot [30 cm] or more depending on the size of the plant and the growth). Buds close to the medium surface generally do not root as they dry out too much; rather the deeper bud unions send out roots at the callus formations. After rooting is complete (after the first year), separate the new plants and transplant them to a lath or shade house for another year of supervised and watered growth. Remove the hilling medium and let the mother plant recover. A strong mother plant can be stool-layered every three to four years without harming it. Of course one must sacrifice the bloom from these propagating plants. By this method several handsome plants can be obtained from one hilling without harm to the mother plant. Stooling-beds were a common sight in many nurseries in the mid-20th century.

Lilacs From Root Shoots or Suckers

Most of the cultivars of *Syringa vulgaris* and its early hybrids produce adventitious buds along the upper root system. Some cultivars are notorious in producing root shoots (even to the point of being a nuisance), while other cultivars rarely produce them. If your lilac is not grafted, these root suckers, which appear a short distance from the main trunks, are identical in every way to the mother plant; this is another good reason why lilacs should not be grafted but be on their own root.

Root shoots or suckers are an excellent way to propagate choice lilacs on a small scale. It would be totally inadequate for large nursery needs. You must wait a year after the sucker appears to allow it to develop some roots of its own, then cut it off, closer to the main trunk than to the sucker since the roots are not always under the sucker stem directly but often some inches away at an angle. Use a sharp spade as the runner of the suckering shoot often is a few inches below the surface and quite heavy, needing some force of the spade to sever it. You can also clear away some

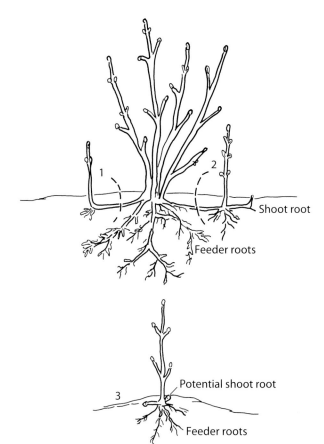

Separating a root shoot, or sucker, from a mother plant. (1) Cut here one year after sucker has appeared. (2) Leave a severed sucker in place one year to form feeder roots. (3) Replant a shoot one year after severing it, when it has sufficient feeder roots to sustain itself. Drawing by John Fiala.

of the soil close to the main stem and sever the runner with pruning shears. After severing it, leave it another year to develop a good root system of its own. The following fall take it up and plant it in a permanent place or a nursery row. You soon will have a strong, new plant identical in every way to the mother plant. Do not cut off the shoot when you first see it or, alas, you will have a stem without any root.

Lilacs from Cuttings

With a little skill and understanding it is possible to grow new lilacs from green cuttings (same season growth). Choose strong new growth, pencil thick if possible, with about four to five pairs of buds. Make your cuttings in late spring when new growth can be snapped off by hand and not bent only or too hardened. The best time for taking green cuttings of the early cultivars will be late May and early June, for

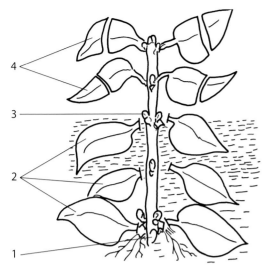

Making softwood cuttings. (1) Cut the base of the cutting just below the lowest set of leaves. New roots will form where the callous grows. (2) Remove the three lowest pairs of leaves at the bud juncture. (3) Insert the cutting into the growing medium, positioning the uppermost pair of leafless buds at ground level. (4) Cut off half of the remaining top leaves. Drawing by John Fiala.

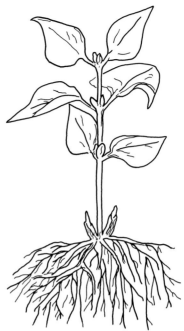

A well-rooted cutting. Drawing by John Fiala.

most others early to mid-June. Much depends upon the climate, local weather, and geographic area. Do not expose fresh cut materials to hot winds or sun; place them in an insulated cooler if many are to be made. Keep the length of cuttings rather uniform—to about 5 inches (13 cm) with four or five pairs of leaves. Make a basal cut just below the last pair of leaves, using a sharp knife. Remove the bottom two or three pairs of leaves at the bud juncture. Treat all cut ends with a rooting compound, following directions for either a liquid dip or a powder dusting. Insert the cutting into the medium, keeping the two lowest pairs of buds in the medium and the third pair just at ground level. The two pairs of cut leaves remain above the medium.

Prepare a good propagating medium. One recipe uses equal parts of vermiculite, sharp (not fine) sand, and shredded sphagnum moss or peat. Many very successful propagators use equal parts of vermiculite and sand with just a handful of peat or good garden loam. Whatever mixture is used it must be capable of holding moisture and yet have excellent aeration and drainage to prevent rotting of the cuttings. Always use a sterile mixture. If vermiculite is used, it must be $\frac{1}{8}$–$\frac{1}{4}$ inch (3–6 mm) in size, not the finely powdered form. Fine vermiculite, like fine sand, will compact and prevent aeration and drainage. Because soil aeration is very important for root development, the medium must be able to retain dampness without becoming soggy, yet provide for a flow of air that is consistent. If larger-grained sharp sand is not available, then substitute very small pea-gravel—never fine sand. Water once and drain well. Now you are ready to set the cuttings.

Place the cuttings vertically in the medium so that the third pair of buds is just even with the surface. Do not pack the medium tightly around the cuttings. Cover the entire container with heavy polyethylene or plastic, either a bag or sheet according to size needed. Use strong wire hoops as a frame to prop up the plastic from inside. If the medium has not been overwatered, the system will operate on its own, requiring only light and heat, 70°F (21°C) daytime and 65°F (18°C) at night. For quickest rooting, an even bottom heat of 70°F from a pre-set heating cable is excellent. Avoid higher temperatures.

Roots will begin to form in 8–12 weeks. Some cultivars and the late-blooming species root a bit faster than *Syringa vulgaris*. If you notice mold growing or leaves blackening or too much water forming in your little plastic greenhouse, something has gone wrong—non-sterile conditions or decay from some source, too much moisture, not enough soil aeration, or too much heat. The situation must be remedied immediately. Open, air, and remove the cause of the mold, dust with a fungicide, then reclose. It is not a bad idea to very lightly dust your cuttings with a fungicide just before you close or cover them with plastic. If cuttings show blackened leaves or buds or stem areas, throw them out and begin all over with more sterile medium and proper procedures.

Rooting Just a Few Lilac Cuttings

A few lilac cuttings, as few as two or three in a single pot, can be propagated with comparative ease. Use any size or shape of container that will fit on a window ledge in a half-shaded window. Thoroughly wash and sterilize the container by soaking it in a solution of 10 to 25 percent household bleach. Then line the container with a clear plastic bag (heavy duty and sterile), placing the bag in the container closed end down (the plastic bag will hold the soil; the container only keeps it together). Be certain there are no holes in the plastic. Fill the bag to the height of the container with damp, but not wet, rooting medium that has been sterilized. Use the medium mentioned previously (equal parts vermiculite, sharp sand, and shredded sphagnum moss or peat). You can sterilize small amounts of medium in a 200°F (93°C) oven for 20–30 minutes, keeping it covered so all the moisture does not evaporate. The sterilized soil must be damp but not wet and yet porous enough to allow for air flow. Loosen the rooting medium as you fill the bag to the proper level. It will take the shape of the container in which the bag is held.

Dust the cuttings lightly with a rooting compound. Making a hole in the soil with a pencil or round ob-

ject, inserting the cuttings into the rooting medium and slightly tighten the area around them left by the hole. If you merely push the cuttings into the loose medium you will rub off all the rooting compound. Tamp the cuttings slightly as you do not want them in an air pocket either. Do not crowd too many cuttings into one pot; three to four cuttings in a 5-inch (13-cm) pot allows enough space for air movement between the cuttings.

Next, draw the plastic bag up and close it tightly at the top. There will be sufficient moisture in the medium to create its own mini-greenhouse atmosphere.

A pot covered with a plastic bag serves as a mini-propagation lab. Drawing by John Fiala.

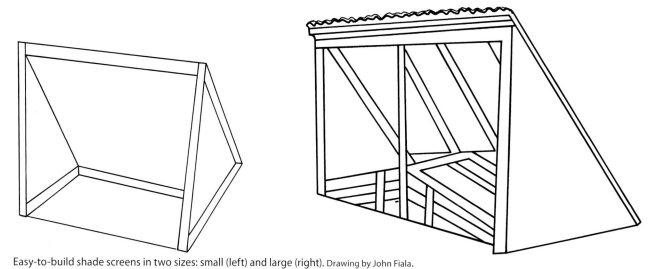

Easy-to-build shade screens in two sizes: small (left) and large (right). Drawing by John Fiala.

Too much water will cause rot and mold. If conditions are correct there is no need to open the plastic at all. Place the container in a shaded window with early morning or late afternoon sun, under artificial lights, or in a lath or shade house. Avoid direct sunlight which will overheat the small plastic greenhouse very quickly and cook or kill the cuttings; in this process they have no outside ventilation.

If shade is needed, construct a simple shade screen that opens to the north or northeast (see figure). It can be used to protect several pots. For a small unit, use a plywood panel 2–3 feet (60–90 cm) high. Paint the inside of the panel white to reflect indirect limited light, and sink the pots into the soil or sand-gravel bottom of the shade screen. For a larger model, make the frame with lumber 2 × 4 or 2 × 2 inches (5 ×10 or 5 × 5 cm). Use plywood panels to make the sides, and corrugated plastic panels for the roof. Paint the sides and roof white, inside and out. The larger model will provide room for several hundred cuttings in trays.

The success of this kind of system rests in using a medium that is only slightly on the damp side, not wet; using a sterile rooting medium and good cuttings; not overheating with high temperature; and protecting the cuttings from direct sunlight. It is relatively simple method, ideal for rooting a few cuttings indoors in a north or west window.

The Halward Method of Propagation Under Mist

A very successful method of rooting cuttings under constant mist has been developed by Ray E. Halward (1917–1989), propagator at Royal Botanical Gardens, Hamilton, Ontario, Canada. The procedure has been summarized by Chris Graham (1986):

1. The misting system is housed in a fiberglass, plastic-lined house, shaded with 46 percent shade saran outside plus burlap shade on the inside. Heating cables in the sand bed are set at 70°F (21°C) during the summer.

2. Cuttings are taken in the latter part of June up to 10 July, but those cuttings taken toward the end of this period will not root as readily as the ones taken earlier.

3. Cuttings are wounded on the bottom one-third in two places, on each side. As many as two and three sets of leaves are retained. Very large leaves at times are reduced in size.

4. The rooting medium is three parts sand and one part peat. Another good mixture is equal parts peat and perlite.

5. The most successful rooting compound is Seradix No. 3 (which is about 75 percent indolebutyric acid); it is mixed with equal parts of Captan 50W [a wettable powdered fungicide].

6. Cuttings are given extra light up to 16 hours a day. They are left until September and then hardened-off.

7. Rooted plants are overwintered in the same area with the heating cable set at 32°F (0°C) to prevent freezing. Plants are potted in early spring and are well started when set out.

Aftercare of Rooted Cuttings

All cuttings, especially those rooted under mist, must be gradually hardened-off. The cutting medium must be replaced by a slightly heavier soil with more nutrients. An excellent planting medium for rooted cuttings can be made by mixing equal parts sharp sand-gravel, good garden soil, and peat-humus. This medium drains well, has plenty of nutrients, and is able to retain some moisture. Never place newly rooted cuttings in heavy clay soils or water-holding sphagnum. The rooted cuttings must not dry out but also have a damp, well-aerated soil similar to the rooting medium. Before watering the cuttings, push your finger into the soil to ascertain how dry it really is. Often the upper surface appears dry but half an inch (1.3 cm) down all is sufficiently damp. Good leaf growth and color indicate healthy conditions. Yellow foliage, poor color, or poor growth can be the result of overwatering, excessive dryness, or unsuitable soil.

If the hardening-off area is in a lath or shade house and there is sufficient room between plants that are growing well, it is best to leave them there for a second year, resulting in larger and stronger plants. Mulch them with well-rotted humus; a bit of sharp sand can be added. After the second year they should be strong plants ready for transplanting to nursery rows or the garden. If they still appear weak and have only modest root growth, leave them for a third or even a fourth year. Much depends on the local climate, the length of the growing season, and soil conditions.

Second-year plants may be ready for potting up and entering the nursery container trade. They are much smaller than grafted plants but saleable, especially if they are of the newer, special cultivars or species. They should be so labeled, "Special—Rooted Cutting of New Cultivar." Container plants tend to dry out much more quickly if not in a deeply mulched, buried holding area.

Always propagate only the better and newer cultivars. Certain cultivars are extremely difficult, if not impossible, to propagate from cuttings, whereas others seem to root no matter when taken and with minimal care. Ordinarily the lavender, pink, and blue lilacs grow and root somewhat faster than the white and very deep purple ones. Tetraploids and dwarfs appear to be the slowest to root and develop in transplantable size plants. 'Rochester' roots slowly and grows poorly for many years before it is established, thus making it an unattractive cultivar for the nursery trade. If one grafts it on white ash and is patient to care for it for five or six years, it is a most desirable cultivar and it should command a premium price.

Research and experimentation in finding more efficient and more productive ways to root lilac cuttings has been done in various places under various conditions. See Coggeshall 1962, Congdon 1965, Bojarczuk 1978a, 1978b, and Haskell et al. 1986 for details.

Grafting Lilacs

Grafting is an old technique used in propagating lilacs. In China and Europe certain species of lilacs were grafted as long ago as the mid-18th century.

It is not known who discovered that lilacs could be grafted on *Ligustrum* (privet) rootstock. Neither is there any record of which privet species was used in China, where 25 *Ligustrum* species and subspecies are native (Chang and Green 1996b), or in Europe, where *L. vulgare* is native, but knowledge of such grafting appears to date back to the late 18th century. In North America, rootstocks of *L. ovalifolium* (California privet, native to Japan) and *L. vulgare* (European privet) were most commonly used. Commercial growers in America and Europe have subsequently searched for rootstocks that are better than privet. When privet rootstock is used as a graft nurse, the lilac scion does not always develop its own roots. This results in a single-stemmed plant that is subject to injury, borers, and incompatibility of scion and rootstock, causing the lilac to die. Furthermore, privet is short lived and sends up sucker growth.

Lilac cultivars have been grafted on *Syringa vulgaris* (common lilac), *S. villosa* (late lilac), and *S. ×persica* (Persian lilac). Each has its own difficulties. *Syringa vulgaris* sends up sucker growth which is indistinguishable from the top-worked cultivar and which eventually takes over the whole plant, spelling death for the cultivar graft. *Syringa villosa* does not allow the scion to form its own roots and will outgrow it. *Syringa ×persica* rootstock is a favored host for root nematodes. Although Gao Runqing et al. (2001) have shown that *S. oblata* and *S. pekinensis* can provide compatible rootstock for *S. vulgaris*, in general, lilacs are unsatisfactory as rootstock, special rootstocks for forcing lilacs being the exception.

Fraxinus (ash) species function best as understock for grafting and starting the lilac on its own roots. Like *Ligustrum*, *Fraxinus* is a woody plant genus closely related to *Syringa* in the Oleaceae (olive family). Both *F. americana* (white ash) and *F. pennsylvanica* (green or red ash) can be used as rootstock. In the first year the ash understock feeds and supports the lilac scion, forcing it to form a strong root callus and its own fibrous roots. After that the ash root falls away and the lilac, now well-rooted, is entirely on its own. At this time the lilacs are lifted and sold or replanted in nursery rows for further growth as two- or three-year-old plants on their own roots.

Saddle Grafts and Cleft Grafts

Saddle grafting or cleft grafting works well with ash rootstock. Both types of graft promote sufficient callus formation by the lilac scion to induce own-root formation.

Grafting is generally done in late fall or in winter. If a greenhouse is available, the late winter months of January and February are most favorable and scions are collected at the time of grafting. When grafting is done in late September to October, the grafts are set out in specially protected beds in a lath or shade house for protection.

For the rootstock, use white ash, privet, or common lilac. For scions always use current season's growth of pencil thickness and at least 5–6 inches long (13–15 cm) with at least three pairs of leaf-buds. Do not use twigs with long internodes (the part between two nodes). Do not pack the scions in damp paper, moss, or similar materials as this will foster mold. Instead, wrap the budwood in a dry, plastic bag to eliminate air and store in a refrigerator, or in a snow bank, until grafts are made.

To prepare a rootstock for saddle grafting, cut the top into a point as shown in the figure below. Then prepare the scion to fit over that point by making two cuts in the shape of an inverted V. Fit the scion over the rootstock and tightly tie the graft with a rubber tie.

To prepare a rootstock for cleft grafting, make two cuts as indicated in the figure (below right). The first cut removes a small piece of the rootstock. The second cut creates a pocket, or cleft, in the rootstock. Next, prepare the scion, again by making two cuts as shown. The first cut removes a small piece of the scionwood to create a pointed end. The second cut merely slits, or makes a slash, in the scion. Insert the twice-cut scion into the twice-cut rootstock and tightly tie the graft with a rubber tie. Make certain there are no air spaces where the scionwood and rootstock meet. The cambium (green, growing skin just below the bark) layers

must join tightly. The success of the graft depends on knitting these two layers together.

For both types of grafting, allow the grafts to callous in damp sphagnum, damp sawdust, or barely damp sand for a week to 10 days at 70°F (21°C). When they have calloused, the grafts may be planted outdoors or transferred to cold storage for spring planting. In the field, all understock root shoots must be cut off immediately or they will outgrow and smother the graft. Be certain to plant up to and including the first buds on the scion. The graft must be covered entirely when it is planted.

In the nursery grafting is done in the winter. One ash root can yield three or four rootstocks, each 5–8 inches (13–20 cm) long, depending on the caliper of the scion. The grafts are dipped in a household-bleach solution or dusted with a horticultural fungicide, then covered with sterile, damp sphagnum moss, more on the dry side than wet, and finally covered with plastic before being placed in a greenhouse or cellar at about

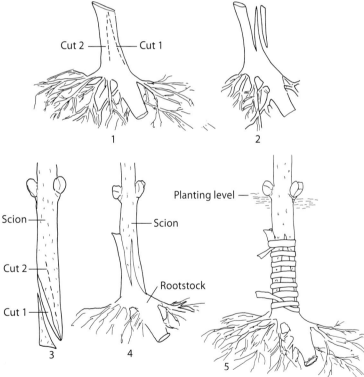

Saddle graft on white ash. After cutting the scion (left top) and understock (left bottom) as indicated, fit the two pieces together (center), and tightly wrap the graft with a rubber tie (right). Drawing by John Fiala.

Cleft graft: (1) Rootstock marked for cutting. Cut 1 removes a small piece of the rootstock; cut 2 does not. (2) Rootstock prepared and ready for scion. (3) Scion after the first cut has been made. Cut 1 removes a small piece of the scion; cut 2 does not. (4) Completed graft with scion inserted into rootstock. The two pieces must fit tightly for the graft to take. (5) Wrapped graft ready for callous formation, after which it may be planted in the ground up to the first buds on the scion. The graft must be covered entirely. Drawing by John Fiala.

65–70°F (18–21°C) where they are kept out of direct sunlight and heat. The grafts must be slightly damp (not wet) to begin the growth process which initiates callus formation. Callus formation requires from four to eight weeks, and during that time the grafts must not be permitted to mold. The grafts are then planted out in a cold-frame or cool greenhouse, or stored very slightly damp for later planting.

Home gardeners can follow the same procedure, making a few grafts and placing them in a pot covered with a plastic bag and set in a shady window in a cool place. For most beginners, however, propagating from cuttings may be more successful than from grafts.

Always use clean, sharp grafting knives without nicked blades to produce clean cuts. Practice cuts on any two twigs, shaping and fitting them together. No one achieves 100 percent success, but with practice and proper management and care of the grafts, at least half should grow.

Green-Graft Cuttings

On a small scale, success may be had in rooting lilac grafts by spring grafting lilac scions on larger ash trees, 3–5 inches (7.5–13 cm) in diameter. After the top of the tree has been entirely removed by making a smooth, horizontal cut, scions are bark-grafted onto the trunk and held in place by electrical tape. The strong, established root system of the ash will force the scions into rapid spring growth (usually done in late April or early May). When the new growth has reached about 6–10 inches (15 to 25 cm), the grafts are unwrapped and will be found to have heavy, white callus growth. Carefully remove the scion with as much white callus adhering as possible, pot it as you would a cutting, and cover with a plastic bag. Root formation is very quick on such green-graft cuttings. Where just a few plants are desired this method works quite well.

Summer Budding of Lilacs

Lilacs may also be propagated by budding, by inserting a bud eye in an understock of a rooted plant. In this method, a single bud is used rather than a scion with several pairs of buds. Thus budding is a more cost-effective method to propagate many new plants from limited stock plants. A single bud will grow an entirely new top of the desired cultivar. If the bud is expected to form its own roots later, the bud-graft must be placed low, near the root of the understock, so it will be covered with soil in which to form roots of its own.

Lilacs are generally budded in the summer when the current year's leaf buds have matured. This usually occurs before roses begin to bud. First prepare the understock by removing most of the growth above the place where the bud is to be inserted, leaving only one or two small branches to keep the sap flowing above the budded area. Never leave any new shoots that appear on the understock below the bud.

Now prepare the cuts. With a sharp budding knife, cut off the bud from the bud stick (see the figure below), leaving a small heel of wood on the bud. Do not peel the bud off, but cut it off the wood. And do not touch the cut surface with your fingers. Make the bud-cut flat, not scooped or dished. Next make a T-shaped cut in the understock, cutting only as deep as the cambium layer. Make sharp, clean cuts with no frayed edges, gently peeling or slipping back the cambium just far enough to insert the prepared bud. Pull

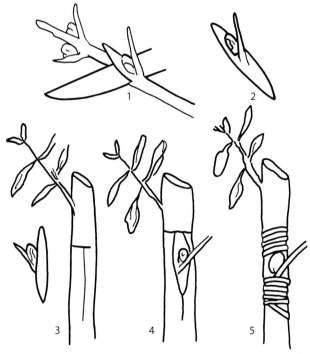

Budding lilacs: (1) Cut the bud eye off with a sharp knife. (2) Bud eye ready for budding. (3) Understock marked for a T-cut where the bud eye will be inserted. Bud eye positioned for insertion. (4) Bud eye inserted into understock. (5) Bud eye and understock wrapped tightly with a rubber tie. Drawing by John Fiala.

the T-cut cambium bark back over the bud, being careful to match the cambium layers exactly.

Fit the two pieces tightly together and wrap the bud securely beginning at the top with either a rubber budding strip or waxed twine. End the wrapping at the bottom of the bud. With practice you can tie the bud in securely either from the top or bottom. Tying a bud from the bottom may prevent rainwater from seeping in.

Within about a week the bud will be either plump and green, indicating it has knitted (or taken), or shriveled and dry, indicating it is a failure. The summer after the bud has united with the understock and begun to grow, remove the remaining top stock.

Most bud failures are due one of the following causes: allowing the bud to dry out before it was inserted or allowing too much air in the budding process by not tightening the tie sufficiently; peeling back too much green cambium so the layers failed to meet; making faulty, careless, frayed cuts; allowing too much wild growth to develop on the understock below the bud or not cutting off all the top stock, both of which can hinder the bud's growth; and overexposing the bud to hot drying winds and hot suns with little ground moisture for the understock. The buds will remain dormant until the following spring.

Producing New Lilac Cultivars

The three ways to produce new cultivars of lilacs are by hybridization, either controlled hand pollination or uncontrolled open pollination; by inducing polyploidy, or increasing the number of chromosomes; and by propagating mutations, or sports, which either occur spontaneously or are induced. Each way is a rather exacting science and art, so each is considered separately. Undoubtedly, the greatest number of new cultivars will be produced by hybridization. Although there have been reports of genetically modified tree crops, we know of no genetically modified lilac cultivars yet.

Hybridizing Lilacs

For those interested in hybridizing lilacs the following suggestions provide a firm basis to proceed in a rational way. Some individuals will gather seed and plant it, hoping for an outstanding new cultivar and, indeed, some few, fine seedlings will come forth from these efforts. Real progress in breeding exceptional new lilacs will come from the hands of those who seriously hybridize, that is, those who hand-pollinate lilacs with a set purpose of selected parents.

Several models or programs of hybridization are proposed here. Each one should include a hybridizing plan with a specific purpose and with special selection of parent materials. Examples are crossing *Syringa vulgaris* 'Rochester' with *S. oblata* subsp. *oblata* 'Alba' to obtain better large-flowering, early-blooming white lilacs; or crossing *S. pubescens* subsp. *patula* with *S. pubescens* subsp. *julianae* to produce low-blooming little-leaved lilacs; or crossing 'Prodige' and 'Rochester' to produce large-flowered, multipetaled deep purple lilacs. Always use only the best gene stock available and choose authenticated plants for parentage.

A program of hybridization also needs to include safeguards for controlled purity of the cross-pollination. Precautions must be set up against insect pollination and wind pollination as well as against self-fertilization.

Hybridization programs also require a schedule for controlled observation of the entire seedling population resulting from the entire seed crop. One specific, singular trait should not be ascribed as a cross characteristic when it appears in only one or two seedlings. Accurate records should be kept of all cross traits and characteristics with total objectivity as to merit or values. Adopt a simple alphanumeric (combination of letters and numbers) breeder's code for your breeder's records, plant labels, and planting-map. Only a combination of these three records will prevent future embarrassment when you are asked about the ancestry of your prize cultivar introduction. Serious plant breeders keep a stud book, which in the long run may provide clues to the inheritance of any given traits. The example on page 260 is from Owen Rogers.

All hybridization programs should establish carefully derived standards for the selection of individual crosses. These should be pursued with complete objectivity, with selection emphasis based both on the merits of genetic inheritance and the general traits of the specific cross. Selectivity for hybridization at times may be quite different from selectivity for the com-

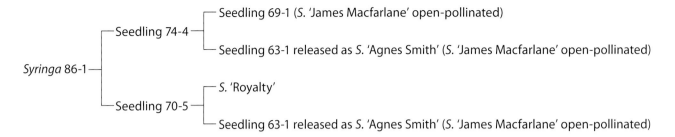

┌─ Seedling 74-4 ┬─ Seedling 69-1 (*S.* 'James Macfarlane' open-pollinated)
│   └─ Seedling 63-1 released as *S.* 'Agnes Smith' (*S.* 'James Macfarlane' open-pollinated)
Syringa 86-1 ┤
│   ┌─ *S.* 'Royalty'
└─ Seedling 70-5 ┴─ Seedling 63-1 released as *S.* 'Agnes Smith' (*S.* 'James Macfarlane' open-pollinated)

Stud book record of the parentage of *Syringa* 86-1 (adapted from Rogers 1994).

mercial market. Very often a winner on the commercial market may have little to offer future generations of hybrids because it is a poor parent. Lilacs 'Sensation' and 'Primrose' are such examples in the area of flower color.

In hybridization two distinct approaches can be taken: one of intensive, selective breeding within a given species (intraspecific breeding), or one of careful crossing of two or more different species (interspecific breeding).

Intraspecific Hybridization

Breeding within a species is simply crossing different cultivars or selections within the same species, or, very strictly, crossing the offspring of special cultivars with each other (sibcrossing). In the many hundreds of cultivars or selections of *Syringa vulgaris* certain crosses have been developed with such strong and set characteristics that they could be considered clonal crosses. Examples are the heavy Lemoine doubles, the large-flowered Havemeyer singles, the multipetaled singles resulting from 'Rochester' ('Rochester' hybrids).

Intraspecific hybridization seeks to select certain special characteristics—size of florets or thyrses, color intensification, low-growing or dwarf habit—and to intensify them by inbreeding. It may also seek to take two different characteristics found one in each parent and combine them with the hope of finding both characteristics in the offspring. An example would be crossing the deep purple of 'Prodige' with the multi-petaled florets and candle-spikes of the white 'Rochester' in hope of producing a deep purple, multipetaled candle-spiked lilac. This kind of hybridization combines unique characters to deepen the color or clarify its brightness, add fragrance, and bring out an earlier or later blooming cultivar. It is interesting to note that Hulda Klager did most of her work with only three *Syringa vulgaris* cultivars. Any character can be intensified to a certain point with continued, careful selective breeding for that factor.

Backcrossing involves crossing the end product of any inbred line back to one of the original or very early parents. Frequently some very outstanding results and intensification of an originally sought-after factor are thus obtained. For example, crossing the

The use of *Syringa vulgaris* 'Rochester' in breeding has given a whole array of new colors, combinations, stripes, stars, eyes, and other forms, including pearled lilacs, softly iridescent and reflecting like mother-of-pearl. B. Peart and M. Walton

third and fourth generation 'Rochester' hybrids back to 'Rochester' would undoubtedly give some very fine 'Rochester' type offspring.

Out-crossing within a given species, such as *Syringa vulgaris*, which has so many diverse cultivars (nearly 2000 named cultivars), involves crossing one clone bred for a special factor, such as floret size, to another bred for a different characteristic, such as special color. Often the infusion of sufficiently different clonal material gives the offspring special vigor. This phenomenon is termed *hybrid vigor*. A common example of hybrid vigor is hybrid corn. In *S. vulgaris* the original and earlier named cultivars of deep purple were marked by weak and poor growth; with the infusion of clonal vigor from other colored lilacs we now have strong-growing very deep purple lilacs such as 'Agincourt Beauty', 'Albert F. Holden', and 'Prodige'. Extensive hybridization work in *S. vulgaris* has been done by the Lemoines, Havemeyer, Eveleens Maarse, Kolesnikov, Fenicchia, and Fiala.

Interspecific Hybridization

Interspecific crosses are those made between two different species or species hybrids within a genus. To date only interspecific hybridization within series *Syringa* has been successful, with the exception of *S. ×diversifolia*, which resulted from a cross between *S. pinnatifolia* (series *Pinatifoliae*) and *S. oblata* (series *Syringa*). The continued interspecific crosses of lilacs will undoubtedly provide some of the most exciting and profitable new lilacs for both hybridizers and commercial growers. These crosses, however, require some of the most difficult work, selectivity, and evaluation. Being the least profitable commercially in the beginning, they eventually should prove their worth in the third and fourth generations. The landmark hybridization by Isabella Preston to produce the remarkable Preston hybrids may not have gained her a fortune, but it has set a foundation of considerable magnitude for others to build upon.

All the horticultural world, especially lilac fanciers, should be aware of the interspecific crosses made by Preston, the Lemoines, and Frank Skinner. These are milestones in lilac hybridizing. Fewer individuals still are aware of the breeding work on *Syringa ×prestoniae* by Władysław Bugała of Kórnik Arboretum, Poland; that by Owen Rogers of University of New

Syringa (Villosae Group) 'Danusia' was bred by Władysław Bugała in Poland from *S. ×prestoniae*. B. Peart and M. Walton

Hampshire, who has worked rather extensively with the beginnings of new double forms of *S. ×prestoniae* and *S. ×josiflexa*; and the work by Donald Egolf in advancing *S. ×hyacinthiflora* at the U.S. National Arboretum, in Washington, D.C. James S. Pringle at Royal Botanical Gardens, Hamilton, Ontario, Canada, crossed some relatively little-worked-with species. Fiala worked with several different and new crosses, some with multibrids (plants having the genetic background of four and five different species). Although all have had some degree of success, results of their work are not yet available to the horticultural trades or private collectors. These efforts should be continued with additional hybridization and considerable selection. There are any number of hybridizing possibilities for new hybridizers in continuing this work of backcrossing, line-breeding, multibrid crossing, and selective breeding.

Through the 19th and 20th centuries, interspecific hybridization concentrated on species in the series *Syringa* (*S. ×hyacinthiflora* of man-made origin; although *S. ×chinensis*, *S. ×laciniata*, and *S. ×persica* are of unknown origin in time and place) and *Villosae* (*S. ×henryi*, *S. ×josiflexa*, *S. ×nanceiana*, *S. ×prestoniae*, and *S. ×swegiflexa*, plus cultivars in the Villosae Group, all of man-made origin). As mentioned earlier, *S. ×diversifolia* involves the series *Pinnatifoliae*. Species in the series *Pubescentes* may still have untapped genetic resources.

Inducing Polyploids in the Genus *Syringa*

Polyploids are plants in which the number of chromosomes has been doubled, tripled, and so on, to varying degrees. Such plants appear in some species in nature, but seem to be naturally absent in others. To date, no polyploid species of *Syringa* have been found in nature.

Significant advance has been made in genera other than *Syringa* with tetraploid and polyploid plants. Many new and often superior forms have thus arisen in horticultural plants available for our gardens.

One of the first individuals to attempt to produce a polyploid lilac was Karl Sax, working at the Arnold Arboretum. Sax reportedly produced a tetraploid *Syringa vulgaris*, which subsequently was lost. Fiala worked for nearly 40 years with various *Syringa* species to produce experimental tetraploids, polyploids, and mixtoploids. He reported obtaining tetraploid hybrids of *S. julianae*, *S. komarowii*, *S. ×prestoniae*, *S. wolfii*, *S. yunnanensis*, and several *S. vulgaris* cultivars and crosses with *S. ×hyacinthiflora* and *S. oblata*, but provided no evidence such as chromosome counts. A few of these hybrids have been named. They include 'Eventide', 'Garden Peace', 'Lark Song', 'Prophecy', 'Spellbinder', and 'Sunrise'. Fiala intended these cultivars primarily for further hybridization rather than as garden lilacs. He indicated that several second- and third-generation seedlings remained under evaluation, but did not record names or breeder's codes, and none of these unnamed selections appears to have been distributed. A third earlier hybridizer is Owen Rogers at the University of New Hampshire. Rogers has done some limited work looking for tetraploids, specializing in the *S. ×josiflexa* hybrids. No tetraploids were found.

Chromosome Counts in *Syringa*

Although the specific chromosome counts of lilac species are not of primary interest to the general lilac fancier, they are of interest to hybridizers. Generally, species will cross only within their own series and with species having identical chromosome counts. The basic number of chromosomes found in *Syringa* are diploid (referred to as $2n$, the lowest possible for the species). Under certain conditions arising either naturally or by the use of specific chemicals, the count on occa-

sion can be doubled, tripled, quadrupled, and so on. Thus we would have $2n$ = diploid, $3n$ = triploid, $4n$ = tetraploid, $5n$ = quintoploid, and so on, increasing the number of the total chromosomes proportionately.

The ordinary (diploid) number of chromosomes in *Syringa* is 44, 46 or 48; the haploid number is $x = 22$, 23, or 24, depending on the species (Darlington and Janaki-Ammal 1945, Darlington and Wylie 1956). Although modern technology in microscopy and photography facilitate the process of counting chromosomes, the high and varying diploid number in *Syringa* is a handicap. All the species and principal lilac hybrids that have been counted to date are presented here in Table 2. No chromosome counts appear to have been reported for *S. ×diversifolia*, *S. ×josiflexa*, *S. mairei*, *S. ×nanceiana*, *S. ×prestoniae*, *S. pubescens* subsp. *julianae*, *S. ×swegiflexa*, and *S. wardii*. The few presumed tetraploids, although so far unconfirmed and unpublished, would follow the tetraploid number for their diploid counterpart. In *S. vulgaris* we find varying diploid counts from 46, 47, to 48. One must be aware that very little chromosome recounting is done once a number has been published. It may be that there are certain groups, especially in *S. vulgaris* and perhaps in *S. oblata*, that vary from the given count. In 1971, a magnificent cultivar of *S. vulgaris* named 'Rochester' was introduced that gives every indication from external characteristics that it could well be a natural tetraploid, but this has still to be confirmed.

Not only is it important to the hybridizer to be able to work with a plant having increased numbers of chromosomes, but this increase may also be expressed in the physical appearance of the tetraploid plant such as thicker, heavier, more leathery leaves; somewhat larger florets and thyrses with deeper color and new hues, often with iridescent tones; thicker flower petals that withstand sun and weather better; more buds, at closer intervals; and often more stamina and resistance to certain diseases and viruses. These traits do not generally appear as dominant until fixed in the third and fourth generations of polyploid crossings. Hence it takes considerable time not only to induce a polyploid but also to carry it on through the next generation to an acceptable garden plant.

As yet no one has done for *Syringa* what the Japanese have done for *Paeonia*, namely, counting chromo-

Table 2. Chromosome counts for the species and principal hybrids of genus *Syringa*.

Subgenus *Ligustrina*

S. reticulata subsp. *reticulata*	2n = 46 (Sax and Abbe 1932)
S. reticulata subsp. *amurensis*	2n = 46 (Tischler 1930, Sax and Abbe 1932)
	2n = 46–48 (Sax 1930)
S. pekinensis	2n = 46 (Chen Jin-Yong, 30 January 2005, pers. comm. to F.V.)

Subgenus *Syringa*, Series *Syringa*

S. vulgaris	2n = 46, 47, 48 (H. Taylor 1945)
	2n = 46 (Uhrikova 1978, Javurkova 1981)
S. oblata	2n = 46 (Sax 1930, H. Taylor 1945)
	2n = 46–48 (Sax and Abbe 1932)
S. oblata subsp. *dilatata*	2n = 46 (Chen Jin-Yong, 30 January 2005, pers. comm. to F.V.)
S. protolaciniata	2n = 46 (Weng and Zhang 1992)
S. ×*chinensis*	2n = 28–40 (Tischler 1908)
	2n = ca. 32 (Tischler 1921–1922)
	2n = 38–40 (Borgenstam 1922)
	2n = 39, 49, 52 (Sax 1930)
S. ×*hyacinthiflora*	2n = 48 (H. Taylor 1945)
S. ×*laciniata*	2n = 44 (Sax and Abbe 1932)
S. ×*persica*	2n = 72–88 (Sax 1930)
	2n = 88 (Tischler 1930)
	2n = 44 (Sax and Abbe 1932)

Subgenus *Syringa*, Series *Pinnatifoliae*

S. pinnatifolia	2n = 48 (Sax 1930, Sax and Abbe 1932)

Subgenus *Syringa*, Series *Pubescentes*

S. pubescens	2n = 48 (Sax 1930, Sax and Abbe 1932)
S. pubescens subsp. *patula*	2n = 48 (Sax 1930, Sax and Abbe 1932, as *S. palibiniana*)
	2n = 46 (Sax 1930, as *S. koehneana*)
S. pubescens subsp. *microphylla*	2n = 48 (H. Taylor 1945)
S. pubescens subsp. *microphylla* var. *potaninii*	2n = 46 (H. Taylor 1945)
S. meyeri	2n = 46 (Sax 1930)
	2n = 46–48 (Sax and Abbe 1932)
S. meyeri var. *spontanea*	2n = 46 (Weng and Zhang 1992)

Subgenus *Syringa*, Series *Villosae*

S. villosa	2n = 46, 48 (Sax and Abbe 1932)
S. emodi	2n = 44 (Tischler 1930)
	n = 23 (Mehra 1976)
S. wolfii	2n = 46 (Sax 1930)
S. josikaea	2n = 44 (Tischler 1930)
	2n = 46, 48 (Sax and Abbe 1932)
S. komarowii	2n = 46 (Sax 1930)
	2n = 46, 48 (Sax and Abbe 1932)
S. komarowii subsp. *reflexa*	2n = 46 (H. Taylor 1945)
S. tomentella	2n = 46, 48 (Sax and Abbe 1932)
S. sweginzowii	2n = 46 (H. Taylor 1945)
S. yunnanensis	2n = 48 (Sax 1930)
S. ×*henryi*	2n = 46 (Sax 1930)

somes of most of the individual cultivars. It would be an enormous task; perhaps only the most outstanding cultivars for which authenticated plants are available could be counted. Undoubtedly, variations will be found. As yet, the field of tetraploid lilacs is an uncharted one that could add another dimension to this already magnificent shrub. The cost of research and the time and tedious work involved are not appealing to most younger researchers. It is a lifetime work and not a task for tinkerers or those easily distracted. Perhaps some financially well-endowed lilac fancier might establish grants for some of this work. Curators of lilac collections must also be urged to keep meticulous records; authenticated plants are essential for this kind of research.

Using Colchicine to Induce Polyploids

In nature polyploids are induced in a variety of ways, for instance, when seeds or plants are frozen in ice under tremendous pressure of weight, or subjected to certain natural vacuums, electrical charges (lightning), or chemical reactions which effect the growing plant cells in mitosis (the time of cell division in the growing plant tissue). In the laboratory various means have been used as well: heat, radiation (gamma rays), and several experimental chemicals. One naturally produced chemical is colchicine ($C_{22}H_{25}O_6N$), an alkaloid in the juice of *Colchicum autumnale* L., naked ladies or meadow saffron (not to be confused with autumn crocus, *Crocus sativus* L., the commercial source of saffron) (Blakeslee and Avery 1937).

In the United States colchicine use is restricted by federal regulation. Similar restrictions may be in effect in other countries. Colchicine is rather expensive, difficult to obtain, and considerably dangerous to use if its fumes are inhaled or if it touches the skin. It is a potent, carcinogenic drug which must not be used by beginners. When proper precautions are followed, colchicine is easy to work with as it is soluble in water, does not disintegrate or contaminate too rapidly, and is reasonably stable in its activity. Use care to keep this solution from becoming diluted by any additional water which will render it too weak to be effective. Colchicine solutions should be stored in dark-colored glass bottles away from sunlight, in a cool place. The solution can be reused several times if not diluted. Keep colchicine out of reach of children.

Best results are obtained by using colchicine at the crucial time of cell division; therefore, it is used only on actively growing material, such as sprouting seedlings or expanding new growth. Near-lethal doses may produce the necessary disruption that could result in longitudinal splitting of chromosomes, producing polyploids, but most of the plants so treated will die, approximately 90 percent, and not all the plants that remain will be polyploid. A few may have mixed numbers of unstable chromosomes (called mixtoploids), and some will divide unevenly and become sterile triploids.

Fiala (1977) found that the most economical and effective use of colchicine in lilacs was with germinating seed or with emerging new growth (by inverting potted lilac plants and immersing the expanding buds and very short new growth in the colchicine solution). Long new growth was too difficult to treat. Fiala also found that most *Syringa* seedlings and growing tissue reacted well to treatments using an aqueous solution containing 0.048 to 0.06 percent colchicine (one gram of colchicine powder dissolved in one liter of distilled water gives a 0.1-percent solution; 0.5 gram per liter gives a workable 0.05-percent solution, which is the most effective strength for treating *Syringa*).

Pre-germinated *Syringa* seeds in active growth—just as the first true leaves begin to unfold—are the best subjects. It is imperative that hard-covered seedcoats, such as in *S. reticulata*, are carefully removed before treatment as these seed-coats greatly inhibit and soak-up additional chemical and thus prolong the process. Allow the seeds to swell, and as they break, before the cotyledons open fully, treat them. The best way to pre-germinate seed is in sterile milled sphagnum moss with some bottom heat of 65–68°F (18–20°C). Do not wash seedlings prior to treatment, as this will dilute the colchicine solution.

With the seedlings in heavy test tubes (glass cigar tubes are ideal), dip them in the colchicine solution until the seedlings are just covered, then cork the tubes. Let the seedlings sit in this solution for 12 to 36 hours; slight stir or shake. The longer the treatment the more lethal the dosage and the more seedlings will die. Pour off the solution (to be reused), and rinse the seedlings a few times. Then place them in a sterile water bath for up to 30 hours or at least equal to the treatment time to rid them of all excess colchicine

Syringa yunnanensis 'Prophecy' is one of several colchicine-induced polyploids created by John Fiala. B. Peart and M. Walton

which will continue to react, if not removed, and kill the seedlings by overexposure.

Wash the seedlings, then plant them in an absolutely sterile, slightly damp medium composed of equal parts of sphagnum, perlite, sharp sand, and sterile potting soil. Dampen and water only with sterile water. Dust with a fungicide. Do not overwater and do not let the seedlings dry out during the crucial three weeks of aftercare. This is the most critical time in which most of the seedlings will die from the overdose of the colchicine in their tissue (resembles the fungus of damping-off). Keep them under artificial lights at no more than 65–70°F (18–21°C) and away from hot sunlight. Most of the seedlings will begin to show the effect of colchicine kill by beginning to rot and die. Remove dying seedlings immediately. The few that survive will have very deep, bright green, thick cotyledons and emerging leaves but will remain static (in inactive growth) for several weeks.

The first leaves to appear are thick, often misshapen, and crinkled. The seedlings are very slow to develop and usually much larger than untreated seedlings which will be on their second and third leaves by the same time. Polyploid growth is very slow, often not more than one or two leaves the first year. Root growth is also very slow, hence winter care is most important. Overwinter in a cool greenhouse where the temperature does not go below freezing. Outdoors or in a lath house, the seedlings generally freeze the first winter, as Fiala learned by sad experience. Only after their second, better the third year, can they be planted out in a sheltered location.

Besides having a slow growth rate, polyploid plants also have very short intervals between buds. Often several buds are found in 1½ inches (4 cm) of stem. Many polyploid seedlings are only a foot (30 cm) high after 10 years. This does not indicate that they are dwarf, but rather that they are still recovering from the shock of treatment. Eventually they will develop stronger roots and begin to grow more normally.

In time the polyploid plants will bloom, but the first blooms will be very disappointing as expectations are always higher than reality. Induced tetraploids and polyploids in the first generation still have only the original pattern of chromosomes; these must be recombined and crossed with other tetraploids to bring out the real variety and potential found in their greatly increased genetic capability. Some of the originally treated plants will have larger flowers with thicker petals and deeper color, but others will be smaller. These treated plants are very mixed genetically and need to settle down. Their tissue is not always stable, so the hybridizer must be on guard for plants reverting back after some years to the original diploid type. Preferably hand-pollinate tetraploids with other tetraploids of a different gene pool for best and fastest results. All tetraploids and polyploids in *Syringa* are still in the experimental stage, but they are on their way to make a name for themselves and claim a spot in our gardens.

Propagating Lilac Mutations or Sports

While new lilac cultivars generally come from hybridization and possibly from induced tetraploids, they can also occur as the result of natural bud mutations or sports. Bud mutations are a disruption of the genetic chains in the chromosome, not the doubling of chromosomes as in polyploids. These disruptions are caused in nature by viruses, heat, radiation, electrical shock, pollution, or unknown factors.

Occasionally bud mutations have arisen in the greenhouse in the process of forcing lilacs for winter bloom by using the hot-water method. Two outstanding cultivars were produced this way in the Netherlands. 'Sensation', a periclinal chimera (an individual composed of two or more genetically different tissues) is a mutation of 'Hugo de Vries' discovered by Dirk Eveleens Maarse. 'Primrose' is a mutation of 'Marie Legraye' found by Gerrit Maarse.

Undoubtedly many bud mutations or sports occur each year in nature but go unnoticed. Some cultivars, such as *Syringa vulgaris* 'Comtesse Horace de Choiseul', are known to have several mutations in bloom of different shades and colors on the same plant. But mutations may cause curious results: leaf variegations of green with white or yellow, red leaf colorations, blos-

som color changes, petal shape, or marginal floret variations such as in 'Sensation' with its white margins.

Most bud mutations, for various reasons not yet understood, appear to be non-genetic; that is, their special characteristics are not transferable through hybridization. Desirable genetic characteristics, however, may remain as hidden recessives that might be intensified through inbreeding. Bud mutations when found must be either rooted as cuttings or grafted to preserve them. When left on the mother plant they most often die by being outgrown by more aggressive growth around them. Fiala once asked noted Dutch hybridist Dirk Eveleens Maarse, why he seemed to find and introduce proportionately more fine lilac sports than other growers. "Because I look a little longer at my lilacs and at the whole plant. I spend more time looking and thinking," was his reply. "There are probably just as many mutations in every large lilac collection, but others do not take time to see them or to root them as a separate plant." The same could be said of seedling crosses and indeed of all hybridization.

Corn geneticist and Nobel Laureate Barbara McClintock (1902–1992) demonstrated what can be accomplished by paying attention to minute genetic elements. In the 1940s and 50s she studied TEs, or transposable elements, that can do unpredictable things in plants and genetics (McClintock 1980). Her work with color genes in corn shows that, even in lilacs, if we were far more observant, we might discover small changes that could be meaningful in the hybridization of new cultivars. We do not pay enough attention to the structures, shades of color, the eyed and striped patterns of floret petals, and we do not intensify them in breeding, therefore many improvements go undiscovered and unused. McClintock showed that color does not always follow predictable patterns. It may be that one of these gene unpredictabilities will some day give us a true yellow or bright red lilac.

CHAPTER TEN

The Lilac Hybridizers of Yesterday, Today, and Tomorrow

N ature has hidden in the genetic make-up of flowers and growing things, marvelous traits and beauty much of which is yet to be unfolded by the work of nature or discovered by the patient genius of man. The lilac is no exception. Gifted individuals have through their dedicated work, understanding, and love of the genus brought forth many new forms, colors, and hybrids over the years. Today we have more and better lilacs available than at any time in history through the efforts of plant explorers, who brought back new species and selections of lilacs, and of lilac hybridizers and nurserymen in many countries, who have constantly sought new and better ways of propagating and growing lilacs.

In the following pages we seek to give a glimpse into the work of the principal lilac hybridizers—the men and women who have made outstanding contributions to the lilac. Knowing a little of their efforts we may better appreciate the loveliness and variety that abound in the large genus we call lilacs. Some of these hybridizers have been giants of genius and labor; others have added to or extended work left undone; several have built the foundations needed by others to continue; a few have discovered, perhaps, only a single lilac cultivar, yet one that has made an outstanding contribution in lilac history. In this chapter, arranged chronologically and geographically, the story of the lilac, the outstanding cultivars and their international heritage, through their originators, will pass the revue.

We have endeavored to include the lilac notables of all countries. In the twentieth century, outside of the former Union of Soviet Socialist Republics and its satellite countries, North America has been the most productive of new developments in hybridization of the lilac. In recent times considerable work in hybridizing *Syringa vulgaris* has been done in the former Soviet Union by Leonid A. Kolesnikov. The availability of

additional plant materials of lilacs from China and Korea in the last few years augurs well for future hybrid development.

In some of the listings in this chapter, cultivar names appear with a year. Preferably this would be the year of introduction of the new cultivar; more often than not, that information is not available. If the cultivar name was registered prior to 1975, there may have been only the original plants; propagation and distribution may have taken place at a later day. Nursery trade catalogs can provide a reliable year of introduction when a complete run of catalogs or price lists is available for a given nursery, such as the Lemoine nursery in France. Announcements of new cultivars in trade magazines and dated flyers are reliable, but second-hand information from books may not be. Amateur lilac breeders and collectors often are not interested in commercial ventures; they give away a few plants to friends and neighbors without recording the year of introduction, and commercial introduction may never happen. The years given in the volume, as in the *International Register and Checklist of Cultivar Names in the Genus Syringa*, remain subject to revision whenever new references turn up.

A Brief History of Plant Genetics and Hybridization

Although we are unable to consider in length the discovery of hybridization and plant breeding, it is an interesting scientific story that was unraveled by many botanists over the centuries. The first mention of hybridization, or the necessity of having two different kinds of trees, pollen-bearing and seed-bearing, is found in Assyrian bas-relief tablets around 883–859 B.C. Hand pollinating of date palms (*Phoenix dactylifera*) was practiced from that time among the Assyrians and Egyptians. It was Rudolph Jakob Camerarius (1665–1721), professor of medicine at Tübingen, Germany, who laid the scientific foundation of plant breeding when he reported on his experiments in *De sexu plantarum epistola* (Camerarius 1694). This botanist appears to have been the first to establish experimentally that pollen is essential to fertilization, and that pollen-producing plants are essentially male and seed-bearing plants female. In his experiments he included the newly discovered Indian corn (*Zea mays*). In 1760 the Imperial Academy of Sciences at St. Petersburg offered a prize for the determination of the problem of sex in plants. It appears that Camerarius' work went unnoticed until fifty years after it was published. The prize was awarded to Carl Linnaeus (or Carl von Linné, the name he used after he was ennobled in 1762) who, in his *De sexu plantarum* (Linnaeus 1760), presented accounts of hybridizing the two goat's beard species, *Tragopogon pratensis* × *T. porrifolius*, and the results.

In 1761, another German botanist, Joseph Gottlieb Koelreuter (also spelled Kölreuter; 1733–1806), who rightly attributed to Camerarius the first discovery of sex in plants and the results of hybridization, published his preliminary reports on some experimentations concerning sex in plants. Koelreuter crossed two tobacco species, *Nicotiana rustica* × *N. paniculata*, producing progeny that was intermediate in its properties but sterile. Koelreuter's work was monumental in its scientific exactness, scope, magnitude, and conclusions. It is a landmark in plant breeding.

Others rapidly followed with published details of experiments on plant sex and hybridization. Philip Miller (1691–1771), from the Chelsea Physic Garden, London, wrote *The Gardeners and Florists Dictionary* in 1724. James Logan (1674–1751), at the time Chief Justice of the Supreme Court of Pennsylvania and a member of the provincial council, experimented with corn, a pioneer step toward hybridization (Logan 1741).

In the 1750s Johann Gottlieb Gleditsch (1714–1786), prefect of the old Berlin Botanical Garden, today's Heinrich von Kleist Park, came to fame for his well-prepared, scientific plant experiment demonstrating the sexuality of plants; it is still regarded one of the finest of its time. In the Botanical Garden, Gleditsch had a pistillate (female) dwarf palm which had never produced fruits. By stagecoach he had pollen brought from Leipzig, obtained from a staminate (male) plant of the same dwarf palm species, and transferred this pollen to the pistil of his female plant. His artificial, or hand pollination was successful, and the palm bore fruit. When the famous dwarf palm died 181 years later, its remains became part of the collection of the Botanical Museum at Berlin-Dahlem. Gleditsch's experiment is referred to as the Berlin Experiment.

Christian Konrad Sprengel (1750–1816), after five years of careful observation of nearly 500 species, published *The Discovered Secret of Nature in the Form and Fertilization of Flowers* (1793). His work contains hundreds of accurate, detailed drawings on plant fertilization in 25 plates. This outstanding scientific work, which ranked among the best, went unnoticed until Charles Robert Darwin mentioned it in his *Origin of Species* (1859). Sprengel's work marked the beginning of modern flower biology, the study and understanding of the relationships between flowers and their pollinators, be they insects, birds, or mammals.

The work of many fine minds and years of scientific experimentation lie behind the art of plant breeding which often is taken for granted. Karl Friedrich von Gärtner (1772–1850) reported about his experiments and observations on the production of hybrids in the plant kingdom in 1837 and in 1849; Wilhelm Olbers Focke (1834–1922) published a 569-page work on plant hybrids in 1881, and Gregor Johann Mendel (1822–1884) wrote about his experiments in plant hybridization in 1866. These and others made advanced and substantial contributions to the science of genetics and modern plant breeding. Readers interested in the history of plant genetics and plant breeding will find that information in *Plant Hybridization Before Mendel* (Roberts 1929). A more recent account is Hans Stubbe's (1965, 1972) summary of the history of genetics up to the point of rediscovery of Mendelian rules.

Development of the Garden Lilac in Western Europe

Prior to 1870 hybridization of lilacs was relatively rare and not yet understood. In 1770 British botanist Richard Weston (1733–1806) recognized two color varieties of the common lilac: *Syringa vulgaris* var. *alba* and *S. vulgaris* var. *purpurea* (the latter known today as 'Marlyensis'). The cultivars, mostly of *S. vulgaris*, were selections made from seedlings planted by nurserymen and garden enthusiasts; these seedlings were grown from seed that had resulted from open (uncontrolled) pollination. Some of the best seedlings were named, and a limited range of colors emerged. Among the most outstanding cultivars were 'Charles X' (pre-1830, single deep purple), 'Azurea Plena' (1843, small double blue, the first reported lilac with double florets), 'Macrostachya' (1874, single pale pink), 'Marie Legraye' (1879, single white), 'Lilarosa' (1887, single pale lavender), and 'Lucie Baltet' (1888, single pale pink).

Mention must be made of some of these early lilac growers who, though not hybridizers, yet introduced some excellent lilacs that have been cherished through the years and remain outstanding today. Many of these earlier cultivars have become the progenitors of our modern lilacs.

Pierre Saugé (1757–1835) established his first nursery in 1807 at the corner of rue de la Santé and rue Léon-Maurice Nordmann in Paris, France. The nursery no longer exists, but the house in which the Saugés lived, formerly at rue de la Santé, number 13, still stands, now part of *Lycée Notre-Dame de France* at that location. It was here that Saugé selected the "Saugé lilac," later known as *Syringa ×chinensis* 'Saugeana'. He did not name the lilac selection for himself; others did. That Saugé and his bride signed their marriage document with an *X* (1 February 1814) indicates they were illiterate. For nurserymen to be illiterate was not uncommon in those days; it explains why Saugé did not write about his new lilac, but others did (Patrice Huet 2004, pers. comm. to F.V.). The confusion about this lilac has been well-recorded by McKelvey (1928). By 1860, the Saugé family nursery had become extinct.

Baltet nursery at Troyes, France, founded in 1720 and active with lilacs from 1842 to 1900, originated the famous lilacs 'Ville de Troyes' (1868), 'De Croncels' (1876), 'Lucie Baltet' (1888), and 'Bleuâtre' (1894). 'Bleuâtre' remains an outstanding blue, much used in hybridizing by Victor Lemoine. 'De Croncels' and 'Lucie Baltet' have a rare coppery coloring or flush while in bud. There is every indication that 'De Cron-

cels', being somewhat a dwarf, having a rare coppery color and a deeper pink-lavender bloom, was the parent of the lovely light pink 'Lucie Baltet', also a dwarf with the same copper glow that has endeared it to the lilac public ever since. Today, more than a century later, it is still one of the most sought after cultivars and a prime choice of hybridizers.

Pierre Cochet the Elder (1803–1853) was a nurseryman at Suisnes (today's Grisy-Suisnes), Seine-et-Marne, France. Although best known for his roses, Cochet was among the early selectors of lilacs. He originated three *Syringa vulgaris* cultivars, 'Philémon' (1840), single dark purple with dark foliage, which received a First Class award in 1855; 'Clara Cochet' (1855), single pink; and 'Scipion Cochet' (pre-1872), single purple with pink margins. All three lilacs are still in cultivation today, at least in collections in North America. Cochet was succeeded in the nursery business by his two sons, Philémon Cochet (1823–1898) and Scipion Cochet (1833–1896) (Patrice Huet 2004, pers. comm. to F.V.).

Francisque Morel (1849–1925) at Lyon, France, is best known for his breeding of *Clematis*. He selected and named the outstanding *Syringa vulgaris* 'Mme F.

Syringa vulgaris 'Ville de Troyes'. B. Peart and M. Walton

Syringa vulgaris 'Clara Cochet'. B. Peart and M. Walton

Morel' (1892), for many years one of the largest floret lilacs of a deep magenta color.

At this time nurserymen were content to plant seeds and, if something new appeared, they selected, propagated, and named the new cultivar. The science of hybridization, although not unknown, was rarely practiced with lilacs. Most nurserymen prior to 1900 did not receive an education in plant genetics but were trained as gardener apprentices—the practice of good garden management, growing and propagating plants. What a college education in botanical genetics is today was relatively unknown to them. A few, however, among them Victor Lemoine, studied genetics on their own; the results of their more scientific approach are evident in the excellent hybrids they produced. It was not until 1870 that Lemoine began hybridization in the true sense of the word, the actual crossing of two named cultivars. Many cultivars still result from seed produced by open (uncontrolled) pollination rather than controlled (deliberate) pollination, though the finest are created by planned hybridization.

Victor Lemoine (1823–1911)

Pierre Louis Victor Lemoine was born on 21 October 1823, and died age eighty-eight on 11 December 1911, at his home in Nancy, France. During his active years as a plantsman, nurseryman, and hybridizer in his little garden nursery in Lorraine province, he probably gave more to horticulture than any other single individual known. He possessed a universal love of plants and had a near intuitive knowledge of and keen vision into what could be hidden in their genetic make-up. This remarkable mental capacity was cou-

pled with a character given to patience, hard work, and persistence. Victor Lemoine so influenced our garden flora that there is hardly a garden today that does not have at least one plant that can be traced to his genius in horticulture. Although Lemoine worked with many plant genera, creating new cultivars of magnificent beauty and worth, he is especially known for his work with lilacs.

Although he had established his nursery in 1849, Lemoine began his lilac work at age 47, around 1870. During the Franco-Prussian War, when the town of Nancy was occupied by Prussian troops, partly as a diversion from the trials of the times and partly out of his own curiosity, he began to turn his spare time to hybridizing lilacs. In 1843 a little-known, small double, bluish lilac, *Syringa vulgaris* 'Azurea Plena', had been discovered and introduced by Gilles Étienne Joseph Libert-Darimont (1804–1875), nurseryman at Thiers-à-Liège, Belgium (C. F. Morren 1853). A bush of this plant had grown for some years in Lemoine's garden; he had early recognized its merits and acquired the plant for future work and study. Lemoine determined to cross this insignificant double lilac, first with the best available single cultivars of *Syringa vulgaris* and then with *S. oblata*, an early-blooming species native to China which he had added to his collection.

Lemoine's eyesight was no longer acute and his hands a bit unsteady from hard work in the nursery, so he enlisted the help of his wife for the actual work as she (Marie Louise Anna Lemoine, née Gomien; b. 1834) was 11 years younger and more physically fit than he. Lemoine began this work with about 30 or so named cultivars of single *Syringa vulgaris* and the small, double 'Azurea Plena' of Libert-Darimont. 'Azurea Plena' was most difficult to work on. The old bush in the Lemoine garden was very tall. The minute, nearly unworkable, florets were composed of many petals without stamens; the twisted pistils were covered by lobes of interior petaloid stamens which were mostly deformed and sterile. Yet this was the plant Lemoine selected as the seed bearer. From her perch atop a step-ladder, his wife pursued the very tedious task of uncovering and finding the best of the deformed pistils to cover with the chosen pollen. Pollen came from several of the best *S. vulgaris* singles then available and from *S. oblata*. Results were ever in

Victor Lemoine. The original photograph by Bartholemy appeared on the front cover of *La Vie à la Campagne* in December 1906.

Syringa vulgaris 'Lemoinei'. B. Peart and M. Walton

doubt. From more than one hundred flowers crossed that first season, only seven seeds were produced. The following year thirty additional fertile seeds were gathered and the work of promise continued.

The Lemoines saw their first results in 1876 when three of the seedlings bloomed. The first received the name of *Syringa hybrida hyacinthiflora plena*. It was a true hybrid between *S. vulgaris* 'Azurea Plena' and *S. oblata*. The thyrses of the new hybrid were well developed, and the florets, although small and a little separated, were double, lilac-blue, very fragrant, and early blooming. The foliage recalled the *S. oblata* autumn purple tints. This plant was put into trade in 1878. Today it is hardly obtainable; because of its historical importance *Syringa* ×*hyacinthiflora* 'Hyacinthiflora Plena' is still growing in some lilac collections.

Syringa vulgaris 'Lemoinei', another cultivar selected from these first seedlings, first flowered for Lemoine in 1877 and was introduced in 1878. It was not a hybrid of *S. oblata* but simply a cross between *S. vulgaris* 'Azurea Plena' and a single *S. vulgaris* cultivar. The florets were double, of good size, and a pure blue-lilac. From that same cross resulted 'Renoncule' and 'Rubella Plena' (1881), and 'Mathieu de Dombasle' (1882).

These first doubles were then crossed without difficulty with the best available singles. In three years the crosses produced wonderful seedlings that were

Syringa vulgaris 'Mathieu de Dombasle'. B. Peart and M. Walton

Syringa vulgaris 'Renoncule'. B. Peart and M. Walton

Syringa vulgaris 'Rubella Plena'. B. Peart and M. Walton

Syringa vulgaris 'Jean Bart'. B. Peart and M. Walton

Syringa vulgaris 'La Tour d'Auvergne'. B. Peart and M. Walton

Syringa vulgaris 'Virginité'. B. Peart and M. Walton

quickly placed into commerce and became known as the French Hybrids: 'Alphonse Lavallée' and 'Michel Buchner' in 1885; 'Lamarck', 'Mons. Maxime Cornu', 'Président Grévy', and 'Pyramidal' in 1886; 'Condorcet', 'La Tour d'Auvergne', 'Léon Simon', and 'Virginité' in 1888; and 'Émile Lemoine' and 'Jean Bart' and in 1889. Most of these cultivars are no longer available commercially, but can be seen in the very large lilac collections. Some of them have been surpassed by later and newer cultivars, but whatever, it was through the genius and work of the Lemoines that a whole new race of giant double lilacs came into being. In their lifetime they had accomplished what seemed an impossible dream (Hirtz 1993).

Émile Lemoine (1862–1943)

The Lemoine nursery, although founded on the plant genius of the father Victor, continued on in greatness through the horticultural skill and ability of his son Paul Émile Prosper Lemoine. This father-son partnership was to prove an outstanding gift to horticulture. The son developed a deep love for the plants his father was hybridizing, especially the lilacs. Émile was born in 1862, eight years before his father began working with lilacs. As a boy Émile helped his father in the hybridizing routines, learning to recognize rare plants and species and what could be expected of them. He was a precocious and bright lad.

By the time Émile was sixteen, he was already sufficiently knowledgeable to assist in the work of hybridizing the second generation of lilacs so painstakingly crossed by his parents. His nimble and quick fingers, and his keen eyesight proved to be a considerable asset to his parents. Many of the transitional lilacs coming from that famous garden at Nancy between the years 1900 and 1911 were probably the work of Émile under his aging father's guidance rather than the direct work of Victor himself.

It is easy to forget this gifted son and attribute most of the work to Victor Lemoine alone, whereas in reality, the bulk of the introductions and hybridizing appears to be the work of Émile Lemoine. Under the name of Victor as hybridizer, perhaps 67 cultivars were introduced prior to 1900. From 1900, when Victor was already 78 years old and in failing health, until his death in 1911, another 64 cultivars were introduced. These are some of the most outstanding cultivars. From 1912 to 1933 (10 years before Émile's death) another 62 cultivars were introduced and are clearly the work of Émile Lemoine. From 1933 to 1968, when the Lemoine nursery closed its doors forever, another 21 cultivars were added, 14 of which were the last work of Émile in collaboration with his son, Henri.

After Émile's death in 1943, seven cultivars were added by Henri Lemoine (1897–1982) bringing to a grand total of at least 214 cultivars over the span of 71 years that originated in this now-famous lilac hybridizing nursery. Of these, 64 should be solely attributed to Victor Lemoine, approximately 140 to Émile, and perhaps 10 to Henri. A wonderful legacy! No more than three, if any, of the Lemoine lilacs are extinct. This record is remarkable, and probably the result of initial good marketing at home and abroad, the quality of the selections and, last but not least, the reputation of the Lemoine nursery.

Neither Victor nor Émile left adequate records of the parentage of their outstanding lilac cultivars. It is known that the single, white 'Marie Legraye' was used as the seed parent crossed with the earliest doubles. From this original cross most of Lemoine's white doubles have come. One, his very finest at that time, Victor named for his faithful hybridizing student and partner, 'Mme Lemoine'. It still ranks among his best. The last lilac Lemoine named, 'Souvenir de Louis

Chasset' in 1955, was a magnificent finale for the family nursery.

After three wars in which Nancy was a battlefield (Franco-Prussian War, 1870–1871; World War I, 1914–1918; and World War II, 1940–1945), it is not surprising that the Lemoines were not well disposed toward Germany and Germans. When Gerd Krüssmann (1910–1980), at the time dendrologist and author at Ludwig Späth nurseries in Berlin, knocked at the gate of the Lemoine nursery for a professional visit, he was turned away (Krüssmann 1937; Krüssmann 1970s, pers. comm. to F.V.).

The Lemoine cultivars encompass every range and shade of color and form. One could plant an entire arboretum of Lemoine lilacs and have one of the most beautiful and outstanding collections found anywhere. However, one must be aware that many of Lemoine's cultivars have been surpassed by some of the newer selections, and that many Lemoine cultivars have been used in further crosses, producing even more outstanding offspring. From a hybridizer's view, some of the finest blue lilacs are still to be found in the really blue Lemoine introductions. Today, crossed with the most modern cultivars, they are showing tremendous promise in pale pastel blues and deeper Wedgwood colors. Beautiful new forms have come from the work of others who have hybridized principally using Lemoine introductions (Havemeyer 1917, L.B. 1917).

Fiala was often asked, "What are the best cultivars introduced by the Lemoines?" To choose the "best" from among more than 214 introductions is difficult if not impossible. Beauty is in the eye of the beholder, and so it is with lilacs; color preferences vary considerably. Some people prefer large single lilacs whereas others are overwhelmed by the large double lilacs that Lemoine so popularized. In the list that follows, Fiala's 40 favorite Lemoine cultivars are starred.

Selected Lilac Introductions of the Lemoines from 1876 to 1953

'Abel Carrière' (*S. vulgaris*), double bluish, 1896
'Alba' (*S.* Villosae Group), single pinkish, 1934 (*S. ×henryi*)
'Albida' (*S.* Villosae Group), single lilac, 1930 (*S. sweginzowii × S. tomentella*)

Syringa vulgaris 'Abel Carrière'. B. Peart and M. Walton

Syringa vulgaris 'Ami Schott'. B. Peart and M. Walton

Syringa vulgaris 'Crépuscule'. B. Peart and M. Walton

Syringa vulgaris 'Ambassadeur'. B. Peart and M. Walton

Syringa vulgaris 'Firmament'. B. Peart and M. Walton

Syringa vulgaris 'Président Grévy'. B. Peart and M. Walton

Syringa vulgaris 'Rustica'. B. Peart and M. Walton

Syringa vulgaris 'Savonarole'. B. Peart and M. Walton

'Alphonse Lavallée' (*S. vulgaris*), double lilac, 1885; RHS Award of Merit 1893
★ 'Ambassadeur' (*S. vulgaris*), single blue, 1930; Certificate of Merit (KMTP) 1932
★ 'Ami Schott' (*S. vulgaris*), double blue, 1933
★ 'Archevêque' (*S. vulgaris*), double deep purplish, 1923; uniquely colored
'Arthur William Paul' (*S. vulgaris*), double purple, 1898
'Banquise' (*S. vulgaris*), double white, 1905
'Belle de Nancy' (*S. vulgaris*), double pinkish, 1891
'Berryer' (*S. ×hyacinthiflora* Early Hybrid-Giraldi), double pinkish with lavender tones, 1913
★ 'Bicolor' (*S. ×chinensis*), single white marked with violet, 1853; synonym *S. ×chinensis* nothof. *bicolor* (Lemoine) Jäger
'Boule Azurée' (*S. vulgaris*), single bluish, 1919

'Boussingault' (*S. vulgaris*), double pinkish, 1896
'Buffon' (*S. ×hyacinthiflora* Early Hybrid-Giraldi), single pinkish, 1921; RHS Award of Merit 1961
★ 'Candeur' (*S. vulgaris*), single white, 1931
★ 'Capitaine Baltet' (*S. vulgaris*), single magenta to pink, 1919
★ 'Capitaine Perrault' (*S. vulgaris*), double pink to lavender, 1925
'Carmen' (*S. vulgaris*), double pinkish, 1918
'Catinat' (*S. ×hyacinthiflora* Early Hybrid-Giraldi), single pinkish, 1922
'Cavour' (*S. vulgaris*), single violet, 1910
'Champlain' (*S. vulgaris*), double violet, 1930
'Charles Baltet' (*S. vulgaris*), double lilac, 1893
'Charles Joly' (*S. vulgaris*), double purple, 1896; RHS Award of Merit
'Charles Sargent' (*S. vulgaris*), double bluish, 1905
'Christophe Colomb' (*S. vulgaris*), single lilac, 1905
'Claude Bernard' (*S. ×hyacinthiflora* Early Hybrid-Giraldi), double pinkish, 1915
'Claude de Lorrain' (*S. vulgaris*), single purple and pinkish, 1889
'Colbert' (*S. vulgaris*), double magenta, 1899

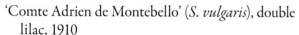

Syringa vulgaris 'Edith Cavell'. B. Peart and M. Walton

Syringa vulgaris 'Miss Ellen Willmott'. B. Peart and M. Walton

Syringa vulgaris 'Mme Lemoine'. B. Peart and M. Walton

'Comte Adrien de Montebello' (*S. vulgaris*), double lilac, 1910

'Comte de Kerchove' (*S. vulgaris*), double magenta, 1899

'Comte Horace de Choiseul' (*S. vulgaris*), double pinkish, 1887

'Comtesse Horace de Choiseul' (*S. vulgaris*), double pinkish, 1891

'Condorcet' (*S. vulgaris*), double magenta, 1888

★ 'Congo' (*S. vulgaris*), single magenta to red, 1896

'Crampel' (*S. vulgaris*), single bluish, 1899

★ 'Crépuscule' (*S. vulgaris*), single blue, 1928

'Dame Blanche' (*S. vulgaris*), double white, 1903

'Danton' (*S. vulgaris*), single purple, 1911

'De Humboldt' (*S. vulgaris*), double violet, 1892

'De Jussieu' (*S. vulgaris*), double lilac, 1891

★ 'De Miribel' (*S. vulgaris*), single deep violet, 1903

'De Saussure' (*S. vulgaris*), double purple, 1903

'Decaisne' (*S. vulgaris*), single bluish, 1910

'Densiflora' (*S. sweginzowii*), single pinkish, 1933

'Descartes' (*S. ×hyacinthiflora* Early Hybrid-Giraldi), single pinkish, 1916

'Desfontaines' (*S. vulgaris*), double magenta, 1906

'Deuil d'Émile Gallé' (*S. vulgaris*), double violet, 1904

'Diderot' (*S. vulgaris*), single purple, 1915

'Diplomate' (*S. vulgaris*), single bluish, 1930

'Doyen Keteleer' (*S. vulgaris*), double lilac, 1895

'Dr Maillot' (*S. vulgaris*), double lilac, 1895

'Dr Masters' (*S. vulgaris*), double pinkish, 1898

'Dr Troyanowsky' (*S. vulgaris*), double lilac, 1901

★ 'Duc de Massa' (*S. vulgaris*), double blue, 1905

'Duplex' (*S. ×chinensis*), double lilac, 1897

★ 'Edith Cavell' (*S. vulgaris*), double white, 1916

'Edmond About' (*S. vulgaris*), double magenta, 1908

'Edmond Boissier' (*S. vulgaris*), single purple, 1906

'Édouard André' (*S. vulgaris*), double pinkish, 1900

'Émile Gentil' (*S. vulgaris*), double bluish, 1915

★ 'Émile Lemoine' (*S. vulgaris*), double lilac, 1889

★ 'Etna' (*S. vulgaris*), single deep reddish purple, 1927

'Étoile de Mai' (*S. vulgaris*), double purple and white, 1905

'Excellens' (*S. pubescens* subsp. *patula*), single white, 1936

'Fénelon' (*S. ×hyacinthiflora* Early Hybrid-Giraldi), single pinkish, 1937

★ 'Firmament' (*S. vulgaris*), single blue, 1932; RHS Award of Merit

'Floréal' (*S.* Villosae Group), single pinkish, 1925 (*S. ×nanceiana*)

'Fraîcheur' (*S. vulgaris*), single white, 1946

'Françisque Morel' (*S. vulgaris*), double lilac, 1896

'Gaudichaud' (*S. vulgaris*), double bluish, 1903

'Général Drouot' (*S. vulgaris*), single lilac, 1890

'Général Pershing' (*S. vulgaris*), double pinkish, 1924; not to be confused with 'General John Pershing' introduced by Dunbar in 1917

'Georges Bellair' (*S. vulgaris*), double magenta, 1900

★ 'Georges Claude' (*S. vulgaris*), double blue, 1935

'Germinal' (*S.* Villosae Group), single magenta, 1939 (*S. ×henryi × S. tomentella*)

'Gilbert' (*S. vulgaris*), single lilac, 1911

★ 'Gismonda' (*S. vulgaris*), double bluish magenta, 1939

'Gloire de Lorraine' (*S. vulgaris*), single magenta, 1876

'Godron' (*S. vulgaris*), double bluish, 1908

'Grand-Duc Constantin' (*S. vulgaris*), double bluish, 1895

'Guizot' (*S. vulgaris*), double lilac, 1897

'Henri Martin' (*S. vulgaris*), double magenta, 1912

'Henri Robert' (*S. vulgaris*), double violet, 1936

'Hippolyte Maringer' (*S. vulgaris*), double lilac, 1909

'Hyacinthiflora Plena' (*S. ×hyacinthiflora*), double bluish, 1878

'Jacques Callot' (*S. vulgaris*), single lilac, 1876

'Jean Bart' (*S. vulgaris*), double pinkish, 1889

'Jean Macé' (*S. vulgaris*), double pinkish, 1915

'Jeanne d'Arc' (*S. vulgaris*), double white, 1902

'Jules Ferry' (*S. vulgaris*), double pinkish, 1907

'Jules Simon' (*S. vulgaris*), double bluish, 1908

Syringa vulgaris 'Monique Lemoine'. B. Peart and M. Walton

Syringa vulgaris 'Souvenir d'Alice Harding'. B. Peart and M. Walton

'Julien Gérardin' (*S. vulgaris*), double lilac, 1916

'Katherine Havemeyer' (*S. vulgaris*), double lavender pink, 1922; RHS Award of Merit 1933 and 1969

'La Lorraine' (*S. ×chinensis*), single magenta, 1899

'La Mauve' (*S. vulgaris*), double pinkish, 1893

'La Tour d'Auvergne' (*S. vulgaris*), double magenta, 1888

'Lamarck' (*S. vulgaris*), double bluish, 1886

★ 'Lamartine' (*S. ×hyacinthiflora* Early Hybrid-Giraldi), single pink, 1911

'Laplace' (*S. vulgaris*), single purple, 1913

Syringa vulgaris 'Capitaine Perrault'. B. Peart and M. Walton

Syringa vulgaris 'Émile Lemoine'. B. Peart and M. Walton

'Lavoisier' (*S. vulgaris*), single pinkish, 1913

'Le Gaulois' (*S. vulgaris*), double lilac, 1884

★ 'Le Nôtre' (*S. vulgaris*), double lilac shades, 1922; uniquely colored

'Le Printemps' (*S. vulgaris*), double pinkish, 1901

'Le Progrès' (*S. ×chinensis*), single lilac, 1903

'Lemoinei' (*S. vulgaris*), double lilac, 1878; RHS First Class Certificate 1884

★ 'Léon Gambetta' (*S. vulgaris*), double lilac, 1907

'Léon Simon' (*S. vulgaris*), double lilac, 1888

'Linné' (*S. vulgaris*), double magenta, 1890

'L'Oncle Tom' (*S. vulgaris*), single purple, 1903

'Louis Henry' (*S. vulgaris*), double magenta, 1894

'Louvois' (*S. ×hyacinthiflora* Early Hybrid-Giraldi), single violet, 1921

'Madame Charles Souchet' (*S. vulgaris*), single bluish, 1949; Certificate of Merit (KMTP) 1952

'Madeleine Lemaire' (*S. vulgaris*), double white, 1928

'Magellan' (*S. vulgaris*), double magenta, 1915

'Marc Micheli' (*S. vulgaris*), double pinkish, 1898

'Marceau' (*S. vulgaris*), single magenta, 1913

'Maréchal de Bassompierre' (*S. vulgaris*), double magenta, 1897

★ 'Maréchal Foch' (*S. vulgaris*), single reddish pink, 1924; RHS Award of Merit 1935

'Maréchal Lannes' (*S. vulgaris*), double bluish, 1910

'Marengo' (*S. vulgaris*), single lilac, 1923

'Marie Finon' (*S. vulgaris*), single white, 1923

'Masséna' (*S. vulgaris*), single magenta, 1923; RHS Award of Merit 1928 and 1930

'Mathieu de Dombasle' (*S. vulgaris*), double lilac, 1882

★ 'Maurice Barrès' (*S. vulgaris*), single blue, 1917

★ 'Maurice de Vilmorin' (*S. vulgaris*), double lilac, 1900

★ 'Maximowicz' (*S. vulgaris*), double violet, 1906

'Michel Buchner' (*S. vulgaris*), double lilac, 1885; RHS Award of Merit 1891

'Milton' (*S. vulgaris*), single purple, 1910

'Mirabeau' (*S. ×hyacinthiflora* Early Hybrid-Giraldi), single lilac, 1911

'Mireille' (*S. vulgaris*), double white, 1904

★ 'Miss Ellen Willmott' (*S. vulgaris*), double white, 1903

Syringa vulgaris 'Le Nôtre'. B. Peart and M. Walton

Syringa vulgaris 'Victor Lemoine'. B. Peart and M. Walton

'Mme Abel Chatenay' (*S. vulgaris*), double white, 1892

★ 'Mme Antoine Buchner' (*S. vulgaris*), double pink, 1909; RHS Award of Merit 1982

'Mme Casimir Périer' (*S. vulgaris*), double white, 1894

'Mme de Miller' (*S. vulgaris*), double white, 1901

'Mme Jules Finger' (*S. vulgaris*), double lilac, 1887

★ 'Mme Lemoine' (*S. vulgaris*), double white, 1890; RHS Award of Merit 1891, 1897, and 1937

'Mme Léon Simon' (*S. vulgaris*), double lilac, 1897

★ 'Monge' (*S. vulgaris*), single red to purple, 1913

'Monique Lemoine' (*S. vulgaris*), double white, 1939; Certificate of Merit (KMTP) 1953, RHS Award of Merit 1958

'Mons. Lepage' (*S. vulgaris*), single bluish, 1889

'Mons. Maxime Cornu' (*S. vulgaris*), double pinkish, 1886

'Mont Blanc' (*S. vulgaris*), single white, 1915

'Montaigne' (*S. vulgaris*), double pinkish, 1907

'Montesquieu' (*S. ×hyacinthiflora* Early Hybrid-Giraldi), single magenta, 1926

'Montgolfier' (*S. vulgaris*), single magenta, 1905

★ 'Monument' (*S. vulgaris*), single white, 1934

'Monument Carnot' (*S. vulgaris*), double pinkish, 1895

★ 'Mrs Edward Harding' (*S. vulgaris*), double magenta, 1922; RHS Award of Merit 1969

'Murillo' (*S. vulgaris*), double purple, 1901

'Naudin' (*S. vulgaris*), double lilac, 1913

'Necker' (*S. ×hyacinthiflora* Early Hybrid-Giraldi), single pinkish, 1920

'Negro' (*S. vulgaris*), single purple, 1899

'Obélisque' (*S. vulgaris*), double white, 1894

★ 'Olivier de Serres' (*S. vulgaris*), double blue, 1909

'Othello' (*S. vulgaris*), single magenta, 1900

'Pallens' (*S.* Villosae Group), single pinkish, 1931 (*S. komarowii* subsp. *reflexa* × ?)

'Pascal' (*S. ×hyacinthiflora* Early Hybrid-Giraldi), single lilac, 1916

'Pasteur' (*S. vulgaris*), single purple, 1903

'Paul Deschanel' (*S. vulgaris*), double magenta, 1924

'Paul Hariot' (*S. vulgaris*), double purple, 1902

'Paul Thirion' (*S. vulgaris*), double magenta, 1915; RHS Award of Merit 1927 and 1969

'Pierre Joigneaux' (*S. vulgaris*), double lilac, 1892

'Planchon' (*S. vulgaris*), double magenta, 1908

'Prairial' (*S.* Villosae Group), single pinkish, 1936 (*S. ×henryi* × *S. tomentella*)

'Président Carnot' (*S. vulgaris*), double lilac, 1890

'Président Fallières' (*S. vulgaris*), double lilac, 1911

★ 'Président Grévy' (*S. vulgaris*), double blue, 1886; RHS Award of Merit 1892

'Président Hayes' (*S. ×chinensis*), single magenta, 1889

'Président Loubet' (*S. vulgaris*), double magenta, 1901

★ 'Président Poincaré' (*S. vulgaris*), double magenta, 1913

'Président Viger' (*S. vulgaris*), double bluish, 1900

'Prince de Beauvau' (*S. vulgaris*), double lilac, 1897

★ 'Prodige' (*S. vulgaris*), single deep reddish purple, 1928

'Pyramidal' (*S. vulgaris*), double lilac, 1886

'Rabelais' (*S. vulgaris*), double white, 1896

'Réaumur' (*S. vulgaris*), single magenta, 1904

'René Jarry-Desloges' (*S. vulgaris*), double bluish, 1905

'Renoncule' (*S. vulgaris*), double lilac, 1881

'Rochambeau' (*S. vulgaris*), single purple, 1919

'Ronsard' (*S. vulgaris*), single bluish, 1912

'Rosace' (*S. vulgaris*), double lilac, 1932

'Rubella Plena' (*S. vulgaris*), double magenta, 1881

★ 'Rustica' (*S. vulgaris*), double lilac, 1950

'Rutilant' (*S.* Villosae Group), single purple, 1931 (*S.* ×*nanceiana*)

'Saturnale' (*S. vulgaris*), single bluish, 1916

★ 'Savonarole' (*S. vulgaris*), double bluish, 1935; uniquely colored

'Sénateur Volland' (*S. vulgaris*), double magenta, 1887

★ 'Siebold' (*S. vulgaris*), double white with yellowish shades, 1906; uniquely colored

★ 'Souvenir d'Alice Harding' (*S. vulgaris*), double white, 1938

'Souvenir de Georges Truffaut' (*S. vulgaris*), double magenta, 1953

'Souvenir de L. Thibaut' (*S. vulgaris*), double pinkish, 1893

'Souvenir de Louis Chasset' (*S. vulgaris*), single magenta, 1953

'Superba' (*S. sweginzowii*), single pinkish, 1915

'Taglioni' (*S. vulgaris*), double white, 1905

'Thunberg' (*S. vulgaris*), double lilac, 1913

'Tombouctou' (*S. vulgaris*), single purple, 1910

'Tournefort' (*S. vulgaris*), double violet, 1887

'Toussaint-Louverture' (*S. vulgaris*), single purple, 1898

'Turenne' (*S. vulgaris*), single purple, 1916

'Turgot' (*S.* ×*hyacinthiflora* Early Hybrid-Giraldi), single pinkish, 1920

'Vauban' (*S.* ×*hyacinthiflora* Early Hybrid-Giraldi), double pinkish, 1913

'Vestale' (*S. vulgaris*), single white, 1910; RHS Award of Merit 1931

'Vésuve' (*S. vulgaris*), single purple, 1916

★ 'Victor Lemoine' (*S. vulgaris*), double pink to lavender, 1906

'Villars' (*S.* ×*hyacinthiflora* Early Hybrid-Giraldi), single lilac, 1920

★ 'Violetta' (*S. vulgaris*), double deep violet, 1916

'Virginité' (*S. vulgaris*), double pinkish, 1888

'Viviand-Morel' (*S. vulgaris*), double lilac, 1902

'Volcan' (*S. vulgaris*), single purple, 1899

'Waldeck-Rousseau' (*S. vulgaris*), double pinkish, 1904

'William Robinson' (*S. vulgaris*), double lilac, 1899

Ludwig Späth Nurseries (1861–1947)

Though founded in 1720 the famous nursery of Ludwig Späth, Berlin-Baumschulenweg, Germany, did not cultivate woody ornamental plants until 1861. As a teenager Franz Ludwig Späth (1839–1913) became interested in arboriculture; he grew apple and pear seedlings, which he would bud and graft. Young Franz apprenticed for one year, after which he completed his secondary school education, studied natural history and botany at the University of Berlin, rounding off his vocational training by working for one year at Adolf Papeleu, Ghent, the best-known, most trend-setting nursery in Belgium at that time; he also traveled to see the leading nurseries in Belgium, England, France, and the Netherlands. When returning home in 1861 he started growing woody plants on a larger scale. Two years later, at the age of 24, Franz succeeded his father as proprietor of Späth nurseries. The nurseries would cultivate a wide range of lilacs, including species, botanical varieties, and cultivars; between 1883 and 1920 they introduced 11 new *Syringa vulgaris* cultivars, all still in cultivation today (Späth 1920). 'Andenken an Ludwig Späth', 'Fürst Bülow', and 'Hyazinthenflieder' resulted from deliberate crosses, the others were chance seedlings.

'Amethyst' (*S. vulgaris*), single pink, 1887

'Andenken an Ludwig Späth' (*S. vulgaris*), single deep magenta, 1883; an outstanding selection even by modern standards; in North America better known as LUDWIG SPAETH; RHS Award of Merit, Certificate of Merit (KMTP) 1966

Syringa vulgaris 'Amethyst'. B. Peart and M. Walton

Syringa vulgaris 'Dr von Regel'. B. Peart and M. Walton

'Dr von Regel' (*S. vulgaris*), single pink with white
   margin, 1883
'Emil Liebig' (*S. vulgaris*), double bluish, 1887
'Frau Berta Dammann' (*S. vulgaris*), single white,
   1883
'Fürst Bülow' (*S. vulgaris*) ('Fuerst Buelow' in North
   America), single purple, 1920; even darker than its
   seed parent, 'Andenken an Ludwig Späth'
'Fürst Lichtenstein' (*S. vulgaris*), single pink, 1887
'Geheimrat Heyder' (*S. vulgaris*), single lilac, 1883
'Geheimrat Singelmann' (*S. vulgaris*), single ma-
   genta, 1887
'Hyazinthenflieder' (*S. vulgaris*), single lilac, 1906;
   not to be confused with *Syringa* ×*hyacinthiflora*
   Rehder, which resulted from the cross *S. oblata* ×
   S. vulgaris
'Professor Sargent' (*S. vulgaris*), single magenta, 1889
'Vergissmeinnicht' (*S. vulgaris*), single lilac to blue,
   1887

In 1912, after earning his doctorate in botany,
Hellmut Ludwig Späth (1885–1945), succeeded his

Syringa vulgaris 'Professor Sargent'. B. Peart and M. Walton

father Franz Ludwig Späth. Späth nurseries flourished
under his leadership. Hellmut Späth was not a Nazi
sympathizer; he voiced his disapproval of the regime,
was arrested in 1944 and sent to concentration camp
Sachsenhausen where he was shot in February 1945
(Sucker 1980, Scholz 1987).

Florent Stepman-Demessemaeker (1856–1915)

Grégoire Léopold Florent Stepman was born in 1856 at Soignies, Belgium. From 1881 to 1883 he was employed by the botanist and orchid grower Jean Jules Linden (1825–1900) in Ghent, and from 1883 to 1889 he worked as horticulturist on the royal estate at Laken. In 1889 he married Marie Josèphe Demessemaeker, daughter of Pierre Jean Demessemaeker, nurseryman at Sint-Jans-Molenbeek. As was the custom in those days, Florent added his wife's maiden name to his family name. Although in the literature con-

Syringa vulgaris 'Docteur Charles Jacobs'. B. Peart and M. Walton

Syringa vulgaris 'Mons. Léon Mathieu'. B. Peart and M. Walton

sulted the name is mostly spelled "De Messemaeker," the 1889 marriage document shows the name as "Demessemaeker" (Marc Imschoot 2003–2005, pers. comm. to F.V.). Additional evidence is the name of a street in Sint-Jans-Molenbeek, "Pierre Jean Demessemaekerstraat." The nursery founded by Jean Demessemaeker in 1860 now became known under the name of Florent Stepman-Demessemaeker. In addition to operating the nursery, Stepman-Demessemaeker was active in a number of horticultural organizations; he also assembled a collection of approximately 250 garden lilacs. Stepman-Demessemaeker died in 1915; his widow appears to have operated the nursery for a few years, selling the property and the lilac collection in the early 1920s. She died in 1935. (Marc Imschoot 2003–2005, pers. comm. to F.V.).

The Stepman-Demessemaeker nursery introduced ten *Syringa vulgaris* cultivars, one of them the beautiful 'Mme Florent Stepman', an excellent white and the top commercial forcing lilac to this day. The survival of the following lilac selections in our gardens attests Stepman-Demessemaeker's good judgment:

'Docteur Charles Jacobs' (*S. vulgaris*), single purple, 1908
'Léon Liberton' (*S. vulgaris*), single lilac
'Léopold II' (*S. vulgaris*), single lilac, 1908
'Mme Florent Stepman' (*S. vulgaris*), single white, 1908; First Class Certificate (KMTP) 1908
'Mons. J. De Messemaeker' (*S. vulgaris*), single purple, 1908; Honor Diploma, Belgium, 1909
'Mons. Léon Mathieu' (*S. vulgaris*), single magenta, 1908
'Mons. van Aerschot' (*S. vulgaris*), single lilac, 1928
'Président Lambeau' (*S. vulgaris*), single pinkish, 1908
'Reine Elisabeth' (*S. vulgaris*), single white, 1909
'Roi Albert' (*S. vulgaris*), single magenta, 1909

Antoine Joseph Klettenberg (1867–1937)

The A.-J. Klettenberg nursery (Grandes Roseraies et Pépinières de Forest), Forest-Brussels, Belgium, introduced 38 named lilac cultivars from 1926 to 1938. Klettenberg founded the firm in 1893 and operated it in partnership with Peter Ferdinant Grave from 1898 to 1901, and with F. Delaruelle-Klettenberg in the 1930s. The firm is now defunct.

Syringa vulgaris 'Souvenir de Claudius Graindorge'. B. Peart and M. Walton

In the autumn 1923 catalog, Klettenberg announced the acquisition of the entire collection of lilacs (approximately 250 cultivars) of the late Florent Stepman-Demessemaeker. Presumably this event marks the beginning of lilac selection work at the Klettenberg nursery; whether these selections are entirely Klettenberg's or in part earlier selections made by Stepman-Demessemaeker is not known (Marc Imschoot, 2003–2005, pers. comm. to F.V.). Only three of the 38 introductions have turned up in our search for lilacs currently in cultivation:

'Madame A. J. Klettenberg' (*S. vulgaris*), double white, 1930

'Souvenir de Claudius Graindorge' (*S. vulgaris*), single pink, 1930

'Souvenir de Gustave Graindorge' (*S. vulgaris*), single purple, 1930

Lilac Cultivars from the Netherlands

Aalsmeer, a town in the province of North Holland, about 15 km southwest of Amsterdam, population 22,000, has the largest flower-auction market in the world and is the center of the Dutch florist industry. Every winter the greenhouse growers at Aalsmeer produce and ship millions of branches of lilacs forced in full bloom. Forcing flowers for domestic and foreign markets is a competitive business; lilac cultivars used in forcing must produce straight stems, full thyrses, and clear colors. It is to be expected that florists and nurserymen have always been alert and on the look-out for cultivars that excel, or perhaps exceed, what was already in cultivation. No wonder new cultivars were reported and introduced in this town. A showplace and showcase for lilacs growing outdoors is the lilac park (Seringenpark) in Aalsmeer. First planted in the 1950s, the collection has been refurbished and updated in the early 2000s. The lilac park is outstanding in May, but the greenhouses are at their best in late December when lilacs are forced into bloom under glass.

While Aalsmeer is the center of florist production, Boskoop, 25 km to the southwest of Aalsmeer, population 14,000, is the center of nursery production. A number of lilac cultivars originated in nurseries in Boskoop. This is not to say that all lilac cultivars selected and named in the Aalsmeer-Boskoop region turned out to be suitable for forcing; most of them were not, but a good number of these cultivars turned out to be good garden lilacs.

In the discussion that follows, the only two true hybridizers are D. Eveleens Maarse and M. Spaargaren. The others are observant growers who spotted bud mutations (sports) and propagated those that appeared to be promising. But first a word about Dutch family names.

Even to a Dutchman the family names Eveleens Maarse, Maarse and Maarsen, and their various generations can be confusing. A few explanations may be in order. Maarse is a very common family name in Aalsmeer; since the choice of Christian names was traditionally quite limited, identical names were not infrequent. Having identical names could be confusing, or even costly where it concerned erroneous business transactions. Solving their particular problem of identical names some generations ago one Maarse added Hzn (son of Hendrik) to his name, while his namesake added Jbzn (son of Jacob) to his name. These distinguishing postscripts have been retained by their respective descendants.

C. B. van Nes and Sons introduced the single purple *Syringa vulgaris* 'C. B. van Nes' in 1901, named for Cornelius B. van Nes, prominent nurseryman, rhododendron breeder and founder of this Boskoop nursery.

Either M. Koster and Sons or Jan van Tol Hzn, Boskoop, may have been the originator or introducer of the single lilac *Syringa vulgaris* 'Hugo Koster'. Introduced in 1914, it became known as an excellent lilac for forcing; the history of this cultivar remains obscure.

The nursery of Felix and Dykhuis (Dijkhuis is the original spelling of the name) introduced the single white *Syringa vulgaris* 'Mme Felix' in 1924. The following year it won two awards: a Silver Gilt Medal, Haarlem, and Certificate First Class (KMTP). It is a forcing lilac in Aalsmeer.

Klaas Keessen Jr. (1847–1916), nurseryman and farmer at Aalsmeer, originated *Syringa vulgaris* 'Hugo de Vries', a single purple. Klaas became father-in-law of Dirk Eveleens Maarse.

The Piet Brothers nursery, operated by Klaas Piet (1863–1941) and Willem Piet (1866–1956), originated *Syringa vulgaris* 'Anna Elisabeth Jaquet', a single purple, sometime prior to 1924; and 'Bloemenlust', a single white, in 1956, grown on a small scale for forcing.

The nursery of J. Eveleens appears to have selected a single bluish sport of *Syringa vulgaris* 'Hugo Koster' in the 1930s. Since the mid-1980s this selection is being grown in Aalsmeer as a forcing lilac under the name 'Dark Koster' (also known as 'Donkere Koster'). This may not be a single clone; mutations of 'Hugo Koster' are not infrequent (G. A. Bunnik, pers. comm. to F.V.).

Dirk Eveleens Maarse Sr. (1881–1975) was born to a nurseryman's family at Aalsmeer. It should be noted that there is no direct relationship between the person Dirk Eveleens Maarse and the nursery of Eveleens and Maarse. After finishing primary school Dirk started working in the nursery and received his initial horticultural training at the Uiterweg-School. When in 1897 the State Horticultural Winter School at Aalsmeer opened its doors, 16-year-old Dirk was admitted to its inaugural class. Upon graduation he spent six months in the United States after which he returned to Aalsmeer to work at his father's nursery, W. Topsvoort, which had a long tradition of producing clipped plants of *Taxus baccata* and *Buxus sempervirens*. Clipped topiary yews, the taller ones often several decades old, were in great demand for formal gardens in the United States and Britain, but World War I wiped out this export market. For some years Dirk had been interested in dahlias, cultivating them between the topiary plants, and he now started to

make his own crosses and selections. In the 1920s he became also interested in lilacs. Based on his breeding experience with dahlias he developed a strategy, which in 1938 allowed him to introduce the first of his lilac novelties, namely, 'Excellent', 'Johan Mensing', and 'Sensation'. Being very conscious of the importance of quality, he made it his policy to introduce only the very best. He would submit his unnamed selections for judgment by the Special Committee of the Dutch equivalent of the Royal Horticulture Society (Koninklijke Maatschappij Tuinbouw en Plantkunde, hereinafter KMTP); only those seedlings and sports that were distinguished with a Certificate of Merit or the prestigious First Class Certificate would be named and introduced commercially (Eveleens Maarse 1954a, 1954b; Paul 1974). In the 1950s Dirk took a leading role in creating the Aalsmeer lilac park, the first substantial collection of lilacs in the Netherlands.

All the Dirk Eveleens Maarse lilacs introduced have proved to be outstanding, and it may well be that his white selections are among the finest. They ought be better known and more widely grown. Since many of these Dutch introductions have not been seen in North America, we are not able to judge them well. In the following list of Dirk's *Syringa vulgaris* introductions, the names of plants in cultivation in North America are starred. Annette Leighton-van Leeuwen, secretary of the Foundation Permanent Judging Committee in Roelofarendsveen, Netherlands, provided information on the KMTP awards.

★ 'André Csizik' (*S. vulgaris*), single magenta, 1950; Certificate of Merit (KMTP) 1950

'Burgemeester Loggers' (*S. vulgaris*), single violet, 1960; Certificate of Merit (KMTP) 1960

★ 'Burgemeester Voller' (*S. vulgaris*), single lavender-blue with a white eye, 1948; Certificate of Merit (KMTP) 1948; large florets

'Directeur Doorenbos' (*S. vulgaris*), single lilac, 1955; Certificate of Merit (KMTP) 1955

'Director General van de Plassche' (*S. vulgaris*), single magenta, 1961

★ 'Excellent' (*S. vulgaris*), single white, 1938; First Class Certificate (KMTP) 1939.

★ 'Flora 1953' (*S. vulgaris*) (often incorrectly listed as 'Flora'), single white, 1953; Award of Merit (KMTP) 1953; large florets, very outstanding

★ 'G. J. Baardse' (*S. vulgaris*), single magenta, 1943; Certificate of Merit (KMTP) 1943, First Class Certificate (KMTP) 1953

'Gerrie Schoonenberg' (*S. vulgaris*), single white, 1948; Certificate of Merit (KMTP) 1948

'Hugo Mayer' (*S. vulgaris*), single bluish, 1950; Certificate of Merit (KMTP) 1950

'J. R. Koning' (*S. vulgaris*), single lilac, 1955; Certificate of Merit (KMTP) 1955

'Johann Mensing' (*S. vulgaris*), single violet, 1938; First Class Certificate (KMTP) 1939

'Jonkheer G. F. van Tets' (*S. vulgaris*), single lilac, 1940; First Class Certificate (KMTP) 1950

'Madame Rosel' (*S. vulgaris*), single lilac, 1953; First Class Certificate (KMTP) 1953

'Maud Notcutt' (*S. vulgaris*), single white; sold to and introduced by R. C. Notcutt, United Kingdom, 1956; whether this selection had an earlier name, prior to being sold to Notcutt, is not known. It is thought to have been of the same parentage as 'Flora 1953'. RHS Award of Merit 1957

'Nanook' (*S. vulgaris*), single white, 1951; Certificate of Merit (KMTP) 1951

'Peerless Pink' (*S. vulgaris*), single pink, 1953; Certificate of Merit (KMTP) 1953

'Riet Bruidegom' (*S. vulgaris*), single white, 1950; Certificate of Merit (KMTP) 1950

★ 'Sensation' (*S. vulgaris*), single deep purple petals edged white, 1938; outstanding, the very first bicolor lilac selected; First Class Certificate (KMTP) 1938

'Treesje Topsvoort' (*S. vulgaris*), single lilac, 1948; Certificate of Merit (KMTP), First Class Certificate (KMTP) 1953

'Voorzitter Dix' (*S. vulgaris*), single magenta 1950; Certificate of Merit (KMTP) 1950, First Class Certificate (KMTP) 1953

'White Superior' (*S. vulgaris*), single white, 1953; Certificate of Merit (KMTP) 1953

Syringa vulgaris 'Hugo Mayer'. B. Peart and M. Walton

Syringa vulgaris 'Jonkheer G. F. van Tets'. B. Peart and M. Walton

Syringa vulgaris 'J. R. Koning'. B. Peart and M. Walton

Syringa vulgaris 'Peerless Pink'. B. Peart and M. Walton

Nurseryman Willem Keessen (1884–1963) of Terra Nova Koninklijke Kwekerij in Aalsmeer, introduced the single white *Syringa vulgaris* 'Helena Agathe Keessen', a mutation of 'Mme Florent Stepman', in 1936.

Aalsmeer florist Gerrit Maarse Jbzn (1885–1978) was the originator of the lilac 'Yellow Wonder', known today as *Syringa vulgaris* 'Primrose'. 'Primrose' was the first foreign developed lilac to be patented in the United States of America (Plant Patent 1108, 24 June 1952); its story is well worth telling. In war-time Holland, in the winter of 1943, in Maarse's hothouse, plants of 'Marie Legraye', a single white lilac, were being forced for bloom. One flowering branch produced four thyrses, one and a half of which bore yellow florets. In a letter dated 30 December 1950 Maarse wrote Richard Maatsch at the University of Hanover, Germany, about the origin of 'Primrose' (Vrugtman & Eickhorst 1981):

All the leaf-buds of the branch in question were removed, as also were the two white and the one partly yellow clusters. That left only the one yellow flower cluster. This was also cut off but not the part below on which small leaf-buds occurred, one of which we hoped would develop. The entire shrub was kept in the hothouse for the spring and the summer and, as was hoped, there developed a small shoot at the place mentioned above. This shoot provided material to allow us to graft ten plants in the following year. To our pleasure they all bloomed yellow.

Anyone familiar with the turmoil of the final years of World War II in the Netherlands will realize that it

is a miracle that this lilac selection survived. The name 'Yellow Wonder' appeared with a description in the 2 July 1949 issue of *The Gardener's Chronicle*, the color of the buds described as pale barium-yellow, *Horticultural Colour Chart* 503/3 (R. F. Wilson 1939, 1942), and the open florets of similar color but slightly paler (Anonymous 1949). Sometime between February 1949 and May 1950 the name was changed to 'Primrose', the name by which this lilac has been known ever since. 'Primrose' received the RHS Award of Merit in 1950, and a First Class Certificate (KMTP) in 1952–1953.

There are occasional reports on sports of 'Primrose' said to have better floret coloration. Two sports have been selected which appear to have a deeper shade of yellow, although opinions on their merits are divided. The first was selected by the late Albert E. Lumley (1902–1981), Amherst, Massachusetts, and has been listed as LUMLEY YELLOW. The second sport was selected at the Holden Arboretum, Kirtland, Ohio, and has been listed as PRIMROSE H; it is marketed in Germany under the registered trademark STERNTALER.

The Maarsen Brothers' nursery in Aalsmeer, operated by Poulus Maarsen (1888–1954) and Gerrit Maarsen (1892–1972), originated 'Prinses Beatrix', a single white, introduced in 1938 and named for Princess Beatrix of the Netherlands, who was born in 1938.

J. D. Maarse and Son, a nursery operated in Aalsmeer by brothers Jacob Maarse (1899–1969) and Albert Maarse (1902–1992), originated 'Gloire d'Aalsmeer', a single white, introduced about 1938.

Ouwerkerk (no information found) introduced the single pink *Syringa vulgaris* 'Annie Ouwerkerk' (occasionally listed as 'Mevr. Annie Ouwerkerk') in 1946.

In 1952 Cornelis Buis (1901–1988) in Aalsmeer introduced *Syringa vulgaris* 'Margaretha', a single white sport of 'Mme Florent Stepman'.

Aalsmeer nurserymen Jaap Maarse Hzn (contemporary) and his son Hendrik Maarse Hzn (contemporary) of the Eveleens and Maarse nursery (no connection to Dirk Eveleens Maarse), and the late Hendrik (Henk) Keessen (1915–1990) and his brother Gerrit Keessen (no dates available) of the Keessen Hameland nursery have been selecting and testing improved clonal lilac rootstock for lilacs produced for green-

Syringa vulgaris 'Helena Agathe Keessen'. B. Peart and M. Walton

house forcing since the early 1980s. In 1994 the Eveleens and Maarse nursery registered plant breeders' rights for *Syringa vulgaris* 'Robuste Albert' (earlier known as 'A1' and 'Robusta') as tissue-culture propagated rootstock.

Martine Spaargaren (1916–1991), daughter to Cornelis Spaargaren Dzn, was born in Aalsmeer and educated at the Boskoop Horticultural School, under the tutelage of dendrologist Boudewijn Karel Boom (1903–1980) and C. Ph. Moerlands. She was hired at the Aalsmeer Experiment Station, where her father was director of horticulture. From 1936 to 1940, under the guidance of Dr. Roodenburg, she participated in the development of cut-flowers for forcing including carnations, gerberas, and lilacs. The *Syringa* crosses were made in 1939, using 'Marie Finon', 'Mme Félix', 'Ruhm von Horstenstein', and 'Königin Luise', but the individual parentages of the final selections are not known. The seed was sown in 1940. In the summer of 1945 the seedlings were prepared for their first test forcing early in 1946. Dirk Eveleens Maarse and W. Maarse (no information on this person) participated in making the initial 15 selections. The first of the final selections were introduced in 1954; one of these was named 'Martine' in honor of its hybridizer (Vrugtman 1999b). Four selections appear to be in cultivation:

'Martine' (*S. vulgaris*), single white, 1954; Certificate of Merit (KMTP) 1954
'Niobe' (*S. vulgaris*), single white, 1958; Certificate of Merit (KMTP) 1958
'Voorzitter Buskermolen' (*S. vulgaris*), single violet, 1954; Certificate of Merit (KMTP) 1954

Syringa vulgaris 'Martine'. B. Peart and M. Walton

'Westend' (*S. vulgaris*), single white, 1956; Certificate of Merit (KMTP) 1956

Albert Maarse (1902–1992) established his nursery in Aalsmeer and was succeeded by his son Jan Maarse (b. 1925). Jan's son-in-law, Gerard Bunnik (b. 1954), took over the operation of the nursery in 1981. In March 2005 Bunnik introduced *Syringa vulgaris* 'Lila Wonder', a single, bi-color, with a violet heart and a white margin. It was the first new forcing lilac introduced in 75 years (Boon 2005; Vrugtman 2005).

Little Known Hardy Lilacs from Scandinavia

Nurseryman Eero ("Eppu") Olavi Viksten (1925–1991), founder of Viksten Nursery, Tammela, Finland, selected and introduced *Syringa* (Villosae Group) 'Tammelan Kaunotar', a single white, in 1990; it is an open-pollinated seedling of *S. josikaea*.

Nurseryman Holger Tolppola (1926–1995), founder of Tolppolas Plantskola KB (1956) of Espoo, Finland, selected and introduced *Syringa* (Villosae Group) 'Holger' in 1975. This single, white selection is probably of open-pollinated *S. josikaea* parentage.

Kimmo L. Kolkka (contemporary), a dendrologist, horticulturist, and nurseryman in Karkkila, Finland, selected *Syringa* (Villosae Group) 'Maria' (*S. ×henryi*), a single white in 1989.

Sirkka-Liisa Peteri (contemporary), who operates a small nursery at Hirvas near Rovaniemi, Finland, not far from the Arctic Circle, found and introduced in the 1980s *Syringa* (Villosae Group) 'Veera', a single, violet, probably *S. ×josiflexa*.

Marjatta Uosukainen (contemporary), director of Laukaa Research and Elite Plant Station in Vihtavuori, Finland, found and introduced *Syringa* (Villosae Group) 'Ainola', a single, dark violet, in about 2001.

Nurseryman Kjell Wickman (contemporary) of Wickmans Plantskola, Närpiö, Finland, selected and introduced *Syringa* (Villosae Group) 'Julia' in 1993, a single pinkish selection of *S. ×henryi*, and *S. josikaea* 'Kjell', a single white in 1998. Wickman's nursery also distributes two *S. vulgaris* cultivars of unknown origin: 'Akkila', a single violet, ca. 2002, and 'Ritoniemi', a single magenta, ca. 2001.

Siri Horntvedt Kjaer (contemporary) of the Department of Plant and Environmental Sciences at Norwegian Agricultural University (now the Norwegian University of Life Sciences), selected and introduced four cultivars in 1985: *Syringa villosa* 'Baldishol', a single violet-pink; *S. josikaea* 'Holte', single magenta; *S. josikaea* 'Moe', single magenta; and *S. josikaea* 'Rå', single violet-bluish. All were selected for winter hardiness and their ability to survive and bloom under the harsh conditions in the garden plots of cottages in the high mountains of Norway. At least two of these cultivars are performing well in the lilac collection at the Reykjavik botanical garden, Iceland.

Two hardy lilacs from Sweden, probably selected at the Balsgård horticultural facility of the Swedish University of Agriculture, are *Syringa josikaea* 'Måttsund', 1980s, single violet; and *S. vulgaris* 'Norrfjärden', pre-1999, double bluish.

Lilac Hybridizing in North America

James Dougall (1810–1888)

The earliest recorded lilac cultivars selected and named in North America appear to be those selected by James Dougall at Windsor Nurseries, Windsor, Ontario, Canada. In 1826 James emigrated from Scotland, joining his elder brother John in Montreal, Upper Canada. Four years later they established a general store, "J. & J. Dougall," at Sandwich Ferry, now Windsor, Ontario. In the 1840s and 1850s James owned and operated first Rosebank Nurseries and later Windsor Nurseries, featuring mostly fruit trees, grape vines, and small fruits, but also some roses and lilacs which he had imported from Europe. Dougall se-

lected and named at least seven cultivars from several thousand open-pollinated seedlings of *Syringa vulgaris*. Four of them were listed in his 1874 Descriptive Catalogue. In the United States three of these cultivars were first offered for sale in 1886 by Ellwanger and Barry of Rochester, New York. 'Prince of Wales', a single dark purple, and 'Princess Alexandra', a double white, can still be found growing in collections (Vrugtman 1982a).

John Dunbar (1859–1927)

John Dunbar was born in Rafford, Elginshire, Scotland. After emigrating to the United States he eventually became assistant superintendent of parks at Rochester, New York. In 1891 he planted about one-hundred lilacs at Highland Botanical Park, whereby began an odyssey which was to make Rochester an early center of lilac cultivars. In four years those first hundred lilacs bloomed with such splendor that they attracted considerable attention. Great crowds soon began to come each May to see the lilacs.

By 1908 Dunbar raised several open-pollinated lilac seedlings of the French Hybrids he had planted at the park. Six years later he grew a second group from the mostly Lemoine cultivars. Due to failing health he retired as assistant superintendent and arboriculturist in 1926. A flower bed surrounded by choice lilacs harbors a bronze plaque honoring the memory of this staunch Scotsman who made lilacs and Rochester famous. He must smile at the annual lilac festivals and parades that pass the spot where the first hundred lilacs and their seedlings bloomed. A

Syringa vulgaris 'Prince of Wales'. B. Peart and M. Walton

John Dunbar and granddaughter, 20 June 1922. Photographer unknown

row of old Dunbar lilacs can still be found blooming each spring to greet the lilac enthusiasts as they climb the path high on the hill.

From his first 75 seedlings which matured just prior to World War I, Dunbar selected 19 to be named—perhaps a few too many. Eight were very well received and entered the commercial trade. Among them was his famous bluish lilac 'President Lincoln' and the deep purple 'Adelaide Dunbar'. From the second group of seedlings he selected about 50 of which 11 were named. For many decades 'President Lincoln' was considered the bluest lilac known, though many of the Lemoine cultivars were indeed bluer. Although the color of 'President Lincoln' is a unique blue-lavender, its greatest fault is the bodyguard of new green shoots so quickly and vigorously thrown up around the bloom as to hide its real beauty as a garden plant. 'President Lincoln' is an open-pollinated seedling of the old 'Alba Virginalis' (pre-1841), also a vigorous grower.

Of his most prized cultivar, 'General Sherman', Dunbar writes, "We consider this cultivar perhaps one of the most beautiful lilacs in cultivation!" Indeed, this open-pollinated seedling of the very old *Syringa vulgaris* 'Marlyensis Pallida' (pre-1864) is an outstanding lilac even today and should be included in every worthwhile collection. In bud a deep lavender, it opens to a pearled creamy, pale lavender—a treasure of beauty. It was Dunbar's choicest which somehow the garden writers and the commercial nurseries missed. Of the 30 cultivars Dunbar named in his lifetime, 12 were available at one time or an-

other from nurserymen. This is a remarkably high record for a hybridizer not growing and selling his own plants. The Dunbar lilacs listed here are currently in cultivation in collections and, where noted, also available in commerce:

'A. B. Lamberton' (*S. vulgaris*), double violet-lavender, 1916

'Adelaide Dunbar' (*S. vulgaris*), double deep-purple, 1916 (commerce)

'Admiral Farragut' (*S. vulgaris*), single lilac, 1923 (commerce)

'Alexander Hamilton' (*S. vulgaris*), violet-lavender, 1923

'Calvin C. Laney' (*S. vulgaris*), single purple, pre-1923 (commerce)

'Clarence D. Van Zandt' (*S. vulgaris*), single purple, 1923

'Elihu Root' (*S. vulgaris*), double magenta, 1923

'General Elwell S. Otis' (*S. vulgaris*), double lilac, 1906

'General Grant' (*S. vulgaris*), single purple, 1917

'General John Pershing' (*S. vulgaris*), double azure lilac, 1917; not to be confused with 'Général Pershing', a double pink introduced in 1924 by the Lemoine nursery

'General Kitchener' (*S. vulgaris*), double bluish, 1917

'General Sheridan' (*S. vulgaris*), double lacy white, 1917; perhaps his best white selection

'General Sherman' (*S. vulgaris*), single pink, 1917 (commerce)

'George W. Aldridge' (*S. vulgaris*), single lilac, 1923

Syringa vulgaris 'General John Pershing'. B. Peart and M. Walton

Syringa vulgaris 'George W. Aldridge'. B. Peart and M. Walton

'Henry Clay' (*S. vulgaris*), showy single white, 1923

'Henry Wadsworth Longfellow' (*S. vulgaris*), double magenta, 1920

'Henry Ward Beecher' (*S. vulgaris*), double lilac, 1923

'Hiram H. Edgerton' (*S. vulgaris*), single purple, 1919

'Joan Dunbar' (*S. vulgaris*), double white, 1923 (commerce)

'Patrick Henry' (*S. vulgaris*), double lilac, 1922

'President Harding' (*S. vulgaris*), single purple, 1923

'President John Adams' (*S. vulgaris*), double white, 1923

'President Lincoln' (*S. vulgaris*), single bluish, 1916 (commerce)

'President Monroe' (*S. vulgaris*), double violet, 1923

'President Roosevelt' (*S. vulgaris*), single purplish red, 1919

'Susan B. Anthony' (*S. vulgaris*), single magenta, 1923 (commerce)

'Thomas A. Edison' (*S. vulgaris*), single purple, 1922

'Thomas Jefferson' (*S. vulgaris*), single pink, 1922

'William C. Barry' (*S. vulgaris*), single pale lavender, 1917 (commerce)

'William S. Riley' (*S. vulgaris*), single magenta, 1922 (commerce)

Syringa vulgaris 'Henry Clay'. B. Peart and M. Walton

Syringa vulgaris 'President Roosevelt'. B. Peart and M. Walton

Syringa vulgaris 'Hiram H. Edgerton'. B. Peart and M. Walton

Syringa vulgaris 'Susan B. Anthony'. B. Peart and M. Walton

Syringa vulgaris 'Thomas Jefferson'. B. Peart and M. Walton

Hulda Klager (1864–1960)

Hulda Thiel was born in Germany on 10 May 1864 and spent her first birthday on the high seas en route to North America. The Thiels pioneered in Wisconsin, then moved on to Minnesota and finally, when Hulda was 13, settled in Lewis County, Washington, near the town of Woodland. In her early teens Hulda married Frank Klager to become a dairyman's wife. Each year their farm was inundated by the flooding Lewis River, so Frank graded a seven foot high embankment, 90 feet square around their home. The flood waters brought fertility to the soil, and on this "floating island" as Hulda called it, she planted her beloved flowers and garden.

Among her duties as a farmer's wife and mother, she somehow found time to study botany and read every available gardening book and catalog. There were but meager funds for new plants and seeds each year, so Hulda saved seeds from her own garden. In time, with her father's death, she and her husband were able to purchase the old family home with 4½ acres of land on the outskirts of Woodland where she first lived. This became their permanent home and the place where she planted and worked for more than 40 years with her lilacs. From the book *New Creations in Plant Life* (Harwood 1905) she learned about the work and methods of Luther Burbank (1849–1926) and the great possibilities in cross-pollinating plants. She visited Burbank in California and corresponded with him. Although she worked with many different kinds of plants, she turned her major efforts to hybridizing lilacs.

In 1905 she began her work with lilacs and in five years had created 14 new cultivars. She had purchased a collection of seven named *Syringa vulgaris* cultivars from an eastern nursery. Of these she discarded two for poor quality of their flowers; another two were destroyed by the horses. The remaining three cultivars became her Magic Three, the cornerstones of her lilac hybridizing work; they were 'Mme Casimir Périer' (Lemoine 1884), a fine double white; 'Président Grévy' (Lemoine 1886), a double blue; and 'Andenken an Ludwig Späth' (Späth 1883), an excellent purple. She crossed these three, cross-pollinating and backcrossing their seedlings. She had definite objectives in mind: to create vigorous, disease-resistant plants; to extend the color range into clear blue, pink, and rose; and to create variations in flower cluster forms and in the size of the florets.

From her Magic Three Hulda Klager originated more than 100 new cultivars; at one time her seedlings grown for observation numbered over 300. The cultivars she introduced were named for neighboring towns and for friends and relatives as they came to visit her gardens. She knew only the two older Lemoine cultivars; it is remarkable that despite her ignorance of any of the newer Lemoine or other introductions she was able, in total isolation, to produce so many new cultivars from an extremely limited gene pool of three lilacs. Perhaps she was misunderstood as a farm woman without skills by some eastern lilac fanciers who heard of her work only indirectly, as most of her best lilacs have never been seen in eastern collections or gardens because of the difficulty in obtaining them.

After her husband's death in 1922, and with the help of their son, Fred (Fritz), Klager produced plants commercially, leaving her little time for hybridizing. Her sales were limited to customers who came to her nursery. There are no inventories or price lists from those years. The earliest documented commercial introduction of eight of her lilacs was by R. M. Cooley (Cooley's Gardens) of Silverton, Oregon, in 1928. These eight cultivars are referred to in McKelvey (1928: 559–563). In 1947 Klager received a citation, "For distinguished achievements in horticulture" from the Oregon Federation of Garden Clubs, and in 1958 the Horticultural Award of the Washington State Federation of Garden Clubs.

Klager had a large number of seedlings ready to be named, many of considerable merit, when the disastrous flood of 1948 destroyed her entire garden, her Magic Three, and all their progeny. Only thirteen of her lilacs had been introduced commercially at that time. Her son died shortly after the flood. At the age of 84 the amazing Hulda declared, "I will remain here where I belong. I will devote the rest of my life in rebuilding the garden; I have faith!" (Collins 1948).

So she did begin anew. Friends, neighbors, former customers, and well-wishers sent out the message to bring back her lilacs and helped rebuild the garden. Hulda's beloved lilacs came back as suckers and plants. And they bloomed as they did before for her twilight years. It is unfortunate, but due to the circumstances, the lack of adequate descriptions, and the time-lapse between Klager's death and the reconstruction of her garden during which few records were maintained, that the identities of the lilac cultivars at the Hulda Klager Gardens cannot be established with certainty. The garden at Woodland, now a State and National Historic Site, blooms with the radiant colors of the Klager lilacs, and the fragrance of peace drifts over her bronze memorial. The Lilac Lady of Woodland died in Woodland in her 96th year in 1960.

The Hulda Klager Lilac Garden Society, a nonprofit organization, administers the 4½-acre property, the lilac collection, and the restored Victorian Thiel-Klager family home and its outbuildings. The Garden was officially opened in 1976 (Vrugtman 1998, 1999c).

The more frequently encountered Klager lilac cultivars are listed here. Of these, the four best are 'City of Gresham', strongly scented; 'Martha', the most fragrant of the Klager lilacs, according to Reva Ballreich; 'My Favorite', Klager's favorite lilac; and 'Ostrander', probably her best selection.

'Abundant Bloomer' (*S. vulgaris*), single pink, 1928
'Alice' (*S. vulgaris*), single lilac, 1928
'Alice Christianson' (*S. vulgaris*), double purple
'Alma' (*S. vulgaris*), single purple, 1932
'Carmine' (*S. vulgaris*), single magenta, 1928
'Celestial Blue' (*S. vulgaris*), single blue, 1930
'City of Chehalis' (*S. vulgaris*), single pink, pre-1953
'City of Gresham' (*S. vulgaris*) (syn. 'Klager Dark Purple'), single purple, 1915
'City of Kalama' (*S. vulgaris*), single purple, 1915
'City of Kelso' (*S. vulgaris*), double pink, pre-1942
'City of Longview' (*S. vulgaris*), double pink, 1930
'City of Olympia' (*S. vulgaris*), single lilac, 1934
'Clara' (*S. vulgaris*), single pink, 1928
'Dillia' (*S. vulgaris*), double white, 1915
'Dresden China' (*S. vulgaris*), single lilac, 1930
'Elizabeth Mills' (*S. vulgaris*), single purple, 1930
'Fluffy Ruffles' (*S. vulgaris*), single lilac, pre-1953
'Frank Klager' (*S. vulgaris*), single purple, pre-1942
'Fred L. Klager' (*S. vulgaris*), single purple, 1930
'Fritz' (*S. vulgaris*), double purple, 1928; plants in cultivation under this name, but single purple, are not true to name

'Hulda' (*S. vulgaris*), single purple, 1929
'Irvina' (*S. vulgaris*), single purple, 1920
'Lillian Lee' (*S. vulgaris*), single pink, 1935
'Mariam Cooley' (*S. vulgaris*), single pink, 1931
'Martha' (*S. vulgaris*), single white, 1930
'Mrs Morgan' (*S. vulgaris*), double pink, 1928
'My Favorite' (*S. vulgaris*), double magenta, 1928
'Old Rose' (*S. vulgaris*), single pink, 1928
'Ostrander' (*S. vulgaris*), double purple, 1928
'Princess Pink' (*S. vulgaris*), single pink, 1938
'R. W. Mills' (*S. vulgaris*), double pink, 1928

'Roland Mills' (*S. vulgaris*), single purple, 1930
'Susanna' (*S. vulgaris*), single white, 1928
'Vivian Evans' (*S. vulgaris*), single lilac, pre-1953
'Weddle' (*S. vulgaris*), double magenta, 1928
'Wm K. Mills' (*S. vulgaris*), single purple, 1930
'Woodland' (*S. vulgaris*), single purple, 1930

Syringa vulgaris 'Clara'. B. Peart and M. Walton

Syringa vulgaris 'Abundant Bloomer'. B. Peart and M. Walton

Syringa vulgaris 'Fred L. Klager'. B. Peart and M. Walton

Syringa vulgaris 'Carmine'. B. Peart and M. Walton

Syringa vulgaris 'Fritz'. B. Peart and M. Walton

Syringa vulgaris 'Old Rose'. B. Peart and M. Walton

Syringa vulgaris 'Ostrander'. John Fiala

Syringa vulgaris 'Vivian Evans'. B. Peart and M. Walton

T. A. Havemeyer (1868–1936)

Theodore Augustus Havemeyer was a highly respected and knowledgeable amateur horticulturist and garden writer interested in gladiolus, iris, lilies, and peonies, but above all, lilacs. About 1910 he visited the Lemoine nursery in Nancy, France, returning home with some of Lemoine's finest new cultivars of *Syringa vulgaris*, an abundance of sage Lemoine advice and knowledge, and a deep love for lilacs that lasted to the end of his life. The Lemoines and their nursery made a lasting impression on Havemeyer. Realizing the exceptional hybridizing work of the Lemoines, Havemeyer turned to improving color and size of single-flowered lilacs. Most of the basic stock he used were the plants he brought from Lemoine. To these he added the finest plants available from the lilac nurseries of his day. These plants became the nucleus of his lilac collection and his future lilac selection work. Havemeyer's 42-acre Cedar Hill Nursery Estate at Brookville, Long Island, New York, at one time numbered 20,000 lilac plants!

During his lifetime Havemeyer selected and named 45 new cultivars of *Syringa vulgaris*. Most of the names of these new lilacs were published in *Lilacs for America*, the Report of the 1953 Lilac Survey Committee of the American Association of Botanical Gardens and Arboretums, chaired by John C. Wister (Wister 1953). An additional 11 Havemeyer seedlings were selected and named by Mark M. Eaton (see also entry under that name); the names of six of these selections were published in *Lilacs for America* 1953, two were registered in 1963, one in 1970, and two names appear never to have been published. One Havemeyer seedling, 'Ellie-Marie', single and lilac, was named by Thomas Sears and is also listed in *Lilacs for America*. Wister (1933) with his wonderful lilac knowledge and experience once wrote of Havemeyer,

Of all the collections of lilacs I have seen either in this country or abroad none can equal that in the garden nursery of Mr. T. A. Havemeyer at Brookville, Long Island . . . It has always seemed to me that the colors of his flowers are brighter than those grown farther inland. Perhaps the moist air from the Sound has much to do with that, for his soil is far from being rich and must require much feeding. His plants are grown in nursery rows and are rather difficult to study because often they are too close together or are difficult to approach through cultivated ground, but all of them are making superb growth and give flowers finer than any I have ever seen elsewhere.

Like Lemoine, Havemeyer named most of his lilacs for horticultural friends, prominent members of society, patrons of horticulture, and members of his own family. One of his finest whites was named 'Carley' for one of his tow-headed granddaughters. Whether he hand-pollinated or planted open-pollinated seed (which is more likely), and what the parent cross or seed pod was for his named varieties, was not recorded nor did he make mention of these facts. Nowhere does Havemeyer claim to have crossed any two particular cultivars so it is to be assumed he gathered seed from plants that he considered to be promising parents and carefully selected the choicest of the thousands of seedlings which resulted. His outstanding success gives testimony to what can be accomplished by trained and careful observation and selection of open-pollinated seedlings. He had a good eye and a fine sense of what he was seeking to accomplish in lilacs. Even in old age when illness forced him to use a wheelchair and he was not able to speak, he selected his lilacs carefully with a nod or shake of his head as he viewed his seedlings.

Some of the Havemeyer lilacs are outstanding as parents for further hybridizing. 'Sarah Sands' crossed with some of our larger floreted, newer lilacs gives seedlings of magnificent old rose and rose-purple shades. 'Carley' is an excellent parent for both size and color. 'Mrs John Davis' is perfection for transmitting both floret size and form. 'True Blue' (considered by John Wister as one of Havemeyer's finest and the best blue lilac) is an exceptional parent for all shades of blue, especially pale and delicate blues. There is a wealth of hybridizing material in the Havemeyer lilacs that has never been used. Many of his finest are relatively unknown after 70 years and should have been offered by nurseries decades ago.

The best of the Havemeyer lilacs in cultivation are listed here:

'Carley' (*S. vulgaris*), single white, enormous panicles, outstanding

'Dawn' (*S. vulgaris*), single bluish lilac; not to be confused with the single pinkish *S.* (Villosae Group) 'Dawn'

'Heather' (*S. vulgaris*), single white

'James Stuart' (*S. vulgaris*), single carmine-rose

'Lady Lindsay' (*S. vulgaris*), single magenta; reddest lilac in bud, recurved and twisted petals; somewhat difficult to grow well

'Mrs A. Belmont' (*S. vulgaris*), single light blue with a pert eye

'Mrs Elizabeth Peterson' (*S. vulgaris*), single two-toned steel-blue and deep purple reverse

Syringa vulgaris 'Dawn'. John Fiala

Syringa vulgaris 'Nancy Frick'. John Fiala

Syringa vulgaris 'Night'. B. Peart and M. Walton

Syringa vulgaris 'Dr Brethour'. B. Peart and M. Walton

'Mrs Flanders' (*S. vulgaris*), single purple; color very fine

'Mrs John S. Williams' (*S. vulgaris*), single bluish-lavender, large florets, enormous panicles; outstanding

'Mrs W. E. Marshall' (*S. vulgaris*), single deep black-purple, perhaps the darkest lilac; small florets but outstanding in color; slow grower

'Mrs Watson Webb' (*S. vulgaris*), single pink-magenta, large florets

'Nancy Frick' (*S. vulgaris*), single pink; of considerable merit

'Night' (*S. vulgaris*), an excellent single deep purple

'Prof. E. H. Wilson' (*S. vulgaris*), double white rosettes, very fine

'Romance' (*S. vulgaris*), single rosy-lavender

'Sarah Sands' (*S. vulgaris*), single deep rich, red-purple; late bloomer (named for his sister-in-law)

'True Blue' (*S. vulgaris*), single outstanding pale blue; remarkable

'Zulu' (*S. vulgaris*), single dark violet; of exceptional size and beauty

Sarah Ida Paterson (1872–1957)

Mrs. T. A., as she was known to friends and neighbors, had an extensive lilac garden at Agincourt, Ontario, Canada. Although she selected only a few new cultivars, all introduced after her death, they were all of good quality. Her three dark purple lilacs, 'Dr Brethour' (1961), 'Frank Paterson' (1961), and 'Helen Schloen' (1962), and the white 'Jimmy Howarth' (1961) are well known in cultivation. Fortunately the clonal material she used was continued on in the work of Leonard Slater.

Leonard Slater (1916–1982)

Leonard Kelvey Slater, Agincourt, Ontario, Canada, carried on the work of Sarah Ida Paterson, producing two outstanding, large-flowered lilacs. His first introduction, *Syringa vulgaris* 'Agincourt Beauty' in 1968, is a lilac of heavy substance with huge deep purple florets, so large they hang like clusters of immense grapes. His second introduction was the magnificent, single white named 'Slater's Elegance' in 1974. These lilacs may be difficult to equal for many years, and like 'Rochester', may set a new mark when used in hybridizing. Both cultivars were patented in the United States in 1975. A third selection, 'Mrs Irene Slater', a single violet, is still awaiting commercial introduction. Leonard Slater was a retiring personality who loved lilacs and set a very high standard for new introductions.

Leonard Slater. John Fiala

Mark Eaton (1900–1992)

Upon Havemeyer's death in 1936, his lilac collection at Cedar Hill was passed on to his friend, Mark Eaton. Under Eaton's direction eleven selections of Havemeyer were named and introduced. Some are among the finest of the Havemeyer lilacs. Only four appear to be still in cultivation, but they are well worth of a place among the best lilacs:

'Hallelujah' (*S. vulgaris*), single magenta, 1954
'Mauve Mist' (*S. vulgaris*), single magenta, 1963
'Serene' (*S. vulgaris*), single pinkish blue
'Snowflake' (*S. vulgaris*), single white, 1965

Rarely does a team such as Havemeyer-Eaton come forth for the good of all. Most of the Havemeyer lilacs were relatively unknown until they were offered to the public through the efforts and nursery of Mark Eaton. Often hybridizers' most mature and best work is done toward the end of their life, and most frequently the best fruit of their work is lost upon their death. The best seedlings are often not evaluated by trustees of estates and discarded.

For his work in promoting the lilac, Mark Eaton was awarded the International Lilac Society's Award of Merit in 1972. Under his direction Lilacland at Glen Head, Long Island, became a lilac specialty nursery, one where the very difficult and choice introductions of considerable merit could be found. Thankfully, though nurseries such as Lilacland (Mark Eaton), Dahliatown (J. Herbert Alexander), and Kingsville (Henry J. Hohman) may have disappeared, a new generation of nurseries and plantspeople have replaced them.

Isabella Preston (1881–1965)

It was in Lancashire, England, that Isabella Preston was born in 1881 and where she took a short course at Swanley Horticultural College for Women in 1906. At the age of 31 she came to Canada. In the autumn of 1912 she enrolled at Ontario Agricultural College in Guelph, under J. W. Crowe, the noted lily breeder. Here she developed *Lilium ×princeps* 'Paul Creelman', an important breakthrough in lily breeding.

In 1920 Preston was hired as a "day laborer" by the Division of Horticulture of the Central Experimental Farm at Ottawa to establish a breeding program of ornamental plants. Well over two years passed before a permanent position as Specialist in Ornamental Horticulture was approved. Preston's assignment included breeding programs with lilies, roses, lilacs, Siberian iris, columbine, and flowering crab apple. Rosybloom flowering crabs, hardy shrub roses, and a series of Siberian iris are but some of the results of her work. Perhaps her most outstanding accomplishments were with lilacs. Her principal lilac work included *Syringa villosa* and *S. reflexa*, resulting in the cross that now bears her name, *S. ×prestoniae*, and the hybrid *S. ×josiflexa* (*S. josikaea* × *S. reflexa*). She named over 50 selections and eventually introduced 47 new cultivars; she described and named another 36 which were never introduced (von Baeyer 1987).

Her original *Syringa villosa* (♀) × *S. reflexa* (♂) crosses made in the spring of 1920 produced 696 seeds; the *S. josikaea* (♀) × *S. reflexa* (♂) crosses produced only a few seeds. The following spring she lined out 299 seedlings, after discarding the 60 seedlings with variegated foliage. From the *S. josikaea* (♀) × *S. reflexa* (♂) cross only one seedling survived which she named 'Guinevere', designating it the nomenclatural type for *S. ×josiflexa*. From 1934 to 1948 she named five open-pollinated seedlings of 'Guinevere'.

In November 1925 Preston wrote to Susan McKelvey of her progress, "In 1924 the majority bloomed and I think this year they all did." She stirred up keen interest at the Arnold Arboretum for both McKelvey and Alfred Rehder visited Ottawa in June 1927 to evaluate her new hybrids. Subsequently, McKelvey (1928) described the Preston hybrid (*Syringa ×prestoniae* McKelvey) in her book naming two cultivars, 'Isabella' for its originator and 'W. T. Macoun' for William Tyrrell Macoun, Dominion horticulturist at the Central Experimental Farm. It should be noted that McKelvey used the alphabetical system in recording parentage of *S. ×prestoniae* as *S. reflexa* × *S. villosa*, which causes considerable confusion to those who follow the nomenclatural convention of placing the female parent first in describing a cross. This convention more easily and more effectively tells the true picture of the cross as *S. villosa* (♀ the seed or pod parent) × *S. reflexa* (♂ the pollen parent). 'Diana', named in 1926, resulted from the reciprocal cross of *S. reflexa* (♀) × *S. villosa* (♂) also made in 1920; it was the only seedling selection named. 'Diana' became the open-pollinated seed parent of 'Romeo', the more widely known cultivar.

Preston also crossed *Syringa vulgaris* 'Negro' with *S.* ×*hyacinthiflora* 'Lamartine'. From this cross she selected three cultivars, two of which, 'Muriel' and 'Norah', are still in cultivation. 'Peggy', resulting from open-pollinated 'Lamartine', also is still in cultivation (Macoun 1928; Cameron 1950, 1955, 1960).

Preston retired in December 1946. After spending a year in Britain she returned to Canada and settled in Georgetown, Ontario. Gardening was her passion; she cultivated and enjoyed many of her own plant creations in her garden. Among the awards and honors bestowed on her was the prestigious Veitch Memorial Medal from the Royal Horticultural Society, "for work in raising good plants" (1938).

The cultivars listed here appear to be in cultivation at the time of writing and are a good selection of the varying shades of color and form produced by these hybrids. The grouping by parentage shows the breeding patterns used by Preston. There are so many named Preston cultivars that are very similar in color, mostly shades of pink and pinkish lavender, that it is difficult to distinguish between them; this has brought about the current trend of using Villosae Group for all cultivars of interspecific parentage within the series *Villosae* (Hoffman 2003).

The best of Preston's *Syringa* ×*prestoniae* cultivars are listed first. Note that, following the currently accepted classification of lilacs (see chapter one), the binomial *S.* ×*prestoniae* McKelvey applies to all hybrids of *S. villosa* with *S. komarowii* in the broad sense, that is, including subsp. *komarowii* and subsp. *reflexa*:

'Audrey' (*S.* Villosae Group), single pinkish, 1928; RHS Award of Merit 1939
'Calphurnia' (*S.* Villosae Group), single lavender, pre-1942
'Desdemona' (*S.* Villosae Group), single blue, 1927; fine
'Elinor' (*S.* Villosae Group), single bluish lavender, 1928; RHS Award of Merit 1951
'Francisca' (*S.* Villosae Group), single purple, 1928; very good
'Isabella' (*S.* Villosae Group), single pinkish lavender, 1928; very fine; RHS Award of Merit 1941

'Juliet' (*S.* Villosae Group), single magenta, 1928; good
'Romeo' (*S.* Villosae Group), single pink, 1938
'Ursula' (*S.* Villosae Group), single pinkish lavender, 1928
'Viola' (*S.* Villosae Group), single purple, 1928; very fine
'W. T. Macoun' (*S.* Villosae Group), single pink, 1927

Syringa (Villosae Group) 'Audrey'. B. Peart and M. Walton

Syringa (Villosae Group) 'Calphurnia'. B. Peart and M. Walton

Syringa (Villosae Group) 'Elinor'. B. Peart and M. Walton

The best among Preston's *Syringa ×josiflexa* (*S. josi-kaea* × *S. komarowii*) cultivars are as follows:

'Bellicent' (*S.* Villosae Group), single pinkish, 1922; RHS First Class Certificate 1946
'Elaine' (*S.* Villosae Group), single white, 1948; very good
'Guinevere' (*S.* Villosae Group), single magenta, 1925
'Lynette' (*S.* Villosae Group), single dark purple, 1938

One selection resulted from open-pollinated *Syringa josikaea*:

'Kim' (*S.* Villosae Group), single violet, 1942; Royal Horticultural Society Award of Merit 1958

Another selection resulted from the cross *Syringa komarowii* × *S. sweginzowii*:

'Carlton' (*S.* Villosae Group), single pink, 1948

From the cross of *Syringa komarowii* subsp. *reflexa* with a misidentified lilac received from Victor Lemoine as *S. wolfii* (Preston 1946), Preston selected:

'Ethel M. Webster' (*S.* Villosae Group), single bright magenta-pink, 1948; very fine

From the cross (*Syringa vulgaris* 'Negro' × *S. ×hyacinthiflora* 'Lamartine') × ?, Preston selected one cultivar:

'Maureen' (*Syringa ×hyacinthiflora*), single lilac, 1936; RHS Award of Merit 1942

William Russel Leslie (ca. 1891–1985)

In the early 1930s Preston sent a number of unnamed lilac seedlings to the Canada Department of Agriculture Research Station at Morden, Manitoba, for further evaluation in the harsher Manitoba climate. Leslie, superintendent at the Station from 1921 to 1956 and in charge of the ornamentals program, made six selections:

'Beacon' (*S.* Villosae Group), single magenta, 1937 (*S. ×prestoniae*)
'Coral' (*S.* Villosae Group), single pinkish, 1936 (*S. ×prestoniae*)
'Dawn' (*S.* Villosae Group), single pinkish to white, 1937 (*S. ×prestoniae*)
'Nocturne' (*S.* Villosae Group), single blue, 1936 (*S. ×prestoniae*)

Syringa (Villosae Group) 'Coral'. John Fiala

Syringa (Villosae Group) 'Juliet'. B. Peart and M. Walton

Syringa (Villosae Group) 'Nocturne'. B. Peart and M. Walton

Syringa (Villosae Group) 'Redwine'. B. Peart and M. Walton

'Redwine' (*S.* Villosae Group), single bright magenta, 1936 (*S.* ×*prestoniae*); good

'Swanee' (*S.* Villosae Group), single white, 1936 (*S.* ×*prestoniae*); whites are rare among the *S.* ×*prestoniae* cultivars)

Frank Skinner (1882–1967)

In 1895, at age 13, Frank Leith Skinner sailed from his native Scotland with his parents who were to settle as cattle ranchers and grain farmers at Dropmore in northwestern Manitoba, Canada. Life in the cold prairie province was rugged and demanding; young Frank received little formal education. An unquenchable interest in and a consuming curiosity about plants was to make him internationally recognized as a botanist, horticulturist, and plant breeder. He was the acknowledged peer of the best-trained horticulturists around the world; many were personal friends and all knew him through his extensive correspondence.

Skinner contracted pneumonia in 1911 and lost the lower lobe of his right lung. He was advised to avoid strenuous activity so he turned his attention more to gardening activities and interests. That year he began his first formal collection of plant materials capable of surviving the harsh prairie conditions. These were the foundations for his hybridizing work and his Hardy Plant Nursery. From 1911 to 1918 he used his spare time to learn about horticulture, collect new plants, correspond with horticulturists, and develop the basics of hybridizing and nursery techniques. He was a self-taught man. He remained a rancher and farmer until 1925 when he decided to commercialize his plant propagating and hybridizing work. Devot-

Frank Skinner. Courtesy of the Skinner family.

ing a number of acres of the ranch at Dropmore to his nursery, he worked to develop new plants hardy to that location in USDA Zone 2b with its extremes of weather and average annual minimum temperatures between −40° and −45°F (−40° and −43°C). Here he worked with many different plants—trees and shrubs, fruits and flowers—producing hardy selections that were rapid-growing as well as drought- and disease-resistant.

In 1947 Skinner married Helen Belle Cumming. They raised five children, one of whom, Hugh Skinner, continued to operate Skinner's Nursery and Garden at Roblin, Manitoba. Frank Skinner received many awards and honors for his work; he was made a Member of the British Empire in 1943, and the University of Manitoba bestowed an honorary doctor of laws in 1947. Although he worked with new selections of hardy trees, shrubs, roses, lilies, herbaceous perennials, and tree and bush fruits with excellent results, one of his primary pursuits was improving the garden lilac.

On his first visit to the Arnold Arboretum in October 1918 Skinner carried back with him seedlings of *Syringa oblata* subsp. *dilatata* and *Syringa pubescens* subsp. *patula* given to him by Charles S. Sargent. The *S. oblata* plants were grown from seed collected by Ernest H. Wilson in the Diamond Mountains of Korea. Neither *S. reflexa* nor *S. sweginzowii* are hardy in the harsh climate of Dropmore, Manitoba. In the spring of 1920 Skinner crossed *S. reflexa* pollen from the Arnold Arboretum on flowers of *S. villosa*. These first attempts were unsuccessful. By coincidence in the same year another Canadian, Isabella Preston, was successful in making the same cross. Skinner had to wait until 1922 when he again received pollen from the Arnold Arboretum to repeat the cross, this time with good results. From the first generation of seedlings Skinner selected and named four cultivars: 'Handel' and 'Hiawatha' introduced in 1932, 'Helen' in 1935, and 'Hecla' in 1936. 'Donald Wyman', introduced in 1944, was grown from seed collected from an open-pollinated *S. ×prestoniae* seedling.

In the spring of 1921 the seedlings of *Syringa oblata* subsp. *dilatata*, obtained from Sargent in 1918 at the Arnold Arboretum, bloomed. Skinner began his famous Early Hybrid crosses that he called "American Hybrids" using various *S. vulgaris* cultivars, which he did not name, as pod parents (♀) and *S. oblata* subsp. *dilatata* as the pollen parent (♂). Eleven years later, in 1932, he introduced the first cultivars, 'Asessippi' and 'Minnehaha'. His final introduction in 1966 was 'Maiden's Blush', which at first he believed to be an interspecific hybrid.

The more outstanding among the 20 cultivars Skinner introduced from *Syringa vulgaris* (♀) and *S. oblata* subsp. *dilatata* (♂) include 'Pocahontas' in 1935, 'Gertrude Leslie' and 'Swarthmore' in 1954, 'Sister Justina' in 1956, 'Mount Baker' and 'The Bride' in 1961, 'Doctor Chadwick' in 1963, and 'Royal Purple' and the outstanding 'Maiden's Blush' in 1966. 'Grace Mackenzie', which Skinner introduced in 1942 as an interspecific hybrid, has since been determined to be one of his Early Hybrids. Although he called his hybrids American lilacs, they belong in *S. ×hyacinthiflora*. Skinner's cultivars with *S. oblata* subsp. *dilatata* parentage are much better garden plants than the *S. ×hyacinthiflora* cultivars with *S. oblata* subsp. *oblata* (formerly known as *S. oblata* var. *giraldii*) parentage. They are not as tall and rangy, and the buds and flowers appear to be somewhat more winter hardy than the cultivars with *S. oblata* subsp. *oblata* as a parent. Their inflorescence appears more open and abundant. The Skinner cultivars have proven themselves for all-round performance.

In 1936 Skinner introduced 'Hedin' (*Syringa villosa* × *S. sweginzowii*), another lovely garden plant. In 1942, he introduced 'Skinneri' (originally named *S. ×skinneri*) from the cross of *S. pubescens* subsp. *patula* with *S. pubescens* subsp. *pubescens*. Sometime before 1949, he introduced *S. ×diversifolia* 'William H. Judd', single white; the history of this selection is not well documented, but it appears that Karl Sax of the Arnold Arboretum made the cross (*S. oblata* × *S. pinnatifolia*) and Skinner grew the plants at his nursery, although this cultivar was never listed in his catalogs.

For more than three decades Skinner enriched our gardens, introducing 144 new cultivars of ornamental plants. Outside of his nursery his only financial aid was a federal grant given when he was 80 years old to record his life experiences. His book, *Horticultural Horizons: Plant Breeding and Introduction at Dropmore, Manitoba* (Skinner 1966), was published just six months before his death in 1967, at the age of 86. He will probably be best remembered for his outstanding and hardy *S. ×hyacinthiflora* cultivars with *S. oblata* subsp. *dilatata* parentage. Should you want only one Skinner introduction, let it be 'Maiden's Blush'. You will be unhappy unless you add 'Pocahontas', and have a pair of lovely lilac maidens. The best of Skinner's *Syringa ×hyacinthiflora* (*S. vulgaris* × *S. oblata* subsp. *dilatata*) cultivars are listed here:

'Asessippi' (*S. ×hyacinthiflora*), single lilac, 1932
'Charles Nordine' (*S. ×hyacinthiflora*), single bluish, 1953
'Churchill' (*S. ×hyacinthiflora*), single, 1945
'Daphne Pink' (*S. ×hyacinthiflora*), single pinkish, 1959
'Doctor Chadwick' (*S. ×hyacinthiflora*), single bluish, pre-1963

Syringa ×hyacinthiflora 'Asessippi'. B. Peart and M. Walton

Syringa ×hyacinthiflora 'Louvain'. B. Peart and M. Walton

Syringa ×hyacinthiflora 'Swarthmore'. B. Peart and M. Walton

Syringa ×hyacinthiflora 'Royal Purple'. B. Peart and M. Walton

Syringa (Villosae Group) 'Handel'. B. Peart and M. Walton

'Evangeline' (*S. ×hyacinthiflora*), double magenta, 1934

'Excel' (*S. ×hyacinthiflora*), single lilac, 1932

'Frazer' (*S. ×hyacinthiflora*), single pinkish, 1945

'Gertrude Leslie' (*S. ×hyacinthiflora*), double white, 1954

'Grace Mackenzie' (*S. ×hyacinthiflora*), single lilac, 1942

'Laurentian' (*S. ×hyacinthiflora*), single bluish, 1945

'Louvain' (*S. ×hyacinthiflora*), single violet, 1962

'Maiden's Blush' (*S. ×hyacinthiflora*), single pinkish, 1966

'Minnehaha' (*S. ×hyacinthiflora*), single pinkish, 1932

'Mount Baker' (*S. ×hyacinthiflora*), single white, 1961; marketed in Germany as SCHNEEWEISSCHEN

'Nokomis' (*S. ×hyacinthiflora*), single lilac, 1934

'Pocahontas' (*S. ×hyacinthiflora*), single purple, 1935

'Royal Purple' (*S. ×hyacinthiflora*), double purple, 1966

'Sister Justina' (*S. ×hyacinthiflora*), single white, 1956

'Swarthmore' (*S. ×hyacinthiflora*), double lilac, 1954

'The Bride' (*S. ×hyacinthiflora*), single white, 1961

'Tom Taylor' (*S. ×hyacinthiflora*), double purple, 1962

The best of Skinner's *Syringa ×prestoniae* (*S. komarowii* × *S. villosa*) cultivars are as follows:

'Donald Wyman' (*S.* Villosae Group), single purple, 1944; grown from seed collected from an open-pollinated *S. ×prestoniae* seedling

'Handel' (*S.* Villosae Group), single pinkish, 1932

'Hecla' (*S.* Villosae Group), single pinkish to white, 1936

'Helen' (*S.* Villosae Group), single pinkish, 1935

'Hiawatha' (*S.* Villosae Group), single magenta, 1932; unique flower formation

'Horace' (*S.* Villosae Group), single magenta, 1932

Syringa (Villosae Group) 'Helen'. B. Peart and M. Walton

Syringa (Villosae Group) 'Hiawatha'. B. Peart and M. Walton

Syringa (Villosae Group) 'Hedin'. John Fiala

From the cross *Syringa villosa* × *S. sweginzowii* Skinner introduced two selections:

'Hedin' (*S.* Villosae Group), single pinkish, pre-1942
'Hunting Tower' (*S.* Villosae Group), single white, pre-1942

Mary Blacklock (1860–1956) and Minerva Castle (1891–1976)

Mary Eliza Blacklock and her partner and successor, Minerva Swann Castle, operated Rowancroft Gardens in Meadowvale, Ontario, Canada. They selected and introduced some outstanding *Syringa vulgaris* cultivars, the very best of which are 'St Joan', 'St Margaret', and 'Violet Glory'. Blacklock and Castle were quiet and retiring individuals, shunning any publicity for their work with lilacs. Though they selected many fine seedlings, only the very best were named and introduced. Castle was given an Award of Merit by the International Lilac Society in 1972, "for outstanding work in hybridizing lilacs and introducing better varieties."

Three *Syringa vulgaris* cultivars were introduced under the name of Blacklock:

'Heavenly Blue' (*S. vulgaris*), single blue, 1943; of great merit and beauty
'St Joan' (*S. vulgaris*), double white, 1957; outstanding
'St Margaret' (*S. vulgaris*), double white, 1957; very fine; marketed in Germany as FRAU HOLLE

Three were introduced under the name of Castle:

'Blue Delight' (*S. vulgaris*), single bluish, 1968
'Violet Glory' (*S. vulgaris*), single deep violet, 1969; with large florets
'White Surprise' (*S. vulgaris*), single white, 1964

Walter Bosworth Clarke (1876–1953)

Walter Clarke founded and developed W. B. Clarke and Company of San Jose, California, as a specialty nursery for ornamental woody plants. He did extensive work in developing and introducing worthwhile lilacs for California, especially Early Hybrids. Many of these are choice garden shrubs to this day. Clarke received a number of horticultural awards for his nursery's introductions and hybridization programs. Among these awards are the Jackson Dawson Memorial Gold Medal from the Massachusetts Horticultural Society in 1945, twelve Awards of Merit conferred by the California Horticultural Society, and an award from the Royal Horticultural Society. Clarke's work with lilacs spanned 35 years.

Of the lilacs selected, named, and introduced by Clarke the following *Syringa ×hyacinthiflora* cultivars may be found in collections and nurseries:

'Alice Eastwood' (*S. ×hyacinthiflora*), double claret purple, 1942; long slim spikes

'Blue Hyacinth' (*S. ×hyacinthiflora*), single medium blue, 1942; large hyacinth-shaped florets

'Bountiful' (*S. ×hyacinthiflora*), single rosy orchid, 1949; bulky thyrses

'Clarke's Giant' (*S. ×hyacinthiflora*), single rosy mauve, 1948; enormous floret size; Royal Horticultural Society Award of Merit 1958

'Esther Staley' (*S. ×hyacinthiflora*), single lilac-pink, 1948; tall grower; Royal Horticultural Society Award of Merit 1961

'Fantasy' (*S. ×hyacinthiflora*), double medium to deep purple, 1960

'Kate Sessions' (*S. ×hyacinthiflora*), single medium purple-mauve to bluish, 1942

'Missimo' (*S. ×hyacinthiflora*), single rosy purple, 1944; large florets with recurved and curled petals

'Pink Cloud' (*S. ×hyacinthiflora*), single soft lavender-pink, 1947

'Pink Spray' (*S. ×hyacinthiflora*), single soft mauve-pink, 1948

'Purple Gem' (*S. ×hyacinthiflora*), single deep violet-purple, 1960

'Purple Glory' (*S. ×hyacinthiflora*), single purple, 1948

'Purple Heart' (*S. ×hyacinthiflora*), single deep violet-purple, 1948; very early, purplish black buds

Syringa vulgaris 'Pink Spray'. B. Peart and M. Walton

Syringa ×hyacinthiflora 'Summer Skies'. B. Peart and M. Walton

Syringa vulgaris 'Blue Hyacinth'. B. Peart and M. Walton

'Splendor' (*S. ×hyacinthiflora*) (synonym 'Purple Splendour'), double deep purplish blue, 1948
'Spring Dawn' (*S. ×hyacinthiflora*), single bluish, 1960
'Summer Skies' (*S. ×hyacinthiflora*), single bluish to soft sky-blue, 1948; orchid buds
'Sunset' (*S. ×hyacinthiflora*) (marketed in Germany as ELFENKÖNIG), double rosy purple, 1949
'Sweetheart' (*S. ×hyacinthiflora*), double soft to deep pink, 1953
'White Hyacinth' (*S. ×hyacinthiflora*), single white, 1948; counterpart of 'Blue Hyacinth'

Clarke also introduced the following *Syringa vulgaris* cultivars:

'Cora Brandt' (*S. vulgaris*), double white, 1947; showy compounded clusters in open panicles
'Early Double White' (*S. vulgaris*), double white, 1944

'May Day' (*S. vulgaris*), single pink, 1966
'Mood Indigo' (*S. vulgaris*), single dark ruddy purple, 1946
'Mountain Haze' (*S. vulgaris*), single purplish blue, 1946
'Peau de Chamois' (*S. vulgaris*), single magenta, 1936

Following Clarke's death in 1953, W. B. Clarke and Company became J. Clarke Nursery Company, operated by James F. Clarke (no dates available). It is clear from the dates of introduction in the preceding list that James introduced some of Walter's selections, such as 'Fantasy', 'May Day', 'Purple Gem', and 'Spring Dawn'. His own selections and introductions are as follows:

'Beth Turner' (*S. vulgaris*), single pink, 1968
'Clarke's Double White' (*S. vulgaris*), double white, 1968
'Old Fashioned' (*S. vulgaris*), single bluish lilac, 1967

Syringa vulgaris 'White Hyacinth'. B. Peart and M. Walton

Syringa vulgaris 'May Day'. B. Peart and M. Walton

Syringa vulgaris 'Cora Brandt'. B. Peart and M. Walton

Syringa vulgaris 'Beth Turner'. B. Peart and M. Walton

Edward James Gardner (1891–1952) and Robert Louis Gardner (1909–1972)

Ed Gardner was the founder and owner-operator of Edw. J. Gardner Nursery at West DePere, Wisconsin; in the late 1940s the nursery was moved to Horicon, Wisconsin, where it was operated until 1972. Ed was a nurseryman who was interested in improving methods of plant propagation. He wrote an article on mist propagation in the 1 May 1941 issue of *American Nurseryman*. He was a member of the American Peony Society and originated several new peony cultivars (Nehrling 1960, Wister 1962). Ed Gardner was also interested in lilacs; Walter Eickhorst reports that Gardner's 1950 price list contained more than 250 names of lilacs. He selected, named, and introduced seven to nine new lilac cultivars.

Robert Louis Gardner was the younger brother of Ed. After Ed's death he became owner-operator of Edw. J. Gardner Nursery. After Robert's death in 1972 the nursery was discontinued (Vrugtman 1998b).

Introduced by the Edw. J. Gardner Nursery and reportedly in cultivation are these *Syringa vulgaris* cultivars:

'Edward J. Gardner' (*S. vulgaris*), double pinkish, pre-1950; also seen listed as 'Edward Gardner', 'Edward J. Gardener', 'Edw. J. Gardner', 'Gardner #443', and marketed in Germany as FLAMINGO

'Jessie Gardner' (*S. vulgaris*), single violet, 1956; also seen listed as 'Gardner #472'

'Lawrence Wheeler' (*S. vulgaris*), single bluish, no date; also seen listed as 'Gardner #509', and 'S. L. Wheeler'

'Leone Gardner' (*S. vulgaris*), single purple, 1956; also seen listed as 'Gardner #451', and 'Leone Hanratty'

Syringa vulgaris 'Leone Gardner'. B. Peart and M. Walton

Syringa vulgaris 'Jessie Gardner'. B. Peart and M. Walton

'Mary Gardner' (*S. vulgaris*), single bluish, 1956; also seen listed as 'Gardner #444', and 'Mary Ann Gardner'

'Mrs R. L. Gardner' (*S. vulgaris*), single purple, 1956; also seen listed as 'Gardner #441', and 'Mrs Robert M. Gardner'

John Paul Rankin (1891–1976)

John Rankin was born in Johnstown, Pennsylvania. He graduated from Ohio Wesleyan College and completed his medical studies at Johns Hopkins Medical School. For several years he taught at Western Reserve Medical School in Cleveland, Ohio, and practiced medicine in Elyria, Ohio. Rankin's avocation was with flowering plants and shrubs. All his life he worked in his spare time in his several acres of gardens. He was a rose and lilac enthusiast.

Personal acquaintance with the Lemoine nursery, John Dunbar, Theodore Havemeyer, Alice Harding, and the lilac growers of his time enabled Rankin to assemble in his collection most of the latest introductions. At one time his lilac collection numbered over a thousand cultivars. He often obtained the original plant, the so-called ortet, of an introduction he deemed worthy. Several original Havemeyer plants were tagged with lead markers on the roots to identify them as ortet; among them were 'Carley', 'Mrs Flanders', 'Mrs John Davis', 'Mrs Watson Webb', and 'True Blue'. Rankin's collection contained lilacs from nearly every breeder of that era, concentrating on cultivars of *Syringa vulgaris*.

Rankin's love for lilacs led him to plant several hundred seedlings in seeking to improve certain color classes suggested to him by John Wister, namely, the violet and lilac colors. At bloom time his Elyria lilac gardens welcomed hundreds of visitors. Among the choicest lilacs were many splendid old cultivars of exceptional quality rarely seen even in collections at public gardens. He spent over forty years collecting, improving, and selecting lilacs with no financial or material recognition. Locally nicknamed the "Lilac Doctor," Rankin was a collector without commercial aspirations, so no dates of introduction exist for his cultivars. When he died, many, if not all, of his lilac selections went to Falconskeape, from where some became "commercial."

Perhaps his best known cultivars are 'Edith Braun', named for his bride-to-be who died shortly before they were to be married, and 'Lewis Maddock', an outstanding pink early hybrid, perhaps the earliest to bloom, named for a trusted garden-keeper. 'Pinkie' and 'White Lace' are also among Rankin's best lilacs. Of the 24 known Rankin lilacs, 10 can be found in collections and occasionally in nurseries:

'Betty Opper' (*S. vulgaris*), double pink

'Caroline Foley' (*S. vulgaris*), single magenta. Because of its extremely strong annual growth, this cultivar has been used by nurserymen as a standard for grafting other cultivars.

'Edith Braun' (*S. vulgaris*), single rich magenta-red-purple

'Edna Dunham' (*S. vulgaris*), single white

'Geraldine Smith' (*S. vulgaris*), single white

'Helen Pellage' (*S. vulgaris*) (often misspelled 'Helen Palagge'), single purple

'Lewis Maddock' (*S. ×hyacinthiflora* Early Hybrid), single light pink

'Pinkie' (*S. vulgaris*), single light pink

'White Lace' (*S. vulgaris*), single white, small florets, heavy blooming, heavy suckering

'White Long Fellow' (*S. vulgaris*), single white

John Rankin, M.D. Courtesy of Clare Short.

Syringa vulgaris 'Geraldine Smith'. B. Peart and M. Walton

J. Herbert Alexander Sr. John Fiala

Syringa vulgaris 'Pinkie'. B. Peart and M. Walton

J. Herbert Alexander Sr. (1893–1977)

John Herbert Alexander grew up in East Bridgewater, Massachusetts, where his father operated a nursery business. Sometime after the end of World War I, Alexander founded his own business, Dahliatown Nurseries, at Middleboro. Originally he specialized in dahlias, but discontinued them when the entire stock was destroyed by fire. He became well known among blueberry growers as a supplier of choice blueberry stock. He also propagated and sold hardy herbaceous perennials, including daylilies. Once he became interested in lilacs, a continuous stream of new or less-known lilac introductions was made available to the public, among them several new selections of his own. Introductions from other breeders included *Syringa vulgaris* 'Beth Turner' (Clarke 1968) and 'Cora Lyden' (Lyden 1963). Alexander had a shrewd eye for lilacs and their inherent qualities. He promoted lilacs wher-

ever and whenever possible. At Dahliatown Nurseries, one could always find something unique and different. Alexander's mind was an encyclopedia of plant knowledge, especially about lilacs.

Plants, shrubs, and trees need not only those who work to perfect them by diligent hybridization and careful selection but, especially and foremost, they need those whose skill and ingenuity can promote and bring them to the public and to the attention of nurserymen. Of the more than 2000 named lilac cultivars, no more than a handful can ever be marketed realistically. Lilacs, like other shrubs and plants, need astute nurserymen to ascertain those of merit, to recognize real quality, old and new, and to make them available to the public. This is an art and special gift that only a few have. Alexander was one of these few. In 1973 he received the International Lilac Society Award of Merit, "For a lifetime of dedication in hybridizing, growing and introducing newer and better forms of lilacs" (Vrugtman 2001).

Following is a listing of Alexander's cultivars, introduced in the 1960s and 1970s, that can be found in collections and in the nursery trade. The seven Villosae Group cultivars in circulation, all from the cross *Syringa* (Villosae Group) 'James Macfarlane' × *S.* (Villosae Group) 'Ethel M. Webster', are difficult to verify since all have been described only as "single pink."

'Alexander's Aristocrat' (*S.* Villosae Group), single pink, 1967
'Alexander's Perfection' (*S.* Villosae Group), single pink, 1969

Syringa (Villosae Group) 'Alexander's Aristocrat'. B. Peart and M. Walton

Syringa (Villosae Group) 'Alice Rose Foster'. B. Peart and M. Walton

Syringa (Villosae Group) 'Alexander's Pink'. B. Peart and M. Walton

Syringa (Villosae Group) 'Ferna Alexander'. B. Peart and M. Walton

under the same name. Plants growing at the Arnold Arboretum, lineages 784-85 and 745-80, are authenticated, and propagules documented to that lineage are true to name.

'Mrs J. Herbert Alexander' (*S.* Villosae Group), single pink, 1970

Cora Lyden (1892–1982)

A love of lilacs led Cora Lindsey Lyden to select and grow new cultivars from open-pollinated seed. Of the selections made in her Maine garden only two cultivars of *Syringa vulgaris* are reportedly in cultivation: 'John's Favorite' (1963), single purple, and 'Cora Lyden' (1963), a delightful double pink.

Fred Lape (1900–1985)

Fred Lape was a botanist, poet, professor of English, journalist, local historian, linguist, horticulturist, and lilac enthusiast. On his Oak Nose Farm in Esperance,

'Alexander's Pink' (*S.* Villosae Group), single pink, 1967

'Alice Rose Foster' (*S.* Villosae Group), single pink, 1968

'Dorothy Ramsden' (*S. vulgaris*), single purple, 1971

'Ferna Alexander' (*S.* Villosae Group), single pink, 1970

'Mary C. Bingham' (*S.* Villosae Group), single pink, 1976. Other selections may have been distributed

Fred Lape. John Fiala

Syringa ×*hyacinthiflora* 'Sweet Charity'. B. Peart and M. Walton

New York, he established the George Landis Arboretum. His book, *A Garden of Trees and Shrubs—Practical Hints for Planning and Planting an Arboretum* (Lape 1965), is a step-by-step guide for estate planters who are beginners. Lape's best lilac origination is *Syringa* (Villosae Group) 'Summer White' (*S.* ×*henryi*), introduced in 1978, a beautiful late-blooming single white lilac. For his translations of Russian lilac publications, Lape received an International Lilac Society Award of Merit in 1974.

Walter Edward Lammerts (1904–1996)
On 5 January 1954, the United States Patent Office issued Plant Patent 1238 to Walter Edward Lammerts, La Cañada, California, for a "lilac plant" released to the nursery trade under the name of 'Lavender Lady', a single pale-purple. With this selection Lammerts achieved a breakthrough that would expand the region in which lilacs could be grown successfully. During the preceding century nurserymen, florists, and horticulturists had learned from experience that cultivars of *Syringa vulgaris* and *S.* ×*hyacinthiflora* required winter chilling, a period of low temperature, to produce a good show of bloom the following spring. Gardeners in mild-winter climates discovered that, although the flower buds for next year's bloom are formed long before winter, their lilacs just would not produce a good show. 'Lavender Lady', however, seemed to ignore this rule. The species affiliation of 'Lavender Lady' remained obscure until it was cleared up in a study by James S. Pringle (1995) at Royal Botanical Gardens, Hamilton, Ontario, who determined it to be a *S.* ×*hyacinthiflora* cultivar. Lammerts used

'Lavender Lady' in his subsequent crosses, successfully producing additional mild-winter lilac cultivars, all of which appear to be still in cultivation:

'Angel White' (*S.* ×*hyacinthiflora*), single white, 1971

'Big Blue' (*S.* ×*hyacinthiflora*), single bluish, 1953. Note that plate 77 in the original edition of this book (Fiala 1988) does not show 'Big Blue' but an unidentified lilac; 'Big Blue' is single and bluish, not single and violet (Vrugtman 1999d).

'Heather Haze' (*S.* ×*hyacinthiflora*), single pink, 1953

'Lavender Lady' (*S.* ×*hyacinthiflora*), single purple, 1954

'Old Lace' (*S.* ×*hyacinthiflora*), single pink, 1953

'Sierra Snow' (*S.* ×*hyacinthiflora*), single white, 1963

'Sweet Charity' (*S.* ×*hyacinthiflora*), single purple, 1953

In 1977 Lammerts received an International Lilac Society Award of Merit, "For his pioneering work in the development of warm-winter-tolerant Lilacs and the introduction of new cultivars for southern areas."

Lammerts developed *Syringa* ×*hyacinthiflora* 'Lavender Lady' while employed at the Descanso estate at La Cañada. He departed from Descanso in 1953, the year prior to the issue of Plant Patent 1238, taking with him some of the unnamed seedlings, and leaving some behind. The Descanso estate was sold and became a public garden, part of the Los Angeles State and County Arboretum (LASCA) system. In the mid-1950s Descanso Gardens employed a horticulturist, John Sobeck (1894–1965). In 1966, the year following Sobeck's death, the superintendent of Descanso Gardens registered 18 new cultivar names for "crosses made by John Sobeck 1955." No records have survived, either at the Los Angeles State and County Arboretum or Descanso Gardens; there is no documentation to indicate whether these cultivars resulted from crosses made by Sobeck, or whether they are selections made from the seedlings left behind by Lammerts in 1953. Nevertheless, they have enriched the garden flora of mild winter regions. Of these 18 *Syringa* ×*hyacinthiflora* cultivars, 11 appear to be in cultivation:

'Blue Boy' (*S.* ×*hyacinthiflora*), single bluish, 1966; not the single bluish *S. vulgaris* 'Blue Boy' introduced by Max Peterson in 2004
'California Rose' (*S.* ×*hyacinthiflora*), single pink, 1966

Syringa ×*hyacinthiflora* 'California Rose'. B. Peart and M. Walton

Syringa ×*hyacinthiflora* 'Sylvan Beauty'. B. Peart and M. Walton

'Chiffon' (*S.* ×*hyacinthiflora*), single lilac, 1966
'Dark Night' (*S.* ×*hyacinthiflora*), single purple, 1966
'Descanso Giant' (*S.* ×*hyacinthiflora*), single lilac, 1966
'Descanso King' (*S.* ×*hyacinthiflora*), single bluish, 1966
'Descanso Princess' (*S.* ×*hyacinthiflora*), single lilac, 1966
'Forrest Kresser Smith' (*S.* ×*hyacinthiflora*), single lilac, 1966
'Guild's Pride' (*S.* ×*hyacinthiflora*), single lilac, 1966
'Sylvan Beauty' (*S.* ×*hyacinthiflora*), single pink, 1966
'White Spring' (*S.* ×*hyacinthiflora*), single white, 1966

Kenneth Warren Berdeen (1907–1987)

Born of Scottish ancestry in Stonington, Maine, Ken Berdeen was a steam and diesel engineer. His interest in lilacs began in 1953 when he purchased five lilacs from Sears and Roebuck. For thirty years he spent all his spare time, and in retirement full time, developing new cultivars of *Syringa vulgaris*. At one time there were more than 2300 lilacs, many his seedlings, on his 60 acre (24 ha) farm at Alewive Road outside Kennebunk. At the time of his death he had pre-selected about 75 seedlings; some of which he had named for his relatives, neighbors, and friends. In 1973 Berdeen received the Award of Merit from the International Lilac Society, "For a lifetime of dedication in hybridizing, growing and introducing newer and better forms of lilacs." (Willard 1981).

Ken Berdeen. John Fiala

Fulfilling an old promise, Ken's granddaughter, Lynette Mascioli, took on the management of the Berdeen lilacs in 1991. A few years later she opened Gramp's Gardens at Alewive Road to the public (McLaughlin 1998). Berdeen had recognized his responsibilities as a plant breeder, albeit an amateur one; in a letter dated 3 December 1976 (pers. comm. to F. V.), he wrote, "I am very reluctant to registering lilacs until they have bloomed several times, and there are so many mediocre plants already registered that I do not want to add more . . . I don't think any plant should be registered until they have bloomed at least five times."

The primary goal is to restore and maintain the lilac collection. In cooperation with Evie King and Roger Coggeshall of Syringa Plus Nurseries at West Boxford, Maine, Berdeen's lilac originations have been evaluated for their garden merit; only the best of his selections are being propagated and offered for sale (Mascioli 1998, pers. comm. to F.V.; Mascioli 2003; King 1998). The best of Berdeen's cultivars are listed here:

'Betsy Bowman' (*S. vulgaris*), single dark purple, 2005
'Brent Sirois' (*S. vulgaris*), double magenta, 2005
'Carolyn Bergen' (*S. vulgaris*), double pink, 2005
'Carolyn Howland' (*S. vulgaris*), single bluish and magenta, 1976
'Chris' (*S. vulgaris*), single purple, 1969
'Cynthia' (*S. vulgaris*), single pinkish, 1971
'Dianah Abbott' (*S. vulgaris*), single light purple, 1976
'Eleanor Berdeen' (*S. vulgaris*), single bluish and pinkish, 1979
'James Berdeen' (*S. vulgaris*), single lilac, 2005
'Jefferson Berdeen' (*S. vulgaris*), double magenta, 2005
'John Kennedy' (*S. vulgaris*), double white, 1982
'Lee Jewett Walker' (*S. vulgaris*), single pinkish, 1981
'Little Bit' (*S. vulgaris*), single pinkish, 1985
'Lucy Bergen' (*S. vulgaris*), single blue, 2005
'Lynette Sirois' (*S. vulgaris*), double bluish, 1968
'Max Peterson' (*S. vulgaris*), double magenta to lilac, 1983
'Olive May Cummings' (*S. vulgaris*), double pinkish to violet, 1979
'Walter's Pink' (*S. vulgaris*), single pinkish, 1987

Syringa vulgaris 'Chris'. B. Peart and M. Walton

Syringa vulgaris 'Dianah Abbott'. John Fiala

Syringa vulgaris 'Eleanor Berdeen'. John Fiala

Syringa vulgaris 'James Berdeen'. B. Peart and M. Walton

Syringa vulgaris 'John Kennedy'. B. Peart and M. Walton

Alvan Roger Grant (1916–2007)

As director of parks at Rochester, New York, Alvan Grant gathered seed of *Syringa vulgaris* 'Edith Cavell', Émile Lemoine's huge double white, then planted in the Highland Botanical Park nursery. In time several seedlings grew, but it was one—small, slow growing, with a heavily textured leaf—that caught the attention of Grant and Bernard Harkness, the park superintendent. It turned out to be an amazing plant indeed! The florets were single yet multipetaled, waxlike and magnificent in bloom with long, well-filled thyrses. In 1971 it was named 'Rochester' to honor the city. As Grant's single contribution to lilacdom it established a new plateau from which a whole new strain of lilacs has emerged.

Grant received the International Lilac Society Award of Merit in 1978 "[f]or a career of service in the Monroe County Parks and the emphasis given to

lilac therein." 'Rochester' has been introduced into the trade on a very limited scale because it is difficult to propagate and grows too slowly to suit most gardeners—it remains a small plant after several years. However, once established on its own roots it is an outstanding lilac. It may be one of the best lilacs ever produced, for its intrinsic beauty and for its extraordinary genetic characters for hybridizing. It is the foundation of the Rochester strain of cultivars developed by Richard A. Fenicchia.

Richard Americo Fenicchia (1908–1997)

Dick Fenicchia was employed by the County of Monroe Department of Parks, Rochester, New York, from 1925 to 1934, when he lost his job because he was not going to change his political affiliation; rehired in 1950 he remained with the Parks until his retirement in 1978; he participated in plant selection and introduction. Lilacs were a new venture in his hybridizing career. The outstanding white, single *Syringa vulgaris* 'Rochester', originated by Alvan R. Grant, is a truly magnificent multipetaled lilac, unique in its heavy, waxlike, textured florets, and enormous straight panicles of white standing like upright candles. A seedling of 'Edith Cavell', it was brought to recognition by Fenicchia, who first saw its possibilities and began to hybridize with it while park superintendent at Highland Botanical Park (Millham 2004).

Richard Fenicchia. John Fiala

Fenicchia successfully pollinated 'Rochester' with select cultivars including 'Mme Charles Souchet', 'Edward J. Gardner' and 'Glory'. From the resulting seeds came a first generation of new lilacs. They were recognized as a whole new strain of multipetaled (primrose form) new hued lilacs. Fenicchia was urged to select the best for exhibit at the International Lilac Society convention in Rochester in 1972. Their merit, and the work of Fenicchia, were recognized. Six of the first-generation seedlings were named: 'Bernard Slavin', 'Bishop McQuaid', 'Dr Edward Mott Moore', 'Dwight D. Eisenhower', 'Frederick Douglass' and 'George Ellwanger'. The seedling rows of first and second generation, also referred to as F_1 and F_2 generation (F standing for *filia* or daughter) of 'Rochester' crosses have produced additional outstanding and diverse progeny. These selections show amazing color variations, ranging from pale pastels to pearled colors not seen before in lilacs. This mother-of-pearl effect is seen on the pale pastel shades of blues and lavenders. Among 'Rochester' seedlings are a number of dwarf and very low growing forms excellent for rock gardens and Japanese gardens.

Hybridization of lilacs at Highland Botanical Park was terminated upon Fenicchia's retirement in 1978, although Dick would continue to keep a keen eye on his seedlings and cuttings in the propagating house. Other hybridizers, taking their cue from his success, have used 'Rochester' in other crosses with similar success. For his work Fenicchia received the International Lilac Society's Director's Award (1972) and two Awards of Merit (1976 and 1988). All who love lilacs will ever be grateful for the hours of work that have given us the Rochester strain of lilacs. Fenicchia's cultivars that can be found in commerce or collections are as follows:

Syringa vulgaris 'Frederick Law Olmsted'. B. Peart and M. Walton

Syringa vulgaris 'Martha Stewart'. B. Peart and M. Walton

'Alvan R. Grant' (*S. vulgaris*), single purple
'Bernard Slavin' (*S. vulgaris*), single white
'Bicentennial' (*S. vulgaris*), single bluish
'Bishop McQuaid' (*S. vulgaris*), single purple
'Blue Diamond' (*S. vulgaris*), single bluish
'Charles Lindbergh' (*S. vulgaris*), single violet to bluish
'Dwight D. Eisenhower' (*S. vulgaris*), single bluish
'Flower City' (*S. vulgaris*), single violet to purple
'Frederick Douglass' (*S. vulgaris*), single magenta

'Frederick Law Olmsted' (*S. vulgaris*), single white
'George Eastman' (*S. pubescens* subsp. *julianae*), single magenta
'Independence' (*S. vulgaris*), single white
'John Dunbar' (*S. vulgaris*), single violet
'Margaret Fenicchia' (*S. vulgaris*), single purple to violet
'Martha Stewart' (*S. vulgaris*), single violet-bluish
'Richard A. Fenicchia' (*S. vulgaris*), double purple to violet
'Sesquicentennial' (*S. vulgaris*), single violet

Betty Stone. John Fiala

Elizabeth (Betty) Stone (no dates)

The late Betty (Mrs. Ralph W.) Stone became interested in lilacs about 1945 and was one of the collaborators in the 1953 Lilac Survey conducted by the Lilac Survey Committee, American Association of Botanical Gardens and Arboretums, under the chairmanship of John C. Wister. By 1970 she had developed a lilac collection at Ashland, Ohio, featuring more than 350 cultivars. Though Stone originated, selected, and named seven *Syringa vulgaris* cultivars, only three appear in cultivation today, namely, 'Anna Nickles', 'Betty Stone', and 'Florence Christine', all described as single and lilac. For her dedicated lilac work Betty Stone received the International Lilac Society Award of Merit in 1980.

Joel Margaretten (1910–1988)

Joel Margaretten, a dentist in Leona Valley, California, was also known for his cattle, his peonies, and especially his thousands of lilacs. In a seemingly impossible area he produced lilacs for the cut-flower market, hybridized lilacs, and developed Margaretten Park, the largest lilac collection in California at the time. His unusual climatic and soil conditions were a challenge and required a very special way of growing lilacs. He wrote (Fiala 1988):

Because of the unusual climate lilacs blossom early, usually before Easter. They last for a week or two, fade and go to seed. The soil is adobe, muddy in the winter and hard as rock in the summer. Except when the ground is frozen, it is almost impossible to cultivate. If there is no rain a power drill is used to get holes dug for planting the lilacs. Normal rainfall, except for 1969–70 is about 2 inches so there is a continual problem with water. Irrigation is a necessity all summer until August, then it is stopped to let the lilacs go dormant. Continued irrigation after that would bring on a new crop of flowers that would abort after a week. Temperatures, even in the winter, can go from 0° F [-18° C] in the morning to 75° F [24° C] by noon. Snow lasts for a day or two, doing more havoc than good. It bends branches down to the ground, freezes the young shoots necessitating more pruning.

Pruning is usually done in the winter when it is easier and more time is available. Pruning is severe to get rid of all dead and crossed branches. The lilacs are kept at 5–6 ft. in height, partly from cutting long stems for the market and to keep them easier to work with. Fertilizer is side dressed. Diesel oil is used for weed control and also cuts down on scale. It also kills any young suckers coming from the ground (You can't have everything!)

Most of the hybrids are grown on terraces. The *Syringa vulgaris* are in fields for tractor work and irrigation. The lilacs bloom fabulously!

Indeed his lilacs were fabulous and we have chosen to repeat his account of his system of growing lilacs for those who feel it is not possible under such circumstances to grow lilacs. Margaretten's system of withholding water during the late summer to induce dormancy may be the answer for many mild-winter-latitude lilac lovers who claim lilacs will not bloom for them for want of cold weather.

Not only was Margaretten an outstanding grower with an excellent collection, but he selected lilacs as well. His first introduction, a double lavender-violet, was named for his wife 'Tita'. For his work with lilacs Margaretten was presented with the International Lilac Society Award of Merit (1975), Honor and Achievement Award (1983), and Director's Award (1987). Margaretten selected and named about 40 new *Syringa vulgaris* cultivars; no evaluations are available. Only two of these cultivars appear to have reached the market; another 16 cultivars are reportedly grown in collections:

Syringa vulgaris 'Leila Romer'. B. Peart and M. Walton

Syringa vulgaris 'Mrs Nancy Reagan'. B. Peart and M. Walton

'Charles Holetich' (*S. vulgaris*), single lilac (collections)

'Don Wedge' (*S. vulgaris*), double lilac (collections)

'Ed Frolich' (*S. vulgaris*), single bluish (collections)

'Fiala Remembrance' (*S. vulgaris*), double white (commerce)

'George Emanuel' (*S. vulgaris*), single violet (collections)

'Leila Romer' (*S. vulgaris*), single bluish (collections)

'Lourene Wishart' (*S. vulgaris*), single bluish and white (commerce)

'Mrs Eleanor Roosevelt' (*S. vulgaris*), single magenta (collections)

'Mrs Katherine Margaretten' (*S. vulgaris*), double bluish (collections)

'Mrs Nancy Reagan' (*S. vulgaris*), double violet (collections)

'Polly Hagaman' (*S. vulgaris*), single bluish and white to bluish (collections)

'President Ronald Reagan' (*S. vulgaris*), double bluish (collections)

'Ray Halward' (*S. vulgaris*), single lilac (collections)

'Reva Ballreich' (*S. vulgaris*), double white (collections); not to be confused with the double pinkish 'Reva Ballreich' by Max Peterson

'Selma Margaretten' (*S. vulgaris*), single bluish (collections)

'Solomon Margaretten' (*S. vulgaris*), double lilac and white (collections)

'Theo Holetich' (*S. vulgaris*), single magenta (collections)

'Tita' (*S. vulgaris*), double pink (collections)

Syringa vulgaris 'President Ronald Reagan'. B. Peart and M. Walton

Syringa vulgaris 'Selma Margaretten'. B. Peart and M. Walton

William Archibald Cumming (1911–1999)

For more than two decades, Bill Cumming was active with new ornamental plants, including lilac cultivars, at the Morden Research Station, Agriculture Canada, in Manitoba. While working with a number of woody plant genera he introduced two excellent *Syringa* Villosae Group lilacs:

William Cumming. Photographer unknown.

Syringa (Villosae Group) 'Minuet'. B. Peart and M. Walton

'Minuet' (*S.* Villosae Group), single purple, a fine low grower (*S.* ×*josiflexa* 'Redwine' × *S.* ×*prestoniae* 'Donald Wyman').

'Miss Canada' (*S.* Villosae Group), single china-rose (*S.* ×*josiflexa* 'Redwine' × *S.* ×*prestoniae* 'Hiawatha')

'Minuet' has three species in its genetic makeup (*S. josikaea*, *S. komarowii*, and *S. villosa*).

Cumming was an authority on lilac hybridization and on the suitability of various cultivars for the different regions of Canada. He received an honorary doctor of science degree from the University of Manitoba in 1972 and was recipient of the International Lilac Society Award of Merit (1972) for his lilac hybrids. He was a brother-in-law to Frank Skinner, the great Canadian lilac hybridizer.

John Fiala (1924–1990)

Reared on an Ohio farm John Leopold Fiala early developed a fondness for plants and horticulture. Before he was 16 he had already planted his own orchard and had an experimental vegetable and flower garden. At 12 he wrote to Arie den Boer asking him all about flowering crabapples, beginning a friendship that lasted until den Boer's death. Fiala's professional career was that of a parish priest in the Cleveland diocese, and a professor of clinical psychology and education at John Carroll University, a Jesuit University in Cleveland. In teaching psychology he needed illustrative materials in genetics, which brought about the continuation of his early work with plants—especially growing seedlings of controlled pollination, and experimenting with colchicine to produce polyploid cultivars—with its attendant observation of inheritances.

From college days Fiala worked with plants on the "little farm plot" allotted to him from the family acres. Here, over a span of 45 years, plant work continued on lilacs, flowering crabapples, peonies, daylilies, buckeyes (*Aesculus*), various nut trees, oaks, and numerous other plants—with the lilacs and crabapples receiving the greatest attention. Though his principal duties in education, church administration, and as his bishop's secretary for parishes demanded most of his time, Fiala continued his work with plants. After his early retirement in 1982 because of serious illness, he continued working with daylilies, crape-myrtles, lilacs, and crabapples in the warmer winters of Florida, bringing plants north each April for the spring and summer work on his "farm acres" known as Falconskeape, at Medina, Ohio.

Lilacs had fascinated Fiala since he was about 25. His lilac work at Falconskeape covered programs such as breeding and selecting for new and better cultivars of *Syringa vulgaris*, especially for a wider range of colors and forms; breeding and selecting new cultivars of *S. ×hyacinthiflora*; working with the lesser-known species and subspecies, particularly *S. pubescens* subsp. *julianae*, *S. komarowii*, *S. wolfii*, and their hybrids with other species.

One cannot hybridize any plant without being indebted to an endless number of horticultural and gardening friends who grow and introduce rare plants and give encouragement and direction. Sometime in the 1950s Fiala read an article on the use of colchicine on plants, producing polyploid plants with larger blooms, and the work done by a Swedish research team using this drug to increase the fruit size of apples. Colchicine ($C_{22}H_{25}O_6N$), an alkaloid, is obtained from naked ladies, *Colchicum autumnale* L. (not to be confused with autumn crocus, *Crocus sativus* L., the commercial source of saffron); it influences mitosis and tissue metabolism. Colchicine was most difficult to obtain. (See chapter nine for information on the use of colchicine.) Fiala's results were meager. Although several new cultivars he introduced are listed as being colchicine-induced polyploid, the chromosome numbers of these cultivars have not yet been independently confirmed ('Aloise', 'Elsie Lenore', 'Eventide', 'Hosanna', 'Kum-Bum', 'Lark Song', 'Little Miss Muffet' and 'Prophecy'). Most rewarding and productive was Fiala's breeding work with newer cultivars of *Syringa vulgaris* such as 'Agincourt Beauty', 'Flora 1953', 'Rochester', 'St Joan', and several others including his own introductions 'Pat Pesata' and 'Professor Robert B. Clark'. Following his own recommendation (Fiala 1988: 163–164), Fiala recorded the parentage of his crosses, making the information available to future lilac hybridizers.

Fiala was a founding member of the International Lilac Society (ILS), which has recognized his work in lilacs with four of its awards, namely Honor and Achievement (1976), President's (1980), Director's (1985), and Arch McKean (1989). He also received the Massachusetts Horticultural Society's Thomas Roland Medal for hybridizing achievements. Many of his introductions are not yet well known. More than 50 named cultivars of lilacs and 42 named flowering crabapples have come from this garden. Some of his early introductions were marketed through Ameri-Hort Research of Medina, Ohio, Karen Tarpey Murray, vice president of marketing and sales, and her husband, Peter Murray.

A number of cultivars of *Syringa vulgaris*, *S. ×hyacinthiflora*, and interspecific hybrids have been named and introduced at Falconskeape Gardens. Only those cultivars that are reportedly being grown in collections and nurseries are listed here. Although Charles Holetich and Bruce Peart recorded performance data on 21 of the 25 Fiala cultivars growing in the Katie Osborne Lilac Garden of Royal Botanical Gardens, Hamilton, Ontario, during the summer of 2003, no summary of results has been published yet (Peart 2004).

The following are cultivars of *Syringa vulgaris* selected by Fiala:

'Albert F. Holden' (*S. vulgaris*), single violet to purple, 1980 ('Sarah Sands' × 'Réaumur')
'Aloise' (*S. vulgaris*), single white, 1986 ('Flora 1953' × 'Flora 1953')
'Arch McKean' (*S. vulgaris*), single magenta, 1984 ('Agincourt Beauty' × 'Rochester')
'Atheline Wilbur' (*S. vulgaris*), double magenta, 1980 (('Rochester' × 'Edward J. Gardner') × 'Rochester')
'Avalanche' (*S. vulgaris*), single white, 1983 ('Flora 1953' × 'Carley')
'Blue Danube' (*S. vulgaris*), single bluish, 1986 ('Rochester' × 'True Blue')

Syringa vulgaris 'Albert F. Holden'. B. Peart and M. Walton

'Blue Delft' (*S. vulgaris*), single bluish, 1982 ('Mrs A. Belmont' × 'Rochester')

'Blue Giant' (*S. vulgaris*), single bluish, 1977 ('Flora 1953' × 'True Blue')

'Bluebird' (*S. vulgaris*), single bluish, 1969 ('Gismonda' × 'Rustica')

'Dr John Rankin' (*S. vulgaris*), single violet, 1979 ('Glory' × 'Flora 1953')

'Drifting Dream' (*S. vulgaris*), double violet, 1985 ('Rochester' × 'Rochester' seedling)

Syringa vulgaris 'Atheline Wilbur'. B. Peart and M. Walton

Syringa vulgaris 'Aloise'. B. Peart and M. Walton

Syringa vulgaris 'Avalanche'. B. Peart and M. Walton

Syringa vulgaris 'Arch McKean'. B. Peart and M. Walton

'Elsie Lenore' (*S. vulgaris*), single pinkish to magenta, 1982 ('Sensation' × 'Sensation')

'Emery Mae Norweb' (*S. vulgaris*), double white, 1980 ('Gismonda' × 'Flora 1953')

'Flow Blue' (*S. vulgaris*), single bluish, 1980 ('True Blue' × 'Mrs A. Belmont')

'Gertrude Clark' (*S. vulgaris*), single white, 1984, ('Rochester' × 'Rochester' seedling)

'Glacier' (*S. vulgaris*), double white, 1981 (('Gismonda' × 'Flora 1953') × 'Rochester')

'Hosanna' (*S. vulgaris*), double violet, 1969 ('Gismonda' × 'Rustica')

'Joel' (*S. vulgaris*), single pinkish, 1981 ('General Sherman' × 'Flora 1953')

'Little Miss Muffet' (*S. vulgaris*), single magenta, 1965 ('Mrs Edward Harding' × 'Macrostachya'); slow growing

'Lois Amee Utley' (*S. vulgaris*), double pinkish, 1986 ('Rochester' × 'Mme Antoine Buchner')

'Lourene Wishart' (*S. vulgaris*), double pinkish, 1980 ('Rochester' × 'Edward J. Gardner')

'Marie Frances' (*S. vulgaris*), single pinkish, 1983 ('Edward J. Gardner' × 'Rochester')

'Midnight' (*S. vulgaris*), single purple, 1984 ('Agincourt Beauty' × 'Violet Glory')

Syringa vulgaris 'Elsie Lenore'. John Fiala

Syringa vulgaris 'Hosanna'. B. Peart and M. Walton

Syringa vulgaris 'Gertrude Clark'. John Fiala

Syringa vulgaris 'Joel'. B. Peart and M. Walton

Syringa vulgaris 'Lois Amee Utley'. B. Peart and M. Walton

'Mollie Ann' (*S. vulgaris*), single magenta, 1981 ('Rochester' × 'Violet Glory')

'Pat Pesata' (*S. vulgaris*), single bluish, 1981 ('Rochester' × 'True Blue')

'Pauline Fiala' (*S. vulgaris*), single violet and white, 1983 ('Sensation' × 'Flora 1953')

'Pixie' (*S. vulgaris*), single white, 1981 ('Rochester' × 'Rochester'); slow growing

'Porcelain Blue' (*S. vulgaris*), single bluish, 1981 ('Rochester' × 'Mrs A. Belmont')

'Professor Robert B. Clark' (*S. vulgaris*), single white to pinkish, 1983 (('Rochester' × 'Edward J. Gardner') × 'Rochester')

'Rhapsody' (*S. vulgaris*), single bluish, 1983 ('Rochester' × 'Mrs A. Belmont')

'Sacrament' (*S. vulgaris*), single white, 1985 ('Rochester' × 'Primrose')

'Sculptured Ivory', single white, 1985 ('Rochester' × 'Primrose')

'Snow Cap', single white, 1985 ('Rochester' × 'Professor Robert B. Clark'); not to be confused with *S. reticulata* 'Elliot' which is trademarked SNOWCAP

'Sonnet' (*S. vulgaris*), single magenta, 1982 ('Mrs A. Belmont' × 'Flora 1953')

Syringa vulgaris 'Marie Frances'. B. Peart and M. Walton

Syringa vulgaris 'Mollie Ann'. B. Peart and M. Walton

Syringa vulgaris 'Sacrament'. B. Peart and M. Walton

Syringa vulgaris 'Pat Pesata'. B. Peart and M. Walton

'Spring Parade' (*S. vulgaris*), single lilac, 1984
  ('Rochester' × unnamed seedling)

'Swansdown' (*S. vulgaris*), single white, 1983 ('Rochester' × 'Atheline Wilbur')

'Tiffany Blue' (*S. vulgaris*), single bluish, 1984 ('True Blue' × 'Mrs A. Belmont')

'Wedgwood Blue' (*S. vulgaris*), single bluish, 1981
  ('Rochester' × 'Mrs A. Belmont')

Syringa vulgaris 'Sonnet'. John Fiala

'Winner's Circle' (*S. vulgaris*), double magenta, 1985
  ('Rochester' × 'Mrs W. E. Marshall')

'Yankee Doodle' (*S. vulgaris*), single purple, 1985
  ('Prodige' × 'Rochester')

Syringa vulgaris 'Wedgwood Blue'. B. Peart and M. Walton

Fiala also selected cultivars of *Syringa* ×*hyacinthiflora*, referred to as Early Hybrids:

'Alice Chieppo' (*S.* ×*hyacinthiflora*), double lilac, 1984 (*S. oblata* subsp. *dilatata* × *S. vulgaris* 'Rochester')
'Mary Short' (*S.* ×*hyacinthiflora*), double pinkish, 1979 ('Pocahontas' × 'Esther Staley')

One selection was made from *Syringa pubescens* subsp. *julianae* and one from *S. oblata*:

'Pink Parasol' (*S. pubescens* subsp. *julianae*), single pinkish, 1983 ('Hers' × 'George Eastman')
'Wild Fire' (*S. oblata*), single lilac, 1984

Fiala also selected several *Syringa* (Villosae Group) cultivars, also referred to as Late Lilacs. Frequently the parentage of these included two or more different species:

'Dancing Druid' (*S.* Villosae Group), single magenta, 1968; presumably ((*S. yunnanensis* × *S. tomentella*) × (*S. komarowii* × (*S. sweginzowii* × *S. tomentella*))) (Vrugtman 1998a; Pringle 2000)
'Eventide' (*S.* Villosae Group), single violet, 1980 ('Garden Peace' × 'Lark Song'); or ((*S. komarowii* × *S. wolfii*) × ((*S. sweginzowii* × *S. tomentella*) × *S. komarowii*)) (Vrugtman 2001)
'Kum-Bum' (*S.* Villosae Group), single violet with golden foliage, 1969 (*S. tomentella* seedling)
'Lark Song' (*S.* Villosae Group), single pinkish, 1968 ((*S. sweginzowii* × *S. tomentella*) × *S. komarowii*)

Syringa (Villosae Group) 'Dancing Druid'. B. Peart and M. Walton

Syringa (Villosae Group) 'Eventide'. John Fiala

'Prophecy' (*S.* Villosae Group), single violet, 1969 (*S. yunnanensis* × *S. yunnanensis*)

'Royal Crown' (*S.* Villosae Group), single lilac, 1958 (*S. sweginzowii* × (*S. sweginzowii* × *S. tomentella*))

The reader may wonder what happened to Fiala's gardens. Falconskeape, the "farm acres," had its beginning in 1969, the year Fiala moved his plants, including the lilacs, to the 56-acre (23-ha) property at 7359 Branch Road, Medina, Ohio. Here he developed his garden and concentrated on breeding and selecting flowering crabapples, lilacs and herbaceous perennials. Aware of his failing health, and concerned about the continuity of Falconskeape Gardens, Fiala registered it as a not-for-profit organization. The gardens were opened for the public in 1988. A members organization, Friends of Falconskeape, was founded. About the same time Ameri-Hort Research was incorporated as the commercial venture to continue breeding, selecting, and marketing Falconskeape ornamental plants. Fiala installed a board of trustees, and turned the day-to-day management of Falconskeape over to Karen Tarpey Murray and Peter Murray.

When Fiala died in December 1990, Falconskeape Gardens and Ameri-Hort Research continued operating under the direction of the board of trustees. Donations, membership, and registration fees for public and private events were to cover operating expenses. However, municipal zoning regulations prohibited the programs and activities that were to sustain Falconskeape Gardens. In December 1993 the Friends of Falconskeape organization was dissolved and the board of trustees disbanded. In May 1994 a 6-acre (2.4-ha) parcel of land was separated and sold to Marc and Julie Dehrmann. This parcel, which had sustained most of the lilacs, still bears the name Falconskeape. Through the cooperation and generosity of the new owners it was possible to collect propagating material and perpetuate some of the Fiala originations.

George Daniels (d. 1995)

George Daniels, a nurseryman with the L. E. Cook Company of Visalia, California, selected and named *Syringa vulgaris* 'Lecburg' in 1993. This single purple sport of 'Monge' has been marketed in the United States by Cook Company under their registered trademark BURGUNDY QUEEN.

Ralph Moore (b. 1907)

Ralph Moore, nurseryman and plant breeder, still actively involved at the age of 100 at Sequoia Nursery in Visalia, California, selected *Syringa vulgaris* 'Monore' in 1987. This single bluish-purple cultivar is marketed in the United States by Monrovia Nursery under their registered trademark BLUE SKIES (Vrugtman 1989).

Donald Egolf (1928–1990)

Don Egolf was one of America's leading hybridizers of woody plants. His work with *Hibiscus, Lagerstroemia, Magnolia, Prunus, Pyracantha,* and *Viburnum* resulted in a number of excellent cultivars, some of which have won awards. He was an extraordinary person gifted with rare insights and talents in both plant research and hybridizing.

In contrast to Egolf's hybridization work on *Viburnum*, which he had started as a graduate student at Cornell University in the 1950s, his interest in *Syringa* was aroused much later at the United States National Arboretum in Washington, District of Columbia. He made an extensive survey of the available cultivars of *S. vulgaris* and *S.* ×*hyacinthiflora*, determining their susceptibility to mildew, a disfiguring, although not fatal, fungus disease of lilacs, which particularly discourages growing them in the warmer middle belt of their range. The objective was to extend the limits of growing good lilacs farther south by selective hybridization, especially in *S.* ×*hyacinthiflora* (*S. vulgaris* × *S. oblata*). In 1980 Egolf received the International Lilac Society's Directors' Award in recognition of his lilac hybridization work at the National Arboretum.

Egolf's tragic death in an automobile accident terminated the *Syringa* breeding program. Three lilac

Donald Egolf. John Fiala

cultivars resulting from his breeding work have been selected and named by Margaret Pooler, who is reviving the lilac hybridization work at the National Arboretum (Pooler, in press). *Syringa* 'Betsy Ross', a single white, was released in 2000. It resulted from a cross using *S. oblata*, collected in 1974 in China, as the male parent, and an unidentified *Syringa* specimen from Highland Botanical Park, Rochester, New York, as the female parent. *Syringa* ×*hyacinthiflora* 'Declaration', a single reddish purple, and *S.* ×*hyacinthiflora* 'Old Glory', a single bluish purple, were both released in 2006. They resulted from the cross *S.* ×*hyacinthiflora* 'Sweet Charity' × *S.* ×*hyacinthiflora* 'Pocahontas' made in 1978.

Syringa ×*hyacinthiflora* 'Betsy Ross'. M. Pooler

Syringa ×*hyacinthiflora* 'Declaration'. M. Peterson

Syringa ×*hyacinthiflora* 'Old Glory'. M. Pooler

University of New Hampshire, Durham

Albert Franklin Yeager (1892–1961) and Elwyn Marshall Meader (1910–1996) introduced *Syringa pubescens* subsp. *patula* 'Miss Kim', a single violet lilac, in 1954. This cultivar, which had been selected from seedlings grown from seed collected by Meader in the Pouk Han Mountains of Korea in 1974, received a Royal Horticultural Society Award of Garden Merit. In 1959 Yeager announced the selection and naming of *Syringa* (Villosae Group) 'Anna Amhoff'. This cultivar of *S.* ×*josiflexa* has pink buds and, in full bloom, white flowers.

Lilac work continued under the direction of Owen Maurice Rogers, who originated *Syringa* (Villosae Group) 'Agnes Smith' (1970) and 'Jesse Hepler' (1981) (*S.* ×*josiflexa*). Rogers directed the development of the research garden. The nursery rows contain promising new breakthroughs, including multipetaled, double, late-blooming lilacs of exceptional quality, vigor and unique floret substance; hybrids of outstanding beauty, miniature plants, unique forms and sizes, colors and beauty; plants to be observed and evaluated for future selection or future breeding programs; only the cream-of-the-crop deserves introduction. *Syringa* (Villosae Group) 86-1 is an unnamed *S.* ×*josiflexa*

selection with double florets that holds promise for future use in hybridizing (Rogers 1994).

Rogers compiled the *Tentative International Register of Cultivar Names in the Genus Syringa L.* while on sabbatical leave in 1975 (Rogers 1976). This tentative lilac register was patterned after *Lilacs for America* (1953); it became the cornerstone of the current *International Register and Checklist of Cultivar Names in the Genus Syringa L.* (Vrugtman 2007c). Rogers has been an active member of the International Lilac Society, serving as president, editor, and in other capacities. Now professor emeritus, Rogers is the recipient of the Director's Award (1979), the Honors and Achievement Award (1984), the Arch McKean Award (1991), and the Distinguished Recognition Award (2001) of the International Lilac Society.

Lilac introductions from the University of New Hampshire include the following, all outstanding lilacs, worthy for every garden with space for them:

'Agnes Smith' (*S.* Villosae Group), single white,
 Rogers 1970; marketed in Germany as MISS USA
'Anna Amhoff' (*S.* Villosae Group), single white,
 Yeager 1959 (*S.* ×*josiflexa*)
'Anne Tighe' (*S. vulgaris*), double purple, Yeager 1945

Owen M. Rogers. John Fiala

Syringa vulgaris 'Anne Tighe'. B. Peart and M. Walton

'James Macfarlane' (*S.* Villosae Group), single pinkish, Yeager 1959 (parentage uncertain)

'Jesse Hepler' (*S.* Villosae Group), single magenta, Rogers 1978 (*S.* ×*josiflexa*)

'Marie Rogers' (*S.* Villosae Group), double white, Rogers 2005

'Mary Blanchard' (*S. vulgaris*), single violet, Yeager 1958

'Maybelle Farnum' (*S.* Villosae Group), single purple, Yeager 1961 (*S.* ×*josiflexa*)

'Miss Kim' (*S. pubescens* subsp. *patula*), single violet, Meader & Yeager 1954

'Nellie Bean' (*S.* Villosae Group), single purple, Yeager 1961 (*S.* ×*josiflexa*)

Royal Botanical Gardens, Hamilton, Ontario, Canada

In the late 1960s James S. Pringle made several interesting crosses of *Syringa yunnanensis* with select cultivars of *S.* ×*prestoniae*, *S. reflexa*, and *S. sweginzowii*, and Joan L. Brown continued this work under Pringle's guidance into the next decade. The interesting hybrids are described elsewhere under the species lilacs. Not only are many of these crosses historic, in that some have never been attempted before, but they are extremely well documented and evaluated by Pringle, something rarely done by other hybridizers (Pringle 1977, 1981).

In 1975 Joan L. Brown crossed *Syringa vulgaris* 'Rochester' with 'Primrose' and 'St Joan', producing some extraordinary white and colored lilacs with large florets and thyrses. One selection, Brown 75116-16, a single purple known to Fiala (1988, p. 106), remained unnamed, was not propagated, and was eventually lost. Brown introduced two other selections, although the Royal Botanical Gardens, Hamilton, had terminated the plant breeding and selecting program in 1992.

'Father John' (*S. vulgaris*), single white, introduced mid-1990s ('Rochester' × 'Primrose')

'McMaster Centennial' (*S. vulgaris*), double white, 1999 ('Primrose' × 'St Joan')

Neal S. Holland

Originated by Neal Holland at his nursery in Harwood, North Dakota, and commercially introduced by Bailey Nurseries of St Paul, Minnesota, are the cultivars in the FAIRYTALE series. They were selected from the cross *Syringa meyeri* 'Palibin' × *S. pubescens* subsp. *microphylla* 'Superba'. Additional cultivars are said to be in the testing stage; the following are commercially available:

'Bailbelle' (marketed as TINKERBELLE), single pinkish, 1999; compact growth habit

'Baildust' (marketed as FAIRY DUST) single pinkish, 2001; slow-growing, compact habit

'Bailina' (marketed as THUMBELINA), single pinkish, 2004; 5–6 feet (1.5–1.8 m) tall and wide

Syringa vulgaris 'Father John'. John Fiala

Syringa vulgaris 'Bailbelle' (TINKERBELLE). B. Peart and M. Walton

'Bailming' (marketed as PRINCE CHARMING), single pinkish, 2004; dwarf-rounded habit

'Bailsugar' (marketed as SUGAR PLUM FAIRY), single pinkish-lilac, 2003; globose, compact habit

J. Giles Waines

Giles Waines, at the Botanic Garden, Riverside Campus of the University of California, initiated a breeding program in 1996. The aim is to produce short-stature plants with attractive foliage, good in size bloom in well-shaped thyrses, bright flower colors, and good fragrance, adapted to California's climate.

Max Peterson

Max Peterson and his wife, Darlene, received the 2004 Directors Award of the International Lilac Society, "For a lifetime of dedicated work in hybridizing, preserving and promoting the Lilac. For their devotion to the cultivation of Meadowlark Hill Lilac Garden, the world's largest private lilac collection." At Meadowlark Hill Lilac Garden, Ogallala, Nebraska, they have selected, named, and distributed the following:

'Beth' (*S. vulgaris*), double white, 1999

'Bridal Memories' (*S. vulgaris*), single white, 1993

'Darlene' (*S. vulgaris*), double pinkish, 1996

'Jeffrey' (*S. vulgaris*), double magenta

'Pink Delight' (*S. vulgaris*), single pinkish, pre-1987

'Red Pixie' (*Syringa*), single magenta to pinkish, ca. 1987; selected from open-pollinated *S. pubescens* subsp. *julianae* 'Hers'; not related to the single white *S. vulgaris* 'Pixie' introduced by Fiala in 1981

'Reva Ballreich' (*S. vulgaris*), double pink, 1988; not to be confused with the double white 'Reva Ballreich' by Joel Margaretten

'Ruby Cole' (*S. vulgaris*), single pink

Peterson also introduced three *Syringa vulgaris* cultivars raised by Henry E. Sass (1910–1982), a farmer and plant breeder at Benson Station, Omaha, Nebraska:

'Blue Boy' (*S. vulgaris*), single bluish, 2004; not *S. ×hyacinthiflora* 'Blue Boy', Sobeck 1966

'Hyperion' (*S. vulgaris*), pre-1987

'Red Giant' (*S. vulgaris*), single magenta, pre-1987

Frank and Sara Moro

The Moros established a nursery and lilac collection in 1990. Select Plus International Nurseries, Québec, Canada, offers a wide selection of lilacs. Frank received a 1998 Award of Merit of the International Lilac Society, "For his enthusiastic efforts in the distribution of lilac species, cultivars, and promotion of lilacs." In 2000 he was the recipient of the Arch McKean Award, "For encouraging the establishment of a lilac Website, and for supplying a great deal of material used on the site." In 2001 the Moros received the Distinguished Recognition Award of the International Lilac Society for establishing a nursery offering the largest selection of named lilacs. Frank is the co-author of a French-language book on lilacs (Giguère and Moro 2005). New lilac selections made and introduced by the Moros are as follows:

'Anastasia' (*Syringa*), single magenta, 1996 (open-pollinated seedling of *S.* 'MORjos 060F' JOSÉE)

'Cameo's Jewel' (*S. reticulata* subsp. *reticulata*), single white, 1995; foliage variegated (open-pollinated seedling of 'Ivory Silk')

'Cinderella' (*S. pubescens* subsp. *patula*), single pinkish, 1998

'Colby's Wishing Star' (*Syringa*), single pinkish, 2003 (open-pollinated seedling of 'MORjos 060F' JOSÉE)

'Corinna's Mist' (*S. ×hyacinthiflora*), single pinkish, 2001; foliage variegated (mutant of 'California Rose')

'Patriot' (*S.* Villosae Group), single purple, 2002 (mutation of *S.* 'Minuet')

'Sleeping Beauty' (*Syringa*), single pinkish, 2001; autumn foliage reddish (*S. pubescens* subsp. *microphylla* 'Superba' × *S. meyeri* 'Palibin')

'Snowstorm' (*S. meyeri*), single pinkish, 2000 (open-pollinated seedling of *S. meyeri* 'Palibin')

Lilac Hybridizing in the Russian Federation and Its Former Satellite Countries

Leonid Kolesnikov was for Russia and its satellite countries what Victor Lemoine was for Western Europe and North America. These were indisputably the pioneers and trendsetters for lilac breeding, but there were, and still are, other lilac originators in the former Soviet Union. Language and communication barriers have kept us from learning much about these breeders and their lilacs; economic and import barriers have kept us from obtaining and growing these lilacs. Charles D. Holetich (1982), with his English translation of the publication by Rubtzov et al. (1980) on "Lilac species and cultivars in cultivation in USSR" and his Romanization of the Russian cultivar names, unlocked this information to the English-speaking world. While working on the transliteration of the cultivar names, Holetich realized that the Romanization tables of American and British style manuals worked only one way, namely, from Cyrillic to Roman script (see, for example, *CBE Style Manual* by the Council of Biology Editors 1972, *ALA-LC Romanization Tables* by Barry 1991, and *Chicago Manual of Style* by the University of Chicago Press Staff 2003). He proposed and published a simple but effective solution. Certain Cyrillic characters are transliterated to English by using two or more Latin characters, such as я = ya, ю = yu, ш = sh, ч = ch, and so on. Whenever this is the case, the Latin characters have been underlined. For example, the Latin ya will transliterate to the Cyrillic я, rather than to the individual characters ы and a. The Romanization of the Cyrillic character щ is underlined twice: shch, distinguishing it from ш = sh and ч = ch appearing side by side. For his contributions Holetich received the Honors and Achievement Award of the International Lilac Society in 1986. The notes that follow are incomplete at best; they are also likely to contain spelling errors and inconsistencies caused by transliterations from Cyrillic to Roman script. There are no reports on evaluation available yet, as few of these cultivars have become available commercially. Following are the more prolific lilac breeders we have learned about. Cultivars that have shown up in collections or commerce are so noted.

Nikolaĭ Kuz'mich Vekhov (1887–1956)

Vekhov worked at the Lesostepnaya Experimental Breeding Station (LOSS), Meshchersk, Lipetsk Region, Stanovliansky district of Russia, from 1925 until his death in 1956. Although we know very little about the man and although the lilac cultivars named by him became known to us only in the late 1980s,

Vekhov must be ranked among the early lilac breeders in Russia. His known *Syringa vulgaris* introductions are listed here:

'Aélita' (*S. vulgaris*), single lilac to purple
'Belaya Noch'' (*S. vulgaris*), double pinkish, 1987
'Elena Vekhova' (*S. vulgaris*), double white, 1952
'Lesostepnaya' (*S. vulgaris*), double pinkish to magenta, 1987
'Nepovtorimaya' (*S. vulgaris*), single lilac to pinkish, 1987
'Nezhnost'' (*S. vulgaris*), double pinkish, pre-1987
'Pamyat' o Vavilove' (*S. vulgaris*), double pinkish, 1987
'Pamyat' o Vekhove' (*S. vulgaris*), double violet, 1972
'Rus' (*S. vulgaris*), single pinkish, 1996
'Russkaya Pesnya' (*S. vulgaris*), double violet, 1996
'Utro Rossii' (*S. vulgaris*), double violet, 1987
'Yunost' (*S. vulgaris*), single lilac to pinkish. 1952
'Zarya' (*S. vulgaris*), double purple

Syringa vulgaris 'Belaya Noch''. T. Poliakova and I. Semyonova

Syringa vulgaris 'Pamyat' o Vekhove'. T. Poliakova and I. Semyonova

Some of Vekhov's lilac work at LOSS appears to have been continued by Valentina Leonidovna Romanova (1927–1991) and M. Egorova (no data available), who introduced *Syringa vulgaris* 'Lipchanka', a violet cultivar.

Leonid Alekseevich Kolesnikov (1893–1973)

Leonid Kolesnikov started out as an amateur grower of lilacs and roses and became a leading specialist and head of the Experimental and Model Selection Nursery. Although he pioneered in the creation of new cultivars of *Syringa vulgaris*, he did not limit his work to hybridizing lilacs but devoted himself to every aspect of their growth and culture. Kolesnikov first planted lilacs in his own garden in 1916. Three years later he sowed seeds of his own hybridizing and began a career devoted to improving the lilac.

Kolesnikov avidly read and studied every available book on botany, especially on methods of breeding, grafting, and planting lilacs. Traveling frequently and widely across the country, he not only acquainted himself with the then-known methods of lilac culture and propagation, but was able to observe firsthand what was being done in the larger nurseries of his time.

The young Kolesnikov made every effort to extend the number of varieties in his garden. By 1923 his collection of lilacs had reached over one hundred named cultivars and his garden began receiving the attention of specialists and scientific researchers. M. P. Nagibins, a researcher at the Botanical Garden of Moscow State University, helped Kolesnikov considerably with botany and botanical research, which in turn led him to the work of K. Timiryazev, N. I. Kichunov, D. D. Artzibashev, Ivan Michurin, Trofim D. Lysenko, and Luther Burbank.

Kolesnikov used almost exclusively Lemoine introductions with one exception. He used 'Alphonse Lavallée', 'Belle de Nancy', 'Berryer', 'Buffon', 'Congo', 'Decaisne', 'Émile Lemoine', 'Jules Simon', 'Katherine Havemeyer', 'Michel Buchner', 'Monge', 'Mme Lemoine', 'Pasteur', 'Président Poincaré', and 'Réaumur', with 'Andenken an Ludwig Späth' being his only non-Lemoine parent plant. After 20 years of patient hybridizing he began to see the real results of his labors. From his seedlings he selected cultivars such as 'K. A. Timiryazev', 'Leonid Leonov', and 'Sumerki'. From these first open-pollinated seedlings he then cross-pollinated those seedlings he deemed best. He particularly liked his named cultivars 'I. V. Michurin', 'M. I. Kalinin', and 'Zarya Kommunizma' as hybridizing materials. He shared with Victor Lemoine a preference for the large floret double lilacs.

Kolesnikov's book, *Lilacs* (1952, 1955), grew out of his hybridizing work and many experiments in lilac grafting, transplanting, and seed propagation. His experiments indicating lilacs could, and perhaps should, be moved in midsummer dry weather, radically altered the traditional and conventional notion on transplanting lilacs. Other experiments indicated that flower color of cultivars of light rose, pinks, lilac-violet, and blue shades are best in soil pH close to neutral, otherwise the colors become "muddy." His fertilizing experiments showed that by using "green water," a heavily manured water and lime solution, on lilacs, five or six flower buds could be induced rather than the traditional two or three. His "green water" is made by putting weeds, green cuttings, grass, and so forth in water, and after all have decayed using the "water" as liquid fertilizer. He determined that one of the best times to transplant lilacs without sacrificing bloom the following year is from 14 to 18 days after florescence. His horticultural ingenuity extended to inventing new budding tools, shears, pruning, and spraying equipment. He strongly believed in Michurinism, the principles and teachings of Ivan V. Michurin (1855–1935). One of Michurin's theories was that acquired characteristics were heritable (Michurin 1949).

Kolesnikov's work was interrupted by wars (as was that of the Lemoine's). In 1939 he participated in the Finnish Campaign. In 1940, his wife, Olimpiada N. Kolesnikova, showed in his absence some of his lilac selections at the All-Union Agricultural Exposition where he was awarded the Diploma of Honor for his work. During one of the enemy air raids, bombs fell in his garden, many of his plants were destroyed, and his wife suffered from mental trauma for the rest of her life. His return to his peaceful lilac pursuits was brief. In 1942 he was again on the battlefield for five months, returning home after being severely wounded. In 1943 he made the cross with 'I. V. Michurin' and 'Belle de Nancy', which gave him his two best lilacs, the double white tinged lavender 'Krasavitsa Moskvy' and the fine double bluish lilac 'Pamyat' o S. M. Kirove'. After the war began the productive years of his lilac work.

Kolesnikov was a curious and knowledgeable man, always searching to understand the ways of nature. He read a great deal and understood plants with a kind of sixth sense. He was ready to share his knowledge with colleagues and visitors whether amateurs or professionals. As an amateur floriculturist Kolesnikov was awarded the Stalin Prize for breeding new lilac cultivars. But there were difficult years ahead. In 1952 Kolesnikov had to turn his property over to the city of Moscow. Because he had been recognized for his breeding work and the lilacs he had created, a nursery was set up to be the new home of his lilacs, and Kolesnikov was appointed its director. But a few years later urban sprawl forced out the nursery; the old lilacs bushes had to be moved again and again, apparently without having been repropagated. It is not surprising that many of them succumbed. In 1966 the old Kolesnikov family home in Moscow was demolished; the garden is no more and some of the surviving lilacs were moved to city parks (David Wilson, 14 March 2005, pers. comm. to F.V.).

At its meeting in Boston in May 1973, the International Lilac Society awarded Kolesnikov its Director's Award for his work with lilacs. Like Lemoine, his lilacs will remain his lasting tribute. Only in recent years have some of Kolesnikov's cultivars become available in North America. Numbers and sources are as yet very limited. Since we have seen only a small portion of Kolesnikov's many introductions, it would be unfair to give a definitive evaluation. Outside of the Main Botanical Garden, Russian Academy of Sciences, Moscow, the single largest collection of Russian lilacs is at Royal Botanical Gardens, Hamilton, Ontario, Canada. The following Kolesnikov cultivars have been reported in cultivation. Note the many that Fiala considered to be outstanding:

'Akademik Burdenko' (*S. vulgaris*), double bluish to lilac

'Akademik Maksimov' (*S. vulgaris*), double purple-pinkish; plants cultivated in North American under this name with single, white flowers are not true to name

'Aleksei Mares'ev' (*S. vulgaris*), single bluish to lilac, 1951; outstanding

'Andryusha Gromov' (*S. vulgaris*), double bluish to lilac

'Dzhavakharlal Neru' (*S. vulgaris*), single purple, 1974; outstanding

'Galina Ulanova' (*S. vulgaris*), single white, 1976; outstanding

'Gastello' (*S. vulgaris*), single bluish to lilac; outstanding

'Golubaya' (*S. vulgaris*), single bluish, pre-1963; outstanding

'Gortenziya' (*S. vulgaris*), single lilac to pinkish, 1930; outstanding

'I. V. Michurin' (*S. vulgaris*), double lilac to pinkish, 1941

'Indiya' (*S. vulgaris*), single lilac, 1955; outstanding

'Izobilie' (*S. vulgaris*), double lilac, pre-1959; outstanding

'K. A. Timiryazev' (*S. vulgaris*), single lilac, 1955

'Kapriz' (*S. vulgaris*), double lilac to pinkish, 1952; outstanding

Syringa vulgaris 'Gastello'. B. Peart and M. Walton

Syringa vulgaris 'I. V. Michurin'. B. Peart and M. Walton

Syringa vulgaris 'Krasnaya Moskva'. B. Peart and M. Walton

Syringa vulgaris 'Leonid Leonov'. T. Poliakova and I. Semyonova

'Komsomolka' (*S. vulgaris*), double lilac, 1974; outstanding

'Krasavitsa Moskvy' (*S. vulgaris*) (marketed in the United States as BEAUTY OF MOSCOW, in Germany as SCHÖNE VON MOSKAU and MÄDCHEN AUS MOSKAU, and in France as BELLE DE MOSCOU), double white, 1974; outstanding

'Krasnaya Moskva' (*S. vulgaris*) (PRIDE OF MOSCOW), single purple, pre-1960; outstanding

'Kremlevskie Kuranty' (*S. vulgaris*), single lilac, 1974

'Leonid Kolesnikov' (*S. vulgaris*), double violet; outstanding

'Leonid Leonov' (*S. vulgaris*), single lilac and violet, 1941; outstanding

'M. I. Kalinin' (*S. vulgaris*), single violet to lilac, 1941

'Marshal Vasilevskiĭ' (*S. vulgaris*), double violet to pink, 1963

'Marshal Zhukov' (*S. vulgaris*), single lilac to magenta, 1948; outstanding

'Mechta' (*S. vulgaris*) (dream), single bluish to lilac, 1941, outstanding, a dependable and heavy bloomer

'Nadezhda' (*S. vulgaris*) (HOPE), double bluish to lilac, pre-1974; outstanding

'Nebo Moskvy' (*S. vulgaris*) (MOSCOW SKY), double bluish to lilac to magenta, 1963

'Nevesta' (*S. vulgaris*), single pinkish; not to be confused with the single white 'Nevesta' from Central Botanical Garden, Kiev, Ukraine; outstanding

'Ogni Moskvy' (*S. vulgaris*), single purple; outstanding

'Olimpiada Kolesnikova' (*S. vulgaris*), double lilac to pinkish, 1941; outstanding

'P. P. Konchalovskiĭ' (*S. vulgaris*), double bluish to lilac, 1956; outstanding

'Pamyat' o Kolesnikove' (*S. vulgaris*), double white, 1974

'Pamyat' o S. M. Kirove' (*S. vulgaris*), double lilac, 1943; very showy large thyrses, outstanding

'Pioner' (*S. vulgaris*), single lilac to pinkish to purple, 1951; outstanding

'Pol' Robson' (*S. vulgaris*), single lilac to bluish, 1965

'Polina Osipenko' (*S. vulgaris*), double white, 1941

'Radzh Kapur' (*S. vulgaris*), single lilac to magenta, 1974

'Sholokhov' (*S. vulgaris*), single lilac to pinkish, pre-1974

'Sorok Let Komsomola' (*S. vulgaris*), single lilac

'Sovetskaya Arktika' (*S. vulgaris*) (RUSSIAN ARCTIC), double white, 1955; outstanding

'Sumerki' (*S. vulgaris*) (twilight), single violet to bluish, 1954

'Utro Moskvy' (*S. vulgaris*) (morning in Moscow), double lilac to pinkish, 1938

'Valentina Grizodubova' (*S. vulgaris*), double pinkish, pre-1974

Syringa vulgaris 'Sholokhov'. John Fiala

Syringa vulgaris 'Doch' Tamara'. T. Poliakova and I. Semyonova

Syringa vulgaris 'Valentina Grizodubova'. B. Peart and M. Walton

'Zarya Kommunizma' (*S. vulgaris*) (marketed in the United States as DAWN OF COMMUNISM), single magenta to purple, 1951; outstanding
'Znamya Lenina' (*S. vulgaris*) (BANNER OF LENIN), single purple to magenta, pre-1959; outstanding
'Zoya Kosmodem'yanskaya' (*S. vulgaris*), single bluish, 1943

Following the death of Leonid Kolesnikov, an additional four of his *Syringa vulgaris* selections appear to have been released by Vladimir D. Mironovich (b. 1904) of Serpukhova, Moscow Region, Russia. We lack further detail.

'Doch' Tamara' (*S. vulgaris*), single pinkish, pre-1994 (collections)
'Moskovskiĭ Universitet' (*S. vulgaris*) (Moscow University), double lilac, pre-1994 (collections)
'Pyatidesyatiletie Oktyabrya' (*S. vulgaris*), single violet to pink, 1986 (collections)
'Velikaya Pobeda' (*S. vulgaris*) (great victory), double, lilac bluish, pre-1994

Nikifor Savel'yevich Stashkevich (1902–1993)

Nikifor Stashkevich, Soviet army colonel and professor at the tank academy in Moscow, befriended Kolesnikov and became an amateur lilac breeder. He originated two cultivars that have been introduced into North American collections.

Syringa vulgaris 'Tankist'. B. Peart and M. Walton

Syringa ×hyacinthiflora 'Nina'. T. Poliakova and I. Semyonova

'Russkaya Krasavit̲s̲a' (*S. vulgaris*), single white, pre-1974 (collections, commerce)

'Tankist' (*S. vulgaris*), single purple, pre-1967 (collections)

Central Botanical Garden, Moscow

Three workers at this garden—Ivan Ivanovi̲c̲h̲ S̲h̲tan'ko (1904–1991), horticulturist from 1946 to 1975; horticulturist Nikolai Leonidovich Mik̲h̲aĭlov; and agriculturist Nina Ivanovna Rybakina—selected several cultivars, some of which can be found in North American collections. In 1977 Mik̲h̲aĭlov received the International Lilac Society's Director's Award, "For dedicated work in promoting the lilac through an internationally known lilac collection and the publication of works designed to extend knowledge of the Lilac in his native country and the world."

'Alenu̲s̲h̲ka' (*S. vulgaris*), single pinkish, S̲h̲tan'ko & Mik̲h̲aĭlov 1956 (collections, commerce)

'Ametist 2' (*S. vulgaris*), single bluish to lilac, S̲h̲tan'ko & Mik̲h̲aĭlov 1956

'Aria' (*S. ×hyacinthiflora*), single bluish to lilac, Mik̲h̲aĭlov & Rybakina 2002

'Elena Rosse' (*S. ×hyacinthiflora*), single lilac to pinkish, Mik̲h̲aĭlov & Rybakina 2002

'Kosmos' (*S. vulgaris*), single violet, S̲h̲tan'ko & Mik̲h̲aĭlov 1956 (collections, commerce)

'Mulatka' (*S. vulgaris*), single magenta, Mik̲h̲aĭlov & Rybakina 1980 (collections, commerce)

'Nikolaĭ Mik̲h̲aĭlov' (*S. vulgaris*), single purple, Mik̲h̲aĭlov & Rybakina 2002

Syringa vulgaris 'Nikolaĭ Mik̲h̲aĭlov'. T. Poliakova and I. Semyonova

'Nina' (*S. ×hyacinthiflora*), double pinkish, Mik̲h̲aĭlov & Rybakina 2002

'Ostankino' (*S. vulgaris*), single bluish, S̲h̲tan'ko & Mik̲h̲aĭlov 1956 (collections)

'S̲h̲kol'nit̲s̲a' (*S. vulgaris*) (schoolgirl), single bluish to lilac, S̲h̲tan'ko & Mik̲h̲aĭlov 1956 (collections)

'Skromnit̲s̲a' (*S. ×hyacinthiflora*), single pinkish to white, Mik̲h̲aĭlov & Rybakina 2002

'Vek' (*Syringa*), double lilac, Mik̲h̲aĭlov & Rybakina 2002

'Yubileĭnay̲a' (jubilee) (*S. vulgaris*), single lilac to pinkish, S̲h̲tan'ko & Mik̲h̲aĭlov 1956 (collections)

Syringa vulgaris 'Ostankino'. B. Peart and M. Walton

Syringa vulgaris 'Shkol'nitsa' B. Peart and M. Walton

Syringa vulgaris 'Yubileĭnaya'. John Fiala

Dendrological Gardens of M. A. Lisavenko Scientific Research Institute for Siberian Horticulture, Barnaul, Siberia

Zinaida Ivanovna Luchnik (1909–1994) and Natal'ya Borisnova Semenyuk (no dates), now retired, originated two selections of *Syringa vulgaris* which have not yet been reported in Western Europe and North America. Lilac work at this institution appears to have been terminated. Following are their selections:

'Altaĭskaya Rozovaya' (*S. vulgaris*), single pinkish, pre-1984

'Kruzhevnitsa' (*S. vulgaris*), double lilac to pinkish, pre-1984

Ufa Botanical Garden, Bashkortostan, Russian Federation

In 1973, Ufa Botanical Garden, Bashkortostan (formerly Bashkiria) released eight *Syringa vulgaris* cultivars selected by horticulturist Aleksandra Sergeyevna Sakharova (1917–1986), none of which have reached Western gardens:

'Agidel' (*S. vulgaris*), single white, 1973

'Aĭgul' (*S. vulgaris*), double lilac to pinkish, 1973

'Alesha' (*S. vulgaris*), single magenta, 1973

'Gul'nazira' (*S. vulgaris*), single pinkish, 1973

'Krasavitsa Bashkirii' (*S. vulgaris*), double lilac to pinkish, 1973

'Nafisa' (*S. vulgaris*), single pink and white, 1973

'Salavat Yulaev' (*S. vulgaris*), double purplish violet, 1973

'Shaura' (*S. vulgaris*), single magenta, 1973

Botanical Garden, Saint Petersburg, Russia

We have little information on E. Potutova at the Saint Petersburg botanical garden and her *Syringa vulgaris* selections, which may not yet have been seen outside Russia:

'Aleksandr Pushkin' (*S. vulgaris*), single violet, pre-1980

'Noktyurn' (*S. vulgaris*), single purple, pre-1980

'Russkiĭ Suvenir' (*S. vulgaris*), single purple, pre-1980

'Serebristyĭ Landysh' (*S. vulgaris*), double white, pre-1980

'Sirenevaya Piramida' (*S. vulgaris*) (silver lily-of-the-valley), single purple, pre-1980

Central Botanical Garden, Minsk, Belarus

Nikolai Vladislavovi<u>ch</u> Smol'ski (b. 1905) and Veronika Fedorovna Bibikova, horticulturists at the Central Botanical Garden in Minsk, originated a number of *Syringa vulgaris* cultivars, most of which have shown up in European and American lilac collections:

'Belorusskie Zori' (*S. vulgaris*), single lilac to pinkish, 1964 (collections)

'Konstantin Zaslonov' (*S. vulgaris*), single magenta, 1964 (collections, commerce)

'Lebedu<u>sh</u>ka' (*S. vulgaris*), single white, 1964 (collections, commerce)

'Lunny Svet' (*S. vulgaris*), double white, 1964 (collections)

'Marat Kaze' (*S. vulgaris*), single bluish, 1964 (collections)

'Min<u>ch</u>anka' (*S. vulgaris*), single violet, 1964 (collections, commerce)

'Pam<u>ya</u>ti A. T. Smol'sko' (*S. vulgaris*), single lilac, 1964 (collections, commerce)

'Partizanka' (*S. vulgaris*), single lilac, 1964 (collections, commerce)

'Pavlinka' (*S. vulgaris*), double purple, 1964 (collections, commerce)

'Polesska<u>ya</u> Legenda' (*S. vulgaris*), single purple, pre-1959

'Svit<u>ya</u>zanka' (*S. vulgaris*), single purple, 1964 (commerce)

'Vera <u>Kh</u>oruz<u>ha</u>ya' (*S. vulgaris*), single lilac to pinkish, 1964 (collections, commerce)

'Za<u>shch</u>itnikam Bresta' (*S. vulgaris*), double white, 1964 (collections, commerce)

'Zor'ka Venera' (*S. vulgaris*), single purple, 1964 (commerce)

Syringa vulgaris 'Konstantin Zaslonov'. T. Poliakova and I. Semyonova

Syringa vulgaris 'Lunnyĭ Svet'. B. Peart and M. Walton

Syringa vulgaris 'Minchanka'. T. Poliakova and I. Semyonova

Syringa vulgaris 'Pavlinka'. T. Poliakova and I. Semyonova

Syringa vulgaris 'Zashchitnikam Bresta'. B. Peart and M. Walton

State Nikita Botanical Gardens, Yalta, Crimea, Ukraine

Vera Nikolaevna Klimenko (1909–1985) worked at the State Nikita Botanical Gardens as horticulturist from 1949 to 1978; her daughter, Zinaida Klimenko, has worked there also as horticulturist since 1958. Alexander Grigor'ev was horticulturist from 1960 to 1986. In the mid to late 1950s these workers selected and named a number of *Syringa vulgaris* cultivars, of which only 'Lesya Ukrainka' has been reported in cultivation in Western Europe:

'Devich'e Schast'e' (*S. vulgaris*), single pinkish to purple, 1955
'Fioletovyĭ Sultan' (*S. vulgaris*), single violet, 1955
'Knipper-Chekhova' (*S. vulgaris*), single purple, 1955
'Krymskaya Krasavitsa' (*S. vulgaris*), single bluish to lilac, 1955
'Krymskaya Lazur'' (*S. vulgaris*), single violet to bluish, 1955
'Lesya Ukrainka' (*S. vulgaris*), single purple, 1955 (commerce); not to be confused with the double white 'Lesya Ukraynka'
'Lilovaya Purga' (*S. vulgaris*), single pinkish, 1955
'Lilovaya Raketa' (*S. vulgaris*), single lilac to pinkish, 1955
'Marsianka' (*S. vulgaris*), single violet, 1955
'Mechta Materi' (*S. vulgaris*), single purple, 1955
'Pamyat' o Chekhove' (*S. vulgaris*), single purple, 1955
'Radost' Pobedy' (*S. vulgaris*), single pinkish violet, 1955
'Sapun-gora' (*S. vulgaris*), single violet, 1955
'Sevastopol'skiĭ Val's' (*S. vulgaris*), single lilac, 1955
'Sirenevyĭ Kaskad' (*S. vulgaris*), single lilac, 1955
'Soyuz-Apollon' (*S. vulgaris*), 1955
'Vesennyaya Krasa' (*S. vulgaris*), single violet to lilac, 1955
'Yaltinskaya Prelest' (*S. vulgaris*), single purple, 1955
'Yuzhanka' (*S. vulgaris*), single purple, 1955
'Yuzhnaya Noch'' (*S. vulgaris*) (southern night), single violet, 1955

Central Botanical Garden, Kiev, Ukraine

Leonid Ivanovich Rubtzov (1902–1980), horticulturist from 1948 to 1980; Valentina Grigorivna Zhogoleva (1923–1980), horticulturist from 1953 to 1980;

Syringa vulgaris 'Bogdan Khmel'nitskiĭ'. B. Peart and M. Walton

Nina Aleksandrovna Lyapunova, horticulturist from 1946 to 1965; and Vasil' Kuz'movich Gorb, horticulturist since 1971, have selected, named, and introduced the following *Syringa vulgaris* cultivars. Most of these have been reported in cultivation in Western Europe and North America:

'Bogdan Khmel'nitskiĭ' (*S. vulgaris*), double pinkish, pre-1980 (collections, commerce)
'Kievlyanka' (*S. vulgaris*), single lilac, 1956 (collections, commerce)
'Lesnaya Pesnya' (*S. vulgaris*), single bluish to lilac, pre-1961
'Lesya Ukraynka' (*S. vulgaris*), double white, pre-1997 (commerce); not to be confused with the single purple 'Lesya Ukrainka'
'Nevesta' (*S. vulgaris*), single white, pre-1961 (commerce?); not to be confused with Kolesnikov's single pinkish 'Nevesta'
'Ogni Donbassa' (*S. vulgaris*) (lights of Dombas), double lilac, 1956 (collections, commerce)
'Poltava' (*S. vulgaris*), single violet to lilac, 1956 (collections, commerce)
'Rozovoe Oblako' (*S. vulgaris*), single lilac to pinkish, 1956 (commerce)

Syringa vulgaris 'Poltava'. B. Peart and M. Walton

Syringa vulgaris 'Taras Bul'ba'. John Fiala

'Taras Bul'ba', double lilac, 1956 (collections, commerce)

'Topaz' (*S. vulgaris*), single violet, Zhogoleva 1976

'Zviozdochka Kieva' (*S. vulgaris*), double white, probably Rubtzov and Zhogoleva pre-1963

Agricultural University, Kharkov, Ukraine

Syringa vulgaris 'S. V. Lavrov', pre-1980, a double lilac, was named for its originator, S. V. Lavrov, horticulturist at the Agricultural University in Kharkov. We have no other information on the originator.

Donetsk Botanical Garden, Donetsk, Ukraine

Sergeĭ Ivanovich Tereshchenko, horticulturist and plant breeder at Donetsk Botanical Garden in the Ukraine, registered five *Syringa vulgaris* cultivars with the State Commission of Ukraine for Sort Testing and Protection of Plants at Kiev:

'Donetskiye Zori' (*S. vulgaris*) (Donetsk dawn), double pinkish, 2002

'Donetsky Souvenir' (*S. vulgaris*) (Donetsk souvenir), single lilac, 2002

'Ogni Donetska' (*S. vulgaris*) (lights of Donetsk), single lilac, 2002

'Professor A. L. Lypa' (*S. vulgaris*), double lilac to pinkish, 2002

'Professor M. L. Reva' (*S. vulgaris*), double lilac to pinkish, 2002

Syringa vulgaris 'Donetskiye Zori'.

Syringa vulgaris 'Donetsky Souvenir'.

Syringa vulgaris 'Ogni Donetska'.

Syringa vulgaris 'Professor A. L. Lypa'.

Syringa vulgaris 'Professor M. L. Reva'.

Kórnik Arboretum and Lilac Cultivars from Poland

The Institute of Dendrology of the Polish Academy of Sciences at Kórnik, about 15 miles (25 km) southeast of Poznan, was established in 1933; it is an institution of higher learning and authorized to confer the academic degree of doctor of biological sciences. The Kórnik Arboretum (Arboretum Kórnickie) adjacent to the castle is a former Italian garden dating back to the 16th century, which was renovated to a French garden in the 18th century. After 1830 the park was enlarged and converted to an arboretum. Today about 3000 species and cultivars of Eurasian and American trees and shrubs are grown on 111 acres (45 ha); the Kórnik Arboretum is one of the richest of its kind in Europe.

The present lilac collection had its beginning in 1926 under the direction of A. Wroblewski. At the outbreak of the World War II, in 1939, the lilac collection at Kórnik numbered 125 taxa. After the war the collection was enlarged with newer introductions from abroad to over 500 species and named cultivars. The soils at the arboretum are composed of light, sandy, rather dry and poor topsoil with underlying peat and clay, not the most desirable soil for *Syringa vulgaris*. Annual precipitation averages 20 inches (500 mm), with long periods of dry weather in the summers. Dry-spells of from four to six weeks are common. Winters are moderate with little snow, though occasionally winter minimum temperatures of −4° to −22°F (−20° to −30°C) have been recorded. Average temperatures for January and July at Kórnik Arboretum are quite similar to those at Royal Botanical Gardens, Hamilton, Ontario, Canada, as are the occasional minimum temperatures. The difference is in the annual precipitation, which at Royal Botanical Gardens averages 35 inches (889 mm).

The lilac collection at Kórnik contains most of the introductions of Mikołaj Karpow-Lipski. Many are reportedly outstanding but are still little known outside of Poland and mostly unavailable in North America. In 1952 Władysław Bugała commenced a program of hybridizing *Syringa ×prestoniae*. The Arboretum is well worth a special visit and the extra time when in Poland. The lilac collection is a demonstration of what can be accomplished despite difficult soil conditions. Located in the arboretum is the Dendrological Museum.

Mikołaj Karpow-Lipski (1896–1981)

Mikołaj Karpow-Lipski was born in Warsaw on 12 October 1896, the son of a railroad employee. In 1910, at age 14, he enrolled in a three-year horticultural school in Warsaw, graduating in 1913. In the autumn of the same year he entered the agricultural and horticultural college at Humán, in Belarus, the most prestigious horticultural college of the Russian Empire of that era.

At the outbreak of World War I Karpow-Lipski was drafted into the Imperial Army. Overtaken by the Russian Revolution in 1917 he served in the so-called East-Corps, fighting the Leninist forces. Sent to Greece with an East-Corps unit he traveled through Western Europe, including Italy, France, and Great Britain. Having already a budding interest in plant breeding, he acquainted himself with the famous tree nurseries of Vilmorin Andrieux in Paris and Victor Lemoine in Nancy.

Following the end of World War I Karpow-Lipski returned to a now independent Poland and found employment in horticulture. He joined the Warsaw horticultural society and kept up to date with the literature on horticulture and plant breeding, including writings in Russian and French. In 1928 he started his own breeding and selecting work soon after which he purchased a 11-acre (4.5-ha) farm in Kończewice, near Toruń. His initial breeding work was with pears; subsequently he branched out to breeding vegetables and herbaceous ornamental plants.

The events of World War II forced him to flee Kończewice and to work in the region known today as West Ukraine. Some of his work was with medicinal plants including selection work on castor bean (*Ricinus communis*).

After the conclusion of World War II Karpow-Lipski returned to his farm. Many original stock plants, hybrids, and selections resulting from his earlier efforts had been destroyed, but a collection of some 80 lilac cultivars acquired from Victor Lemoine had survived. He started anew, concentrating as in earlier years on tree fruits, vegetable crops such as rhubarb and tomatoes, and herbaceous perennials including gladiolus and peonies. Karpow-Lipski began breeding lilacs in 1947, using as breeding stock primarily 'Capitaine Baltet', 'Madame Lemoine', 'Maréchal Foch', 'Masséna', 'Michel Buchner', 'Président Poincaré', and 'Victor Lemoine'. From the progeny of about 1600 seedlings he selected and named more than 40 new cultivars.

Of the 32 known named Karpow-Lipski cultivars only 12 appear to be grown in North America. Władysław Bugała, formerly director of the Institute of Dendrology and the Kórnik Arboretum of the Polish Academy of Sciences, and a successful lilac breeder himself, considers 'Chmurka', 'Kardynał' and 'Stefan Makowiecki' to be the best of the Karpow-Lipski originations:

'Biała Anna' (*S. vulgaris*) (white Anna), single white, 1971 (collections, commerce)

'Bogdan Przyrzykowski' (*S. vulgaris*), double magenta, 1961 (collections, commerce)

'Dr W. Bugała' (*S. vulgaris*), single pinkish, 1962 (collections)

'Fale Bałtyku' (*S. vulgaris*) (wave of the Black Sea), single bluish, 1961 (collections)

'Fryderyk Chopin' (*S. vulgaris*), single magenta, 1958 (collections)

'Kapitan Teliga' (*S. vulgaris*), single purple to violet, 1973 (collections)

'Kardynał' (*S. vulgaris*), double purple to violet, 1986 (commerce)

Syringa vulgaris 'Bogdan Przyrzykowski'. B. Peart and M. Walton

Syringa vulgaris 'Prof. Jósef Brzeziński'. B. Peart and M. Walton

Syringa (Villosae Group) 'Basia'. B. Peart and M. Walton

'Konstanty Karpow' (*S. vulgaris*), single pinkish, 1953 (collections)

'Pomorzanka' (*S. vulgaris*), single pinkish, 1962 (commerce)

'Prof. Edmund Jankowski' (*S. vulgaris*), single bluish, 1958 (collections)

'Prof. Jósef Brzeziński' (*S. vulgaris*), double pinkish, 1958 (collections)

'Stefan Makowiecki' (*S. vulgaris*), single magenta, 1958 (collections)

Władysław Bugała (b. 1924)

During the 1950s and 1960s, working at the Kórnik Arboretum in Poland, Władysław Bugała has selected and named nine open-pollinated seedlings from many thousands of seedlings of late-blooming *Syringa ×prestoniae*. Being second-generation seedlings of two Preston cultivars suggests what can be accomplished by diligent selection (Bugała 1995).

A promising hybridizing program could be undertaken, using Bugała's model, crossing some of the best Preston cultivars, selecting the very best, and backcrossing these selections. There is an untapped gene pool in the Preston cultivars. Undoubtedly many excellent cultivars would result.

Bugała received the 2003 Directors' Award, "For a lifetime of dedicated work in hybridizing the Ottawa Lilac [*Syringa ×prestoniae*] and selecting new and better cultivars, for writing papers on lilacs, and for assistance in making Polish lilac cultivars internationally available." Bugała's introductions from open-pollinated 'Octavia' and 'Ursula' are as follows (all are available in collections, a few in commerce also):

'Agata' (*S.* Villosae Group), single deep purple buds opening to rosy lilac, 1970; originally named 'Diana' (collections)

'Basia' (*S.* Villosae Group), single deep pink opening to pink, 1970; very showy (collections, commerce)

'Danusia' (*S.* Villosae Group), single deep red buds opening to pink, 1971; a heavy bloomer (collections, commerce)

'Esterka' (*S.* Villosae Group), single deep carmine-rose opening to light pink, 1970; outstanding in color (collections, commerce)

'Goplana' (*S.* Villosae Group), single carmine-pink opening to light pink, 1970 (collections, commerce)

'Jaga' (*S.* Villosae Group), single light violet fading to lavender, 1970; very large panicles (collections, commerce)

'Jagienka' (*S.* Villosae Group), single deep purple opening to lavender-violet, 1970; an early bloomer (collections, commerce)

'Nike' (*S.* Villosae Group), single deep purple opening to bright purple, 1970; a very showy late bloomer (collections, commerce)

'Telimena' (*S.* Villosae Group), single pale pink turning to white, 1970; very large, glossy leaves (collections, commerce)

Adolf Vaigla (1911–2001)

Adolf Vaigla lived through turbulent times. When he was born on 1 January 1911, Estonia was part of the Russian Empire. The revolution of 1917 brought self-government to the Estonians, but the sovereignty gained by Estonia in 1920 lasted just over 20 years. In

1940 the Soviets occupied the Baltic republics. Estonia regained independence from the Union of Soviet Socialist Republics some 50 years later in 1991.

Working in the orchard owned by his elder brother was young Adolf's first horticultural experience. He later shifted to growing vegetables for family use and for sale. From 1927 until 1929 he attended basic horticultural school at Vahi. Here Adolf met three people who became his role models for life: August Mätlik, professor (lecturer) at the University of Tartu; Karl Robert Tavel, who had extensive practical horticultural experience in countries outside Estonia; and Arvid Vilms, his elder school friend, who apprenticed in the nursery Willi at Tartu and, many years later when employed at Sheridan Nurseries in Ontario, Canada, was to become Vaigla's "Canadian connection" and the source of some of his lilac breeding stock.

In the spring of 1930 Vaigla became garden superintendent at Väimela agricultural school. Later, in 1936, after military service, he was appointed head of the technical training department of the Räpina Gardening College. Besides his work as an instructor Vaigla continued his own studies, earning a master's diploma in 1937, completing his studies in 1940, and qualifying as vocational teacher in horticulture in 1941. Later, in 1956, Vaigla earned a diploma in agronomy. The major part of his working life Vaigla spent in Räpina. He was an expert in every sector of agriculture and horticulture, and his influence on development of agricultural and horticultural practices, and on scientific development has been a significant one. His major achievements are in the acclimatization of garden plants and corn (*Zea maize*). It was Vaigla's friend Arvid Vilms who sent him selected lilac seed from Canada and later alerted staff at Royal Botanical Gardens, Hamilton, to his lilac cultivar selections (Arvid Vilms, 1960s, pers. comm. to F.V.).

Vaigla's 23 cultivars are growing at Räpina Gardening College and the botanical garden at the University of Tartu, although descriptive information is not available for all of them. A few cultivars have been reported from collections elsewhere, and some are listed commercially. Vaigla's selections of *Syringa vulgaris* are listed here:

'Aino' (*S. vulgaris*), single violet to bluish, 1970 (commerce)

'Andres' (*S. vulgaris*), single lilac to pinkish, 1969 (commerce)

'Elsa Maasik' (*S. vulgaris*), single purple (collections, commerce)

'Helgi' (*S. vulgaris*), double violet-pinkish

'Jaanika' (*S. vulgaris*)

'Kannika' (*S. vulgaris*)

'Kristjan' (*S. vulgaris*)

'Leenu' (*S. vulgaris*), double purple-pinkish

'Liina' (*S. vulgaris*), double pinkish, 1946 (commerce)

'Roosi' (*S. vulgaris*)

'Saima' (*S. vulgaris*), single violet-purple, 1952 (commerce)

'Silja' (*S. vulgaris*), double violet-pink, 1969 (commerce)

'Silvi Vrait' (*S. vulgaris*)

'Tiina' (*S. vulgaris*), single pinkish magenta, 1969 (commerce)

Vaigla also introduced several cultivars of *Syringa* ×*hyacinthiflora*:

'Arvid Vilms' (*S.* ×*hyacinthiflora*), single lilac-pink, 1955 (collections, commerce)

'Jaan' (*S.* ×*hyacinthiflora*), single magenta, 1990 (commerce)

'Kivi Ats' (*S.* ×*hyacinthiflora*), single magenta, 1956 (commerce)

'Laine' (*S.* ×*hyacinthiflora*), single pink, 1985 (commerce)

'Martin' (*S.* ×*hyacinthiflora*)

'Rauno' (*S.* ×*hyacinthiflora*)

'Vaiga' (*S.* ×*hyacinthiflora*), single pink, 1970 (commerce)

Pēteris Upītis (1896–1976)

Pēteris Upītis was born 19 May near Jumurda in the Cēsis district of Latvia. In childhood he developed an interest in horticulture, which became his life's greatest love. He studied at the Priekui Agricultural School until 1913, after which he continued his education by visiting the larger horticultural centers of Europe. Lively correspondence with horticulturists all over the world and the exchange of information and seeds continued all his life. After graduating from Agricultural School he returned to his parents' farm where he planted an orchard and started a laboratory for soil and fruit biochemical content analyses. World War II brought it all to an end.

In the autumn of 1945 Upītis started anew at the Latvian Academy of Agriculture, registering and studying fruit landraces. He traveled throughout Latvia on his bike, collecting and describing the most interesting fruit tree seedlings. At Dobele he found fertile soil for a garden on the site of the former Vārna nursery. This became the base for an experimental farm. In 1957 Upītis commenced planting his own gardens. Working with 24 horticultural crops, he bred and introduced apricots, apples, pears, plums, cherries, filberts, walnuts, quinces, raspberries, strawberries, and other fruits. He also bred lilacs. His *Syringa vulgaris* 'Esības Prieks', 'Gaiziņkalns', 'Liega', and 'Māte Ede Upītis' are well known in Latvia and abroad.

Upītis was also an artist at heart whose hobbies included photography, poetry, and music. Dobele became a visiting place for artists and writers. In 1976 the small laboratory building in which he worked became a museum. One hundred seventy-four lilac accessions grow in the museum's gardens, about half of which are of Latvian origin. Upītis named 41 selections of *Syringa vulgaris*. Unfortunately, he did not record the parentage of his lilac selections. 'Liega' and 'Mazais Princis' have been given plant breeders' rights protection in Latvia from 2004 to 2029. There are uncertainties about the correct spelling of some names and for many no description is available. Some of his cultivars are available in collections:

'Atmiņu Maurs' (*S. vulgaris*), double violet, 1950

'Bērzes Krasts' (*S. vulgaris*), single pinkish violet, 1970

'Daudzpusīgais Zemzaris' (*S. vulgaris*), single violet, 1963

'Dobeles Meitene' (*S. vulgaris*), single white, 1980

'Dobeles Sapņotājs' (*S. vulgaris*), double purple to violet, 1950

'Esības Prieks' (*S. vulgaris*), single violet to purple, 1950

'Eterena' (*S. vulgaris*), double white, 1972

'Gaistošais Sapnis' (*S. vulgaris*), single violet and white, 1972

'Gaiziņkalns' (*S. vulgaris*), double purple, 1958

'Imants Ziedonis' (*S. vulgaris*), single violet, 1975

'Jaunā Ausma' (*S. vulgaris*), single purple, 1970

'Jaunkalsnavas Nakts' (*S. vulgaris*), single bluish violet, 1958

'Jēra Maigums' (*S. vulgaris*), double violet, 1970

'Kaisma' (*S. vulgaris*), single violet, 1970

'Kristīne Baltpurviņa' (*S. vulgaris*), single white, 1970

'Liega' (*S. vulgaris*), double white, 1970

'Maija Viešņa' (*S. vulgaris*), single purple-pink, 1991

'Māte Ede Upītis' (*S. vulgaris*), single white, 1963

'Mazais Princis' (*S. vulgaris*), single white, 1989

Syringa vulgaris 'Gaistošais Sapnis'. B. Peart and M. Walton

Syringa vulgaris 'Liega'. B. Peart and M. Walton

'Mirklja Vara' (*S. vulgaris*), single pinkish violet, 1970
'Pārsteigums' (*S. vulgaris*), single violet and white, 1950
'Pērļu Zvejnieks' (*S. vulgaris*), single white, 1968
'Sārtais Viesis' (*S. vulgaris*), single pinkish violet, 1970
'Smaidošais Laiks' (*S. vulgaris*), single violet, 1970
'Tev Jaunība' (*S. vulgaris*), single violet, 1970
'Tēvzeme' (*S. vulgaris*), single white, 1965
'TTT' (*S. vulgaris*), single purple to violet, 1970
'Uscītīgais Dunkers' (*S. vulgaris*), double purple, 1969
'Vasaras Svētki' (*S. vulgaris*), single violet, 1965
'Vēstule Solveigai' (*S. vulgaris*), single magenta, 1968; plants grown in Latvia under this name appear to be mostly 'Vasaras Svētki' (Raymond Cinovskis, 4 January 1991, pers. comm. to F.V.)
'Vidzemes Debesis' (*S. vulgaris*), single violet, 1965
'Vīrietis Labākajos Gados' (*S. vulgaris*), single purple to violet, 1970
'Vita' (*S. vulgaris*), double violet, 1970
'Vitālais Sebris' (*S. vulgaris*), double light purple-pink, 1970
'Vīzija' (*S. vulgaris*), single violet, 1970
'Zaiga' (*S. vulgaris*), double violet, 1970
'Zilais Kalns' (*S. vulgaris*), single light purple-violet, 1970

Laimonis Karklins

Laimonis Karklins of Kegums, Latvia, has submitted 45 of his lilac selections for evaluation at the Dobele Horticultural Station, including 'Pērle', a double pink (see photo on page 8); and 'Santa', a single violet-pink. Reports are not yet available.

Botanical Garden, Tashkent, Uzbekistan

Lyubov' Kononovna Kravchenko (no dates) selected and named several *Syringa vulgaris* cultivars prior to 1980. Lilacs are no longer grown at the Botanical Garden, and none of the Kravchenko cultivars appear to have reached Western Europe or North America yet:

'Konfetti' (*S. vulgaris*), double lilac to magenta
'P. K. Ozolin' (*S. vulgaris*), double pinkish
'Pozdnyaya Vishnevaya' (*S. vulgaris*), double magenta

'Radostnaya' (*S. vulgaris*), single pinkish
'Valentina Tereshkova' (*S. vulgaris*), double pinkish

Botanical Garden, Kazakhstan Academy of Sciences, Almaty, Kazakhstan

Information about A. F. Mel'nik, V. G. Rubanik, and Boris K. Dyagilev, horticulturists at the Botanical Garden in Almaty, Kazakhstan, and about the *Syringa vulgaris* cultivars they introduced sometime prior to 1993 is incomplete. None of these selections have been reported yet from lilac collections in Europe and North America. The lilac breeding program at the Botanical Garden appears to have been discontinued in the 1990s, and by 2004 the entire collection had been reduced to the following 10 cultivars:

'Akademik Sakharov' (*S. vulgaris*), white
'Antonia Mel'nik' (*S. vulgaris*), double pinkish
'Belosnezhka' (*S. vulgaris*)
'Brilliant' (*S. vulgaris*), single purple, Rubanik & Dyagilev
'Chokan Volikhanov' (*S. vulgaris*)
'Hantengri' (*S. vulgaris*), double bluish to lilac
'Luch Vostoka' (*S. vulgaris*), double pinkish, large florets, pre-1980
'Medeo' (*S. vulgaris*), single pinkish
'Mirnoe Nebo' (*S. vulgaris*), double bluish
'Rassvet' (*S. vulgaris*) (dawn), single violet
'Samal' (*S. vulgaris*)
'Sholpan' (*S. vulgaris*), double bluish to lilac
'Snezhnii Kom' (*S. vulgaris*), single white
'Vesenii Motiv' (*S. vulgaris*), double pinkish

Syringa vulgaris 'Snezhnii Kom'. T. Poliakova and I. Semyonova

Kazakhstan Pedagogical Institute, Almaty,
Kazakhstan,

Mar'yam Galimovna Sagitova (1923–2001), senior lecturer at the ABAY Kazakhstan Pedagogical Institute, with the assistance of her husband, Tadeush Vikent'evich Dzevitsky (1918–2000), their son Oleg and their daughter Milada Tadeushevna Dzevitskaya, evaluated some 300 lilac seedlings from 1945 to 1991. About 32 selections were named, three of which were registered in 1991 with the statutory registration authority of the Russian Federation, and eight in 1994 with the statutory registration authority of Kazakhstan. *Syringa vulgaris* 'General Panfilov', a double purple-violet, was named in 1994 but not registered. Other selections have remained unnamed. The Institute's lilac collection no longer exists; the site was cleared in 2004. Information on distribution of these cultivars to collections or commerce is not yet available. The names of the lilacs that have received statutory registration are as follows:

'Akku' (*S. vulgaris*), single white, 1994
'Almaatinka' (*S. vulgaris*), double bluish purple, 1994
'Gul'der' (*S. vulgaris*), double light magenta, 1994
'Maĭgul' (*S. vulgaris*), single purple with light pink shade, 1994; white dot on the lower side of the petals; fading to a lighter, smoky shade
'Mar'yam' (*S. vulgaris*), single, light purple with pinkish shade, 1994; fading to a silvery shade
'Milada' (*S. vulgaris*), single light pinkish purple with crimson shade, 1994
'Oleg' (*S. vulgaris*), double light pinkish purple, 1994; outer corolla more intensely colored than inner
'Podarok Mame' (*S. vulgaris*), single pale purple with pinkish shade, 1991; fading to bluish violet
'Serezha' (*S. vulgaris*), single dark purple, 1994; fading to violet
'Suyunshi' (*S. vulgaris*), single light purple, 1991
'Tadeush' (*S. vulgaris*), single dark magenta, 1991

Lilac Hybridizing in China

In the 1980s we became aware of a lilac breeding and selecting program at Beijing Botanical Garden in China. One cultivar had been sold to a garden in Japan, and the name of it appeared on an inventory list. We traced its origin to Beijing. The lilac program had its beginning prior to the Cultural Revolution (1966–1976). Fortunately, lilacs are quite resilient; a good number of plants survived the years of neglect to become the foundation for the revived program.

The following cultivars have been selected, named, and registered by Zang Shu-Ying, professor and horticulturist, and Fan Ying-Han, horticulturist, at Beijing Botanical Garden:

'Chang Tong Bai' (*S. oblata*), single white, 1984
'Chun Ge' (*S. vulgaris*), double pinkish purple, 1984
'Luo Lan Zi' (*S. ×hyacinthiflora*), double violet, 1984
'Si Ji Lan' (*Syringa*), single bluish to purplish magenta, 1989 (*S. meyeri* × *S. pubescens* subsp. *microphylla*)
'Wan Hua Zi' (*S. oblata*), single purple, 1984
'Xiang Xue' (*S. ×hyacinthiflora*), double white, 1984
'Zi Yun' (*S. ×hyacinthiflora*), double violet, 1984

In the 1990s Dong Bao-Hua of the Beijing Botanical Garden and Institute of Botany and Chen Jun-Yu (b. 1917) of the Beijing Forestry University discovered a mutation of *Syringa pekinensis* with pale golden yellow flowers which has been named 'Bei Jing Huang' (Zhang and Cui 2000), meaning "golden garden."

We are still waiting to see these cultivars become available in the nursery trade. Although the modern pinyin transcription from Chinese characters to Roman script has been used for the Chinese cultivar names, they may not be spelled exactly the same way if and when they make their entry in North America or Europe.

CHAPTER ELEVEN

The Lilac in Art and Design

Photographic technology came into being in the 18th century and has developed ever since. It has enabled us to depict lilacs in black and white and in color, as prints and as slides. More recently, digital photography facilitates electronic transmission and the storage of pictures in the computer and on compact disk. However, the plant photographer has not replaced the graphic artist and botanical illustrator. Lilacs have appeared in drawings, paintings, woodcuts, ceramics, coins, and postage stamps.

Early Illustrations

H. Walter Lack (2000) researched the discovery and rediscovery of the lilac and documented early illustrations of lilacs in detail. Three very early original illustrations of *Syringa vulgaris* are known today. The first is a drawing in the collection of plant drawings assembled by Conrad Gesner (1516–1565), a physician in Zürich, Switzerland. This drawing is at the University Library in Erlangen, Germany, as MS 2386, folio 302r (Zoller et al. 1991). A watercolor, part of the *Codice Erbario* of Pietro Antonio Michiel (1510–1576), patrician of Venice, is at the Marciana National Library in Venice, Italy, as blue book no. 4 (De Toni 1940). The third illustration, also a watercolor, was painted around 1560 and is part of the *Erbario Dipinto* assembled by Italian naturalist Ulissi Aldrovandi (1522–1607), first director of the Bologna botanical garden in 1568 (Maioroli et al. 1995). The watercolor is at the University Library, Bologna, Italy, in *Iconographia plantarum*, volume 9, figure 356. While the dates of these three illustrations could not be precisely determined, since no items were added to these collections after the death of their respective owners, the Erlangen drawing must be pre-1565, the Venice watercolor pre-1576, and the Bologna watercolor pre-1601.

The earliest printed illustration is the colored woodcut of *Syringa vulgaris*, which appeared in Pier Andrea Mattioli's *Commentarii* (1565) in which the artist depicted the unlikely occurrence of flowers and fruits on the same branch. Presumably Mattioli had not yet seen a lilac plant and may have based his woodcut on a painting and a description (Johnston 2001). Later editions of the *Commentarii* display a different woodcut depicting a flowering branch without the seed capsules; this is the black-and-white woodcut commonly reproduced and referred to as the earliest known illustration of a lilac (as in Coats 1963, Vrugtman 1973) but erroneously dated 1565. For more detailed information consult the paper by Lack (2000) and summaries of it in German by Thorsten Lichtblau (2001) and Zvezdana Poeplau (2002).

About 1600 the bishop-prince Konrad of Germany commissioned the German apothecary and botanist Basilius Besler (1561–1629) to execute a work describing the plants in the palace gardens at Eichstätt. The resulting work, *Hortus Eystettensis*, was published in Nuremberg in 1613. Plate 1 shows *Syringa vulgaris*, left (II) a mauve lilac, "*Syringa coerulea Lusitanica Lilac Matthioli*," and right (III) a white lilac, "*Syringa flore cenerei coloris Aschenfarber Spanischer Springe-Baum*." The original drawings are in the University Library, Erlangen, Germany (Besler 1613, Stafleu and Cowan 1976).

Paintings and Prints

The Old Picture Gallery (Alte Pinakothek), one museum in the Bavarian State Picture Galleries (Bayerische Staatsgemäldesammlungen) of Munich, Germany, has in its collection a 1616–1617 painting by Peter Paul Rubens (1577–1640) and Jan Brueghel the Elder (1568–1626) titled "Madonna in a Garland of

Flowers" (oil on oak, inventory number 331/3883). The garland, painted by Brueghel, shows two lilac branches with purplish blue flowers (one on the right and one on the left) and, elsewhere (in the lower part of the garland), white lilacs. This may very well be the earliest appearance of a lilac in a flower painting (van Raalte 1963; Klaus Herder, 2002, pers. comm. to F.V.; Patrice Huet, 2004, pers. comm. to F.V.; Néret 2004).

With its entry in Western European gardens and, some time later, in North American gardens, the lilac also appeared more often in flower paintings. Mitchell (1973) gives numerous examples including, in chronological order, Alexandre François Desportes (1661–1743, French), still-life pictures; Pieter Casteels (1684–1749, Flemish), flower piece 1721; Johann Baptist Hälszel (1712–1777, German), flower piece 1771; Jacobus Linthorst (1745–1815, Dutch), *Pret à bonheur* flower piece 1808; Antoine Berjon (1754–1843, France), flower piece; Elise Bruyère (1776–1842, French), *Groupe de fleurs dans un vase d'albâtre oriental*, completed by Jean-A. Chazal (1793–1853, French), a pupil of Gérard van Spaendonck; Albertus Jonas Brandt (1788–1821, Dutch), flower piece; François Lepage (1796–1871, French), flower piece; Josef Knapp (ca. 1800–1867, Austrian), flower painting 1836; Eugène Claude (1841–1922, French), *Basket of lilac*; Mary Cassatt (1844–1926, American), impressionistic flower piece about 1889; Louis-Alexandre Cabié (1853–1939, France), still-life; Raoul-Henry Maucherat de Longpré (b. 1859, French), *Lilas*, 1877; and Georges-Léon Dufrénoy (1870–1943, French), lilacs.

The Bibliothèque Centrale of the Muséum National d'Histoire Naturelle, Paris, France, in its famous vellum collection has a watercolor of a white *Syringa vulgaris* (18: f. 36) painted about 1650 by Nicholas Robert (1614–1685) for Louis XIV (Lack 2000). A native of France, Robert stands out as one of the early botanical illustrators. Jean Baptiste Gaston d'Orléans (1608–1660), brother of Louis XIII, had commissioned Robert to document his collection of rare plants on vellum, one of the plants being the common lilac. After Gaston's death, Robert's work continued under sponsorship of Louis XIV (Mitchell 1973).

A 1785 flower piece by Gérard van Spaendonck (1746–1822) contains a single, flowering branch of *Syringa vulgaris* in the lower right-hand corner of the

painting. Foliage, flower buds, and florets are clear and sharp in detail. It is not surprising that Mitchell (1973) described Spaendonck as "perhaps the most accomplished painter of flowers in all mediums, oil, gouache, and watercolor; and clearly possessed the gifts to be a good teacher whose pupils perpetuated his style far into the nineteenth century." Born in the Netherlands, Spaendonck apprenticed in Antwerp and moved to Paris in 1769. In 1780 he was appointed professor of flower painting at the Jardin du Roi, the present-day Muséum National d'Histoire Naturelle, and became professor of iconography in 1793. He also contributed to the royal vellum collection initiated by Robert.

Cornelis van Spaendonck (1756–1840), pupil and collaborator of Gérard, followed his older brother to Paris in 1873. He became an accomplished painter of flowers. In 1795, he painted an alabaster vase on a marble table filled with various fruits and a lilac branch (Hardouin-Fugier and Grafe 1989).

When Jean Henri Jaume Saint-Hilaire (1772–1845) came to Paris about 1800, he studied under Gérard van Spaendonck. Jaume combined his study of botany with the art of illustration, becoming a scientific illustrator in the true sense of the term. Among the plates in his 1825 treatise of cultivated trees and shrubs of France we find one titled "Common Lilac" (*Syringa vulgaris*), another "Hybrid Lilac" (*S. ×chinensis*), and a third "Persian Lilac with Laciniated Leaves" (*S. ×laciniata*).

Following up on the lilac theme in botanical illustration, and taking a fast-forward to the 20th century, we cannot fail to mention freelance artist Elsie Margaret Stones (b. 1920) and her chromolithograph of *Syringa meyeri* 'Palibin' (Green 1979). Born in Australia, she studied at Swinburne Art School and the

Lilac detail from Gérard van Spaendonck's *Basket and Vase of Flowers*, 1785. F. Vrugtman

National Gallery School in Melbourne, prior to moving to England in 1951. Some 400 of her watercolors were reproduced in *Curtis's Botanical Magazine* alone (Blunt and Stearn 1994).

Readers interested in botanical illustrations of lilacs may want to search in the six-volume *Index Londinensis* (Stapf 1929–1931), which lists illustrations of flowering plants, ferns, and fern allies. Otto Stapf (1857–1933) was born in Austria, studied botany in Vienna, and was appointed keeper of the herbarium at Royal Botanic Gardens, Kew, in 1890. He was editor of *Curtis's Botanical Magazine* from 1922 until his death. Providing more recent coverage is the two-volume *Flowering Plant Index of Illustration and Information* compiled by Richard Isaacson (1979, 1982), librarian at the Andersen Horticultural Library, Minnesota Landscape Arboretum, Chanhassen, Minnesota. Not to be overlooked are the lilac illustrations in the *Flora of China* (Chang and Green 1996a).

Postcard of Hans Sachs under a lilac by Ernst Kutzer. Used by permission of Sven Fricke.

Ernst Kutzer (1880–1965), following his studies at the Art Academy in Vienna, became an accomplished illustrator of children's books, textbooks, and picture books. He wrote and illustrated more than 50 titles, and his illustrations appeared in more than 600 books. Some of the posters and postcards he created are still highly priced. One postcard in a series inspired by the operas of Richard Wagner shows Hans Sachs, the cobbler in Die Meistersinger, in front of his home under a lilac tree. It is there that Sachs sings, "*Was duftet doch der Flieder, so mild, so stark und voll!*" The "Flieder Monolog," as it is known, takes place in act two, scene three. The postcard was printed about 1908 in Graz, Austria.

Woodcuts and Wood Engravings

German-American artist Gustave Baumann (1881–1971) emigrated to the United States in 1891. He studied at the Art Institute of Chicago and at the College of Arts and Crafts (Kunstgewerbeschule) in Munich. In 1918 he moved to New Mexico. One of his color woodcuts, "A Lilac Year" (30.5 × 31 cm; 1949) is in the collection of the Museum of Fine Arts, Museums of New Mexico, Santa Fe, New Mexico.

Dutch-Canadian artist Gerard Brender à Brandis (b. 1942) emigrated to Canada in 1947. After studying fine arts at McMaster University, Hamilton, Ontario, he set up a studio, first at Carlisle and later at Stratford, Ontario. Gaining national and international recognition as wood engraver and bookwright, Brender à Brandis is perhaps best known for his botanicals. The wood engraving "White Lilacs" is reproduced in his book *Wood, Ink and Paper* (Brender à Brandis 1980).

Ceramics

The Dutch flower painters Gérard and Cornelis van Spaendonck, mentioned earlier in this chapter, worked for the Sèvres porcelain factory in Paris. Lilacs have appeared on Sèvres porcelain, as documented by this auction listing once posted on the Internet, "A pair of Louis Philippe Sèvres porcelain floral dessert plates, 1845, circular, each painted to the central circular reserve with a still life of a basket of flowers including lilac, roses, and convolvulus, upon a marble ledge, within a plain gilt band frame, the border with a continuous trail of flowering pink roses against a gilt banded ground, both with printed Louis Philippe initials in green beneath a crown."

The Royal Doulton Company has a dinnerware set named "Lilactime," referring to color, not design. The pattern shows white scrolls on a lilac band. A lovely platter made by Thomas China of Germany, however, has gorgeous white, pink, blue, and purple lilacs in the center (Thomas pattern 7392). And Royal Albert Fine China has introduced Lilac Lane Platinum, a stunning dinnerware set featuring dark purple lilacs against a white background with gold trim.

Coins

In 1998, Franktown Township of Beckwith, Ontario, Canada, issued a $5 (Canadian) Municipal Trade Token. Designed by Serge Pelletier (b. 1960), the token is 38 mm in diameter, plain edged, and enameled. The 1000 tokens in circulation are enameled antique bronze. Also issued were 200 collector tokens, of which 100 are silver plated enameled and 100 gold plated enameled. The design features lilac florets and buds. This trade token made history in the numismatic world as the first circulating enameled token. The tokens were sold out three days after their production was announced. Pelletier is a graduate of the Laval University's school of visual arts in Québec, Canada. He is a painter, sculptor, goldsmith, and writer (Vrugtman 2004f).

Postage Stamps

Postage stamps with flower designs make extraordinarily interesting collections. Stamps with lilac designs were issued in France in 1959, in the United States in 1982, in Canada in 1991 and 2007, and perhaps in additional countries. The following are a few examples.

On 17 January 1959, the French postal authority issued the 15-franc Floralies Parisiennes 1959 stamp.

It shows the Arc de Triomphe with a vignette including lilacs, rhododendron, roses, fuchsias, violets, and many other plants. The copper-plate engraving was made by Pierre Gaudon.

Quantity: 6,000,000
Dimensions: $^9/_{10} \times 1^2/_5$ inches (22 × 36 mm); vertical
Perforations: 13

On 14 April 1982, the United States Postal Service issued the 20-cent New Hampshire purple finch and lilac stamp in its Birds and Flowers of the Fifty States series designed by American artists Arthur B. Singer (1917–1990) and his son Alan D. Singer (b. 1950). The lilac is the state flower of New Hampshire. Another stamp in the series honoring Idaho's bird and flower identifies the blossom shown as "Syringa." The plant shown is *Philadelphus lewisii*, mock orange or syringa, syringa being the common name used for this genus in western North America.

Purple finch and lilac stamp honoring New Hampshire in 1982. F. Vrugtman

On 22 May 1991, Canada Post Corporation issued a series of five 40-cent commemorative stamps featuring public gardens. One of the stamps shows a vista of Royal Botanical Gardens' Rock Garden with lilac branches in the lower foreground. The stamps were introduced to mark the 50th anniversary of Royal Botanical Gardens. The designs were created by David Wyman, based on illustrations by Gerard Gauci; the contemporary artists live in Toronto, Ontario, Canada.

Quantity: 3,000,000 (of each individual design)
Dimensions: $1^1/_5 \times 1^3/_5$ inches (30.5 × 40 mm); vertical
Perforations: 13+

Finnish stamp featuring lilac in 2006.
F. Vrugtman

Canadian postage stamps featuring public gardens in 1991.
F. Vrugtman

On 4 March 2004 the U.S. Postal Service issued a 37-cent Garden Bouquet stamp. White lilacs and pink roses make up the bouquet, which is a reproduction of a chromolithograph probably printed in Germany circa 1880 to 1900. The artist and engraver are unknown. Richard Sheaff of Scottsdale, Arizona, was the designer and art director for the stamp.

Quantity: 750,000,000

In 2006, on the 150th anniversary of the Finnish stamp, Finland issued several first-class non-denomi-

national stamps. One of these showed a purple lilac twig in bloom. The original artwork was painted by Leena Airikkala. The Åland Islands (between Finland and Sweden) and the Ukraine have also issued lilac stamps in recent years. No doubt other countries will do so in the future.

On 1 March 2007, Canada Post Corporation issued two 52-cent stamps featuring lilacs. One stamp features the white-flowered *Syringa vulgaris* 'Princess Alexandra', the oldest Canadian hybrid, and the other shows the purple *S.* (Villosae Group) 'Isabella'. The stamps were designed by Isabelle Toussaint based on photographs taken at the Central Experimental Farm lilac collection where *S.* (Villosae Group) 'Isabella' was originated by Isabella Preston.

Quantity: 10,000,000
Dimensions: 1³⁄₁₀ × 1 inch (34 mm x 25.6 mm); horizontal
Perforations: 13+

Lilac stamps from Canada in 2007.
F. Vrugtman

APPENDIX A
Noted Plant Explorers and Taxonomists
of *Syringa*

This is by no means a definitive list; we may have missed some important people and included some marginal ones. Nevertheless, the toils and efforts of the individuals mentioned here have contributed to the knowledge of the genus *Syringa* and the diversity of lilacs in our gardens. The two primary sources of information consulted on spelling of names and dates of birth and death are *Zander Handwörterbuch der Pflanzennamen* (Encke et al. 1984) and *Index of Botanists* (Harvard University Herbaria 2001).

Aitchison, James Edward Tierney (1836–1898); English surgeon, botanist, and plant explorer, who served as a major in the Bengal army.

Anderson, Edgar (1897–1969); American botanist and writer.

Bai Pei-Yu (b. 1938); Chinese botanist.

Baring, Charles (b. 1937); second Lord Howick of Glendale, founder of Howick Arboretum (Alnwick, Northumberland, England), plant collector in India and Nepal.

Bartholomew, Bruce Monroe (b. 1946); American botanist, member of the 1980 Sino-American Botanical Expedition to western Hubei, China.

Bean, William Jackson (1863–1947); English botanist, Royal Botanic Gardens, Kew, Richmond, England.

Bell, Andrew C. (contemporary); American botanist, collected *Syringa* during an expedition to Yunnan and Sichuan, China, in 1997.

Berezovski, Mikhail M. (19th century); Russian zoologist, traveled with Grigoriĭ Potanin in China from 1891 to 1894.

Blinkworth, Robert (19th century); English plant explorer in Asia in the 1830s, collected for Nathaniel Wallich, director of the East India Company's botanic gardens at Calcutta.

Blume, Carl Ludwig von (1796–1862); Dutch botanist and first director of the Rijksherbarium, Leiden, Netherlands.

Boerhaave, Hermann (1668–1738); Dutch physician and patron of Carl Linnaeus, listed *Syringa vulgaris* (as *S. caerulea*) in his 1710 *Index Plantarum* (p. 252).

Bonvalot, Pierre Gabriel Édouard (1853–1933); French plant collector in China.

Borbás, Vincźe von (1844–1905); Hungarian botanist.

Borzan, Želimir (b. 1940); Croatian dendrologist, photographer, and author; professor at the Faculty of Forestry, University of Zagreb who explored the native range of *Syringa vulgaris* and *S. josikaea* with Charles Holetich.

Boufford, David (b. 1941); American botanist, member of the 1980 Sino-American Botanical Expedition to western Hubei, China.

Brandis, Sir Dietrich (1824–1907); German botanist who worked for the British Forest Service in India from 1855 to 1883.

Bretschneider, Emil V. (1833–1901); physician to the Russian legation in Beijing, botanist, and plant collector.

Bristol, Peter W. (contemporary); American horticulturist, member of the North America–China Plant Exploration Consortium collecting in China in 1994.

Bunge, Alexander von (1803–1890); Russian physician, botanist, and plant explorer in northern China and other areas of Asia.

Bureau, Louis Édouard (1830–1918); French botanist; director of the herbarium at the Muséum d'Histoire Naturelle in Paris, France.

Cesalpino, Andrea (1519–1603); Italian physician, botanist, physiologist, author of *De plantis* (1583), founder and director (1553–1592) of the botanical garden at the University of Pisa.

Chang Mei-Chen (b. 1933); Chinese plant taxonomist and specialist on Oleaceae.

Chen Xin-Lu (contemporary); Chinese botanist and taxonomist, collected lilacs in China in the 1990s.

Clark, Robert B. (1914–2005); American botanist and close associate of Fiala who wrote or compiled certain sections of Fiala's original lilac book.

Clarke, William Smith (1826–1886); American agriculturist and botanist, explored the flora of Japan from 1876 to 1877 while president of the Agricultural College at Sapporo.

Cornu, Marie Maxime (1843–1901); French botanist.

Curtis, William (1746–1799); English horticulturist, founder and publisher of *Curtis's Botanical Magazine*, London, a source of illustrations of *Syringa* species.

David, Armand (1826–1900); French Jesuit missionary-botanist and plant explorer in China.

Decaisne, Joseph (1807–1882); Belgian botanist who worked at the Jardin des Plantes, Paris.

Delavay, Jean Marie (1834–1895); French Jesuit missionary-botanist and plant explorer in China.

Diels, Friedrich Ludwig Emil (1874–1945); German botanist, director of the Botanic Garden and Botanical Museum Berlin-Dahlem, prolific writer, author of *Die Flora von Central-China* (1901).

Dorsett, Palemon Howard (1862–1943); American plant collector for the U.S. Department of Agriculture, Bureau of Plant Industry, Washington, D.C.

Dumont de Courset, Baron George(s) Louis Marie (1746–1824); French botanist and horticultural writer.

Farrer, Reginald John (1880–1920); English plant explorer in China and horticultural writer.

Forrest, George (1873–1932); Scottish botanist and plant explorer in China.

Fortune, Robert (1812–1880); English horticulturist, writer, and plant explorer in China and other areas of Asia.

Franchet, Adrien René (1834–1900); French botanist at the Jardin des Plantes, Paris, worked on many of the plant collections sent home by French plant collectors in Asia, including Armand David and Jean Marie Delavay.

Garnier, Marie Joseph François (19th century); French naval officer and plant collector in China in the 1860s.

Gill, William John (1843–1882); British plant collector in China.

Giraldi, Giuseppe (d. 1901); Italian missionary and plant explorer in China.

Green, Peter Shaw (b. 1920); English plant taxonomist, specialist in Oleaceae, Royal Botanic Gardens, Kew, England.

Hara, Hiroshi (1911–1986); Japanese botanist, University of Tokyo, studied the flora of eastern Himalaya and Nepal.

Hatusima, Sumihoko (b. 1906); Japanese botanist.

Hermann, Paulus (1640–1695); Dutch physician and botanist, explorer of the flora of Sri Lanka, director of the botanical garden at the University of Leiden from 1680 to 1695, listed *Syringa vulgaris* (as *Syringa coerulea*) and *Syringa ×persica* (as *Syringa Persica foliis integris*) in his 1687 publication.

Hesse, Hermann Albrecht (1852–1937); German nursery owner in Weener (Ems), Lower Saxony, Germany.

Heuffel, János A. (1800–1857); Hungarian botanist and physician, reported on native habitat of *Syringa vulgaris* in 1831.

Hoffman, Marco H. A. (contemporary); Dutch horticultural taxonomist, Boskoop, Netherlands.

hort. Latin for *hortorum* (of gardens) or *hortulanorum* (of gardeners), used in former times for botanical epithets for which the author was unknown. Some of these epithets became cultivar epithets after 1953, with the introduction of the *ICNCP* (Stearn 1953).

Hosie, Alexander (d. 1905); English (?) plant collector in China in the 1880s.

Incarville, Pierre Nicholas le Cheron d' (1706–1757); French Jesuit missionary-botanist and plant explorer in China.

Jacquin, Joseph Franz von (1766–1839); Austrian botanist.

Jäger, Hermann (1815–1890); German physician and botanist.

Jovanovič, Branislav (contemporary); botanist, Belgrade University, who described and named three botanical varieties of *Syringa vulgaris* in 1980 with Emilia Vukicevič.

Kingdon-Ward, Francis (1885–1958); English plant collector, collected a herbarium specimen in 1914 from which was described the legendary *Syringa pinetorum*, which is still waiting to be rediscovered.

Kirchner, Georg (1837–1885); German gardener and botanist.

Kirilov, Porfirij Jevdokimovic (1801–1864); Russian physician to the 11th Ecclesiastical Mission at Beijing, explored for plants ca. 1821–1842.

Kitaibel, Pál (Paul) (1757–1817); Hungarian botanist, discovered ca. 1800 a new lilac and proposed the name *Syringa prunifolia*, which was never published. This lilac was later named *S. josikaea* by Joseph Jacquin.

Koch, Karl Heinrich Emil (1809–1879); German botanist, dendrologist, and pomologist.

Koehne, Bernhard Adalbert Emil (1848–1918); German teacher and botanist.

Komarov, Vladimir Leontievich (1869–1945); Russian plant explorer and botanist, initiator of the *Flora of the USSR* (*Flora SSSR*), who traveled and collected in Manchuria and Korea from 1893 to 1895.

La Rue, Carl Downey (1888–1955); American botanist, University of Michigan, in 1948 studied lilacs growing on Mackinac Island, Michigan.

Lack, Hans Walter (b. 1949); Austrian botanist, researched and documented the story of the discovery and rediscovery of the common lilac, *Syringa vulgaris*.

Lancaster, Charles Roy (b. 1937); English horticulturist, made several collecting trips to China between 1981 and 1986.

Léveillé, Augustin Abel Hector (1863–1918); French botanist.

Lindley, John (1799–1865); English botanist, secretary of the Royal Horticultural Society, London, for forty years.

Lingelsheim, Alexander von (1874–1937); German botanist.

Linnaeus, Carl (1707–1778); Swedish biologist, physician, and botanist, who founded binomial nomenclature, the starting point of present-day nomenclature, author of *Genera Plantarum* (1737) and *Species Plantarum* (1753). Also known as Carl von Linné after he was ennobled in 1762.

Loddiges, George (1784–1846); English nurseryman and botanist, son of Conrad Loddiges, a Dutch immigrant who founded a well-known nursery in Hackney, near London, England.

Ma Yu-Chuan (b. 1916); Chinese botanist.

Maack, Richard (1825–1886); Russian botanist and plant collector in China and other areas of Asia.

Maire, Édouard-Ernest (1848–1932); French plant collector in China.

Maximowicz, Karl Johann (1827–1891); Russian botanist, plant collector in China, and author.

McKelvey, Susan Delano (1883–1964); American botanist and author of *The Lilac* (1928).

McNamara, William A. (contemporary); Quarryhill Botanical Garden (Glen Ellen, California), plant collector in India and Nepal.

Meng Zheng-Gui (contemporary); collected *Syringa mairei* in Yunnan in 2003.

Meyer, Frank Nicholas (1875–1918); Dutch-American botanist and plant explorer, who collected in China and other areas of Asia for the U.S. Department of Agriculture, Bureau of Plant Industry, Office of Foreign Seed and Plant Introduction, Washington, D.C.

Meyer, Paul W. (b. 1952); American horticulturist, member of the North America–China Plant Exploration Consortium collecting in China in 1994.

Miller, Philip (1691–1771); English gardener, botanist, and author of *The Gardeners Dictionary* (1768) in which he described *Syringa laciniata* as a true species.

Moldenke, Harold Norman (1909–1996); American botanist.

Möllendorf, Otto F. von (1848–1903); German botanist and plant collector in China.

Mordant de Launey, Jean Claude Mien (ca. 1750–1816); botanist and librarian at the Jardin des Plantes, Paris.

Morse, Warner J. (1872–1931); American plant collector for the U.S. Department of Agriculture, Bureau of Plant Industry, Washington, D.C.

Munting, Abraham (1626–1683); Dutch botanist and physician, who described *Syringa* ×*persica* (as *Jasminum persicum*) and *S. vulgaris* (as *Syringa Arabum flore coeruleo*) in 1672.

Nakai, Takenoshin (1882–1952); Japanese plant taxonomist.

Orléans, Henri d' (1867–1901); French prince, who collected plants with Pierre Bonvalot in China.

Pampanini, Renato (1875–1949); Italian botanist.

Persoon, Christiaan H. (1761–1836); Dutch-German botanist, who lived in France.

Potanin, Grigorii N. (1835–1920); Siberian-Russian writer and plant explorer, who made four trips to China, including one for the Russian Geographical Society from 1891 to 1894.

Prince, William Robert (1795–1869); American botanist, plant explorer, and owner of Prince Nursery (1737–1850), Flushing-Landing, Long Island, New York.

Pringle, James Scott (b. 1937); American-Canadian plant taxonomist and expert on *Syringa*, at Royal Botanical Gardens, Hamilton, Ontario, Canada.

Purdom, William (1880–1921); English plant explorer in China and other areas of Asia for the Veitch nursery, Chelsea, England, and subsequently for the Arnold Arboretum, Jamaica Plain, Massachusetts.

Qu Shi-Zeng (b. 1926); Chinese botanist.

Radde, Gustav F. R. J. von (1831–1903); German-Russian biologist, founder-director of a Caucasian museum in Tbilisi (Georgia), and plant collector in Siberia from 1855 to 1859.

Rehder, Alfred (1863–1949); German-American botanist, dendrologist, author, and curator of the Arnold Arboretum of Harvard University from 1918 to 1940.

Reichenbach, Heinrich Gottlieb Ludwig (1793–1879); German botanist and director of the Hamburg (Germany) botanical garden.

Renault, Bernard (1836–1904); French botanist and horticulturist.

Rochel, Anton (1770–1847); Hungarian botanist at the University of Budapest, who reported *Syringa vulgaris* growing in western Romania in 1828.

Rock, Joseph F. C. (1884–1962); Austrian-American linguist, botanist, and plant explorer, who collected for Arnold Arboretum, Jamaica Plain, Massachusetts.

Royle, John Forbes (1798–1858); English physician, botanist, superintendent of East India Company botanic garden at Saharanpur, Uttar Pradesh, India, from 1823 to 1832, subsequently professor at King's College, London, England.

Ruprecht, Franz J. I. (1814–1870); Austrian-Russian plant taxonomist, who wrote about the flora of Russia in 1857.

Schmidt, Franz (1751–1834); Austrian nurseryman who first used the name *Syringa "Chinensis"* in print, but without description.

Schneider, Camillo Karl (1876–1951); German dendrologist, plant taxonomist, landscape architect, and writer, who traveled in western China in 1913 and worked at the Arnold Arboretum, Jamaica Plain, Massachusetts, from 1915 to 1918.

Schur, Philipp J. F. (1799–1878); Austrian teacher, pharmacist, and botanist.

Sibthorp, John (1758–1796); British botanist who in 1794 rediscovered the native range of *Syringa vulgaris*.

Smith, Harald (Harry) Karl August (1889–1971); Swedish botanist in Uppsala, who collected plants in China.

Smith, Sir William Wright (1875–1956); Scottish botanist, director of Royal Botanic Garden, Edinburgh, Scotland, from 1922 to 1956, made extensive collecting trips in the Himalaya Mountains.

Sontag, A. (19th century); collected plants in Korea from 1894 to 1895.

Soulié, Jean André (1858–1905); French Jesuit missionary-botanist and plant collector in China.

Spongberg, Stephen Alan (b. 1942); American botanist, member of the 1980 Sino-American Botanical Expedition to western Hubei, China, also collected in China in 1997.

Sprenger, Carl Ludwig (1846–1917); German nurseryman, plant breeder, and botanist, who established a nursery in Naples, Italy, in 1877 and in his final years was superintendent of the German Kaiser's garden on the Greek island of Corfu.

Szeczenyi (19th century); plant collector in China in the 1880s.

Tang Tsin (1897–1984); Chinese botanist.

Tatarinov, Aleksander (1817–1886); Russian plant collector in China from 1840 to 1850.

Tournefort, Joseph Pitton de (1656–1708); French botanist at the Jardin des Plantes, Paris, from 1688 to 1708 who devised a classification for plants that was used in France for almost a century.

Turczaninov, Nicolai Stepanovič (1796–1864); Russian plant taxonomist.

Vahl, Martin (1749–1804); Danish botanist and student of Carl Linnaeus.

Velenovský, Josef (1858–1949); Czech botanist.

Verdoorn, Frans (1906–1984); Dutch bryologist, biohistorian, and publisher of *Chronica Botanica* from 1935 to 1962.

Vrugtman, Freek (b. 1927); Dutch-Canadian horticultural botanist, and author; International Lilac Registrar, International Cultivar Registration Authority for *Syringa* L. (Oleaceae), Royal Botanical Gardens, Hamilton, Ontario; compiler of the *International Register and Checklist of Cultivar Names in the Genus* Syringa (1976–).

Vukicević, Emilia (contemporary); botanist, Belgrade University, who described and named three botanical varieties of *Syringa vulgaris* in 1980 with Branislav Jovanović.

Wallich, Nathaniel (1786–1854); Danish-English physician, botanist, plant explorer in Asia, director of the East India Company's botanic gardens at Calcutta.

Weston, Richard (1733–1806); English botanist who recognized two color varieties of the common lilac.

Willdenow, Carl Ludwig von (1765–1812); German botanist, director of the Botanic Garden and Botanical Museum Berlin-Dahlem, Germany.

Wilson, Ernest H. (1876–1930); English-American botanist and plant collector in China for James Veitch and Sons nursery, Chelsea, England, from 1899 to 1902, and subsequently for Arnold Arboretum, Jamaica Plain, Massachusetts, from 1906–1919.

Wister, John Caspar (1887–1982); American horticulturist and landscape architect; prolific horticultural writer; International Lilac Registrar 1956–1975; founding member of the International Lilac Society, 1971.

Yaltirik, Faik (b. 1930); Turkish botanist at the Forestry Department of the University of Istanbul at Bahceköy.

Zhou Si-Quang (b. 1937); Chinese botanist.

APPENDIX B
Lilac Hybridizers and Originators

This annotated alphabetical list is based on the *International Register and Checklist of Cultivar Names in the Genus Syringa*, Appendix D, "Annotated Alphabetical List of Lilac Cultivar Originators," compiled by Freek Vrugtman, International Lilac Registrar (Vrugtman 2007c). It includes all known lilac cultivar originators. However, since not every lilac cultivar name that has appeared in print during the past 250 years has been referred to in this volume, not every originator's name will have appeared in this book either. Only brief identifications are made; precise data on originators are not always known or available.

Alexander Sr., J. Herbert (1893–1977); nurseryman, Dahliatown Nurseries (defunct), Middleboro, Massachusetts.

Alexander III, John H. (contemporary); plant propagator, Arnold Arboretum of Harvard University, Jamaica Plain, Massachusetts.

Anderson, Edgar Shannon (1897–1969); botanist, United States.

Arboretum Norr, Luelå, Sweden.

Audibert nursery (19th century); operated by brothers in Tonnelle near Tarascon, Provence, France, but now defunct.

Bachtell, Kris R. (contemporary); American horticulturist, Morton Arboretum, Lisle, Illinois, and member of the North America–China Plant Exploration Consortium collecting in China in 1994.

Bakker and Sons nursery, J. C.; founded in 1949 in Saint Catharines, Ontario, Canada.

Baldwin, Clarence Earl (1876–1970); nurseryman, Baldwin Rose Gardens nursery (defunct), Omaha, Nebraska.

Ballreich, Reva (b. 1925); lilac collector, Idyllwood, California.

Balsgård; Elitplantstationen Balsgård, Sweden.

Balet nursery; founded in 1720 in Troyes, Champagne-Ardenne region, France, and active with lilacs from 1842 to 1900 but now defunct.

Barankiewicz, Henryk (contemporary); nurseryman, Stary Pożóg, Lublin, Poland.

Barbier nursery; operated by nurseryman Albert Barbier (1845–1931) in Orléans, France; at times the nursery was known as Transon Brothers nursery.

Barnes Jr., Franklin Lockwood, and Alice Gee (Mrs. Franklin L.) Barnes (contemporary); fruit farmers, Julian, California.

Barnes, Laura Leggett (Mrs. Albert C.) (1873–1966); horticulturist, Merion Station, Pennsylvania.

Barry, Patrick (1816–1890); nurseryman, Mount Hope Nurseries, Rochester, New York. (Ellwanger and Barry)

Baudriller (no dates); nurseryman, Gennes, Maine-et-Loire, France.

Becker, Gilbert (1909–1968); farmer, Climax, Michigan.

Behnsch, Reinhold (d. 1912); nurseryman, Dürrgoy near Breslau, Silesia, Germany (now Wrocław, Poland).

Bellion, Claude (contemporary); nurseryman, Pépinières Minier, Beaufort-en-Vallée, Maine-et-Loire, France.

Berdeen, Kenneth Warren (1907–1987); steam engineer, Kennebunk, Maine.

Berniau, L. (no dates); nursery owner, Orléans, France.

Bertin âiné, or Bertin père (ca. 1808); horticulturist, Boulevard de la Reine, Versailles, France.

Bibikova, Veronika Fedorovna (contemporary); horticulturist, Central Botanical Garden; Minsk, Belarus. (Smol'skiĭ and Bibikova)

Billiard, Ch. (no dates); nurseryman, Fontenay-aux-Roses near Paris, France.

Blacklock, Mary Eliza (1860–1956); nurserywoman, Rowancroft Gardens (defunct), Meadowvale, Ontario, Canada.

Block, Allan F. (contemporary); nurseryman, Romulus, Michigan.

Boice, Dorothy Wardell (Mrs. Van Ness L.) (no dates); Friendly Acres, Salt Point, New York.

Boughen, Ron (contemporary); nurseryman, Ron Boughen Nursery, Valley River, Manitoba, Canada.

Brahy-Ekenholm, Joseph (1815–1873), and Adrienne Marie Ekenholm (1794–1879); amateur horticulturists, Herstal near Liège, Belgium.

Brand, Archie Mack (1871–1953); lawyer, horticulturist, and peony breeder, Faribauld, Minnesota. Archie's father, Oliver Franklin Brand (1844–1921), established Brand Peony Farm in 1868. The company operated for 110 years under various names and owner-managers. Archie joined the firm in 1899. Myrtle G. Gentry (1882–1972) was the owner-operator from 1953 to 1956. Brothers Archibald P. Tischler and Robert W. Tischler (1911–2007) owned and operated Brand Peony Farm from 1956 to 1976, then started Tischler Peony Garden in Faribauld.

Briot, Pierre Louis ("Charles") (1804–1888); nurseryman at a government nursery, Trianon-Versailles, France.

Bron, Ed (contemporary); nurseryman, Bron and Sons Nursery, Grand Forks, British Columbia, Canada.

Brown, Joan Leslie (contemporary); plant breeder from 1974 to 1981 at Royal Botanical Gardens, Hamilton, Ontario, Canada.

Bruchet (no dates); nurseryman, St Rambery-sur-Loire, Loire, France.

Bugała, Władysław (b. 1924); horticulturist and plant breeder, Kórnik Arboretum of the Polish Academy of Sciences, Kórnik, Poland.

Buis, Cornelis (1901–1988); florist in Aalsmeer, Netherlands, in the C. Buis and Sons nursery started by his father and later operated by his mother.

Bunnik, Gerard (b. 1954); nurseryman, Firma Alb. Maarse, Aalsmeer, Netherlands. See Maarse and Son nursery for more details.

Case, Bernard Orville (1866–1936); farmer and nurseryman, Fruit Valley (now a neighborhood in Vancouver), Washington.

Cassegrain (20th century); floriculturist at Pépinières Grandes Roseraies, Orléans, France.

Castle, Minerva Swann (1891–1976); nurserywoman, Rowancroft Gardens (defunct), Meadowvale, Ontario, Canada.

Chapman, Colin (contemporary); keeper of a National Collection of Lilacs at Wyvestone, Suffolk, England,

under the umbrella of the National Council for the Conservation of Plants and Gardens.

Chen Jun-Yu (b. 1917); Beijing Forestry University, Beijing, China. (Dong and Chen)

Chenault, Léon (1853–1930) and his son Raymond Chenault (no dates); nurserymen, Orléans, France.

Child, Harold L. (1897–1991); millwright machinist, Dixfield, Maine.

Clark, Robert Brown (1914–2005); botanist, Meredith, New Hampshire.

Clarke Nursery; established in San Jose, California, as W. B. Clarke nursery by Walter B. Clarke (1876–1953), becoming J. Clarke nursery when operated by James F. Clarke (contemporary).

Cleaves, Kenneth (contemporary); Lincolnville, Maine.

Cochet the Elder, Pierre (1803–1853); nurseryman and rosarian, Suisnes (now Grisy-Suisnes), Seine-et-Marne, France.

Cumming, William Archibald (1911–1999); horticulturist, Agriculture and Agri-Food Canada, Morden Research Centre from 1955 to 1975, Morden, Manitoba, Canada.

Daniels, George (d. 1995); nurseryman, L. E. Cooke Company, Visalia, California.

Darimont (no dates); horticulturist, Liège, Belgium.

Dauvesse nursery, Orléans, France.

De Belder, Robert (1921–1995), and Jelena De Belder-Kovačič (1925–2003); amateur horticulturists and proprietors of Arboretum Kalmthout and Domain Hemelrijk in Essen, Belgium.

de Wilde, Robert C. (contemporary); marketing manager, Doylestown, Pennsylvania.

Delbard, Georges (1906–1995); nurseryman and plant breeder, Delbard S.C.A., Commentry, Allier, France.

Delcor, François (1879–1969); nurseryman, Pépinière Delcor (now defunct), Lebbeke, Belgium.

Descanso Gardens, La Cañada-Flintridge, California.

Dingle Plants and Gardens; Margaret Handley (no dates; contemporary); Stamford, Lincolnshire, United Kingdom.

Dong Boa-Hua (contemporary); professor, Beijing Botanical Garden and Institute of Botany, Beijing, China. (Dong and Chen)

Dorsett, Palemon Howard (1862–1943); agricultural plant explorer for the U.S. Department of Agriculture, Bureau of Plant Industry, Washington, D.C.

Dougall, James (1810–1888); nurseryman, merchant, and politician, who operated Windsor Nurseries, Windsor, Ontario, Canada.

Draps, Jean Baptiste Léopold (1882–1956); horticulturist and nurseryman, who operated the Draps-Tomaes nursery from 1922 to 1950 in Vilvoorde and Koningsloo, near Brussels, Belgium.

Dubois (no dates); plant breeder, France.

Dunbar, John (1859–1927); horticulturist and assistant superintendent of parks from 1891 to 1926 for the County of Monroe, Department of Parks, Rochester, New York.

Dyagilev, Boris K. (contemporary); horticulturist, Botanical Garden, Kazakhstan Academy of Sciences, Almaty, Kazakhstan. (Mel'nik, Rubanik, and Dyagilev; Rubanik and Dyagilev)

Dzevitskaya, Milada Tadeushevna (contemporary); daughter of Mar'yam Sagitova, Almaty, Kazakhstan, who with her mother introduced new lilac hybrids. (Sagitova and Dzevitskaya)

Dzevitsky, Tadeush Vikent'evich (1918–2000); electrical engineer, contractor, and lilac breeder, Almaty, Kazakhstan; married to Mar'yam Sagitova. (Sagitova and Dzevitsky)

Eaton, Mark Miller (1900–1992); proprietor of Lilac Land, Glen Head, New York. (Havemeyer and Eaton)

Egolf, Donald (1928–1990); plant breeder, United States Department of Agriculture, U.S. National Arboretum, Washington, D.C. (Egolf and Pooler)

Egorova, M. (no dates); Lesostepnaya Experimental Breeding Station (LOSS), Meshchersk, Lipetsk Region, Russia. (Romanova and Egorova)

Eichler nursery, Moritz (pre-1940); a defunct nursery, Chemnitz, Saxony, Germany.

Ellwanger, George (1816–1906); nurseryman, Mount Hope Nurseries, Rochester, New York. (Ellwanger and Barry)

Engler (no dates); probably Firma Blumenland Engler, Leipzig-Miltitz, Saxony, Germany.

Eveleens Maarse Sr., Dirk (1881–1975); nurseryman, W. Topsvoort nursery, Aalsmeer, Netherlands.

Eveleens nursery, J.; Aalsmeer, Netherlands.

Fan Ying-Han (contemporary); horticulturist, Beijing Botanical Garden and Institute of Botany, Beijing, China. (Zang and Fan)

Farr, Bertrand H. (1863–1924); nurseryman, Farr Nursery, Wyomissing, Pennsylvania.

Felix and Dykhuis nursery; founded in 1887 by B. B. C. Felix (no dates) and Dikhuis (no dates), as the name was originally spelled, in Boskoop, Netherlands.

Fenicchia, Richard Americo (1908–1997); horticulturist with the County of Monroe, Department of Parks, Rochester, New York.

Fiala, John L. (1924–1990); American Jesuit priest, clinical psychologist, amateur horticulturist, plant breeder, proprietor of Falconskeape, and partner in Ameri-Hort Research (defunct), Medina, Ohio.

Flemer III, William (d. 2007); nurseryman and plant breeder, Princeton Nursery, Princeton, New Jersey.

Fleming, Robert Alexander (1924–2005); horticulturist, Horticultural Research Station of Ontario, Vineland Station, Ontario, Canada.

Franklin, Alonzo Berry (1858–1944); nurseryman, Minneapolis, Minnesota.

Franklin, Mabel Lucille (1892–1987); horticulturist, Minnetonka, Minnesota.

Fröbel, Karl Otto (1844–1906); nurseryman and plant breeder, Fröbel Nursery, Zürich, Switzerland.

Gardner Nursery, Edward J.; operated by nurseryman brothers Edward James Gardner (1891–1952) and Robert Louis Gardner (1909–1972), Horicon, Wisconsin.

Gathoye, François (1807–1859); nurseryman, Bayards lez-Liège, Belgium.

Gielis, Louis (20th century); Brussels, Belgium.

Gireoud, Friedrich August Hermann (1821–1896); horticulturist, Sagan, Silesia, Germany (now Zagan, Poland), and Berlin, Germany.

Gorb, Vasil' Kuz'movich (contemporary); horticulturist since 1971 at Central Republic Botanical Garden, Kiev, Ukraine. (Rubtzov, Zhogoleva, Lyapunova, and Gorb)

Gorshkovitch; perhaps from Belarus.

Goscote Nurseries, Cossington, Leicestershire, England.

Gouchault, Auguste (1851–1936); nurseryman, Orléans, France.

Gram, Kai Jorgen Arthur (1877–1961); botanist, University of Copenhagen, Denmark.

Grant, Alvan Roger (1916–2007); horticulturist, County of Monroe, Department of Parks, Rochester, New York.

Grigor'ev, Alexander Grigor'evich (contemporary); horticulturist from 1960 to 1986 at the State Nikita Botanical Gardens, Yalta, Crimea, Ukraine.

Grunewald, Friedrich Wilhelm (1864–1933); nurseryman, Zossen, Brandenburg, Germany.

Hancock, Marcus Leslie (1892–1977); nurseryman, Woodland Nurseries, Mississauga, Ontario, Canada.

Hathaway Nurseries, Visalia, California.

Hauck, Cornelius John (1893–1967); industrialist and horticulturist, of Cincinnati, Ohio, who donated his horticultural library and 8-acre (3.2-ha) estate, Sooty Acres (now Hauck Botanic Garden), to the city.

Havemeyer, Theodore Augustus (1868–1936); industrialist, amateur horticulturist, and plant breeder, who established a nursery at Brookville, Long Island, New York. In 1937 his widow, Katherine S. Havemeyer, was the proprietress of the nursery, known as Cedar Hill Nursery. (Havemeyer and Eaton) (Havemeyer and Sears).

Hawkins, Roy Frank (1886–1972); farmer, La Porte City, Iowa.

Heard, William Russell (1916–1995); landscape architect and nurseryman, Heard Gardens, Johnston, Iowa.

Heeren Jzn, K., florists, Aalsmeer, Netherlands.

Henry, Louis (1853–1903); horticulturist at the Jardin des Plantes, Paris.

Henry, Mary Gibson (Mrs. John Norman) (1884–1967); horticulturist, Gladwyne, Pennsylvania.

Herman, Dale E. (contemporary); research horticulturist, North Dakota State University, Fargo.

Herrmann, John (contemporary); nurseryman, John Herrmann Nursery, Waterford, Ontario, Canada.

Hers, Joseph (1884–1965); Belgian railroad official and amateur botanist, who collected seeds and herbarium specimens for the Arnold Arboretum in northern China from 1910 to 1924.

Hetz, Charles W. (1906–1953); nurseryman, Fairview Evergreen Nurseries, Fairview, Pennsylvania.

Hilborn, Ernest Carroll (1876–1953); nurseryman, Northwest Nursery Company, Valley City, North Dakota.

Hildreth, Aubrey Clare (1893–1975); horticulturist, U.S. Department of Agriculture, Denver, Colorado. (Dorsett, Morse, and Hildreth)

Hillier and Sons nursery; established in 1864 in Winchester, Surrey, England, by Edwin Hillier (d. 1926); succeeded by sons Edwin Lawrence Hillier (1865–1944) and Arthur Richard Hillier (b. 1877); succeeded by Sir Harold George Hillier (1905–1985), son of Edwin Lawrence Hillier; succeeded by sons John

George Hillier (contemporary) and Robert Hillier (contemporary). The Hilliers are the founders of Jermyns Gardens and Arboretum at Ampfield, Romsey, Hampshire, England.

Hodgdon, Philip B. (d. 1978); teacher and nurseryman, Hamesbest Nursery (defunct), Randolph Center, Vermont.

Hohman, Henry J. (1896–1974); nurseryman, Kingsville Nurseries (defunct), Kingsville, Maryland.

Holland, Neal S. (contemporary); horticulturist and plant breeder at North Dakota State University, Fargo, proprietor of Sheyenne Garden nursery in Harwood, North Dakota.

Horntvedt, Siri (Kjaer) (contemporary); horticulturist at Agricultural University of Norway in Ås, now the Norwegian University of Life Sciences.

Hoser, Peter (1857–1939); horticulturist, Warsaw, Poland.

Hughes, Wayne and Millie (contemporary); aerospace engineer, Cambridge Springs, Pennsylvania.

Jacob-Makoy, Lambert (1790–1873); doyen of Belgian horticulture; nurseryman, Firma L. Jacob-Makoy (ca. 1810–1861) and Firma L. Jacob-Wayne (1861–1873), Liège, Belgium.

Karolin's, Alimonies (contemporary); amateur plant breeder, Begums, Latvia.

Karpow-Lipski, Mikołaj (1896–1981); amateur plant breeder, Kończewice near Chełmza, Poland.

Keaffaber, Merle Lowell (1928–1988), and Anna Mae Keaffaber (1921–1994); Perrysburg, Ohio.

Keessen Jr., Klaas (1847–1916); nurseryman and farmer in Aalsmeer, Netherlands, son of the first Keessen nurseryman, Willem Keessen (1814–1893).

Keessen, Willem (1884–1963); fifth-generation nurseryman in, Aalsmeer, Netherlands.

Kelly Brothers Nursery (no dates), New York.

Kelsey Highland Nursery (defunct 1958), Boxford, Massachusetts. (Wilson and Kelsey)

Kettler, Fred Henry (1876–1956); nurseryman, Fred Kettler Nursery, Platteville, Wisconsin.

Kircher, Konrad (contemporary); nurseryman, Kircher Baumschulen (defunct 2006), Bad Zwischenahn, Lower Saxony, Germany.

Klager, Hulda Thiel (1864–1960); amateur horticulturist and plant breeder, Woodland, Washington.

Klehm, Roy G. (contemporary); nurseryman, Beaver Creek Nursery, Poplar Grove, Illinois.

Klettenberg, Antoine Joseph (1867–1937); nurseryman, Grandes Roseraies et Pépinières de Forest, Brussels, Belgium, from 1893 to ca. 1939; operated in partnership with Peter Ferdinant Grave from 1898 to 1901, and with F. Delaruelle-Klettenberg in the 1930s. Shortly after the death of Florent Stepman in 1915 Klettenberg acquired Stepman's collection of about 250 lilac cultivars.

Klimenko, Vera Nikolaevna (1909–1985); horticulturist at the State Nikita Botanical Gardens, Yalta, Crimea, Ukraine, from 1949 to 1978. (Klimenko, Klimenko, and Grigor'ev).

Klimenko, Zinaida Konstantinovna (contemporary); horticulturist at the State Nikita Botanical Gardens in Yalta, Crimea, Ukraine, since 1958 (Klimenko, Klimenko, and Grigor'ev)

Kolesnikov, Leonid Alekseevich (1893–1973); amateur plant breeder, Moscow, Russia. (Kolesnikov and Mironovich)

Kolkka, Kimmo L. (contemporary); dendrologist, horticulturist, and nurseryman, Karkkila, Finland.

Kopp, Emil (contemporary); Sinzheim near Baden-Baden, Baden-Württemberg, Germany.

Koster and Sons, M.; nursery in Boskoop, Netherlands.

Kravchenko, Lyubov' Kononovna (contemporary); horticulturist, Botanical Garden, Tashkent, Uzbekistan.

Krsnak, Jimmy (contemporary); Anderson Nurseries, Wentworth South Dakota; formerly Seed and Fertilizer Section, South Dakota Department of Agriculture, Pierre, South Dakota.

Lambert, Peter (1859–1939); nurseryman and rose hybridizer, Trier, Rhineland-Palatinate, Germany.

Lambrechts, Pierre (contemporary); Waterloo, Belgium.

Lammerts, Walter Edward (1904–1996); horticulturist, geologist, and plant breeder, Freedom, California.

Lape, Fred (1900–1985); poet, writer, and horticulturist, who founded George Landis Arboretum, in Esperance, New York.

Larsen, Carl Aryan (1902–1984); draftsman, Salt Lake City, Utah.

Lavrov, S. V. (contemporary); horticulturist, Agricultural University, Kharkov, Ukraine.

Lecointe; a nurseryman, Louveciennes, near Versailles, France.

Lederman, Anton Cornelius (1877–1962); German-American nurseryman, Wheaton Nurseries, Wheaton, Illinois; originally spelled Ledermann.

Legraye, Marie Anne Victoire (1840–1879); gardener-florist, who founded her own shop in Liège, Belgium.

Lemke, August Henry (1868–1946); dentist in Wausau, Wisconsin.

Lemoine nursery (1849–1965); founded in Nancy, France, by Pierre Louis Victor Lemoine (1823–1911), and subsequently operated by his son Paul Émile Prosper Lemoine (1862–1943) and grandson Henri Lemoine (1897–1982).

Leroy, André (1801–1875); nurseryman, Angers, France.

Leslie, William Russel (ca. 1891–1985); superintendent from 1921 to 1956, Morden Research Station, Canada Department of Agriculture, Morden, Manitoba, Canada. (Preston and Leslie)

Libert-Darimont, Gilles Étienne Joseph (1804–1875); nurseryman, member of the Royal Horticulture Society of Liège, and son of Étienne Joseph Libert (1771–1845), who established greenhouses and a nursery about 1809 in Liège, Belgium.

Liberton, Léon Louis Théodore (b. 1865); probably amateur horticulturist, Louvain, Belgium.

Löbner, Max (1869–1947); horticulturist and educator at the Higher State Institute for Horticulture in Pillnitz-Dresden, Saxony, and at the Horticulture Institute and Laboratory in Friesdorf-Bonn, North Rhine-Westphalia, Germany.

Loddiges, Conrad (1738–1826); Dutch nurseryman, father of George Loddiges, and founder of a well-known nursery in Hackney, near London, England.

Lombarts, Petrus (Pierre) Arnoldes Franciskus Maria (1873–1949); nurseryman, Koninklijke Boomkwekerijen Pierre Lombarts, Zundert, North Brabant, Netherlands.

LOSS, or Lesostepnaya (Forest-Steppe) Experimental Breeding Station, Meshchersk, Lipetsk Region, Russia. (Romanova and Egorova) (Vekhov)

Luchnik, Zinaida Ivanovna (1909–1994); horticulturist at the Dendrological Gardens of M. A. Lisavenko Scientific Research Institute for Siberian Horticulture in Barnaul, Altai, Russia. (Luchnik and Semenyuk)

Lumley, Albert Ernest (1902–1981); educator and politician, who began growing and collecting lilacs in 1950 in Pelham near Amherst, Massachusetts.

Lyapunova, Nina Aleksandrovna (contemporary); horticulturist from 1946 to 1965 at Central Republic Botanical Garden, Kiev, Ukraine. (Rubtzov, Zhogoleva, and Lyapunova)

Lyden, Cora Lindsey (1892–1982); wife of John L. Lyden, North Monmouth, Maine.

Maarse, Hendrik (1900–1971); nurseryman, Aalsmeer, Netherlands.

Maarse and Son nursery, J. D.; operated by brothers Jacob Maarse (1899–1969) and Albert Maarse (1902–1992) in Aalsmeer. Albert's son, Jan Maarse (b. 1925), succeeded his father as nursery manager. In 1981 Jan's son-in-law, Gerard Bunnik (b. 1954), became manager.

Maarse Jbzn, Gerrit (1885–1978); florist, G. Maarse Jbzn nursery, Aalsmeer, Netherlands.

Maarsen Brothers nursery, P. and G.; operated by Poulus Maarsen (1888–1954), and Gerrit Maarsen (1892–1972) in Aalsmeer, Netherlands.

Machet and Josem nursery (no dates), Châlons-sur-Marne, Marne, France.

Mahaux, Jean (no dates); amateur horticulturist, Brussels, Belgium.

Margaretten, Joel (1910–1998); dentist, cattle rancher, and lilac grower, Leona Valley, California.

Mathies, John (contemporary); nurseryman, Cannor Nurseries, Chilliwack, British Columbia, Canada.

Mathieu, Léon Jean Armand Ghislain (1832–1916); amateur horticulturist, Louvain, Belgium; name variant Matthieu.

McLean Jr., William L. (no dates), Pennsylvania.

Meader, Elwyn M. (1910–1996); horticulturist and plant breeder, University of New Hampshire, Durham; in 1947 collected seed of *Syringa pubescens* subsp. *patula* in the Pouk Han Mountains, Korea, from which 'Miss Kim' was eventually selected and introduced. (Meader and Yeager)

Mel'nik, A. F. (contemporary); plant breeder, Botanical Garden, Kazakhstan Academy of Sciences, Almaty, Kazakhstan. (Mel'nik, Rubanik, and Dyagilev)

Meyer, Frank Nicholas (Frans Nicholaas Meijer) (1875–1918); Dutch-American botanist and plant explorer (ca. 1905–1918) for the U. S. Department of Agriculture, Bureau of Plant Industry, Office of Foreign Seed and Plant Introduction, Washington, D.C. (Meyer and Fiala)

Mezitt, Ed (no dates), and R. Wayne Mezitt (contemporary); nurserymen, Weston Nurseries, Hopkinton, Massachusetts.

Michie, Alex (no dates); horticulturist, Cedar Hill Nursery, Brookville, Long Island, New York. (Havemeyer and Michie)

Michurin, Ivan Vladimirovich (1855–1935); famed Russian horticulturist and plant breeder, Koslov (renamed Michurinsk in 1932), Russia.

Mikhaĭlov, Nikolai Leonidovich (contemporary); horticulturist, Central Botanical Garden, Moscow, Russia. (Mikhaĭlov and Rybakina) (Shtan'ko and Mikhaĭlov)

Mironovich, Vladimir Davydovich (b. 1904); Soviet army officer, Serpukhova, Moscow Region, Russia; founder of the Syringarium at Moscow State University in 1974. (Kolesnikov and Mironovich)

Moore, Ralph (b. 1907); nurseryman and plant breeder, Sequoia Nursery, Visalia, California.

Morel, Françisque (1849–1925); nurseryman and plant breeder, primarily of *Clematis*, in Lyons, Rhône, France.

Morel, Georges Michel (1916–1973); plant physiologist, virologist, and biochemist, Le Chesnay, Yvelines, France.

Morey, Dennison (contemporary); plant breeder, primarily of roses, and head of the breeding program for Jackson and Perkins in California.

Moro, Frank, and Sara Moro (contemporary); nurserymen, Select Plus International Lilac Nursery, Mascouche, Québec, Canada.

Morse, Warner Jackson (1872–1931); agricultural plant explorer for the U. S. Department of Agriculture, Bureau of Plant Industry, Washington, D.C. (Dorsett, Morse, and Hildreth)

Nelen, Louis (20th century); nurseryman, Essen, Belgium.

Nelson, Caspar I. (1886–1970); bacteriologist, North Dakota Agricultural College, Fargo, North Dakota.

Nijnatten, André van (contemporary); nurseryman, André van Nijnatten Zundert B.V., Zundert, North Brabant, Netherlands.

Nollent (no dates); probably France.

Oakes, Walter Warren (1928–2005); auditor and lilac enthusiast, Dixfield, Maine.

Olbrich, Stephan (d. 1932); horticulturist, Fröbel Nursery, Zürich, Switzerland.

Oliemans Brothers nursery, H. and J. (no information); Aalsmeer, Netherlands.

Oliver, A. A. (no dates); Mount Eden, California.

Olsen, Aksel (1887–1982); nurseryman, Kolding, Denmark. (Olsen and Gram).

Ordnung, Emanuel (1863–1933); horticulturist, Fürstlich Lobkowitz'sche Baumschulen (nursery defunct), Eisenberg, Austria (Czech: Jezeři).

Oudin nursery (circa 1846; no information); Lisieux, Calvados, France.

Ouwerkerk nursery (ca. 1940s); Aalsmeer, Netherlands.

Parsons Sr., Samuel Brown (1819–1909); nurseryman, Flushing, Long Island, New York.

Paterson, Sarah Ida (1872–1957); lilac gardener, Agincourt, Ontario, Canada. Nicknamed "Mrs. T. A."

Pépinières Minier; a nursery operated by Claude Bellion (contemporary) in Beaufort-en-Vallée, Maine-et-Loire, France.

Peteri, Sirkka Liisa (contemporary); nurseryman, Hirvas near Rovaniemi, Finland.

Peterson, Max and Darlene (contemporary); farmers and lilac collectors, Meadowlark Hill Lilac Garden, Ogallala, Nebraska.

Pfitzer Sr., Wilhelm (1821–1905); nurseryman who established W. Pfitzer nursery in 1844 in Stuttgart, Baden-Württemberg, Germany.

Phair, Philip DeWitt (1871–1965); lawyer, Presque Isle, Maine.

Piet Brothers nursery; established by nurserymen Klaas Piet (1863–1941) and Willem Piet (1866–1956) in Aalsmeer, Netherlands.

Pillow, James Parton (1861–1927); accountant, Cold Spring-on-Hudson, New York.

Pokluda, Joseph John (contemporary); nurseryman, Sheridan Nurseries, Norval, Ontario, Canada.

Polin, Edward Gustus (1884–1971); farmer, Fultonville, New York.

Pooler, Margaret R. (contemporary); geneticist, Floral and Nursery Plants Research Unit, U. S. National Arboretum, Washington, D.C. (Egolf and Pooler)

Poscharsky, Oskar (1856–1914); nurseryman, Laubegast near Dresden, Saxony, Germany.

Potutova, E. (contemporary); Saint Petersburg Botanical Garden, Russia.

Preston, Isabella (1881–1965); horticulturist and plant breeder at the Central Experimental Farm, Canada Department of Agriculture, Ottawa, Ontario, from 1920 to 1948. (Preston and Leslie)

Rankin, John Paul (1891–1976); physician and lilac collector, Elyria, Ohio.

Renaud (19th century); horticulturist, Nantes, Loire-Atlantique, France.

Robinson, Edward George (1900–1992); nurseryman and plant breeder, Gaybird Nursery, Wawanesa, Manitoba, Canada.

Rogers, Owen Maurice (contemporary); horticulturist and plant geneticist, University of New Hampshire, Durham.

Rolph, Henry (Harry) Macdonald (1886–1977); farmer, Markham, Ontario, Canada.

Romanova, Valentina Leonidovna (1927–1991); horticulturist, Lesostepnaya Experimental Breeding Station (LOSS), Meshchersk, Lipetsk Region, Russia. (Romanova and Egorova)

Rottert, H. (no dates); nurseryman, Germany.

Rubanik, V. G. (contemporary); Botanical Garden, Kazakhstan Academy of Sciences, Almaty, Kazakhstan. (Rubanik and Dyagilev) (Mel'nik, Rubanik, and Dyagilev)

Rubtzov, Leonid Ivanovich (1902–1980); horticulturist, Central Republic Botanical Garden, Kiev, Ukraine, from 1948 to 1980. (Rubtzov and Zhogoleva) (Rubtzov, Zhogoleva, and Lyapunova)

Ruliffson, Raymond J. (1876–1956); cemetery inspector at Mount Hope Cemetery and nurseryman at Gracewood Lilac Garden, Rochester, New York.

Rybakina, Nina Ivanovna (contemporary); agriculturist, Central Botanical Garden, Moscow, Russia, from 1968 to 1988. (Mikhaïlov and Rybakina)

Sagitova, Mar'yam Galimovna (1923–2001); docent and lilac breeder, ABAY Kazakhstan Pedagogical Institute, Almaty, Kazakhstan, from 1945 to 1991. (Sagitova and Dzevitskaya) (Sagitova and Dzevitsky)

Sakharova, Aleksandra Sergeyevna (1917–1986); horticulturist, Ufa Botanical Garden, Bashkortostan, Russian Federation.

Santa Ines nursery, Nos near Santiago, Chile.

Sass, Hans Peter (1868–1949); German-American farmer and plant breeder, Midwest Gardens, Elkhorn, Nebraska.

Sass, Henry E. (1910–1982); farmer and plant breeder, Benson Station, Omaha, Nebraska.

Sass, Jacob (1872–1945); German-American farmer and plant breeder, Benson Station, Omaha, Nebraska.

Saugé, Pierre (1757–1835); florist, who established his first shop in 1807 in Paris, France.

Sax, Karl (1892–1973); cytologist, plant breeder, and director of Arnold Arboretum of Harvard University from 1947 to 1954, Jamaica Plain, Massachusetts. (Sax and Skinner)

Schichtel Sr., George V. (contemporary); nurseryman, Schichtel's Nursery, Orchard Park, New York.

Schloen, John (1907–1979); horticulturist, Brooklin, Ontario, Canada.

Schmidt, Gábor (contemporary); professor and horticulturist, Corvinus University, Budapest, Hungary.

Schweikart, Hans (contemporary); nurseryman, Schweikart Baumschulen, Hattersheim, Hessen, Germany.

Scott, Edith Wilder (Mrs. Arthur Hoyt) (1876–1960); Media, Pennsylvania.

Seabury, Alton (no dates); Little Compton, Rhode Island.

Sears, Thomas W. (20th century); horticulturist, Glen Head, New York.

Semenyuk, Natal'ya Borisnova (contemporary); plant breeder, Dendrological Gardens of M. A. Lisavenko Scientific Research Institute for Siberian Horticulture, Barnaul, Siberia. (Luchnik and Semenyuk)

Shtan'ko, Ivan Ivanovich (1904–1991); horticulturist, Central Botanical Garden, Moscow, Russia, from 1946 to 1975. (Shtan'ko and Mikhaĭlov)

Simon, F. H. (no dates); nurseryman, Pépinière Francisque Simon, Charbonnières-les-Bians, Rhône, France.

Simon-Louis, Léon Louis (1834–1913); nurseryman, Pépinière Simon-Louis, Plantières near Metz, Lorraine, France.

Skinner, Frank L. (1882–1967); nurseryman and plant breeder, Skinner's Nursery, Roblin, Manitoba, Canada. (Sax and Skinner)

Slater, Leonard Kelvey (1916–1982); amateur horticulturist, Agincourt, Ontario, Canada.

Slavin, Bernard H. (1874–1960); horticulturist and park superintendent from 1890 to 1940 for County of Monroe Department of Parks, Rochester, New York.

Slock, Liévin (1832–1901); gardener, Jette St Pierre, Brussels, Belgium.

Smol'skiĭ, Nikolai Vladislavovich (b. 1905); horticulturist, Central Botanical Garden, Minsk, Belarus. (Smol'skiĭ and Bibikova)

Sobeck, John (1894–1965); horticulturist, Descanso Gardens, Los Angeles State and County Arboretum, La Cañada, California.

Spaargaren, Martine (1916–1991); plant breeder, Test Garden of Rijks Horticultural Winter School in Aalsmeer, Netherlands, from 1936 to 1940

Späth nursery (1720–1949); operated by various family members including Johan Ludwig Carl Späth (1793–1883), Franz Ludwig Späth (1861–1947), and Franz's son, Hellmut Ludwig Späth (1885–1945), in Berlin, Germany.

Stashkevich, Nikifor Savel'yevich (1902–1993); army colonel and educator at tank academy, amateur lilac breeder, Moscow, Russia.

Stepman-Demessemaeker, Grégoire Léopold Florent (1856–1915); horticulturist and nurseryman, Anderlecht and Sint-Jans-Molenbeek, Brussels, Belgium. Note that although in the literature consulted the name is mostly spelled "De Messemaeker," the 1889 marriage document shows the name as "Demessemaeker." Additional evidence is the name of a street in Sint-Jans-Molenbeek, "Pierre Jean Demessemaekerstraat."

Stone, Elizabeth (20th century); amateur gardener and wife of Ralph Stone, Ashland, Ohio.

Stropkey, John G. (1909–1970); nurseryman, John G. Stropkey and Sons, Painesville, Ohio.

Taffler, Stephen (d. 2005); horticulturist and author, Berkhamsted, Herfordshire, United Kingdom.

Temple, F. L. (19th century); nurseryman, Shady Hill Nurseries (defunct), Cambridge, Massachusetts.

Tereshchenko, Sergeĭ Ivanovich (contemporary); horticulturist and plant breeder, Donetsk Botanical Garden, National Academy of Sciences, Donetsk, Ukraine.

Theidel, Richard Paul (1890–1979); nurseryman, Littleford Nursery, Downers Grove, Illinois, and Hinsdale Nursery, Hinsdale, Illinois.

Thomayer, František Josef (1856–1938); landscape architect, pomologist, and nurseryman at Thomayerovy Stromové Školky nursery in Říčany, near Prague, Czechoslovakia (now Czech Republic).

Tischler, Robert W. (1921–1994), businessman and nurseryman, Faribault, Minnesota. Tischler owned and operated Brand Peony Farm 1968–1980. See also Brand, A. M.

Tolppola, Holger (1926–1995); nurseryman, Tolppolas Plantskola, Espoo, Finland.

Towson Nursery (no dates), Towson, Maryland.

Transon Brothers nursery, Orléans, Loiret, France. Operated by nurserymen Paul (1833–1909) and Eugène Transon (1837–1909); at times also known as Barbier and Sons.

Tulp and Son nursery, Piet (contemporary); nurseryman, Aalsmeer, Netherlands.

United States Department of Agriculture, Natural Resources Conservation Service, Plant Materials Center, Bismarck, North Dakota.

Uosukainen, Marjatta (contemporary); horticulturist and director, Laukaa Research and Elite Plant Station of MTT Agrifood Research Finland, Vihtavuori, Finland.

Upītis, Pēteris (1896–1976); head plant breeder at the Dobele Horticultural Plant Breeding Experimental Station, Latvia, from 1963 to 1976.

Upton, Edward A. (1875–1959); pharmacist and nurseryman, Upton Nursery Company, Detroit, Michigan.

Vaigla, Adolf (1911–2001); horticulturist, Räpina Gardening College, Räpina, Estonia.

van der Bom, Th. (19th century); Oudenbosch, North Brabant, Netherlands.

van Houtte, Louis Benoît (1810–1876); horticulturist, La Pinte-lez-Gand, ca. 1839–1951, botanist, educator, explorer, plant breeder; publisher and editor of the 23-volume *Flore des serres et des jardins de l'Europe* (1845–1880), Ghent, Belgium.

van Nes, J. H.; nurseryman, C. B. van Nes and Sons nursery, Boskoop, Netherlands.

van Tol Hzn, Jan, (1872–1960); architect, musician, lawyer, and nurseryman, Jan van Tol nursery, Boskoop and Gouda, Netherlands.

Vandendriessche, Henri (1875–1938); horticulturist and florist, Nivelles, Belgium.

Vekhov, Nikolaĭ Kuz′mich (1887–1956); horticulturist, Lesostepnaya Experimental Breeding Station (LOSS) from 1925 to 1956, Meshchersk, Lipetsk Region, Russia.

Verhoeven, Henri (20th century); Brussels, Belgium.

Viehmeyer, Glenn (1900–1974); horticulturist from 1943 to 1966 at the West Central Research and Extension Center, University of Nebraska, North Platte, Nebraska.

Viksten, Eero ("Eppu") Olavi (1925–1991); nurseryman and founder of Viksten Nursery, Tammela, Finland.

The nursery is currently operated by Viksten's sons Markku, Mikko, and Jukka.

Waines, J. Giles (contemporary); geneticist and director of the botanic gardens and herbarium at the University of California, Riverside.

Wallace, John Alexander (1899–1986); nurseryman, Beaverlodge Nursery, Beaverlodge, Alberta, Canada.

Wandell, Willet N. (contemporary); nurseryman and plant breeder, Discov-Tree Landscape, Oquawka, Illinois.

Wickman, Kjell (contemporary); nurseryman, Wickmans Plantskola, Närpiö, Finland.

Wiles, H. N. (no dates); Dayton, Ohio.

Wilke nursery, Rudolf (1847–ca. 1950); Berlin, Germany. Operated by nurserymen Wilhelm Ernst Wilke (1878–1938) and Paul Wilke (1885–1945).

Willmott Jr., John (1775–1834); nurseryman, Lewisham Nursery, John Willmott and Company, Kent, England.

Wolfhagen (mid-19th century); nurseryman, Halle, Saxony-Anhalt, Germany.

Yeager, Albert Franklin (1892–1961); plant breeder, University of New Hampshire, Durham, New Hampshire. (Meader and Yeager)

Zampini, James W. (contemporary); nurseryman, Lake County Nursery, Perry, Ohio.

Zang Shu-Ying (contemporary); horticulturist and plant breeder, Beijing Botanical Garden and Institute of Botany, Beijing, China. (Zang and Fan)

Zhang Zhiming (contemporary); director, Beijing Botanical Garden and Institute of Botany, Beijing, China.

Zhogoleva, Valentina Grigorivna (1923–1980); horticulturist, Central Republic Botanical Garden, Kiev, Ukraine, from 1953 to 1980. (Rubtzov, Zhogoleva, and Lyapunova; Rubtzov and Zhogoleva)

Zhue, Li-huan (contemporary); Department of Forestry, Northeast Forestry University, Harbin, Heilongjiang, China.

The World's Noteworthy Lilac Collections, Gardens, and Nurseries

The collections, gardens, and nurseries are listed to encourage readers to view lilacs in their own areas and perhaps even visit those farther away when opportunity arises. This is by no means a definitive list; we are certain to have missed some important ones, and included some marginal ones, or some that have declined since first reported. Inclusion of a lilac collection or lilac nursery in this list does not give it special status or endorsement by the International Lilac Society; correct identification of the lilacs and the correct use of names is the responsibility of the individuals in charge of these collections and nurseries. We have not been able to visit many of the foreign countries to view their collections and do not have knowledge of all of them; we often rely on information from correspondents, or information in print or on the Internet. The International Lilac Society would welcome information and pictures of places of lilac interest from readers who want to share with its members and correspondents.

Australia

Garroorigana, New South Wales. Near Goulburn, this 1857 national heritage homestead has one of the oldest gardens in the area, dating back at least to the 1870s. Although the exact year of the first lilac planting is not known, it is estimated to have been in the early 1900s (Jenny Macdougall, 2005, pers. comm. to F.V.).

Goulburn Lilac City Festival, New South Wales. Since the early 1950s Goulburn has celebrated an annual lilac festival each October. Not only is it claimed to be the longest continuously run celebration in Australia, it also appears to be the only one of its kind in Australia. The committee that puts on the festival actively promotes the planting of lilacs on public lands and private properties throughout the city and has raised fund for this purpose; local nurseries are cooperating in this effort by propagating suitable, early-flowering lilac selections.

Lottah Nursery, Tom Thekathyil, Lottah, Tasmania. Features the most extensive collection of lilacs in Australia. Offers a wide selection of lilac cultivars for sale.

Austria

Praskac Pflanzenland, c/o Franz Praskac, Tulln/Donau. Nursery featuring lilacs.

Saint Marc Cemetery (Friedhof Sankt Marx), Leberstrasse, Vienna. Inaugurated in 1784 and closed down in 1874, the cemetery covers about 15 acres (6 ha) and is the only remaining cemetery of the Biedermeier period (1815–1848). It is the final resting place of Wolfgang Amadeus Mozart (1756–1791). Today it is an island of peace and quiet amid a busy city. It is said to have the highest density of lilacs in Vienna and to be well worth a visit during April and May when the lilacs are in bloom.

VitroPlant Pflanzen-Biotechnologie, Klosterneuburg. Nursery specializing in micropropagation.

Belarus

Central Botanical Garden, Belarus Academy of Sciences, Minsk.

Belgium

Arboretum Kalmthout, Kalmthout. Established as a tree plantation in the 1800s but now owned by Antwerp province and open to the public as a botanical garden.

Pépinière le Try, c/o Dominique de Witte, Céroux. Nursery specializing in lilacs and other shrubs.

Canada

There are no lilacs in Syringa Provincial Park. Located in south central British Columbia near the southeastern end of the Lower Arrow Lake, which is a part of the Columbia River, the park was named for Syringa Creek. The creek was named for the syringa, or mock orange, *Philadelphus lewisii*, a shrub that is indigenous to the area. The common name syringa is widely used in western North America for the genus *Philadelphus*, which is not related to the genus *Syringa*.

Lilac Collections

Centennial Lilac Garden, Niagara Parks Commission, Niagara Falls, Ontario.

Central Experimental Farm, Ottawa, Ontario. The first woody plant collections at the Farm were established in 1889. Out of the original 465 acres (182 ha) purchased for use as an experimental farm in 1886, 65 acres (26 ha) were set aside for an arboretum to test the hardiness of plants from around the world and their suitability to the Canadian climate; this is the oldest planting of its kind in Canada. The initial planting in the fall of 1889 included 15 lilacs (Saunders and Macoun 1899); two plants of this original planting, *Syringa vulgaris* var. *alba* and var. *purpurea* are still there (Speirs 2005). Later a further 361 acres (146 ha) were added to the Farm and lilacs were planted throughout. The Farm, operated by Agriculture and Agri-Food Canada, became a Canadian Heritage Site in 1998. Lilacs take a special place at the Farm—Isabella Preston worked here from 1920 until 1948, creating many lilac cultivars. Maintenance and curatorship of the lilacs, undertaken by the Friends of the Central Experimental Farm in partnership with Agriculture and Agri-Food Canada, commenced in 2000. As of 2005 the Farm grew more than 800 lilacs, representing at least 318 different species and cultivars.

Devonian Botanic Garden, University of Alberta, Edmonton, Alberta.

Golden Prairie Arboretum, Alberta Horticultural Research Centre, Brooks, Alberta.

Jardin botanique de Montréal (Montreal Botanic Garden), Montréal, Québec.

Katie Osborne Lilac Garden, Royal Botanical Gardens, Hamilton, Ontario. Established in the 1960s, this garden has one of the larger collections of lilacs. During its years of development, it obtained lilac plants, scions, and cuttings from collections and hybridizers all over the world. In time its role changed, and from the late 1970s into the early 2000s it functioned as a dependable and reliable source of *Syringa* propagules, and custodian of the lilac gene pool. In 1993 the Historic Sites and Monuments Board of Canada designated Royal Botanical Gardens an Historic Site, stating,

> This important botanical garden is distinguished by its first-class horticultural collection. Originating in the late 1920s, it developed as a series of discrete gardens and a wildlife conservation area within an urban context. Some of Canada's most talented landscape architects, botanists, and plant curators have collaborated on the garden, imparting an overall unity and aesthetic appeal. In 1975, Royal Botanical Gardens was designated the International Registration Authority for the names of cultivated lilacs in honour of its world-renowned lilac collection.

Morden Research Centre, Agriculture and Agri-Food Canada, Morden, Manitoba. The research station, or Morden Arboretum as it was known in its earlier days, has a long tradition of testing ornamental plants including lilacs for climatic and edaphic conditions of the Canadian Prairies (Davidson et al. 2003). About a dozen new lilac cultivars were introduced from this research station.

Patterson Garden Research Station, University of Saskatchewan, Saskatoon.

University of British Columbia, UBC Botanical Garden and Centre for Plant Research, Vancouver, British Columbia.

University of Guelph, The Arboretum, Guelph, Ontario.

Private Lilac Collections and Plantings

Blackman's Secret Garden, c/o Linda Blackman, Tête Jaune Cache ("Yellow Head"), Robson Valley, British Columbia. The lilacs in this deep forest garden on the banks of the Fraser River are in bloom about mid-June.

Cap-à-l'Aigle, Village des lilas, La Malbaie, Charlevoix County, Québec. A German horticulturist donated to the hamlet of Cap-à-l'Aigle a collection of 1000 different cultivars of lilacs; planting commenced in 2002; 200 lilacs have been planted in the garden overlooking the Saint Lawrence River. Cap-à-l'Aigle makes up part of the World Biosphere Reserve. The hamlet holds an annual lilac festival.

Culp Farm, c/o Bonnie Culp, Dunster, Robson Valley, British Columbia. The Farm features an extensive lilac collection, which is in bloom about mid-June.

Frank Skinner Arboretum Trail, Dropmore, near Roblin, Manitoba. Development of the Trail commenced in 1993. The trail planting features some of the hardy plants introduced and developed by Frank L. Skinner.

Franktown, Ontario. Franktown features acres of naturalized lilacs. In 1998 Franktown, the Lilac Capital of Ontario, issued a five dollar Municipal Trade Token. The Franktown Lilac Festival has been an annual event since it began in 1995.

Lindsay, Ontario. Lilacs of Lindsay, in partnership with the City of Kawartha Lakes Parks and Recreation Department, has established a lilac plantation in the Logie Street Park in Lindsay and other locations throughout the city. The Logie Street Park contains about 120 cultivars of lilacs.

T. R. B. Watson Arboretum, Blithe Hill Nurseries, c/o Jean S. Watson, Orangeville, Ontario. The Arboretum, started in 1981, has been enriched by the Millennium Collection of lilacs, featuring a wide selection of European and North American cultivars.

Nurseries Featuring Lilacs

Blithe Hill Nurseries, c/o Jean S. Watson, Orangeville, Ontario.

Fox, Eugene ("Gene"), Millet, Alberta.

Jefferies Nurseries, c/o Wilbert and Sharon Ronald, Portage la Prairie, Manitoba.

Reimer's Nurseries, c/o Paul Reimer, Chilliwack, British Columbia. Wholesale growers.

Select Plus International Nursery, c/o Frank and Sara Moro, Mascouche, Québec. Maintains an assortment of more than 1000 lilac cultivars.

Van's Nurseries, c/o Bill Van der Zalm, Ladner, British Columbia. Wholesale growers of container lilacs.

Lilac Festivals

Calgary, Alberta. On the last Sunday in May the annual Lilac Festival is held in Calgary.

Cap-à-l'Aigle, Québec. This hamlet in La Malbaie, Charlevoix County, holds its festival Le Temps des Lilas usually in early to mid June.

Franktown, Ontario. Since the first Franktown Lilac Festival was held in 1995, it has become an annual event.

Hamilton, Ontario. An annual Lilac Festival is held at Royal Botanical Gardens, Hamilton, usually on the 3rd or 4th weekend in May.

Lindsay, Ontario. Lilacs of Lindsay hosts an annual Lilac Festival which takes place about the last weekend in May.

China

Beijing Botanical Garden, Institute of Botany, Chinese Academy of Sciences, Beijing. Founded in 1956 the botanical garden developed rapidly during its initial decade, but collections declined during the Cultural Revolution (1966–1976). Lilac breeding and selecting work, commenced in the 1950s, was resumed in the late 1970s by Shu-Ying Zang and Ying-Han Fan. The 8¾-acre (3.5-ha) Lilac Garden provides space for indigenous taxa of *Syringa* and for cultivars to be used in the breeding program.

Harbin Forest Botanical Garden, Harbin, Heilongjiang. Established in 1957 on the site of a small nursery, the garden now covers 335 acres (134 ha) and is the "lung" of the big industrial city of Harbin. Harbin is situated on the banks of the Songhua Jiang, or Amur River, which lends its name to the Amur tree lilac, *Syringa reticulata* subsp. *amurensis*.

Huhehaote Botanical Garden, Huhehaote, Nei Mongol. This appears to be most northern lilac collection in China.

Croatia

Arboretum Lisičine (Hrvatske šume), Voćin, Slavonia. The Arboretum's current collection of 40 lilac cultivars will be enlarged to about 170 in the near future.

Hrvatske šume, Zagreb, Uprava šuma Podružnica Požega, Kutjevo. This nursery has 170 different lilac taxa, mainly cultivars; individual plants are grown in a large plot providing scions and cuttings for plant production.

National Park Brijuni, Forestry Nursery (Šumski rasadnik), Fažana. There are 35 different lilac cultivars in the collection. At the time of writing plant propagation had not yet been initiated and no plants are offered for sale yet.

University of Zagreb, Faculty of Science, Department of Biology, Botany and Botanical Gardens, Zagreb. The botanical garden in Zagreb has approximately 10 different cultivars. Through the garden's nursery production program, plants in the collections are propagated and sold.

Vrtni centar Iva, Štefanec, Čakovec. Private nursery with a collection of 41 taxa and cultivars; each taxon is represented by a single plant providing cuttings for plant production.

Denmark

Arboretum Hørsholm of the Royal Veterinary and Agricultural University, Hørsholm.

Heide's Planteskole, c/o Ole Heide, Thisted. Lilac collection and nursery consisting of 480 cultivars, many of them little-known introductions from Eastern Europe.

England
National Collections of Lilacs

The National Council for the Conservation of Plants and Gardens (NCCPG) seeks to conserve, document, promote, and make available Britain and Ireland's great biodiversity of garden plants for the benefit of horticulture, education, and science. Collection holders undertake to preserve, grow, propagate, document, and make available the plants in their chosen group. Currently there are three National Collections of Lilacs are registered.

Brighton and Hove Council, Withdean Park, Peacock Lane, Environmental Department, Brighton, Sussex. Currently there are about 320 botanical taxa and cultivars in Brighton's collection. Philip Williamson received the 2003 President's Award of the International Lilac Society, "For your leadership in the restoration of the NCCPG National Collection of Lilacs at Withdean Park Brighton and Hove, England."

Leeds City Council, The Lilac Walk at Golden Acre Park, Otley Road, Bramhope, Leeds, Yorkshire. The Lilac Walk features about 10 botanical taxa and 95 cultivars.

Norman's Farm, c/o Mr. and Mrs. Colin Chapman, Wyverstone, Stowmarket, Suffolk. This 5-acre (2-ha) garden features 25 botanical taxa and about 480 cultivars of lilacs. Colin received the International Lilac Society's President's Award in 1996, "For his service to the Society by promoting the lilac in Great Britain and in Europe" and the Arch McKean Award in 2000 "For his many published articles and for his tireless efforts in promoting the lilac in Europe."

Arboreta and Botanical Gardens with Lilac Collections

The Lilac Garden, **Royal Botanic Gardens, Kew**, Richmond, Surrey. Renovated in 1993 and comprising 105 accessions of species and cultivars, the lilac collection is displayed in 10 beds, illustrating the development of the modern garden lilac.

Royal Horticultural Society Garden, Wisley, Woking, Surrey.

Sir Harold Hillier Gardens, Ampfield, Romsey, Hampshire. About 70 accessions of lilac species and cultivars.

Private Lilac Collection

Christopher Lane, The Granary, Callaways Lane, Newington, Sittingbourne, Kent.

Nursery Featuring Lilacs

Gobbett Nursery, c/o Gordon C. J. Link, Farlow, near Kidderminster, Worcestershire. Offers about 30 different lilacs.

Estonia

Botanical Garden, University of Tartu, Tartu, Estonia.

Finland

Helsinki. The city flower is *Syringa vulgaris*, which was brought to Finland in the late 1720s. Although their origin is unknown, many lilacs grow in the parks and gardens of Helsinki.

France
Arboreta and Botanical Gardens with Lilac Collections

Jardin Botanique du Montet (Conservatoire et Jardins Botaniques de Nancy), c/o Jean-François Gonot, Villers-lès-Nancy, Lorraine. Through the initiative of Pierre Valck and Jean-François Gonot, former curator and current curator respectively, a collection of lilac cultivars that originated in the Lemoine nursery is being assembled and maintained at this garden.

Les Jardins de Brocéliande, c/o Gerard Brière, Route de Montfort, Breal-Sous, Montfort, Bretagne. The lilac collection began in 1994 through the initiative of Jean-François Hervé. Of the 60-acre (24-ha) park, 5 acres (2 ha) are dedicated to *Syringa* and display some 400 cultivars.

Lilac Collections in Public Parks

L'arboretum de l'école du Breuil, Bois de Vincennes, Paris.

Le Jardin de Bagatelle, Bois de Boulogne, Paris.

Parc Départemental des Lilas, rue Lemerle Vetter, Vitry-sur-Seine near Paris. For almost two centuries, from the mid-18th century to the mid-20th century, Vitry-sur-Seine was the center of the French lilac forcing industry. One of the park's eco-museum features is the collection of about 700 lilac cultivars.

Germany
Lilac Collections in Public Gardens

Botanical Garden Rombergpark, Dortmund, Westphalia. After the government took over Späth Arboretum, Gerd Krüssmann retained his interest in lilacs (Krüssmann 1947). He became director of the Botanical Garden Rombergpark, Dortmund (1949 through 1974), where he assembled a new lilac collection and proposed a scheme for test plantings and evaluation (Krüssmann 1960a, b). Priorities changed after Krüssmann's retirement and the lilac collection has fallen in decline.

Institut für Stauden und Gehölze, Fachbereich Landschaftsarchitektur, Fachhochschule Weihenstephan, Freising, Bavaria. The lilac collection at Weihenstephan, on the Agricultural Campus of the Technical University Munich, was still flourishing in the late 1960s and 70s under the directorship of Richard Hansen. It contained about 50 species and cultivars at that time. In recent years the lilacs have suffered from neglect and have almost disappeared.

Späth Arboretum, Berlin-Baumschulenweg, Berlin. Situated in the Russian occupation zone following World War II, the well-known collection at this arboretum was assembled by the Späth dendrologists Karl Frost (no dates) and Gerd Krüssmann (1910–1980), fell in decline when the Ludwig Späth nursery was expropriated, and became a state-owned firm.

Nurseries Featuring Lilacs

Oberlausitzer Baum- und Rosenschulen Löbau, Löbau, Saxony.

Piccoplant Mikrovermehrungen, c/o Elke Haase, Oldenburg, Lower Saxony. Propagating about 100 lilac cultivars and producing about 480,000 plants annually via micro-propagation, this nursery is probably the largest European producer of lilacs and has established strong connections in China, India, and North America. Although primarily wholesale, at the time of writing about 35 cultivars are available via online retail at www.fliedertraum.de; as the nursery operation is expanding, the number of available cultivars should reach 100. The website is in German and presents descriptive information and guidelines for planting, pruning, and fertilizing lilacs.

Lilac Plantings in Cities and Towns on Private Property

Bad Frankenhausen, Thuringia. *Syringa vulgaris* accompanied the introduction of viticulture on the hills of this region in the 16th century, but did not gain prominence until the beginning of the 19th century, when an outbreak of *Phylloxera vitifoliae* ruined the vineyards. The lilacs, however, persisted and prospered on the hills. Where vineyards prosper, there is an annual wine festival. Bad Frankenhausen was no exception. Peasants, traders, craftsmen, and entertainers would come from near and far. Following the economic setback, the city fathers needed another good cause for a festival, and so the Lilac Festival was born. The Festival prospered until 1945. After reunification of Germany, the Lilac Festival was revived in 1992 in the old tradition. Highlights of the festival include election of a Lilac Queen, who must give evidence of her knowledge about the city and about lilacs, and give a musical rendition; the planting of a lilac tree; and a parade.

Friesack, Brandenburg. Friesack earned its nickname *Fliederstadt* (Lilactown) as a result of the efforts of the local beautification club, founded in 1897, whose members planted lilacs along roads and squares. The lilacs bloomed in May and the healthy climate of the rural surroundings soon attracted vacationers from Berlin.

Pillnitz, near Dresden, Saxony. The New Palace, constructed between 1818 and 1826, features an inner court with a unique planting of 90 lilacs on standard rootstock.

They appear to not be the original plants, but the historic layout has been maintained.

Iceland

Reykjavik Botanical Garden, Reykjavik. The common lilac flowers in July.

Japan

Botanic Garden Hokkaido University, Sapporo, Hokkaido. The garden features a lilac collection.

Kawashima Park, Sapporo, Hokkaido. Opened in 1999, one of the main features of this public park is its collection of about 200 lilac species and cultivars.

Odor Park, Sapporo, Hokkaido. The lilac is the official flower of the city of Sapporo. The Odor Park Lilac Festival is celebrated annually. Visitors are given seedlings to plant in this public park. Other events include flower shows, concerts, and sketching sessions.

Kazakhstan

Almaty, formerly Alma-Ata. The name of this city alludes to the native crab apple *Malus sieversii*. Alma-Ata has been translated by different authors as "Mother of Apples," "Father of Apples," or "abundant in apples." Almaty is also a city of lilacs and the hometown of Mar'yam Sagitova, who selected about 32 new cultivars at the ABAY Kazakhstan Pedagogical Institute between 1945 and 1991. Unfortunately, the Institute's lilac collection no longer exists; the site was cleared in 2004–2005.

Botanical Garden, Kazakhstan Academy of Sciences, Almaty. In the 1980s and early 1990s, the team of Mel'nik, Rubanik, and Dyagilev developed several new lilac cultivars at this garden but reportedly lilacs no longer grow at this site.

Latvia

National Botanic Gardens, Salaspils.
State Agency Latvia State Institute of Fruit Growing, Dobele. Formerly the Dobele Horticultural Plant Breeding Experimental Station, the Upitis Garden, as it is popularly known in Latvia, features the largest lilac collection in the country—174 species and cultivars.

This is the garden where Peter Upītis developed and tested his lilac and fruit cultivars from 1957 to 1976. A museum on the grounds features Upītis's life's work in plant breeding and the history of fruit culture in Latvia.

Lithuania

Botanical Gardens of Vilnius University, Vilnius.

The Netherlands
Universities and Research Stations with Lilac Collections

Botanical Garden Belmonte, Wageningen University, Wageningen. Lilacs are part of the collection of Oleaceae (olive family).

Botanical Gardens of Utrecht University, Fort Hoofddijk, De Uithof, Utrecht. The National Plant Collection of the Netherlands came into being in 1988. It is coordinated and controlled by the Dutch Botanic Gardens Foundation (Stichting Nationale Plantencollectie), with the aim to reduce excessive duplications. Collections are distributed over 17 participating botanical gardens and arboreta. The genus *Syringa* was assigned to the University of Utrecht Botanical Garden in 2001; the collection is classified for "in-depth specialization." By 2007 the collection comprised 32 botanical taxa and 35 cultivars. One part of the collection is located in Fort Hoofddijk, the other at the arboretum in Doorn, which is also the evaluation site for new selections of *S. reticulata*.

Display Garden "De Oirsprong." Oirshot. The organization of Dutch Plant Collections was initiated by the nurserymen of Boskoop and coordinates about 80 special collections which are open to the public. E. van Vugt and Cor van Gelderen are keepers of the organization's lilacs. There are 45 different lilacs displayed here; *Syringa vulgaris* cultivars are excluded.

Research Station for Nursery Stock, Boskoop. For many years woody plant cultivar trials were an integral part of ornamental plant research at the Station. Most of the lilacs growing at the Station have now been moved to the Botanical Gardens of Utrecht University. Recent research on *Syringa* has been carried out by Ronald C. Snijder (Snijder 1999) and Marco H. A. Hoffman (Hoffman 2000, 2003).

Historical Lilac Collections

Historical Garden Aalsmeer, c/o Cees van Dam, Aalsmeer. The 2½-acre (1-ha) garden demonstrates and interprets the horticultural history of Aalsmeer from 1650 until about 1940. The collection of about 40 lilac cultivars represents the assortment grown for forcing in local greenhouses. A significant number of lilac cultivars originated in this area.

Seringenpark, Aalsmeer. The triangular, 7½-acre (3-ha) lilac park, originally designed by garden and landscape architect Christiaan Peter Broerse (1902–1995), laid out and planted from 1946 to 1952, was for many years the primary lilac collection in the country. The spring 1951 inventory lists 163 species and cultivars (Seringenpark 1951). From 2000 to 2004 the collection was rejuvenated and updated.

Nurseries Featuring Lilacs

Firma C. Esveld, Boskoop. Esveld offers about 100 species and cultivars, including a few recent introductions.

Heesterkwekerij Mars, Luttenberg. The nursery specializes in lilacs and offers about 30 cultivars for sale.

Pieter Zwijnenburg Jr., Boskoop. The Zwijnenburg nursery offers well over 250 species and cultivars of lilacs.

Norway

Landsnes Planteskole, c/o Arild Johan Landsnes, Asker. The nursery features lilacs and a collection of more than 170 cultivars.

Poland

Botanical Garden of the University Maria Curie-Sklodowska, Lublin.

Kórnik Arboretum, Institute of Dendrology, Polish Academy of Sciences, Kórnik. The lilac collection includes more than 500 species and named cultivars. (See chapter ten for more details.)

Warsaw University Botanic Garden, Warsaw. In 1818 Czar Alexander I of Russia presented Warsaw University with the Royal Garden, situated between Lazienki and Belvédère Palace, for the purpose of creating a botanic garden. Michal Szubert (1787–1860), professor of botany, was appointed its first director, a position he held until 1846. The planting of lilacs along the central avenue, designed by Szubert, is said to be the most beautiful feature of the Warsaw Botanic Garden to this day.

Russia

Botanic Gardens, Stavropol, Stavropol Krai. Named for V. V. Skriptchinsky.

Botanical Gardens, Moscow State University, Moscow. Named for Mikhail V. Lomonosov.

Central Siberian Botanical Gardens, Russian Academy of Sciences, Novosibirsk, Siberia.

Lesostepnaya Experimental Breeding Station (LOSS), Meshchersk, Lipetsk Region, Stanovliansky district. LOSS is also host to the oldest Russian lilac nursery, established in the 1920s. Nikolaï Vekhov was its head from 1925 to 1950. Subsequently, it was managed by Valentina Romanova from 1950 to 1991. At the time of writing Antonina Minayeva is the director.

Lisavenko Scientific Research Institute for Siberian Horticulture, Botanical Garden and Arboretum, Barnaul, Altai Krai.

N. V. Tsitsin Main Botanical Garden, Russian Academy of Sciences, Moscow. The most extensive lilac collection in the Russian Federation, with the primary focus on *Syringa vulgaris* cultivars.

Scotland

Royal Botanic Garden, Edinburgh. There appear to be about 45 accessions in the collection, a number of which are native collections from China.

Slovakia

Arborétum Borová hora, Technical University, Zvolen.

South Korea

Kwangnung Arboretum, Forestry Research Institute, Seoul. The lilac collection consists mainly of native taxa.

Sweden

Stiftelsen Trädgårdsodlingens, Elitplant-stationen, Kristianstad. Producer of certified nursery stock.

Ukraine

Botanical Garden, National Academy of Sciences, Donetsk. The Garden features about 140 cultivars of *Syringa vulgaris* and *S. ×hyacinthiflora*, mostly introductions of Lemoine in France, the Russian Leonid Kolesnikov, and the Belarusian breeders Nikolai Smol'skiĭ and Veronika Bibikova. The collection has provided the gene pool for the hybridizing and selecting program of Sergeĭ Tereshchenko.

Central Botanical Garden, National Academy of Sciences, Kiev. Having a major lilac collection at their disposal, horticulturists Leonid Rubtzov, Valentina Zhogoleva, Nina Lyapunova, and Vasil' Gorb developed and introduced new cultivars.

Russkaya Usad'ba (Russian Farmstead), c/o Sergey Terekhov, Donetsk. This nursery specializes in the production of cultivars originated by Leonid Kolesnikov and Nikolaĭ Vekhov.

State Nikita Botanical Garden, Yalta, Crimea. Vera Klimenko, her daughter, Zinaida Klimenko, and Alexander Grigor'ev have contributed to the development of new lilac cultivars.

United States of America

The North American Plant Collections Consortium (NAPCC), a program of the American Public Gardens Association, is a network of botanical gardens that take official responsibility for collecting and preserving specific plant groups and the genetic resources they represent. NAPCC member collections may focus on any plant group, large or small, and can include plants that are rare or endangered in the wild, or are from areas with difficult or restricted access, exhibit disease and pest resistance, are adaptable to a range of environmental conditions, or have significant ornamental or historical value.

Arboreta and Botanical Gardens with Lilac Collections

Arnold Arboretum of Harvard University, Jamaica Plain, Massachusetts. Arnold Arboretum has the top lilac research collection of living plants and herbarium specimens in North America. A score of plant collectors, geneticists, horticulturists, propagators, and taxonomists at the Arboretum have advanced the knowledge of the genus *Syringa* and of the cultivation of lilacs; the combination of Arnold Arboretum and lilacs conjures names such as J. Herbert Alexander, Edgar Anderson, Alfred Fordham, Joseph Hers, Richard A. Howard, Jianhua Li, Susan D. McKelvey, Frank N. Meyer, William Purdom, Alfred Rehder, Joseph F. C. Rock, Charles S. Sargent, Karl Sax, Camillo K. Schneider, and Ernest H. Wilson. On Lilac Sunday the Arboretum is open from dawn to dusk.

Bickelhaupt Arboretum, Clinton, Iowa. The lilac collection has been laid out along a meandering trail. Of special interest are the newer, disease-resistant cultivars and the semidwarf collection of Neal Holland's FAIRYTALE lilacs.

Chicago Botanic Garden, Glencoe, Illinois. There are about 50 lilacs in the living plant collections.

Denver Botanic Gardens, Denver, Colorado. The Heirloom Garden pays tribute to early plant pioneers. The garden design incorporates purple, the color that characterizes the lilac collection, and its complementary color, yellow. The colors silver and white, and textural plants such as *Artemisia* and *Yucca* complete the scheme.

Emma Watson Lilac Garden, Fernwood Botanical Gardens and Nature Preserve, Niles, Michigan. There are about 50 different lilacs in the Emma Watson Lilac Garden.

Eureka College, Lilac Arboretum, Eureka, Illinois. Around 1900, graduates of the College began a tradition of sending lilac cultivars back to the campus from abroad. Although the Arboretum went through a period of decline, interest has been rekindled, and new lilacs are planted each spring.

Holden Arboretum, Kirtland, Ohio. With 3100 acres (1240 ha) Holden is the largest arboretum in the United States. Its Lilac Walk is laid out on 7 acres (2.8 ha) featuring a collection of about 260 lilacs in a well-landscaped setting.

Howard Taylor Lilac Collection at the Mary Flagler Cary Arboretum, Millbrook, New York. The collection was dedicated in 1961 and is now one of the special collections of the Institute of Ecosystem Studies, a division of the New York Botanical Garden.

Landis Arboretum, Esperance, New York. There are about 50 different lilacs in the Arboretum, which was established by Fred Lape. Lilacs had his special interest.

Louisa Clark Spencer Lilac Collection, Brooklyn Botanic Garden, Brooklyn, New York. Although the date of establishment of the first lilac planting at Brooklyn Botanic Garden is not known, the collection included more than 100 cultivars in 1917.

Missouri Botanical Garden, Saint Louis, Missouri.

Morris Arboretum of the University of Pennsylvania, Philadelphia, Pennsylvania.

Morton Arboretum, Lisle, Illinois. Established in 1986, Chicagoland Grows is a partnership among the Chicago Botanic Garden, the Morton Arboretum, and the Ornamental Growers Association of Northern Illinois. One of its introductions is *Syringa pekinensis* 'Morton', trademarked as China Snow.

New York Botanical Garden, Bronx, New York. Located near the Rose Garden is the T. A. Havemeyer Lilac Collection, with 90 different cultivars varying in colors from white and pale blue to lavender and deepest purple.

Polly Hill Arboretum, West Tisbury, Martha's Vineyard, Massachusetts. More than 60 lilac species and cultivars are represented in this collection.

Quarryhill Botanical Garden, Glen Ellen, California. Quarryhill Botanical Garden maintains one of the largest collections of scientifically documented wild source temperate Asian plants in North America, including lilacs.

Scott Arboretum of Swarthmore College, Swarthmore, Pennsylvania. Scott Arboretum was established in 1929. The lilac collection was initiated by John C. Wister, who first wrote about it in April 1938. It was the center point from which the 1941 and 1953 Lilac Surveys were conducted, and where the International Cultivar Registration Authority for the genus *Syringa* was first established in 1956.

Tyler Arboretum, Media, Pennsylvania. It is here that John Caspar Wister (1887–1982) planned and laid out his second collection of lilacs. Wister was the Arboretum's first director, from 1946 until 1968.

United States National Arboretum, Washington, D.C. Established in 1927 the Arboretum is administered by the USDA Agricultural Research Service. Its mission is to serve the public need for scientific research, education, and gardens that conserve and showcase plants to enhance the environment.

Universities and Research Stations with Lilac Collections

Bernheim Arboretum and Research Forest, Clermont, Kentucky.

Botanic Garden of Smith College, Northampton, Massachusetts.

Cornell Plantations, Cornell University, Ithaca, New York.

Earl G. Maxwell Arboretum, University of Nebraska-Lincoln, Lincoln, Nebraska.

Hidden Lake Gardens of Michigan State University, Tipton, Michigan.

Longenecker Gardens, University of Wisconsin Arboretum, Madison, Wisconsin.

Lyle E. Littlefield Ornamentals Trial Garden, University of Maine, Orono, Maine. Littlefield Garden was founded in the early 1960s by Lyle E. Littlefield, then professor of horticulture. The mission of the Garden is to obtain, plant, and evaluate as wide a range as possible of ornamental plants with potential for use in the northern landscape. Since it was founded, the Garden has amassed a collection of over 2500 woody and herbaceous plants. All of them receive extensive evaluation for winter hardiness, ornamental characteristics, cultural requirements, and overall potential for the landscape. The collection contains 180 lilacs.

Minnesota Landscape Arboretum, Chaska, Minnesota. Part of the Department of Horticultural Science within the College of Agricultural, Food and Environmental Sciences at the University of Minnesota, the Arboretum provides a community and a national resource for horticultural and environmental information, research and public education; it develops and evaluates plants and horticultural practices for cold climates. Their 150-plus lilacs bloom in early May.

Red Butte Garden, University of Utah, Salt Lake City, Utah.

United States Department of Agriculture Plant Introduction Station at Glenn Dale, Maryland. Hundreds of new plants are introduced each year to the United States; some of these plants are sent to the Glenn Dale Station for extensive testing for potential disease and pest contamination. In addition, the Plant Introduction records are a valuable source of information on these plant introductions.

University of California at Irvine South Coast Research and Extension Center, Irvine, California.

University of California at Riverside Botanic Gardens, Riverside, California. The two University of California collection sites complement each other; Irvine, between the Santa Ana Mountains and the Pacific Ocean, has a coastal climate, whereas Riverside, on the Santa Ana River, has a drier and warmer interior climate.

University of Idaho Arboretum and Botanical Garden, Moscow, Idaho. European and Asian lilac collections.

University of New Hampshire, Department of Plant Sciences, Durham, New Hampshire. Plant collections are initiated, grow, and reach their peak; but once they lose their purpose, or people lose interest in them, they decline. This teaching, research, and breeding collection is suffering from old age and from honey-fungus (*Armillaria mellia*) infection. Restarting the collection at a fresh site with repropagated plants would be the only answer.

University of Vermont Horticultural Farm, South Burlington, Vermont.

Lilac Collections in Public Parks

Arbor Lodge State Historical Park and Arboretum, Nebraska City, Nebraska. Displayed along the Max and Darlene Peterson Lilac Walk and in additional beds are more than 280 lilacs.

Descanso Gardens, La Cañada, California. Walter Lammerts created some of his mild-winter tolerant lilac cultivars here and they are now featured in the gardens.

Duniway Park, Portland, Oregon. Bernard Case (1866–1936) operated a walnut farm in Fruit Valley, now a community in Vancouver, Washington. He was also interested in lilacs and assembled a collection. Following his death the Portland Garden Club purchased Case's lilacs and planted them in Duniway Park. The approximately 1-acre (0.4 ha) Lilac Garden holds about 225 plants of 125 cultivars (Vrugtman 1993).

Ewing Park Lilac Arboretum and Children's Forest, Des Moines Botanical Center, Des Moines, Iowa.

Highland Botanical Park, Monroe County Parks Department, Rochester, New York. Designed by Frederick Law Olmsted, the Park is a completely planned arboretum. Planted in 1894, it features the nation's largest collection of lilacs, more than 1200 shrubs representing 500 varieties, and is the home of Rochester's famous Lilac Festival. The Park is operated by the Monroe County Parks Department, where horticulturists John Dunbar, Richard Fenicchia, Alvan Grant, and Bernard Slavin developed and introduced their new lilac cultivars.

John A. Finch Arboretum, Spokane, Washington. The 65-acre (26-ha) park features 2000 trees and shrubs, including 65 groups of lilacs. The plantings date from 1949.

Lasdon Park and Arboretum, Somers, New York. The lilac collection, started in 1999, comprises a selection of species lilacs, *Syringa vulgaris* cultivars, and early- and late-blooming cultivars. Lasdon is operated by the Westchester County Department of Parks, Recreation, and Conservation.

Lilacia Park, Park District of Lombard, Lombard, Illinois. Lombard owes its lilac collection to Colonel William Plum (1845–1927). In the 1870s he and his wife, Helen Williams Plum, settled in the new village of Lombard, where he purchased land on the corner of Park and Maple. The estate would eventually be known as Lilacia. The Plums became enamored with lilacs while visiting the Lemoine nursery in Nancy, France. The present collection of lilacs in Lilacia began with two cultivars, 'Michel Buchner', a double light purple, and 'Mme Casimir Périer', a double white, purchased at Lemoine's. Colonel Plum passed away in 1927, leaving his land to the people of Lombard as a public park and, in memory of his wife, his house as a "free public library and reading rooms."

Manito Park Lilac Garden, Spokane, Washington. The Park is noted for its lilacs.

Nell Singer Lilac Walk, Central Park, New York City. Created in 1970, the Lilac Walk was conceived and financed by philanthropist Nell Singer. It is bordered on the south by the north fence of the Sheep Meadow. A plaque at the site reads: "Even during periods of harsh conflict and confrontation the delicate beauty and fragrance of the lilac have been faithful annual reminders of lovelier aspects in human relations. In tribute to those aspects, this Lilac Walk is Dedicated to the People of the City of New York."

New Jersey State Botanical Garden at Skylands, Ringwood State Park, Ringwood, New Jersey.

Wentworth-Coolidge Lilac Festival, Portsmouth, New Hampshire. The lilac is the official state flower of New Hampshire. The original lilacs were imported to New Hampshire from England in the 1750s by the Royal Governor, Benning Wentworth, to display at his mansion just outside the city. Each May the grounds of Wentworth-Coolidge Mansion bloom with the clonal descendants of the original lilacs. The resulting Lilac Festival has been drawing larger crowds each year. Lilac experts offer lectures and demonstrations; visitors can purchase lilacs and related products and sign up for a historic house membership or summer classes. Regrettably, this historic lilac collection is infected with honey-fungus (*Armillaria mellia*).

Lilacs in Cities and Towns on Private Property

Camden, Maine.

Cooperstown, New York. Wonderful old lilacs are planted everywhere.

Lombard, Illinois. Known as the Lilac Village. The city holds an annual lilac festival.

Mackinac City, Mackinac Island, Michigan.

Portsmouth, New Hampshire.

Rochester, New Hampshire.

Spokane, Washington. Known as the Lilac City in the West.

Woodstock, Vermont. Lilacs line Main Street.

Private Lilac Collections

Butternut Hill Farm, Hampden, Maine. The late Roger F. Luce (1920–2002), educator, historian, and horticulturist, collected and cultivated many plants, including lilacs. Some lilacs were grown from seed brought back from his trips to China.

Erickson's Nursery and Landscape, c/o Brian Erickson, Brainerd, Minnesota.

Falconskeape, c/o Marc and Julie Dehrmann, Medina, Ohio. Fiala started his collection here in 1969; this is where he developed his new cultivars.

Gramp's Gardens, Berdeen's Lilacs, c/o Lynette Mascioli, Kennebunk, Maine.

Hamesbest Garden, c/o Jean Kerle, Randolph Center, Vermont. Established in 1980–1981 by Gertrude Hodgdon (1902–1992) in honor of her husband Philip B. Hodgdon (1902–1978), teacher and nurseryman. Their daughter continues taking care of the Garden and its 125 different lilacs.

Howard and Carolyn Merrill, Alfred, Maine.

Hulda Klager Lilac Gardens, Hulda Klager Lilac Society, Woodland, Washington. The garden where Klager developed her new lilac cultivars is now a National Historic Site.

Lake Street Garden Center, c/o Tim Wolfe, Salem, New Hampshire.

Lilac Farm, c/o Wayne and Millie Hughes, Cambridge Springs, Pennsylvania. When official retirement came in 1988, Wayne and Millie changed their focus from aerospace to lilacs, adding to their collection and selecting a few of their own.

Lilacland, c/o James Lumley, Pelham, Massachusetts. When Albert E. Lumley (1902–1981) discovered that soil conditions on his property were not favorable for tree fruits, but well-suited for lilacs, he made the switch in the 1950s and never looked back. Now maintained by his son, the collection contains about 300 lilac cultivars and is open to visitors from about 15 May to 15 June.

Longwood Gardens, Kennett Square, Pennsylvania.

Margaretten Park, c/o Mrs. Tita Margaretten, Palmdale, California.

McLaughlin Garden, South Paris, Maine. The Bernard McLaughlin estate is a wonderful display of lilacs surrounded by hundreds of combinations of hostas. The McLaughlin Foundation sponsors an annual Lilac Festival each spring.

Meadowlark Hill Garden, c/o Max and Darlene Peterson, Ogallala, Nebraska. One of the most extensive and well-documented collections on the Great Plains, it has inspired others to grow and enjoy lilacs. In May 2004 the Petersons received the International Lilac Society's Director's Award, "For a lifetime of dedicated work on hybridizing, preserving and promoting the Lilac. For their devotion to the cultivation of Meadowlark Hill Lilac Garden, the world's largest private Lilac collection."

Mountain View Lilacs, c/o Karla Davis, Woodlake, California. This is the mirror-collection of the lilacs originally assembled by Reva Ballreich at Idyllwild, California, from the early 1980s until 2004; the collection is in the care of Ballreich's daughter.

Pie in the Sky, Sabra and Robert Gilbert, Hyde Park, New York. In 2005 the pie-shaped field near the top of a mountain in the Catskills, hence the name, provides growing space for a collection of about 175 lilac cultivars.

Samuel J. Harper, Kennebunk Pond, Lyman, Maine.

Shelburne Museum, Shelburne, Vermont. The museum buildings are set in 45 acres (18 ha) of landscaped grounds, featuring about 400 lilacs representing 90 cultivars.

Stampe Lilac Garden (Duck Creek Park), Davenport, Iowa.

Stanley M. Rowe Arboretum, Indian Hill, Cincinnati, Ohio.

Strawbery Banke Museum, Portsmouth, New Hampshire. Incorporated in the museum village is the Goodwin Mansion, once the residence of New Hampshire Governor Ichabod Goodwin (1794–1882) and his wife Sarah Parker Rice Goodwin (d. 1896). Lilacs were among Sarah's favorite flowers. The historic gardens of the museum village feature a number of older, mostly unnamed lilac selections. In the olden days lilac suckers would be dug up and transplanted to a friend or relative's garden.

Sunny Field, c/o William H. Horman, Emmett, Michigan.

Syringa Plus, c/o Evelyn King and Roger Coggeshall, West Newbury, Massachusetts. A collection of well over 300 cultivars, hybrids, and species, including selections that are still being observed and evaluated.

Wedgewood Park, c/o Vera and Don Wedge, Albert Lea, Minnesota.

Nurseries Featuring Lilacs

Arbor Village Farm Nursery, c/o Lanny Rawdon and Derrick Rawdon, Holt, Missouri.

Bailey Nurseries, Saint Paul, Minnesota.

Briggs Nursery, Olympia, Washington. This wholesale (micro-propagation) nursery propagates about 60 lilac cultivars, with an annual production of about 700,000 plants.

Carroll Gardens, c/o Alan Summers, Westminster, Maryland.

E. C. Browns' Nursery, Christopher Wilson, Thetford Center, Vermont.

Erickson's Nursery and Landscape, c/o Brian Erickson, Brainerd, Minnesota.

Fieldstone Gardens, Vassalboro, Maine.

Forest Farm, Ray and Peg Prag, Williams, Oregon.

Fox Hill Nursery, c/o Eric and Jennifer Welzel, Freeport, Maine.

Garden of Eder Nursery, c/o Michael and Kathy Eder, Franklinville, Wisconsin.

Heard Gardens, c/o Robert and Mary Anne Rennebohm, West Des Moines, Iowa. Honoring the tradition established by its founder William (Bill) R. Heard (1916–1995), this nursery continues to grow lilacs.

Hulda Klager Lilac Gardens, Hulda Klager Lilac Society, Woodland, Washington.

King's Tree Farm and Nursery, Route 133, West Boxford, Massachusetts.

Knight Hollow Nursery, c/o Deborah McCown, Middleton, Wisconsin. A micro-propagation nursery.

Lake Street Garden Center, c/o Tim Wolf, Salem, New Hampshire.

Lilac Creek Nursery, c/o Doug O'Reilly, Eden, New York.

Lilac Hill Nursery, c/o Edward (Ted) F. Collins, Victor, New York.

Microplant Nurseries, Gervais, Oregon. The Nurseries routinely propagate about 35 lilac cultivars and will propagate new selections on contract.

Mountain Shadow Nursery, Olympia, Washington. A micro-propagation nursery.

Rabbit Run Nursery, c/o Thomas Nelson, Rochester, Massachusetts.

Sheyenne Garden, c/o Neal S. Holland, Harwood, North Dakota.

Spring Meadow Nursery, c/o Dale and Liz Deppe, Grand Haven, Michigan.

Syringa Plus, c/o Evelyn King and Roger Coggeshall, West Newbury, Massachusetts. A small nursery with a large assortment, featuring about 150 older and newer cultivars.

Wedge Nurseries, Albert Lea, Minnesota.

Lilac Festivals

Challis, Idaho. The Challis Area Lilac Festival is held annually in May and June; it hosts many events, including a Lilac Parade.

Eureka College, Eureka, Illinois. A Lilac Festival and Fine Arts Faire is held each spring, with lilac horticultural demonstrations at the site.

Lisbon, New Hampshire. The Annual Lisbon Lilac Festival in New Hampshire's White Mountains is held in May. It is a celebration of New Hampshire's state flower, featuring a parade, carnival rides, street vendors, golf tournament, fireworks and much more.

Lombard, Illinois.

Mackinac Island, Michigan. The Chamber of Commerce on Mackinac Island hosts an annual 10-day Lilac Festival from about early to mid June.

Portsmouth, New Hampshire. Each May a lilac celebration is held at Wentworth-Coolidge Mansion. Some of the first lilacs imported from Europe were planted here in the mid-1700s by Benning Wentworth. Visitors can learn all about lilacs and purchase cuttings from descendants of the original lilacs. The Saturday afternoon event includes house tours, art gallery displays, lectures, and the chance to walk the grounds along Portsmouth's Little Harbor.

Rochester, New York. The Rochester Lilac Festival is the largest of them all. It also has one of the largest displays of lilacs, boasting 500 cultivars on over 22 acres (8.8 ha) in Highland Botanical Park. The festival lasts for two weeks and includes a wide range of events, exhibits, 10-km races, craft displays, bands and concerts, and much more.

Shelburne, Vermont. An annual Lilac Festival is held in mid to late May.

Spokane, Washington. The Spokane Lilac Association organizes the Annual Lilac Festival and the Grand Lilac Parade, scheduled for the third Saturday in May.

Woodland, Washington. From the last week of April through the first week of May the Lilac Festival is held at the Hulda Klager Lilac Gardens.

Wrightwood, California. The Wrightwood Lilac Festival and Garden Tour is held annually in mid-May.

Glossary

Abaxial The side of an organ away from the axis or center of the axis; dorsal

Acuminate An acute apex whose sides are somewhat concave and taper to a protracted point

Acute Sharp, ending in a point, the sides of the tapered apex essentially straight or slightly convex

Adaxial The side of an organ toward the axis; ventral

Anther The pollen-bearing part of the stamen, borne at the top of the filament or sometimes sessile

Apex (pl. **apices**) The tip or distal end

Apiculate Terminated by an *apicula*, a short, sharp, flexible point

Appressed Closely and flatly pressed against; adpressed

Asexual propagation Vegetative propagation; propagation of plants without fertilization (pollination); cuttings, grafting, micropropagation

Attentuate Showing a long, gradual taper, applied to bases or apices of parts

Barbate Bearded; having hair tufts

Callus The cells that appear on cut surfaces when a plant is wounded and which gradually cover and seal the damaged area

Calyx The outer whorl of a floral envelope, composed of the sepals, which may be distinct, or connate in a single structure

Capsule A dry fruit resulting from the maturing of a compound ovary (or more than one carpel), usually opening at maturity by one or more lines of dehiscence; the lilac fruit is a two-celled capsule

Caudate Bearing a tail-like appendage

Cernuous Drooping

Chimera A plant or plant part composed of two or more genetically different types of cells; see also graft chimera, periclinal chimera, and variegated

Ciliolate Minutely marginally fringed with hairs

Conspicuous Obvious to the eye; noticeable

Corolla The inner circle or second whorl of a floral envelope

Cross To cause to interbreed (verb); the act of hybridization (noun)

Cucullate With hoodlike sepals or petals

Cultivar International abbreviation of the words *cultivated variety*; an assemblage of plants that has been selected for a particular attribute or combination of attributes and that is clearly distinct, uniform, and stable in these characteristics and that when propagated by appropriate means retains those characteristics

Cuneate Wedge-shaped; triangular, with the narrow end at the point of attachment, as the bases of leaves or petals

Cyme A broad, more or less flat-topped, determinate flower cluster, with central flowers opening first

Cymose Bearing cymes or cymelike

Cytokinins (CK) A class of plant growth substances (plant hormones) active in physiological processes such as promoting cell division, cell growth, and cell differentiation

Dentate With sharp, spreading, rather coarse indentations or teeth that are perpendicular to the margin

Distal Pertaining to the end of any structure farthest from the point of attachment

Epidermal Pertaining to the epidermis, the outermost protective layers of cells of roots, stems, leaves, and flowers

Farinose Covered with a fine powdery coating or dust

Fascicled Bundled

Filiform Threadlike; long and very slender

Funnelform Formed like a funnel

Genus The principal category in the nomenclatural hierarchy between family and species

Glabrescent Becoming glabrous

Glabrous Not hairy

Glaucescent Somewhat glaucous

Glaucous Bluish green

Globose Spherical or globe-shaped

Graft chimera A plant whose tissues consist of two genetically different cells in intimate association, formed when a bud developing from the region of a graft contains tissues of both scion and rootstock. *Syringa* 'Correlata' is a graft chimera that developed from a graft of *S.* ×*chinensis* + *S. vulgaris*

Graft union The location of the graft

Grafting The (usually deliberate) fusion of tissues from two or more different plants

Hierarchy The categories of taxa arranged in order according to their rank

Hose-in-hose double Lilac florets where there are two or more corollas but fully functional reproductive parts

Hybrid The result of a cross between differing plants

Hybrid formula The names of the parent plants of the hybrid linked with a multiplication sign (×)

Inflorescence The basic architectural unit of the flower-producing portion of the plant

Interspecific hybridization Pertaining to the progeny of two or more individuals of different species

Intraspecific hybridization Pertaining to the progeny of two or more individuals of the same species

Laciniate Slashed into narrow, pointed lobes

Lanate Woolly, with long, intertwined, curly hairs

Lanceolate Lance-shaped; much longer than broad; widening above the base and tapering to the apex

Lateral On or at the side

Lenticellate Having corky spots (lenticels) on young bark, corresponding to epidermal stomata

Lobate Divided into lobes

Multiplication sign (×) The indication of hybrid origin

Mutation A spontaneous or engineered, relatively permanent change in hereditary material involving either a physical change in chromosome relations or a fundamental change in genes and occurring either in germ cells or in somatic cells but with only those in germ cells being capable of perpetuation by sexual reproduction

Oblique Slanting; unequal sided

Obovate The reverse of ovate, the terminal half broader than the basal

Obtuse Blunt or rounded at the end

Ortet The original single plant from which a clone ultimately derives (the term *clonotype* has been used occasionally in North America)

Ovate With an outline like that of a hen's egg, the broader end below the middle

Palmate Lobed or divided or ribbed in a palmlike fashion

Panicle An indeterminate branching raceme; an inflorescence in which the branches of the primary axis are racemose and the flowers pedicellate

Pedicel The stalk of one flower in a cluster

Pedicellate Supported by a pedicel

Periclinal chimera A chimera in which tissues of one genetic type completely surround tissues of another genetic type; occurs by bud mutation where epidermal cell layers have genetically different structure than the deeper positioned cell layers, effecting variegation of foliage or florets

Petaloid Petal-like; in color and shape resembling a petal

Petiolate Supported by a petiole

Petiole Leaf stalk

pH The negative logarithm of the effective hydrogen-ion concentration or hydrogen-ion activity in gram equivalents per liter used in expressing both acidity and alkalinity on a scale whose values run from 0 to 14 with 7 representing neutrality, numbers less than 7 increasing acidity, and numbers greater than 7 increasing alkalinity

Pilose Shaggy with soft hairs

Pinnate Feather-formed; with the leaflets of a compound leaf placed on either side of the rachis

Plant patent A grant of right, available in certain countries, which provides a means of control over a new plant's propagation, use, and sale for a given period

Pollen Spores or grains borne by the anther, containing the male element

Provenance The known geographic origin of plants or seed

Puberulent Minutely pubescent; the hairs soft, straight, erect, scarcely visible to the unaided eye

Puberulous Somewhat puberulent

Pubescent Covered with soft, short hairs; downy

Rachis (pl. **rachides** or **rachises**) Axis bearing flowers or leaflets

Radial double Lilac florets that have more than the basic number of corolla lobes and fully functional reproductive parts; also referred to as multipetaled

Reflexed Abruptly recurved or bent downward or backward

Reniform Kidney-shaped

Reticulate Netted

Rooting compound A hormone-based chemical compound that assists in root formation

Rootstock Understock

Rubber ties Strips of rubber of various width used in grafting and budding

Rugose Wrinkled, usually covered with wrinkles, the venation seeming impressed into the surfaces

Scion The shoot containing buds that is used for grafting

Selfing, to self To pollinate with pollen from the same flower or plant; to undergo self-pollination

Sibcrossing Crossing (cross-pollinating) the offspring of related cultivars with each other

Somatic Pertaining to the purely bodily part of the plant, excluding the reproductive parts

Species (singular and plural) The basic category in the nomenclatural hierarchy

Sport See *mutation*

Stamen The pollen-bearing organ of a seed plant, typically composed of anther and filament

Staminode double Lilac florets where reproductive parts turned petaloid in some degree, but only one corolla

Stigma (pl. **stigmata**) The portion of the pistil which receives the pollen

Style The more or less elongated part of the pistil between the ovary and the stigma

Subcordate Tending to be heart-shaped

Subcoriaceous Tending to be leathery

Subcylindric Somewhat shaped like a cylinder

Subglabrous Somewhat or slightly glabrous

Subsessile Nearly sessile; with almost no stalk

Subspecies (subsp.) The category in the nomenclatural hierarchy between species and variety

Taxon (pl. **taxa**) A taxonomic entity or group of any rank; a taxon includes all its subordinate taxa

Terminal Situated at the end

Thyrse A type of inflorescence in which an elongate, indeterminate main axis bears numerous lateral branches, each the principal axis of a cymose subdivision; the typical lilac inflorescence

Topovariant A distinguishable group of plants grown from seed from a given provenance

Truncate Appearing as cut off at the end; the base or apex nearly or quite straight across

Understock The living material upon which a scion is grafted which, at some point, is reduced to leave only root tissues beneath the scion

Valvate Opening by valves

Variegated, variegation Having markings of different colors or diversity of colors on the foliage or florets, such as in *Syringa vulgaris* 'Aucubaefolia' (foliage) or *S. vulgaris* 'Sensation' (florets)

Variety (var.) The secondary category on the nomenclatural hierarchy between species and form; *var.* stands for *varietas*, *f.* stands for *forma*

Venation Veining; arrangement or disposition of veins

Villous Provided with long and soft, not matted, hairs; shaggy

Literature Cited

Albrecht, Hans Joachim. 2005. Die Sorten der *Syringa* Villosae-Gruppe. *Gartenpraxis* 31(3): 8–12.

Alexander III, John Herbert. 1992. Fifty of the best lilacs for the gardens of New England. *Lilacs* 21(1): 18.

Alexander III, John Herbert. 1996. Would a lilac by any other name smell so sweet? A search for fragrance. *Arnoldia* 56(1): 25–28.

Alexander III, John Herbert. 1999. Take a new look at lilacs. *Fine Gardening* 66 (March–April): 32–37.

American Association of Botanical Gardens and Arboreta. 2001. *North American Plant Collections Consortium. Membership Directory and Handbook.* Kennett Square, Pennsylvania: American Association of Botanical Gardens and Arboreta.

Anderson, Edgar, and Alfred Rehder. 1935. New hybrids from the Arnold Arboretum. *Journal of the Arnold Arboretum* 16: 358–363.

Anonymous. 1912. *Syringa sweginzowii. Arnold Arboretum Bulletin* 59.

Anonymous. 1949. A yellow lilac. *The Gardeners' Chronicle* 3260 (2 July): 1.

Apostolova, Iva, and Ljubka Slavova. 1997. *Compendium of Bulgarian Plant Communities Published Between 1891 and 1995.* Sofia: Institute of Botany, Bulgarian Academy of Sciences.

Bachtell, Kris R. 1991. Peking lilac (*Syringa pekinensis*). *Morton Arboretum Quarterly* 27(1): 10–12.

Bai Pei-Yu. 1979. Some new taxa of Oleaceae from Tibet, China. *Acta Botanica Yunnanica* 1(1): 151–156.

Bailey, Liberty Hyde. 1902. *The Standard Cyclopedia of American Horticulture.* 4 vols.

Barry, Randall K., editor. 1997. *ALA-LC Romanization Tables: Transliteration Schemes for Non-Roman Scripts.* Washington, D.C.: U.S. Library of Congress. http://www.loc.gov/catdir/cpso/roman.html. Accessed 13 May 2000.

Bartrum, Douglas. 1959. *Lilac and Laburnum.* London: John Gifford.

Bean, William Jackson. 1910. *Kew Bulletin of Miscellaneous Information* 23: 176.

Bean, William Jackson. 1980. *Trees and Shrubs Hardy in the British Isles*, 8th ed. London: John Murray.

Belanger, Eva, and Gilles M. G. C. Souchet. 2005. Monographie d'une Forcerie de Lilas à Vitry / Seine (Val de Marne). École du Louvre. (unpublished notes)

Belon, Pierre. 1553. Les Observations de Plusieurs Singularités et Choses Mémorables Trouvés en Grèce, Asie, Judée, Egypte, Arabie et Autres Pays Estrangers. Paris: G. Corrozet.

Belorusets, E. Sh. 1990. *Siren'* [lilac]. Kiev: Urozhaĭ.

Bennett, Jennifer. 2002. *Lilacs for the Garden.* Buffalo: Firefly Books.

Besler, Basilius. 1613. *Hortus Eystettensis.* Nuremberg.

Betts, Edwin M., editor. 1944. *Thomas Jefferson's Garden Book, 1766–1824.* Philadelphia: American Philosophical Society.

Bibikova, Veronika F. 1974. Skreshchivaemost' razichnykh vidov sirini. *Byulleten' Glavnogo Botanicheskogo Sada* 92: 34–40.

Bilov, V. N., Ivan I. Shtan'ko, and Nikolai V. Mikhaĭlov. 1974. *Siren'* [lilac]. Moscow: Nauka.

Blakeslee, Albert Francis, and Amos Geer Avery. 1937. Methods of inducing doubling of chromosomes in plants. *Journal of Heredity* 28: 393–411.

Blunt, Wilfrid, and William Thomas Stearn. 1994. *The Art of Botanical Illustration*, ed. 2. Woodbridge: Antique Collectors' Club.

Boerhaave, Hermann. 1710. *Index Plantarum.* Lyons.

Bojarczuk, Krystyna. 1978a. Propagation of green cuttings of lilac (*Syringa vulgaris* L.) cultivars using various substances stimulating rooting. *Arboretum Kórnickie* 23: 53–100. (in Polish with English summary)

Bojarczuk, Krystyna. 1978b. Anatomical and physiological studies on lilac (*Syringa vulgaris* L.) cuttings during their rooting. *Arboretum Kórnickie* 23: 101–120. (in Polish with English summary)

Boom, B. K. 1957. *Jaarboek van de Nederlandse Dendrologische Vereniging* 20: 113–114.

Boon, Patricia. 2005. Een wonder van een sering. *De Telegraaf* (17 April): T25.

Borbás, Vinczé von. 1882. *Erdészeti Lapok* [Forestry papers], 883.

Borgenstam, E. 1922. Zur Zytologie der Gattung *Syringa* nebst Erörterungen über den Einfluss äusserer Faktoren auf die Kernteilungsvorgänge. *Arkiv för Botanik utgevet av Kungliga Svenska Vetenskapsakademien* 17(15): 1–27.

Brandis, Dietrich. 1874. *The Forest Flora of North-West and Central India: A Handbook of the Indigenous Trees and Shrubs of Those Countries*. London: William H. Allen.

Brender à Brandis, Gerard. 1980. *Wood, Ink and Paper*. Toronto: Porcupine's Quill.

Bretschneider, Emil V. 1898. *History of European Botanical Discoveries in China*. Bristol, United Kingdom: Ganesha Publishing.

Brickell, Christopher David, Bernard Rene Baum, Wilbert L. A. Hetterscheid, Alan Christopher Leslie, John McNeill, Piers Trehane, Freek Vrugtman, and John H. Wiersema, editors. 2004. *International Code of Nomenclature for Cultivated Plants* Regnum Vegetabile 144.

Brummit, Richard Kenneth. 1992. *Vascular Plant Families and Genera*. Richmond: Royal Botanic Gardens, Kew.

Brummit, Richard Kenneth, and C. E. Powell, editors. 1992. *Authors of Plant Names: A List of Authors of Scientific Names of Plants, with Recommended Standard Forms of Their Names, Including Abbreviations*. Richmond: Royal Botanic Gardens, Kew.

Buckley, Arthur. 1982. Lilacs at Ottawa. *Lilacs* 11(1): 10–20.

Bugała, Władysław. 1955. The Ottawa lilac and its varieties. *Arboretum Kórnickie* 1: 131–141. (in Polish with English summary)

Bugała, Władysław. 1964. Lilacs in the Kórnik Arboretum and their acclimatization to date. *Arboretum Kórnickie* 9: 59–96. (in Polish with English summary)

Bugała, Władysław. 1995. New cultivars of *Syringa ×prestoniae* in the Kórnik Arboretum. *Lilacs* 24(4): 90–91.

Bunge, Alexander von. 1833. *Syringa oblata* (as *Syringa chinensis*). *Mémoires des Savants Etrangers de l'Académie Imperiale des Sciences de St Petersbourg*, sixth series, 2: 116 (1835). (in Latin)

Bureau, Louis É., and Adrien Franchet. 1891. *Syringa tomentella*. Plantes nouvelles du Thibet et de la Chine occidentale receuillies pendant le voyage de M. Bonvalot et du Prince Henri d'Orléans en 1890. *Journal de Botanique* 5: 103 (1 April), 160 (May 16).

Caldwell, Billy E., editor. 1989. Intellectual Property Rights Associated with Plants. American Society of Agronomy Special Publication 52. Madison, Wisconsin: Crop Science Society of America.

Camerarius, Rudolph J. 1694. *De sexu plantarum epistola*. Tübingen, Germany.

Cameron, D. F. 1950. Ornamental plant breeding. Progress Report. Division of Horticulture, Central Experimental Farm, Ottawa 1934–48. Ottawa: Canada Department of Agriculture.

Cameron, D. F. 1955. Ornamental plant breeding. Progress Report. Division of Horticulture, Central Experimental Farm, Ottawa 1949–53. Ottawa: Canada Department of Agriculture.

Cameron, D. F. 1960. Ornamental plant breeding. Progress Report. Division of Horticulture, Central Experimental Farm, Ottawa 1954–58. Ottawa: Canada Department of Agriculture.

Caprio, Joseph M. 1957. Phenology of lilac bloom in Montana. *Science* 126(3287): 1344–1345.

Caprio, Joseph M., M. D. Magnuson, and H. N. Metcalf. 1970. Instructions for phenological observations of purple common lilac and red berry honeysuckle. Circular 250. Western Region Research Publication. Bozeman: Montana Agricultural Experiment Station, Montana State University.

Cesalpino, Andrea. 1583. *De plantis libri XVI*. Florence: Giorgio Marescotti.

Chang Mei-Chen, and Chen Xin-Lu. 1990. Studies on Chinese *Syringa*: 1. Investigatio et Studium Naturae 10: 32–40.

Chang Mei-Chen, and Peter S. Green. 1996a. *Syringa*. In *Flora of China*. Eds. Z. Y. Wu and P. H. Raven. St. Louis: Missouri Botanical Garden. 15: 280–286.

Chang Mei-Chen, and Peter S. Green. 1996b. *Ligustrum* Linnaeus. In *Flora of China*. Eds. Z. Y. Wu and P. H. Raven. St. Louis: Missouri Botanical Garden. 15: 299.

Chang Mei-Chen, and Qu Shi-Zeng. 1992. *Syringa pubescens*. *Flora Reipublicae Popularis Sinica* 61: 2–222.

Chapman, Colin. 2001. European newsletter—Post scriptum. *Lilacs* 30(4): 112.

Chen Congzhou. 1984. Shuo yuan [on Chinese gardens]. Bilingual edition, Chinese and English. Shanghai: Tongji University Press.

Clark, Robert Brown. 1977. Lilac phenology. *International Lilac Society* 3(5): 5.

Coats, Alice M. 1963. *Garden Shrubs and Their Histories.* London: Vista Books.

Coggeshall, Roger G. 1962. Hybrid lilacs from softwood cuttings. *American Nurseryman* (15 June): 7–8.

Collins, Dean. 1948. A lifetime with lilacs. *Flower Grower* 35(11): 830.

Congdon, M. 1965. Timing and its relation to cutting selection. Combined Proceedings, East–West Regions, of the International Plant Propagators Society 15: 230–232.

Cornu, Marie M. 1888. *Revue Horticole*, p. 492, plate.

Council of Biology Editors. 1972. *CBE Style Manual.* 3rd edition. Arlington, Virginia: American Institute of Biological Sciences.

Cui Hong-Xia, Jiang G.-M., Niu S.-L., Li Y.-G., Jiang C.-D., Liu M.-Z., and Gao L.-M. 2004. Gas exchanges of an endangered species *Syringa pinnatifolia* and a widespread congener *S. oblata. Photosynthetica* 42(4): 529–534.

Curtis, William. 1793. *Syringa vulgaris*—common lilac. *Curtis's Botanical Magazine*, series 1, 6: plate 183.

Cutler, Sandra McLean. 1997. *Dwarf and Unusual Conifers Coming of Age—A Guide to Mature Garden Conifers.* North Olmsted: Barton-Bradley Crossroads.

Dahlström, Svante. 1960. Under almar och lindar. *Promenader* 2: 161–169. Turku, Finland.

Darlington, Cyril D., and Edavalath K. Janaki-Ammal. 1945. *Chromosome Atlas of Cultivated Plants.* London: Allen and Unwin.

Darlington, Cyril D., and Ann P. Wylie. 1956. *Chromosome Atlas of Flowering Plants.* New York: Macmillan.

Darlington, William. 1849. *Memorials of John Bartram and Humphry Marshall.* Facsimile edited by Joseph Ewan. New York: Hafner, 1967.

Darwin, Charles Robert. 1859. *The Origin of Species by Means of Natural Selection, or The Preservation of Favoured Races in the Struggle for Life.* London: John Murray.

Davidson, Campbell G., Richard J. Enns, and Susanne Enns (Gobin). 1994. Landscape Plants at the Morden Arboretum: A Compilation of the Landscape Plants That Have Been Tested at the Agriculture and Agri-Food Canada Research Centre, Morden, Manitoba, Canada.

Davis, Malcolm Bancroft, and Isabella Preston. 1938. The lilac in Canada. Ornamental Flowering Trees and Shrubs. London: Report of the Royal Horticultural Society Conference, pages 135–140, figures 42–44.

De Belder, Jelena. 1998. *Het leven begint in de herfst— Vier seisoenen in het Arboretum Kalmthout.* Warnsveld: Terra / Lannoo.

Decaisne, Joseph. 1878. Monographie des genres *Ligustrum* et *Syringa. Nouvelles Archives du Muséum d'Histoire Naturelle*, séries 2, 2: 1–45. Paris: Masson.

De Toni, E. 1940. Pietro Antonio Michiel. I cinque libri de piante Codice Marciano trascizione e commento. Venezia: Reale Istituto de Scienze, Lettere ed Arti.

Dhar, Uppeandra, and P. Kachroo. 1983. *Alpine Flora of Kashmir Himalaya.* Jodhpur: Scientific Publishers.

Diels, Ludwig. 1901. *Syringa microphylla.* Die Flora von Central-China. Nach der vorhandenen Literatur und neu mitgeteiltem orignal Material. *Botanische Jahrbücher für Systematik, Pflanzengeschichte und Pflanzengeographie* 29: 531.

Dubé, P. A., L. P. Perry, and M. T. Vittum. 1984. Instructions for phenological observations: Lilac and honeysuckle. Vermont Agricultural Experiment Station Bulletin 692.

Dvorak, Joseph, Jr. 1978. *A Four-Year Study at Lilac Park, the Morton Arboretum.* Special Scientific Publication of the International Lilac Society.

Eigsti, O. J., and P. Dustin Jr. 1955. *Colchicine in Agriculture, Medicine, Biology and Chemistry.* Ames: Iowa State College Press.

Encke, Fritz, Günther Buchheim, and Siegmund Seybold. 1984. *Zander Handwörterbuch der Pflanzennamen*, 14th edition. Stuttgart: Ulmer.

Eveleens Maarse, Dirk. 1954a. Fliedersorten für die Treiberei. *Gartenwelt* 54(23).

Eveleens Maarse, Dirk. 1954b. Some remarks on my new lilacs. *Dendron* 1: 11–13.

Federov, A. A., editor. 1969. *Chromosome Numbers of Flowering Plants.* Leningrad: Izdatel'stvo Nauka.

Fiala, John Leopold. 1977. Colchicine treatment in the genus *Syringa. Lilacs* 6(1): 18–21.

Fiala, John Leopold. 1988. *Lilacs: The Genus* Syringa. Portland: Timber Press.

Fiala, John Leopold. 1994. *Flowering Crabapples: The Genus* Malus. Portland: Timber Press.

Flemer III, William. 1984. Island and median-strip planting. *Arnoldia* 44(4): 20.

Fletcher, Harold R., John Scott Lennox Gilmour, George Hill Mathewson Lawrence, Elbert Luther Little Jr., Gunnar Nilsson-Leissner, and Roger (Marie Vincent Philippe Leveque) de Vilmorin, editors. 1958. *International Code of Nomenclature for Cultivated Plants*. Regnum Vegetabile 10.

Focke, Wilhelm Olbers. 1881. *Die Pflanzenmischlinge: Ein Beitrag zur Biologie der Gewächse*. Berlin: Bornträger.

Fordham, Alfred J. 1959. Propagation and care of lilacs. *Arnoldia* 19: 36–45.

Franchet, Adrien René. 1891. *Syringa yunnanensis. Revue Horticole* 191: 308, 332.

Fu, Li-kuo, editor. 1992. *China Plant Red Data Book: Rare and Endangered Plants*, Volume 1. Beijing: Science Press.

Gao, Runqing, Liu Jianbin, Chen Xinlu, and Xing Jinhong. 2001. Studies on asexual propagation technique of lilac. *Journal of Beijing Agricultural College* 16(2): 31–35. (in Chinese)

Gärtner, Karl Friedrich von. 1837, 1849. Versuche und Beobachtungen über die Bastarderzeugung im Pflanzenreich. Stuttgart.

Giguère, Rock, and Frank Moro. 2005. *Les Lilas: Les Meilleurs Choix, les Plus Beaux Fleurs, Tous les Conseils pour Les Cultiver*. Montréal: Les Éditions de l'Homme.

Gilmour, John Scott Lennox, F. R. Horne, Elbert Luther Little Jr., Frans Antonie Stafleu, and Richard Hook Richens, editors. 1969. *International Code of Nomenclature for Cultivated Plants—1969*. Regnum Vegetabile 64.

Goethe, Johann Wolfgang von. 1810. *Zur Farbenlehre*. Tübingen, German.

Goldblatt, Peter, and Dale E. Johnson, editors. 1996. Index to Plant Chromosome Numbers 1992–1993. Monographs in Systematic Botany from the Missouri Botanical Garden 58.

Goldman-Huertas, Benjamin Michael. 2005. An update on the lilac family tree. *Lilacs* 34(4): 120–122.

Gould, Charles J., and Worth E. Vassey. 1977. Lilacs resistant to bacterial blight. *Lilacs* 6(1): 48–57.

Grae, Ida. 1974. *Nature's Colors: Dyes from Plants*. New York: Macmillan.

Graham, Chris. 1986. Lilac propagation at Royal Botanical Gardens. *Lilacs* 15(1): 18–21.

Green, James L. 1984. Lilac—Year-round cut flower?—Dual-purpose plant? *Ornamentals Northwest Archives* 8(2): 13–19.

Green, Peter Shaw. 1979. *Syringa meyeri* var. *meyeri* 'Palibin'. *Curtis's Botanical Magazine* 182: 117–120, plate 778.

Green, Peter Shaw. 1984a. The Chinese "common" lilac. *The Plantsman* 6(1): 12–13.

Green, Peter Shaw. 1984b. *Syringa oblata. Lilacs* 13(1): 9–10.

Green, Peter Shaw. 1989a. Review of *Lilacs: The Genus* Syringa, by John L. Fiala. *Kew Magazine* 6(2): 90–92.

Green, Peter Shaw. 1989b. The laciniate-leaved lilacs. *Kew Magazine* 6(3): 116–124, plate 132.

Green, Peter Shaw. 1995. Proposal to reject the name *Syringa buxifolia* Nakai (Oleaceae). *Taxon* 44(4): 636.

Green, Peter Shaw, and Chang Mei-Chen. 1995. Some taxonomic changes in *Syringa* L. (Oleaceae), including a revision of series *Pubescentes. Novon* 5(4): 329–333.

Green, Peter Shaw, and H. J. Fliegner. 1991. When is a privet not a lilac? *Kew Magazine* 8: 58–63, plate 171.

Green, Thomas. 1993. Plants under attack by MLOs—Mycoplasma-like organisms. *Morton Arboretum Quarterly* 29(2): 28–32.

Gressley, David. 2000. Japanese tree lilacs. *Lilacs* 29(3): 84–85.

Greuter, Werner, John McNeill, Fred Rogers Barrie, Hervé-Maurice Burdet, Vincent Demoulin, Tarciso S. Filgueiras, Dan Henry Nicolson, Paul Claude Silva, Judith Ellen Skog, Piers Trehane, Nicholas J. Turland, and David L Hawksworth, editors. 2000. *International Code of Botanical Nomenclature* (Saint Louis Code). Regnum Vegetabile 138.

Griffiths, H. M., Wayne A. Sinclair, Christine D. Smart, and Robert E. Davis. 1999. The phytoplasma associated with ash yellows and lilac witches'-broom: *Candidatus Phytoplasma fraxini. International Journal of Systematic Bacteriology* 49(4): 1605–1614.

Grodzinskogo, A. M. 1985. Ornamental plants for outdoor and indoor areas. Kiev: Naukova Dumka. (*Syringa*, pages 301–310; in Russian)

Grohmann, Fritz. 1974. Oleaceae. In *Flora of West Pakistan*, 59. Eds. Eugene Nasir and Syed Irtifaq Ali. Islamabad: National Herbarium.

Gromov, Andrey. 1963. *Siren'*. Moscow: Moskovskii Rabochii.

Hansen, Mary Ann. 2000. Powdery mildew-resistant woody ornamentals. Publication 450-616, Department of Plant Pathology, Physiology and Weed Science. Blacksburg: Virginia Polytechnical Institute and State University.

Hara, Hiroshi. 1941. *Syringa reticulata. Journal of Japanese Botany* 17: 21.

Hara, Hiroshi, Arthur Oliver Chater, and Leonard Howard John Williams. 1982. *An Enumeration of the Flowering Plants of Nepal* 3: 82. London: British Museum (Natural History).

Harding, Alice. 1933. *Lilacs in My Garden: A Practical Handbook for Amateurs*. New York: Macmillan.

Hardouin-Fugier, Elisabeth, and Etienne Grafe. 1989. *French Flower Painters of the 19th Century: A Dictionary*. Edited by Peter Mitchell. London: Philip Wilson.

Harms, Friedrich. 1897. *Flieder und Asparagus*. Lehrbuch de Anzucht, Kultur und Treiberei des Flieders, sowie der Grosskultur der Schnittgrün-Asparagus. Beschreibung der besten Sorten und deren lohnenste Verwendung. Erfurt: Ludwig Möller.

Harms, Friedrich. 1902. *Möller's Deutsche Gärtner-Zeitung* 8: 3.

Harnborne, J. B., and Peter Shaw Green. 1980. A chemotaxonomic survey of flavonoids in leaves of the Oleaceae. *Journal of the Linnean Society*, Botany 81: 155–167.

Hartmann, Hudson T., Dale E. Kester, Fred T. Davies Jr., and Robert L. Geneve. 2002. *Hartmann and Kester's Plant Propagation: Principles and Practices*, 7th edition. Upper Saddle River: Pearson Prentice Hall.

Harvard University Herbaria. 2001. Index of Botanists. http://cms.huh.harvard.edu/databases/botanist_index.html.

Harwood, William Sumner. 1905. *New Creations in Plant Life: An Authoritative Account of the Life and Work of Luther Burbank*. New York: Macmillan.

Haskell, David, Owen Rogers, and Douglas Routley. 1986. Etiolation and tissue culture as lilac propagation techniques. *Lilacs* 15(1): 45–50.

Hatusima, S. 1938. *Syringa wolfii* var. *hirsuta*. Bulletin of the University Forest, Kyushu Imperial University, Fukuoka 10: 103.

Havemeyer, Theodore A. 1971. How the modern lilac came to be: Recounting the story of Mr. Lemoine's work as told by himself. *The Garden Magazine*, pp. 232–233.

Hawksworth, David L. 1994. *A Draft Glossary of Terms Used in Bionomenclature*. Monograph 9. Paris: International Union of Biological Sciences.

Hedge, Ian, and Per Wendelbo. 1970. A note on the rhododendrons of Afghanistan. *The Rhododendron and Camellia Year Book* 24: 179.

Hedrick, Ulysses Prentiss. 1950. *A History of Horticulture in America to 1860*. New York: Oxford University Press.

Heinze, Woldemar, and Detlef Schreiber. 1984. Eine neue Kartierung der Winterhärtezonen für Gehölze in Europa. *Mitteilungen der Deutschen Dendrologischen Gesellschaft* 75: 11–56. (in German with English summary)

Hemsley, William Botting. 1906. A new Chinese lilac with pinnate leaves. *Gardeners' Chronicle*, series 3, 39: 68.

Henry, Louis. 1894. *Syringa oblata. Le Jardin* 8: 162.

Henry, Louis. 1900. Crossings made at the Natural History Museum of Paris from 1887 to 1899. *Journal of the Royal Horticultural Society* 24: 218–236.

Henry, Louis. 1901. *Syringa affinis. Journal de la Société Nationale d'Horticulture de France*, séries 4, 2: 731.

Hermann, Paul. 1687. Catalogus horti Academici Lugundo Batavi. Leiden: Cornelius Boutestein.

Hesse, Hermann. 1935. Nursery catalog, p. 76.

Heuffel, János A. 1831. *Syringa vulgaris*. In *Flora, oder Allgemeine Botanische Zeitung Regensburg* 14(1): 399.

Hibben, Craig R. 1986. Progress report on lilac witches'-broom research. *Lilacs* 15(1): 35–38.

Hibben, Craig R. 1991. Relatedness of mycoplasma-like organisms associated with ash yellows and lilac witches'-broom. *Plant Disease* 75(12): 1227–1230.

Hibben, Craig R. 2005. Lilac witches'-broom. *Lilacs* 34(1): 17.

Hibben, Craig R., C. A. Lewis, and J. D. Castello. 1985. Mycoplasmalike organisms identified in lilacs with witches'-broom disease. *Lilacs* 14(1): 11–18.

Hibben, Craig R., C. A. Lewis, and J. D. Castello. 1986. Mycoplasmalike organisms, cause of lilac witches'-broom. *Plant Disease* 70: 342–345.

Hibben, Craig R., J. T. Walker, M. P. Taylor, and J. C. Allison. 1977. Lilacs resistant to leaf-roll necrosis and powdery mildew. *Lilacs* 6(1): 35–47.

Hildebrandt, Virginia. 1986. Lilac propagation by tissue culture: Academic to commercial. *Lilacs* 15(1): 25–34.

Hildebrandt, Virginia, and Patricia M. Harney. 1983. In vitro propagation of *Syringa vulgaris* 'Vesper'. *Hort-Science* 18: 432–434.

Hirtz, François. 1993. *Victor Lemoine, un grand nom de l'horticulture mondiale.* Thesis, Diplôme d'Etat de Docteur en Pharmacie, Université de Nancy.

Hoffman, Marco H. A. 2000. *Syringa vulgaris*—sortimentsonderzoek. *Dendroflora* 37: 60–96. (in Dutch with English and German summaries)

Hoffman, Marco H. A. 2003. *Syringa* Villosae Groep—Sortimentsonderzoek en keuringsrapport. *Dendroflora* 39: 104–119. (in Dutch with English and German summaries)

Hoffman, Marco H. A. 2004. *Syringa* Villosae Group—first cultivar group in *Syringa*. *Lilacs* 33(1): 25–27.

Holetich, Charles Dragutin. 1982. English translation of *Lilac Species and Cultivars in Cultivation in USSR*, by Leonid I. Rubtzov, Nikolai L. Mikhaïlov, and Valentina G. Zhogoleva. *Lilacs* 11(2): 1–38.

Holetich, Charles Dragutin. 1995. *The Katie Osborne Lilac Garden.* Horticultural Leaflet 1. Hamilton: Royal Botanical Gardens.

Hopp, R. J., and B. O. Blair. 1973. Plant phenology in eastern and central North America: I. Development of networks and preliminary results. Vermont Agricultural Experiment Station Bulletin 677.

Hopp, R. J., B. O. Blair, and R. P. Hickin. 1973. Plant phenology in eastern and central North America: II. Phenological observations on lilac 'Red Rothomagensis'. Vermont Agricultural Experiment Station Bulletin 678.

Howard, Richard A. 1959. A booklet on lilacs from Russia. *Arnoldia* 19: 31–35.

Howard, Richard A. 1965. Susan Delano McKelvey, 1883–1964. *Journal of the Arnold Arboretum* 46: 45–47.

Howard, Richard A. 1980. E. H. Wilson and the "nodding lilac." *Lilacs* 9: 13–15.

Howard, Richard A., and George K. Brizicky. 1965. The translation and transliteration of cultivar names with some notes on lilacs. *American Association of Botanical Gardens and Arboreta Quarterly Newsletter* 64: 15–21.

Ihne, Egon. 1885. Karte der Aufblühzeit von *Syringa vulgaris* in Europa. *Botanisches Centralblatt* 21: 85–88, 116–121, 150–155.

Irvine, Susan A. 1995. *Perfume: The Creation and Allure of Classic Fragrances.* New York: Crescent Books.

Isaacson, Richard T. 1979. *Flowering Plant Index of Illustration and Information.* Boston: G. K. Hall.

Isaacson, Richard T. 1982. *Flowering Plant Index of Illustration and Information, 1979–1981.* Cleveland: Garden Center of Greater Cleveland.

Jackson, Donald, and Dorothy Twohig, editors. 1978. *The Diaries of George Washington.* Volume 4, *The Papers of George Washington.* Charlottesville: University Press of Virginia.

Jäger, Hermann. 1865. *Syringa* ×*chinensis* nothof. *bicolor. Die Ziergehölze* (Ornamental trees and shrubs). Weimar, Germany.

Jaume Saint-Hilaire, Jean Henri. 1825. *Traité des arbrisseaux et des arbustes cultivés en France et en pleine terre.* Paris: J. H. Jaume Saint-Hilaire.

Javurkova, V. 1981. Chromosome number reports 73. *Taxon* 30: 856–857.

Johannsen, Wilhelm Ludvig. 1900. *Das Äther-Verfahren beim Frühtreiben mit besonderer Berücksichtigung der Fliedertreiberei.* Jena.

Johnston, Stanley. 2001. Images of lilacs. http://members.aol.com/arbexhibit/lilac.htm. Accessed 9 June 2004.

Jovanović, Branislav, and Emilia Vukicević. 1980. Lilac (*Syringa vulgaris* L.) variables on the serpentines of the river Ibar ravine. Unpublished English translation by Janos Berenji, Yugoslavia, without Latin descriptions (Berenji, January 2005, pers. comm. to F. V.).

Jull, Laura. 2006. *Lilacs for Cold Climates.* Publication A3825. Madison, Wisconsin: University of Wisconsin-Extension, Cooperative Extension. [Also available on the Internet at http://learningstore.uwex.edu/Lilacs-for-Cold-Climates-P1176C94.aspx?UserID=561479.]

Kalva, Vladimir. 1980. *Ceriņi.* Riga: Liesma.

Kalva, Vladimir. 1988. *Sirelid.* Riga: Valgus.

Kang, K. H., and C. S. Chang. 1998. Systematic study of *Syringa* (Oleaceae) in Korea. *Korean Journal of Plant Taxonomy* 28(3): 249–279.

Karpow-Lipski, Mikołaj. 1958. New Polish varieties of lilacs. *Arboretum Kórnickie* 3: 99–108. (in Polish with English summary)

Keeler, Harriet. 1969. *Our Northern Shrubs and How to Identify Them.* New York: Dover.

Kelsey, Harlan P., and William A. Dayton, editors. 1942.

Syringa. In *Standardized Plant Names: A Revised and Enlarged Listing of Approved Scientific and Common Names of Plants and Plant Products in American Commerce or Use*. American Joint Committee on Horticultural Nomenclature. Harrisburg: J. Horace McFarland. 332–333, 613–617.

Kihara, H. 1957. *Fauna and Flora of Nepal Himalaya: Scientific Results of the Japanese Expeditions to Nepal Himalaya 1952–1953*. Kyoto: Fauna and Flora Research Society, Kyoto University. 1: 204.

Kim, K.-J., and R. K. Jansen. 1998. A chloroplast DNA phylogeny of Lilacs (*Syringa*, Oleaceae): Plastome groups show a strong correlation with crossing groups. *American Journal of Botany* 85(9): 1338–1351.

King, Evie, and Roger Coggeshall. 1998. Our work with the Ken Berdeen lilacs in Kennebunk, Maine. *Lilacs* 27(2): 49–50.

Kochieva, E. Z., N. N. Ryzhova, O. I. Molkanova, Alexandr M. Kudryavtsev, Vladimir P. Upelniek, and Irena B. Okuneva. 2004. The genus *Syringa*: Molecular markers of species and cultivars. *Russian Journal of Genetics* 40(1): 30–32. (in Russian, with English summary on pages 37–40)

Koehne, Bernhard A. E., and Alexander von Lingelsheim. 1910. *Syringa sweginzowii. Repertorium Specierum Novarum Regni Vegetabilis*. Centralblatt für Sammlung und Veröffentlichung von Einzeldiagnosen neuer Pflanzen 8: 9.

Koelreuter, Joseph Gottlieb. 1761–1766. Vorläufige Nachricht von einigen das Geschlecht der Pflanzen betreffenden Versuchen und Beobachtungen, nebst Fortsetzungen 1, 2 und 3. Leipzig.

Kolesnikov, Leonid. 1955. *Lilac*. Moscow: Foreign Languages Publishing House. (translated from the Russian edition published by the Moscow Worker Publishing House, Moscow, 1952)

Komarov, Vladimir L. 1900. Trudy Glavnago Botanicheskago Sada. *Acta Horti Petropolitani* 18: 146 (Conspectus Flora Korea 2: 10).

Krijger, Dik. 2003. Screening sortiment trekseringen—Screening van een inernationaal sortiment van Seringen ter verbeting van het bedrijfsresultaat op trekheesterbedrijven en behoud van cultuurlandschappelijke waarden van de Aalsmeerse bovenlanden. Glastuinbouw: Praktijkonderzoek Plant & Omgeving.

Kronfeld, E. M., 1918. Flieder und Holunder. *Mitteilungen der Deutschen Dendrologischen Gesellschaft* 27: 209–228.

Krüssmann, Gerd. 1937. *Die Laubgehölze: Verzeichnis und Beschreibung der in Deutschland winterharten Laubgehölze, ein Nachschlagebuch für Gärtner, Forstleute und Gartenfreunde sowie zum Gebrauch an Fachschulen*. Unter Mitwirking von Karl Frost. Berlin: Paul Parey.

Krüssmann, Gerd. 1947. Das Fliedersortiment. *Deutsche Baumschule* 1: 70–71.

Krüssmann, Gerd. 1960a. Vorarbeiten für eine Flieder-Sichtung. *Deutsche Baumschule* 12(3): 57–71; 12(4): 89–108.

Krüssmann, Gerd. 1960b. Fliederprüfung in Dortmund am 19. Mai 1960. *Deutsche Baumschule* 12(8): 213–214.

Kudryatseva, V. M., and V. F. Bibikova. 1969. O prichinakh neskreshivaemosti pri otdalennoi gibridzatsii sireni. *Byulleten' Glavnogo Botanicheskogo Sada* 73: 51–54.

Kyte, Lydiane, and John Kleyn. 1996. *Plants from Test Tubes*. 3d ed. Portland, Oregon: Timber Press.

L. B. 1917. Victor Lemoine, plant hybridist: an appreciation. *The Garden Magazine*, p. 234.

Lack, H. Walter. 2000. Lilac and horse-chestnut: Discovery and rediscovery. *Curtis's Botanical Magazine*, series 6, 17(2): 109–141.

Lack, H. Walter, and David J. Mabberley. 1998. *The Flora Graeca Story: Sibthorp, Bauer, and Hawkins in the Levant*. Oxford: University Press.

Lammens, Edmond, and Adolphe Buyssens. 1970. *Floriculture: Généralitéset Plantes de Plein Air*. Brussels: De Boeck.

Lape, Fred. 1965. *A Garden of Trees and Shrubs: Practical Hints for Planning and Planting an Arboretum*. Ithaca: Cornell University Press.

La Rue, Carl D. 1948. The lilacs of Mackinac Island. *American Midland Naturalist* 39(2): 505–508.

Lasseigne, Francis Todd. 2004. *Physiological Responses of Selected Taxa of* Salvia, Taxus, Cephalotaxus, *and* Syringa *to Heat and/or Flooding*. Ph.D. Thesis, North Carolina State University.

Le Blon, Jakob Christof. 1725. *Coloritto or the Harmony of Colouring in Painting, Reduced to Mechanical Practice*. London. Facsimile edition. New York: Van Nostrand Reinhold, 1980.

Lemoine, Émile. 1900. Hybrids between the common lilac and the laciniated Persian lilac. *Journal of the Royal Horticultural Society* 24: 299–311.

Lemoine, Émile. 1903–1904. On the use of ether and chloroform for the forcing of shrubs, and of lilacs in particular. *Journal of the Royal Horticultural Society* 28: 45.

Lemoine, Victor. 1853. Catalogue 8, p. 6. Nancy, France.

Lemoine, Victor. 1878. *Syringa hyacinthiflora plena.* Catalogue 78, p. 6. Nancy, France.

Lemoine, Victor. 1896. Catalogue 134, p. 9. Nancy, France.

Léveillé, A. A. Hector. 1910. *Feddes Repertorium Specierum Novarum Regni Vegetabilis.* Zeitschrift für Systematische Botanik 8: 285.

Léveillé, A. A. Hector. 1916. *Catalogue des Plantes du Yun-Nan,* 181.

Li, Jian-Hua, John H. Alexander III, and Zhang Dong-Lin. 2002. Paraphyletic *Syringa* (Oleaceae): Evidence from sequences of nuclear ribosomal DNA ITS and ETS regions. *Systematic Botany* 27(3): 592–597.

Lichtblau, Thorsten. 2001. Flieder und Rosskastanie: Entdeckung und Wiederentdeckung. http://www.fu-berlin.de/presse/fup/archiv/pdw01/pdw_01_033.html. Accessed 16 February 2003.

Lindley, John. 1859. *Syringa oblata. Gardeners' Chronicle,* p. 868.

Lingelsheim, Alexander von. 1920. In *Das Pflanzenreich.* Ed. A. Engler. Leipzig: W. Engelmann. 4: 243(1–2).

Linnaeus, Carl. 1737. *Genera Plantarum.* Stockholm.

Linnaeus, Carl. 1753. *Species Plantarum.* 2 vols. Stockholm.

Linnaeus, Carl. 1760. Disquisitio de sexu plantarum ab Academia Imperiali Scientiarum Petropolitana praemio ornata. *Amoenitates Academicae* 10: 100–131.

Logan, James. 1741. Experimenta et meletemata de plantarum generatione nec non canonum pro inveniendis refractionum, tum simplicium, tum in lentibus duplicium focis demonstrationes geometricae. Leyden: C. Haak.

Loudon, John Claudius. 1835–1838. *Arboretum et Fruticetum Britannicum, or, The Trees and Shrubs of Britain, Native and Foreign, Hardy and Half-Hardy, Pictorially and Botanically Delineated, and Scientifically and Popularly Described; with Their Propagation, Culture, Management,* 2 vols. London: Longman, Orme, Brown, Green and Longmans.

Luneva, Z. S., Nikolai L. Mikhaǐlov, and E. A. Sudakova. 1989. *Siren'.* Moscow: VO Agronromizdat.

Ma Yu-Chuan, and Zhou Si-Quang. 1981. *Syringa pinnatifolia* var. *alashanensis. Flora Intramongolica* 5: 412.

McClintock, Barbara. 1980. Modified gene expressions induced by transposable elements. In *Mobilization and Reassembly of Genetic Information.* Eds. W. A. Scott, R. Werner, D. R. Joseph, and Julius Schultz. Miami Winter Symposium. New York: Academic Press. 17: 11–19.

McCown, Brent H. 1983. Micropropagation of ornamental plants. *Lilacs* 12(1): 38–44.

McCown, Deborah D. 1989. Micropropagation of lilacs. *Lilacs* 18(4): 104–106.

McKelvey, Susan Delano. 1925. *Syringa rugulosa. Journal of the Arnold Arboretum* 6: 152.

McKelvey, Susan Delano. 1927. *Syringa* ×*prestoniae. Horticulture,* new series 5(15): 302.

McKelvey, Susan Delano. 1928. *The Lilac—A Monograph.* New York: Macmillan.

McKelvey, Susan Delano. 1934. *Syringa rugulosa. Journal of the Arnold Arboretum* 15: 302.

McLaughlin, Susan. 1998. Berdeen: Granddaughter works to restore his heirloom lilacs. *People, Places and Plants* 3(2): 73–76.

Macoun, William Tyrrell. 1928. New ornamental plants originated in the Division of Horticulture: *Syringa.* Division of Horticulture. Report of the Dominion Horticulturist for the year 1928. Ottawa: Canada Department of Agriculture. 53–58.

Magnol, Pierre. 1697. *Hortus regius monspeliensis, sive, Catalogus plantarum quae in Horto regio monspeliensi demonstrantur.* Montpellier.

Maioroli, A., et al. 1995. Catalogazione e prime classificazioni. *Flortecnica* 12, Supplement, pages 105–366.

Marsolais, J. V., J. S. Pringle, and B. N. White. 1993. Assessment of random amplified polymorphic DNA (RAPD) as genetic markers for determining the origin of interspecific lilac hybrids. *Taxon* 42: 531–537.

Martin, Susan F., and Kim Tripp. 1997. *Growing Conifers: Four-Season Plants.* New York: Brooklyn Botanic Garden.

Marzell, Heinrich, and Heinz Paul. 1979. *Syringa vulgaris.* In *Wörterbuch der deutschen Pflanzennamen.* Volume 4, *Sabadilla–Zygophyllum.* Wiesbaden: Franz Steiner. 546–564.

Mascioli, Lynette. 1998. Remembering Ken Berdeen. *Lilacs* 27(2): 47–48.

Mattioli, Pier Andrea. 1565. *Commentarii in sex libros Dioscoridis de medica materia.* Venezia: Ex Officina Valgrisiana.

Maximowicz, Karl Johann. 1859. Primitiae florae amurensis. Versuch einer Flora des Amurlandes. Mémoires Présentés a l'Académie Impériale des Sciences de St. Pétersbourg par Divers Savans et Lus dans ses Assamblées 9: 1–504.

Mehra, Pran Nath. 1976. *Cytology of Himalayan Hardwoods*. Calcutta (now Kolkata): Sree Saraswaty Press.

Mendel, Gregor Johann. 1866. *Versuche über Pflanzenhybriden*. Verhandlungen des Naturforschenden Vereins in Brünn. Abhandlungen 1865. 4: 3–47.

Meyer, Friedrich. 1952. *Flieder*. Stuttgart: Ulmer.

Michurin, Ivan V. 1949. *Selected Works*. Moscow: Foreign Languages Publishing House. (first published in 1934 as Transactions of the I. V. Michurin Plant-Breeding Station 2).

Miller, Philip. 1724. *The Gardeners and Florists Dictionary, or A Complete System of Horticulture; to Which Is Added a Catalogue of Curious Trees, Plants and Fruits*, 2 volumes. London: Charles Rivington.

Miller, Philip. 1768. *The Gardeners Dictionary*, 8th edition. London.

Millham, Kent. 2004. Richard Fenicchia: Great plantsman and hybridizer. *Lilacs* 33(4): 111–113.

Minocha, Subhash C. 1979. Lilacs in test tubes: Potential for cloning of lilacs by cell and tissue culture. *Lilacs* 8(1): 12–19.

Mitchell, Peter. 1973. *European Flower Painters*. London: Adam and Charles Black.

Moldenke, Harold N. 1956. *Syringa ×lamartina*. *Phytologia* 5: 341.

Moore, N. (Hannah) Hudson. 1904. *Lilacs*. New York: Frederick A. Stokes Company. 130–160.

Moore, Raymond John, editor. 1973. *Index to Plant Chromosome Numbers 1967–1971*. Regnum Vegetabile 90.

Mordant de Launey, Jean C. M. 1805. *Syringa rothomagensis. Le Bon Jardinier*. 584.

Morin, P. 1621. Catalogue des Plantes Rares Qui se Trouvent à Present dans Son Jardin.

Moro, Frank, and Corinna Moro. 2003. Variegated late lilacs. *Lilacs* 32(4): 155.

Morren, Charles F. A. 1853. *Syringa vulgaris* 'Azurea Plena'. Bulletins de l'Académie Royale des Sciences, des Lettres et des Beaux Arts de Belgique 1: 273.

Munsell Color Company. 1952. *Munsell Color Charts for Plant Tissues*. Baltimore: Munsell Color.

Munting, Abraham. 1672. *Jasminum Persicum foliis integris*. Waare Oeffening der Planten. Amsterdam.

Murashige, Toshio. 1974. Plant propagation through tissue cultures. *Annual Review of Plant Physiology* 25: 135–166.

Murray, Edward. 1968. Oleaceae. In *Flora Iranica–Flora des iranischen Hochlandes und der umrahmenden Gebirge: Persien, Afghanistan, Teile von West-Pakistan, Nord-Iraq, Azerbaidjan, Turkmenistan*. Ed. Karl Heinz Rechinger. Graz: Akademische Druck- und Verlagsanstalt. 52: 2.

Nakai, Takenoshin. 1909–1911. *Flora Koreana*, 2 volumes. Tokyo: Imperial University of Tokyo.

Nakai, Takenoshin. 1918. *Syringa buxifolia*. *Botanical Magazine* (Tokyo Botanical Society) 32: 128–131.

Nakai, Takenoshin. 1922. *Syringa palibiniana* var. *kamibayashii. Flora Sylvatica Koreana* 10: 52, pl. 22.

Nakai, Takenoshin. 1926. *Syringa pubescens*. *Botanical Magazine* (Tokyo Botanical Society) 40: 148.

NatureServe. 2006. NatureServe Explorer: An online encyclopedia of life [web application]. Version 6.1. NatureServe, Arlington, Virginia. Available http://www.natureserve.org/explorer. Accessed 30 March 2007.

Nehrling, Arno, and Irene Nehrling. 1962. *Peonies, Outdoors and In*. New York: Hearthside Press.

Néret, Gilles. 2004. *Peter Paul Rubens 1577–1640. L'Homère de la Peinture*. Köln: Taschen.

Olmsted, Frederick Law, Frederick V. Coville, and Harlan P. Kelsey. 1923. *Standardized Plant Names: A Catalogue of Approved Scientific and Common Names of Plants in American Commerce*. Salem: American Joint Committee on Horticultural Nomenclature. 263–264, 484–488.

Palibin, Ivan Vladimirovich. 1900. *Ligustrinum patulum*. *Acta Horti Petropolitani* 18: 156.

Pampanini, Renato. 1910. *Syringa oblata* var. *hupehensis. Nuovo Giornale Botanico Italiano*, new series, 17: 690.

Parkinson, John. 1629. *Paradisi in Sole Paradisus Terrestris*. London: Humfrey Lownes and Robert Young. (in English)

Parkinson, John. 1640. *Theatrum botanicum*. London: T. Cotes. (in English)

Paul, L. 1974. Er is in zeventig jaar wel veel veranderd in Aalsmeer. *Vakblad voor de Bloemisterij* 29(17): 31.

Peart, Bruce. 2004. Lilac evaluation for 2003. *Lilacs* 33(3): 88.

Poeplau, Zvezdana. 2002. Wie der Flieder nach Mittel-europa kam. FU-Botaniker weist die Herkunfts-geschichte des Flieders nach. http://www.fu-berlin.de/presse/fup/archiv/pdw02/pdw_02_025.html. Accessed 23 January 2003.

Pooler, Margaret. 2006. New lilacs from the U. S. National Arboretum. *Lilacs* 34(4): 116–117.

Potter, H, C. M. 1913. Forcing lilacs for Easter. *The Canadian Florist* 8(23): 231.

Preil, W. 2002. In vitro Produktion 1991–2000 der kom-merziellen Laboratorien des ADIVK. Bundesanstalt für Züchtungsforschung an Kulturpflanzen. Institut für Zierpflanzenzüchtung. http://www.adivk.de/adivk5.html. Accessed 26 February 2005.

Preston, Isabella. 1946. Some new hybrid lilacs. *Garden-ing Illustrated* (December).

Pringle, James S. 1975. The concept of the cultivar. *Jour-nal of Arboriculture* 1: 30–34.

Pringle, James S. 1976. Some effects of thermal-neutron radiation on seeds of *Syringa*. *Lilacs* 5(1): 1–24.

Pringle, James S. 1976–1977. The concept of the cultivar. *Pacific Horticulture* 37(3): 38–44; 37(4): 23–26; 38(1): 21–25; 38(2): 46–48.

Pringle, James S. 1977. Interspecific hybridization experi-ments in *Syringa* series Villosae (Oleaceae). *Baileya* 20(2): 49–91.

Pringle, James S. 1978a. Nomenclatural notes on *Syringa* series *Villosae* (Oleaceae). *Baileya* 20(3): 93–103.

Pringle, James S. 1978b. Notes on *Syringa tigerstedtii* (Oleaceae). *Baileya* 20(3): 104–114.

Pringle, James S. 1978c ["1977"]. Notes on the italiciza-tion and spelling of botanical names: A guide for nat-uralists and horticulturists. *Gardens Bulletin*, Royal Botanical Gardens 31: 13–14.

Pringle, James S. 1978d. Notes on the confusing and recurrently misapplied names in *Syringa*. *Lilacs* 7(1): 50–70.

Pringle, James S. 1981. A review of attempted and reported interseries and intersubgeneric hybridization in *Syringa* (Oleaceae). *Baileya* 21(3): 101–123.

Pringle, James S. 1983a. A summary of the currently accepted nomenclature at the specific and varietal lev-els in *Syringa*. *Lilac Newsletter* 9(3): 1–6.

Pringle, James S. 1983b. What is a type specimen? *Lilac Newsletter* 9(5): 1–3.

Pringle, James S. 1983c. Nomenclature of the Amur lilac, *Syringa reticulata* var. *amurensis* (Oleaceae). *Phytologia* 52(5): 285–287.

Pringle, James S. 1984. Effective and valid publication of scientific names. *Lilac Newsletter* 10(1): 2–4.

Pringle, James S. 1990. An updated summary of cur-rently accepted botanical nomenclature at the specific and varietal levels in *Syringa*. *Lilacs* 19(4): 75–80.

Pringle, James S. 1994. Linnaeus and binomial nomencla-ture. In *Canada's Royal Garden: Portraits and Reflec-tions*. Ed. Norman S. Track. Toronto: Viking Press. 55–57.

Pringle, James S. 1995. The classification of *Syringa* 'Lav-ender Lady'. *Lilacs* 24(4): 97–99.

Pringle, James S. 1996. Notes on *Syringa vulgaris* and *S.* ×*hyacinthiflora*. *Lilacs* 25(2): 56–60.

Pringle, James S. 1997. An updated summary of classifi-cation in *Syringa* at the ranks of species, subspecies, and variety. *Lilacs* 26(1): 19–26.

Pringle, James S. 2000. Inconsistent accounts of the ancestry of *Syringa* 'Dancing Druid'. *Lilacs* 29(3): 86–89.

Qu Shi-Zeng, and Chen Xin-Lu. 1989. *Syringa chuanx-iensis*. *Bulletin of Botanical Research* (China) 9(3): 39.

Radde, Gustav. 1861. *Berichte über Reisen im Süden von Ost-Sibirien*. Beiträge zur Kenntniss des Russischen Reiches und der angrenzenden Länder Asiens 23: 574, 606, 625, 629, 633, 635, 636.

Rajora, O., and M. Rahman. 2003. Microsatellite DNA and RAPD fingerprinting, identification and genetic relationships of hybrid poplar (*Populus* ×*canadensis*) cultivars. *Theoretical and Applied Genetics* 106(3): 470–477.

Randeni, Gamini. 1990. Survey of cultivar fingerprinting techniques for possible future application in the genus *Syringa*. *Lilacs* 19(4): 81–83.

Rehder, Alfred. 1899. *Möller's Deutsche Gärtner-Zeitung* 14: 206.

Rehder, Alfred. 1902. *Syringa*. In *The Standard Cyclope-dia of American Horticulture*. Ed. Liberty Hyde Bailey. New York: Macmillan. 4: 1763.

Rehder, Alfred. 1926. New species, varieties and combi-nations from the herbarium and the collections of the Arnold Arboretum. *Journal of the Arnold Arboretum* 7: 34.

Rehder, Alfred. 1945. *Journal of the Arnold Arboretum* 26: 74, 77.

Rehder, Alfred. 1949a. *Manual of Cultivated Trees and Shrubs Hardy in North America Exclusive of the Subtropical and Warmer Temperate Regions*, second edition. New York: Macmillan. (*Syringa*, pp. 777–783)

Rehder, Alfred. 1949b. *Bibliography of Cultivated Trees and Shrubs Hardy in the Cooler Temperate Regions of the Northern Hemisphere*. Jamaica Plain: Arnold Arboretum of Harvard University. (*Syringa*, pages 564–570)

Reichenbach, H. G. L. 1830. *Syringa josikaea*. Iconographia botanica, seu, Plantae criticae: Icones plantarum rariorum et minus rite cognitarum, indigenarum exoticarumque, iconographia et supplementum, . . . 8: 32, number 1049, plate 780.

Resink, A. J. 1907. Der Tee. In *Kulturpflanzen der Weltwirtschaft*. Eds. Otto Heinrich Warburg and J. E. van Someren Brand. Leipzig: R. Voigtländer. 217–255.

Ridgway, Robert. 1912. *Color Standards and Color Nomenclature*. Washington, D.C.: Robert Ridgway.

Rijsewijk, Vincent van. 1994. Teeltduur sering kan twee jaar korter. *De Boomkwekerij* 45: 24–25.

Roberts, Herbert Fuller. 1929. *Plant Hybridization Before Mendel*. Princeton: Princeton University Press.

Rochel, A. 1828. Plantae Banatus rariores, iconibus et descriptionibus illustratae. Praemisso tractatu phytographico et subnexis additamentis in terminologiam botanicam. Pestini [Budapest]: L. Landerer de Füskút.

Rock, Joseph F. C. 1925–1926. Notes and photographs on plant explorations to China. Arnold Arboretum Archives. (unpublished documents)

Rogers, Owen Maurice. 1976. *Tentative International Register of Cultivar Names in the Genus* Syringa. Research Report 49, New Hampshire Agricultural Experiment Station. Durham: University of New Hampshire.

Rogers, Owen Maurice. 1994. Parentage of 86-1. *Lilacs* 23(4): 107.

Rogers, Owen Maurice. 1998. Is your lilac single or double? *Lilacs* 27(3): 78–79.

Routley, Douglas. 2003. Do your clothes smell lilac fresh? *Lilacs* 32(2): 59–60.

Royal Horticultural Society. 1966. *Royal Horticultural Society Colour Chart*. London: Royal Horticultural Society.

Royal Horticultural Society. 1986. *Royal Horticultural Society Colour Chart*. London and Leiden: Royal Horticultural Society and Flower Council of Holland.

Royal Horticultural Society. 1995. *Royal Horticultural Society Colour Chart*. London: Royal Horticultural Society.

Royal Horticultural Society. 2001. *Royal Horticultural Society Colour Chart*. London: Royal Horticultural Society.

Royle, John Forbes. 1839. *Syringa emodi*. Illustrations of the Botany and other Branches of the Natural History of the Himalayan Mountains, and the Flora of Cashmere. 2 vols. London: W. H. Allen. 1: 267; 2: plate 65, figure 2.

Rubanik, V. G., A. F. Mel'nik, and Z. I. Parshina. 1977. Siren', *Syringa* L. Alma-Ata: Kaĭnar.

Rubtzov, Leonid I., Nikolai L. Mikhaĭlov, and Valentina G. Zhogoleva. 1980. *Lilac species and cultivars in cultivation in USSR*. Kiev: Naukova Dumka. (in Russian)

Rubtzov, Leonid I., Valentina G. Zhogoleva, and Nina A. Lyapunova. 1961. *Syringarii* [lilac garden]. Kiev: Central Republic Botanical Garden, Academy of Sciences Ukrainian Soviet Socialist Republic.

Ruprecht, Franz Josef Ivanovich. 1857. Die ersten botanischen Nachrichten über das Amurland, Abtheilung I. Beobachtungen von Maximowicz, über die wichtigen Bäume und Sträucher, p. 120 et sequentes, und Anhang: Novae species herbaceae. Ibidem p. 209 et sequentes, Abtheilung II. Bäume und Sträucher, beobachtet von Richard Maack, ibidem p. 257 et sequentes. *Bulletin de la Classe Physico-Mathématique de l'Académie des Sciences de Saint-Pétersbourg*, séries 2, 15: 371.

Sabeti, Habibollah. 1976. *Forests, Trees and Shrubs of Iran*. Teheran: Ministry of Agriculture and Natural Resources, National Agricultural and Natural Resources Research Organization. (in Farsi, in Arab script)

Sargent, Charles Sprague. 1888. Notes upon lilacs. *Garden and Forest* 1(19): 220–222.

Sargent, Charles Sprague, editor. 1911–1917. *Plantae Wilsonianae: An Enumeration of the Woody Plants Collected in Western China for the Arnold Arboretum of Harvard University During the Years 1907, 1908, and 1910 by E. H. Wilson*, 3 volumes. Cambridge, Massachusetts: University Press. 1: 301; 3: 433.

Sargent, Charles Sprague. 1912. *Syringa oblata*. Arnold Arboretum Bulletin 23 (12 May).

Sargent, Charles Sprague. 1917. *Syringa microphylla*. *Arnold Arboretum Bulletin* 3 (6 November): 64.

Saunders, William, and William Tyrrell Macoun. 1899. Catalogue of the Trees and Shrubs in the Arboretum and Botanic Garden at the Central Experimental Farm, Ottawa. Bulletin 2, second series. Ottawa.

Sax, Karl. 1930. Chromosome number and behavior in the genus *Syringa*. *Journal of the Arnold Arboretum* 11(1): 7–14.

Sax, Karl. 1945. Lilac species hybrids. *Journal of the Arnold Arboretum* 26: 79–84, plate 1.

Sax, Karl. 1947. Plant breeding at the Arnold Arboretum. *Arnoldia* 7: 9–12.

Sax, Karl. 1950. Rootstocks for lilacs. *Arnoldia* 10: 57–60.

Sax, Karl, and Ernst C. Abbe. 1932. Chromosome numbers and the anatomy of the secondary xylem in the Oleaceae. *Journal of the Arnold Arboretum* 13: 37–48.

Schneider, Camillo K. 1903. *Wiener Illustrierte Garten-Zeitung* 28: 105.

Schneider, Camillo K. 1907–1912. *Illustriertes Handbuch der Laubholzkunde: Charakteristik der in Mitteleuropa heimischen und im Freien angepflanzten Angiospermen Gehölz-Arten und Formen mit Ausschluss der Bambuseen und Kakteen*, 2 volumes and index. Jena: Gustav Fischer.

Schneider, Camillo K. 1910. *Syringa. Repertorium Specierum Novarum Regni Vegetabilis*. Centralblatt für Sammlung und Veröffentlichung von Einzeldiagnosen neuer Pflanzen 9: 80–82.

Schneider, Camillo K. 1911. Ein Beitrag zur Kenntnis der Gattung *Syringa. Mitteilungen der Deutschen Dendrologischen Gesellschaft* 20: 226–230.

Schneider, Frits. 1964. Kruising en selectie. *Jaarboek Proefstation voor de Boomkwekerij te Boskoop 1963*: 108–111.

Schofield, Edmund A. 1987. A life redeemed: Susan Delano McKelvey and the Arnold Arboretum. *Arnoldia* 47(4): 9–23.

Scholz, Hildemar, editor. 1987. *Botany in Berlin*. On the occasion of the XIV International Botanical Congress. Berlin: Botanic Garden and Botanical Museum Berlin-Dahlem.

Schopmeyer, Clifford S., technical coordinator. 1974. *Seeds of Woody Plants in the United States*. Agriculture Handbook 450. Washington, D.C.: U.S. Department of Agriculture, Forest Service.

Schur, Philipp J. F. 1866. *Enumeratio Plantarum Transsilvaniae*, 451.

Seringenpark. 1951. Het Seringen Park te Aalsmeer. Gemeente Aalsmeer. Lijst van soorten en variëteiten Seringen in het Seringenpark te Aalsmeer. Netherlands.

Shephard, Sue. 2003. *Seeds of Fortune: A Gardening Dynasty*. New York: Bloomsbury.

Shishkoff, Nina. 2006. Susceptibility of selected lilac (*Syringa* L.) cultivars to *Phytophthora ramorum*, the sudden oak death pathogen. *Phytopathology* 95: S160.

Sinclair, Wayne A. 1996. Ash yellows and lilac witches'-broom: Phytoplasmal diseases of concern in forestry and horticulture. *Plant Disease* 80(5): 468–475.

Sinclair, Wayne A., and Helen M. Griffiths. 1994. Ash yellows and its relationship to dieback and decline of ash. *Annual Review of Phytopathology* 32: 49–60.

Skinner, Frank Leith. 1949. New lilacs. *Horticulture* 27(5): 181.

Skinner, Frank Leith. 1966. *Horticultural Horizons: Plant Breeding and Introduction at Dropmore, Manitoba*. Winnipeg: Manitoba Department of Agriculture and Conservation.

Skinner's nursery. 1948. Catalog 12.

Skoog, F., and C. O. Miller. 1957. Chemical regulation of growth and organ formation in plant tissue cultured in vitro. *Symposium of the Society for Experimental Biology* 11: 118–131.

Skvortsov, Boris V., and Wei Wang. 1958. Tchen ngo Liou. *Illustrated Flora of Ligneous Plants of Northeast China*, 566.

Smith, Harald K. A. 1948. *Lustgården* 28–29: 105–110.

Smith, William W.. 1916a. *Syringa wardii. Notes from the Royal Botanic Garden, Edinburgh* 9: 132.

Smith, William W. 1916b. Note on *Parasyringa*, a new genus of Oleaceae. *Transactions of the Botanical Society of Edinburgh* 27: 93–96.

Snijder, Ronald C. 1999. *Sortimentsonderzoek* Syringa vulgaris *L.: Beschrijving en identificatie van cultivars*. Thesis, Landbouwuniversiteit, Wageningen. (in Dutch with English summary)

Song, C. S., R. Z. Xu, and Q. H. Zhang. 1989. *Rare and Endangered Plants in China*. Beijing: China Forest Press. (in Chinese)

Souchet, Charles. 1931. Le forçage du lilas. *La Revue Horticole* 1931: 329–332.

Späth, L. 1920. *Späth-Buch 1720–1920* [seed and nursery trade catalog]. Berlin: L. Späth.

Speirs, Joan. 2005. Proposed introduction dates for some Villosae Group lilac cultivars originated in Canada. *Lilacs* 34(4): 123–124.

Spence, Jonathan D. 1996. *God's Chinese Son: The Taiping Heavenly Kingdom of Hong Xiuquan*. New York: W. W. Norton.

Spongberg, Stephen A. 1984. Cultivar registration at the Arnold Arboretum. *The Bulletin—American Association of Botanical Gardens and Arboreta* 18(3): 88–89.

Sprengel, Christian K. 1793. *Das entdeckte Geheimniss der Natur im Bau und in der Befruchtung der Blumen* [The Discovered Secret of Nature in the Form and Fertilization of Flowers]. Berlin.

Stafleu, Frans A., and Richard S. Cowan. 1976. *Taxonomic Literature*, 2nd edition, Volume 1, *A–G*. Regnum Vegetabile 94.

Stapf, Otto. 1924. *Syringa potaninii. Curtis's Botanical Magazine* 150: plate 9060.

Stapf, Otto. 1929–1931. *Index Londinensis to Illustrations of Flowering Plants, Ferns, and Fern Allies*, 6 volumes. Oxford: Clarendon Press.

Starcs, K. 1926. *Cerines* (*Syringa* L.). Därzkopibas.

Starcs, K. 1928. Übersicht über die Arten der Gattung *Syringa* L. *Mitteilungen der Deutschen Dendrologischen Gesellschaft* 40: 31–49.

Stearn, William Thomas, editor. 1953. *International Code of Nomenclature for Cultivated Plants*. London: Royal Horticultural Society.

Steltenkamp, Robert J. 1979. Perfumery notes: A review of lilac. *Perfumer and Flavorist* 4(5): 1, 3–5.

Stewart, Ralph Randles. 1972. An annotated catalogue of the vascular plants of West Pakistan and Kashmir. In *Flora of West Pakistan*. Eds. Eugene Nasir and S. I. Ali. Islamabad, National Herbarium. Karachi: Fakhri Printing Press.

Strekalov, I. F., and N. I. Potapova. 2001. *Siren'*. Moscow: Fiton+.

Stubbe, Hans. 1965. *Kurze Geschichte der Genetik bis zur Wiederentdeckung der Vererbungsregeln Gregor Mendels*, 2nd edition. Jena: Fischer Verlag.

Stubbe, Hans. 1972. *History of Genetics: From Prehistoric Times to the Rediscovery of Mendel's Laws*. Cambridge: Massachusetts Institute of Technology Press.

Sucker, Ulrich. 1980. Zur Geschichte der Dendrologie und des Späthschen Arboretums in Berlin. *Wissenschaftliche Zeitschrift der Humboldt-Universität zu Berlin, Mathematisch-Naturwissenschaftliche Reihe* 68a: 65–69.

Sytsema, Wietze. 1962. Bloei van sering aan afgesneden takken. *Mededelingen van de Landbouwhogeschool te Wageningen, Nederland* 62(2): 1–57.

Sytsema, Wietze. 1969. Influence of growth retardants on flower bud initiation of lilac. *Acta Horticulturae* 14: 205–207.

Taylor, H. 1945. Cyto-taxonomy and phylogeny of the Oleaceae. *Brittonia* 5(4): 337–367.

Taylor, Jane. 1990. Four Lemoine genera: *Syringa, Philadelphus, Deutzia, Weigela. The Plantsman* 11(4): 225–240.

Taylor, Judith M. 2004. The legacy of Victor Lemoine. *Rare Book Review* 31(5): 42–44.

Taylor, Judith M., and Harry M. Butterfield. 2003. *Tangible Memories: Californians and Their Gardens 1800–1950*. Philadelphia: Xlibris Corporation.

Temple, F. L. 1887. *Pyrus spectabilis, Parkmani*, and Chinese Weeping Lilac.

Tereshchenko, Sergeĭ Ivanovich. 2003. Sireni na yugo-vostoke Ukrainy [lilacs in southeastern Ukraine]. Donetsk: Weber.

Theis, Nina. 2007. Progress report on the lilac fragrance study. (unpublished report)

Tischler, Georg Friedrich Leopold. 1908. Zellstudien an sterilen Bastardpflanzen. *Archiv für Zellforschung* 1: 33–151.

Tischler, Georg Friedrich Leopold. 1921–1922. Allgemeine Pflanzenkaryologie. 9. Die Chromosomen und ihre Bedeutung für Stammes- und Erblichkeitsforschung. In *Handbuch der Pflanzenanatomie*. Ed. Karl Linsbauer. Berlin: Verlag Bornträger. 2(1): 521–683.

Tischler, Georg Friedrich Leopold. 1930. Über die Bastardnatur des persischen Flieders. *Zeitschrift für Botanik* 23: 150–162.

Tournefort, Joseph Pitton de. 1694. *Élémens de Botanique ou Méthode pour Connoître les Plantes*. Paris.

Trehane, Piers, Christopher D. Brickell, Bernard Rene Baum, Wilbert L. A. Hetterscheid, Alan Christopher Leslie, John McNeill, Stephen A. Spongberg, and Freek Vrugtman, editors. 1995. *International Code of Nomenclature for Cultivated Plants—1995*. Regnum Vegetabile 133.

Trehane, Piers. 2001. Trademarks are not names! *Lilacs* 30(4): 105–109.

Tucker, Arthur O., Michael J. Maciarello, and Sharon S. Tucker. 1991. A survey of color charts for biological descriptions. *Taxon* 40: 201–214.

Turczaninov, Nikolai S. 1840. *Syringa pubescens. Bulletin de la Société Impériale des Naturalistes de Moscou* 13: 73.

Uhrikova, Anna. 1978. Index of chromosome numbers of Slovakian flora. Part 6. *Acta Facultatis Rerum Naturalium Universitatis Comenianae, Botanica, Bratislava* 26: 1–42.

University of Chicago Press Staff. 2003. *The Chicago Manual of Style.* 15th edition. Chicago: University of Chicago Press.

Upton, Edward A. 1980. *The Edward A. Upton Scrapbooks of Lilac Information*, Volumes 1, 2. Reprinted by the International Lilac Society Corporation.

Upton, Edward A. 1986. *The Edward A. Upton Scrapbooks of Lilac Information*, Volumes 3, 4. Reprinted by the International Lilac Society Corporation.

Upton, Edward A. n.d. Lilacs: A Scrap Book. Volumes 5, 6. (unpublished manuscripts)

USDA. 1990. USDA Plant Hardiness Zone Map. Miscellaneous Publication 1745. Washington, D.C.: U.S. Department of Agriculture, Agricultural Research Service.

USDA. 2005. *Woody Plant Seed Manual.* Agricultural Handbook. Washington, D.C.: U.S. Department of Agriculture, Forest Service. http://www.nsl.fs.fed.us/wpsm. Accessed 16 February 2005.

Vahl, Martin. 1804–1805. *Syringa villosa.* Enumeratio Plantarum in partibus Siaellandiae septentrionalis et orientalis 1: 38.

van den Berg, A. J. 1988. Teelt van seringen (Syringa). *Bloementeeltinformatie* 33.

van Raalte, Dirk. 1963. *Handboek der bloemisterij: ten dienste van het Middelbaar en Hoger Tuinbouwonderwijs en de praktijk.* 2nd volume, 3rd edition. Doetinchem: C. Misset N.V. (*Syringa*, pages 427–453).

Vasil'ev, V. N. 1952. Oleaceae. In *Flora of the USSR.* Eds. B. K. Shishkin and E. G. Bobrov. English translation, 1967. Israel Program for Scientific Translation. (*Syringa*, 18: 356–387)

Velenovský, Josef. 1894. Sitzungsberichte der königlichen böhmischen Gesellschaft der Wissenschaften. *Mathematisch-Naturwissenschaftliche Classe* (Prague) 1993 (37): 43.

Verdoorn, Frans, editor. 1944. Ghiselin de Busbeck (Busbequius), Ogier. *In* On the aims and methods of biological history and biography with some notes for the collaborators of the Index Botanicorum. *Chronica Botanica* 8: 441–444, with wood cut by Melchior Lorichs, 1557.

Vittum, M. T., and R. J. Hopp. 1979. The N.E.- 95 lilac phenology network. In *Phenology, an Aid to Agricultural Technology.* Ed. R. J. Hopp. Vermont Agricultural Experiment Station Bulletin 684. 1–5.

von Baeyer, Edwinna. 1987. The horticultural odyssey of Isabella Preston. *Canadian Horticultural History* 1(3): 125–175.

Vrugtman, Freek. 1973. The garden lilac. *The Garden's Bulletin* 27(1): 1–6, figure 1. Royal Botanical Gardens, Hamilton, Canada.

Vrugtman, Freek. 1975. Lilac registration and its implications. *Lilacs* 4: 13–15.

Vrugtman, Freek. 1980a. *Syringa oblata* 'Cheyenne', Hildreth 1971. *Lilac Newsletter* 6(4): 11–13.

Vrugtman, Freek. 1980b. *Syringa vulgaris* 'Stadtgärtner Rothpletz', Fröbel 1905. *Lilac Newsletter* 6(3): 3.

Vrugtman, Freek. 1982a. James Dougall, 1810–1888. *Lilacs* 11(1): 28–32.

Vrugtman, Freek. 1982b. Why register cultivar names? *Lilacs* 11(1): 37–38.

Vrugtman, Freek. 1984a. Valid publication of new cultivar names of lilacs. *Lilac Newsletter* 10(1): 1–3.

Vrugtman, Freek. 1984b. Cultivar description and cultivar identification. *Lilac Newsletter* 10(5): 1–3.

Vrugtman, Freek. 1988. Lilac registration 1986–87. *HortScience* 23(3): 458.

Vrugtman, Freek. 1989. Corrigenda: Lilac registration 1986–87. *HortScience* 24(3): 435–436.

Vrugtman, Freek. 1990a. Lilac registration 1989. *HortScience* 25(6): 618.

Vrugtman, F. 1990b. Addenda and corrigenda to the tentative international register of cultivar names in the genus *Syringa* (1976). Contribution 73. Hamilton, Ontario: Royal Botanical Gardens.

Vrugtman, Freek. 1993. Bernard Orville Case and the lilacs of Duniway Park. *Lilacs* 22(4): 122.

Vrugtman, Freek. 1996. *Syringa oblata* var. *dilatata* (Nakai) Rehder 'Nakai'—An invalid name? From the registrar's desk. *Lilacs* 25(2): 37–38.

Vrugtman, Freek. 1998a. The Rankin lilacs reviewed; T. A. Havemeyer's lilacs reviewed. From the registrar's desk. *Lilacs* 27(1): 19–31.

Vrugtman, Freek. 1998b. *Syringa* L. 'Dancing Druid', Fiala 1969 of what parentage? *Lilacs* 27(3): 88.

Vrugtman, Freek. 1998c. The Hulda Klager Lilacs reviewed; The Klager lilacs listed by Fr. Fiala. *Lilacs* 27(3): 69–88.

Vrugtman, Freek. 1998d. The Gardner brothers and their lilacs. *Lilacs* 27(3): 89–90.

Vrugtman, Freek. 1999a. The Maarse(n)s of Aalsmeer and their lilacs. *Lilacs* 28(4): 105–112.

Vrugtman, Freek. 1999b. Martine Spaargaren [1916–1991] and the Proefstation introductions. *Lilacs* 28(4): 103–104.

Vrugtman, Freek. 1999c. The Hulda Klager Lilacs reviewed (addendum). *Lilacs* 28(3): 69–80, 28(4): 112.

Vrugtman, Freek. 1999d. *Syringa ×hyacinthiflora* 'Big Blue', Lammerts 1953. *Lilacs* 28(4): 99–113.

Vrugtman, Freek. 2001a. John Herbert Alexander, Sr.—An outstanding lilac grower and nurseryman. *Lilacs* 30(3): 92–95.

Vrugtman, Freek. 2001b. A brief note about *Syringa* 'Eventide'. *Lilacs* 30(4): 113.

Vrugtman, Freek. 2003a. Mikołaj Karpow-Lipski—A Polish hybridizer of distinction. From the registrar's desk. *Lilacs* 32(2): 51–58.

Vrugtman, Freek. 2003b. 'Nakai'. Corrections, updates and comments. From the registrar's desk. *Lilacs* 32(4): 151–152.

Vrugtman, Freek. 2003c. Lilac cultivar name registration 2002. *HortScience* 38(6): 1301.

Vrugtman, Freek. 2004a. Lilac cultivar name registration 2003 (*Syringa* Villosae Group). *HortScience* 39(6): 1524.

Vrugtman, Freek. 2004b. *Syringa* (Villosae Group) 'Charisma' and 'Shantelle'—Phytoplasma induced lilac cultivars. *Lilacs* 33(4): 114–115.

Vrugtman, Freek. 2004c. Do you have *Syringa pinetorum* growing in your collection? *Lilacs* 33(4): 121–122.

Vrugtman, Freek. 2004d. *Syringa pubescens* subsp. *patula* 'De Belder', De Belder & Fiala 1988. *Lilacs* 33(4): 123.

Vrugtman, Freek. 2004e. *Syringa oblata* var. *donaldii*—Not a validly published name. *Lilacs* 33(4): 120–121.

Vrugtman, Freek. 2004f. The Franktown lilac tokens. *Lilacs* 33(4): 120.

Vrugtman, Freek. 2005a. *Syringa reticulata* subsp. *pekinensis* 'Jin Yuan', a new cultivar from China. *Lilacs* 34(1): 12–13.

Vrugtman, Freek. 2005b. Lilac cultivar name registrations 2004. *HortScience* 40(6): 1597.

Vrugtman, Freek. 2007a. *Syringa vulgaris* 'Lila Wonder', Bunnik 2006. *Lilacs* 36(1): 20–22.

Vrugtman, Freek. 2007b. *Syringa villosa* 'Legacy', USDA-NRCS Bismarck 1999. *Lilacs* 36(2): 75–77.

Vrugtman, Freek. 2007c. International Register and Checklist of Cultivar Names in the Genus *Syringa* L. [Oleaceae]. "Work-in-Progress" Lilac Register. Contribution 91. Hamilton, Ontario, Royal Botanical Gardens. Issued on CD-ROM.

Vrugtman, Freek, and Walter E. Eickhorst. 1981. The history of *Syringa vulgaris* 'Primrose'. *Lilacs* 9(1): 28–30.

Walker, J. T., C. R. Hibben, and J. C. Alison. 1975. Cultivar ratings for susceptibility and resistance to the leaf-roll necrosis disorder of lilac. *Journal of the American Society for Horticultural Science* 100(6): 617–631.

Wallich, Nathaniel. 1831. A numerical list of dried specimens of plants in the East India Company's botanic garden at Calcutta. (unpublished manuscript)

Weng R.-F., and Zhang M.-Z. 1992. Chromosome numbers in Chinese Oleaceae I. *Investigatio et Studium Naturae* 12: 66–77.

Weston, Richard. 1770. *Botanicus Universalis et Hortulanus* 1: 289.

Whittle, Tyler. 1970. *The Plant Explorers*. Philadelphia: Chilton Book Company. (reprinted in 1997, New York: Lyons Press)

Willard, L. F. 1981. The lilac man. *Yankee Magazine* (April): 93, 176, 177.

Willdenow, Carl L. von. 1796. *Berliner Baum-Zeitung*, 378.

Wilson, Ernest Henry. 1917. *Aristocrats of the Garden*. New York: Doubleday, Page and Company. 213–229.

Wilson, Ernest Henry. 1919. *Journal of the Arnold Arboretum* 1: 41.

Wilson, Robert F. 1939, 1942. *Horticultural Colour Chart*, 2 volumes. London: British Colour Council and Royal Horticultural Society.

Wister, John Caspar. 1927. A lilac checklist. *National Horticultural Magazine* 6(1): 1–16.

Wister, John Caspar. 1930. *Lilac Culture*. New York: Orange Judd.

Wister, John Caspar. 1933. Where the country's finest lilacs grow. *Horticulture* 11(22): 175–176.

Wister, John Caspar. 1938. Lilacs at Swarthmore. *Gardeners' Chronicle of America* 42(4): 96.

Wister, John Caspar, editor. 1942. *Syringa*. In *Standardized Plant Names*, second edition. Eds. H. P. Kelsey and W. A. Dayton. American Joint Committee on Horticultural Nomenclature. Harrisburg, New York: J. Horace McFarland. 613–617.

Wister, John Caspar, editor. 1942. Lilacs for America: Report of the 1941 Lilac Survey Committee of the American Association of Botanical Gardens and Arboretums. Swarthmore, Pennsylvania: Arthur Hoyt Scott Horticultural Foundation.

Wister, John Caspar, editor. 1943. Lilacs for America: Report of the 1941 Lilac Survey Committee of the American Association of Botanical Gardens and Arboretums. Revised and corrected. Swarthmore, Pennsylvanis: Arthur Hoyt Scott Horticultural Foundation.

Wister, John Caspar. 1951. Additions to lilac survey. *News Letter* (American Association of Botanical Gardens and Arboretums) 7: 3–9.

Wister, John Caspar, editor. 1953. Lilacs for America: Report of the 1953 Lilac Survey Committee of the American Association of Botanical Gardens and Arboretums. Swarthmore, Pennsylvania: Arthur Hoyt Scott Horticultural Foundation.

Wister, John Caspar, editor. 1962. *The Peonies*. Washington, D.C.: American Horticultural Society.

Wolfe, David W. 2004. Climate change impacts on Northeast agriculture and farmer adaptation. In *Proceedings, Climate Change and Northeast Agriculture: Developing an Education Outreach Agenda.* Ed. D. W. Wolfe. Symposium held 17 November 2004, Cornell Cooperative Extension, Ithaca, New York. 16–23.

Wolfe, David W., Mark D. Schwartz, Alan N. Lakso, Yuka Otsuki, Robert M. Pool, and Nelson J. Shaulis. 2004. Climate change and shifts in spring phenology of three horticultural woody perennials in the northeastern USA. Abstract. *International Journal of Biometeorology.* http://biometeorology.org. Accessed 14 February 2005.

Wu, Z. Y., and P. H. Raven, eds. 1996. *Flora of China,* vol. 15, *Myrsinaceae through Loganiaceae.* St. Louis: Missouri Botanical Garden Press.

Yaltirik, Faik. 1976. *Türkiye'deki Doğal Oleaceae Taksonlarinin Sistematik Revizyonu.* Istanbul.

Yaltirik, Faik. 1978. Oleaceae. In *Flora of Turkey and the East Aegean Islands.* Ed. Peter Hadland Davis. Edinburgh: Edinburgh University Press. 6: 145–158.

Yeager, Albert F. 1950. Breeding improved horticultural plants. II. Fruits, nuts, and ornamentals. New Hampshire Agricultural Experiment Station Bulletin 383.

Yeager, Albert F., E. B. Risley, Elwyn M. Meader, and Radcliffe B. Pike. 1959. Breeding and improving ornamentals. New Hampshire Agricultural Experiment Station Bulletin 461: 11–13.

Yip, Joseph K. L., and Patrick C. C. Lai. 2005. The Nationally Rare and Endangered Plant, *Aquilaria sinensis:* Its status in Hong Kong. http://www.hkherbarium.net/Herbarium/topics/Aquilaria/Aquilaria_E.htm.

Young, J. M., C. T. Bull, S. H. De Boer, G. Firrao, L. Gardan, G. E. Saddler, D. E. Stead, and Y. Takikawa. 2005. *International Standards for Naming Pathovars of Phytopathogenic Bacteria.* http://www.isppweb.org. Accessed 11 March 2005.

Zhang Dong-Lin, and Michael Dirr. 2004. Potential new ornamental plants from China. *Southern Nursery Association Research Conference Proceedings* 49: 607–609.

Zhang Lin-Hai, Robert Ballard, and Sriyani Rajapakse. 2002. Generation of SSR markers for rose genetic mapping and cultivar fingerprinting. http://www.intlpag.org/10/abstracts/PAGX_P215.html. Accessed 26 March 2005.

Zhang Shu-Ying, and Cui Hong-Xia. 2000. *Lilac.* Shanghai: Shanghai Science Technical Press. (in Chinese)

Zoller, Heinrich, Martin Steinmann, and Karl Schmid, editors. 1991. *Conradi Gesneri Historia Plantarum.* 2 volumes only. Dietikon-Zürich: U. Graf.

Index of Scientific Plant Names

Boldface numbers indicate photo pages. *Italic* numbers indicate main entry pages.

Ligustrina (subgenus), *67–74*
Ligustrina amurensis, see *Syringa reticulata* subsp. *amurensis*
   var. *mandshurica*, see *Syringa reticulata* subsp. *amurensis*
   var. *pekinensis*, see *Syringa pekinensis*
Ligustrum, 34, 67
Ligustrum mairei, see *Syringa mairei*
Ligustrum patulum, see *Syringa pubescens* subsp. *patula*
Ligustrum reticulatum, see *S. reticulata* subsp. *reticulata*
Oleaceae, *18*
Pinnatifoliae (series), *88–90*
Pubescentes (series), *90–105*
Syringa (genus), *20–25*, 37
Syringa (subgenus), *75–121*
Syringa (series), *75–88*
Syringa adamiana, see *S. tomentella*
Syringa affinis, see *S. oblata* subsp. *oblata* 'Alba'
   var. *giraldii*, see 'Giraldii' (*S. oblata*)
Syringa afghanica, *83*
Syringa alborosea, see *S. tomentella*
Syringa amurensis, see *S. reticulata* subsp. *amurensis*
   var. *japonica*, see *S. reticulata* subsp. *reticulata*
   var. *major*, 22
   var. *pekinensis*, see *S. pekinensis*
   var. *rotundifolia*, see *S. reticulata* subsp. *amurensis*
Syringa bretschneideri, see *S. villosa*
Syringa buxifolia, see *S. protolaciniata*
Syringa ×*chinensis*, *83–85*, **84**, **202**
   var. *alba*, 22, 84
   nothof. *bicolor*, 22, 275
   nothof. *duplex*, 22
Syringa chuanxiensis, see *S. mairei*
Syringa ×*clarkiana*, 22
Syringa +*correlata*, 22, 84

Syringa debelderi, see *S. pubescens* subsp. *patula* 'De Belder'
Syringa debelderorum, see *S. pubescens* subsp. *patula* 'De Belder'
Syringa dilatata, see *S. oblata* subsp. *dilatata*
   var. *alba*, see *S. oblata* subsp. *dilatata*
   f. *alba*, see *S. oblata* subsp. *dilatata*
   var. *longituba*, see *S. oblata* subsp. *dilatata*
   var. *pubescens*, see *S. oblata* subsp. *dilatata*
   var. *rubra*, see *S. oblata* subsp. *dilatata*
   var. *violacea*, see *S. oblata* subsp. *dilatata*
Syringa ×*diversifolia*, 90
Syringa dubia, 22
Syringa emodi, *106–107*
Syringa fauriei, see *S. reticulata* subsp. *amurensis*
Syringa ×*fialiana*, 22
Syringa filicifolia, 22
Syringa formosissima, see *S. wolfii*
   var. *hirsuta*, see *S. wolfii*
Syringa giraldiana, see *S. pubescens* subsp. *microphylla*
Syringa giraldii, see *S. oblata* subsp. *oblata*
Syringa glabra, see *S. komarowii* subsp. *komarowii*
Syringa ×*henryi*, *116–117*
Syringa ×*heterophylla*, 23
Syringa hirsuta, see *S. wolfii*
   var. *formosissima*, see *S. wolfii*
Syringa hupehensis, 23
Syringa ×*hyacinthiflora*, 30, *85–86*, **211**, **246**, 301
Syringa hybrida hort., 23
Syringa hybrida hort. ex Bean, 23
Syringa ×*hybrida* W. R. Prince, 23
Syringa japonica, see *S. reticulata* subsp. *reticulata*
Syringa josikaea, *44–47*, **45**, **46**, 108, 138, 152

Syringa ×*josiflexa*, *117–118*, 299
Syringa julianae, see *S. pubescens* subsp. *julianae*
Syringa koehneana, see *S. pubescens* subsp. *patula*
Syringa komarowii, *108–111*, **109**, 162, 174
   subsp. *komarowii*, *108–110*, **109**
   subsp. *reflexa*, *110–111*, **111**, 162
   var. *reflexa*, see *S. komarowii* subsp. *reflexa*
   var. *sargentiana*, see *S. komarowii* subsp. *komarowii*
Syringa ×*laciniata*, *86–87*, **87**, 138
Syringa ×*lamartina*, 23
Syringa ×*lemoineiana*, 23
Syringa luminifera, 23
Syringa mairei, *103–104*
Syringa meyeri, 32, *102–103*, 138
   var. *meyeri*, *102–103*
   var. *spontanea*, 103
     f. *alba*, see *S. meyeri* var. *spontanea*
     f. *spontanea*, 103
Syringa microphylla, see *S. pubescens* subsp. *microphylla*
   var. *alba*, see *S. meyeri* var. *spontanea*
   f. *alba*, see *S. meyeri* var. *spontanea*
   var. *giraldiana*, see *S. pubescens* subsp. *microphylla*
   var. *minor*, 23
Syringa ×*nanceiana*, 47, 119
Syringa oblata, *75–81*
   subsp. *oblata*, *76–78*, **77**
   var. *affinis*, see *S. oblata* subsp. *oblata* 'Alba'
   var. *alba*, see *S. oblata* subsp. *oblata*
   subsp. *dilatata*, *78–81*, **79**
     f. *pendula*, 23
   var. *dilatata*, see *S. oblata* subsp. *dilatata*
   var. *donaldii*, 23, 80
   var. *giraldii*, see *S. oblata* subsp. *oblata*
   var. *hupehensis*, see *S. oblata* subsp. *oblata*

Syringa palibiniana, see *S. pubescens*
    subsp. *patula*
      var. *kamibayashii*, 24
Syringa patula, see *S. pubescens* subsp.
    patula
Syringa pekinensis, 32, *72–74*, **73**
Syringa persica Brandis, 22
Syringa ×persica L., **87**, *87–88*, 152,
    226
    var. *laciniata*, 24
Syringa pinetorum, *104–105*
Syringa pinnatifolia, *88–90*, **89**
    var. *alashanensis*, see *S. pinnatifolia*
Syringa potaninii, 24
Syringa ×prestoniae, *119–121*, *297–*
    299, 302, 342
Syringa ×pringleiana, 24
Syringa protolaciniata, *81–82*
Syringa pteridifolia, 24
Syringa pubescens, 32, *90–102*, 138
    subsp. *pubescens*, 33, *90–92*, **92**
      var. *hirsuta*, see *S. pubescens* subsp.
        patula
    subsp. *julianae*, 32, 33, *92–95*, **93**,
      152
    subsp. *microphylla*, 32, *96–99*
      var. *microphylla*, *96–97*, **97**
      var. *flavanthera*, *97*
      var. *potaninii*, **98**, *98–99*, 163
    subsp. *patula*, 32, **99**, *99–101*, 138,
      190
      var. *tibetica*, see *S. pubescens* subsp.
        microphylla
Syringa pulchella, 25

Syringa ×quatrobrida, 24
Syringa reflexa, see *S. komarowii* subsp.
    reflexa
Syringa rehderiana, see *S. tomentella*
Syringa reticulata, 32, *67–71*
    var. *amurensis*, see *S. reticulata*
      subsp. *amurensis*
    subsp. *reticulata*, *67–71*, **68**, 134,
      233
    subsp. *amurensis*, 33, *71*, **71**, **72**, 134
    var. *mandshurica*, see *S. reticulata*
      subsp. *amurensis*
    subsp. *pekinensis*, see *S. pekinensis*
Syringa rhodopea, *144*; see 'Rhodopea'
    (*S. vulgaris*)
Syringa robusta, see *S. wolfii*
    var. *rupestris*, see *S. wolfii*
Syringa rothomagensis, 25
Syringa rugulosa, see *S. mairei*
Syringa sargentiana, see *S. komarowii*
    subsp. *komarowii*
Syringa schneideri, see *S. pubescens*
    subsp. *microphylla*
Syringa sempervirens, 25
Syringa siberica, 25
Syringa ×sinensis, 25
Syringa ×skinneri, see 'Skinneri' (*S.*
    pubescens)
Syringa suspensa, 25
Syringa ×swegiflexa, *121*, **121**
Syringa ×sweginbretta, 25
Syringa sweginzowii, 32, *112–114*, **114**
Syringa ×swegitella, 25
Syringa tetanoloba, see *S. sweginzowii*

Syringa tibetica, 116
Syringa tigerstedtii, see *S. sweginzowii*
Syringa tomentella, 112
    var. *rehderiana*, see *S. tomentella*
Syringa ×tribrida, 25
Syringa trichophylla, see *S. pubescens*
    subsp. *microphylla*
Syringa ×varina, 25
Syringa velutina, see *S. pubescens* subsp.
    patula
Syringa verrucosa, see *S. pubescens*
    subsp. *julianae*
Syringa villosa, 49, *105–106*, **106**
    "Giraldi," see 'Giraldii' (*S. oblata*)
    var. *glabra*, see *S. komarowii* subsp.
      komarowii
    var. *rosea*, see *S. villosa*
Syringa Villosae Group, *21–22*, 30,
    116, 298
Syringa vulgaris, **18**, **19**, **30**, 32, *37–43*,
    38, **39**, 75, **202**, **241**, **248**
    number of cultivars, 26
    var. *oblata*, see *S. oblata* subsp. *oblata*
Syringa wardii, 105
Syringa wilsonii, see *S. tomentella*
Syringa wolfii, **107**, *107–108*, 174
    var. *hirsuta*, 108
Syringa wulingensis, see *S. pubescens*
    subsp. *pubescens*
Syringa yunnanensis, *114–115*, **115**
    var. *pubicalyx*, see *S. yunnanensis*
Villosae (series), *1–22*, 32, *105–121*,
    298

Index of Lilac Cultivar Names

Boldface numbers indicate photo pages. *Italic* numbers indicate main entry pages.

'A. B. Lamberton' (*S. vulgaris*), **175**, *175*, 289

'A. M. Brand' (*S. vulgaris*), **175**, *175*

'Abel Carrière' (*S. vulgaris*), 273, **274**

'Abundant Bloomer' (*S. vulgaris*), 292, **293**

'Ada' (*S.* ×*hyacinthiflora*), *172*

'Adelaide Dunbar' (*S. vulgaris*), *175*, **176**, 289

'Admiral Farragut' (*S. vulgaris*), 289

'Adriana' (*S.* Villosae Group), *152*

'Aélita' (*S. vulgaris*), 329

'Agata' (*S.* Villosae Group), **152**, *152*, 342

'Agidel' (*S. vulgaris*), 335

'Agincourt Beauty' (*S. vulgaris*), **135**, *135*, 296

'Agnes Smith' (*S.* Villosae Group), *117*, **117**, 134, 326

'Aïgul' (*S. vulgaris*), 335

'Aino' (*S. vulgaris*), 343

'Ainola' (*S.* Villosae Group), 287

'Akademik Burdenko' (*S. vulgaris*), 331

'Akademik Maksimov' (*S. vulgaris*), 331

'Akademik Sakharov' (*S. vulgaris*), 345

'Akkila' (*S. vulgaris*), 287

'Akku' (*S. vulgaris*), 346

'Alba' (*S. komarowii* subsp. *reflexa*), *111*, *134*

'Alba' (*S. oblata* subsp. *oblata*), 50, **60**, 77, *77*

'Alba' (*S.* ×*persica*), *88*

'Alba' (*S.* Villosae Group), *116*, 273

'Alba' (*S. yunnanensis*), *115*

'Alba Grandiflora' (*S. vulgaris*), **26**

'Alba Virginalis' (*S. vulgaris*), 289

'Albert F. Holden' (*S. vulgaris*), *188*, **318**, 318

'Albida' (*S.* Villosae Group), 32, **114**, *134*, 273

'Albīns' (*S. vulgaris*), 345

'Aleksandr Pushkin' (*S. vulgaris*), 335

'Alekseĭ Mares'ev' (*S. vulgaris*), **139**, *139*, 331

'Alenushka' (*S. vulgaris*), *154*, 334

'Alesha' (*S. vulgaris*), *175*, 335

'Alexander Hamilton' (*S. vulgaris*), 289

'Alexander's Aristocrat' (*S.* Villosae Group), 308, **309**

'Alexander's Perfection' (*S.* Villosae Group), 308

'Alexander's Pink' (*S.* Villosae Group), **309**, 309

'Alice' (*S.* Villosae Group), **186**, *186*

'Alice' (*S. vulgaris*), 292

'Alice Chieppo' (*S. vulgaris*), *147*, 323

'Alice Christianson' (*S. vulgaris*), 292

'Alice Eastwood' (*S.* ×*hyacinthiflora*), **172**, *172*, 304

'Alice Rose Foster' (*S.* Villosae Group), *163*, **309**, 309

'Alma' (*S. vulgaris*), 292

'Almaatinka' (*S. vulgaris*), 346

'Aloise' (*S. vulgaris*), *126*, 318, **319**

'Alphonse Lavallée' (*S. vulgaris*), **147**, *147*, 275, **222**

'Altaĭskaya Rozovaya' (*S. vulgaris*), 335

'Alvan R. Grant' (*S. vulgaris*), 314

'Ambassadeur' (*S. vulgaris*), *139*, **274**, 275

'Amethyst' (*S. vulgaris*), 280, **281**

'Ametist 2' (*S. vulgaris*), **147**, *147*, 334

'Ami Schott' (*S. vulgaris*), *139*, **274**, 275

'Amor' (*S. vulgaris*), **166**, *166*

'Anabel' (*S.* ×*hyacinthiflora*), **160**, *160*

'Anastasia' (*Syringa*), 328

'Andenken an Ludwig Späth' (*S. vulgaris*), 29, *175*, **176**, 280, 291

'André Csizik' (*S. vulgaris*), **166**, *166*, 284

'Andres' (*S. vulgaris*), 343

'Andryusha Gromov' (*S. vulgaris*), 331

'Angel White' (*S.* ×*hyacinthiflora*), **133**, *133*, 310

'Anna Amhoff' (*S.* Villosae Group), **118**, *118*, 134, 326

'Anna Elisabeth Jaquet' (*S. vulgaris*), *175*, **176**, 284

'Anna Nickles' (*S. vulgaris*), **147**, *147*, 315

'Anne Shiach' (*S. vulgaris*), *175*, **176**

'Anne Tighe' (*S. vulgaris*), *175*, **326**, 326

'Annie Ouwerkerk' (*S. vulgaris*), 286

'Antonia Mel'nik' (*S. vulgaris*), 345

'A1', see 'Robuste Albert' (*S. vulgaris*)

'Arch McKean' (*S. vulgaris*), *166*, 318, **319**

'Archevêque' (*S. vulgaris*), *177*, 275

'Archiduchesse Charlotte' (*S. vulgaris*), *154*

'Aria' (*S.* ×*hyacinthiflora*), 334

'Ariel' (*S.* Villosae Group), *138*

'Arthur William Paul' (*S. vulgaris*), *177*, *177*, 275

'Arvid Vilms' (*S.* ×*hyacinthiflora*), 343

'Asessippi' (*S.* ×*hyacinthiflora*), **200**, **301**, 301,

'Atheline Wilbur' (*S. vulgaris*), *188*, 318, **319**

'Atmiņu Maurs' (*S. vulgaris*), 344

'Aucubaefolia' (*S. vulgaris*), **191**, *191*

'Audrey' (*S.* Villosae Group), **298**, 298

'Aurea' (*S. emodi*), **106**, *107*, 192

'Aurea' (*S. vulgaris*), *191*

'Avalanche' (*S. vulgaris*), *126*, 318, **319**

'Azurea Plena' (*S. vulgaris*), **246**, 269

'Bailbelle' (*Syringa*), 197, **327**, 327

'Baildust' (*Syringa*), 197, 327

'Bailina' (*Syringa*), 197

'Bailming' (*Syringa*), 197, 328

'Bailsugar' (*Syringa*), 197, 328

'Baldishol' (*S. villosa*), 34, 288

Banner of Lenin, see 'Znamya Lenina' (*S. vulgaris*)

'Banquise' (*S. vulgaris*), *126*, **127**, 275

'Basia' (*S.* Villosae Group), *163*, **342**, 342

'Beacon' (*S.* Villosae Group), 299
BEAUTY OF MOSCOW, see 'Krasavitsa
    Moskvy' (*S. vulgaris*)
'Bei Jing Huang', see 'Jin Yuan' (*S.
    pekinensis*)
BEIJING GOLD, see 'Zhang Zhiming'
    (*S. pekinensis*)
'Beijing Huan', see 'Jin Yuan' (*S. pekin-
    ensis*)
'Belaya Noch'' (*S. vulgaris*), **329**, 329
BELLE DE MOSCOU, see 'Krasavitsa
    Moskvy' (*S. vulgaris*)
'Belle de Nancy' (*S. vulgaris*), 275
'Bellicent' (*S.* Villosae Group), **118**,
    118, 299
'Belorusskie Zori' (*S. vulgaris*), **147**,
    147, 336
'Belosnezhka' (*S. vulgaris*), 345
'Bernard Slavin' (*S. vulgaris*), *126*, 314
'Berryer' (*S.* ×*hyacinthiflora*), **160**,
    160, 275
'Bērzes Krasts' (*S. vulgaris*), 344
'Beth' (*S. vulgaris*), 328
'Beth Turner' (*S. vulgaris*), **305**, 305
'Betsy Bowman' (*S. vulgaris*), 312
'Betsy Ross' (*S.* ×*hyacinthiflora*), **325**,
    325
'Betty Opper' (*S. vulgaris*), 307
'Betty Stone' (*S. vulgaris*), *148*, 315
'Biała Anna' (*S. vulgaris*), 341
'Bicentennial' (*S. vulgaris*), 314
'Bicolor' (*S.* ×*chinensis*), *83*, *133*, 275
'Big Blue' (*S.* ×*hyacinthiflora*), *145*, 310
'Birchwood' (*S. oblata* subsp. *dilatata*),
    80
'Bishop McQuaid' (*S. vulgaris*), *177*,
    314
'Bleuâtre' (*S. vulgaris*), *139*, 269
'Bloemenlust' (*S. vulgaris*), *126*, 284
'Blue Angel' (*S. vulgaris*), *139*
'Blue Boy' (*S.* ×*hyacinthiflora*), *145*,
    311
'Blue Boy' (*S. vulgaris*), 328
'Blue Danube' (*S. vulgaris*), *139*, *139*,
    318
'Blue Delft' (*S. vulgaris*), *188*, 319
'Blue Delight' (*S. vulgaris*), **139**, *139*,
    303
'Blue Diamond' (*S. vulgaris*), 314
'Blue Giant' (*S. vulgaris*), **140**, 319
'Blue Hyacinth' (*S.* ×*hyacinthiflora*),
    304, 304
BLUE SKIES, see 'Monore' (*S. vulgaris*)
'Bluebird' (*S. vulgaris*), *139*, 319
'Bluets' (*S. vulgaris*), **140**, *140*

'Bogdan Khmel'nitskiĭ' (*S. vulgaris*),
    338, 338
'Bogdan Przyrzykowski' (*S. vulgaris*),
    341, 341
'Botaniste Pauli' (*S. vulgaris*), *166*
'Boule Azurée' (*S. vulgaris*), **140**, *140*,
    275
'Bountiful' (*S.* ×*hyacinthiflora*), *160*,
    304
'Boussingault' (*S. vulgaris*), 275
'Brent Sirois' (*S. vulgaris*), 312
'Bridal Memories' (*S. vulgaris*), 328
'Bright Centennial' (*S. vulgaris*), **166**,
    166
'Brilliant' (*S. vulgaris*), 345
'Buffon' (*S.* ×*hyacinthiflora*), *160*, **161**,
    275
'Burgemeester Loggers' (*S. vulgaris*),
    135, *135*, 284
'Burgemeester Voller' (*S. vulgaris*), *135*,
    284
BURGUNDY QUEEN, see 'Lecburg' (*S.
    vulgaris*)

'C. B. van Nes' (*S. vulgaris*), *177*, 283
'California Rose' (*S.* ×*hyacinthiflora*),
    311, 311
'Calphurnia' (*S.* Villosae Group), **298**,
    298
'Calvin C. Laney' (*S. vulgaris*), **177**,
    177, 289
'Cameo's Jewel' (*S. reticulata* subsp.
    reticulata), *68*, *192*, 328
'Candeur' (*S. vulgaris*), *126*, 275
'Capitaine Baltet' (*S. vulgaris*), *166*,
    167, **214**, 275
'Capitaine Perrault' (*S. vulgaris*), *158*,
    275, **278**
'Carley' (*S. vulgaris*), *127*, **214**, 295
'Carlton' (*S.* Villosae Group), *121*, *163*,
    299
'Carmen' (*S. vulgaris*), 275
'Carmine' (*S. vulgaris*), 292, **293**
'Caroline Foley' (*S. vulgaris*), 307
'Carolyn Bergen' (*S. vulgaris*), 312
'Carolyn Howland' (*S. vulgaris*), 312
'Carolyn Mae' (*S. vulgaris*), **148**, *148*
'Catawba Pink' (*S. vulgaris*), **154**, *154*
'Catinat' (*S.* ×*hyacinthiflora*), *160*, **161**,
    275
'Cavour' (*S. vulgaris*), *135*, 275
'Celestial Blue' (*S. vulgaris*), 292
'Centenaire de la Linneenne' (*S. vul-
    garis*), *148*
'Champlain' (*S. vulgaris*), **135**, *135*, 275

'Chang Tong Bai' (*S. oblata*), 346
'Chantilly Lace' (*S. reticulata*), *68*, **69**,
    192, *192*
'Charisma' (*S.* ×*prestoniae*), 235
'Charles Baltet' (*S. vulgaris*), 275
'Charles Holetich' (*S. vulgaris*), 316
'Charles Joly' (*S. vulgaris*), **177**, *177*,
    275
'Charles Lindbergh' (*S. vulgaris*), 314
'Charles Nordine' (*S.* ×*hyacinthiflora*),
    145, *145*, 301
'Charles Sargent' (*S. vulgaris*), **140**,
    140, 275
'Charles X' (*S. vulgaris*), 269
'Charlotte Morgan' (*S. vulgaris*), *166*,
    167
'Charm' (*S. vulgaris*), **154**, *154*
'Charmian' (*S.* Villosae Group), *152*,
    153
'Cheyenne' (*S. oblata* subsp. *dilatata*),
    80, *80*, 146
'Chiffon' (*S.* ×*hyacinthiflora*), 311
'China Gold' (*S. reticulata*), *69*, *192*
CHINA SNOW, see 'Morton' (*S. pekin-
    ensis*)
'Chinese Magic' (*Syringa*), *133*
'Chokan Volikhanov' (*S. vulgaris*), 345
'Chris' (*S. vulgaris*), *177*, **312**, 312
'Christophe Colomb' (*S. vulgaris*),
    148, *148*, 275
'Chun Ge' (*S. vulgaris*), 346
'Churchill' (*S.* ×*hyacinthiflora*), *160*,
    161, 301
'Cinderella' (*S. pubescens* subsp. *patula*),
    99, 328
'City of Chehalis' (*S. vulgaris*), 292
'City of Gresham' (*S. vulgaris*), 292
'City of Kalama' (*S. vulgaris*), 292
'City of Kelso' (*S. vulgaris*), 292
'City of Longview' (*S. vulgaris*), 292
'City of Olympia' (*S. vulgaris*), 292
'Clara' (*S. vulgaris*), 292, **293**
'Clara Cochet' (*S. vulgaris*), 269, **270**
'Clarence D. Van Zandt' (*S. vulgaris*),
    289
'Clarke's Double White' (*S. vulgaris*),
    305
'Clarke's Giant' (*S.* ×*hyacinthiflora*),
    304
'Claude Bernard' (*S.* ×*hyacinthiflora*),
    161, *161*, 275
'Claude de Lorrain' (*S. vulgaris*), 275
'Cleaves' (*S. pekinensis*), *73*
'Coerulea Superba' (*S. vulgaris*), *139*

'Col. Wm. R. Plum' (*S. vulgaris*), **177**, *177*

'Colbert' (*S. vulgaris*), 275

'Colby's Wishing Star' (*Syringa*), 328

'Cole' (*S. reticulata*), *69*, *134*

'Comte Adrien de Montebello' (*S. vulgaris*), 276

'Comte de Kerchove' (*S. vulgaris*), 276

'Comte Horace de Choiseul' (*S. vulgaris*), **158**, *158*, 276

'Comtesse Horace de Choiseul' (*S. vulgaris*), 276

'Condorcet' (*S. vulgaris*), 276

'Congo' (*S. vulgaris*), **167**, *167*, 276

Copper Curls, see 'SunDak' (*S. pekinensis*)

'Cora Brandt' (*S. vulgaris*), **305**, 305

'Cora Lyden' (*S. vulgaris*), *154*, 309

'Coral' (*S.* Villosae Group), *163*, **299**, 299

'Corinna's Mist' (*S. ×hyacinthiflora*), *192*, 328

'Corinne' (*S. vulgaris*), **167**, *167*

'Correlata' (*Syringa*), 84

'Crampel' (*S. vulgaris*), 276

'Crayton Red' (*S.* Villosae Group), *117*

'Crépuscule' (*S. vulgaris*), *140*, **274**, 276

'Cynthia' (*S. vulgaris*), *154*, **155**, 312

'Dame Blanche' (*S. vulgaris*), 276

'Dancing Druid' (*S.* Villosae Group), *174*, **323**, 323

'Danton' (*S. vulgaris*), *178*, 276

'Danusia' (*S.* Villosae Group), **261**, 342

'Daphne Pink' (*S. ×hyacinthiflora*), **161**, *161*, 301

'Dappled Dawn' (*S. vulgaris*), **191**, *191*

'Dark Koster' (*S. vulgaris*), **228**, 284

'Dark Night' (*S. ×hyacinthiflora*), **184**, *184*, 311

'Darlene' (*S. vulgaris*), 328

'Daudzpusīgais Zemzaris' (*S. vulgaris*), 344

'Dawn' (*S.* Villosae Group), 299

'Dawn' (*S. vulgaris*), *140*, **295**, 295

DAWN OF COMMUNISM, see 'Zarya Kommunizma' (*S. vulgaris*)

'De Belder' (*S. pubescens* subsp. *patula*), **100**, *100–101*

'De Croncels' (*S. vulgaris*), *178*, *178*, 269

'De Humboldt' (*S. vulgaris*), 276

'De Jussieu' (*S. vulgaris*), 276

'De Miribel' (*S. vulgaris*), **135**, *135*, 276

'De Saussure' (*S. vulgaris*), **178**, *178*, 276

'Decaisne' (*S. vulgaris*), **140**, *140*, 276

'Declaration' (*S. ×hyacinthiflora*), **325**, 325

'Delreb' (*S. vulgaris*), 30

'Densiflora' (*S. sweginzowii*), 276

'Descanso Giant' (*S. ×hyacinthiflora*), 311

'Descanso King' (*S. ×hyacinthiflora*), **145**, *145*, 311

'Descanso Princess' (*S. ×hyacinthiflora*), 311

'Descartes' (*S. ×hyacinthiflora*), 276

'Desdemona' (*S.* Villosae Group), **146**, *146*, **224**, 298

'Desfontaines' (*S. vulgaris*), 276

'Deuil d'Émile Gallé' (*S. vulgaris*), 276

'Deviche Schast'e' (*S. vulgaris*), 338

'Diana' (*S.* Villosae Group), 297

'Dianah Abbott' (*S. vulgaris*), *178*, **312**, 312

'Diderot' (*S. vulgaris*), **178**, *178*, 276

'Dillia' (*S. vulgaris*), 292

'Diplomate' (*S. vulgaris*), *140*, 276

'Directeur Doorenbos' (*S. vulgaris*), **148**, *148*, 284

'Director General van de Plassche' (*S. vulgaris*), 284

'Dobeles Meitene' (*S. vulgaris*), 344

'Dobeles Sapņotājs' (*S. vulgaris*), 344

'Doch' Tamara' (*S. vulgaris*), **333**, 333

'Docteur Charles Jacobs' (*S. vulgaris*), **282**, 282

'Doctor Chadwick' (*S. ×hyacinthiflora*), **146**, *146*, 301

'Don Wedge' (*S. vulgaris*), 316

'Donald Wyman' (*S.* Villosae Group), *186*, 301, 302

'Donaldii' (*S. oblata* subsp. *dilatata*), **80**, *80–81*, **249**

'Donetskiye Zori' (*S. vulgaris*), **339**, 339

'Donetsky Souvenir' (*S. vulgaris*), **339**, 339

'Donkere Koster', see 'Dark Koster' (*S. vulgaris*)

'Dorothy Ramsden' (*S. vulgaris*), 309

'Downfield' (*S. vulgaris*), **167**, *167*

'Doyen Keteleer' (*S. vulgaris*), 276

'Dr Brethour' (*S. vulgaris*), *178*, **296**, 296

'Dr Edward Mott Moore' (*S. vulgaris*), *135*, 314

'Dr John Rankin' (*S. vulgaris*), *136*, 319

'Dr Lemke', see 'No. 71' (*S. vulgaris*)

'Dr Maillot' (*S. vulgaris*), 276

'Dr Masters' (*S. vulgaris*), 276

'Dr Troyanowsky' (*S. vulgaris*), 276

'Dr von Regel' (*S. vulgaris*), **281**, 281

'Dr W. Bugała' (*S. vulgaris*), 341

'Dresden China' (*S. vulgaris*), 292

'Drifting Dream' (*S. vulgaris*), 319

'DTR 124' (*S. pekinensis*), *73*

'Duc de Massa' (*S. vulgaris*), **140**, *140*, 276

'Duplex' (*S. ×chinensis*), *83*, 276

'Dusk' (*S. vulgaris*), **178**, *178*

'Dwight D. Eisenhower' (*S. vulgaris*), *140*, **141**, 314

'Dzhavakharlal Neru' (*S. vulgaris*), **179**, *179*, 331

'Early Double White' (*S. vulgaris*), *127*, 305

'Ed Frolich' (*S. vulgaris*), 316

'Eden' (*S. vulgaris*), *167*

'Edith Braun' (*S. vulgaris*), **179**, *179*, 307

'Edith Cavell' (*S. vulgaris*), *127*, **276**, 276, 313

'Edmond About' (*S. vulgaris*), 276

'Edmond Boissier' (*S. vulgaris*), **179**, *179*, 277

'Edna Dunham' (*S. vulgaris*), 307

'Édouard André' (*S. vulgaris*), 277

'Edward J. Gardner' (*S. vulgaris*), **158**, *158*, 306

86-1 (*S.* Villosae Group), 260, 326

'Elaine' (*S.* Villosae Group), **134**, *134*, 299

'Eleanor Berdeen' (*S. vulgaris*), *141*, **312**, 312

'Elegantissima' (*S. emodi*), *107*, *133*

'Elena Rosse' (*S. ×hyacinthiflora*), 334

'Elena Vekhova' (*S. vulgaris*), 329

ELFE, see 'Dark Night' (*S. ×hyacinthiflora*)

ELFENKÖNIG, see 'Sunset' (*S. ×hyacinthiflora*)

'Elihu Root' (*S. vulgaris*), 289

'Elinor' (*S.* Villosae Group), **146**, *146*, **298**, 298

'Elizabeth Mills' (*S. vulgaris*), 292

'Ellie-Marie' (*S. vulgaris*), 294

'Elliott' (*S. reticulata*), *69*, 321

'Elsa Maasik' (*S. vulgaris*), 343

'Elsie Lenore' (*S. vulgaris*), *158*, **320**, 320

'Emery Mae Norweb' (*S. vulgaris*), *127*, 320

'Emil Liebig' (*S. vulgaris*), 281

'Émile Gentil' (*S. vulgaris*), **141**, *141*, 277

'Émile Lemoine' (*S. vulgaris*), *148*, 277, **278**

'Engler Weisser Traum' (*S. vulgaris*), 228

'Enid' (*S.* Villosae Group), *163*

'Epaulettes' (*S. pubescens* subsp. *julianae*), **95**, *174*

'Esības Prieks' (*S. vulgaris*), 344

'Esterka' (*S.* Villosae Group), *163*, 342

'Esther Staley' (*S.* ×*hyacinthiflora*), *172*, **173**, 304

'Eterena' (*S. vulgaris*), 344

'Ethel Child' (*S. vulgaris*), *179*

'Ethel Dupont' (*S. vulgaris*), *179*

'Ethel M. Webster' (*S.* Villosae Group), **163**, *163*, 299

'Ethiopia' (*S. vulgaris*), **179**, *179*

'Etna' (*S. vulgaris*), *179*, 277

'Étoile de Mai' (*S. vulgaris*), *179*, 277

'Evangeline' (*S.* ×*hyacinthiflora*), 33, 302

'Eventide' (*S.* Villosae Group), *138*, **323**, 323

'Excel' (*S.* ×*hyacinthiflora*), **152**, *152*, **153**, 302

'Excellens' (*S. pubescens* subsp. *patula*), **100**, *101*, *134*, 277

'Excellent' (*S. vulgaris*), **127**, *127*, 284

FAIRY DUST, see 'Baildust' (*Syringa*)

FAIRYTALE series, 197, 327

'Fałe Bałtyku' (*S. vulgaris*), **141**, *141*, 341

'Fantasy' (*S.* ×*hyacinthiflora*), *172*, **173**, 304

'Father John' (*S. vulgaris*), *127*, **327**, 327

'Fénelon' (*S.* ×*hyacinthiflora*), **161**, *161*, 277

'Ferna Alexander' (*S.* Villosae Group), **309**, 309

'Fiala Remembrance' (*S. vulgaris*), 316

'Fioletovyĭ Sultan' (*S. vulgaris*), 338

'Firmament' (*S. vulgaris*), *141*, **274**, 277

Flamingo, see 'Edward J. Gardner' (*S. vulgaris*)

'Flora', see 'Flora 1953' (*S. vulgaris*)

'Flora 1953' (*S. vulgaris*), **127**, *127*, **195**, 284

'Floréal' (*S.* Villosae Group), *47*, **119**, *119*, 277

'Florence Christine' (*S. vulgaris*), 315

'Flow Blue' (*S. vulgaris*), *141*, 320

'Flower City' (*S. vulgaris*), *179*, 314

'Fluffy Ruffles' (*S. vulgaris*), 292

'Forrest Kresser Smith' (*S.* ×*hyacinthiflora*), 311

'Fountain' (*S.* Villosae Group), *121*, **163**, *163*

'Fraîcheur' (*S. vulgaris*), **128**, *128*, 277

'Francisca' (*S.* Villosae Group), **186**, *186*, 298

'Françisque Morel' (*S. vulgaris*), 277

'Frank Klager' (*S. vulgaris*), **180**, *180*, 292

'Frank Meyer' (*S. oblata*), *77–78*, 134

'Frank Paterson' (*S. vulgaris*), **180**, *180*, 296

'Fraser' (*S.* × *hyacinthiflora*), **162**, *162*

'Frau Bertha Dammann' (*S. vulgaris*), 281

FRAU HOLLE, see 'St Margaret' (*S. vulgaris*)

'Frazer' (*S.* ×*hyacinthiflora*), 302

'Fred L. Klager' (*S. vulgaris*), 292, **293**

'Fred Payne' (*S. vulgaris*), **136**, *136*

'Frederick Douglass' (*S. vulgaris*), *167*, 314

'Frederick Law Olmsted' (*S. vulgaris*), **220**, **314**, 314

'Fritz' (*S. vulgaris*), 292, **293**

'Fryderyk Chopin' (*S. vulgaris*), *168*, 341

'Fürst Bülow' (*S. vulgaris*), **180**, *180*, 281

'Fürst Lichtenstein' (*S. vulgaris*), 281

'G. J. Baardse' (*S. vulgaris*), *168*, 285

'Gaistošais Sapnis' (*S. vulgaris*), **344**, 344

'Gaiziņkalns' (*S. vulgaris*), *1*, 344

'Galina Ulanova' (*S. vulgaris*), **128**, *128*, 331

'Garden Peace' (*S.* Villosae Group)

'Gastello' (*S. vulgaris*), **331**, 331

'Gaudichaud' (*S. vulgaris*), 277

'Geheimrat Heyder' (*S. vulgaris*), 281

'Geheimrat Singelmann' (*S. vulgaris*), 281

'Général Drouot' (*S. vulgaris*), 277

'General Elwell S. Otis' (*S. vulgaris*), 289

'General Grant' (*S. vulgaris*), 289

'General John Pershing' (*S. vulgaris*), **289**, 289

'General Kitchener' (*S. vulgaris*), 289

'General Panfilov' (*S. vulgaris*), 346

'Général Pershing' (*S. vulgaris*), *158*, 277

'General Sheridan' (*S. vulgaris*), **128**, *128*, 289

'General Sherman' (*S. vulgaris*), *188*, **189**, 289

'George Eastman' (*S. pubescens* subsp. *julianae*), *93–94*, **94**, *162*, 314

'George Ellwanger' (*S. vulgaris*), 314

'George Emanuel' (*S. vulgaris*), 316

'George W. Aldridge' (*S. vulgaris*), **289**, 289

'Georges Bellair' (*S. vulgaris*), **168**, *168*, 277

'Georges Claude' (*S. vulgaris*), *141*, 277

'Geraldine Smith' (*S. vulgaris*), *128*, 307, **308**

'Germinal' (*S.* Villosae Group), **174**, *174*, 277

'Gerrie Schoonenberg' (*S. vulgaris*), *128*, **129**, 285

'Gertrude Clark' (*S. vulgaris*), *128*, **320**, 320

'Gertrude Leslie' (*S.* ×*hyacinthiflora*), 126, **133**, *133*, 301, 302

'Gilbert' (*S. vulgaris*), 277

'Giraldii' (*S. oblata*), 78

'Gismonda' (*S. vulgaris*), **168**, *168*, 277

'Glacier' (*S. vulgaris*), *128*, 320

'Gloire d'Aalsmeer' (*S. vulgaris*), *128*, 286

'Gloire de Lorraine' (*S. vulgaris*), 277

'Glory' (*S. vulgaris*), **168**, *168*

'Godron' (*S. vulgaris*), 277

'Golden Eclipse' (*S. reticulata*), **69**, *69*, 192

'Golubaya' (*S. vulgaris*), *141*, 331

'Goplana' (*S.* Villosae Group), **164**, *164*, 342

'Gortenziya' (*S. vulgaris*), **148**, *148*, 331

'Grace' (*S.* ×*hyacinthiflora*), *184*, **185**

'Grace Mackenzie' (*S.* ×*hyacinthiflora*), 301, 302

'Grand-Duc Constantin' (*S. vulgaris*), 277

'Guild's Pride' (*S.* ×*hyacinthiflora*), 311

'Guinevere' (*S.* Villosae Group), 46, **118**, *118*, 174, 297, 299

'Guizot' (*S. vulgaris*), 277

'Gul'der' (*S. vulgaris*), 346

'Gul'nazira' (*S. vulgaris*), 335

'Hallelujah' (*S. vulgaris*), **180**, *180*, 297

'Handel' (*S. Villosae Group*), 301, **302**, 302

'Hantengri' (*S. vulgaris*), 345

'Heather' (*S. vulgaris*), *128*, **129**, 295

'Heather Haze' (*S. ×hyacinthiflora*), 310

'Heavenly Blue' (*S. vulgaris*), *141*, 303

'Hecla' (*S. Villosae Group*), 301, 302

'Hedin' (*S. Villosae Group*), 301, **303**, 303

'Helen' (*S. Villosae Group*), 301, 302, **303**

'Helen Pellage' (*S. vulgaris*), 307

'Helen Schloen' (*S. vulgaris*), **180**, *180*, 296

'Helena Agathe Keessen' (*S. vulgaris*), **286**, 286

'Helgi' (*S. vulgaris*), 343

'Heloise' (*S. Villosae Group*), *164*

'Henri Martin' (*S. vulgaris*), 33, **148**, *148*, 277

'Henri Robert' (*S. vulgaris*), **136**, *136*, 277

'Henry Clay' (*S. vulgaris*), **290**, 290

'Henry Wadsworth Longfellow' (*S. vulgaris*), **168**, *168*, 290

'Henry Ward Beecher' (*S. vulgaris*), 290

'Herman Eilers' (*S. vulgaris*), 154

'Hers' (*S. pubescens* subsp. *julianae*), *94–95*, **95**, 162

'Hiawatha' (*S. Villosae Group*), 301, 302, **303**

'Hippolyte Maringer' (*S. vulgaris*), **149**, *149*, 277

'Hiram H. Edgerton' (*S. vulgaris*), **290**, 290

'Holger' (*S. Villosae Group*), 287

'Holte' (*S. josikaea*), 34, 288

'Holy Maid' (*S. vulgaris*), 155

HOPE, see 'Nadezhda' (*S. vulgaris*)

'Horace' (*S. Villosae Group*), 302

'Hosanna' (*S. vulgaris*), *136*, **320**, 320

'Hugo de Vries' (*S. vulgaris*), 284

'Hugo Koster' (*S. vulgaris*), **228**, 283, 284

'Hugo Mayer' (*S. vulgaris*), *141*, **285**, 285

'Hulda' (*S. vulgaris*), 293

'Hunting Tower' (*S. Villosae Group*), **134**, *134*, 303

'Hyacinthiflora Plena' (*S. ×hyacinthiflora*), 277

'Hyazinthenflieder' (*S. vulgaris*), 281

'Hyperion' (*S. vulgaris*), 328

'I. V. Michurin' (*S. vulgaris*), *155*, **331**, 331

'Imants Ziedonis' (*S. vulgaris*), 344

'Independence' (*S. vulgaris*), 314

'Indiya' (*S. vulgaris*), **149**, *149*, 331

'Irvina' (*S. vulgaris*), 293

'Irving' (*S. Villosae Group*), *164*

'Isabella' (*S. Villosae Group*), *120*, *120*, 153, 297, 298

IVORY PILLAR, see 'Willamette' (*S. reticulata*)

'Ivory Silk' (*S. reticulata*), *69–70*, *70*, *134*, **236**

'Izobilie' (*S. vulgaris*), *149*, 331

'J. R. Koning' (*S. vulgaris*), **285**, 285

'Jaan' (*S. ×hyacinthiflora*), 343

'Jaanika' (*S. vulgaris*), 343

'Jacques Callot' (*S. vulgaris*), *149*

'Jaga' (*S. Villosae Group*), *138*, 342

'Jagienka' (*S. Villosae Group*), **153**, *153*, 342

'James Berdeen' (*S. vulgaris*), 312, **313**

'James Macfarlane' (*S. Villosae Group*), **164**, *164*, 327

'James Stuart' (*S. vulgaris*), **168**, *168*, 295

'Jane Day' (*S. vulgaris*), **181**, *181*

'Jaunā Ausma' (*S. vulgaris*), 344

'Jaunkalsnavas Nakts' (*S. vulgaris*), 344

'Jean Bart' (*S. vulgaris*), **272**, 277

'Jean Macé' (*S. vulgaris*), 277

'Jeanne d'Arc' (*S. vulgaris*), 277

'Jefferson Berdeen' (*S. vulgaris*), 312

'Jeffrey' (*S. vulgaris*), 328

'Jēra Maigums' (*S. vulgaris*), 344

'Jesse Hepler' (*S. Villosae Group*), *118*, **118**, 327

'Jessica' (*S. Villosae Group*), *138*, *138*

'Jessie Gardner' (*S. vulgaris*), *136*, **306**, 306

'Jimmy Howarth' (*S. vulgaris*), 296

'Jin Yuan' (*S. pekinensis*), *73*

'Joan Dunbar' (*S. vulgaris*), 290

'Joel' (*S. vulgaris*), **320**, 320

'Johan Mensing' (*S. vulgaris*), 285

'John Dunbar' (*S. vulgaris*), *128*, **129**, 314

'John Kennedy' (*S. vulgaris*), 312, **313**

'John's Favorite' (*S. vulgaris*), 309

'Jonkheer G. F. van Tets' (*S. vulgaris*), **285**, 285

JOSÉE, see 'MORjos 060F' (*Syringa*)

'Jules Ferry' (*S. vulgaris*), 277

'Jules Simon' (*S. vulgaris*), *141*, **142**, 277

'Julia' (*S. Villosae Group*), *117*, 287

'Julien Gérardin' (*S. vulgaris*), 277

'Juliet' (*S. Villosae Group*), 298, **299**

'K. A. Timiryazev' (*S. vulgaris*), 331

'Kabul' (*S. protolaciniata*), *82*

'Kaisma' (*S. vulgaris*), 344

'Kannika' (*S. vulgaris*), 343

'Kapitan Teliga' (*S. vulgaris*), 341

'Kapriz' (*S. vulgaris*), **149**, *149*, 331

'Kardynał' (*S. vulgaris*), 341

'Käte Härlin' (*S. vulgaris*), 128

'Kate Sessions' (*S. ×hyacinthiflora*), *162*, 304

'Katherine Havemeyer' (*S. vulgaris*), **158**, *158*, 277

'Katherine Jones' (*S. ×hyacinthiflora*), *173*

'Kievlyanka' (*S. vulgaris*), 338

'Kim' (*S. Villosae Group*), **138**, *138*, 299

'Kivi Ats' (*S. ×hyacinthiflora*), 343

'Kjell' (*S. josikaea*), 287

'Klmone' (*S. pubescens* subsp. *patula*), 30, 197

'Knipper-Chekhova' (*S. vulgaris*), 338

'Komsomolka' (*S. vulgaris*), **149**, *149*, 332

'Konfetti' (*S. vulgaris*), 345

'Königin Luise' (*S. vulgaris*), *128*, 287

'Koningsloo' (*S. vulgaris*), 136

'Konstantin Zaslonov' (*S. ×hyacinthiflora*), *158*, **336**, 336

'Konstanty Karpow' (*S. vulgaris*), **158**, *158*, 342

'Kosmos' (*S. vulgaris*), **136**, *136*, 334

'Krasavitsa Bashkirii' (*S. vulgaris*), 335

'Krasavitsa Moskvy' (*S. vulgaris*), **189**, 332

'Krasnaya Moskva' (*S. vulgaris*), *181*, **332**, 332

'Kremlevskie Kuranty' (*S. vulgaris*), *149*, 332

'Kristīne Baltpurviņa' (*S. vulgaris*), 344

'Kristjan' (*S. vulgaris*), 343

'Kruzhevnitsa' (*S. vulgaris*), 335

'Krymskaya Krasavitsa' (*S. vulgaris*), 338

'Krymskaya Lazur' (*S. vulgaris*), 338

'Kum-Bum' (*S. Villosae Group*), 323

'La Lorraine' (*S.* ×*chinensis*), *83*, 172, 277
'La Mauve' (*S. vulgaris*), 277
'La Tour d'Auvergne' (*S. vulgaris*), **272**, 277
'Lady Lindsay' (*S. vulgaris*), *168*, **169**, 295
'Laine' (*S.* ×*hyacinthiflora*), 343
'Lamarck' (*S. vulgaris*), 277
'Lamartine' (*S.* ×*hyacinthiflora*), **85**, **221**, 277, 298
'Laplace' (*S. vulgaris*), **181**, *181*, 277
'Lark Song' (*S.* Villosae Group), *164*, **247**, 323
'Laurentian' (*S.* ×*hyacinthiflora*), **146**, *146*, 302
'Lavaliensis' (*S. vulgaris*), 155
'Lavender Lady' (*S.* ×*hyacinthiflora*), *184*, **185**, 310
'Lavender Lassie' (*S.* ×*hyacinthiflora*), *184*
'Lavoisier' (*S. vulgaris*), 278
'Lawrence Wheeler' (*S. vulgaris*), *141*, 306
'Le Gaulois' (*S. vulgaris*), 278
'Le Nôtre' (*S. vulgaris*), *136*, 278, **279**
'Le Printemps' (*S. vulgaris*), 278
'Le Progrès' (*S.* ×*chinensis*), 278
'Lebedushka' (*S. vulgaris*), *128*, 336
'Lecburg' (*S. vulgaris*), 324
'Lee Jewett Walker' (*S. vulgaris*), **155**, *155*, 312
'Leenu' (*S. vulgaris*), 343
'Leila Romer' (*S. vulgaris*), **316**, 316
'Lemoinei' (*S. vulgaris*), **271**, 278
'Léon Gambetta' (*S. vulgaris*), **150**, *150*, 278
'Léon Liberton' (*S. vulgaris*), 282
'Léon Simon' (*S. vulgaris*), 278
'Leon Wyczółkowski' (*S. vulgaris*), *168*
'Leone Gardner' (*S. vulgaris*), **306**, 306
'Leonid Kolesnikov' (*S. vulgaris*), 332
'Leonid Leonov' (*S. vulgaris*), *150*, **332**, 332
'Léopold II' (*S. vulgaris*), 282
'Léopold III' (*S. vulgaris*), *181*
'Lesnaya Pesnya' (*S. vulgaris*), 338
'Lesostepnaya' (*S. vulgaris*), 329
'Lesya Ukrainka' (*S. vulgaris*), 338
'Lesya Ukraynka' (*S. vulgaris*), 338
'Lewis Maddock' (*S.* ×*hyacinthiflora*), **162**, *162*, 307
'Liega' (*S. vulgaris*), **16**, **344**, 344
'Liina' (*S. vulgaris*), 343

'Lila Wonder' (*S. vulgaris*), 287
'Lilarosa' (*S. vulgaris*), **155**, *155*, **209**, 269
'Lillian Lee' (*S. vulgaris*), 293
'Lilovaya Purga' (*S. vulgaris*), 338
'Lilovaya Raketa' (*S. vulgaris*), 338
'Linné' (*S. vulgaris*), 278
'Lipchanka' (*S. vulgaris*), *136*
'Little Bit' (*S. vulgaris*), 312
'Little Miss Muffet' (*S. vulgaris*), *159*, **198**, 320
'Lois Amee Utley' (*S. vulgaris*), *155*, 320, **321**
'L'Oncle Tom' (*S. vulgaris*), **198**, 278
'Louis Henry' (*S. vulgaris*), 278
'Lourene Wishart' (*S. vulgaris*), *155*, 316, 320
'Louvain' (*S.* ×*hyacinthiflora*), **302**, 302
'Louvois' (*S.* ×*hyacinthiflora*), *138*, 278
'Luch Vostoka' (*S. vulgaris*), 345
'Lucie Baltet' (*S. vulgaris*), **155**, *155*, **195**, 269
'Lucy Bergen' (*S. vulgaris*), 312
LUDWIG SPAETH, see 'Andenken an Ludwig Späth' (*S. vulgaris*)
'Lullaby' (*S. vulgaris*), **150**, *150*
LUMLEY YELLOW (*S. vulgaris*), 286
'Lunnyĭ Svet' (*S. vulgaris*), 336, **337**
'Luo Lan Zi' (*S.* ×*hyacinthiflora*), 346
'Lutèce' (*S.* Villosae Group), *47*, **117**, *117*, 138
'Lutens' (*S. vulgaris*), **192**
'Lynette' (*S.* Villosae Group), *186*, 299
'Lynette Sirois' (*S. vulgaris*), 312

'M. I. Kalinin' (*S. vulgaris*), **136**, *136*, 332
'Macrostachya' (*S. vulgaris*), *155*, **156**, 269
'Madame A. J. Klettenberg' (*S. vulgaris*), 283
'Madame Charles Souchet' (*S. vulgaris*), *139*, *141*, **142**, 278
'Madame Hankar-Solvay' (*S. vulgaris*), *141*
'Madame Rosel' (*S. vulgaris*), 285
MÄDCHEN AUS MOSKAU, see 'Krasavitsa Moskvy' (*S. vulgaris*)
'Madeleine Lemaire' (*S. vulgaris*), *128*, **129**, 278
'Magellan' (*S. vulgaris*), **169**, *169*, 278
'Maiden's Blush' (*S.* ×*hyacinthiflora*), **86**, **122**, **123**, *162*, 301, 302
'Maiennacht' (*S. vulgaris*), *155*

'Maĭgul' (*S. vulgaris*), 346
'Maija Viešņa' (*S. vulgaris*), 344
'Maître Georges Hermans' (*S. vulgaris*), *169*
'Marat Kazeĭ' (*S. vulgaris*), *141*, 336
'Marc Micheli' (*S. vulgaris*), 278
'Marceau' (*S. vulgaris*), **169**, *169*, 278
'Maréchal de Bassompierre' (*S. vulgaris*), 278
'Maréchal Foch' (*S. vulgaris*), **169**, *169*, 278
'Maréchal Lannes' (*S. vulgaris*), *141*, **142**, 278
'Marengo' (*S. vulgaris*), 278
'Margaret Fenicchia' (*S. vulgaris*), *181*, 314
'Margaret Rice Gould' (*S. vulgaris*), **181**, *181*
'Margaretha' (*S. vulgaris*), 286
'Margot Grunewald' (*S. vulgaris*), *141*, **142**
'Maria' (*Syringa* Villosae Group), 287
'Mariam Cooley' (*S. vulgaris*), 293
'Marie Finon' (*S. vulgaris*), *128*, **129**, 287
'Marie Frances' (*S. vulgaris*), *155*, 320, **321**
'Marie Legraye' (*S. vulgaris*), *128*, **129**, 269, 286
'Marie Marcelin' (*S. vulgaris*), **159**, *159*
'Marie Rogers' (*S.* Villosae Group), *118*, 327
'Marlyensis' (*S. vulgaris*), 227, 269
'Marlyensis Pallida' (*S. vulgaris*), **150**, *150*, 289
'Marshal Vasilevskiĭ' (*S. vulgaris*), *155*, **156**, 332
'Marshal Zhukov' (*S. vulgaris*), **150**, *150*, 332
'Marsianka' (*S. vulgaris*), 338
'Martha' (*S. vulgaris*), 292, 293
'Martha Kounze' (*S. vulgaris*), **156**, *156*
'Martha Stewart' (*S. vulgaris*), **314**, 314
'Martin' (*S.* ×*hyacinthiflora*), 343
'Martine' (*S. vulgaris*), **287**, 287
'Mary Blanchard' (*S. vulgaris*), 327
'Mary C. Bingham' (*S.* Villosae Group), 309
'Mary Gardner' (*S. vulgaris*), 307
'Mary Short' (*S.* ×*hyacinthiflora*), **208**, 323
'Mar'yam' (*S. vulgaris*), 346
'Masséna' (*S. vulgaris*), **169**, 278

'Māte Ede Upītis' (*S. vulgaris*), 344
'Mathieu de Dombasle' (*S. vulgaris*), **271**, 278
'Måttsund' (*S. josikaea*), 288
'Maud Notcutt' (*S. vulgaris*), 130, 285
'Maureen' (*S. ×hyacinthiflora*), **211**, 299
'Maurice Barrès' (*S. vulgaris*), *141*, **142**, 278
'Maurice de Vilmorin' (*S. vulgaris*), **150**, *150*, 278
'Mauve Mist' (*S. vulgaris*), **223**, 297
'Max Löbner' (*S. ×hyacinthiflora*), *184*, **185**
'Max Peterson' (*S. vulgaris*), 312
'Maximowicz' (*S. vulgaris*), *136*, **137**, 278
'May Day' (*S. vulgaris*), **305**, 305
'Maybelle Farnum' (*S.* Villosae Group), **186**, *186*, 327
'Mazais Princis' (*S. vulgaris*), 344
'McMaster Centennial' (*S. vulgaris*), 327
'Mechta' (*S. vulgaris*), **143**, *143*, 332
'Mechta Materi' (*S. vulgaris*), 338
'Medeo' (*S. vulgaris*), 345
'Melissa Oakes' (*S. vulgaris*), *156*
'Metensis' (*S. ×chinensis*), 33
'Michel Buchner' (*S. vulgaris*), **151**, *151*, 278
'Midnight' (*S. vulgaris*), 320
'Midwest Gem' (*S. vulgaris*), **159**, *159*
'Milada' (*S. vulgaris*), 346
'Mildred Luetta' (*S. vulgaris*), **181**, *181*
'Milton' (*S. vulgaris*), 278
'Minchanka' (*S. vulgaris*), *2*, 336, **337**
'Minister Dąb-Kociol' (*S. vulgaris*), *143*
'Minnehaha' (*S. ×hyacinthiflora*), 301, 302
'Minuet' (*S.* Villosae Group), **317**, 317
'Mirabeau' (*S. ×hyacinthiflora*), **85**, 278
'Mireille' (*S. vulgaris*), 278
'Miriam Cooley' (*S. vulgaris*), *159*
'Mirklja Vara' (*S. vulgaris*), 345
'Mirnoe Nebo' (*S. vulgaris*), 345
'Miss Aalsmeer' (*S. vulgaris*), *181*
MISS AMERICA, see 'Agnes Smith' (*S.* Villosae Group)
'Miss Canada' (*S.* Villosae Group), **164**, *164*, 317
'Miss Ellen Willmott' (*S. vulgaris*), *130*, **276**, 278
'Miss Kim' (*S. pubescens* subsp. *patula*), 64, **101**, *101*, 138, **205**, 326, 327

MISS SUSIE, see 'Klmone' (*S. pubescens* subsp. *patula*)
MISS USA, see 'Agnes Smith' (*S.* Villosae Group)
'Missimo' (*S. ×hyacinthiflora*), *173*, 304
'Mister Big' (*S. vulgaris*), *169*
'Mme Abel Chatenay' (*S. vulgaris*), **130**, *130*, 279
'Mme Antoine Buchner' (*S. vulgaris*), **156**, *156*, 279
'Mme Casimir Périer' (*S. vulgaris*), **227**, 279, 291
'Mme de Miller' (*S. vulgaris*), 279
'Mme F. Morel' (*S. vulgaris*), **169**, *170*, 269–270
'Mme Felix' (*S. vulgaris*), **130**, *130*, 284, 287
'Mme Florent Stepman' (*S. vulgaris*), **130**, *130*, 282, 286
'Mme Jules Finger' (*S. vulgaris*), 279
'Mme Lemoine' (*S. vulgaris*), *130*, **215**, **276**, 279
'Mme Léon Simon' (*S. vulgaris*), 279
'Mme Léopold Draps' (*S. vulgaris*), *130*
'Mme Pierre Verhoeven' (*S. vulgaris*), *181*
'Moe' (*S. josikaea*), 34, 288
'Mollie Ann' (*S. vulgaris*), *151*, 321, **322**
'Monge' (*S. vulgaris*), **182**, *182*, 279, 324
'Monique Lemoine' (*S. vulgaris*), *130*, **277**, 279
'Monore' (*S. vulgaris*), **29**, **220**, 324
'Mons. J. De Messemaeker' (*S. vulgaris*), 282
'Mons. Léon Mathieu' (*S. vulgaris*), **282**, 282
'Mons. Lepage' (*S. vulgaris*), 279
'Mons. Maxime Cornu' (*S. vulgaris*), 279
'Mons. van Aerschot' (*S. vulgaris*), 282
'Mont Blanc' (*S. vulgaris*), 126, 279
'Montaigne' (*S. vulgaris*), **156**, *156*, 279
'Montesquieu' (*S. ×hyacinthiflora*), *173*, *173*, 279
'Montgolfier' (*S. vulgaris*), 279
'Monument' (*S. vulgaris*), *130*, 279
'Monument Carnot' (*S. vulgaris*), 279
'Mood Indigo' (*S. vulgaris*), *136*, 305
'MORjos 060F' (*Syringa*), 29, 103, 328
'Morton' (*S. pekinensis*), 73–74

'Moskovskiĭ Universitet' (*S. vulgaris*), 333
MOSCOW SKY, see 'Nebo Moskvy' (*S. vulgaris*)
'Mother Louise' (*S. vulgaris*), *130*
'Mount Baker' (*S. ×hyacinthiflora*), **133**, *133*, 301, 302
'Mountain Haze' (*S. vulgaris*), 305
'Mrs A Belmont' (*S. vulgaris*), 139, *143*, 295
'Mrs Edward Harding' (*S. vulgaris*), **170**, *170*, 279
'Mrs Eleanor Roosevelt' (*S. vulgaris*), 316
'Mrs Elizabeth Peterson' (*S. vulgaris*), *143*, 295
'Mrs Flanders' (*S. vulgaris*), *182*, 296
'Mrs Harry Bickle' (*S. vulgaris*), **157**, *157*
'Mrs Irene Slater' (*S. vulgaris*), 296
'Mrs J. Herbert Alexander' (*S.* Villosae Group), 309
'Mrs John S. Williams' (*S. vulgaris*), *151*, 296
'Mrs John W. Davis' (*S. vulgaris*), *170*, 295
'Mrs Katherine Margaretten' (*S. vulgaris*), 316
'Mrs Morgan' (*S. vulgaris*), 293
'Mrs Nancy Reagan' (*S. vulgaris*), **316**, 316
'Mrs R. L. Gardner' (*S. vulgaris*), *182*, 307
'Mrs Trapman' (*S. vulgaris*), 188
'Mrs W. E. Marshall' (*S. vulgaris*), **182**, *182*, 296
'Mrs Watson Webb' (*S. vulgaris*), **170**, *170*, 296
'Mulatka' (*S. vulgaris*), 334
'Muriel' (*S. ×hyacinthiflora*), *184*, 298
'Murillo' (*S. vulgaris*), *182*, 279
'My Favorite' (*S. vulgaris*), 292, 293

'Nadezhda' (*S. vulgaris*), **143**, *143*, 332
'Nafisa' (*S. vulgaris*), 335
'Nakai' (*S. oblata* subsp. *dilatata*), *81*
'Nancy Frick' (*S. vulgaris*), **295**, 296
'Nanook' (*S. vulgaris*), *130*, 285
'Naudin' (*S. vulgaris*), 279
'Nebo Moskvy' (*S. vulgaris*), **143**, *143*, 332
'Necker' (*S. ×hyacinthiflora*), 279
'Negro' (*S. vulgaris*), *182*, 279, 298
'Nellie Bean' (*S.* Villosae Group), *186*, 327

'Nepovtorimaya' (*S. vulgaris*), 329
'Nevesta' (*S. vulgaris*) Kolesnikov, 332
'Nevesta' (*S. vulgaris*) Rubtzov, Zhogoleva & Lyapunova, 332, 338
'Nezhnost'' (*S. vulgaris*), 329
'Night' (*S. vulgaris*), **296**, 296
'Nike' (*S.* Villosae Group), **138**, *138*, 342
'Nikolaĭ Mikhaĭlov' (*S.* ×*hyacinthiflora*), **334**, 334
'Nina' (*S.* ×*hyacinthiflora*), **334**, 334
'Niobe' (*S. vulgaris*), 287
'No. 71' (*S. vulgaris*), *143*
'Nocturne' (*S.* Villosae Group), **299**, 299
'Nokomis' (*S.* ×*hyacinthiflora*), *152*, **153**, 302
'Norah' (*S.* ×*hyacinthiflora*), *152*, **153**, 298
'Norrfjärden' (*S. vulgaris*), 288
'Noktyurn' (*S. vulgaris*), 335
'Nouveau' (*S.* ×*diversifolia*), *90*

'Oakes Double White' (*S. vulgaris*), *130*, **131**
'Obélisque' (*S. vulgaris*), 279
'Octavia' (*S.* Villosae Group), 342
'Ogni Donbassa' (*S. vulgaris*), *151*, 338
'Ogni Donetska' (*S. vulgaris*), 339, **340**
'Ogni Moskvy' (*S. vulgaris*), 332
'Old Fashioned' (*S. vulgaris*), 305
'Old Glory' (*S.* ×*hyacinthiflora*), **325**, 325
'Old Lace' (*S.* ×*hyacinthiflora*), 310
'Old Rose' (*S. vulgaris*), 293, **294**
'Oleg' (*S. vulgaris*), 346
'Olimpiada Kolesnikova' (*S. vulgaris*), **157**, *157*, 332
'Olive May Cummings' (*S. vulgaris*), **159**, *159*, 312
'Olivier de Serres' (*S. vulgaris*), *143*, **216**, 279
'Orchid Beauty' (*S.* ×*chinensis*), *83*, **84**, 172
'Orchid Chiffon' (*S.* ×*hyacinthiflora*), *162*
'Ostankino' (*S. vulgaris*), 334, **335**
'Ostrander' (*S. vulgaris*), *188*, 292, 293, **294**
'Othello' (*S. vulgaris*), 279

'P. K. Ozolin' (*S. vulgaris*), 345
'P. P. Konchalovskiĭ' (*S. vulgaris*), **143**, *143*, 332

'Palibin' (*S. meyeri*), *102–103*, **103**, 162, **190**, **197**, **202**
'Pallens' (*S.* Villosae Group), 279
'Pallida' (*S. josikaea*), **47**, *138*
'Pamyat' o Chekhove' (*S. vulgaris*), 338
'Pamyat' o Kolesnikove' (*S. vulgaris*), 332
'Pamyat' o S. M. Kirove' (*S. vulgaris*), **151**, *151*, 332
'Pamyat' o Vavilove' (*S. vulgaris*), 329
'Pamyat' o Vekhove' (*S. vulgaris*), **329**, 329
'Pamyati A. T. Smol'skoĭ' (*S. vulgaris*), 336
'Panna Dorota Goła<curlicue>becka' (*S. vulgaris*), 130
'Pārsteigums' (*S. vulgaris*), 345
'Partizanka' (*S. vulgaris*), 336
'Pascal' (*S.* ×*hyacinthiflora*), **33**
'Pasteur' (*S. vulgaris*), **182**, *182*, 279
'Pat Pesata' (*S. vulgaris*), *188*, 321, **322**
'Patricia' (*S.* ×*hyacinthiflora*), **173**, *173*
'Patrick Henry' (*S. vulgaris*), 290
'Patriot' (*S.* Villosae Group), 328
'Paul Deschanel' (*S. vulgaris*), **170**, *170*, 279
'Paul Hariot' (*S. vulgaris*), **182**, *182*, 279
'Paul Thirion' (*S. vulgaris*), **170**, *170*, 279
'Paulina' (*S.* Villosae Group), *120*, 186
'Pauline Fiala' (*S. vulgaris*), *136*, 321
'Pavlinka' (*S. vulgaris*), 336, **337**
'Peau de Chamois' (*S. vulgaris*), 305
'Peerless Pink' (*S. vulgaris*), **285**, 285
'Peggy' (*S.* ×*hyacinthiflora*), **146**, *146*, 298
'Pendula' (*S. pekinensis*), **74**, *74*, *134*
'Pērle' (*S. vulgaris*), **8**, 345
'Pērļu Zvejnieks' (*S. vulgaris*), **5**, 345
'Philémon' (*S. vulgaris*), 269
PHILLIP ADAMS, see 'Kum-Bum' (*S. tomentella*)
'Pierre Joigneaux' (*S. vulgaris*), 279
'Pink Cloud' (*S.* ×*hyacinthiflora*), **173**, *173*, 304
'Pink Delight' (*S. vulgaris*), 328
'Pink Lace' (*S. vulgaris*), **157**, *157*
'Pink Mist' (*S. vulgaris*), **157**, *157*
'Pink Parasol' (*S. pubescens* subsp. *julianae*), *95*, *162*, 323
'Pink Spray' (*S.* ×*hyacinthiflora*), **304**, 304
'Pinkie' (*S. vulgaris*), 307, **308**
'Pioner' (*S. vulgaris*), **151**, *151*, 332

'Pixie' (*S. vulgaris*), 321
'Planchon' (*S. vulgaris*), **170**, *171*, 279
'PNI 7523' (*S. reticulata*), *70*
'Pocahontas' (*S.* ×*hyacinthiflora*), **86**, *138*, 301, 302
'Podarok Mame' (*S. vulgaris*), 346
'Pol' Robson' (*S. vulgaris*), 332
'Polesskaya Legenda' (*S. vulgaris*), *183*, 336
'Polina Osipenko' (*S. vulgaris*), 332
'Polly Hagaman' (*S. vulgaris*), 316
'Poltava' (*S. vulgaris*), 338, **339**
'Pomorzanka' (*S. vulgaris*), *157*, 342
'Porcelain Blue' (*S. vulgaris*), *188*, **189**, 321
'Pozdnyaya Vishnevaya' (*S. vulgaris*), 345
'Prairial' (*S.* Villosae Group), *47*, **164**, *164*, 279
'Président Carnot' (*S. vulgaris*), 279
'Président Fallières' (*S. vulgaris*), 279
'Président Grévy' (*S. vulgaris*), *144*, **275**, 279, 291
'President Harding' (*S. vulgaris*), 290
'Président Hayes' (*S.* ×*chinensis*), *83*, **84**, 279
'President John Adams' (*S. vulgaris*), 290
'Président Lambeau' (*S. vulgaris*), 282
'President Lincoln' (*S. vulgaris*), **144**, *144*, 289, 290
'Président Loubet' (*S. vulgaris*), 171, 280
'President Monroe' (*S. vulgaris*), 290
'Président Poincaré' (*S. vulgaris*), **171**, *171*, 280
'President Ronald Reagan' (*S. vulgaris*), **316**, 316
'President Roosevelt' (*S. vulgaris*), **290**, 290
'Président Viger' (*S. vulgaris*), 280
PRIDE OF MOSCOW, see 'Krasnaya Moskva' (*S. vulgaris*)
'Primrose' (*S. vulgaris*), 130, **189**, *189*, **221**, 286
PRIMROSE H (*S. vulgaris*), 130, 286
PRIMROSE L (*S. vulgaris*), *130*
'Prince Baudouin' (*S. vulgaris*), *171*
PRINCE CHARMING, see 'Bailming' (*Syringa*)
'Prince de Beauvau' (*S. vulgaris*), 280
'Prince of Wales' (*S. vulgaris*), 151, **288**, 288
'Princess Alexandra' (*S. vulgaris*), 288
'Princess Pink' (*S. vulgaris*), 293

'Prinses Beatrix' (*S. vulgaris*), 286
'Priscilla' (*S. vulgaris*), **171**, *171*
'Prodige' (*S. vulgaris*), **183**, *183*, 280
'Prof. E. H. Wilson' (*S. vulgaris*), *130*, **131**, 296
'Prof. Edmund Jankowski' (*S. vulgaris*), *144*, 342
'Prof. Hoser' (*S. vulgaris*), **144**, *144*
'Prof. Jósef Brzeziński' (*S. vulgaris*), **342**, *342*
'Professor A. L. Lypa' (*S. vulgaris*), 339, **340**
'Professor M. L. Reva' (*S. vulgaris*), 339, **340**
'Professor Robert B. Clark' (*S. vulgaris*), *189*, 321
'Professor Sargent' (*S. vulgaris*), **281**, 281
'Prophecy' (*S. Villosae Group*), **265**, 324
'Purple Gem' (*S. ×hyacinthiflora*), *184*, 304
'Purple Glory' (*S. ×hyacinthiflora*), *184*, **185**, 304
'Purple Haze' (*Syringa*), *82*, *82*
'Purple Heart' (*S. ×hyacinthiflora*), *184*, 304
'Purple Splendour', see 'Splendor' (*S. ×hyacinthiflora*)
'Pyatidesyatiletie Oktyabrya' (*S. vulgaris*), 333
'Pyramidal' (*S. vulgaris*), 280

'Quadricolor' (*S. vulgaris*), 192
'Quartet' (*S. Villosae Group*), **164**, *165*

'R. W. Mills' (*S. vulgaris*), 293
'Rå' (*S. josikaea*), 34, 288
'Rabelais' (*S. vulgaris*), 280
'Radiance' (*S. vulgaris*), *157*
'Radost' Pobedy' (*S. vulgaris*), 338
'Radostnaya' (*S. vulgaris*), 345
'Radzh Kapur' (*S. vulgaris*), **171**, *171*, 332
'Rassvet' (*S. vulgaris*), 345
'Rauno' (*S. ×hyacinthiflora*), 343
'Ray Halward' (*S. vulgaris*), 316
'Réaumur' (*S. vulgaris*), **171**, *171*, 280
'Red Feather' (*S. vulgaris*), *171*
'Red Giant' (*S. vulgaris*), 328
'Red Pixie' (*Syringa*), 328
'Red Rothomagensis' (*S. ×chinensis*), 28, **31**, *32*, *83–84*
'Redwine' (*S. Villosae Group*), **300**, *300*

REGENT, see 'PNI 7523' (*S. reticulata*)
REGENT BRAND, see 'PNI 7523' (*S. reticulata*)
'Reine Elisabeth' (*S. vulgaris*), 282
'René Jarry-Desloges' (*S. vulgaris*), *144*, 280
'Renoncule' (*S. vulgaris*), **271**, 280
'Reva Ballreich' Margaretten (*S. vulgaris*), 316
'Reva Ballreich' Peterson (*S. vulgaris*), 328
RÊVE BLEU, see 'Delreb' (*S. vulgaris*)
'Rhapsody' (*S. vulgaris*), *189*, 321
'Rhodopea' (*S. vulgaris*), *139*, *144*
'Richard A. Fenicchia' (*S. vulgaris*), 314
'Riet Bruidegom' (*S. vulgaris*), *130*, **131**, 285
'Ritoniemi' (*S. vulgaris*), 287
'Robusta', see 'Robuste Albert' (*S. vulgaris*)
'Robuste Albert' (*S. vulgaris*), 229, 287
'Rochambeau' (*S. vulgaris*), 280
'Rochester' (*S. vulgaris*), *130*, **260**, 313
'Roi Albert' (*S. vulgaris*), 282
'Roland Mills' (*S. vulgaris*), 293
'Romance' (*S. vulgaris*), **159**, *159*, 296
'Romeo' (*S. Villosae Group*), **165**, *165*, 298
'Ronsard' (*S. vulgaris*), 280
'Roosi' (*S. vulgaris*), 343
'Rosace' (*S. vulgaris*), 280
'Rosea' (*S. yunnanensis*), *115*, **115**
ROSENROT, see 'Maiden's Blush' (*S. ×hyacinthiflora*)
ROSARÖD, see 'Maiden's Blush' (*S. ×hyacinthiflora*)
'Royal Crown' (*S. Villosae Group*), 324
'Royal Purple' (*S. ×hyacinthiflora*), 301, **302**, 302
'Royalty' (*S. Villosae Group*), **116**, *118*, **186**, *186*, **234**
'Rozovoe Oblako' (*S. vulgaris*), 338
'Rubella Plena' (*S. vulgaris*), **272**, 280
'Rubra' (*S. josikaea*), **46**, *47*
'Ruby Cole' (*S. vulgaris*), 328
'Ruhm von Horstenstein' (*S. vulgaris*), **171**, *171*, 287
'Rus' (*S. vulgaris*), 329
RUSSIAN ARCTIC, see 'Sovetskaya Arktika' (*S. vulgaris*)
'Russkaya Krasavitsa' (*S. vulgaris*), 334
'Russkaya Pesnya' (*S. vulgaris*), *136*, **137**, 329

'Russkiĭ Suvenir' (*S. vulgaris*), 335
'Rustica' (*S. vulgaris*), **275**, 280
'Rutilant' (*S. Villosae Group*), *47*, *119*, **119**, 280

'S. V. Lavrov' (*S. vulgaris*), *151*, 339
'Sacrament' (*S. vulgaris*), 321, **322**
'Saima' (*S. vulgaris*), 343
'Saint Jerzy Popieluszko' (*S. vulgaris*), *172*
'Salavat Yulaev' (*S. vulgaris*), 335
'Samal' (*S. vulgaris*), 345
'Santa' (*S. vulgaris*), 345
'Sapun-gora' (*S. vulgaris*), 338
'Sarah Sands' (*S. vulgaris*), **183**, *183*, **209**, 296
'Sārtais Viesis' (*S. vulgaris*), 345
'Satin Cloud' (*S. vulgaris*), *131*
'Saturnale' (*S. vulgaris*), *145*, 280
'Saugeana' (*S. ×chinensis*), 28, 33, **84**, *84*, 269
'Savonarole' (*S. vulgaris*), *145*, **275**, 280
SCHNEEWEISSCHEN, see 'Mount Baker' (*S. ×hyacinthiflora*)
SCHÖNE VON MOSKAU, see 'Krasavitsa Moskvy' (*S. vulgaris*)
'Scipion Cochet' (*S. vulgaris*), 269
'Sculptured Ivory' (*S. vulgaris*), *131*, 321
'Sea Storm' (*S. vulgaris*), *145*
'Selma Margaretten' (*S. vulgaris*), **316**, 316
'Sénateur Volland' (*S. vulgaris*), 280
'Sensation' (*S. vulgaris*), **190**, *190*, **216**, 285
'Sentinel' (*S. pubescens* subsp. *julianae*), *174*
'Serebristyĭ Landysh' (*S. vulgaris*), 335
'Serene' (*S. vulgaris*), 33, 297
'Serezha' (*S. vulgaris*), 346
'Sesquicentennial' (*S. vulgaris*), *136*, 314
'Sevastopol'skiĭ Val's' (*S. vulgaris*), 338
'Shantelle' (*S. Villosae Group*), 235
'Shaura' (*S. vulgaris*), 335
'Shkol'nitsa' (*S. vulgaris*), 334, **335**
'Sholokhov' (*S. vulgaris*), 332, **333**
'Sholpan' (*S. vulgaris*), 345
'Si Ji Lan' (*Syringa*), 346
'Siebold' (*S. vulgaris*), *190*, 280
'Sierra Snow' (*S. ×hyacinthiflora*), 310
Signature, see 'Sigzam' (*S. reticulata*)
'Sigzam' (*S. reticulata*), *70*
'Silja' (*S. vulgaris*), 343

'Silver King' (*S. vulgaris*), **190**, *190*
'Silvi Vrait' (*S. vulgaris*), 343
'Sireneva̯a Piramida' (*S. vulgaris*), 335
'Sirenevy̆ Kaskad' (*S. vulgaris*), 335, 338
'Sister Justina' (*S. ×hyacinthiflora*), 126, **133**, *133*, 301, 302
'Skinneri' (*S. pubescens*), *102*, 301
'Skromni̯sa' (*S. ×hyacinthiflora*), 334
'Slater's Elegance' (*S. vulgaris*), **131**, *131*, 296
'Slavin' (*S. komarowii* subsp. *reflexa*), **111**, *111*
'Sleeping Beauty' (*Syringa*), 328
'Smaidošais Laiks' (*S. vulgaris*), 345
'Snezhni̯ Kom' (*S. vulgaris*), **345**, 345
'Snow Cap' (*S. vulgaris*), 321
'Snow Shower' (*S. vulgaris*), **131**, *131*
'Snow White' (*S. vulgaris*), 229
Snowcap, see 'Elliott' (*S. reticulata*)
'Snowdrift' (*S. Villosae Group*), *134*
'Snowflake' (*S. vulgaris*), 297
'Snowstorm' (*S. meyeri*), 328
'Solomon Margaretten' (*S. vulgaris*), 316
'Sonnet' (*S. vulgaris*), *151*, 321, **322**
'Sorok Let Komsomola' (*S. vulgaris*), 332
'Souvenir d'Alice Harding' (*S. vulgaris*), *132*, **277**, 280
'Souvenir de Claudius Graindorge' (*S. vulgaris*), **283**, 283
'Souvenir de Georges Truffaut' (*S. vulgaris*), *172*, 280
'Souvenir de Gustave Graindorge' (*S. vulgaris*), 283
'Souvenir de L. Thibaut' (*S. vulgaris*), 280
'Souvenir de Louis Chasset' (*S. vulgaris*), *172*, 280
'Souvenir de Mevrouw Dr Kenis' (*S. vulgaris*), *137*
'Souvenir de Mme Louis Gielis' (*S. vulgaris*), *132*
'Sovet̯ska̯a Arktika' (*S. vulgaris*), **132**, *132*, 332
'So̯uz-Apollon' (*S. vulgaris*), 338
'Spellbinder' (*S. Villosae Group*), **165**, *165*
'Splendor' (*S. ×hyacinthiflora*), *184*, 305
'Spring Dawn' (*S. ×hyacinthiflora*), *146*, 305
'Spring Parade' (*S. vulgaris*), 322
'Springtime' (*S. Villosae Group*), *165*

'St Joan' (*S. vulgaris*), *132*, **213**, 303
'St Margaret' (*S. vulgaris*), **132**, *132*, 303
'Stadtgärtner Rothpletz' (*S. vulgaris*), *183*
'Stefan Makowiecki' (*S. vulgaris*), **172**, *172*, 342
'Stephanie Rowe' (*S. vulgaris*), **157**, *157*
STERNTALER, see Primrose H (*S. vulgaris*)
SUGAR PLUM FAIRY, see 'Bailsugar' (*Syringa*)
'Sumerki' (*S. vulgaris*), **144**, *145*, 322
SUMMER CHARM, see 'DTR 124' (*S. pekinensis*)
'Summer Skies' (*S. ×hyacinthiflora*), **174**, *174*, 305
'Summer Snow' (*S. reticulata*), *70*
'Summer White' (*S. Villosae Group*), **117**, *117*, 134–135, 310
'SunDak' (*S. pekinensis*), *74*
'Sundak', see 'SunDak' (*S. pekinensis*)
'Sunrise' (*S. Villosae Group*), 113, 199, 247, 262
'Sunset' (*S. ×hyacinthiflora*), *174*, 305
'Superba' (*S. pubescens* subsp. *microphylla*), **97**, *97*, 163
'Superba' (*S. sweginzowii*), 112, **114**, *114*, 280
'Susan B. Anthony' (*S. vulgaris*), **290**, 290
'Susanna' (*S. vulgaris*), 293
'Suyun̯shi' (*S. vulgaris*), 346
'Svit̯azanka' (*S. vulgaris*), 336
'Swanee' (*S. Villosae Group*), **134**, *135*, 300
'Swansdown' (*S. vulgaris*), *132*, 322
'Swarthmore' (*S. ×hyacinthiflora*), 301, **302**, 302
'Sweet Charity' (*S. ×hyacinthiflora*), **310**, 310
'Sweetheart' (*S. ×hyacinthiflora*), **174**, *174*, 305
'Sylvan Beauty' (*S. ×hyacinthiflora*), **311**, 311

'Tadeu̯sh' (*S. vulgaris*), 346
'Tadeusz Kościuszko' (*S. vulgaris*), 151
'Taff's Treasure' (*S. ×persica*), *88*, 192
'Taglioni' (*S. vulgaris*), *132*, 280
'Talisman' (*S. vulgaris*), *172*
'Tammelan Kaunotar' (*S. Villosae Group*), 287
'Tankist' (*S. vulgaris*), **334**, 334

'Taras Bul'ba' (*S. vulgaris*), **339**, 339
'Telimena' (*S. Villosae Group*), **165**, *165*, 342
'Tev Jaunība' (*S. vulgaris*), 345
'Tēvzeme' (*S. vulgaris*), 345
'The Bride' (*S. ×hyacinthiflora*), **86**, 126, *134*, 301, 302
'Theo Holetich' (*S. vulgaris*), 316
'Thomas A. Edison' (*S. vulgaris*), 290
'Thomas Jefferson' (*S. vulgaris*), 290, **291**
THUMBELINA, see 'Bailina' (*Syringa*)
'Thunberg' (*S. vulgaris*), 280
'Tiffany Blue' (*S. vulgaris*), **190**, *190*, 322
'Tiina' (*S. vulgaris*), 343
TINKERBELLE, see 'Bailbelle' (*Syringa*)
'Tita' (*S. vulgaris*), 315, 316
'Tom Taylor' (*S. ×hyacinthiflora*), *184*, **185**, 302
'Tombouctou' (*S. vulgaris*), 280
'Topaz' (*S. vulgaris*), **137**, *137*, 339
'Touch of Spring' (*S. ×hyacinthiflora*), *138*
'Tournefort' (*S. vulgaris*), 280
'Toussaint-Louverture' (*S. vulgaris*), **183**, *183*, 280
'Treesje Topsvoort' (*S. vulgaris*), 285
'Triste Barbaro' (*S. vulgaris*), *183*
'True Blue' (*S. vulgaris*), 139, **144**, *145*, 295, 296
'TTT' (*S. vulgaris*), 345
'Turenne' (*S. vulgaris*), 280
'Turgot' (*S. ×hyacinthiflora*), 280

'Ukraina' (*S. vulgaris*), **160**, *160*
'Ursula' (*S. Villosae Group*), *120*, 165, 298, 342
'Uscītīgais Dunkers' (*S. vulgaris*), 345
'Utro Rossii' (*S. vulgaris*), 329
'Utro Moskvy' (*S. vulgaris*), **160**, *160*, 332

'Vaiga' (*S. ×hyacinthiflora*), 343
'Valentina Grizodubova' (*S. vulgaris*), 332, **333**
'Valentina Tere̯shkova' (*S. vulgaris*), 345
'Variegata' (*S. emodi*), *107*, 192
'Vasaras Svētki' (*S. vulgaris*), 345
'Vauban' (*S. ×hyacinthiflora*), **162**, *162*, 280
'Veera' (*Syringa Villosae Group*), 287
'Vek' (*Syringa*), 334

'Velikaya Pobeda' (*S. vulgaris*), 333
'Vera Khoruzhaya' (*S. vulgaris*), 336
'Vergissmeinnicht' (*S. vulgaris*), 281
'Veseniĭ Motiv' (*S. vulgaris*), 345
'Vesennyaya Krasa' (*S. vulgaris*), 338
'Vesper' (*S. vulgaris*), **183**, *183*
'Vestale' (*S. vulgaris*), 132, 280
'Vēstule Solveigai' (*S. vulgaris*), 345
'Vésuve' (*S. vulgaris*), *183*, 280
'Victor Lemoine' (*S. vulgaris*), 151, **279**, 280
'Victorie' (*S. vulgaris*), 228
'Vidzemes Debesis' (*S. vulgaris*), 345
'Villars' (*S. ×hyacinthiflora*), 280
'Ville de Troyes' (*S. vulgaris*), **269**, 269
'Viola' (*S.* Villosae Group), *186*, 298
'Violet Glory' (*S. vulgaris*), *137*, 303
'Violetta' (*S. vulgaris*), *137*, *137*, 280
'Virginité' (*S. vulgaris*), **272**, 280
'Vīrietis Labākajos Gados' (*S. vulgaris*), 345
'Vita' (*S. vulgaris*), 345
'Vitālais Sebris' (*S. vulgaris*), 345
'Vivian Evans' (*S. vulgaris*), 293, **294**
'Viviand-Morel' (*S. vulgaris*), 280
'Vīzija' (*S. vulgaris*), 345
'Volcan' (*S. vulgaris*), **183**, *183*, 280
'Voorzitter Buskermolen' (*S. vulgaris*), 287
'Voorzitter Dix' (*S. vulgaris*), **172**, *172*, 285

'W. T. Macoun' (*S.* Villosae Group), *120*, *297*, 298

'Waldeck-Rousseau' (*S. vulgaris*), 280
'Walter's Pink' (*S. vulgaris*), 312
'Wan Hua Zi' (*S. oblata*), 346
WATER TOWER, see 'Morton' (*S. pekinensis*)
WATERTOWER, see 'Morton' (*S. pekinensis*)
'Weddle' (*S. vulgaris*), 293
'Wedgwood Blue' (*S. vulgaris*), *145*, **239**, 322, **323**
'Westend' (*S. vulgaris*), 287
'White Hyacinth' (*S. ×hyacinthiflora*), **305**, 305
'White Lace' (*S. vulgaris*), **132**, *132*, 307
'White Long Fellow' (*S. vulgaris*), 307
'White Spring' (*S. ×hyacinthiflora*), 311
'White Superior' (*S. vulgaris*), 285
'White Surprise' (*S. vulgaris*), 303
'White Swan' (*S. vulgaris*), **132**, *132*
'Wild Fire' (*S. oblata* subsp. *dilatata*), *81*, **81**, 323
'Willamette' (*S. reticulata*), *70*
'William C. Barry' (*S. vulgaris*), 290
'William H. Judd' (*S. ×diversifolia*), *90*, 301
'William Robinson' (*S. vulgaris*), *151*, 280
'William S. Riley' (*S. vulgaris*), 290
'Winner's Circle' (*S. vulgaris*), 322
'Wittbold Variegated' (*S. vulgaris*), 191
'Wm K. Mills' (*S. vulgaris*), 293
'Woodland' (*S. vulgaris*), 293

'Woodland Blue' (*S. vulgaris*), **145**, *145*
'Woodland Violet' (*S. vulgaris*), *184*

'Xiang Xue' (*S. ×hyacinthiflora*), 346

'Yaltinskaya Prelest' (*S. vulgaris*), 338
'Yankee Doodle' (*S. vulgaris*), 322
'Yellow Wonder', see 'Primrose' (*S. vulgaris*)
'Yubileĭnaya' (*S. vulgaris*), 334, **335**
'Yunost' (*S. vulgaris*), 329
'Yuzhanka' (*S. vulgaris*), 338
'Yuzhnaya Noch' (*S. vulgaris*), 338

'Zaiga' (*S. vulgaris*), 345
'Zarya' (*S. vulgaris*), 329
'Zarya Kommunizma' (*S. vulgaris*), **172**, *172*, 333
'Zashchitnikam Bresta' (*S. vulgaris*), 336, **337**
'Zhang Zhiming' (*S. pekinensis*), *74*
'Zi Yun' (*S. ×hyacinthiflora*), 346
'Zilais Kalns' (*S. vulgaris*), 345
'Znamya Lenina' (*S. vulgaris*), **184**, *184*, 333
'Zor'ka Venera' (*S. vulgaris*), 336
'Zoya Kosmodem'yanskaya' (*S. vulgaris*), 333
'Zulu' (*S. vulgaris*), **184**, *184*, 296
'Zviozdochka Kieva' (*S. vulgaris*), 339

General Index

Boldface numbers indicate photo pages.

Aalsmeer Flower Auction, 283
Afghan lilac, see *Syringa protolaciniata*
Agricultural University, Kharkov, Ukraine, 339
Aitchison, James E. T., 65, 352
albino seedlings, 74, 248
Alexander III, John H., 82, 357
Alexander Sr., J. Herbert, 297, **308**, 308–309, 357
American hybrid lilac, see *Syringa ×hyacinthiflora*
Ameri-Hort Research, 318, 324
Amur tree lilac, see *Syringa reticulata* subsp. *amurensis*
Anderson, Edgar S., 198, 352, 357
Andrieux, Vilmorin, 341
animal damage, 242–243
anthocyanins, 124
Arboretum Hørsholm, 369
Arboretum Lisičine, 368
Arboretum Kalmthout, 366
Arboretum Norr, 357
armillaria root rot, 233–234
Arnold Arboretum, 64, 200, 207, 301, 373
Audibert nursery, 357
autumn leaf color of lilacs, 190–191
autumn seed pod color, 191
azaleas as companion plants, 215

Bachtell, Kris R., 66, 357
bacterial blight, 231
Bai Pei-Yu, 352
Bailey, Liberty Hyde, 52
Bakker and Sons nursery, 357
Baldwin, Clarence E., 357
Ballreich, Reva, 357
Balsgård Elitplantstationen, 357
Baltet nursery, 269, 357
Barankiewicz, Henryk, 357
Barbier nursery, 357
Baring, Charles, 66, 352

Barnes, Alice G., 357
Barnes Jr., Franklin L., 357
Barry, Patrick, 357
Bartholomew, Bruce M., 66, 352
Bartram, John, 40
Baudriller, 357
Bean, William J., 352
Becker, Gilbert, 357
beds, preparing soil, 203, 217–218
Behnsch, Reinhold, 357
Beijing Botanical Garden and Institute of Botany, 346, 368
Beijing Forestry University, 346
Bell, Andrew C., 66, 352
Bellion, Claude, 357
Berdeen, Kenneth W., **311**, 311–312, 357
Berezovski, Mikhail M., 52, 113, 352
Berniau, L. 357
Bertin, 357
Bibikova, Veronika F., 336, 357
Billiard, Ch., 357
birds, 84, 120, 197, 205, 235, 238, 245
Blacklock, Mary E., 303, 357
blights, 231
Blinkworth, Robert, 49, 65, 352
Block, Allan F., 191, 357
bloom sequence of species, 31
blueberrying (twiggy growth), 223
Blume, Carl L. von, 352
Boerhaave, Hermann, 352
Boice, Dorothy W., 358
Bonvalot, Pierre G. E., 65, 352
Borbás, Vinczé von, 352
borers and lilacs, 236–237
Borzan, Želimir, 352
Botanic Garden and Botanical Museum Berlin-Dahlem, 268
Botanical Garden, Kazakhstan Academy of Sciences, Almaty, 345, 371
Botanical Garden, Saint Petersburg, 335
Botanical Garden, Tashkent, Uzbekistan, 345
Botanical Society of America, 66

Boufford, David, 66, 352
Boughen, Ron, 358
Brahy-Ekenholm, Joseph, 358
Brand, Archie M., 358
Brandis, Sir Dietrich, 352
Bretschneider, Emil V., 72, 352
Briot, Pierre L. ("Charles"), 358
Bristol, Peter W., 64, 66, 352
broadleaf lilac, see *Syringa oblata*
Bron, Ed, 358
Brooklyn Botanic Garden, 89, 374
brooming disease, 240
Brown, Joan L., 327, 358
Bruchet, 358
budding, 258–259
Bugała, Władysław, 340, 341, 342, 358
Buis, Cornelis, 286, 358
Bunge, Alexander von, 49, 65, 352
Bunnik, Gerard, 287, 358
Bureau, Louis É., 352
Busbecq, Count de, 38–39

Camerarius, Rudolph J., 268
Case, Bernard O., 358
Cassegrain, 358
Castle, Minerva S., 303, 358
Centennial Lilac Garden **205**, 367
Central Botanical Garden, Kiev, 338–339, 373
Central Botanical Garden, Minsk, 336
Central Botanical Garden, Moscow, 334
Central Experimental Farm, Ottawa, 367
Cesalpino, Andrea, 352
Chang Mei-Chen, 353
Chapman, Colin, 358
Chen Jun-Yu, 346, 358
Chen Xin-Lu, 66, 353
Chenault, Léon, 358
Chenault, Raymond, 358
Child, Harold L., 358
China, lilacs from, 48–49, 50–52, 62–63

Chinese Academia Sinica, 66
Chinese lilac, see *Syringa ×chinensis*
Chinese tree lilac, see *Syringa pekinensis*
chromosome counts, 262–264
cicadas, 237–238
Clark, Robert B., 353, 358
Clarke Nursery, 358
Clarke, James F., 305
Clarke, Walter B., 303
Clarke, William S., 353
Cleaves, Kenneth, 358
cleft grafts, 256–257
climate, 17, 31, 33, 193
cluster types, 43
Cochet the Elder, Pierre, 269, 358
Coggeshall, Roger, 312, 377
colchicine, 264–266, 318
cold tolerance, 33–36
color charts, 124–125
color classification and classes, 125
    bluish (III), *139–146*, 187
    lilac (IV), *147–153*, 187
    magenta (VI), *165–174*, 188
    pinkish (V), *153–165*, 187–188
    purple (VII), *175–186*, 188
    violet (II), *135–138*, 187
    white (I), *126–135*, 187
color in lilacs, 122
common lilac, see *Syringa vulgaris*
companion plants, 207–216
conifers as companion plants, 207–208
Cornu, Marie M., 353
Cox, Euan H. M., 61–62
crabapples as companion plants, 175, 208–210
cultivar fingerprinting, 27–28
cultural practices, 74, 315
Cumming, William A., **317**, 317, 358
Curtis, William, 353
cut flowers, 230
cut-leafed lilac, see *Syringa ×laciniata*
cuttings for propagation, 252–256

Daniels, George, 324, 358
Darimont, 358
Darwin, Charles, 268
Dauvesse nursery, 358
David, Armand, 52, 65, 72, 353
De Belder, Robert, 66, 100, 358
De Belder-Kovačič, Jelena, 66, 100, 358
de Wilde, Robert C., 358
Decaisne, Joseph, 353
deer damage, 242

Delavay, Jean Marie, 52, 65, 353
Delbard, Georges, 358
Delcor, François, 358
Dendrological Gardens of M. A. Lisavenko Scientific Research Institute for Siberian Horticulture in Barnaul, Altai, Russia, 335
Descanso Gardens, 310, 311, 358, 375
Devonian Botanic Garden, 367
Diels, Friedrich L. E., 353
Dingle Plants and Gardens, 346
diseases of lilacs, 241–235
Dobele Horticultural Plant Breeding Experimental Station, 371
dogwoods as companion plants, 210–211
Donetsk Botanical Garden, 339, 373
Dong Boa-Hua, 346
Dorsett, Palemon H., 66, 353, 358
Dougall, James, 288, 359
drainage, 217–218
Draps, Jean Baptiste L., 359
Dubois, 359
Dumont de Courset, Baron G. L. M., 353
Dunbar, John, **288**, 288–290, 307, 359
dwarf Korean lilac, see *Syringa meyeri*
dwarf lilacs, 102, 190, 194, 197, 269, 327
Dyagilev, Boris K., 345, 359
Dzevitskaya, Milada T., 346, 359
Dzevitsky, Tadeush V., 346, 359

early blooming lilac, see *Syringa oblata*
early flowering lilac, see *Syringa ×hyacinthiflora*
Early Hybrid lilacs, 301, 303, 323
Eaton, Mark M., 294, 297, 359
Egolf, Donald, **324**, 324–325, 359
Egorova, M., 330, 359
Eichler nursery, Moritz, 359
Ekenholm, Adrienne M., 358
Ellwanger, George, 359
Engler, 359
Eveleens Maarse Sr, Dirk, 226, 284, 287, 359
Eveleens nursery, J., 284, 359
Ewing Park, 200, 207

Falconskeape, **210**, 318, 324, 376
fall webworm, 239–240
Fan Ying-Han, 346, 359
Farr, Bertrand H., 359
Farrer, Reginald J., 59, 61–62, 353
Felix and Dykhuis nursery, 284, 359

Fenicchia, Richard A., **313**, 313–314, 359
Fiala, John L., 317–324, 359
flavonoids, 124
Flemer III, William, 71, 359
Fleming, Robert A., 359
floral arrangements, **230**
floret formation, 42
flower types in lilacs, 43
flowering cherries as companion plants, 211–212
forcing lilacs, 226–229
Forrest, George, 56, 60–61, 65, 353
Fortune, Robert, 50, 65, 353
fragrance in lilacs, 32–33
Franchet, Adrien R., 353
Franklin, Alonzo B., 359
Franklin, Mabel L., 359
French Hybrids, 272
Fröbel, Karl O., 359
frost damage, 240–241

Gardner Nursery, Edward J., 306, 359
Gardner, Edward J., 306
Gardner, Robert L., 306
Garnier, Marie J. F., 353
Gärtner, Karl F. von, 268
Gathoye, François, 359
genetics, 267–268
Gentry, Myrtle G., 358
Gielis, Louis, 359
Gill, William J., 353
Giraldi, Giuseppe, 52, 65, 353
Gireoud, Friedrich A. H., 359
Gleditsch, Johann G., 268
Golden Prairie Arboretum, 367
gold-leaved lilacs, 191
Gorb, Vasil' K., 338, 359
Gorshkovitch, 35
Goscote Nurseries, 359
Gouchault, Auguste, 359
graft incompatibility, 242
grafting, 34, 256–258
Gram, Kai J. A., 359
Grant, Alvan R., 313, 359
Grape Hill Gardens, **196**, **209**
Grave, Peter F., 282
Green, Peter S., 353
green-graft cuttings, 258
Grigor'ev, Alexander G., 338, 359
Grunewald, Friedrich W., 360

habitat of lilacs, 38, 217
Halward Method, 255
Hancock, Marcus L., 360

Handel-Mazzetti, Heinrich, 52
Hara, Hiroshi, 353
Harbin Forest Botanical Garden, 368
hardiness, 33–36
Harding, Alice, 307
Harkness, Bernard, 313
Hathaway Nurseries, 360
Hatusima, Sumihoko, 353
Hauck, Cornelius J., 360
Havemeyer, Theodore A., 294–296, 297, 307, 360
Hawkins, Roy F., 360
Heard, William R., 360
hedges, 47, 202
Heeren Jzn, K., 360
Henry, Augustine, 52, 53
Henry, Louis, 75, 360
Henry, Mary G., 360
Herman, Dale E., 360
Hermann, Paulus, 353
Herrmann, John, 360
Hers, Joseph, 59, 66, 94, 360
Hesse, Hermann A., 353
Hetz, Charles W., 360
Heuffel, János A., 38, 353
Highland Botanical Park, **204**, **216**, 313–314, 375
Hilborn, Ernest C., 360
Hildreth, Aubrey C., 360
Hillier and Sons nursery, 360
Hillier Gardens, 369
Himalayan lilac, see *Syringa emodi*
Hodgdon, Philip B., 360
Hoffman, Marco H. A., 22, 116, 353
Hohman, Henry J., 297, 360
Holden Arboretum, 64, 200, **222**, 373
Holetich, Charles, 226, 329
Holland, Neal S., 327–328, 360
hornets, 238–239
Horntvedt, Siri (Kjaer), 360
Hoser, Peter, 360
Hosie, Alexander, 353
hostas as companion plants, 175, 213–214
Hughes, Millie, 360
Hughes, Wayne, 360
Huhehaote Botanical Garden, 368
Hungarian lilac, see *Syringa josikaea*
hyacinth lilac, see *Syringa ×hyacinthiflora*
hybridizing, 246, 259–261

Incarville, Pierre N. le Cheron d', 49, 65, 72, 353
insect pests, 235–240

International Lilac Registrar, 27
interspecific hybridization, 261
intraspecific hybridization, 260

Jacob-Makoy, Lambert, 360
Jacquin, Joseph F. von, 353
Jäger, Hermann, 353
Japanese beetle, 239
Japanese tree lilac, see *Syringa reticulata*
Jardin des Plantes, Paris, 64
Jefferson, Thomas, 41
Jovanović, Branislav, 353

Karklins, Laimonis, 345
Karpow-Lipski, Mikołaj, 340, 341–342, 360
Karolin's, Alimonies, 360
Katie Osborne Lilac Garden, 367
Kazakhstan Pedagogical Institute, 346, 371
Keaffaber, Anna Mae, 360
Keaffaber, Merle Lowell, 360
Keessen, Gerrit, 286
Keessen, Hendrik, 286
Keessen Jr, Klaas, 284
Keessen, Willem, 286, 360
Kelly Brothers Nursery, 360
Kelsey Highland Nursery, 360
Kettler, Fred H., 360
King, Evelyn (Evie), 312, 377
Kingdon-Ward, Francis, 56, 59, 66, 353
Kircher, Konrad, 360
Kirchner, Georg, 353
Kirilov, Porfirij J., 50, 65, 72, 354
Kitaibel, Pál (Paul), 354
Kjaer, Siri H., 287
Klager, Hulda T., 291–293, 360, 376
Klehm, Roy G., 360
Klettenberg, Antoine J., 282–283, 361
Klimenko, Vera N., 338, 361
Klimenko, Zinaida K., 338, 361
Koch, Karl H. E., 354
Koehne, Bernhard A. E., 354
Koelreuter, Joseph G., 268
Kolesnikov, Leonid A., 328, 330–333, 361
Kolkka, Kimmo L., 287, 361
Komarov, Vladimir L., 55, 65, 354
Komarov Botanical Institute and Garden, 64
Kopp, Emil, 360
Korean lilac, see *Syringa pubescens* subsp. *patula*

Kórnik Arboretum, 40, 342, 372
Koster and Sons nursery, M., 283, 361
Kravchenko, Lyubov' K., 345, 361
Krsnak, Jimmy, 361
Krüssmann, Gerd, 275
Kutzer, Ernst, **349**

La Rue, Carl D., 354
Lack, Hans W., 354
Lambert, Peter, 361
Lambrechts, Pierre, 361
Lammerts, Walter E., 310–311, 361
Lancaster, C. Roy, 66, 354
Landis Arboretum, 310, 373
landscaping with lilacs, 193
Lape, Fred, 309–310, **310**, 361
Larsen, Carl A., 361
Late Lilacs, 323
lath houses, 249, 252, 254
Laurent, Sébastien, 227
Lavrov, S. V., 361
layering of lilacs, 251
leaf miner, 238
leaf necrosis, 240
Lecointe, 361
Lederman, Anton C., 361
Legraye, Marie Anne V., 361
Lemke, August H., 361
Lemoine, Émile, 272–273
Lemoine, Henri, 273
Lemoine, Marie Louise Anna, 270
Lemoine, Victor, 139, 270–272, **271**, 330
Lemoine nursery, 273, 294, 307, 341, 361
Leroy, André, 361
Leslie, William R., 299–300, 361
Lesostepnaya Experimental Breeding Station (LOSS), 329, 361, 372
Léveillé, Augustin A. H., 354
Libert-Darimont, Gilles É. J., 270, 361
Liberton, Léon L. T., 361
Lilac Performance Form, 225
Lilacia Park, **194**, 375
Lilacland, **196**, 200, **211**, 297, 376
Lindley, John, 354
Lingelsheim, Alexander von, 354
Linnaeus, Carl, 17, 268, 354
Löbner, Max, 361
Loddiges, Conrad, 361
Loddiges, George, 354
Logan, James, 268
Lombarts, Petrus (Pierre) A. F. M., 361
Los Angeles State and County Arboretum, 310, 311

LOSS, see Lesostepnaya Experimental Breeding Station
Loudon, John C., 17
Luchnik, Zinaida I., 335, 361
Lumley, Albert E., 286, 361
Lyapunova, Nina A., 338, 361
Lyden, Cora L., 309, 362

Ma Yu-Chuan, 354
Maack, Richard, 50, 65, 71, 354
Maarse and Son nursery, J. D., 286, 362
Maarse Jbzn, Gerrit, 286, 362
Maarse, Albert, 286, 287
Maarse, Hendrik, 286, 362
Maarse, Jaap, 286
Maarse, Jacob, 286
Maarse, Jan, 287
Maarse, W., 287
Maarsen, Gerrit, 286, 362
Maarsen, Poulus, 286, 362
Machet and Josem nursery, 362
Mackinac Island lilacs, 40–41, **41**
Macoun, William T., 297
magnolias as companion plants, 212
Mahaux, Jean, 362
Maire, Édouard-Ernest, 66, 354
Manchurian tree lilac, see *Syringa reticulata* subsp. *amurensis*
Margaretten, Joel, 315–316, 362
Margary, August, 51
Mascioli, Lynette, 312
Mathies, John, 362
Mathieu, Léon J. A. G. M., 51, 55, 65, 71, 354, 362
McKelvey, Susan D., 26, 27, 124, 354
McLaughlin estate, Bernard, **214**, **215**, 376
McLean Jr, William L., 362
McNamara, William A., 66, 354
Meader, Elwyn M., **64**, 66, 101, 326, 362
Meadowlark Hill Lilac Garden, **200**, 328, 376
Mel'nik, A. F., 345, 362
Mendel, Gregor J., 268
Meng Zheng-Gui, 354
Meyer lilac, see *Syringa meyeri*
Meyer, Frank N., 59–60, 65, 66, 77, 354, 362
Meyer, Paul W., 66, 354
Mezitt, Ed, 362
Michie, Alex, 362
Michurin, Ivan V., 330, 362
micropropagation, 250

Mikhaïlov, Nikolai L., 334, 362
mildew, 232–233
Miller, Philip, 268, 354
Mironovich, Vladimir D., 333, 362
Moldenke, Harold N., 354
mole damage, 243
Möllendorf, Otto F. von, 354
Montreal Botanic Garden, 367
Moore, Ralph, 324, 362
Mordant de Launey, Jean Claude M., 354
Morden Research Centre, 317, 367
Morel, Françisque, 269–270, 362
Morel, Georges M., 362
Morey, Dennison, 362
Moro, Frank, 328, 362
Moro, Sara, 328, 362
Morse, Warner J., 66, 354, 362
mouse damage, 243
mower damage, 243–244
Munting, Abraham, 354
Murray, Karen, 318, 324
Murray, Peter, 318, 324

Nakai, Takenoshin, 354
naming lilacs, 17, 26–27
National Council for the Conservation of Plants and Gardens, 369
Nelen, Louis, 362
Nelson, Caspar I., 362
nematodes, 238
Nijnatten, André van, 362
Nollent, 362
North America–China Plant Exploration Consortium, 66
North American Plant Collections Consortium, 373
North Dakota State University, 74
nothospecies, 26

Oakes, Walter W., 362
Olbers, Wilhelm, 268
Olbrich, Stephan, 362
Oliemans Brothers nursery, H. and J., 362
Oliver, A. A., 362
Olsen, Aksel, 362
Ordnung, Emanuel, 362
Orléans, Henri d', 50, 65, 354
ortet (plant), 307
Oudin nursery, 363
Ouwerkerk nursery, 286, 363

Pampanini, Renato, 354
Parsons Sr, Samuel B., 363

Paterson, Sarah I., 296, 363
Peking lilac, see *Syringa pekinensis*
peonies as companion plants, 212, 215
Pépinières Minier, 363
Performance Form
Persian lilac, see *Syringa ×persica*
Persoon, Christiaan H., 354
Peteri, Sirkka L., 287, 363
Peterson, Darlene, 328, 363
Peterson, Max, 328, 363
Pfitzer Sr, Wilhelm, 363
Phair, Philip D., 363
phenology, 31–32
phytophthora blight, 232
Piet Brothers nursery, 284, 363
Piet, Klaas, 284, 363
Piet, Willem, 284, 363
Pillow, James P., 363
plant explorations, 49–67
plant hunters, 52–62
plant tags, 224, 244
Pokluda, Joseph J., 363
Polin, Edward G., 363
pollution and lilacs, 240
polyploids, 262–266
Pooler, Margaret R., 325, 363
Poscharsky, Oskar, 363
Potanin, Grigoriï N., 49, 52, 54–55, 65, 354
Potutova, E., 335, 363
Pouk Han Mountains (Korea), 64, 326
powdery mildew, 232–233
Pratt, Antwerp, 51
Preston lilac, see *Syringa ×prestoniae*
Preston, Isabella, 119, 297–299, 363
Prince, William R., 354
Pringle, James S., 327, 355
pruning lilacs, 220–221
Przewalski, Nikolai M., 187, 51
Purdom, William, 59, 65, 355

Qu Shi-Zeng, 355

rabbit damage, 243
Radde, Gustav F. R. J. von, 71, 355
Rankin, John P., **307**, 307, 363
record keeping, 224
Rehder, Alfred, 355
Reichenbach, Heinrich G. L., 355
rejuvenating lilacs, 202, 222
Renaud, 363
Renault, Bernard, 355
Robinson, Edward G., 363
Rochel, Anton, 38, 355

Rock, Joseph F. C., **50**, 50, 56–58, 66, 355
Rogers, Owen M., **326**, 326, 363
Rolph, Henry (Harry) M., 330, 363
Romanova, Valentina L., 330, 363
root shoot propagation, 252
Rottert, H., 363
Royal Botanic Garden, Edinburgh, 372
Royal Botanic Gardens, Kew, 64, 369
Royal Botanical Gardens, Hamilton, 64, **198**, **207**, 318, 327, 330, 367
Royal Horticultural Society, London, 64, 124–125
Royal Horticultural Society Garden, Wisley, 369
Royle, John F., 355
Rubanik, V. G., 345, 363
Rubtzov, Leonid I., 338, 363
Ruliffson, Raymond J., 363
Ruprecht, Franz J. I., 72, 355
Rybakina, Nina I., 334, 363

saddle grafts, 256–257
Sagitova, Mar'yam G., 346, 363
Sakharova, Aleksandra S., 335, 363
Santa Ines nursery, 363
Sargent, Charles S., 53, 300
Sass, Hans P., 363
Sass, Henry E., 328, 363
Sass, Jacob, 363
Saugé, Pierre, 269, 363
Saugé lilac, see 'Saugeana' (*S. ×chinensis*)
Sax, Karl, 75, 301, 363
scale on lilacs, 235–236
Schichtel Sr, George V., 363
Schloen, John, 364
Schmidt, Franz, 355
Schmidt, Gábor, 364
Schneider, Camillo K., 52, 60, 65, 355
Schur, Philipp J. F., 355
Schweikart, Hans, 364
Scott, Edith W., 364
Seabury, Alton, 364
Sears, Thomas W., 364
seed propagation, 245–246, 248
Select Plus International Lilac Nursery, 328, 368
Semenyuk, Natal'ya B., 335, 364
Seringenpark, 372
Shelburne Museum gardens, **205**, 377
Shtan'ko, Ivan I., 334, 364
Sibthorp, John, 38, 355
Simon, F. H., 364

Simon-Louis, Léon L., 364
Sino-American Botanical Expedition, 66
site selection, 193–194
Skinner, Frank L., **300**, 300–303, 364
Slater, Leonard K., **296**, 296, 364
Slavin, Bernard H., 364
Slock, Liévin, 364
Smith, Harald (Harry) K. A., 52, 66, 355
Smith, Sir William Wright, 59, 355
Smol'skiĭ, Nikolai V., 336, 364
Sobeck, John, 311, 364
soil, 218–220
Sontag, A., 56, 65, 355
Souchet, Charles, 227
Souchet, Julien, 227
Soulié, Jean André, 355
Spaargaren, Martine, 287, 364
Späth nursery, 273, 280–281, 364
Späth, Franz Ludwig, 280
Späth, Hellmut Ludwig, 281
Späth Arboretum, 370
Spongberg, Stephen A., 66, 355
sports, propagation of, 266
Sprengel, Christian K., 268
Sprenger, Carl L., 355
stamps with lilacs, **350**, **351**
Stashkevich, Nikifor S., 333, 364
State Nikita Botanical Gardens, 338, 373
stem blight, 232
Stepman-Demessemaeker, Grégoire L. Florent, 282, 364
Stone, Elizabeth, **315**, 315, 364
stool layering, 251–252
Stropkey, John G., 364
suckers, 252
sudden oak death, 232
summer budding, 258–259
sun and lilacs, 220
Swedish University of Agriculture, 288
Szeczenyi, 355

Taffler, Stephen, 364
Tang Tsin, 355
Tatarinov, Alexander, 72, 355
taxonomy of lilacs, 20–22
Temple, F. L., 364
Tereshchenko, Sergeĭ I., 339, 364
Theidel, Richard P., 364
Thomayer, František J., 364
thyrse types, 42
Tischler, Archibald P., 358

Tischler, Robert W., 358, 364
tissue culture, 250–251
Tolppola, Holger, 287, 364
Tournefort, Joseph P. de, 355
Towson Nursery, 364
trade designations, 28–29
trademark names, 29–30
Transon Brothers nursery, 364
transplanting lilacs, 222
tree lilacs, 67, 74–75
Tulp and Son nursery, Piet 364
Turczaninov, Nicolai S., 355
Tyler Arboretum, **221**, 374

Ufa Botanical Garden, 335
understocks for grafting lilacs, 256
United States Department of Agriculture, 365, 374
United States National Arboretum, 207, 324, 325, 374
University of British Columbia, Vancouver, 367
University of California, Riverside, 328, 375
University of Guelph Arboretum, **197**, **202**, 367
University of New Hampshire, 64, 326, 375
University of Saskatchewan, 367
University of Tartu, 369
University of Tokyo, 64
University of Zagreb, 368
Uosukainen, Marjatta, 287, 365
Upītis, Pēteris, 343–345, 365
Upton, Edward A., 365

Vahl, Martin, 355
Vaigla, Adolf, 342–343, 365
van der Bom, Th., 365
van Houtte, Louis B., 365
van Nes and Sons nursery, C. B., 283
van Nes, J. H., 365
van Spaendonck, Gérard, lilac paintings of, **348**
van Tol Hzn, Jan, 283, 365
Vandendriessche, Henri, 365
variegated leaves, 191–192
Veitch nursery, Chelsea, England, 52, 64
Vekhov, Nikolaĭ K., 329–330, 365
Velenovský, Josef, 355
Verdoorn, Frans, 355
Verhoeven, Henri, 365
verticillium wilt, 232
Viehmeyer, Glenn, 198, 365

Viksten, Eero ("Eppu") O., 287, 365
Vilms, Arvid, 343
Vrugtman, Freek, 355
Vukicević, Emilia, 355

Waines, J. Giles, 328, 365
Wallace, John A., 356, 365
Wallich, Nathaniel, 49
Wandell, Willet N., 365
Warren and Son Nursery, 42
Washington, George, 41
weed killers, 244
Wentworth lilacs, **40**, 376

Weston, Richard, 135, 268, 356
Wickman, Kjell, 287, 365
Wickmans Plantskola, 287
Wiles, H. N., 365
Wilke nursery, Rudolf, 365
Willdenow, Carl L. von, 356
Willmott Jr, John, 365
Wilson, Ernest H., 37, 49, 52–54, **54**,
    65, 66, 300, 356
wind-chill chart, 241
Wister, John C., 124, 356
witches'-broom of lilacs, 234–235, 240
Wolfhagen, 365

Yaltirik, Faik, 356
Yeager, Albert F., 75, 326, 365
Yunnan lilac, see *Syringa yunnanensis*

Zampini, James W., 365
Zang Shu-Ying, 346, 365
Zhang Zhiming, 365
Zhogoleva, Valentina G., 338, 365
Zhou Si-Quang, 356
Zhue Li-huan, 365